D1476593

Computer Architecture

Computer Architecture

Pipelined and Parallel Processor Design

Michael J. Flynn
Stanford University

Jones and Bartlett Publishers
Boston   London

Editorial, Sales, and Customer Service Offices
Jones and Bartlett Publishers
One Exeter Plaza
Boston, MA 02116
1-800-832-0034
617-859-3900

Jones and Bartlett Publishers International
7 Melrose Terrace
London W6 7RL
England

Library of Congress Cataloging-in-Publication Data

Flynn, Michael J., 1934 –
    Computer architecture : pipelined and parallel processor design /
Michael J. Flynn.
        p.   cm.
    Includes bibliographical references and index.
    ISBN 0-86720-204-1
    1. Computer architecture. 2. Microprocessors--Design and
construction. I. Title.
    QA76.9.A73F58   1995
    004.2'2--dc20   94-41225
                                                                 CIP

Printed in the United States of America
99 98 97 96 95   10 9 8 7 6 5 4 3 2 1

Contents

Preface

Computers have changed markedly over the last decade. Features, performance, and memory sizes representing a computer that filled a room with equipment and cost millions of dollars a decade ago now sit on the top of a desk. This revolution has been brought about by the enabling technology of very large scale integrated circuits (VLSI). Yet, the revolution still goes forward. Increasingly, precise lithography enables even faster and more elaborate computers (processors plus memory).

These faster processors enable, in turn, a myriad of advanced complex systems controlled by multiple embedded computers. They also enable the significant enhancement of human life through the amplification of human intelligence. This is an exciting time for computer designers.

For all the excitement surrounding developments in the field, the presentation of the ideas used in developing computing processors has also undergone an evolution. A traditional way of presenting computer design has been to study existing examples of computers—a type of computer appreciation. The problem with this is that it falls short in understanding of design, because it is never possible to fully understand the tradeoffs that the design team had to face in concluding the implementation of their design. Moreover, many of these constraints have radically changed, so that the approaches taken to design have also changed. Techniques used to design the minicomputers of a decade ago are now totally obsolete. Techniques used to design mainframes are now largely incorporated into the current generation of microprocessors and will be superceded in the next generation of microprocessors.

This text is used at Stanford as the last in a series of texts for a one-year graduate-level course on computer architecture and organization. This material, especially the last half of the book, represents the most advanced material that a typical student sees before directly encountering the design process. In order to prepare the student for processor design, it is necessary to understand the tradeoffs that must be made and the tools that are available to make these tradeoffs during the design process. Rather than review the details of existing machines, this text takes an approach that abstracts the essential elements of processor design and stresses a design methodology. This includes:

- Design concepts.
- Design target data.
- Evaluation tools, especially those using basic probability theory and simple queueing theory.

This book stresses the nature of design tradeoffs through the use of extensive design studies and examples, and the use of analytic tools in making these tradeoffs.

There is a debate in the engineering design community on the relative merits of evaluation by analysis versus evaluation by simulation. Both techniques have a place, but surely analytic analysis takes precedence, at least in an academic treatment of the subject. The design space for computer architectures is enormous. Unless the space can be shrunk by making tradeoffs using analytic approximations and analytic evaluations, it would be hopeless to arrive at an optimum design. As pointed out by a number of researchers, simulation based upon small kernel programs frequently gives erroneous results. The problem with analysis, of course, is that analysis can be very complex. The underlying assumptions of the analysis (a certain probability distribution, etc.) are frequently not met. I have chosen a first-order analytic approach that we use reasonably consistently throughout this text. This approach targets the most obvious bottleneck or constraint in the system, represents that constraint in analytic form, and then studies the effect of that bottleneck on the rest of the system. This, coupled with conservative design data (what I have called the *design target data*, following the usage of Alan Smith), enables reasonably sophisticated studies of tradeoffs in complex design situations.

The last chapter, Processor Studies, could be a subtitle for the entire book. This chapter brings together many of the exercises and studies used throughout the chapters into a study of two complex design situations. As the reader will see, minor variations of many of the parameters in these studies could lead to significantly different conclusions than those presented. Concepts, data, and evaluation form the bedrock of any reasonable design study.

This book has a lengthy history. It was started about ten years ago, and has undergone ten "editions" over these years as course notes for EE382 at Stanford. Advances in the field kept me always one year away from a final edition. But, in doing so, it helped me to rethink both the content and presentation of materials many times, and, as a result, I have tried to abstract the essentials and stress design methodology. Indeed, the text avoids extensive compendiums of current features of various processors or technologies, just as it stresses concepts that underlie these processor designs.

How to Contact the Author

Comments on the book and error detection may be directed electronically to flynn@ee.stanford.edu, or mailed by way of the Electrical Engineering Department, M/C 4055, Stanford, CA 94305.

Acknowledgments

Any work of this scope has had many helping hands. Originally, the chapter 5 material was conceived around published materials by Alan Smith (whose work I admire). As time went by, it was clear that his treatment had to be redone, but I have followed his design target miss data (DTMR data) in spirit. I have also had the opportunity to use unpublished material by George E. Rossmann and B. Rau. Again, it was my original intention to publish an edition much earlier. Their early contributions are now largely incorporated into several of the chapters in this book. I would like also to acknowledge generations of students who have contributed mightily to this project. I mention a few below.

George Zalewski, Tim Wood, Bill Wong, Verdi Wahjosoedibjo, Radha Vaidyanathan, Benjamin Jui-Shen Tseng, Thomas Truong, Evan Torrie, Manu Thapar, Jon Sweedler, Kartik Subbarao, Brad Stone, Steven Speer, Vijayaraghavan Soundararajan, Polly Siegel, Eric Schwarz, Marc Schaub, Jim Richard, Brent Rasmussen, Arjun Prabhu, Peter Potrebic, Amol Patel, Bob Odineal, Kevin Nowka, Kianoosh Naghshineh, Michael Murray, Albert Mu, Dario Meluzzi, Devin Martin, Robert Mardjuki, Bill Lynch, Jack Loh, Albert Liddicoat, Bob Kutter, Ashok Kumar, Tsuneki Kojima, Scott Johnson, David Harris, Ricardo Gonzalez, Mike Frey, Todd Erdner, Van T. Dam, Brett Coon, Walter Clark, Jim Christy, Cheng Hwee Chee, David Chappell, Chip Chapin, Kashun Chan, Kashun Chan, David Carroll, Brian Carlton, Joe Butler, Amir Ben-Efraim, Hesham Al-Twaijry.

I have also received significant help from external reviewers. I especially acknowledge the detailed review of chapter 8 by Professor Josep Torrellas at the University of Illinois. Other reviewers also helped considerably. They include:

Professor Dharma Agrawal	North Carolina State University
Professor Yitzhak Birk	Technion University
Dr. Pradeep Dubey	IBM T. J. Watson Research Center
Professor Mark Evans	University of Michigan
Professor R. J. Flynn	NY Polytechnic University
Professor Kai Hwang	University of Southern California
Professor V. Milutinovic	University of Belgrade
Professor Trevor Mudge	University of Michigan

Professor Tadao Nakamura	Tohoku University
Professor Janak Patel	University of Illinois
Professor Yale Patt	University of Michigan
Professor Timothy Pinkston	University of Southern California
Professor H. C. Torng	Cornell University

Special Acknowledgements

The following people made direct major contributions to the indicated chapters or areas.

Chapter 1	Kevin Rudd (editing and examples)
Chapter 3	George Rossmann (commercial data)
Chapter 4	George Rossmann (original organization), Larry Brisson (Study 4.9, interlocks)
Chapter 5	Tin-Fook Ngai (data presentation), Gerald Luiz (logical inclusion section)
Chapter 6	Bob Rau (organization) and Fung Lee (models)
Chapter 7	Brian Bray (reorder buffers)
Chapter 8	Andrew Zimmerman (bus-based protocols), David Glasco (networked protocols)
Chapter 9	Fung Lee (models), Kathy Richardson (I/O data)
Chapter 10	Kevin Rudd, Khaled Zakharia (Study 1), Steve Fu (Study 2)
Appendices A, B, D	Steve Fu
Appendix C	Tin-Fook Ngai
Appendix F	Andrew Zimmerman
Overall	Susan Gere assembled, edited, rendered, formatted, and produced countless drafts of the manuscript and delivered the final product. Kevin Rudd served as advisor, Fontmaster, and hacker-of-TEX extraordinaire. Marsha Finley gave expert help during the final manuscript preparation.

Typographical Notes

This book was typeset using the Lucida fonts designed by Bigelow and Holmes (9.5 on 12 pt) and was formatted under LATEX 2$_\varepsilon$—aided considerably by the many wonderful macro packages described in The LATEX Companion (Addison-Wesley, 1994) by Goosens, Mittelbach, and Samarin. The graphics, drawn from countless sources, were made possible in their present (relatively) beautified forms thanks in part to the timely development of Adobe's Acrobat Distiller.

Trademarks

The following are the trademarks of the following organizations:

WE 32100 is a trademark of AT&T.
Control Data 6600/7600 and Cyber series are trademarks of CDC.
Alpha, PDP-8/10/11 and VAX are trademarks of Digital Equipment Corp.
M-1800 is a trademark of Fujitsu.
PA-RISC and Precision architecture are trademarks of Hewlett-Packard.
M-880 is a trademark of Hitachi Corp.
System 360/370/390, Enterprise, and RS/6000 are trademarks of IBM.
Intel iAP x86 and Pentium are trademarks of Intel Corporation.
R-series is a trademark of MIPS.
M88000/M680x0 are trademarks of Motorola Corporation.
Univac 1108 is a trademark of Sperry Corporation.
SPARC is a trademark of SUN Microsystems.
Lucida is a trademark of Bigelow and Holmes Inc. (Y&Y).

Chapter 1

An Introduction to Architecture and Machines

The most important influences on the design of a computing machine or processor are the instruction set (or sets) executed and the technology used in its implementation. In order to understand the machine design process, one must first understand the instruction set and the function of each instruction.

The term *computer architecture* [16] is usually used to describe the instruction set together with major implementation details such as bus structure, storage type, register type, etc. While the instruction set implies many of these implementation details, the *implementation* is separate from the architecture, since the implementation is the mechanism that executes or interprets the instruction (Figure 1.1). If an instruction specifies 16 general-purpose registers, most implementations have at least 16 registers. Implementations that have significantly more or fewer than this number are interesting exceptions, which we consider later in this book. Our primary interest in this chapter is to review the concepts and requirements implied by instruction sets, since they form the basis for intelligent machine design.

The term *architecture* includes the instruction set, which yields an interpretable program representation. Multiple implementations of the System 370 instruction set, the VAX [32, 31], the Motorola M680x0, the Intel iAP x86 [58], and the RISC instruction sets (such as SPARC) illustrate the various cost–performance technology tradeoffs possible in creating a machine.

One of the longest-lived instruction sets is the IBM mainframe System/360 (S/360), introduced in 1963 [140, 141, 142, 143]. Although over the years it has been relabeled (S/370, S/370 ESA, Enterprise system, and System/390) and extended, the S/360 core instruction set remains unchanged and probably will continue for some time. Over the years, perhaps 100 different machines have implemented this core instruction set, including manufacturers such as IBM (S/370, 30X0 models, Enterprise system, etc.), Amdahl (V series), Hitachi (H series), Fujitsu, and others. For general-purpose usage, the hallmark of a good instruction set is its ability to provide efficient (cost–performance) machine implementations across wide variances in technology (both hardware and software). As well as being long-lived,

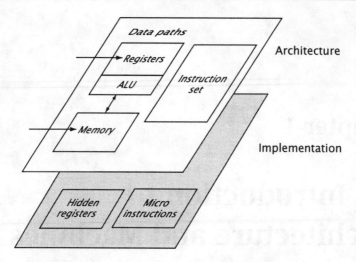

Figure 1.1 A two-level view of a computer architecture and its implementation.

a well-designed instruction set ought to allow for multiple machine implementations at various cost–performance points, to accommodate different user budgets and needs.

Occasionally, a seemingly well-designed instruction set may become difficult to implement because of unforeseen shifts in technology. The DEC VAX series (late 1970s) was an impressive extension of their earlier PDP-11 series instruction set introduced in 1968. Its instruction set provided an elaborate operational vocabulary that minimized the number of bits needed to represent or execute a program. For the technology of the '70s, this was of significant advantage; memory was an expensive part of the machine. Unfortunately, in order to achieve this code density, the instruction size and interpretation were highly variable. This was not a problem for the simple unpipelined machine implementations of the '70s, but became a significant hurdle for complex pipelined implementations 10 or 15 years later. Moreover, the cost of memory and cache has significantly decreased over the years, decreasing the value of code density. The VAX instruction set (and PDP-11) paradigm has also significantly influenced instruction set designers of contemporary (circa 1980) machines such as the Motorola M680x0 series and (to a lesser extent) the Intel 8086.

RISC instruction sets of the '80s were developed for microprocessors in part to overcome the complex implementations required by VAX-type instruction sets. RISC instruction sets used simple fixed-size instructions that facilitated implementation for complex pipelined machines. Code density was regarded as unimportant, since it complicated instruction decoding. With the advent of on-chip caches for microprocessors, optimization of memory usage is now more important, so code density may be the next hurdle for RISC implementations.

There are *always* tradeoffs in instruction set design. A well-designed instruction set allows variability in implementation technology and is less sensitive to technological changes. As time goes by, even a well-designed set must undergo changes—additions to accommodate new functionality and perhaps a de-emphasis of older features. Thus, at any moment, a successful architecture includes an instruction set consisting of:

- A core of frequently used instructions.

- Some features extending or correcting limitations in the original design.

- Some instructions no longer expected to be used (either superseded or "out of vogue"), which remain for reasons of compatibility.

This book is not intended as a historical retrospective of instruction sets. Rather, our approach is to stress the underlying principles in computer architecture: recognizing various generic instruction set types, similarities, and (essential) differences. Our primary purpose is to study *processor design*: the realization of efficient implementations *given* an instruction set and architectural limitations (cache size, etc.); but of necessity we will also study the effect of variations in architecture on the implementation efficiency (cost and performance). There are a number of books which provide a more introductory treatment to processor design—see [271, 127, 123] and [296].

1.1   Some Definitions and Terms

- A *state* is a particular configuration of storage (i.e., registers or memory), and a *state transition* is a change in that configuration.

- A *cycle* is the time between state transitions. If the storage being reconfigured is registers, we have an *internal* or *machine cycle*. If the storage is memory, we have a *memory cycle*.

- A *command* is a function that, when applied to a particular state, generates the next state. *Command* is a generic term used to describe various types of instructions.

- A *process* is a sequence of commands and an initial state. In a sense, a process is a *macro command*, since it applies to an initial state and generates a final state.

- A *machine*[1] is a set of commands and storage together with an implementation that causes the state transitions determined by the command (Figure 1.1).

- The *storage* is the range and domain of the commands. A machine's storage is only that storage referred to by its instruction set. If the instruction set cannot refer to a hidden register, it is not part of the storage, but rather part of the implementation.

The implementation that interprets the instruction can itself be a machine (that is, have instruction set, storage, and implementation); if so, the original (outermost) machine is called the *image* (or the micro-) *machine* and

---

[1]A *computer* then is a machine that can modify the sequence of commands being executed, i.e., its control flow. We use the terms machine and computer interchangeably.

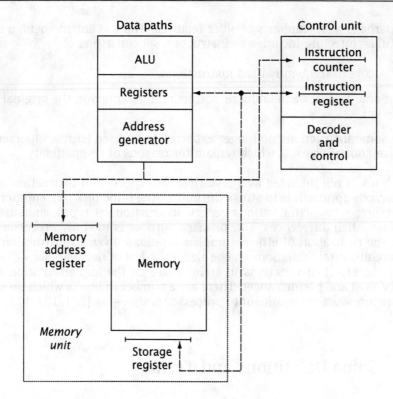

Figure 1.2   Basic units of a processor and (some) paths.

Figure 1.3   The instruction.

the implementation that interprets the commands is called the *host machinehost* (or the macro-) *machine*.

The set of all image commands and storage is defined as the *architecture of the machine*. By convention, image commands are called *instructions* or, if the distinction is important, *image instructions*, and the commands comprising the host are called *microinstructions* or *host instructions*.

The basic functional units of a processor are shown in Figure 1.2. The control unit contains all the registers and decoding hardware required to interpret the current instructions (in the instruction register). This hardware controls the sequence of actions in the data paths to provide correct instruction execution. The *data paths* consist of the ALU (arithmetic logical unit), any other specialized execution units (floating-point, etc.), address generation hardware, data and address registers, and the interconnections between these subunits. The memory unit is the last major processor unit. It includes an input address register, an output storage register, and the memory itself.

Table 1.1 Notation for microprograms and state transitions.

$R_1 \leftarrow R_2$	Copy contents of R_2 into R_1.
SR $\leftarrow$ Mem [MAR] or Memory read	Memory read operation: the contents of the address in memory address register (MAR) fetched into the memory output storage register (SR).
Mem [MAR] $\leftarrow$ SR or Memory write	Memory write operation: data in the storage register (SR) copied into the location specified by the address in the memory address register (MAR).
PC $\leftarrow$ $*$ + 1 or PC $\leftarrow$ PC+1	The current value $*$ in the program counter is incremented by 1.
MAR $\leftarrow$ $[R_X]$ + $[R_B]$ + D	Contents of register specified by R_X plus contents of register specified by R_B plus D are transferred to the MAR. $[R_X]$ indicates that R_X is a register address.

The instruction (Figure 1.3) is a vector of bits partitioned into fields. These fields identify properties of, or actions to be taken by, an instruction, including:

1. Format.

2. Object address (identifiers)—the "A," "B," and "C" fields in Figure 1.3.

3. Operation—the "OP" in Figure 1.3.

4. Sequence control.

Some fields (or actions) may be missing from an instruction either because they are implied or are unnecessary. Notation for describing actions within instruction execution is shown in Table 1.1.

1.2   The Machine: Interpretation and Microprogramming

Management of the interpretation process is the responsibility of the decoder (a part of the implementation mechanism). The process of interpreting or executing an instruction begins with the decoding of the opcode field from the instruction. The decoder activates storage and registers for a series of state transitions that correspond to the action of the opcode. The image machine storage consists of registers and memory, which are both explicitly stated in the instruction and implicitly defined by the instruction. Explicit registers include:

1. General purpose registers (GPR).

2. Accumulators (ACC).

3. Address registers (index or base registers).

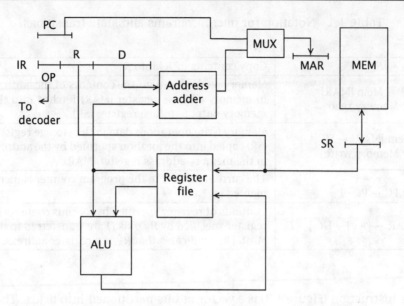

Figure 1.4   Some processor registers and data paths. *R* indicates a register in the register file, *D* an address displacement.

Implicit registers consist of the following (Figure 1.4):

1. Program or instruction counter (PC). Most instruction formats imply the next instruction in sequence as the current location plus the length of the current instruction.

2. Instruction register (IR). This register holds the instruction being interpreted or executed. Decoding is performed on the opcode held in this register.

3. Memory address register (MAR). This is the address register for a memory operation.

4. Storage register (SR). This is sometimes referred to as the *memory buffer register*, and contains the data used in the memory (to or from) operation.

5. Special use registers—usage depending on instruction.

Data paths connect the output of one register to the input of another, and may include combinatorial logic. The opcode generally defines which of the many data paths are used in execution. The collection of all opcodes defines the data paths required by a specific architecture. A register may be connected to multiple output destination registers and accepts input from one of several source registers in any one cycle. A register output (Figure 1.5) is gated to various destinations with which it can communicate in a single cycle. The activation of a particular data path is done through a *control point*. The activation and definition of every control point in the processor for every cycle of operation is the responsibility of the instruction decoder, which may be implemented directly or as a microprogram storage (Figure 1.6).

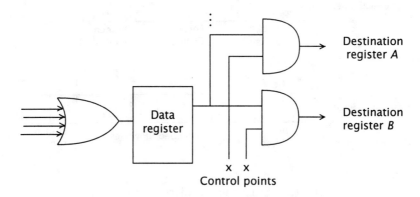

Figure 1.5   Register output gating.

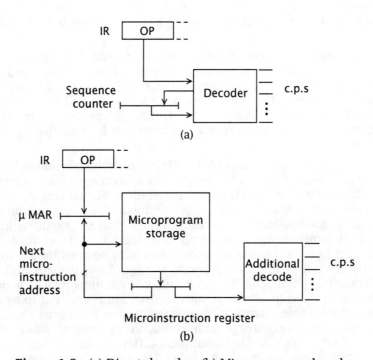

Figure 1.6   (a) Direct decoder. (b) Microprogram decoder.

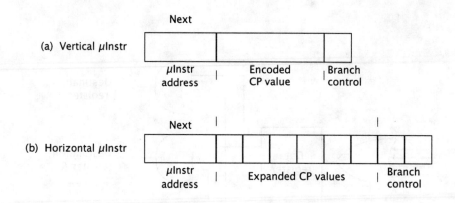

Figure 1.7 Examples of microinstructions.

Whether the decoder that manages interpretation is microprogrammed or directly decoded involves subtle tradeoffs in the host machine design. Direct decoders (Figure 1.6a) are designed by using combinatorial logic (usually PLAs) to represent the various desired control point actions. The logical inputs come from the opcode (the type of instructions to be performed), the sequence counter (a small counter to keep track of which cycle within an instruction's execution is being activated), and some test information from the data registers (e.g., sign of a value) to correctly set the next control action.

Microprogrammed decoders (Figure 1.6b) are designed using ROM (read-only memory), sometimes complemented with RAM (read/write random access memory). The opcode provides an initial address to an entry (microinstruction), which specifies the control point values as well as the expected address of the next microinstruction. During the process of instruction execution, the next microinstruction address may be modified by test information.

In microprogrammed machines [291, 305], the microinstruction defines the control point values required throughout the system as well as controls the sequencing of the interpretation of an operation. Sequencing can be performed either in-line or with the explicit address of the next microinstruction in the sequence. Microinstruction formats typically explicitly include the next microinstruction address. In most machines, the control points are encoded in some fashion in microinstruction representation, making more efficient use of the microprogram storage. Some designs highly encode the control point actions so that only a few actions may be activated in a particular cycle. This type of microinstruction is referred to as a *vertical* microinstruction (Figure 1.7a) and requires an additional decoder to process the encoded control point information. In contrast, other designs partition control point actions into many different classes, any of which can be activated within any given cycle. This type of microinstruction is referred to as a *horizontal* microinstruction (Figure 1.7b).

Table 1.2 provides a qualitative comparison between the two approaches. Direct decoders are usually fast and small, but may complicate the design process, especially for certain operating system functions (security, con-

Table 1.2   Direct or hardwired control vs. microprogrammed control: comparative decoder features.

Attribute	Hardwired Decoders	Microprogrammed Decoders
Speed	Fast	Slower
Chip area efficiency	Uses least area	Uses more area
Ease of change, additions	Somewhat difficult	Easier
Ability to handle large/complex instruction sets	Somewhat difficult	Easier
Ability to support operating systems and diagnostic features	Very difficult (unless anticipated during design)	Easy
Where used	Mostly RISC microprocessors	Mainframes, some microprocessors
Instruction set size	Usually under 100 instructions	Usually over 100 instructions
ROM size	—	2^K-10^K by 40–200 bit microinstructions

figuration management, etc.) or machine diagnostics. Microprogrammed decoders are usually used in these environments. Note that a slower decoder does not necessarily mean a slower machine, as other paths in the machine may be the determining speed factor.

The cycle time of the machine is determined by the time it takes to move data from one register to another through intervening combinatorial logic. For machines with particularly long or elaborate combinatorial logic in the data paths, it is possible to distinguish short paths from long and to define multiples of the original clock to manage these long paths, as discussed later.

1.3   The Instruction Set

Computers deal with many different kinds of data in many different ways. There are probably as many variations of data representations as there are processor implementations. Additionally, the operations available to perform the requisite data manipulations are often subtly different on different processors and frequently use different assembly syntax. All of these factors make choosing a data and instruction representation system that is generally acceptable difficult at best.

> *This section aims at providing a basic understanding of the key concepts involved. Both data types and instruction set designs are presented from a "birds-eye view," and comparisons between some of the major alternatives currently in use are considered to place the choices in perspective.*

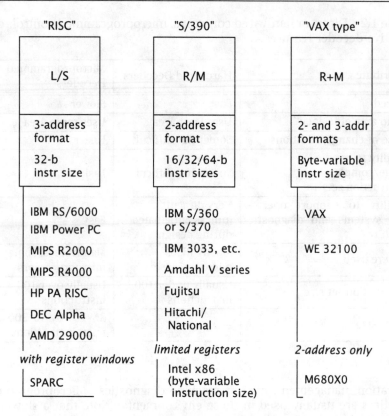

Figure 1.8   Generic and actual architectures.

Processor design issues are closely bound to the instruction set. Instruction set analysis data based on existing machines affects many of these design issues. However, innovative processor designs are constantly being introduced into the marketplace. These may be based on existing instruction sets, on extensions to existing instruction sets, or on entirely new instruction sets. In order to provide an analysis in the face of changing instruction set details, three generic instruction approaches are described. This avoids dealing with machine artifacts and peculiarities and still allows the presentation of data representative of different architecture types. These generic approaches have a recognizable correspondence to the marketplace: they share features of many available machines, both mainframe and microprocessor (Figure 1.8).

Consistent with most modern machines, each of these generic approaches is based upon a register set to hold operands and addresses. Among processors of general interest, the register set size varies from 8 to 32 words, each word consisting of 32 bits. For our generic processor approach, when floating-point arithmetic operations are available in the architecture, an additional set of floating-point registers is assumed to be also available. In early microprocessor architectures, the floating-point registers and associated floating-point execution hardware were provided as a coprocessor—a separate chip with close coupling to the microprocessor. More recently, mi-

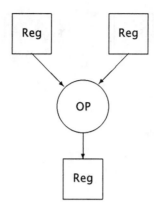

Figure 1.9 The L/S architecture. L/S format: all operands for ALU operations must lie in registers.

croprocessors integrate floating-point hardware and registers on the processor chip.

Our generic approaches assume a program status word, which consists of various types of control status information, including condition codes (described later) set by the instruction. With this common core, the three instruction set types are:

1. The L/S, or Load–Store architecture.

2. The R/M, or Register–Memory architecture.

3. The R+M, or Register-plus-Memory architecture.

Figure 1.8 relates these instruction set types to common machines provided by the better known manufacturers.

The L/S architecture   describes many of the RISC (reduced instruction set computer) microprocessors (IBM RS/6000, MIPS R-series, Hewlett–Packard's PA-RISC, Sun Microsystem SPARC, Motorola M88000). All values must be loaded into registers before an execution can take place. An ALU **ADD** instruction must have both operands and result specified as registers (three addresses). Thus, an **ADD** with one operand in memory is not allowed (Figure 1.9). The purpose of the RISC architecture is to establish regularity of execution and ease of decoding in an effort to improve overall performance. RISC architects have tried to reduce the amount of complexity in the instruction set itself and regularize the instruction format so as to simplify decoding of the instruction. A simpler instruction set with straightforward timing is more readily implemented.

The R/M or **Register–Memory architectures**   include instructions that can operate both on registers and with one of the operands residing in memory. Thus, for the R/M architecture, an **ADD** instruction creates the sum of a register value and a value contained in memory, putting the result into the same register (two addresses), This use of a memory value is not allowed in the L/S architecture (Figure 1.10).

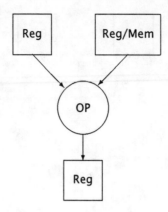

Figure 1.10 The R/M architecture. R/M format: one source operand may lie in memory, the other source operand must be a register that also serves as the destination (a *two-address* format, sometimes called *one and one-half address* because of the preceding limitation). Character-based operations are an exceptional case. Their format is Mem OP Mem → Mem.

For our R/M architecture, the result of a simple (e.g., integer or floating-point) ALU operation must go to the register that was used as an operand source (Figure 1.10). The R/M architectures generally trace their evolution to the IBM System 360 introduced in 1963 (later System 370, the 3XXX models, Enterprise system, and S/390); there have been many variations on this basic architecture style. Most general-purpose modern mainframe computers follow the R/M style (IBM, Amdahl, Hitachi, Fujitsu, etc., which all use the IBM instruction set), as well as several microprocessor architectures (Intel x86 series). There are many variant architectures included within the R/M designation. We use data from IBM mainframe environments as representative of the R/M architecture. The applicability of this data to Intel-type machines is very approximate, since Intel uses byte-variable instructions, has selected instructions with memory destinations, and uses special implied registers. Our R/M architecture anticipates some variability in instruction size: we assume that the register-to-register operations are 16 bits, while the register-to-memory operations are 32 bits.

R+M or **Register-plus-Memory architectures**   allow formats to include operands that are either in memory or in registers. Thus, for example, an ADD may have all of its operands in registers or all of its operands in memory, or any combination thereof. The R+M architecture generalizes the formats of R/M (Figure 1.11). The outstanding example of the R+M architecture is Digital Equipment's VAX series of machines. VAX is an extension of the older PDP-11 introduced in the late 1960s and generalizes the use of the register set through the use of register modes, which are described later. The use of an extended set of formats and register modes allows a powerful and varied specification of operands and operation type within a single instruction. Microprocessors such as the Motorola M680x0 series or the ATT WE 32100 also belong to the R+M architecture class, although they do not have instruction set capability as extensive as VAX. Unfortunately, format and mode variability complicates the decoding process so that the

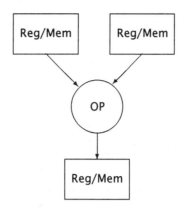

Figure 1.11 The R+M architecture. R+M format: operands may lie in either register or memory. Three operands are independently specified (three-address) and each may specify either register or memory. Formats also include the two-address type where one source operand address (register or memory) is the same as the destination.

process of interpretation of generalized instructions can be slow (but R+M architectures make excellent use of memory/bus bandwidth).

The L/S type of processor architecture uses fixed-size instructions (typically 32 bits) with uniform field interpretation (size typically 32 bits) and with a regular execution sequence. At the other extreme, the R+M architecture frequently uses compact and flexible representation of program actions. Instruction flexibility as represented by the R+M architecture provides a more compact representation—fewer bits to fetch instructions for execution, fewer numbers of instructions to execute—while the more restrictive L/S architecture provides a more rapid execution of each instruction, but executes more instructions. Because of its emphasis on pipelined processors, this text stresses the L/S architectures and R/M architectures, as they are the most natural candidates for pipeline implementations. Current R+M architectures are more difficult to realize in pipeline implementations because of their extensive use of variable operand specifiers (the operand modes). While it would be possible to create more regular implementations of R+M architectures, perhaps equally suited for pipelining, these are not yet common in the marketplace.

1.4   Basic Data Types

One of the most important aspects of an architecture is the format (size, shape, and structure) of the data values that are operated on by the instruction set. The *data type* defines the format and use of data objects and implies the operations that are valid for each type. For most familiar machines, the different data types can be broken down into the following classes (Figure 1.12):

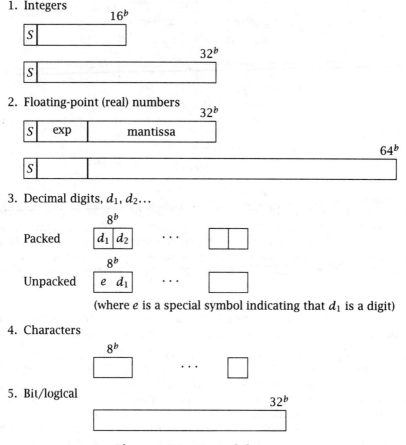

Figure 1.12   Typical data types.

1. Integers (signed or unsigned whole numbers).

   Integers are the fundamental data type used in computers. Other numeric data types may be readily assembled using this data type.[2] Different formats may be used to represent signed numbers, by far the most common of which is the two's-complement representation. This is the representation formed by using $-a = 0 - a$.[3] The advantage of this format is that no special care need be taken with numbers after conversion (which does, however, require a subtraction) is complete. Less common is the one's-complement representation that is formed by $-a = \text{NOT } a$.[4] This representation is much easier for converting between formats, but has several undesirable properties—not the least of which is that -0 does not have the same pattern as $+0$ (or unsigned $0 = +0$).

---

[2]Actually, *bit strings* form the basis for computer arithmetic. However, as bit strings do not provide any numeric functionality, their use as a basis for operations is fine for actual hardware (where *everything* is really a bit string), but complicates any practical discussion of arithmetic.

[3]More formally, for an n bit binary number, $-a = (2^n - a) \bmod 2^n$, where $2^{n-1} > |a|$.

[4]Or $-a = (2^n - 1 - a) \bmod (2^n - 1)$. The dual representations of zero (all 1's or all 0's) occur because $0 \equiv (2^n - 1) \bmod (2^n - 1)$.

Table 1.3   Comparison of floating-point specifications.

	IBM S/390	VAX	IEEE Standard
	S = Short	S = Short	S = Short
	L = Long	L = Long	L = Long
Word length	S: 32 bits	S: 32 bits	S: 32 bits
	L: 64 bits	L: 64 bits	L: 64 bits
Exponent	7 bits	8 bits	S: 8 bits
			L: 11 bits
Significand	S: 6 digits	S: (1)+23 bits	S: (1)+23 bits
	L: 14 digits	L: (1)+55 bits	L: (1)+52 bits
Bias of exponent	64	128	S=127, L=1023
Radix	16	2	2
Hidden "1"	No	Yes	Yes
Radix point	Left of Fraction	Left of hidden "1"	Right of MSB†of frac.
Range of Fraction	$(1/16) \leq F < 1$	$0.5 \leq F < 1$	$1 \leq F < 2$
F representation	Signed magnitude	Signed magnitude	Signed magnitude
Approximate max. positive number	$16^{63} \simeq 10^{76}$	$2^{126} * \simeq 10^{38}$	$2^{1024} \simeq 10^{308}$ (L)
Precision	S: $16^{-6} \simeq 10^{-7}$	S: $2^{-24} \simeq 10^{-7}$	$S: 2^{-23} \simeq 10^{-7}$
	L: $16^{-14} \simeq 10^{-17}$	L: $2^{-56} \simeq 10^{-17}$	L: $2^{-52} \simeq 10^{-16}$

*Approximate maximum positive number, excluding reserved exponent representations.
†MSB—most significant bit.

2. Reals (both fixed- and floating-point representations).

Fixed point consists of both integer and fractional portions of fixed sizes that are manipulated much as integers (they are often called *scaled integers*), and yet represent non-integral values. The advantage of fixed-point numbers is that they provide real values with no overhead other than conversion over their limited range (determined by the fixed field sizes). One benefit of this representation is that the numbers may be treated in the software as if they were integers. Floating-point numbers are represented by a fractional value with an exponent multiplier. These numbers require significant conversion as well as care during some operations to ensure that numbers are "compatible" both before and after the operation (called *normalization*). The main advantage of floating-point numbers is the large range of numbers available—the IEEE double precision format can represent numbers from 2.2×10^{-308} up to 1.8×10^{308}. For comparison, a 64^b fixed-point number would have a maximum representation of about 10^{20}.

Floating-point numbers have a number of different representations; the most common systems include those used in System 390, VAX, and the IEEE floating point standard [144]. Most floating-point numbers fit in either a word (32 bits, or short floating representation), or a 64-bit double word operand. Floating-point numbers contain a sign specification, a representation of the fraction (mantissa or significand), and the exponent representation—either exponent plus sign or a characteristic in an excess code representation. A number of other aspects of a floating-point number are implied, i.e., understood by both the hardware and the programmer. These include the radix and the position at the radix point (analogous to the decimal point) as well as the use of the "hidden one." Since a normalized floating-point number always has a nonzero (i.e., a one) leading bit (with radix equal two), this bit may be implied to be one. Then only the remaining bits of the fraction need to be stored as data, thus saving a bit and allowing an extra bit of fraction significance. Some details of floating-point representations are shown in Table 1.3. Usually floating-point numbers are represented as

where char = biased exponent (characteristic). If char has p bits, then bias is typically $\frac{1}{2}$ (radix)^p and char = exponent + bias.[5] For example, in a system with bias = 128, the exponent of -3 is represented as 125. Use of this representation (rather than, say, two's-complement) allows very small numbers to have small absolute exponents and zero to have a zero exponent.

Thus, a number x is interpreted as

$$x = (-1)^s \times (\text{Radix})^{\text{char-bias}} \times (1).\text{mantissa},$$

where radix, bias, hidden "1," and radix point are all implied.

For example, the following are computational results and stored results (underlined data are stored as the mantissa):

(a) IBM S/390

Computed result 0.0101XXXX is stored as (.)<u>0101XXXX</u>, since no hidden "1" is used and "0101" is a normalized leading digit in *hexadecimal.*

(b) VAX

Computed result 0.0101XXXX is normalized to 0.101XXXX (with exponent decremented by one) and stored as (.)(1)<u>01XXXX</u>.

(c) IEEE

Computed result 0.0101XXXX is normalized to 1.01XXXX (with exponent decremented by two), then stored as (1)(.)<u>01XXXX</u>.

3. Decimals.

Decimal numbers represent the bulk of the calculations performed by business applications, as they can represent decimal (base 10) numbers with no loss of precision through data conversion. This format has two major problems. The first is that the implementation of decimal operations is slow, since the numbers are stored, one digit per byte, in ASCII ("unpacked") format or in two digit per byte binary coded decimal (BCD, or "packed") format, neither of which is natural for most machines to perform calculations. (See Figure 1.13.) Many of the early microprocessors, however, included specific instructions

---

[5]It is $2^{p-1} - 1$ for the IEEE standard.

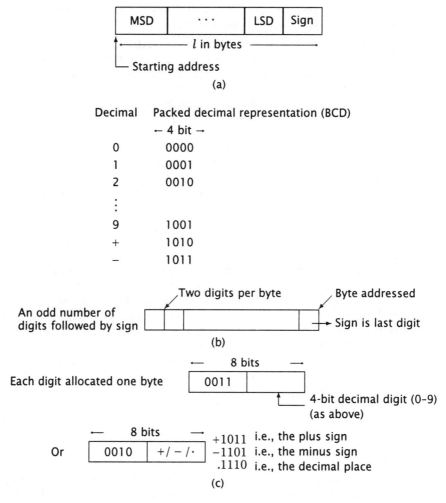

Figure 1.13   Decimal representation (ASCII). (a) Decimal number consists of a string of bytes in either packed (b) or unpacked (c) format. MSD/LSD indicate most/least significant digit.

to deal with these numbers, and often high-end business machines (e.g., the IBM mainframes) implement a number of features to allow these numbers to be efficiently processed. The second problem is that there is no representation standard and manufacturers choose different implementations for storing and processing decimal data (i.e., length indicators, etc.).

4. Characters.

Character strings are simply a sequence of a variable number of bytes. The length of the character string in bytes is specified in the instruction where this data representation is supported. The 256 representations available in a byte are defined by the ASCII standard format as representing various upper and lower case alphanumeric symbols together with special characters. The character string may be used to represent decimal or text information.

Numeric representation, especially as a standard (transportable) representation, involves many potentially damaging complications. For the most part, there is only minimal interest in being able to transfer binary data images between different machines, mostly due to the significant differences that are clearly present between implementations. Therefore, despite the increase in data space requirements, the majority of numerical data is represented in text form (using *characters*), which is easy[6] to convert. This is obviously true, as there are only two major conventions to be concerned with—IBM's EBCDIC (Extended Binary Coded Decimal Interchange Code) and the subsequently developed ASCII (American Standards Code for Information Interchange).

However, as one might expect, compatibility is not any more achievable for characters than it is in other areas. The incompatibility is due to a number of very subtle differences. Some machines use one end-of-line character, some use another, some use both (of course, in one order or the other—and it *does* matter!). Additionally, some use 6-bit ASCII (no lower case), others use 7-bit ASCII, and others use 8-bit ASCII (sometimes for parity, other times for additional information). Another incompatibility results from the problem of byte ordering (the Big-endian vs. Little-endian debate). Byte ordering is determined by whether the high (most significant) byte or the low byte is stored first (at the lowest address in memory)—for example, SUN SPARC and Motorola 680x0 use high-byte ordering ("Big-endian"), while DEC and Intel use low-byte ordering ("Little-endian"). Some machines, such as the MIPS processors, have user-selectable byte ordering, and many machines provide conversion instructions to aid the transfer of data.

5. Bits.

Binary bits are easy: no one *really* expects the interpretation of strings of bits to be consistent across machines and so no one really tries. These values are arbitrarily sized (although most machines limit them to the word size for the machine). They are also used to represent vectors of single-bit elements, which may be tested and changed (sometimes using dedicated instructions, often using only logical operations such as AND, OR, and NOT). There are two main applications for bit strings, of which only the first—communication with and control of input/output devices—is common. This application is a very low level communications process and is rarely of any interest for communicating between different machines. (Often even different hardware implementations of the same basic machine architecture use different input/output specifications.) The second application is in packing data to make the most efficient use of space. This is of concern in a few specific applications (such as a `packed record` in Pascal).

The preceding classes are not wholly disjoint, as character strings may represent decimal numbers, and reals may be manipulated as bit vectors (and integers) for format conversion. In many implementations, the integer and

---

[6]The alert reader will sense a calamity in the making for those foolish individuals who actually *believe* that anything in compatibility is *easy*.

floating-point representations for zero are the same—a bit vector of all 0 digits—whereas the decimal form is often represented as the character "0" followed by a length code of 1, or as the character string "0.0" followed by a length code of 3 and a sign digit; and yet, despite the different formats, all of these representations are equivalent to the same actual value!

Clearly, different processors have completely different data representations. Some representations are based on speed, others on compactness, and others seemingly on sheer perversity. For example, the Cray series of processors uses a proprietary floating-point representation that has as its main virtue the speed of the implementation, but has many representation anomalies (e.g., the number "one" multiplied by a very large number may cause an overflow). Almost every manufacturer has used at least one unique floating-point number format through the years. At one time, CDC supported at least five different (non-compatible) floating-point representations on their product line. It is only recently that new designs have started standardizing on a floating-point standard (IEEE Floating Point Standard, STD-754-1985), which was developed to standardize at least the *behavior* if not the actual storage allocation. Unfortunately, even this "standard" has different implementations depending on the level of adherence to the standard.

This text does not deal further with the details of number representation or execution unit design. While data representation issues may be significant secondary issues in determining processor performance, the influence is difficult to assess at the level of analysis performed in this text. In fact, any actual performance difference may only be determined by using actual traces from the processors. For example, certain data representations may facilitate conversions between representations, but may be computationally time-consuming. However, if the anticipated target application involves many conversions with sparsely distributed calculations, there may be a significant performance advantage in using this format. Another problem is that a data representation may have awkward side effects that require the elongation of the minimum cycle time or the addition of an extra cycle to process. This also has a significant impact on the overall performance of the machine. Each case must be considered on its own merit with regard to the known or expected target application.

Some issues concerning data formats are directly relevant to a discussion of processor performance. Knowledge of the various classes of data is required to construct an instruction set (examined in the next section). Additionally, certain properties of data representation (such as operand length) are significant in determining processor performance. For example, the longer the operand, the longer the instruction may take to execute.

Most processors define operand sizes in terms of words or bytes. The most common word size currently is 32 bits, but there are still many 8- and 16-bit machines in common use and 64-bit machines are available as well. There are also some more obscure word sizes in the marketplace. Most of these are older machines (such as the DEC PDP-8 at 12 bits, the DEC PDP-10 and the Univac 1108 at 36 bits, and the CDC Cyber 70 at 60 bits), with most new designs being restricted to word sizes of powers of 2, typically 32 or 64 bits. These figures represent the typical parameters corresponding to "mainstream" machines.

The IEEE Floating Point Standard and Its Users

While it is beyond the scope of this book to go into the details of the IEEE standard, the standard represents a significant contribution to improved accuracy of representation, completeness, and operational power. (For example, the IEEE standard supports four rounding modes—round to nearest, truncate, round positive, and round negative, in contrast to most machines with either no or one single rounding option.) The standard introduced the notion of denormalized numbers—a technique to preserve the accuracy and integrity of very small numbers, rather than set them to zero as done in other machines. The standard defines and supports square root, data conversion operations, and other operations which are not always found in floating-point operational repertoire. As a necessary consequence, the IEEE standard is somewhat difficult to implement. It is complex, and requires designers to add extra hardware to complete the full formation of resultant products, etc.

There are some ironies in all this. The IEEE standard is used with almost all microprocessor architectures, including the R/M (Intel x86) and all of the L/S architectures (the RISC microprocessors). Use of the IEEE standard with the RISC processors is particularly interesting. The IEEE standard at first glance appears to be the antithesis of the principles incorporated in the RISC machine design philosophy. It is complex and time-consuming, in both design time and execution time. It is exactly what the RISC machine philosophy was developed to overcome. Yet because it is a standard, few designers have even noted the philosophic inconsistency or irony in it all. It represents the adoption of two conflicting design styles or fashions.

There is yet another irony. The IEEE standard, with its extensive rounding support and support for data integrity, is most valuable in large-scale scientific computations which may go on for hours on the largest and most sophisticated of computers. The standard is least valuable in smaller workstation-type applications whose execution time rarely exceeds several minutes. Yet the supercomputer designers, such as Cray Corporation, use a very crude floating-point format supporting a minimum accuracy (minimum rounding flexibility) philosophy in the interest of speed. Most large scientific computations are carried out on supercomputers like the Cray by users who seem to prefer the reduced floating-point capability with perhaps reduced accuracy if providing high speed. Yet those workstation users who have access to the fully featured floating-point standard rarely have applications that really exercise its facilities.

Table 1.4 Orthogonal properties. Orthogonal instruction sets define *all* operations for *all* data types (all "x"s, below).

Operations	Half-word Integer—Short	Word Integer—Long	Double-word Floating-Point	
Add	x	x	x	
Subtract	x	x	x	
Multiply	x	x	x	
Divide	x	x	x	
Shift right	·	·	·	
Shift left	·	·	·	
AND	·	·	·	
OR	·	·	·	
NOT	·	·	·	
⋮				

The default precision of a machine is typically one *natural word* in size. A natural word is the word size that a machine *uses* as its normal word size. For example, the IBM S/390 series has a natural word size of 32 bits and older entries in the Intel x86 series have a natural word size of 16 bits. Many machines also provide operations on larger and smaller word sizes. (Frequent forms are half-word and long- or double-word, although other forms are possible.) The natural word size may be different from the hardware word size. For example, the Motorola 680x0 is advertised as a 32-bit processor and readily manipulates 32-bit values (its natural word size). However, the physical word size for many early implementations of this instruction set is 16 bits, since the internal data paths and logic are all 16 bits wide. Thus, the performance of a particular processor can be less than that of other 32-bit processors, which require an extra cycle to make a second pass through the logic unit to generate a double-length result. It is, however, significantly faster than the competing 16-bit processors, where the extra precision is required to be explicitly implemented in software.

1.5   Instructions

1.5.1   Classes of Operations

In many modern machines, the operation vocabulary (instruction set) has become rather extensive, as the number of standard operations is large and the variations in parameters (including addressing modes) are many. If all actions are defined for all data types, the instruction set is said to have the *orthogonal property* (Table 1.4). Most machines include a common core of operations that include:

- Integer arithmetic:

   add, subtract, multiply, divide,

- Logical:

    and, or, not, xor, shift, rotate,

- Control transfer:[7]

    jump, branch, trap.

Many machines have included additional instructions that many still consider to be part of the common core of operations:

- Floating-point arithmetic:

    add, subtract, multiply, divide, square root

- Bit manipulations:

    extract, insert, test, set, clear

- Comparison tests:

    less than or equal to, odd parity, carry

Depending on the application of the machine, operations may be included for character translation and coding (IBM S/390), decimal number manipulation (many business-targeted machines), enhanced math support (including transcendental and other functions), and so forth. Many machines even provide combination instructions (such as test and branch, multiply then add, etc.).

The addition of complex instructions to a machine has come back to haunt some designers. The DEC VAX, the Intel x86, and the Motorola 680x0 included a complex set of instructions to provide comprehensive facilities for the programmer. As the later models of these machines have been developed, many of the more complex (and less frequently used) instructions have been moved outside of a highly streamlined core processor to a separate microprogrammed processor or left entirely to software emulation. As the relative use of these instructions is very low, the practice of restricting the core processor to the commonly used operations has led to significant performance improvements in the majority of applications. Of course, those processes that use the emulated instructions frequently show dramatic performance degradation.

There is considerable diversity between machines with regard to simple operations alone. Figure 1.14 illustrates the situation for the ADD operation. Some machines have several different varieties of instructions to account for specific cases, such as unsigned or extended precision instructions. For example, as shown in Table 1.5, the IBM S/390 has about 10 ADD instructions, while the VAX has more than 25 different forms for ADD instructions. VAX programming is not for the faint of heart! In contrast, the MIPS R2000 has only four ADD instructions. The R2000 is closely coupled with the R2010 floating-point unit, which provides several additional ADD operations. The variety of types of ADD is shown for each machine in Tables 1.6–1.8.

---

[7]In this text, *jump* and *branch* are synonymous, with *branch* the preferred usage.

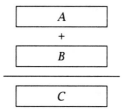

Figure 1.14 The ADD instruction. It might seem that there would be only a limited number of variations in creating the sum of two numbers.

Table 1.5 Some ADD operations in various machines.

IBM S/390	A, AR, AE, AD, AER, ADR, AP, AL, ALR
VAX	ACBB, ACBD, ACBF, ACBG, ACBH, ACBL, ACBW, ADAWI, ADDB2, ADDB3, ADDF2, ADDF3, ADDG2, ADDG3, ADDH2, ADDH3, ADDL2, ADDL3, ADDP4, ADDP6, ADDW2, ADDW3, ADDWC, AOBLEQ, AOBLSS.
MIPS R2000	ADD, ADDI, ADDIU, ADDU
R2010*	ADD.S, ADD.D

* The R2010 is the floating-point coprocessor for the R2000.

Table 1.6 A list of the principal ADD instructions in S/390 (R+M).

R+M data type designators

A	Add (32^b) integers (RM: Memory to Register)
AR	Add (32^b) integers (RR: Register to Register)
AE	Add Floating Point—32^b (RM)
AD	Add Floating Point—64^b (RM)
AER	AE (RR)
ADR	AD (RR)
AP	Add decimal, packed
AL	Add "logical"—32^b unsigned integers (RM)
ALR	AL (RR)

Table 1.7   A list of some ADD instructions in VAX machines (R+M).

B	=	Byte (1B)
W	=	Word (2B)
L	=	Long word (4B)
F	=	(32b)
D	=	(64b)
G	=	special type floating-point format (64b)
H	=	(128b)
ADDW2		Add integer "Word"—2 address
ADDW3		Add integer "Word"—3 address
ADDWC		Add integer (16 bits) With Carry
AOBLEQ		Add One and Branch Less than or Equal
AOBLSS		Add One and Branch Less than

Add, compare, and branch on integer—B, W, L:

ACBB	B (8 bits)
ACBW	W (16 bits)
ACBL	L (32 bits)

Add, compare, and branch on floating point—F, D, G, H:

ACBF	F (32 floating point)	
ACBD	D (64 floating point)	
ACBG	G (64 special floating point format)	
ACBH	H (128 special floating point format)	
ADAWI	Add Aligned Word Interlock	
ADDB2	Add B	—2 address
ADDB3		—3 address
ADDF2	Add F	—2 address
ADDF3		—3 address
ADDG2	Add G	—2 address
ADDG3		—3 address
ADDH2	Add H	—2 address
ADDH3		—3 address
ADDL2	Add L	—2 address
ADDL3		—3 address
ADDD2	Add D	—2 address
ADDD3		—3 address
ADDP4	Add Packed 4-byte operand	
ADDP6	Add Packed 6-byte operand	

Table 1.8   A list of the principal ADD instructions found in MIPS machines (L/S).

ADD	Add 32b integers
ADDU	Add 32b unsigned integers
ADDI	Add integers using an immediate operand
ADDIU	Add unsigned integers using an immediate operand
ADD.S	Floating-point—single precision
ADD.D	Floating-point—double precision

Table 1.9   Some mnemonics for an ADD instruction. (The purpose is to add two integer words contained in two registers, R1 and R2, and put the result in R1.)

S/390	AR	R1, R2
MIPS Co. R2000	ADD	R1, R1, R2
VAX	ADDL2	R2, R1
Intel 80386	ADD	EAX, EBX
M680x0	ADD.L	D2, D1

1.5.2   Instruction Mnemonics

Another problem in analyzing machines is that the instruction *mnemonics*, or assembly representation, are even less consistent than operations. For example, one early machine[8] used the mnemonic TAD to represent subtraction because it emphasized the number representation in use on that machine. (In a two's-complement number system, subtraction can be thought of as Two's complement ADdition.) Most machines use a variation of SUB for SUBtraction.

Unfortunately, although there have been several attempts, no standard for instruction set mnemonics has been adopted. Each vendor uses its own assembly language syntax, often creating obscure glyphs for no particular reason. Sometimes, as with the Intel 8080, the mnemonics have been copyrighted, making compatibility or even similarity subject to copyright infringement.

Not only are the mnemonics inconsistent (Table 1.9), but some machines have adopted the convention that the destination is the first parameter, while others have adopted the convention that the destination is the last parameter. A few have even tried to define algebraic-like assembly language constructs. A few examples of instructions implementing the simple addition $A = B + C$ follow:

> *Example 1:*   ADD   A, B, C
> *Example 2:*   ADD   B, C, A
> *Example 3:*   A = B + C

---

[8]The DEC PDP-8.

These examples do not reflect the variation in mnemonics, but only a few variations in operand specification. The preceding instructions take three arguments: two source and one destination. This is not always the case; many times it is necessary to duplicate one of the arguments because the two-argument instructions are really of the form B = B + C, which generates a similar result (B + C), but destroys one of the arguments (B, the first source) in the process. This kind of result is typical of the R/M machine type, and the three-argument instructions are typical of the L/S machine type. Many R+M machine types have both two- and three-argument instructions.

The latest attempt to standardize the assembly language mnemonics is the IEEE Working Group for IEEE P694 [26],[9] which, like its predecessors, has not met with much success in the industry. There are several reasons for this. A standard removes much of the distinction between different machines. Certainly, the actual set of implemented operations would be different, but a careful programmer might never have to know what machine was being worked on. This could be a marketing crisis! Another problem is that there really is no accepted core of operations. Certainly, addition, multiplication, etc., are present in any machine, but some machines implement combined instructions (the VAX ACBW combines an addition (16 bits), a comparison, and a branch all in one instruction!), register sets are varied in number, nomenclature, and qualities (some machines even implement a register set organized as a *stack* of register subsets to improve context switch performance), and so on. Each machine (at the assembly level) is very different, making a standard a herculean task.

1.5.3   General Machine Conventions

This book follows the spirit of the proposed IEEE standard mentioned before. We define only a few basic operation mnemonics. This will, hopefully, provide a clear understanding of the *intent* of the examples as well as instill a sense of simplicity that the reader may remember as the proud parent of a new processor instruction set.

The convention followed in this book is simple. Instruction mnemonics consist of an operation and a data type specification concatenated together with a "." separating the two portions of the mnemonic for clarity. Thus, an integer word addition is written ADD.W (or simply ADD, if there is no ambiguity) and a floating-point multiplication is written MPY.F. A similar format is used for branch conditions in place of the data type specification, so that a branch on less than or equal to would be written BC.LE. The mnemonics and modifier fields are chosen for simplicity and would, of course, be more complicated if the instruction to be represented were:

> ...multiply the sine of the first operand by the arctangent of the second operand and add it to the contents of the destination operand, branching on less than or equal to the value of the third operand to a target address continued in the fourth operand.

For the most part, the mnemonics used in this book are limited to the ones listed in Tables 1.10, 1.11, and 1.12. Special cases are explained in the text when required. These tables are not intended to be complete. They

---

[9]Not to be confused with the IEEE floating point standard, STD-754-1985.

Table 1.10   Instruction set mnemonic elements.

Mnemonic	Operation
ADD	Addition
SUB	Subtraction
MPY	Multiplication
DIV	Division
INC	Increment
DEC	Decrement
CMP	Compare
MOVE	Decimal (.P) or Character (.C) Move
CLR	Clear (a register)
LD	Load (a register from memory)
ST	Store (a register to memory)
LDA	Load address (generated by instr) into register
LDM	Load multiple registers
STM	Store multiple registers
MOVE	Move (register to register or memory to memory)
SHL	Shift Left
SHR	Shift Right
BR	Unconditional Branch
BC	Conditional Branch
BAL	Branch and Link
BALR	Branch to Register and Link

merely indicate some of the generic operations used throughout the text and provide a general framework.

Many commercial assemblers allow the programmer to specify the operand, and the assembler infers the data type from its knowledge of the operands. Thus, if the location someLoc were defined to be a double-precision floating-point value, then the instruction LD R15, someLoc would generate the identical code as LD.D R15, someLoc. Additionally, when there is no explicit type information in the instruction, as in MPY R2, R14, R4, the assembler assumes that the data type is a standard machine word, and thus the instruction generated is the same as MPY.W R2, R14, R4. In this book, the goal is clarity, and thus a formal data type is usually appended to the operation mnemonic.

Register usage is clear from context—a binary operation (such as addition) is a three-operand instruction if there are three operands, a two-operand instruction if there are two operands, and similarly for unary operations. The first register (or memory address) specified is the destination; this reflects the similarity with algebraic notation. Thus, the instructions specified by DIV.W A, B would generate the result $A = A$ DIV B, and those specified by NOT.W A, B would generate the result $A = $ NOT B. These conventions are summarized in Table 1.13.

Table 1.11   Data type modifiers (OP.modifier).

Modifier	Data Type
B	Byte (8 bits)
UB	Unsigned Byte (8 bits)
H	Half Word (16 bits)
UH	Unsigned Half Word (16 bits)
W	Word (32 bits)
UW	Unsigned Word (32 bits)
F	Floating Point (32 bits)
D	Double Precision Floating Point (64 bits)
C	Character or Decimal in an 8-bit format
P	Decimal in a packed (4-bit) format

Table 1.12   Branch conditions—BC.CC.

CC	Condition	CC	Condition
T	True (always)	LE	Less Than or Equal
F	False (never)	LT	Less Than
V	Overflow	EQ	Equal
C	Carry or Borrow	NE	Not Equal
PE	Even Parity	GE	Greater Than or Equal
PO	Odd Parity	GT	Greater Than

Table 1.13   Three conventions used in this book: ALU instruction.

Case 1	OP.X Destination, Source 1, Source 2
	(three operand format)
	or
Case 2	OP.X Destination, Source
	(if only two operands are specified)
	or
Case 3	OP.X Destination/Source 1, Source 2
	(here OP uses two source operands
	and rewrites the result in the source 1 location)

(OP indicates an ALU operation and X indicates a data type/size. Case 1 is used in L/S machines, case 3 in R/M. The OP type distinguishes case 2 from the others. The R+M machines use all three cases. The formats are distinguished implicitly by OP or explicitly by a special OP identifier, e.g., ADD2 or ADD3.)

Store (ST) and move (MOVE) instructions are, to a degree, synonymous. We use STORE when the source argument is a register and the destination is memory. Thus,

    ST A,R1

places the contents of (general register) R1 in memory location A, and

    ST.F A,R1

places the contents of floating register R1 in memory location A.

We use the MOVE construct in a more general way. Usually, MOVE implies that both source and destination operands are in memory, or both are in registers. Thus,

    MOVE A,B

would replace (the word at memory location) A with (the word at memory location) B. Commonly, MOVE is used for strings of characters or decimal numbers. Thus,

    MOVE.C A,B

moves the character string starting at memory location B to A. There is usually a length component associated with A and B, so that we probably should indicate

    MOVE.C (l_1, l_2) A,B,

where l_1 and l_2 are the byte lengths of A and B, respectively. For purposes of this text, we frequently do not need to make these specifications, so that in MOVE.C A,B, the lengths of A and B are assumed to be defined earlier and known.

There is a special type of move associated with decimal arithmetic, called ZMOVE:

    ZMOVE.P A,B.

This decimal move (packed format) operation requires that $l_1 \geq l_2$ and that all leading digits of l_1 (the destination, or A in the above) be zeroed out. For strings, MOVE.C and ZMOVE.P are the two most frequently encountered operations.

MOVE can have a role for all register operands moving a value from one register to another, so that

    MOVE.F R1,R2

has the same effect as moving the value in floating-point register R2 to R1.

Table 1.14   Conventions used in this book: branches.

BR	Target (an unconditional branch to the instruction contained in target).
BC	Target (a conditional branch without a specific condition code identified).
BC.CC	Target (same as BC).
BC.NE	Target (a conditional branch with a condition code specified).
BCT.NE	R1, Target (a conditional branch used for loop control. A count in R1 is decremented; if the result is ≠ 0 control goes to the target).
BAL	Target (an unconditional branch that saves the current IC in an implied register).
BALR	R_{target} (same as BAL except that the target instruction *location* (address) is contained in R_{target}).

1.5.4   Branches

Branches (sometimes called *jumps*) determine program control flow. We distinguish between unconditional BR and conditional BC, since this represents an important timing difference in our later analysis. The BC tests the state of the condition code, or CC, which consists of (usually) four bits that reside in the program status word (PSW) described later. We assume that the condition code is set by each ALU instruction (some machines cause even load and store instructions to set the CC); see Figure 1.15. The condition code also records one of four results (encoded in four bits); that is, specifying whether the condition setting instruction had generated:

1. A positive result.

2. A negative result.

3. A zero result.

4. A result that overflowed.

Conditions of interest to us are presented in Table 1.12. Branch conventions are outlined in Table 1.14.

Clearly, we could construct BR from BC.T using the BC instruction (i.e., BR is the same as BC.T). We choose to explicitly distinguish between these instructions, as they each have significantly different timing implications for a design.

In supporting the branch-on-condition instruction, most architectures include a group of compare instructions (CMP), which simply compare two values, either both in registers (L/S) or various combinations of operands in register and in memory (in the R/M or R+M architectures) to force the setting of a condition code. The compare instruction is an arithmetic compare (it interprets the sign bits), whereas compare logical is a logical, or unsigned, comparison (CMP.U) that treats operands as unsigned quantities.

Setting the condition code

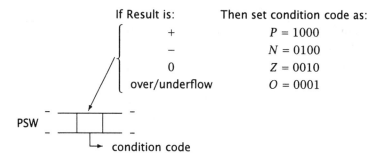

	If Result is:	Then set condition code as:
	+	$P = 1000$
	−	$N = 0100$
	0	$Z = 0010$
	over/underflow	$O = 0001$

PSW

condition code

Using the condition code

Mask

| BC | |

A BC instruction uses a mask to test for a particular condition or combination of conditions. The four-bit mask is ANDed with the four condition code states, $PNZO$; these result bits are then ORed to determine the outcome. If the result is "1," the branch is taken (i.e., is successful); if the result is "0," the branch is not taken and sequencing continues in line.

Mask = 0000	is no op, since all conditions are masked out—producing 0s from the ANDing operation.
Mask = 1111	is unconditional branch, since the previous computation must have produced *some* result (P, N, Z, O) and at least one mask AND condition will be true.
Mask = 1010	selects the condition P or Z, and branch is taken if result is ≥ 0 (e.g., BC.GE).
Mask = 0110	Similarly, the condition selected is N or Z, and branch is taken if result is ≤ 0 (e.g., BC.LE).

Figure 1.15   Examples of setting and using the condition code.

Many architectures include special support for loop control by branch-on-count-type instructions. In branch-on-count (BCT), the contents of a specified register are decremented by one and then tested. If the contents are nonzero, control transfers to the second operand address. The condition code is both untested and unaffected. This can be generalized where an arbitrary value can be used in place of the "one" used in the BCT. An index value contained in a register is added to a first operand register, and the result is compared to an unnamed implied register. If the new sum is less than or equal to the contents of the implied register, transfer of control takes place to the address specified by the third operand; otherwise, control passes to the next instruction in sequence. This add, compare, and branch sequence is in the VAX instruction repertoire. RISC processors forego these extended loop control instructions, since they can be synthesized from sequences of ALU and branch-on-condition instructions.

Table 1.15   Addressing mode summary.

Mode	Specification	Explanation
Register	R*X*	Register *X*
Memory	ADDR	Address specified by ADDR
Indirect	[R*X*]	Address specified by the contents of R*X*
Indexed	OFFSET[R*X*]	Address specified by OFFSET plus contents of R*X*
Immediate	#*val*	The value *val*

1.5.5   Register Sets and Addressing Modes

Another area where there is virtually no hope of standardization is in *referencing* data. The simplest form of data addressing is accessing registers. While most processors use numbered registers, some processors (such as the Intel x86 series) use named registers,[10] and others (such as the Motorola 680x0 series) use several different sets of numbered registers, each with a different specifier.

Some instructions use implied registers that are not named by the instruction, but are used nonetheless. The most common instructions of this sort are jump and branch instructions—the PC register is inferred from the instruction. Older microprocessor architectures, such as the Intel x86 series, used many implicit register references.

As was mentioned earlier, even the order of register arguments for an instruction varies. Often, registers may be part of the general-purpose register set but have predefined meanings. The most common predefined register used in such a way is the stack pointer. More recently, processors have begun to define register 0 to have the value "0." This has several advantages. First, 0 is a commonly used value in both data (for example, in comparisons) and memory reference (as in a 0 index or offset) instructions. Additionally, having a 0 value removes the need for special operations (such as a move or a clear of the destination). Consider the following four operand instructions:

```
ADD.W   R3, R0, #14h   ;load the value 14 (hexadecimal) into R3
ADD.W   R6, R0, R1     ;move R1 to R6
SUB.W   R0, R11, R8    ;compare R11 and R8 (condition code
                       ;to be tested later)
AND.B   R0, R5, #02h   ;test for bit 1 set (condition code
                       ;to be tested later)
```

Each of the preceding instructions can functionally replace a completely unrelated instruction (e.g., CMP.W with SUB.W), thus reducing the number of instructions required and therefore the complexity of the machine.

Table 1.15 summarizes the modes that this text uses. Note that when specific values are not necessary, italicized prototypes (R_d for destination, R_{s1}

[10]The Intel x86 actually has different names for registers to distinguish between different data types—thus, EAX is a 32-bit register, AX is the low 16 bits of the EAX register, and AH and AL are the high and low bytes of the AX register.

Table 1.16   Operand value format summary.

#*val*d	The decimal value *val*
#*val*h	The hex value *val*
#*val*b	The binary value *val*
#*val*q	The octal value *val*
'*char*'	The value of the character *char*

and R_{s2} for sources) are used to specify general cases in the text. Thus, ADD.x R_d, R_{s1}, R_{s2} is a general addition and ADD.x   R5, R11, R0 is a specific add using registers 5, 11, and 0. The usage of the .x suffix indicates that no specific addressing mode is being used but that any compatible mode would work. Table 1.16 summarizes the operand representations used in this book.

One point to note is that many machines do not differentiate between memory, indirect, and indexed addressing modes—when using only a 0 offset, the result is the same as if a simple indirect mode were used, and using only a 0 index is the same as a simple memory mode (within the address limitation of the offset field), i.e.:

$$0[R_X] = [R_X]$$

and

$$X = X[0].$$

Many more modes are possible, including secondary memory indirections and multiple index sources. One very common complex instruction includes automatic incrementing and decrementing of the value in a register or memory address in conjunction with a reference. These instructions are frequently used in implementing loops and stacks and are occasionally found in some computer languages.[11] Although there are definite connections between architectures and computer languages, often a well-designed "general-purpose" computer outperforms a "language-based" computer in many applications. This is often due to the overhead of implementing high-level language constructs in hardware. For the most part, in this text we limit ourselves to the basic modes specified in the table. When the use of more complex addressing modes is required, explanations are provided on an as-needed basis.

1.5.6   Instruction Code Examples

This section attempts to tie together the earlier sections on instruction set characteristics. We show several short fragments from an R/M machine, an L/S machine, and an R+M machine. As a first example, the following code fragment implements a vector summation (for an R/M architecture):

---

[11] The C programming language includes pre- and post-increment and -decrement instructions which correspond directly to these addressing modes.

```
entry:   LD.W  R1, xCounter          ;get x size from memory
         LD.W  R2, xBaseAddress      ;get the base value
         LD.W  R3, #0                ;initialize sum to 0
loop:    ADD.W R3, [R2]              ;add next element
                                     ;in memory to sum
         ADD.W R2, #wordSize         ;point to next element
         SUB.W R1, #1                ;decrement length counter
                                     ;and check for end of list
         BC.NE loop                 ;and continue until done
         ST.W  xSumAddress, R3       ;now write out the sum
         END
```

There are several details to note about the preceding example. First, the instructions are all in two-operand format. Thus, the ADD.W R3, [R2] instruction is equivalent to ADD.W R3, O[R2]—the "O" is understood to be the offset if not specified. This in turn is equivalent to $R3 = R3 + [R2]$. Secondly, the instruction ADD.W R2, #wordSize must manually specify the increment, as the processor does not know the actual word size pointed to by the register. In fact, it does not even know that the value contained in the register is really an address. Finally, we could easily have dropped the .W from the OP since the use of 32-bit words is understood.

A variation of the preceding program using an L/S machine might look like this:

```
entry:   LD.W   R1, xCounter          ;get x size from memory
         LD.W   R2, xBaseAddress      ;and get the base value
         LD.W   R3, #0                ;initialize sum to 0
loop:    LD.W   R4, [R2]              ;get next word from memory
         ADD.W  R3, R3, R4            ;add next element to sum
         ADD.W  R2, R2, #wordSize     ;point to next element
         SUB.W  R1, R1, #1            ;decrement length counter
                                       and check for end of list
         BC.NE  loop, R1              ;and continue until done
         ST.W   xSumAddress, R3       ;now write out the sum
         END
```

Several points should be noted about this example. First, all operands are three-operand format, with the exception of memory references. Second, there is no dedicated compare instruction—the comparison is actually a simple test of the register contents for "0," and indicated in the condition code. Some machines (such as a VAX) would rewrite the two instructions to add the element and increment the pointer into one instruction such as ADD.W R3, [R2++], which automatically increments the address by one data unit (in this case, one word size). The advantage of this is that it combines two instructions, saving memory and cache space. The entire program could have been rewritten much more succinctly on an R+M machine. Taking advantage of the features of a complex instruction set, consider the following code:

```
entry:    LD.W      R1, xCounter          ;get x size from memory
          LD.W      R2, xBaseAddress      ;get the base value
          CLR.W     xSumAddress           ;initialize sum to 0
loop:     ADD.W     xSumAddress, [R2++]   ;add next element to sum
          BCT.NE    R1, loop              ;and continue until done
          END
```

There is an instruction to load an address into a register (LD.W), an instruction to clear a memory location (CLR.W), an instruction that decrements a register and branches if not zero (BCT.NE), and an instruction with an an addressing mode that uses a register as an index value and then increments it by the appropriate amount based on the data type specified. However, there are other considerations in machine design that make the R+M approach less attractive. For example, in order to perform these instructions without penalty, an additional adder might be required to perform the address increment without conflicting with other instructions (such as the following BCT.NE instruction, which performs both a subtract (by one word size) and an effective address calculation). Thus, the actual utility of such an instruction (although common in many machines) must be considered on a case-by-case basis.

Several final simplifications should be noted. First, there is no use of BC.T—this is used sparingly in this text, as statistically it is an uncommon instruction. Second, there is no consideration whether the branch to loop is relative to the program counter or absolute (relative to some special base register). Code that references absolute addresses must always be run at *exactly* the same locations and may therefore be less versatile. Either of these alternatives could expand the address modes specified in Table 1.15. Third, no detailed consideration of condition codes is made. It is assumed that appropriate condition codes are used. The timing of condition code[12] setting is extremely important for program branching, as we shall also see.

1.5.7   Other Instruction Set Issues

System States and Sequencing

Rather than distribute various pieces of control information throughout the processor, modern instruction sets tend to collect them into a single *program status word* (PSW), thus facilitating change of control operations (supervisor call—i.e., call to the operating system—interrupt, etc.).

The PSW (Figure 1.16) usually includes both user-defined control information, such as:

1. Condition code: defining whether the result of the preceding instruction was = 0, > 0, < 0, or overflow.

2. Current instruction address (if not, as in VAX, in a specified register).

---

[12]Some of the first "RISC" machines did away with condition codes entirely—the sole conditional branch mechanism was to test a register for 0 (very fast to implement) and then to provide a collection of test and set instructions to store the truth or falsity in a destination register. This has become less common as other hardware and software techniques have increased the performance of branches without eliminating condition codes.

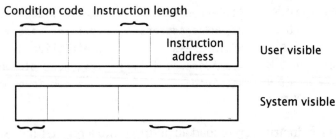

Figure 1.16   An example of a program status word (PSW).

3. Current instruction length: the number of bytes to be added to the PC.

4. Mask bits to enable or disable floating-point/fixed point/decimal over-flow.

5. Odd or even parity information.

and system information pertaining to the particular user:

1. User id: a pointer to the address regions that belong to this particular user.

2. Protection information.

3. Supervisor/user state: an indication of whether the user program or the operating system is being run.

4. Wait/run state: an indication of whether useful work is being performed.

5. Machine check mask enable: if an error occurs, processing may either cease or continue (perhaps to retry an operation or to run a diagnostic program).

6. I/O channel mask(s): a particular program may not wish to be interrupted to be notified that certain I/O information is available.

Mainframes generally have a large PSW that includes all of the preceding features, while most microprocessers have a simpler PSW, including user-defined condition code, user-enabled arithmetic masks, trap indicator for program debugging, and a system-defined access code to indicate the level of privilege of the routine that called the current process.

Sequencing: Task-to-Task and Task-to-Supervisor

Control must pass from one program module to another in an orderly fashion, and when its execution is complete, control must be returned to the program module that called it. Three types of events may force program control to move from one module to another:

1. An instruction that explicitly calls another module.

2. A trap—an unusual data condition that arises during the course of the execution of a module and that implicitly calls the operating system or a service module. (Also, special or undefined opcodes can be used as traps to support particular operating systems functions.)

3. An interrupt—a concurrently executing process module or an external event that notifies the executing module of an event of mutual interest. For example, the power supply system may be able to notify (interrupt) a program several milliseconds before power fails, allowing some measure of data recovery.

For our purposes, we are concerned only with the control that the instruction set exercises on the sequencing of modules to realize program execution. The simplest type of program transfer is branch and link (BAL) in System/390 or branch to subroutine (BSB) in VAX. In either of these instructions, the program counter is saved in a designated register and an unconditional branch is executed to a destination specified in the instruction.

A generalization of this is a call instruction found on VAX (CALLG). Not only does control pass to a new location, but an argument list is also specified in the instruction in the form of a pointer. This points to the first of several arguments that have been prepared by the calling module for use by the caller. In SPARC, the passing of arguments is accomplished simply by moving a register window. As will be discussed later, windowing consists of a series of overlapping register sets within which arguments are prepared by the calling module. These arguments are prepared in the upper end of the caller's register set space; when control passes, these same registers become the lower part of the callee's register set.

Frequently a user procedure must call on the operating system for service: e.g., request for additional memory, a call to the supervisor, or a call causing a change of mode (kernel executive, supervisor, user).

Usually, most architectures are more similar than different insofar as their control structure is concerned; the differences that do exist reflect the amount of information contained in the PSW, or the number of states available to distinguish among users and various levels of protection.

1.5.8   Program Size

Program size (static or dynamic) is determined by the number of instructions involved and the size of each instruction. The type and variability of instruction formats play a key role in both of these qualities. Figure 1.17 shows the various instruction sizes assumed for each of the prototypical architectures used in the text. Our R+M prototype is only a rough approximation of a machine such as a VAX, whose instruction size is byte-variable from 1 to 19 bytes!

We designate each format by the number and types of addresses it specifies. Thus, the L/S architecture has two basic formats: RRR (specifying three distinct registers for an ALU operation) and RM (specifying a register and a memory address, perhaps including offset and base register). All L/S

L/S Machine:

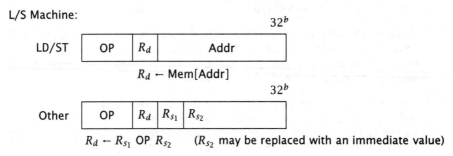

R/M—three basic instruction sizes (using two address format):

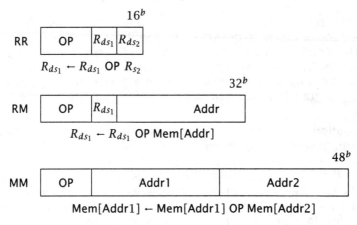

Figure 1.17 Instruction size for various instruction formats L/S and R/M.

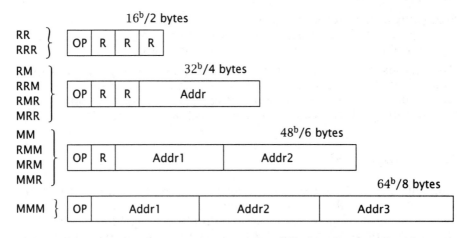

Figure 1.18 Assumed instruction size for differing formats for the R+M architecture. Current examples of R+M machines use byte-variable instructions (VAX, M680x0, etc.). For our purposes, we assume a simpler R+M instruction layout of four basic sizes, 16 through 64 bits, differing by the number of memory (or literal) specifiers required. In dealing with R+M byte-variable instruction sets, the reader should interpret the preceding sizes as the expected instruction sizes for each of the indicated formats.

instructions are a single word (32 bits) in size. In R/M, the source and destination are the same register, designated R_{ds1}. The R+M includes many more formats; the variety is shown in Figure 1.18. In Figures 1.17 and 1.18, the address represents space for base and index register indicators as well as a memory address or offset value.

Even when the format is known, other details, such as the operand addressing mode, may in actual situations determine an instruction's size. For example,

```
OP  R1, [R2]
```

may in some R/M or R+M machines be representable in a 16-bit RR format while in other machines be (implicitly) representable as

```
OP  R1, O[R2]
```

that is, in a 32-bit R/M format. We usually assume that such non-direct register mode requires the "RM" format. Thus, in an R/M machine,

```
OP   R1, [R2]
OP   R1, #value
LDA  R1, disp[Rbase, Rindex]
```

all require the 32-bit RM format. The LDA instruction simply loads the indicated address into R1, where disp indicates an address displacement, R_{base} a base register, and R_{index} an index register.

1.6   Addressing and Memory

Addressing in modern machines consists of several levels of address mappings [69, 70, 161]. Each level (the user program, the operating system, or the hardware manager) provides special services for the user.

Generally, we can describe three levels of addressing (Figure 1.19):

1. The *process* or *user program level.* At this level, the primary concern is with the efficient representation of user statements.

2. The *system level.* The primary concern is with multiple processes sharing a fixed address space. Issues include relocation and protection.

3. The *memory level.* This is the set (or sets) of physical locations used to interpret level 1 and 2 addresses. The primary concern is with access time. A memory manager is responsible for the prediction of localities (or *working sets*) that are about to be used so that they can be readied (accessed) by the processor.

1.6.1   Process Addressing

The designer must provide the user with facilities for efficiently addressing a large number of objects. In almost all modern processors, the basic

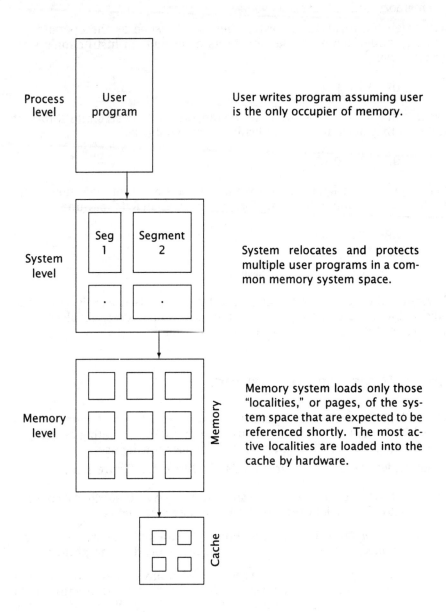

Process level — User program — User writes program assuming user is the only occupier of memory.

System level — Seg 1 | Segment 2 — System relocates and protects multiple user programs in a common memory system space.

Memory level — Memory — Memory system loads only those "localities," or pages, of the system space that are expected to be referenced shortly. The most active localities are loaded into the cache by hardware.

Cache

Figure 1.19   Three levels of addressing.

address resolution is to the byte. In order to maintain a bit-efficient instruction layout in memory, processors adopt an offset + base (offset[R_B]) address format. The base value contained in R_B defines the starting point of a region of user memory. Within this region, items are addressed by the *offset*. Indexing and literal facilities also reduce cache size, providing for offset[R_B, R_X] or #value. Index values contained in R_X usually represent a dimension of the data structure underlying the data being processed. Often these offsets are adjusted by multiplying by the reference size, as in an array subscript. This is relatively fast, as this multiplication is typically a power of 2 and may be performed using a shift instead of an actual multiplication. We assume our processors have these facilities without concerning ourselves with the details of how they are specified (i.e., the bit allocation) in the instruction layout.

The Curse of Register Modes!

Register modes provide an orderly arrangement for specifying the use of a register. They were regarded as a significant improvement in minicomputer instruction set design when introduced in 1967 by DEC in the PDP-11.

They can have an unfortunate consequence for pipelined processor designs, however, especially when the size of the instruction being executed *depends* on the specified mode. Here the starting point of the next instruction or even the next operand is unknown until both the opcode and subsequently the register mode are decoded.

This *significantly* complicates the advanced fetching and alignment of yet-to-be-executed instructions.

Often (especially in R+M processors) extended address facilities are made available in the instruction by the use of address mode bits. An elaborate set mode bit is found in VAX (see Table 1.17) and M680x0 family processors. As not all modes are used with the same frequency, various mode subsets or other arrangements (encoding mode information in the opcode or including special mode bytes) have also been popular.

1.6.2   System Addresses and Segmentation

Most modern system applications require the cooperation of multiple independently written programs (processes). Each process must be relocated and protected with respect to other processes to insure both correct operation and that errant processes are restricted to their own scope.

The basic mechanism usually employed to accomplish this is a *segmented address space*. The overall address space is broken up into units (segments), each with its own *base and bound* register (Figure 1.20). The operating system (itself operating in a segment) manages the collection of these registers (sometimes called control registers). The upper bits of the user (process) address can be used to address different segments. A typical segmented address computation is shown in Figure 1.21. The upper process address (6 to 8 bits) addresses a segment table (in registers or memory). The base

Table 1.17 VAX register modes. Specifier in hexadecimal.

Mode	Specifier	Description
Short Literal	0–3	The literal value is contained in bits 0 through 5 of the operand specifier.
Index	4	The effective address of the operand is formed by first calculating the effective address of the array base, and then adding the value of the index register multiplied by the size of each array element.
Register	5	The register contains the operand.
Register Deferred	6	The register contains the address of the operand.
Autodecrement	7	Register is decremented by the size of the operand in bytes and then used as the address of the operand.
Autoincrement	8	Register is used as the address of the operand and then incremented by the size of the operand in bytes.
Autoincrement Deferred	9	Address in register is a pointer to the effective address of the operand. Register is incremented by 4 after being used to access the effective address.
Byte Displacement	A	Displacement is sign-extended to 32 bits and added to the register to form the effective address.
Byte Displacement Deferred	B	Displacement is sign-extended to 32 bits and added to the register to form a pointer to the effective address.
Half-Word (16^b) Displacement	C	Displacement is sign-extended to 32 bits and added to the register to form the effective address.
Half-Word Displacement Deferred	D	Displacement is sign-extended to 32 bits and added to the register to form a pointer to the effective address.
Long Displacement	E	Displacement is added to the register to form the effective address.
Long Displacement Deferred	F	Displacement is added to the register to form a pointer to the effective address.

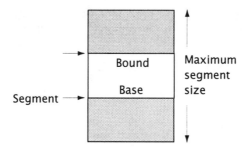

Figure 1.20   Segmented address.

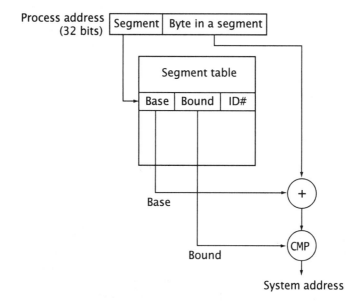

Figure 1.21   Segmented address computation.

address is added to the lower (or some of the lower) bits of the process address, providing a relocated address. This relocated address is compared to a segment bound address to ensure the reference is within the allocated segment size. Typically, maximum segment sizes range from 1–64 MB, although some architectures support 256 MB (the IBM PowerPC) and HP supports "spaces" of up to 4 GB.

The system process must have all the addressing facilities of a user process, *plus* the access to segment and/or control registers to control the behavior of all of the processes in the system.

1.6.3   Memory Space

Memory space involves the physical arrangement of memory regions or localities in the memory hierarchy. There are basically three parameters that the system observes: the memory space *latency*, memory space *bandwidth*, and memory space *size*.

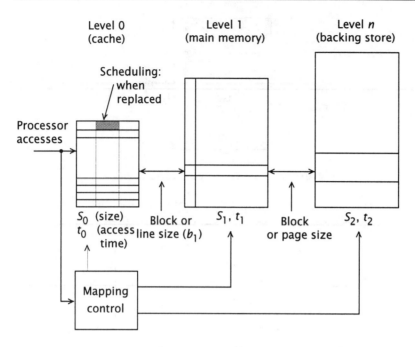

Figure 1.22   Memory space.

Latency is the time for a particular request to be completed. *Bandwidth* refers to the number of requests supplied per unit time. In order to provide large memory spaces with desirable access time (latency) and bandwidths, modern memory systems employ multiple levels of storage (Figure 1.22). Smaller, faster levels have greater cost per bit than larger, slower levels. If there are n levels in the storage hierarchy, then the levels may be ordered by their size and access time from S_0, t_0 for the smallest, closest level to S_{n-1}, t_{n-1} for the largest level. The goal of a good memory system design is to provide the processor with an effective memory space of S_{n-1} with an access time close to t_0. How well this goal is achieved depends on a number of factors—the physical characteristics of the device used in each level as well as the behavioral properties of the processes being executed.

Typically, the actual physical memory space consists of a three-level hierarchy consisting of a cache (L_0), a main memory (L_1), and a disk or backing storage (L_2), which contains the entire virtual memory space. Typical size (S) and access time ratios (t) are:

$$\frac{S_1}{S_0} \sim 10 - 100, \qquad \frac{t_1}{t_0} \sim 10,$$

$$\frac{S_2}{S_1} \sim 10 - 100, \qquad \frac{t_2}{t_1} \sim 10,000.$$

Associated with both the L_0 storage (the cache) and the L_1 storage (main memory) are the corresponding tables T_0 and T_1. T_1 contains the *working set* of S_2 (the disk)—those disk localities that have been recently referenced and are contained in main memory [25, 69]. T_1 is the same as the page table shown in Figure 1.23. T_0 is completely managed by the hardware in a way transparent even to the operating system, and it contains a working set of

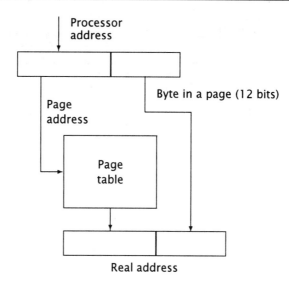

Figure 1.23   Paging process.

L_1—those localities (called *lines*) of L_1 that have been recently referenced by the program. Thus, the overall action by the system consists of the generation of a *virtual effective address*, its translation into a *real address* (a main memory address), and the use of this real address to access the T_0 table to find the entry in the cache for the desired value.

Paging and caching are the mechanisms to support the efficient management of the memory space. Caches are discussed in detail in Chapter 5. Paging is the mechanism by which the operating system brings fixed-size blocks (or pages)—a typical size is 4^{KB}—into main memory. Pages are fetched from backing store (usually disk) on demand (or as required) by the processor. When a referenced page is not present, the operating system is called and makes a request for the page, then transfers control to another process, allowing the processor resources to be utilized while waiting for the return of the requested information.

Figure 1.23 shows a simplified paged memory access. The resultant address (the "real address") is used to access the cache and main memory. The low-order (least significant) 12 bits address a particular location in a 4,096-byte page. The upper bits address a page table (in memory) that (1) determines whether this particular partial page lies in memory and (2) translates the upper address bits if the page is present.

1.7   Virtual to Real Mapping

Usually, the tables performing address translation are in memory, and a mechanism for the translation called the *translation lookaside buffer* (TLB) must be used to speed up this translation. The TLB is a simple register system usually consisting of between 64 and 256 entries. Several of the bits of the virtual address are used as an address into this table. The entry in the table contains the real address, the real upper portion of the physical

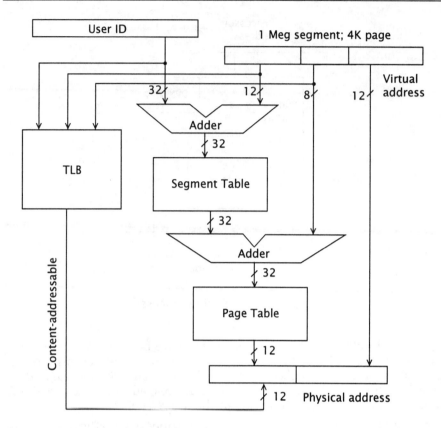

Figure 1.24 A simple virtual (32-bit) to real mapping, producing a 24-bit physical address. The user ID comes from PSW or a related control register.

address in memory, as well as the other bits of the virtual address that have been mapped into this particular location. These residual virtual bits must be compared to the corresponding bits of the virtual reference to ensure that the correct entry has been selected. Since multiple virtual addresses map into the same TLB location, references may occasionally fail to be properly translated, indicated by an invalid comparison. This causes a TLB fault or a not in TLB action to occur, which requires an access to each of the tables in memory and the formation of a correct virtual-to-real translation for that particular virtual address.

Figure 1.24 shows a simple virtual to real memory mapping using a 32-bit process effective address. Each user has an ID, an identifier given to it by the system, which acts as an overall "base" for that user's address space. The user ID defines a base register. This register is pointed to by the PSW. The user ID contains a base address that defines the starting point for the segment table belonging to this particular user. For the simple example shown in Figure 1.24, we assume that the user has one-megabyte segments. With a 32-bit address space, there are $2^{12} = 4,096$ user segments. The upper 12 bits of the user virtual address define one of the user segments. The addition of these upper 12 bits to the 32-bit base address specifies an entry into the segment table that is contained in memory. The segment table, as previously described, contains a base address and a bound for the particular segment identified by the virtual address. It also indicates whether this segment is currently active in memory, and perhaps indicates certain communications and other rights belonging to this user segment. There are 2^8 = 256 4,096-byte pages that are possible in the particular segment selected. Only a certain number of these are active at any one time. The segment table base plus the 8-bit page offset of a page within a segment defines an entry into the page table associated with that particular segment. The page table defines whether or not that particular page is in memory at this time, and also produces the location in memory of that particular page. The output of the page table (12 bits in the case of the example in Figure 1.24) completes the address translation as long as both segment table and page table indicate valid entries. As a simple example, suppose a certain system has a segment table base located in (real) memory at the 32^b address (in hex) 00100000, and suppose a particular user is allocated segments starting at 00000012. This is the user ID.

Now suppose that user produces a virtual address (in hex) of $15010AAB$. Now (real) location 00100012 + 150 = 00100162 is accessed. Suppose it produces:

> Page Table Base: $00A00111$.

Now (real) location $00A00111 + 10 = 00A00121$ is accessed, and it contains $00000BBB$. The leading 5 (hex) digits are ignored, so that the final real address is $BBBAAB$ (a 24-bit address). Note that the segment table base and the page table base are assumed to be real (24-bit) addresses. The upper two hex digits are ignored.

The overall process of accessing the user ID, segment table, and page table, plus performing the appropriate additions of index values, is a time-consuming process—frequently on the order of 20–30 cycles. The TLB is the bypass that takes virtual page information, virtual segment information, and user ID information, while also accessing a small associative memory (or set-associative memory). If an entry is found, the process of accessing the segment table and page table is not required. Rather, the translation has already been completed at some prior time and the real address bits can be replaced in the physical address from the table lookaside buffer. Accessing the TLB is equal to or less than a single machine cycle.

1.8   Basic Instruction Timing

In this section, we discuss *what happens* and *when* during instruction execution. For simple machines, once an instruction set has been defined and the basic functional units determined, the interaction, execution sequence, and timing can be studied.

Functional units usually include:

- Cache.

- Memory (including buffering and access units).

- ALU.

- Address arithmetic (or address generate) unit.

- TLB (may be included in address arithmetic unit).

- Instruction decoder.

Each time one of these units is accessed or employed, an instruction execution event occurs, which occupies one or more cycles.

Simple machines implement instruction execution serially one instruction at a time. Further, they serially use the functional units that the machine comprises. We call machines that serially execute instructions using functional units as defined by the instruction set *well-mapped machines.* The process of instruction execution for such machines usually consists of the following events and sub-events (assuming R/M machine):

Instruction Fetch

- Generate a real instruction address from the value stored in the PC.
- Access the cache.
- Access memory if a cache miss occurs.
- Move the word fetched from the cache/memory (in the SR) to the IR.

Instruction Decode

- Determine instruction type and addressing modes.
- Fetch register operands.

Data Fetch

- Generate a real data address from the offset in the instruction plus base and/or index values.
- Access the cache.
- Access memory if a cache miss occurs.

Execute

- Use ALU to operate on SR and other specified register.

Update Registers

- Adjust PC to point to the next instruction.
- Store result of ALU operation in register.

Of course, many other events also *might* happen, but usually do not. All this is best understood by some examples.

1.8.1   Examples of Well-mapped Machine Instruction Timing

The examination of a machine is not unlike the examination of the insides of a mechanical watch: it is easy to be overwhelmed by the detail, yet over 90% of the process execution time is spent using only a few data paths in very ordinary ways. It is the attempt here to bring simplicity and understanding to the execution process rather than to provide absolute completeness. Therefore, details such as setting up the condition code, memory bounds checking, interrupt checking, etc., are omitted. Actions are fit into the designated cycles. Only the most essential data paths are shown and only the most common instructions are evaluated. We assume that the cycle time has already been established.

Study 1.1   Performance Evaluation

For the following two problems assume a well-mapped R/M processor with the data paths as shown in Figure 1.25. The cache access time is two cycles (one for directory, one for array access). The cache miss time is six cycles (one for cache directory access and five to access memory). It takes two cycles (abbreviated by "~" hereafter) to generate the address (1~ to calculate address, 1~ for TLB). Also, assume there are no TLB misses.

1. (a)   Write the R/M code to execute the statement

$$A := B + C,$$

where A, B, and C are normalized, short floating-point numbers (.F) resident in memory. Assume the BASE address is memory address #D.

```
SUB    R3,R3            ;zero index register
LDA.W  R1, 0D[R3,R0]    ;load inst R1 with BASE
LD.F   R4, 04[R3,R1]    ;load B
ADD.F  R4, 08[R3,R1]    ;add C
ST.F   0[R3,R1], R4     ;store result in A
```

(b)   Develop the detailed instruction timing for the code in problem (a). Assume both code and data are resident in main memory and ALU execution requires two cycles.

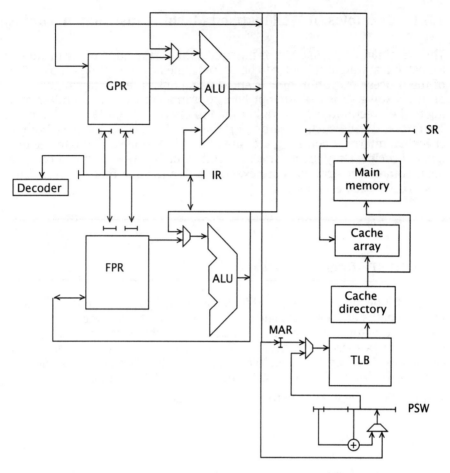

Figure 1.25   Data paths for a nonpipelined R/M processor.

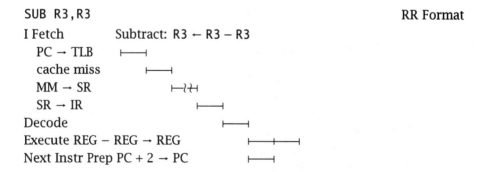

SUB R3,R3   RR Format

I Fetch   Subtract: R3 ← R3 − R3
  PC → TLB   ├──┤
  cache miss   ├──┤
  MM → SR   ├┤┤
  SR → IR   ├──┤
Decode   ├──┤
Execute REG − REG → REG   ├──┼──┤
Next Instr Prep PC + 2 → PC   ├──┤

Note 1   This instruction could be eliminated by using R0 as the index register in instruction sets where R0 always contains zero. We have assumed that a cache miss occurred during instruction fetch. The miss is assumed to bring a line of instructions into the cache, including the subsequent instructions.

We assume that the cache line is sufficiently large to contain the remainder of the instructions. Also note that since this instruction occupies two bytes, we increment the address in the PC by two byte positions to indicate the starting point of the next instruction.

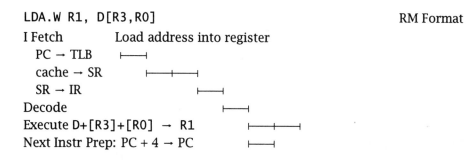

```
LDA.W R1, D[R3,R0]                                    RM Format
```
I Fetch   Load address into register
  PC → TLB
  cache → SR
  SR → IR
Decode
Execute D+[R3]+[R0] → R1
Next Instr Prep: PC + 4 → PC

Note 2   Note that this instruction uses an RM format because it contains a register and a memory address. It does not use the memory address to access memory. We assume R0 contains zero.

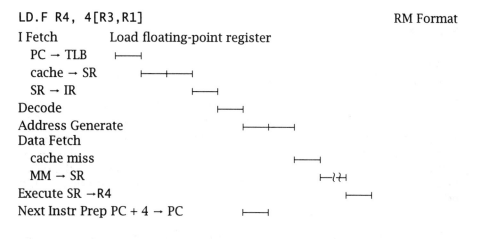

```
LD.F R4, 4[R3,R1]                                     RM Format
```
I Fetch   Load floating-point register
  PC → TLB
  cache → SR
  SR → IR
Decode
Address Generate
Data Fetch
  cache miss
  MM → SR
Execute SR →R4
Next Instr Prep PC + 4 → PC

Note 3   The data address generate includes time to access the TLB. A cache miss occurs presumably because this is the first reference to the data region. It is assumed that subsequent data references are in the cache.

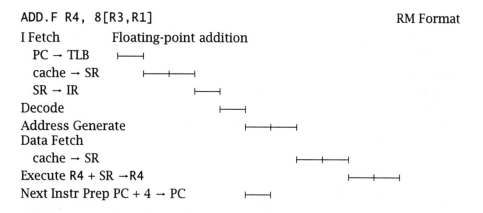

```
ADD.F R4, 8[R3,R1]                                    RM Format
```
I Fetch   Floating-point addition
  PC → TLB
  cache → SR
  SR → IR
Decode
Address Generate
Data Fetch
  cache → SR
Execute R4 + SR →R4
Next Instr Prep PC + 4 → PC

ST.F O[R3,R4], R4   RM Format

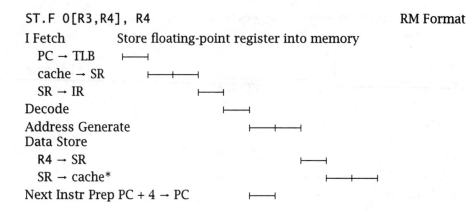

I Fetch   Store floating-point register into memory
  PC → TLB
  cache → SR
  SR → IR
Decode
Address Generate
Data Store
  R4 → SR
  SR → cache*
Next Instr Prep PC + 4 → PC

Note 4 We assume a "copyback" strategy for writes to the cache. If the cache strategy were "write through," then the store would need 5 cycles of main memory access. These cache strategies are explained more fully in Chapter 5.

Summary

To execute this code fragment:

Number of instructions = 5 (1 RR, 4 RM).

Code size is the sum of the sizes of the single RR instruction—2 bytes plus the four RM instructions (each 4 bytes), a total of 18 bytes.

The number of cycles to execute this sequence of instructions is simply the sum of the instruction times (11, 7, 14, 11, and 10 cycles)—a total of 53. If there were no cache, this sum would increase to 77 cycles. On the other hand, if there were a cache and it had no misses, the execution time would be 45 cycles.

2.   Assuming both code and data are resident in cache, show timing for (a) BCT R1, TARGET and (b) BAL R1, TARGET.

(a)   BCT

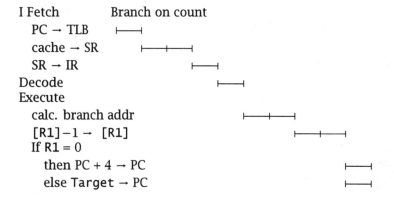

I Fetch   Branch on count
  PC → TLB
  cache → SR
  SR → IR
Decode
Execute
  calc. branch addr
  [R1]−1 → [R1]
  If R1 = 0
    then PC + 4 → PC
    else Target → PC

(b)   BAL

```
I Fetch          Branch and link
   PC → TLB        ⊢——⊣
   cache → SR          ⊢——⊢——⊣
   SR → IR                  ⊢——⊣
Decode                        ⊢——⊣
Execute
   PC + 4 → PC                    ⊢——⊣
   PSW →R1                           ⊢——⊣
   Target → PC                          ⊢——⊣
```

1.8.2   Overlapped and Pipelined Processors

In our well mapped machine of the preceding section, instruction execution proceeded sequentially by cycle. it is possible to speed up instruction execution, and hence improve performance, by overlapping the execution of instructions. Once an instruction has, for example, been decoded and begins to generate a data address, we can begin fetching the next instruction.

In the limit we could begin fetching a new instruction each cycle, in a pipeline or production line fashion.

Machines that concurrently execute a small number (say, 2 or 3) of instructions are called *overlapped* machines. Machines that execute multiple instructions by fetching and/or decoding a new instruction each cycle are called *pipelined* machines. Much of the remainder of this book is concerned with pipelined machines.

1.9   Conclusions

The instruction set, including the data types that it describes, is an important basis for the implementation of any machine. Efficient implementations of the instruction set take into account the objects and actions described by the instructions.

An instruction consists of format, operation, addresses, and sequence control information. This information may be either represented implicitly or explicitly encoded into the instruction, creating a myriad of possible instruction set combinations. For a variety of reasons, most modern machines are based upon general-purpose register sets that contain many of the data arguments used by the instructions. For purposes of assessing code density, cache effectiveness, and general timing properties of an instruction set, we partition most modern instruction sets into one of three classes:

1. The L/S, or load-store class, which includes most of the RISC machines.

2. The R/M, or register–memory machines, which include the IBM System/390 and, more loosely, the Intel x86 series of instruction sets.

3. The R+M, or register-plus-memory architecture, which includes the DEC VAX and, more loosely, the Motorola 680x0 class of machines.

While the partitioning is only approximate, it is important to recognize that fundamental differences in instruction set formats, as represented by these classes, lead to significantly different levels of code density and implementation tradeoffs.

In dealing with addressing and memory, three levels of address mapping can be distinguished:

1. The processor, or user level, which is the address space visible to the user.

2. The system address space, which is the address space visible to the operating system.

3. The memory space, which is the address space visible to the hardware.

These three levels of mapping involve different tradeoffs and different considerations that must be carefully integrated for an efficient overall mapping mechanism.

Given a well-defined instruction set and the basic timing parameters of a processor (internal cycle time, definition of the cycle, and memory timing considerations), it is generally possible to predict instruction timing. There is an expected sequence of actions associated with the interpretation of each instruction. When an implementation executes the expected sequence, we describe that implementation as a *well-mapped* design.

1.10   Historical Development of Computers by Format Class

In terms of modern machines, the instruction set that has had the most impact has been IBM's System/360 [40, 41], which dominates the mainframe marketplace even today as IBM's System/390. It is our prototypical R/M machine. System/360 introduced the notion of general-purpose registers and multiple registers to hold fixed-point register values and addresses, coupled with a separate set of multiple registers to hold floating-point values. Other innovations of the day were byte-addressing, use of a program status word, condition codes, and user–system states. While a number of these items can be found in vestigial form in even earlier machines, System/360 with its market dominance organized these concepts and influenced later instruction set designers in significant ways.

Contemporary with the introduction of System/360 was the introduction of the Control Data 6600 in 1964. This was another very popular and widely recognized machine. It was one of the earliest load–store architectures, built about three types of register sets: address registers, integers, and floating-point registers. The 6600 series was a quite successful entry into the scientific marketplace and evolved over many years as a popular instruction set and was extended by Control Data in its 7600 and Cyber series machine lines.

The earliest L/S processor and what we now might call RISC processor was developed in the late 1970s at IBM research laboratories as the experimental 801 computer; see Radin [239]. It differed from the CDC 6600 in that it had uniform instruction size (32 bits) and it integrated the address and integer registers into a single set of 32 registers. Our L/S architecture, consistent with most mainframe and microprocessor usage, keeps floating-point registers separate from the other registers. On microprocessors, these floating-point registers were envisioned to be implemented in an associated co-processor. The first university-based L/S machine (and first use of the term *RISC*) was the RISC-1 work done at the University of California at Berkeley [230]. Further evolution of the RISC-1 led to RISC-2 and the introduction of register windows. RISC-2 was the basis for Sun Microsystems' SPARC instruction set. Other early RISC processor designs include Hewlett-Packard's Precision architecture, PA-RISC [183, 38], and the MIPS developed at Stanford [126], which became the basis for the MIPS R2000 and successor processors.

The register–memory architectures are dominated by the IBM mainframes, with program-compatible rival offerings from companies such as Amdahl, Hitachi, and Fujitsu. These architectures are a direct evolution of the System/360 architecture, extended over the years to include virtual addressing, enhanced storage capability, capability for addressing very large address spaces, etc. We have included in Figure 1.8 the Intel x86 series as an R/M machine. The Intel x86 series is an extension of its earlier microprocessor efforts such as its 8080 and 8086 [58], and it differs significantly from most other machines presented in this text. While it follows the R/M format, it does not have general-purpose registers. Rather, it uses a number of registers with designated special purposes. While it has 16 registers and one would expect that adequate software support would produce code whose characteristics would generally resemble a prototypical R/M, this correlation is only very approximate.

In 1967, Digital Equipment introduced its well-known PDP-11 series of 16-bit minicomputers [30]. This two-address instruction set accessed values and memory through the use of eight general-purpose registers. Memory was usually accessed indirectly through the registers. The registers had multiple functions. The exact function was determined by use of an associated register mode field. Each register specification had an associated 3-bit mode identifying one of eight possible uses of the designated registers. In 1978, DEC introduced a 32-bit extension called the VAX line. This is the motivation for our prototypical R+M architecture. VAX introduced a robust set of instruction formats, including register and memory formats for two- and three-address instructions. VAX designers continued the use of the register modes introduced in the PDP-11, as the VAX was to be upward-compatible from the PDP-11. The resultant design had byte-variable instructions with excellent code-density properties (described in Chapter 2); but the use of register modes required multiple sequential decoding operations to complete the interpretation of a single instruction. (See "The Curse of Register Modes" on page 41.) This had the unfortunate side effect of significantly complicating the pipelined implementations of the VAX instruction set. The Motorola M68000 series includes some but not all of the variability of instruction formats contained in VAX. For example, it allows a result to be stored either in a register or in memory. Much of the M68000 instruction set seems to have also been at least influenced by PDP-11. It is, however, a design separate from VAX, and data presented later in this text for VAX would only approximate the behavior expected of the Motorola 68000.

1.11   Annotated Bibliography

A great deal has been written about instruction sets and their relative merit. A standard reference work that collects earlier instruction set literature is Siewiorek et al. [257]. This book is a compendium of papers on well-known instruction sets up to about 1980. Included in this work are descriptions of System/360 [15] and its extensions [47]. Also included are papers describing the PDP-11 [30] and the CDC 6600 [281]. These three systems—System/360, PDP-11, and the CDC 6600—significantly influenced instruction set design through the latter 1970s and into the early 1980s. Many of the conventions adopted by these processors found their way, in one form or another, into early microprocessor design.

One area of continuing discussion is the relationship between the external environment—high-level language, operating system, etc.—and instruction sets. Particularly comprehensive books that include a treatment of this subject are Myers [213], Tanenbaum [276], and Dasgupta [65].

There are many works describing the architecture of the Motorola 68000 and Intel x86 series microprocessors. Bronson and Silver [44] include treatment of both, as does Wakerly [298]. There are numerous books describing the instruction sets of the various microprocessors. These include Hilf and Nausch for the 68000 series [128] and Crawford and Gelsinger describing programming of the Intel 386 [62].

Stallings [270] has edited a collection of the principal papers describing the RISC processor development. The R2000 processor is described by Kane [152], and HP's Precision architecture is described by Lee [183].

There are a number of works on arithmetic that include a discussion of various data formats. These include Hwang [137] and Waser and Flynn [300]. The IEEE floating point standard has been described in [144].

Early definitive papers on various aspects of memory include the work of Gibson on cache [102], Dennis on segmentation [71], and Denning on paging [68]. Most standard basic texts on computer organization and architecture include a complete treatment of memory hierarchies, microprogramming, and detailed aspects of computer implementation. Some of the better known standard works on computer organization include Hayes [123], van de Goor [296], Stallings [269], Hamacher et al. [119], and Murray [211].

Additional Reading

On Specific Machine Approaches

VAX Architecture Reference Manual. Digital Equipment Corp., Maynard, MA, Doc. EK-VAXAR-RM-002, 1983.

G. M. Amdahl, G. A. Blaauw, and F. P. Brooks, Jr. Architecture of the IBM System/360. *IBM Journal of Research and Development,* 8(2):87–101, April 1964.

J. S. Birnbaum and W. S. Worley, Jr. Beyond RISC: high-precision architecture. *Hewlett-Packard Journal,* 36, August 1985.

J. L. Hennessy, N. Jouppi, F. Baskett, and J. Gill. MIPS: a VLSI processor architecture. *Proceedings, CMU Conference on VLSI Systems and Computations,* pages 337–346, October 1981.

G. Radin. The 801 minicomputer. *Proceedings, Symposium on Architectural Support for Programming Languages and Operating Systems,* pages 39–77, ACM, New York, March 1982.

G. Bronson and H. Silver. *32-Bit Microprocessors: A Primer Plus.* Advanced Technology Series. AT&T, Indianapolis, 1988.

J. E. Smith and S. Weiss. PowerPC 601 and Alpha 21064: A Tale of two RISCs. *IEEE Computer,* June 1994, pages 46–58.

S. Weiss and J. E. Smith. Power and PowerPC: Principle, Architecture, and Implementation. Morgan Kaufmann, San Francisco, 1994.

On Computer Design Background Review

S. Dasgupta. *Computer Architecture: A Modern Synthesis* (Two volumes). Wiley, New York, 1989.

C. Hamacher, Z. Vranesic, and S. Zaky. *Computer Organization.* McGraw-Hill, New York, 3rd edition, 1990.

J. Hayes. *Computer Architecture and Organization.* McGraw-Hill, New York, 1988.

J. L. Hennessy and D. A. Patterson. *Computer Architecture: A Quantitative Approach.* Morgan Kaufmann, San Mateo, CA, 1990.

W. Murray. *Computer and Digital System Architecture.* Prentice-Hall, Englewood Cliffs, NJ, 1990.

W. Stallings. *Computer Organization and Architecture: Principles of Structure and Function.* Macmillan, New York, 2nd edition, 1990.

A. J. van de Goor. *Computer Architecture and Design.* Addison-Wesley, Reading, MA, 1989.

J. Wakerly. *Microcomputer Architecture and Programming.* J. Wiley, New York, 1989.

On Computer Arithmetic

K. Hwang. *Computer Arithmetic: Principles, Architecture, and Design.* Wiley, New York, 1978.

American National Standards Institute. An American National Standard: IEEE standard for binary floating-point arithmetic, 1988. ANSI/IEEE Standard No. 754.

S. Waser and M. Flynn. *Introduction to Arithmetic for Digital Systems Designers.* Holt, Rinehart and Winston, New York, 1982.

1.12   Problem Set

1. Discuss the probable advantages and disadvantages of using microprogrammed instruction decode.

2. Consider the following simple L/S processor (see Figure 1.16).

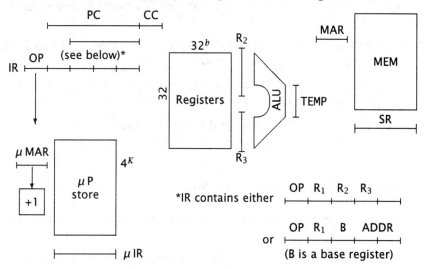

Its instruction layout is similar to the "generic RISC" discussed in this chapter. Its microinstruction consists of two leading bits to define the microinstruction type, and is followed by additional ICP or address information.

For these ("00") microinstructions only the μMAR (microprogram address register) is incremented (+1) at the end of the execution of the microinstruction. If the leading microinstruction bits (bits 1, 2) are "00," then the remaining bits specify ICPs that indicate the following functions:

bit 3	gate PC → MAR
bit 4	memory read [MAR] → SR
bit 5	memory write SR → [MAR]
bit 6	gate R2 → ALU
	and gate R3 → ALU
	and gate ALU → TEMP

bits 7-9   specify one of eight ALU operations:
                              000   ADD
                              001   SUB
                              010   AND
                              011   OR
                              100   NOT
                              101   EXCLUSIVE OR
                              110   SHIFT RT
                              111   SHIFT LEFT

bit 10   gate TEMP → R1

bit 11   gate IR⟨ADDR⟩ → ALU
          and gate [B] → ALU
          and gate ALU → TEMP

bit 12   gate TEMP → MAR

bit 13   gate TEMP → PC

bit 14   gate SR → IR

bit 15   increment PC; PC+1 → PC

bit 16   gate SR → R1

bit 17   gate PC → R2
          and gate IR⟨ADDR⟩ → R3
          and gate ALU → TEMP

If the leading microinstruction bits are "01," then the opcode bits of the IR are loaded into the lowest eight bits of the μMAR and the upper bits are cleared and the indicated address is fetched into the μIR (microinstruction register). The opcode bits in the IR thus form a pointer to a table (the first 256 entries in microprogram storage). Each entry specifies the address of the microprogram routine executing the designated op.

If the leading microinstruction bits are "10," then an unconditional branch occurs in the microcode. The lowest 12 bits of the microinstruction are gated to the micromemory address register (μMAR).

If the leading microinstruction bits are "11," then a conditional branch occurs. The microinstruction contains an address test vector. If any of the specified tests are satisfied, the branch is taken and the address is placed in the microinstruction address register; otherwise, sequencing continues in line.

The test vector tests:

1. TEMP overflow (carryout).

2. TEMP negative.

3. TEMP zero.

4. Value in R2 is NEG.

5. Value in R3 is NEG.

6. CC bits in IR "AND"ed with the CC bits in PSW and then "OR"ed. Result is a "1."

Write the microcode and show instruction timing (through the fetch of the next instruction) for the following instructions, assuming that the instruction is already in the IR:

(a) ADD R1, R2, R3   (absolute—i.e., unsigned—numbers)

(b) LD   R2,#A (the immediate value, A, is stored in the address portion of the IR)

(c) LD   R2, Addr[R3]

Assume memory access = memory write time = 3 cycles.

3. Repeat problem 2 for BC.NE Target [R3]
                          ST   Addr [R3, R1]
                          SUB   R1, R2, R3

4. Extend the processor (data paths and ICPs) described in problem 2 to execute

    MPY R1, R2, R3

Then show the microcode and timing.

5. Suppose the microcode access time is overlapped with the c.p. control of the data path. Microinstructions must now be fetched one cycle early. What will be the effect on the following image instructions?

    (a) BC.NE Target [R2]

    (b) LD   R2, Addr [R1]

Assume the overlap facility allows cycles to execute at $\frac{1}{2}$ the time indicated in problems 2–4. Do either of these instructions require extra cycles (more than the unoverlapped host machine)?

6. Evaluate the effects of the following proposed host improvements on cycle count on various instructions considered in problems 2 and 3.

    (a) Reduce memory access/store time to two cycles.

    (b) Use a three-ported register set (i.e., eliminate TEMP and allow R1 op R2 → R3 in one cycle).

7. Suppose an interrupt occurs in problem 2 after an I-fetch but before instruction execution has occurred.

    A special interrupt bit is set. Extend the host machine (microinstruction, etc.) to handle this and describe the resulting action.

8. A certain computation results in the following (hexadecimal) representation:

    Fraction   +1.FFFF... ,
    Exponent (unbiased)   +F (radix = 2).

Show the floating-point representation for the preceding in:

    (a) IBM long format.

    (b) IEEE short format.

    (c) IEEE long format.

9. Represent the decimal numbers (i) +123, (ii) −4321, and (iii) 00000 (zero is represented as a positive number) as:

   (a) Packed decimal format (in hex).

   (b) Unpacked decimal format (in hex).

   Assume a length indicator (in bytes) is specified in the instruction. Show lengths for each case.

10. The roots of a quadratic equation are:

$$\frac{-b \pm \sqrt{b^2 - 4ac}}{2a}.$$

   Write the assembly code for finding the two roots. The initial values of a, b, and c are stored in Addr [R1], Bddr [R1], Cddr [R1], where R1 contains a base value that must be loaded. The results are to be stored in ROOT1[R1] and ROOT2[R1]. You may assume a square root instruction (SQRT). Using the general mnemonics presented in this chapter,

   (a) Write the R/M code.

   (b) Write the L/S code.

11. Repeat study 1.1 with a hardware square-root instruction using L/S and R/M instruction sets. Find the number of cycles, assuming: (a) all instructions and arguments are in memory with access time of five cycles, and (b) all instructions are in memory with access time of one cycle. Assume arithmetic operations take a single cycle. Discuss the sensitivity of each architecture to memory access time.

12. One can use a vertical microinstruction to point to a horizontal microinstruction (sometimes called a *nanoinstruction*). The vertical microinstruction consists of a pointer into the horizontal microstorage. Discuss the space–time tradeoff for such a system. Create a model and evaluate.

Chapter 2

The Basics: Time, Area, and Instruction Sets

2.1 Introduction

The tradeoff of cost and performance is fundamental to any system design. Different designs result either from the selection of different points on the cost-performance continuum, or from differing assumptions about the nature of cost or performance.

In this chapter, we deal with three conceptual areas. The first area is *time*, which includes partitioning instructions into events or cycles, basic pipelining mechanisms used in speeding up instruction execution, and cycle time as a parameter for optimizing program execution. Second, we discuss *area*. The cost or area occupied by a particular feature is another important aspect of the architectural tradeoff. Third, *instruction sets* affect both performance and implementation. Instruction sets that require more implementation area are less valuable than instruction sets that use less—unless, of course, they can provide commensurately better performance. Long-term *cost-performance ratio* is the basis for most design decisions. By looking at instruction sets and their implementation requirements, we can draw some conclusions about the cost effectiveness of some architectural choices. The goal of this chapter is to provide a basis for cost-performance evaluation as it affects instruction set decisions.

The chapter begins with the *machine cycle*—specifically, how much delay is incurred in a cycle, how instruction execution is partitioned into cycles, and how clocking can be made reliable. We next look at pipelined machines: machines that overlap the execution of multiple instructions in order to speed up program execution. For such processors, we can approximately determine the optimum cycle time. Nothing in machine design is "free," so a cost (area) model is introduced to assist in making instruction set tradeoffs. This model is restricted to on-chip or microprocessor-type tradeoffs, but it illustrates a type of model that the designer must use in all machine designs. Finally, we look at the instruction set data relative to high-level language program actions, and then at tradeoffs between instruction code density and register size.

2.2   Time

The notion of time receives considerable attention from processor designers. It is the basic measure of performance; but breaking actions into cycles and reducing both cycle count and cycle times are important but inexact sciences. The partitioning of actions into cycles can "make or break" a design. Many a design was crippled by an unanticipated "extra" cycle required by a basic action such as cache access.

Overall, there is only a limited theoretical basis for cycle selection and the resultant partitioning of instruction execution into cycles. Much design is done on a pragmatic basis. This section covers some more commonly used models of cycle time determination and instruction execution time partitioning.

In this section, we look at some techniques for instruction partitioning, that is, techniques for breaking up the instruction execution time into manageable and fixed time cycles. In a pipelined processor, data flows through stages much as items flow on an assembly line. At the end of each stage, a result is passed on to a subsequent stage and new data enter. Within limits, the shorter the cycle time, the more productive the pipeline. The partitioning process has its own overhead, however, and very short cycle times become dominated by this overhead. Simple cycle time models can optimize the number of pipeline stages. Reliable operation is another issue that the designer must keep in mind. This includes the clocking approach itself, the relationship between the clock pulses that sample data into registers, and the determination of whether or not there are hazards for data entering registers. Finally, we look at the concept of a minimum achievable cycle time and what it takes to realize such a cycle.

Cycle time is the essential quantum—the building block—of pipeline processor design.

2.2.1   The Nature of a Cycle

A *cycle* is the basic time quantum for processing or communicating information within a machine. A cycle is defined as the time between state transitions. The designer determines the cycle time by finding the worst-case (maximum) time to accomplish a meaningful event (or operation) across the most frequently used data paths. This time must be sufficient for data to be safely sampled into designated destination registers (Figure 2.1). Less frequently used paths that require more time to complete than this require multiple cycles.

A cycle may begin with the new value of the sequence counter or microinstruction address being entered into the decoder. The decoder then provides a control vector (set of control point values) to its output register (or the microinstruction register, for microprogrammed machines). This control vector (or microinstruction) defines a control value that may be further decoded so that each control point has a distinct value. These control points are then applied to the various data path output register gates and combinatorial logic throughout the system (Figure 2.1). This allows data from source registers to propagate through designated combinatorial logic into the in-gating of the destination register. Finally, after a suitable setup

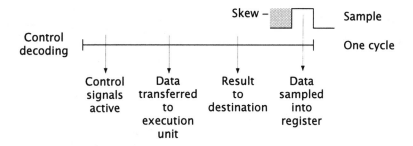

Figure 2.1 Possible sequence of actions within a cycle.

time, all registers may be sampled by an edge or pulse produced by the clocking system.

Frequently, the control decoding and accessing of control point values for the next cycle are overlapped with the application of control signals for the current cycle. See also problem 2 in Chapter 1.

In a synchronous system, the cycle time is usually determined by assuming the worst-case times for each step or action within the cycle. Finally, the clock itself may not arrive at the anticipated time (due to propagation or loading effects). We call the maximum deviation from the expected time of clock arrival the (uncontrolled) *clock skew*. In the alternative asynchronous system, the cycle time is determined by the completion of the event of interest. A *completion signal* must be generated, which then allows the next operation to commence activity. Asynchronous clocking is not generally used within pipelined processors because of the completion signal overhead and pipeline timing constraints.

2.2.2 Partitioning Instruction Execution into Cycles

The execution of an instruction consists of a sequence of events or actions specified by the instruction semantics. In Chapter 1, we assumed that the time required for each event had been nicely packaged into one or more cycles. In this section, we look at this partitioning problem.

Instruction execution has at least the following actions, which are usually executed in sequential order:

1. Instruction Fetch (IF): the cycles required to fetch the contents of the address in the instruction counter into the instruction register (IR).

2. Decode (D): the cycles required to initialize the interpretation (execution) process.

3. Register Fetch (RF): the cycle to fetch register operands.

4. Address Generate (AG): the cycles required to generate the effective memory address of the data operand or the target instruction (in the case of branch).

5. Translate (T).

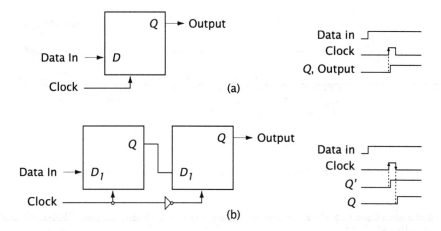

Figure 2.2   Edge-triggered clocks. (a) Single rank. (b) Dual rank.

6. Data Fetch (DF) or Target Instruction Fetch (TIF): the cycles required to fetch the designated information from the memory system.

7. Execute (EX): the cycles required to perform the operation designated by the instruction.

8. Put Away (PA) or Writeback: the time to write a result in a designated register. Sometimes this action is included in the last EX cycle.

Each of the preceding functional actions is allocated one or more processor cycles, although some of these functions may be concurrent—typically, *decode* and *register fetch* occur during the same cycle. For simple processors, the designer determines the time required for each functional event (the worst-case path through each functional unit) and then defines a cycle time based on (perhaps) the average of the various maximum functional times. Units that require more than this time are allocated multiple cycles. This may or may not be an optimum arrangement depending on the effects of quantization of cycle time on the other units. The goal is to minimize the overall instruction execution time.

2.2.3   Clocking Overhead and Reliable Clocking

The type of clocking—the way data is sampled into storage elements—is another important part of processor design. The clock is responsible for entering or sampling data into the register in a synchronously clocked system. The time between corresponding clock actions is the cycle time.

Several variations of synchronous clocking are possible, depending on how data is sampled into the register and how the register is originally designed. Registers are of two basic forms (single rank and dual rank), and have two distinct clock triggering mechanisms (level triggered and edge triggered). A *single-rank register* transmits the input data to the output soon (perhaps two gate delays) after it has been enabled (triggered) by the clock (Figure 2.2a). A *dual-rank register* consists of two latches—an input and an output latch (Figure 2.2b). When the clock is initially enabled, the data-in

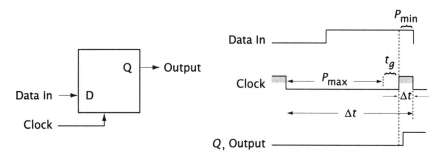

Figure 2.3   Idealized simple clock.

signal is stored in the input latch. When the clock is disabled, the output of the first latch is transferred to the output latch, and soon after is available as output data. The enabling or triggering mechanism can be either the clock level (*level triggered*) or the rise or fall transaction of the clock (*edge triggered*, Figures 2.2a and 2.2b).

The clocking overhead is the additional delay in the worst-case delay path due to register delay and the clock. Suppose we define the following terms:

P_{max}: maximum delay in logic without clock overhead (C)

P_{min}: minimum delay in the shortest logic path

t_w: clock pulse width

Δt: cycle time

t_g: register data setup time

t_d: register output delay after data and clock are enabled

C: clock overhead

For a conventionally clocked system (Figure 2.1):

$$\Delta t = P_{max} + C.$$

Figure 2.3 illustrates conceptual clocking for simple processors. The timing for C is:

$$C = t_g + t_w \quad \text{(assuming } t_w > t_d\text{)}.$$

Most processors use a *transparent clock* (Figure 2.4). This clocking eliminates t_w from C by moving the sample forward in the cycle by t_w. This improves the clock overhead to:

$$C = t_g + t_d,$$

while with a dual-rank edge-triggered clock, data enters rank one on the rising edge of the clock and is available at the output (rank two) on the falling edge. So:

$$C = t_g + t_d + t_w.$$

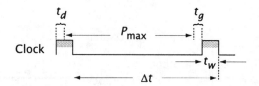

Figure 2.4   Single-rank, transparent clocking.

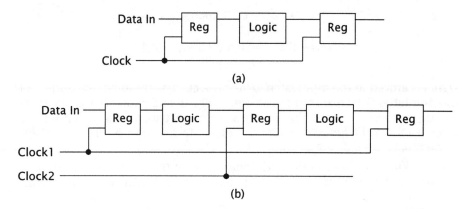

Figure 2.5   Clocks. (a) Single phase. (b) Two-phase.

The single-rank register is fast and has lower cost, but the dual-rank register has clocking advantages. It avoids the logical hazard caused when $P_{min} < t_w$. In the single-rank register (level-sensitive), it is possible for "fast path" data to arrive at the data input of the register while the clock is still enabled (during t_w). This would cause no problem for the dual-rank register.

Figure 2.3 shows a conventional arrangement where a single phase clock is used to enter data into the register after it has transited the logic. Typically, the registers are of simple design; when the clock is high, data on the data-in line is sampled into the register. The register is enabled by the clock in the case of a level-sensitive single-rank register. Such clocking must satisfy some constraints (Figure 2.3).

First, the clock pulse width (t_w) must be long enough both to ensure distribution across the entire system (pulse shrinkage is frequently a problem) and to ensure that the data-in is properly latched into the register when the clock is enabled (t_w > register hold time).

Second, the time between clock pulses, t_m, must be sufficiently long to ensure that the worst possible logic path delay between any two registers is valid when the data-in is sampled at the receiving register ($t_m > P_{max}$).

A third constraint is clock hazard: t_w (the pulse width) must not be longer than the minimum possible path across the logic between two registers, P_{min}. Otherwise, when such a path is enabled, new data being latched into the sending register is transmitted a cycle early into the receiving register ($t_w < P_{min}$).

An alternative clocking technique is to use a multiphased clock. Here, multiple separate clock lines replace the single clock. These separate clock lines (actually, clock-phase lines) enable successive logic stages (Figure 2.5). The

Figure 2.6   Single-phase, level-sensitive clock.

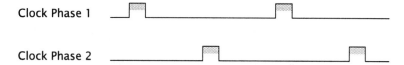

Figure 2.7   Two-phase, level-sensitive clock.

design is arranged so that the two clocks do not overlap (Figure 2.7), and the logic is partitioned so that adjoining registers are clocked on separate phases of the clock. In a two-phase, level-sensitive clocking scheme, short paths cannot affect the proper entry of data into the register. Thus, only the first two constraints apply.

With the transparent single-rank register and a single- or multi-phase clock, it is possible to propagate the register output data as soon as it is available, and begin a new "cycle"—actually a clock phase. Thus, for this case

$$C = t_g + t_d.$$

If the arrival of the clock is not carefully controlled, a time ambiguity called *uncontrolled clock skew* is introduced. If the arrival time of the clock is $\pm\delta$, then the clock period (cycle) must be extended by 2δ (the sum of the earliest and latest deviations). This increases C to

$$C = t_g + t_d + 2\delta.$$

Single-rank, transparent clocking is preferred for most clocking arrangements, as it provides a minimum of complexity in the design and minimizes the clock overhead (Figure 2.8). Edge-triggered clocks are also used, and they also serve to minimize the fast path logical hazard. Such paths become a problem only when there is a significant amount of clock skew between the two registers.

Most modern systems, both mainframe and microprocessors, use multi-phase level-sensitive clocking.

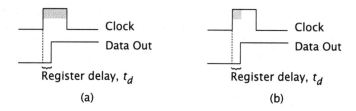

Figure 2.8   Level-sensitive (a) and edge-triggered (b) clocks acting on registers (or latches).

(a) Typical Instruction Execution

(b) Pipelined Execution

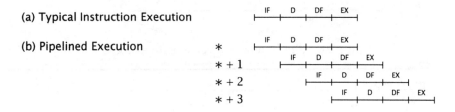

Figure 2.9   Pipelined processors.

2.2.4   Pipelined Processors

Optimizing the partitioning of instructions into cycles is only one way to speed up program execution. Another approach uses concurrency of instruction execution. One could, for example, begin fetching the next instruction as soon as the current instruction had been decoded. An extension to this is the pipelined machine, where as soon as one instruction is begun, i.e., decoded, the next instruction is decoded. We fetch, decode, and execute one instruction each cycle.

Pipelined machine instruction execution is shown in Figure 2.9. Suppose we have a very simple instruction execution process consisting of four cycles:

> IF — Instruction fetch from cache into the IR
> D — Decode instruction
> DF — Data fetch from either memory or register set
>   (ignoring address generation, etc.)
> EX — Execute operation

Pipelined machines attempt to keep each pipeline segment busy all the time. As soon as the first instruction completes the IF cycle, the next instruction is fetched, etc., much as would happen in an assembly line. Pipelined instruction execution can significantly speed up program running time. If the pipeline has four segments or stages, the maximum speedup is four times the well-mapped machine.

Of course, speed has a price—pipelined processors are complex and costly and one never really achieves the four-times speedup. Still, such processors are cost-effective overall as long as chip area accommodates the required added complexity. Almost all recently introduced microprocessors are pipelined.

A basic optimization for the pipeline processor designer is the partitioning of the pipeline into concurrently operating segments. The more segments, the higher the maximum speedup. However, each new segment carries clocking overhead with it, which adversely affects performance.

2.2.5   Optimum Pipelining

If we ignore quantization effects we can determine an optimal cycle time, Δt, and hence the degree of functional segmentation for a simple pipelined

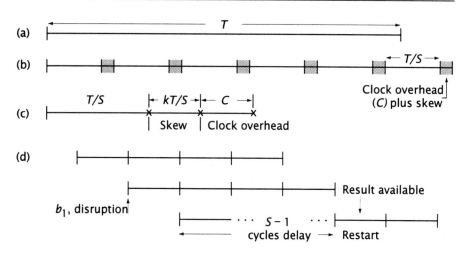

Figure 2.10 Optimal pipelining. (a) Unclocked instruction execution time, T. (b) T is partitioned into S segments. Each segment requires $C + \frac{(k)T}{S}$ clocking overhead and skew. (c) Clocking overhead and its effect on cycle time T/S. (d) Effect of a pipeline disruption (or a *stall* in the pipeline).

processor. Our analysis is based on the work of Kunkel and Smith [175] and Dubey and Flynn [77].

Assume that the total time to execute an instruction without latches or pipeline segments is T nanoseconds (Figure 2.10a). Now T is to be segmented into S segments to allow clocking and pipelining. The ideal delay through a segment is $T/S = T_{seg}$. Associated with each segment are two types of partitioning overhead:

1. A fixed clock overhead time C (in ns), including data setup and hold.

2. A variable linear "stretching" factor k that increases the segment delay (T/s) by a factor of $(1 + k)$. Assume $0 \leq k \leq 1$. This accounts for such effects as clock skew (Figure 2.10b). As cycles (T/s) get larger, more complex functions are incorporated into the cycle. This increases clock distribution difficulties and hence clock skew.

Therefore, the actual cycle time (Figure 2.10c) of the pipelined processor is the ideal cycle time T/S plus the overhead:

$$\Delta t = \frac{T}{S} + \frac{kT}{S} + C = (1 + k)\frac{T}{S} + C.$$

Now consider our idealized pipelined processor. If there are no code interruptions, it processes instructions at the rate of one per cycle; but interruptions can occur (primarily due to incorrectly guessed or unexpected branches, as we shall see in more detail in Chapter 4). Suppose these interruptions occur with frequency b and have the effect of invalidating the $S - 1$ instructions prepared to enter, or already in, the pipeline (representing a "worst-case" disruption, Figure 2.10d). As we shall see in Chapter 4, there are many different types of pipeline interruption, each with a different effect, but this simple model illustrates the effect of disruptions on performance.

Considering pipeline interruption, the performance of the processor is:

$$\text{Performance} = \frac{1}{1 + (S - 1)b} \text{instructions per cycle.}$$

The throughput (G) can be defined as:

$$
\begin{aligned}
G &= \frac{\text{performance}}{\Delta t} \text{ instructions/ns} \\
&= \left(\frac{1}{1 + (S - 1)b} \right) * \left(\frac{1}{(1 + k)(T/S) + C} \right).
\end{aligned}
$$

If we find

$$\frac{dG}{dS} = 0,$$

we can find S_{opt}, the optimum number of pipeline segments [77]:

$$S_{\text{opt}} = \sqrt{\frac{(1 - b)(1 + k)T}{bC}}.$$

Once an initial S has been determined, the total instruction execution latency (T_{instr}) is:

$$
\begin{aligned}
T_{\text{instr}} &= T + S \times \text{(clocking overhead)} \\
&= T + S \left(\frac{kT}{S} + C \right) \\
&= T(1 + k) + SC,
\end{aligned}
$$

$$\text{or}$$

$$S \left((1 + k)T_{\text{seg}} + C \right) = S\Delta t.$$

Finally, we compute the throughput performance G in (million) instructions per second.

Suppose $T = 120\,\text{ns}$ and $b = 0.2$, $C = 5\,\text{ns}$, $k = 0.1$. Then $S_{\text{opt}} \doteq 10$ stages. Figure 2.11 illustrates the effect of pipeline disruptions b on S_{opt} for these machine parameters.

Of course, S_{opt} as determined is simplistic—functional units cannot be arbitrarily divided, integer cycle boundaries must be observed, etc. Still, determining S_{opt} as before can serve as a design starting point or as an important check on an otherwise empirically optimized design.

The preceding discussion considers a number of pipeline segments S on the basis of performance. Each time a new pipeline segment is introduced, additional cost is added which is not factored into the analysis. Each new segment requires additional registers and clocking hardware. Because of this, the optimum number of pipeline segments (S_{opt}) ought to be thought of as a probable upper limit to the number of useful pipeline segments that a particular processor can employ. At the very early stages of any design, when only the estimates for the delay through the various units are known, the initial partitioning of actions into pipeline stages might begin as follows:

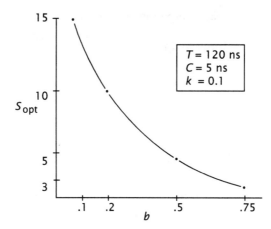

Figure 2.11   Effect of fraction of pipeline interruptions (*b*) on optimum number of pipeline segments (S_{opt}).

1. Estimate *b* from instruction set and machine organization characteristics and *k* from technology considerations, usually $k < .1$; in the absence of detailed information use $k = 0.05$.

2. Using path delay data, determine *T*. Find *C* based on clock design and register delay.

3. Compute S_{opt}. Try various smaller values of *S*, and hence larger Δt, to find the cycle time that minimizes the quantization effects discussed in the next section.

   The following study uses what we have learned so far to create an allocation of actions to pipeline segments.

Study 2.1   Optimum Pipelining

In a certain processor, each instruction requires a number of actions. These actions and their corresponding delays are listed in table 2.1. The delays listed are the nominal values before taking into account any side effects of clock skew and pipeline stage partitioning.

Assume that each pipeline segment requires a clock overhead of 4 ns and a skew factor $k = 0.05$; also, the unit delays can be combined into pipeline stages, but can be subdivided into smaller stages only in the case of I-decode (max of 2 6-ns segments) and Execute (into 3 segments, partitioned 7, 7 and 8 ns).

1. Compute the optimum number of segments (S_{opt}), assuming a branch frequency $b = 0.2$.

   First, we compute *T*, the sum of all execution phase times.

$$T = 4 + 6 + 10 + 3 + 12 + 9 + 3 + 6 + 10 + 3 + 22 + 2$$
$$= 90 \text{ ns.}$$

Table 2.1   Pipeline actions and delays.

I fetch includes	
PC → MAR	4 ns
cache directory access	6 ns
cache data access	10 ns
data transfer to IR	3 ns
I decode	12 ns
Address Generate	9 ns
Address → MAR	3 ns
D fetch includes	
cache directory access	6 ns
cache data access	10 ns
data transfer to ALU	3 ns
Execute includes	
R → ALU → R	22 ns
Register Put Away	2 ns

We are given:

$$k \;\; = \;\; \text{clock skew}$$
$$= \;\; 0.05$$

and

$$C \;\; = \;\; \text{setup and register delay times   (assuming a level-sensitive single-rank register with multiple phase clock)}$$
$$= \;\; 4 \, \text{ns}$$

and

$$b \;\; = \;\; \text{branch frequency}$$
$$= \;\; .2.$$

Then, as a first approximation, the optimum number of pipeline segments (S_{opt}) is:

$$S_{opt} \;\; = \;\; \sqrt{\frac{(1-b)(1+k)T}{bC}} = \sqrt{\frac{(.8)(1.05)(90)}{(.2)(4)}} = 9.7.$$

As discussed earlier, S_{opt} is usually an "upper limit" on a possible number of segments; we initially round down so that

$$S_{opt} \;\; = \;\; 9.$$

2. Partition the actions into approximately S_{opt} segments.

   We begin by partitioning the actions into possible segments (Figure 2.12(a)), using as a rough rule (not a maximum) the expected time per segment,

   $$T_{seg} = \text{time per segment} = 10.0\,\text{ns}.$$

   We label each stage with the principal action that occurs within it.

   Note that some stages (e.g., 2 and 3) will not "fit" into the target $T_{seg} = 10\,\text{ns}$, but they do not greatly exceed T_{seg}.

3. We now compute the total instruction execution time based on several trial cycle times.

   In the preceding partition, the worst stage delay was 13 ns (stage 2), excluding clocking effects. So now let us use $T_{seg} = 13$ ns:

   $$
   \begin{aligned}
   \Delta t &= \text{cycle time} = \text{max stage time} + \text{overheads} \\
            &= (1 + k)T_{seg} + C \\
            &= (13\,\text{ns})(1.05) + 4 = 17.65\,\text{ns} \\
   T_{inst} &= (\text{stages})(\Delta t) = (9)(17.65\,\text{ns}) \\
   T_{inst} &= 159\,\text{ns}.
   \end{aligned}
   $$

   We could also try a minimum partition of (say) $T_{seg} = 9$ ns:

   $$
   \begin{aligned}
   \Delta t &= \text{a stage time} + \text{overheads} \\
            &= 9(1.05) + 4 = 13.5\,\text{ns} \\
   T_{inst} &= (\text{stages that fit in 9\,ns})(\Delta t) + (\text{stages that do not fit})(2\Delta t) \\
            &= (3)(13.5) + (6)(2)(13.5) \\
   T_{inst} &= 202.5\,\text{ns}.
   \end{aligned}
   $$

   At the other extreme, if we tried a coarser partition such as $T_{seg} = 20$ ns, we would have Figure 2.12(b), which creates a cycle of:

   $$\Delta t = (20\,\text{ns})(1.05) + 4 = 25\,\text{ns}$$

   and a total instruction execution time of:

   $$T_{inst} = (5 \text{ stages})(25\,\text{ns/stage}) = 125\,\text{ns}.$$

4. We now compute the expected performance G in million instructions per second for each trial cycle used previously.

   The performance for each partition can be computed:

   $$G = \left(\frac{1}{1 + (S - 1)b} \right) \left(\frac{1}{(1 + k)(T_{seg}) + C} \right)$$

   $$G(T_{seg} = 13\,\text{ns}) = \frac{1}{1 + (8)(.2)} \cdot \frac{1}{17.65\,\text{ns}}$$

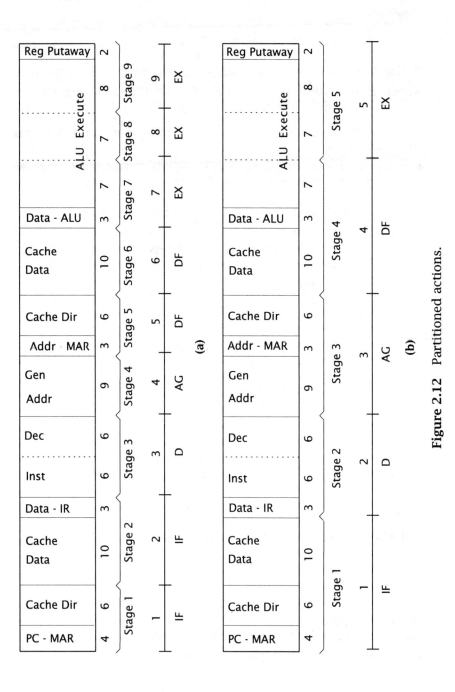

Figure 2.12 Partitioned actions.

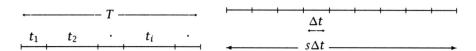

Figure 2.13 Cycle time quantization. T is the total unquantized instruction execution delay, $s\Delta t$ is the quantized instruction execution delay.

$$G(13\,\text{ns}) = 21.8\ \text{MIPS}$$
$$G(9\,\text{ns}) = \frac{1}{1 + (14)(.2)} \cdot \frac{1}{13.5\,\text{ns}}$$
$$G(9\,\text{ns}) = 19.5\ \text{MIPS}$$
$$G(20\,\text{ns}) = \frac{1}{1 + 4(.2)} \cdot \frac{1}{25\,\text{ns}}$$
$$G(20\,\text{ns}) = 22.2\ \text{MIPS}.$$

While the $T_{\text{seg}} = 13\,\text{ns}$ and $20\,\text{ns}$ partitions give practically the same performance, the $20\,\text{ns}$ is clearly to be preferred, since it is a less complex design with fewer pipeline stages.

Generalizing the preceding, we compute S_{opt}, but use it only as a rough guideline in the partitioning process. It is also rather an "upper limit" for the number of segments, since the complexity (and cost) of additional pipeline segmentation makes such segmentation (beyond S_{opt}) impractical. The designer ought to consider several segment times in the range from T/S_{opt} through (at least) $2T/S_{\text{opt}}$, observing (1) performance sensitivity and (2) resultant design complexity. The larger the number of segments, the more complex the design.

2.2.6   Cycle Quantization

Usually, larger functional units can be segmented into pipeline stages, but segmentation cannot occur across segments. This gives rise to a loss of performance due to *cycle quantization*. This is the time lost to fitting functional unit delays into fixed cycle times. In the previous example (study 2.1), we can combine I-decode and Address Generate into a cycle ($12 + 9 = 21\,\text{ns}$), but we cannot combine an I-decode with (say) half of the AG.

In general, in order to minimize instruction execution delay, one must minimize the time wasted due to cycle quantization and cycle overhead. That is, if the unit delay for the ith unit is t_i and if the total unquantized instruction delay is T, then

$$T = \sum_i t_i.$$

After clocking, execution occurs at the clock rate (Δt), and if instruction execution requires s cycles (or time $s\Delta t$), then, ignoring k (as shown in

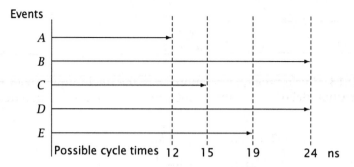

Figure 2.14   Where to put the cycle boundary.

Figure 2.13):

$$s\Delta t \;\geq\; T + sC$$
$$s\Delta t - T \;=\; s(t_m + C) - T$$
$$=\; st_m + sC - T,$$

where t_m is simply $\Delta t - C$, the time between clocks. There are two distinct overheads here; sC is the clocking overhead and it grows as s grows. The other overhead is:

$$st_m - \sum_i t_i,$$

or the quantization overhead. Presumably, if t_m were made small and s correspondingly large, then

$$s_i t_m - t_i \to 0 \qquad \text{for all } i,$$

where s_i is the smallest integer to make the above equal to or greater than zero. The overall effect of quantization is

$$st_m - T.$$

In reducing t_m to reduce quantization overhead, we increase s and hence increase the clocking overhead. There is a delicate balance between the two overheads, as illustrated in the following study.

Study 2.2   Cycle partitioning

Suppose a processor's instruction execution requires a sequence of five events (Figure 2.14) A, B, C, D, and E, with respective delays of:

A	12 ns
B	24 ns
C	15 ns
D	24 ns
E	19 ns

The total unpartitioned execution time is simply the sum of the events, $T = 94$ ns. We assume that each event can be segmented.

For this study, we assume a fixed clocking overhead of 2 ns. We ignore skew effects, i.e., $k = 0$. If we selected a $12 + 2 = 14$ ns cycle time, each of B, C, D, and E would take two cycles for execution (nine total). The clocking overhead is simply the fixed clock overhead times the number of cycles. The quantization overhead is the difference between the total partitioned instruction execution time and the sum of T and the clocking overhead. Continuing for various cycle times, we can tabulate the alternatives for total execution time. Assuming $b = 0.2$, we can then compute G as in study 2.1. We can compute $S_{opt} = 13.7$, but clearly any cycle time less than 14 ns $(12 + 2)$ has excessive quantization overhead. Thus, we start with $S = 9$.

Cycle time	Required # cycles	Clocking overhead	Quantization overhead	Total instr execution	G in MIPS
14 ns	9	18 ns	14 ns	126 ns	27.5
17 ns	8	16 ns	26 ns	136 ns	24.5
21 ns	7	14 ns	39 ns	147 ns	21.6
26 ns	5	10 ns	26 ns	130 ns	21.4

Here, 14 ns is the preferred cycle time and $S = 9$.

Note, however, that if $B = 30$ ns and $D = 30$, then $T = 106$ and $S_{opt} = 14.6$. We would again start with cycle time = 14 ns and new $S = 11$.

Cycle time	Required # cycles	Clocking overhead	Quantization overhead	Total instr execution	G in MIPS
14 ns	11	22 ns	26 ns	154 ns	23.8
17 ns	8	16 ns	14 ns	136 ns	24.5
21 ns	7	14 ns	27 ns	147 ns	21.6
26 ns	7	14 ns	62 ns	182 ns	17.5

Now a 17-nanosecond cycle is optimum.

2.2.7 Wave Pipelining: The Ultimate Limit on Pipelined Processor Cycle Time

What is the fastest cycle time, and how can one go about achieving it?

In the foregoing discussion, cycle time is determined by the maximum delay through a pipeline segment. This time can be reduced by ensuring that the minimum pipeline segment delay is close to the maximum.

It may seem strange that very fast cycle times can be achieved by adding delay to the minimum path through a logic segment (P_{min}). Rather than resort to exotic techniques to minimize the maximum delay (P_{max}) through a pipeline segment, we can, if we have good control on the minimum delay, use this delay as a sort of storage. This allows "waves" of unlatched data to proceed through the various pipeline segments—hence the term "wave"

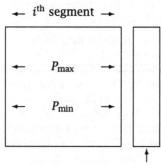

Figure 2.15   The ith pipeline segment.

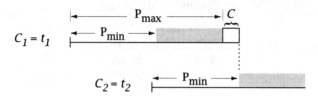

Figure 2.16   Stage propagation delay.

pipelining to describe the use of minimum delay to reduce cycle time. We exclude the register delay from both P_{max} and P_{min}.

Let us define C as the *delay due to clocking*, which consists of both setup and register delay time for the input data. For the sake of this discussion, we ignore the effects of clock skew (i.e., we assume $k = 0$). Suppose the first data item set enters the ith stage (Figure 2.15) at absolute time t_1. What is the earliest time (t_2) at which we can safely enter a second data set?

$$t_2 + P_{\text{min}} \geq t_1 + P_{\text{max}} + C.$$

That is, the second data set can be entered into the ith stage *after* the first data set has a guarantee of being safely stored into the register (Figure 2.16). Thus,

$$t_2 - t_1 \geq P_{\text{max}} - P_{\text{min}} + C.$$

The cycle time Δt is the minimum difference between t_2 and t_1, i.e., $\Delta t = t_2 - t_1$, so

$$\Delta t \geq P_{\text{max}} - P_{\text{min}} + C.$$

For any segment i:

$$\Delta t_i = P_{\text{max}_i} - P_{\text{min}_i} + C_i = (P_{\text{max}} - P_{\text{min}} + C)_i.$$

Next, we determine the worst (or maximum) Δt_i across all segments. That is,

$$\text{Min cycle time} = \{\max (\Delta t_i)\}.$$

For registers using transparent clocking and with no hold time, we can use

$$C = t_g + \max(t_d) - \min(t_d),$$

where (as before) t_g = setup time, and $\max(t_d)$ and $\min(t_d)$ are the maximum and minimum output delays after the clock is enabled. Again, this assumes both that the uncontrolled clock skew and the hold time are zero. The usual case for transparent latches is that the hold time is zero. For a more complete analysis of C for various latches and timing assumptions, see Klass [165] and Wong [309].

"Wave" pipelining does *not* shorten the longest path or the total instruction execution delay, $\sum(P_{max} + C)_i$. It simply increases the rate at which data is processed. Since the $P_{max} + C$ delay is unchanged, and the clock is reduced, the time at which the clock occurs must be adjusted.

Suppose a particular pipeline segment has $P_{max} = 10$ ns and $P_{min} = 7$ ns, with $C = 2$ ns. Rather than waiting for $P_{max} + C = 10 + 2 = 12$ ns, we can be assured that we can bring in another pair of operands—another wave of data—7 ns before the conclusion of the first 12 ns period. This may be done without interfering with the clocking of the first pair of data into a register. The second data will simply not arrive until the first data has been sampled properly into a storage element. With respect to this single pipeline segment, we can reduce the cycle time to $\Delta t = P_{max} - P_{min} + C = 10 - 7 + 2 = 5$ ns. Clearly, as we continue the analysis across multiple pipeline segments, the worst segment—the segment with the longest cycle time—must be the one that is used for the system. Data can only be accepted and produced at the rate commensurate with the slowest segment in the pipeline. To use storage in the form of minimum delay as a factor in design to improve cycle time requires careful management of the time at which the clock occurs to sample data into registers. No longer will clock signals be arranged to arrive at exactly the same time throughout all storage elements in this system. While normally clock signals are expected to arrive at all stages at the same time—without clock skew—constructive clock skew plays an important part in allowing the achievement of minimum cycle time.

Suppose we have a synchronously clocked machine whose state is sampled by the rising clock signal. We use $CK \uparrow$ to indicate the initial relative time ($t = 0$) for clock action at the beginning of the pipeline. Then $CS_i \uparrow$ indicates the amount of relative time change (skew) that the ith pipeline stage has with respect to $CK \uparrow$. The clock for the ith stage must be skewed by $CS_i \uparrow$:

$$CS_i \uparrow = \left[\Sigma_{j=1}^i (P_{max} + C)_j \right] \bmod \Delta t,$$

where $(P_{max} + C)_j$ is the sum of P_{max_j} and clocking delay C. This represents the total maximum delay through the segment of the pipeline. Skewing the clock by $CS_i \uparrow$ insures that the clock samples the data at a time equal to the maximum delay required to reach this i^{th} segment point. This is shown as follows:

$\leftarrow \quad P_{max1} + C \quad \rightarrow$	$\leftarrow P_{max2} + C \rightarrow$	$\cdot$	

$CK \uparrow$ $CS_1 \uparrow$ $CS_i \uparrow$
at $t = 0$

The total time for execution through all S stages of the pipeline is called the *latency*.

$$\text{Latency} = \sum_{j=1}^{S} (P_{\max} + C)_j.$$

EXAMPLE 2.1

Suppose we have the following three-segment pipeline:

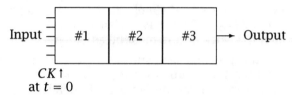

$$CK \uparrow$$
$$\text{at } t = 0$$

with $C = 2$ ns.

Segment #1	$P_{\max 1} = 10$ ns
	$P_{\min 1} = 7$ ns
Segment #2	$P_{\max 2} = 13$ ns
	$P_{\min 2} = 8$ ns
Segment #3	$P_{\max 3} = 12$ ns
	$P_{\min 3} = 9$ ns

The respective segment cycle times are:

$$\begin{aligned}
\Delta t_1 &= 10 - 7 + 2 = 5 \\
\Delta t_2 &= 7 \\
\Delta t_3 &= 5 \\
\max(\Delta t_i) &= 7.
\end{aligned}$$

The clock should be skewed (with respect to $t = 0$ inputs):

$$\begin{aligned}
CS_1 \uparrow &= (10 + 2) \bmod 7 = 12 \bmod 7 = 5 \\
CS_2 \uparrow &= (12 + 13 + 2) \bmod 7 = 27 \bmod 7 = 6 \ (\text{or } -1 \text{ ns}) \\
CS_3 \uparrow &= (27 + 12 + 2) \bmod 7 = 41 \bmod 7 = 6 \ (\text{or } -1 \text{ ns}).
\end{aligned}$$

The data from the first segment of the pipeline is not latched into the second stage until 12 ns after its entry into the first stage. If we designate the beginning of clock activation at the entry to segment #1 as $t_0 = 0$, then this is the time when data begins to flow in the first segment. At 12 ns later the clock should be in a similar position with respect to the entry of the second pipeline segment. Even though the rate is 7 ns, the occurrence of the clock must be purposely skewed so that the data occurring on the maximum delay path is safely clocked into the storage element at the end of the first segment. Thus, the clock must be skewed by 5 ns ($5 + 7 = 12$). Skewing a 7 ns clock by 5 ns (i.e., delaying it by 5 ns) is exactly the same as having it occur 2 ns earlier than the reference clock. Now data, in order to be safely clocked into the second segment register, can experience a delay of $10 + 2 + 13 + 2$, or 27 ns. Using a 7 ns clock that is referenced to $t_0 = 0$, this is 1 ns earlier than the fourth clock ($4 \times 7 - 1 = 27$ ns).

◆

Thus, constructive skewing of the clock, as illustrated previously, allows the fastest possible synchronous cycle times. As in any pipelined system, no useful results appear at the output until the pipeline is full.

Using P_{min} delays and constructive clock skew (CS↑) as shown in the preceding improves the cycle time by using the P_{min} delay to act as a storage element. Extensive use of such techniques is still largely a research area. Wong [311] reports being able to attain a clock speedup of 2.5 by using these techniques. For most of this text, we assume a cycle time defined by P_{max} without taking advantage of P_{min}.

Notice that uncontrolled clock skew in a wave pipelined system can have an even greater effect on cycle time than in a conventionally clocked system. If the uncontrolled skew in the arrival of the clock is $\pm\delta$, its effect on C can be

$$C = t_d + t_g + 4\delta.$$

2.3   Cost–Area

Much of this book is devoted to understanding issues of *performance*. Included in this is the analysis of various memory configurations and processor design choices. Determining performance is relatively straightforward. A basic measure of performance is the product of the cycle time, the number of cycles per instruction (the CPI), and the number of instructions that an architecture executes (particularly in relation to another architecture).

Determining the *goodness* of a processor design is much more difficult. A good design is not simply the fastest possible processor implementation. Implementation and performance must be balanced with cost. A good design achieves an optimum cost-performance tradeoff at a particular target performance.

Moreover, there are a host of other issues that are secondary to the design itself, but directly influence the program cost and hence the product cost. These same issues may influence the marketability of the product. Some of these issues include:

- Compatibility.

- Applicability to the marketplace.

- Upgradability.

- Design time.

- Reliability.

Consider the issue of compatibility. Companies such as IBM, DEC, Intel, and Motorola have generally retained design features, instructions, and even data types that may have effectively been made obsolete by the introduction of more powerful or more robust design attributes. Older instruction types and data types are retained to preserve the portability of programs to the newer processor. This enhances the user acceptability of the design and lowers user cost in adopting the new product. Similarly, the notion of an architecture family is very important in design, sales, and marketing so that a product may be extended later as needs arise to include the possibility of enhanced performance. Yet upgradability as well as compatibility have distinct design costs, as provisions must be made for each design feature. Each feature included affects design time and time to market, whether directly as part of the principal design attributes or indirectly to support compatibility, upgradability, serviceability, or other requirements. Design time represents a fixed cost and a call on design resources, as well as possibly delaying access to a particular market. The more complex the design and the more attributes to be considered, the longer the design cycle and the more design resources and fixed cost required.

Let us explore the costs in more detail. There are two types of cost: fixed cost and the marginal cost of manufacture. Most designers, in the absence of other information, think of cost in terms of the marginal cost to manufacture the next processing unit. The fixed cost includes the engineering cost of both hardware and software, engineering charges for building VLSI masks, charges for both CAD equipment and software, OS and computer software development, and manufacturing tooling expense. On top of this is an allocation for general management and overhead, as well as for marketing development effort. Once the product has been developed, manufacturing commences; but the cost of manufacturing per unit is determined by a learning curve. Early units are necessarily more expensive than later units, both to build and to maintain. After a while the manufacturing process itself becomes more tuned to a particular product and becomes more efficient at producing and testing the product.

Finally, the marginal cost to manufacture is still only one component in the marginal cost to deliver a product. The cost to deliver includes transportation, sales, general marketing, warranty service, and documentation costs.

2.3.1   Area

A processor designer generally has little control over many of the aforementioned fixed or variable costs. It is largely in the area of marginal manufacturing costs that design tradeoff is possible. From time to time throughout this text, when we discuss the issue of cost–performance, it is in this narrow marginal sense. The designer must be aware that the marginal cost–performance we address here cannot be done at the expense of a significant side effect on either the fixed costs or the other variable costs. For example, a significant increase in the complexity of a design may directly affect its serviceability or its documentation costs, or even the hardware development effort and time to market. These effects must be kept in mind, even when it is not possible to accurately quantify the extent of the particular side effects.

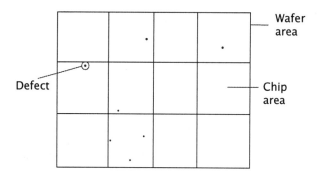

Figure 2.17   Defect distribution on a wafer.

Almost all modern designs are based upon silicon technology in one or another VLSI format. Given a set of VLSI technology parameters, there are two primary determinants of cost:

1. Pins (and package).

2. Silicon area occupied.

It would not be inaccurate to look at the problem of modern processor design as a problem of dealing with islands of logic connected only by a limited number of connection paths, terminated through a limited number of pins and bonding pads. Since the bandwidth on these connections is limited, the total amount of data that can be transmitted is also limited. Regardless of how fast the logic executes, there remains an upper limit to the usefulness of the insular computation bounded by the communications bandwidth available for interchip communications.

Processor Area

Most processors are implemented on one or a few chips, each housing a die about 10–15 mm on a side. These die are produced in bulk from a larger wafer, perhaps 15–21 cm in diameter (about 6–8 inches). Initially, the concern with limited chip area may seem unwarranted. One could simply expand the chip size and produce fewer chips on a wafer, and with these larger chips accommodate any desirable feature or function that the designer might wish to include. Unfortunately, neither the silicon wafers nor processing technologies are perfect. Defects randomly occur over the wafer surface (Figure 2.17). Large chip areas require an absence of defects over that area. If chips are too large for a particular processing technology, there will simply be no yield at all. Defects will be found on all the die on a particular wafer. Figure 2.18 illustrates yield vs. chip area.

It is important to note that a good design is not necessarily one that immediately produces maximum yield. Reducing the area of a design below a certain critical amount has only a marginal effect on yield, which at that point is simply determined by the percentage area affected by defects. Additionally, small designs waste area because there is a required separation between adjacent die on a wafer, so smaller die size simply means a larger amount of area dedicated to interstitial unused wafer area.

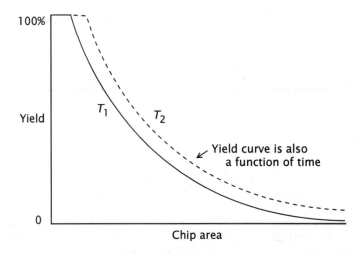

Figure 2.18   Yield vs. chip area at various points in time.

Semiconductor technology has made significant advances in recent years. Both manufacturing and design processes have been improved. Improvements in the design process, largely due to improved photolithography, allow larger amounts of processor logic to be included in a constant area. Designs are limited by the resolution of the photolithography or the ability to define distinct geometries on the wafer surface. Because of optical resolution, and even the wavelength of light itself, devices, connections, etc., on a die have edge irregularities. Thus, the underlying feature that is produced must be large enough (have sufficient area) to insure correct operation. For this reason, the concept of *minimum feature size*, or *geometric limit*, is an important parameter to any designer. For our purposes, we may regard the minimum feature size as the minimum transistor length. The smaller the minimum feature size, the more transistors can be implemented in a given area.

The area available to a designer, on the other hand, is largely a function of the manufacturing processing technology. This includes the purity of the silicon crystals, the absence of dust and other impurities, and the overall control of the diffusion and process technology. Improved manufacturing technology allows larger die to be realized with higher yields. Both photolithography technology and process technology are constantly improving. Processor designs are frequently not readily scalable to use these improvements. Rather, at a certain point a design team embarks on a completely new design to take advantage of improvements in technology. For the processor designer, there is a delicate design decision to be made early on: what die area and what lithography ought we to use to achieve a product with a maximum program life and maximum market impact? The conservative designer is not always a winner in this tradeoff. While the resultant (smaller) design may achieve excellent yields early in its product life, these yields generally will not improve much over product life and the design may be easily surpassed by competitive groups who wait a little longer and then have improved lithography or larger die area available to them for their designs. The successful designer must be aggressive enough in anticipating the movement of technology so that, although early designs may have

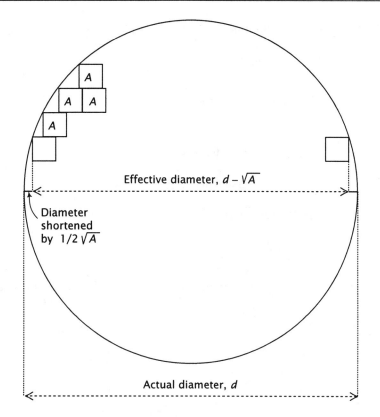

Figure 2.19   Number of die (of area A) on a wafer of diameter d.

low yield (but certainly greater than zero, one hopes), with the advance of technology the design life is extended and the yield greatly improves, thus allowing the design team to amortize fixed costs over a broad base of products.

Suppose a die with square aspect ratio has area A. About N of these die can be realized in a wafer of diameter d (see Figure 2.19):

$$N \approx \frac{\pi}{4A}(d - \sqrt{A})^2.$$

Suppose there are N_G good chips and N_D point defects on the wafer. Even if $N_D > N$, we might expect several good chips, since the defects are randomly distributed and several defects would cluster on defective chips, sparing a few good chips.

Following the analysis of Ghandi [100], suppose we add a random defect to a wafer; N_G/N is the probability that the defect ruins a good die. In other words, the change in the number of good die (N_G), with respect to the change in the number of defects (N_D), is

$$\frac{dN_G}{dN_D} = -\frac{N_G}{N}$$

$$\frac{1}{N_G}dN_G = -\frac{1}{N}dN_D.$$

The yield can be determined as

$$\text{Yield} = \frac{N_G}{N} = e^{-N_D/N}.$$

This describes a Poisson distribution of defects.

Now

$$N_D = \text{Number of wafer defects,}$$

so that if ρ_D is the defect density per unit area, then

$$N_D = \rho_D(\text{wafer area})$$
$$N_D = \rho_D \left(\frac{\pi d^2}{4} \right).$$

For large wafers $d \gg \sqrt{A}$, the diameter of the wafer is significantly larger than the die side and

$$(d - \sqrt{A})^2 \approx d^2$$

and

$$\frac{N_D}{N} = \rho_D A,$$

so that

$$\text{Yield} = e^{-\rho_D A}.$$

Figure 2.20 shows die yield as a function of $\rho_D \cdot A$, the Poisson defect distribution. This is known to be a somewhat pessimistic model of yield; a more accurate estimate is also shown. For the processor designer, the issue is area. Doubling the area has significantly more effect on yield for already large $\rho_D \cdot A$ (i.e., ≈ 5–10 or more). Thus, the large die designer gambles that technology will lower ρ_D in time to provide a sufficient yield for a profitable product.

Die Cost

Die cost is determined by area in two ways. One, as die area increases, fewer die are realized from a fixed size wafer. Two, as per our previous discussion, as the die area increases the yield decreases. This combination of effects is illustrated in the following example:

EXAMPLE 2.2

Assume a wafer has diameter of 21 cm and costs \$5,000 for a particular production run. Compute the cost per die for die area = 2.3 cm^2 and for 1 cm^2 if $\rho_D = 1$ defect/cm^2.

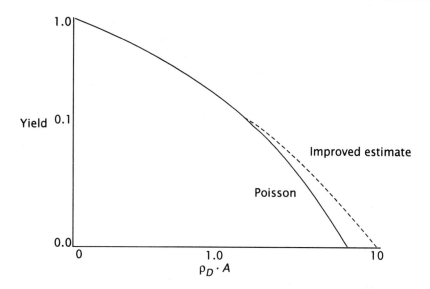

Figure 2.20 Yield vs. wafer defects for Poisson distributed defects. The improved estimate is based on the work of Murphy [210]. See also Walker [299].

The total number of die realized by the 21-cm wafer is

$$N = \frac{\pi}{4A}(d - \sqrt{A})^2.$$

For 2.3 cm² die,

$$N = 130 \qquad (d = 21, \ A = 2.3),$$

and for 1.0 cm² die,

$$N = 314 \qquad (d = 21, \ A = 1).$$

The yield is ($\rho_D = 1$ defect/cm²).

$$Y = \frac{N_G}{N} = e^{-\rho_D A}.$$

For 2.3 cm²:

$$Y = 0.1 \qquad (A = 2.3, \ \rho_D = 1).$$

For 1.0 cm²:

$$Y = 0.37 \qquad (A = 1, \ \rho_D = 1).$$

So, since

$$N_G = N \cdot Y \text{ and } N = \frac{\pi}{4A}(d)^2,$$

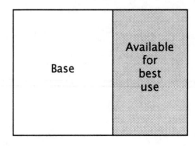

Figure 2.21   Maximizing the marginal utility of area.

for

$$A = 2.3\,\text{cm}^2$$
$$N_G = .1 \times 130 = 13$$
$$\text{Effective cost per die} = \frac{\text{Cost per wafer}}{N_G}$$
$$= \frac{\$5,000}{13} = \$385.$$

For

$$A = 1.0\,\text{cm}^2,$$
$$N_G = 116,$$
$$\text{and effective cost per die} = \$43$$

—roughly doubling the die area may increase the die cost almost 10 times!

◆

Area of Processor Sub-Units

Within a microprocessor, the amount of area a particular sub-unit of a design occupies is a primary measure of its cost. In making design choices or in evaluating the relative merits of a particular design choice, it is frequently useful to use the principle of *marginal utility*: assume we have a complete base design and some additional pins/area available to enhance the design. We select that design enhancement that best uses the available pins and area (Figure 2.21). Several times in this text we consider the principle of marginal utility as it applies to several design alternatives. In the absence of pinout information, we assume that area is a dominant factor in a particular tradeoff.

In dealing with area, the obvious unit appears to be *distance*[2]—either *mils*[2] or *millimeters*[2]. However, because photolithography and geometries' resulting minimum feature sizes are constantly shifting, this is not as desirable a unit as would first appear. The need for a dimensionless distance unit was recognized early. Mead and Conway [194] proposed the unit λ, the fundamental resolution, the distance by which a geometric feature on any one layer of implementation may stray from another geometric feature.

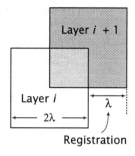

Registration

Figure 2.22   Device with registration uncertainty.

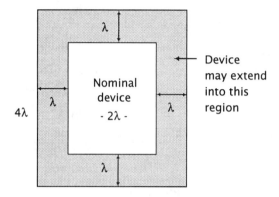

Figure 2.23   Registration uncertainty for a device.

The minimum size for a diffusion region would be 2λ with a necessary allowance of 3λ between adjacent diffusion regions. Thus, a single transistor is $4\lambda^2$, positioned in a minimum region of $25\lambda^2$.

If we start with a device $2\lambda \times 2\lambda$ (Figure 2.22), then a device of nominal $2\lambda \times 2\lambda$ can extend to $4\lambda \times 4\lambda$ (Figure 2.23). Then we need at least 1λ isolation from any other device or $25\lambda^2$ for the overall device area.

For us, the minimum feature size (f) is the length of one polysilicon gate, or the length of one transistor, $f = 2\lambda$. Clearly, we could define our design in terms of λ^2, as in the preceding, and any other processor feature (gate, register size, etc.) can be expressed as a number of transistors (plus interstitial area, other componentry, etc.). Thus, the selection of the area unit is arbitrary to a point. However, we would like to choose a unit that represents primary architectural tradeoffs. While an ALU bit is probably as reasonable as any arbitrary measure of area, adders and data paths are usually fixed portions of a processor design; moreover, areas such as register size, cache size, and TLB size are areas where the designer has more discretion. Thus, for our purposes, we have selected the register bit equivalent (**rbe**) as being the basic area measure. In practical designs, the six-transistor register cell represents about $2700\lambda^2$. This is significantly more than six times the area of a single transistor, since it includes other components, connections, and necessary inter-bit isolating spaces.

One **rbe** equals the area of a bit storage cell. Even in the context of a MOS-based VLSI technology, there is no universal bit storage cell. Our unit **rbe**

Table 2.2   Summary of relative areas.

Item Size in **rbe**	
1 register bit (**rbe**)	1.0 **rbe**
1 static RAM bit as used in an on-chip cache	0.6 **rbe**
1 CAM bit as used in a fully associative cache directory	2.0 **rbe**
1 DRAM bit as used in a large DRAM array	0.1 **rbe**
rbe corresponds to: in feature size, f in resolution, λ	1 **rbe** = $675 f^2$ 1 **rbe** = $2700 \lambda^2$

Item A corresponds to $1 \, mm^2$ with $f = 1\mu$.	Size in A Units
$1A$	$= f^2 \times 10^6$ (f in microns)
$1A$	$= 1481$ **rbe**
A "3-ported" register (2 read–1 write, 32×32^b) is $(32 + 6) * (32 + 6)$ $= 1444$ **rbe**	$\approx 1A \, (= 0.975A)$
A 4KB direct mapped cache with 16^B lines and 24^b tag (directory entry) would have:	
Data bits	$= 4096 \times 8 = 32,768$
Tag bits	$= \frac{4096}{16} \times 24 = 6144$
Cache size	$= 195 + .6[32,768 + 6,144]$ $= 23{,}542$ **rbe**
Total	$= 15.9A$

is referenced to a six-transistor static cell with high bandwidth—a register bit isolated from its input/output circuitry. A six-transistor static cell with lower bandwidth would use less area and a DRAM-bit cell would use still less. Empirically, they would have the relationship shown in Table 2.2.

Static RAM cells are used to reduce the area of on-chip caches at the expense of bandwidth and access time. In this book, all on-chip storage (cache, buffers, etc.) exclusive of registers themselves is assumed to be static cells unless otherwise noted. Other choices such as "fast" DRAM, etc., can readily be scaled.

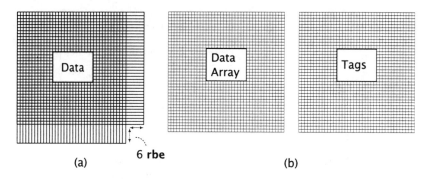

Figure 2.24   Data and tag area model. (a) shows the layout of a register set. (b) shows a cache consisting of data array plus directory.

2.3.2   Data Storage

Some of the more important parts of the chip for area modeling are the register set/cache/buffer areas of the chip, since these are the most frequent targets of design tradeoffs. The register set is an integral part of the data path of the system, but the total area that it occupies is not simply the number of bits that the register set stores. Register sets are usually referred to as *dual* or *three-ported registers.* They allow the user to access two words in one cycle and to return a value to a third word in the register set. Actually, these cells usually consist of one dedicated read port and a time-multiplexed read-and-write port, since the write occurs at the end of the cycle and the reads occur at the beginning of the cycle. These three-ported register buffers have both bit line sense amplifiers and control line drivers that occupy area in addition to the data array itself. It has been empirically determined [207] that the sense amplifiers and drivers add approximately six **rbe** to each dimension of the data buffer (Figure 2.24a). Thus, for a "three-ported" register set, we have the following area relationship:

Area of register = (number of regs + 6)(bits per reg + 6) **rbe**.

A 16-word-by-32-bit register set has approximately 1.6 **rbe** per bit of data stored. If the same register set size were doubled to 32 words by 32 bits, it would have 1.4 **rbe** per data bit.

Caches use smaller cells; thus, for cache storage using static cells, the following relationship has been determined [206]:

Area of cache = $195 + 0.6K_1$(data bits) $+ 0.6K_2$(tag bits) **rbe,**

where 195 **rbe** is allocated to control (e.g., a small PLA), and K_1 and K_2 are area overhead associated with particular cache organizations. Each of K_1 and K_2 is of the form 1 + (cache parameters/cache size). As cache size increases, these overhead factors (K_1, K_2) asymptotically approach one [231].

As shown in Figure 2.24, caches include more than the data array. The cache must also allocate storage for address tags and other information such as dirty bits, valid bits, a comparator, and control logic (Figure 2.24b). These items are discussed in more detail in Chapter 5.

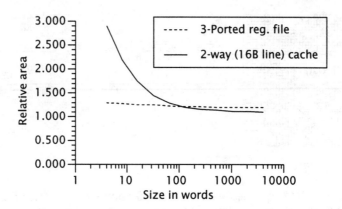

Figure 2.25 Area of on-chip data memory (cache and register file) as a function of memory capacity.

To illustrate the usefulness of the area model, consider a tradeoff between register area and cache area [207]. Figure 2.25 shows a crossover point at about 128 words. Below this point, *three-ported* registers occupy less area per word, while beyond 128 words (512 bytes) a cache, depending on its organization, occupies less area per word (or bit or byte).

The **rbe** model is a simplification. It generally matches the observed area (mean error 9% [207]) occupied by actual designs. For example, the **rbe** model is susceptible to error because it does not model several parameters such as the aspect ratio—the ratio of height to width of a particular storage unit.

Study 2.3   A Baseline Microprocessor Area Model

The key to efficient microprocessor design is *chip floor planning*. The process of chip floor planning is not much different from the process of floor-planning a residence. Each functional area of the processor must be allocated sufficient room for its implementation. Functional units that frequently communicate must be placed close together. Sufficient room must be allocated for connection paths.

To illustrate possible tradeoffs that can be made in optimizing the chip floor plan, we introduce in this section a baseline microprocessor with designated areas for various functions. The area model is based upon empirical observations made of existing chips, design experience, and, in some cases, logical deduction (e.g., the relationship between a floating-point adder and an integer ALU). The processor described here ought not to be considered optimal in any particular sense, but rather a typical example of a number of microprocessors in the marketplace today.

The Starting Point   The microprocessor design process begins with an understanding of the parameters of the semiconductor process. Suppose we expect to be able to use a manufacturing process that has or will have a

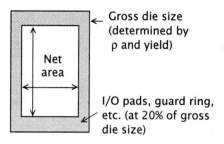

Figure 2.26   Net die area.

defect density of one defect per square centimeter; for economic reasons, we target an initial yield of 10%.

$$Y = e^{-\rho_D A},$$

where $\rho_D = 1$ defect/cm^2, $Y = 0.1$. Then

$$A \doteq 230\,\text{mm}^2 = 2.3\,\text{cm}^2.$$

In other words, the gross chip area available to us is 230 mm^2. This is the total die area of the chip, but such things as pads for the wire bonds that connect the chip to the external world, drivers for these connections, and power supply lines all act to decrease the amount of chip area available to the designer. In general, we allow 20% of the chip area—usually around the periphery of the chip—to accommodate these functions:

$$\begin{aligned} &\text{Pads + Guard Ring + Pad Drivers + Power Supply}\\ &\quad = \quad 20\% \text{ of } 230\,\text{mm}^2 = 46\,\text{mm}^2. \end{aligned}$$

Hence, the net area is 184 mm^2. This is the net area available to the microprocessor designer.

Feature Size   The smaller the feature size, the more logic that can be accommodated within a fixed area. As we discussed earlier, the **rbe** has been empirically determined to be approximately 2700 λ^2. Assume we have a process whose minimum feature size is one micron. Therefore,

$$f = 1\mu$$

and

$$f = 2\lambda,$$

or

$$\lambda = \frac{f}{2}$$

and

$$\lambda^2 = \frac{f^2}{4}.$$

Thus,

$$1 \textbf{ rbe} = 2,700\lambda^2 \doteq 675f^2.$$

The integer registers are assumed to be 32 registers by 32 bits and three-ported. This means that the integer register set occupies

$$38 \times 38 = 1,444 \textbf{ rbe},$$

or

$$1,444 \textbf{ rbe} \times 675\mu^2/\textbf{rbe} = 0.97,\text{mm}^2.$$

At this point, we define a unit of area (A) equal to $f^2 \times 10^6$ (f in microns) or $1\,\text{mm}^2$ with $f = 1$. This corresponds to 1,481 **rbe**. Thus, our three-ported register set occupies $0.97,\text{mm}^2$ or $.97A$, which we round to $1A$. Empirically, it has been determined that the integer ALU for 32-bit operands occupies about the same area as a 32×32-bit register set, so the integer ALU occupies $1A$.

The Architecture   Most instruction sets have basically the same operand vocabulary (excepting very early RISC machines, which accommodated very few operations, or some mainframe architectures (especially VAX) that accommodated a very large number of operations and variants). For our baseline, we select a modern (early 1990s) type of microprocessor: a load/store (L/S) architecture with 32 registers, each of 32 bits, with an integrated floating-point unit and corresponding instruction set. The floating-point unit is expected to be accommodated on-chip. In the style of current microprocessors, our baseline will be pipelined with a short pipeline, such as four or five stages, which will serve to minimize the delays due to branches. The instruction set affects the total available area only slightly. Its primary influence is through the area required for the register set. The decoder itself is allocated $1A$; a more or less elaborate decoder will not greatly affect the total amount of area available to the designer. Any of the following paths:

- Integer ALU

- Cache access

- Instruction decoder

- Register access

may determine the cycle time. Ideally, the designer works to achieve the situation where perhaps several of the preceding simultaneously limit cycle time.

An Area Model   The following is a breakdown of the area required for various functional units used in the baseline processor.

Unit	Area
Integer ALU (32^b)	$1.0A$
Bypass	$0.15A$
Integer reg.	$1.0A$
Shifter	$0.5A$
Incrementor	$0.4A$
I-fetch/PC unit	
PC chain	
Cache miss logic	$0.85A$
2 TLBs (Assumes use of PID)	
32^b virtual to 24^b real	$2 \times 3A$
Decode + control	$1.0A$
Cache controller	$1.0A$
Bus logic	$2.0A$
Store buffer + bypass	$1.0A$
Load/store byte support	$0.2A$
Clock generator	$1.0A$
Subtotal integer	$16.1A$

Most of the preceding data is empirically determined. The TLB requires some discussion, as it occupies almost a third of the base area of the integer processor. The dual TLBs (one for IF and one for DF/DS) are assumed to consist of single-ported register sets (i.e., one TLB bit = 1 **rbe**). This is consistent with fast TLB access requirements. Each TLB is assumed to be 2-way set associative with a total of 128 entries (64×2). Each entry (4^{KB} pages) has a 14-bit virtual address tag ($32^b - 12^b$ *(byte in a page address)* – 6^b *(TLB entry address)*) and a 12-bit real address ($24^b - 12^b$). Also, the entry contains a 4-bit PID (process ID number) and 4 bits of control information (LRU, R/W, etc.). See Chapter 5 for further discussion. Summing up, this gives 34 bits/entry or about 4,352 **rbe** per TLB (34×128). From our earlier discussion, we know that 1,481 **rbe** occupies $1\,\text{mm}^2 = 1A$. Thus, including MUX and comparitors, a single TLB occupies about $3A$. We assume that two TLBs will be used: one for data fetching and one for instruction fetching. Since instruction fetches frequently are simply in-line fetches, it might be possible to have both instructions and data share the same TLB. However, for the moment we choose not to do that, and show two separate TLBs. This correspondingly implies that we have two separate caches, an I-cache and a D-cache.

Floating Point   It has been empirically determined that a floating-point adder occupies the area corresponding to 13.5 times the integer ALU. For our floating-point multiplier, we assume a high-speed two-pass multiplier, which will occupy 1.5 times the floating-point adder area. The divider uses the multiplier hardware. This combination provides a performance of the following:

FADD	3 cycles
FMPY	3 cycles
FDIV	15 cycles,

which occupies an area of:

FP register file	$1A$
FP adder	$13.5A*$
FP multiplier = 1.5 adder	$20.3A*$
Support for divide	$3.0A$
Subtotal FP	$37.8A$

*Includes register bypass support, as discussed in Chapter 4.

The subtotal for the floating-point hardware then is $37.8A$, or $37.8\,\text{mm}^2$.

Latches, Buses, and (Interunit) Control   For each of the functional units, there is a certain amount of overhead to accommodate nonspecific storage (latches), interunit communications (buses), and interunit control. This is allocated as 10% for overhead for latches and 40% overhead for buses, clocking, and overall control. These overhead factors in microprocessor floor planning correspond to actual residential floor planning. They are analogous to the allowances for corridors (communications buses) and for closets (storage—latches).

Latches (10% of FP and integer)	$53.9 \times 0.1 = 5.4A$
Bus and control (40% of FP and integer)	$53.9 \times 0.4 = 21.6A$

Total Processor Area   We can now summarize the area required for the processor as follows:

Integer processor (net)	$16.1\ A$
Floating-point hardware (net)	$37.8\ A$
Latches and buses	$27\ A$
Processor area	$80.9\ A$

Cache Area   Out of our net area of $184\,\text{mm}^2$, the processor occupies an area of $80.9\,\text{mm}^2$. This leaves $103.1\,\text{mm}^2$ available for cache. However, bits and pieces that may be unoccupied on the chip are not always useful to the cache designer. These pieces must be collected into a reasonably compact area that accommodates efficient cache designs.

For example, where the available area has a large height-to-width (aspect) ratio, it may be significantly less useful than a more compact or square area. In general, at this early stage of microprocessor floor planning, we allocate another 10% overhead to aspect ratio mismatch. This leaves a net available area for cache of $92.8\,\text{mm}^2$.

From our earlier discussion, we see that 1,481 **rbe** can be accommodated in $1\,\text{mm}^2$. This means that approximately 137,437 **rbe** is available for the cache (1481×92.8). Since each cache bit only occupies 0.6 **rbe**, we have about 229,000 bits or 28.6 Kbytes available for cache. Out of this must come both the data array and the cache directory (Figure 2.27).

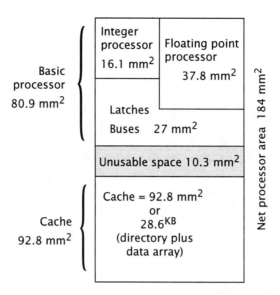

Figure 2.27   A baseline die floorplan.

Summary of Area Design Rules:

1. Compute target chip size from target yield and defect density.

2. Compute die cost and determine whether satisfactory.

3. Compute net available area. Allow 20% (or other appropriate factor) for pins, guard ring, power supplies, etc.

4. Determine the **rbe** size from the minimum feature size. Then determine register set size and ALU.

5. Continue allocating area until the core processor size is determined.

6. Subtract core processor size (5) from net available area (3). This is the die area available for processor optimization.

2.4   Technology State of the Art

Tables 2.3 and 2.4 illustrate some of the current technology parameters for a few representative workstations and mainframes.

There is a general misconception that mainframe processors are "big" while workstation processors are "small." The processor (only) in a typical mainframe uses about 40–100 chips and occupies less than $1/2$ ft^3. Mainframes are usually configured with 4–8 processors, vector facilities, large memory, and extensive I/O, usually packaged in a large frame.

The workstation processor usually fits a single die, but requires a large number of support chips for memory and I/O. A big difference between workstations and mainframes is in the cooling and power requirements. Workstations are air-cooled with modest power supply requirements. Mainframes

Table 2.3   Microprocessor statistics.

Microprocessor	Transistors (millions)	Die Size	Pins	Clock (MHz)	Cache Size	Technology (Metal Layers)
DEC21064	1.7	234 mm	431	200	8K-I/8K-D	0.75μ CMOS (3)
DEC 21164	9.3	298 mm	499	300	8K-I/8K-D/96K-L2	0.5μ CMOS (4)
HP PA7200	1.3	210 mm	540	120	0K-I/2K-D	0.55μ CMOS (3)
IBM PowerPC 601	2.8	120 mm	304	66	32K-U	0.6μ CMOS (4)
IBM PowerPC 603	1.6	85 mm	240	80	8K-I/8K-D	0.5μ CMOS (4)
IBM PowerPC 604	3.6	196 mm	304	80	16K-I/16K-D	0.5μ CMOS (4)
IBM PowerPC 620	6.9	311 mm	625	133	32K-I/32K-D	0.5μ CMOS (4)
Intel 486DX2	1.2	81 mm	168	66	8K-U	0.8μ CMOS (3)
Intel Pentium	3.3	163 mm	273	100	8K-I/8K-D	0.6μ BiCMOS (4)
MIPS R4000SC	1.3	184 mm	447	100	8K-I/8K-D	0.8μ CMOS (2)
MIPS R10000	5.9	298 mm	527	200	32K-I/32K-D	0.5μ CMOS (4)
Motorola 88110	1.3	225 mm	299	50	8K-I/8K-D	0.8μ CMOS (3)
SUN SuperSparc	3.1	256 mm	293	40	20K-I/16K-D	0.7μ BiCMOS (3)
SUN UltraSPARC	4.2	315 mm	521	167	16K-I/16K-D	0.5μ CMOS (4)

Table 2.4 High-speed mainframe technology (c. 1990/91).

Model	IBM 900	Hitachi M-880[a]	Fujitsu M-1800
Cycle time	9 ns	8 ns	7 ns
Number of processors	6	4	8
Basic technology	All use ECL (usually $f = 0.7\mu$, 4-layer metal); about 70–100 ps/gate delay or about 200–300 ps with line delay, etc. Each chip dissipates 20–30 watts!		
ECL gates/chip	5^K	12^K	15^K
Die size	—	12×12 mm	13×13 mm
Chips per module (module is frequently called MCM—multichip module)	100	41	144 on 52 layer board
Module size	—	10.6×10.6 cm	24.5×24.5 cm
Processor	Complete processor uses about 4 MCM's	Processor (excluding cache, etc.) is one module	Processor and cache and memory management is one board (141 chips)
Gates/processor	500,000–1,000,000	Same	Same
Basic with cache, etc.	1–2.5 million gates	Same	Same
Power	1–4 KW/processor, cooled using chilled water		

[a]The Hitachi 3800 announced in 1994 has a cycle time of 2 ns and uses improved versions of this same technology.

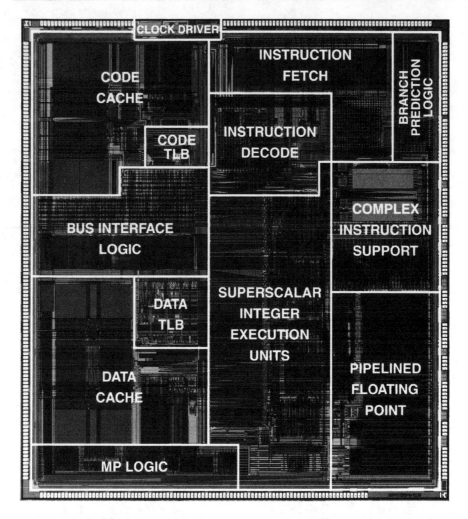

Figure 2.28 The Intel Pentium, iCOMP Index 815. This 100 Mhz processor uses $f = 0.6\mu$ and 4-layer metal BiCMOS. The chip size is 12.7×12.7 mm, or 163 mm^2. Photo courtesy of the Intel Corporation.

cover a spectrum from small air-cooled systems to the high-end examples cited in Table 2.4. Two state-of-the-art microprocessors are shown in Figures 2.28 and 2.29. These photomicrographs also show area allocation for various functions.

The following example illustrates one approach to high-speed mainframe technology.

Mainframe Example: Hitachi M-880

The basic processor (instruction processor) fits on a module (10.6 cm $\times$ 10.6 cm—about 4 inches on a side) and houses about 40 die, each containing up to 12^K gates and each consuming about 20 watts. In order to cool the module (800 watts), the chips are sealed in helium gas and chilled water is

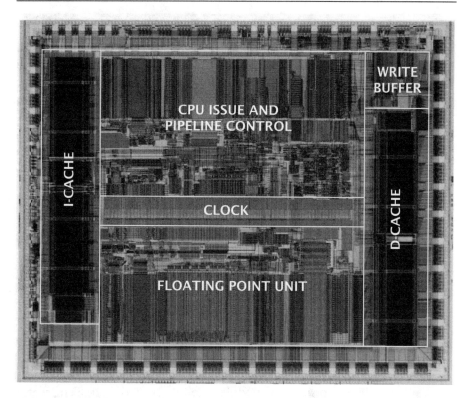

Figure 2.29   The DEC Alpha. This processor achieves 200 MHz with f = 0.75 and 3-layer CMOS. Chip area is 234 mm^2. Photo courtesy of Digital Equipment Corporation.

pumped across the water jacket on the top of the module. (See Figure 2.30.)

The total four-processor system with cache, memory, and I/O control fits on two large processor boards, each holding 20 modules (Figure 2.31.)

2.5   The Economics of a Processor Project: A Study

> *The following study should serve as background information for processor design students about the overall project economics of building computers. It is somewhat humbling to note the relatively small role of the processor in the system in terms of cost and development effort. Yet the processor is the engine that drives the rest of the system—the part most visible to the customer, hence the part that ought to receive a great deal of attention.*

Study 2.4   The $100 Million Project: Will It Make a Profit?

This is a study in the project economics of a modern processor system. For the moment, the technical details of the processor itself are relatively

Figure 2.30 Hitachi processor module. Module is 10.6 × 10.6 cm, water cooled, and has up to 41 ECL chips. Photo courtesy of Hitachi Corp. [168].

unimportant. We can assume that the project is for the development of a network file or compute server for some unspecified environment.

Any project begins with a project plan. This plan has several aspects:

1. The technical specifications. These include a complete set of functional specifications that are to be met by the proposed system, together with an estimate of the expected performance and the component count/ultimate manufacturing costs.

2. Market analysis. This analysis is a study of the users' other suppliers (the competition) in the marketplace; what user needs are, what solutions are currently (or are expected to be) available, together with prices and the expected lifetime of the program.

We assume that the project plan has led us to believe that the proposed product could be sold for an average of $10,000 per unit, achieving sales of 10,000 units over a six- or seven-year period. We further assume that the ultimate cost to manufacture the processor is $1,000 (materials plus labor). As a profit margin, the ratio of selling price to marginal cost for production of 10:1 may seem generous, indeed, guaranteed to produce an enormous profit. However, as we shall see, a gross profit margin of even 10:1 may be insufficient to produce any profit at all, depending on the number of units sold and the size of the fixed-cost investment in product development.

The project may be broken up into time phases.

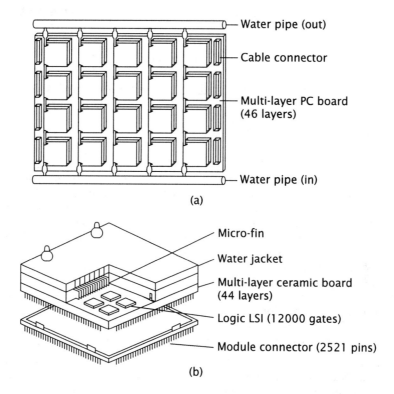

(a)

(b)

Figure 2.31 Hitachi M-880 (a) processor board and (b) module. The four-processor system with I/O controller and I/O interface uses two such boards. Each board is 73 × 53 cm. Figure courtesy of Hitachi Corp. [168].

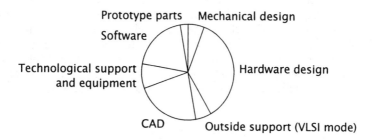

Figure 2.32 Initial development cost—total $18 million.

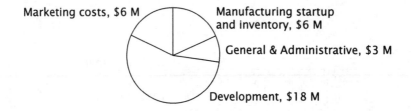

Figure 2.33   Phase I (initial phase) fixed cost estimate—total $33 million.

2.5.1   Phase 1: Development

Depending on its complexity, a processor takes anywhere from 12 to 30 months of development effort before the first unit can be shipped from manufacturing (first customer ship, or FCS, is an important milestone in any program). During this phase, the bulk of the fixed costs are assumed by the project. Initial development costs as shown in Figure 2.32 consist of a good deal more than simple hardware design. Assuming that this is indeed a new product, and not an evolutionary design based on an earlier product design, it is reasonable to expect 24 months to first customer ship. Even a fairly spartan project, consisting of perhaps 30–40 hardware and software designers, CAD design and support personnel, etc., incurs between $9 million and $12 million of salary and indirect costs out of a probable total development cost of $15–20 million. Even so, that does not include all of the fixed costs incurred during this development phase.

Development phase costs also include manufacturing startup costs, inventory costs, and initial marketing and sales costs, as well as general and administrative overhead, as shown in Figure 2.33. The marketing costs include obvious items such as market research, strategic market planning, pricing studies, competitive equipment analysis, etc., as well as the more obvious sales commissions, sales planning, and advertising costs. Manufacturing startup cost is a variable area. We could spend more money here, for example, in automation and test equipment, and achieve a higher-quality product and lower the ultimate cost. On the other hand, if it is essential to keep the fixed costs low, manufacturing startup cost can be reduced by subcontracting out special tooling production and assembly requirements. General and administrative (G & A) "overhead" includes a proportional share of the "front office"—the executive management, personnel department (human resources), financial office, and other costs. Frequently, G&A overhead is included in an indirect charge on development and manufacturing salaries. We have chosen to break it out here to distinguish it from these other charges. Development costs assumed here are simply salaries plus those charges that support an individual designer in an office environment, such as rent, heat, light, secretarial/administrative services, etc.

2.5.2   Phase 2: Early Manufacturing

In the beginning of the manufacturing process, unit cost remains high. It is not until about a thousand units are shipped, perhaps six months to a year into the program, that the marginal manufacturing cost can even begin to approach the ultimate manufacturing costs (Figure 2.34). In addition to the

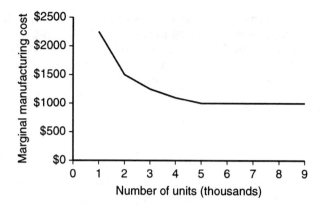

Figure 2.34   Manufacturing learning curve.

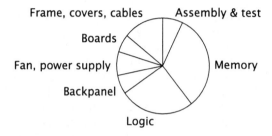

Figure 2.35   Marginal (ultimate) cost to produce processor system.

expected high costs for assembly and testing during this phase, there are usually several iterations with various vendors—of power supplies, boards, mechanical hardware or memory—to ensure the most reliable, available (for inventory), and best-quality goods from the supplier at the most reasonable cost. Problems with vendors as well as building a parts inventory (or assuring a just-in-time supplier) are manufacturing/purchasing issues that must be addressed during the early manufacturing phase.

2.5.3   Phase 3: Production

During this phase, manufacturing hits its stride and produces units at a cost increasingly approaching the ultimate manufacturing cost. However, the marginal cost to *produce* a unit (Figure 2.35) is not necessarily the same

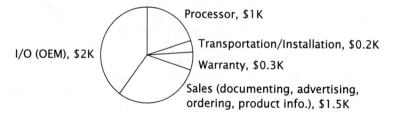

Figure 2.36   Ultimate processor cost in dollars.

as the marginal cost to *deliver* a unit (Figure 2.36). Note the relatively minor position of the processor logic itself in Figure 2.35. A significant amount of hardware cost is accounted for by frames, cables, covers, boards, and power supplies. It is this mechanical and electromechanical hardware that is *influenced by* processor design, but not directly *accounted for* by a particular design. For example, less dense logic that spreads across several boards and consumes a great deal of power increases the overall project manufacturing cost out of proportion to its own intrinsic cost (due to power supply, interconnections, cooling, etc.). Similarly, the marginal cost to deliver a processor is significantly greater than the cost of the processor itself, as it includes market support, transportation, warranty costs, sales, documentation, and ordering costs as well as delivery of associated I/O products. I/O products are generally procured OEM (original equipment manufacturer)— that is, from an OEM supplier at a discount of perhaps 50% off the list price. The sales representative attempts to sell the I/O equipment at list price, presumably with varying success, as a large customer will have direct access to the OEM supplier itself. In any event, it is assumed that the OEM sales are excluded from the total project, since they contribute little, conservatively, to the overall profit of the project. Of course, during the third phase of the project, that is, the production phase, software and hardware development must continue. Design flaws reported by service personnel must be attended to. In order to extend the life of the product, additional functionality and features—perhaps performance enhancements in hardware and software—must be made available, perhaps taking advantage of new logic parts unavailable to the original designer. A good deal of this continuing development effort is focused on extending the life of the product and broadening its market applicability.

2.5.4   Phase 4: All Good Things Must Come to an End

Despite continuing development effort, the product cycle closes when new products have been introduced that generally supersede the capacity/functionality/performance of the existing products. Hitherto we have said nothing about service other than recognizing warranty costs. This is because equipment service is its own profit center. Customers purchase service either through a contract or as required, and through these service calls the service department remains a profitable sub-venture. Long after the last machine has been shipped from the factory, the service department retains a parts inventory to support the product.

The bottom line is: did the project make a profit? From the preceding, it is easy to see how sensitive the project is to the product life and to the number of products shipped. If market forces or competition are aggressive and produce rival systems with expanded functionality and performance, the project life may be shortened and deliver only 5,000 units. This could be disastrous even though the ultimate manufacturing cost has been reached well within the 5,000-unit schedule; there are simply not enough units over which to amortize the fixed costs to ensure profit. On the other hand, if competition is not aggressive and the follow-on development team is successful in enhancing the product and continuing its attractiveness in the marketplace, the project can be one of those rare jewels in a company's repertoire, bringing fame to the designers and smiles to the stockholders.

2.6   Instruction Sets: Processor Evaluation Metrics

The instruction set of a processor represents the processor as a user sees it. Instructions define actions, which are partitioned into cycles. The sum of all these cycles represents program execution.

There are four basic issues that determine overall program execution time:

1. The cycle time. This is primarily a function of the implementation technology and secondarily a function of the instruction set and the size of the units specified by it (register set size, floating-point capability, etc.).

2. Cache and memory size and bandwidth. This is primarily a function of the available chip area and the number of chips involved in the implementation. Secondarily it also is a function of the instruction set.

3. The per-instruction execution time—the CPI or number of cycles per instruction. This is primarily determined by the definition of the cycle and the requirements of the instruction set. It is closely related, however, to the average memory access time, which is determined by cache size and/or memory configuration.

4. Number of instructions required to execute a program. This is determined by the instruction set and the compiler.

The instruction set, then, is the fabric that brings together cycle time and area into a general model of processor performance. There are probably few areas within the computer systems field that create as much controversy as the relative merits of one particular instruction set selection vs. another. Even when purely economic issues such as compatibility, design time, etc., are ignored, controversy still exists—as witnessed by discussion a few years ago of the RISC versus CISC (reduced vs. complex instruction set computer) approaches [270, 193]. Even from a technical point of view, there are many decisions involved in creating an instruction set and an implementation. Moreover, it is difficult to isolate a single factor as being primary in determining performance or cost. A machine is measured in many different ways, and its overall effectiveness depends on all aspects of the system—program size, number of instructions, cycle time, cycles per instruction, and cost (effective use of hardware). Even after the design is complete, the compiler technology plays a dominant role in determining the effectiveness of the features included in the machine.

The issue is not one of simply adding useful features to the instruction set (e.g., more registers), but of making those marginal additions to a machine that realize the best performance per unit of cost. Within a chip, this can be expressed as an area optimization problem: given a marginal increase in area on a base design, what is the best use of area in terms of performance? For a microprocessor, the penalty for using more area than can be accommodated on a single chip is severe, often doubling the cost. In a multichip "mainframe" machine, the additional cost for adding a feature may be more manageable. It is not surprising that the notion of marginal utility of a feature has been much more important in microprocessors than in

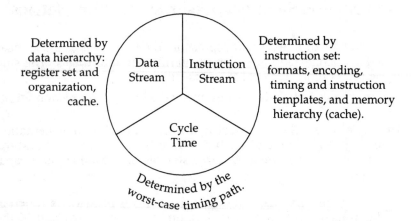

Figure 2.37   Basic performance constituents.

mainframes—hence the concern with instruction set cost-performance optimization. With larger chip areas available for microprocessor implementation, other related issues such as cache size and effectiveness become more pressing.

In the next section, we examine efforts at:

1. Instruction set comparisons.

2. Evaluation of differences in instruction sets.

3. Limits and tradeoffs in instruction set design. We especially look at the optimization of the instruction set code density and the tradeoffs in the register–cache system as a function of die area.

2.6.1   Program Execution

Program execution requires a certain number of processor cycles. The size of a cycle and the number of cycles are primary metrics for machine performance. Unfortunately, it is difficult to predict *a priori* the effects of a particular design choice on cycle time or the number of cycles. We try to manage this problem by creating a processor model in which we can separately examine certain dimensions of the overall processor design space. Three important constituents of performance (Figure 2.37) are:

1. The instruction stream—the dynamic activity of the instruction set in the execution of a program.

2. The data stream—the dynamic activity of data accessing during the execution of a program.

3. The processor cycle.

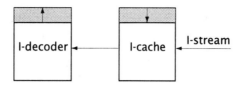

Figure 2.38 I-stream tradeoff: increasing the instruction encoding increases the I-decoder size (area), but decreases the I-cache size (area).

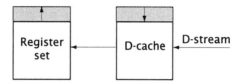

Figure 2.39 D-stream tradeoff: similarly, increasing the register set size decreases the D-cache size.

The Instruction Stream   Increasing the number of formats reduces the number of instructions executed. Increasing the degree of encoding of an instruction set reduces the average size of an instruction. Decreasing the number of instructions executed and the size of the average instruction decreases the number of memory accesses required to execute a particular program (Figure 2.38). These factors improve program execution. On the other hand, such improvements increase the size of the instruction decoder (they require more area, which may increase the cycle time) and require more sophisticated compilers. Moreover, multiple instruction sizes and multiple instruction formats create difficulty in managing the overlapping or pipelined execution of instructions. This extra decode area, for example, must be traded off against the extra instruction cache size that results from a poorly encoded instruction set. The designer must find an optimum balance for the application environment.

The Data Stream   A large register set reduces the read and write requests to memory, but adding registers has a limited usefulness beyond a certain point—as we shall see later, each additional register is less valuable than a register in the initial complement of registers. Moreover, in a user environment with frequent interrupts (such as realtime or multitasking applications) that result in the saving and restoring of these registers, these additional registers can become a burden. There is a tradeoff between enlarging the register set size and using the area for other items such as a small data cache. A large register set size decreases read and write traffic to memory (Figure 2.39). However, a small register size with a data cache occupying the equivalent amount of area may provide better overall performance.

Cycle Time Considerations   Many things affect cycle time, which is determined by the longest path through the processor logic. The longest delay path varies from implementation to implementation, but it is usually found in one of the following areas:

1. Access time to cache.

2. Access time to a register set.

3. Register set access plus ALU function time.

4. Instruction decode time.

Given the functional unit delays and clock times, we can begin the process of pipeline partitioning, as discussed earlier in this chapter.

2.6.2   Instruction Set Comparisons

Intelligent conclusions about a particular design decision cannot be made until that choice is evaluated. We begin by comparing instruction sets.

Some of the earliest attempts at instruction set comparison developed the notion of *overhead instructions*—instructions that appear in the object code because of *architectural considerations*, not because of any algorithmic or source-level requirements. For example, load and store instructions typically are overhead instructions, while add and multiply instructions, corresponding to actions in high-level languages, are not. Instructions can be grouped into classes [91]:

1. F-type, or functional, instructions that *transform* data (such as ALU-type operations). These generally correspond one to one to actions specified by higher level languages.

2. M-type, or data movement, instructions that *position* data for later use (e.g., Load or Store). For many programs, these instructions are required by the instruction set, not the source program.

The ratio of the occurrence of overhead instructions to the occurrence of functional instructions defines one measure of the overall effectiveness of an architecture, the *M-ratio*. The M-ratio is the ratio of data movement instructions (overhead—not required by the high-level language) to functional instructions:

$$\text{M-ratio} = \frac{\text{Number of M-type instructions}}{\text{Number of F-type instructions}}.$$

For S/370, the M-ratio was 2.9 (Flynn [91]), while for DEC-10, the M-ratio was 1.6 (Lunde [187]).

P-type, or procedural, instructions can also be defined to include those instructions that alter or modify instruction sequencing (branches, calls, etc.). Similarly, a *P-ratio* can be defined as follows:

$$\text{P-ratio} = \frac{\text{Number of P-type instructions}}{\text{Number of F-type instructions}}.$$

A breakdown of M, F, and P instruction class frequencies and ratios averaged over many programs for some vintage (early 1970s) architectures is given in Table 2.5.

Table 2.5 Operator use for some older R/M architectures.

Architecture	Processor	% F	% M	% P	M-ratio	P-ratio
R/M	S/370	15.3	45.1	39.6	2.9	2.6
R/M	DEC-10	26.7	42.6	30.5	1.6	1.1
R/M	PDP-11	13.7	35.5	50.8	2.6	3.7

These overhead analysis efforts were naturally limited. For one, they focused on scientific programs. In commercial programs, the object of a program might be to move data; hence, an apparent overhead instruction would really be a functional instruction (as in the case of a Sort program). A more comprehensive approach would be more valuable, but such studies are still useful. They implicitly assume that there is an invariant baseline number of operations (F-type) that is only a function of the program and not a function of architecture.

This viewpoint of "overhead" instructions leads naturally to the concept of a *language-oriented* machine. These machines attempt to (largely) eliminate overhead instructions by having instructions in one-to-one correspondence with high-level language actions. The Burroughs Corp. was a leader in developing machines of this type, especially machines targeted to the ALGOL language [28, 221, 222].

In another approach, Cragon [61] provides an analysis of various normalized machines, including register set machines, stack machines, and the various memory architectures. These hypothetical machines were compared on the basis of probable program size, instruction count, and cycle count. (See problem 16 at the end of this chapter.)

Perhaps the most extensive comparative analysis of instruction sets was done as part of the computer family analysis (CFA) for the Department of Defense computer selection effort [196, 97]. This study was used in creating a standard instruction set for Department of Defense procurement (MIL-STD-1750A). More than twenty parameters were studied on a variety of existing architectures. While most of these parameters simply determined the presence of a feature (e.g., floating-point arithmetic), the S, M, and R measures are significant quantitative measures of instruction set performance:

S: Measure of memory usage—the number of bytes used to represent a test program.

M: Measure of execution time—the number of bytes transferred between memory and processor during execution of a test program.

R: Measure of execution time—the number of bytes transferred among internal registers during the execution of a test program.

The S measure includes all instructions, indirect addresses, and temporary work areas required by the program. The only memory excluded from S is the storage required to hold the actual data structures or parameters specified in the test program.

The basic model underlying the CFA measures is one of measuring the "cost" of occupying memory during program execution. The S measure measures the size of the program representation. The M measure measures the number of bits that must be moved around from and to memory or other storage elements to ensure the execution of the program. Ultimately, the three measures represent a form of space–time product that determines how well a processor has used its memory.

Studying Instruction Sets

Nothing illustrates the changing nature of computer design more than the CFA study and the resulting Department of Defense "standard architecture"—the MIL-STD-1750A. The CFA study [196] was a careful analysis of then (early 1970s) contemporary architectures. Considering more than twenty parameters, the study spanned issues such as code density, instruction set features, memory hierarchies, support, and ease of "assembly-level" programming. Study data provided valuable input into the definition of the 1750A, meant to be a standard architecture for future generations of DOD computers.

By the time the 1750A was defined and released, it was already obsolete! It was a 16-bit architecture, and the industry had begun defining 32-bit machines and microprocessors. There is an important moral here. It is insufficient to simply understand the past, however valuable such data may be. It is only when historical analysis can be coupled with realistic expectations of future technological developments that we have the basis for intelligent and long-lived computer design.

Some Comparative Results

Ideally, we would have some idea as to how much improvement is possible in an architecture. Measures can be defined based only on the high-level language (HLL) representation of the program that characterizes its static and dynamic behavior [93]. Under certain conditions, these measures represent a bound on certain aspects of program execution, and can be used as a baseline for comparing instruction sets.

These were developed to be architecture-independent measures of a program. The measures determine the smallest representation of a high-level language program and the minimal amount of "work" to execute that program.

How well do typical machines compare to the HLL baseline? The answer depends upon several things, only one of which is the instruction set itself.

Huck [135, 136] has conducted probably the most extensive analysis of familiar machines benchmarked to the HLL measures. His analysis is based on a series of scientific test programs, and his data on static program size is presented in Table 2.6. The HP Precision Architecture (PA RISC) is used as a representative L/S machine in these analyses. The most notable aspect of Huck's measurements is that they were carefully controlled using the same

Table 2.6 Static program sizes relative to HLL measures [136]: (a) simple compiler; (b) optimized compiler.

Architecture Class	Architecture		Size
Reference	"HLL" machine		1.00
Stack	P-code	Pascal	10.12
R/M	S/370	Fortran Hopt1	6.23
R+M	VAX UNIX	Fortran	6.40

(a)

Architecture Class	Architecture	Size
L/S	PA RISC	5.30
R/M	S/370	5.50
R+M	VAX/VMS	2.92

(b)

test program suite and essentially the same level of compilation strategies across all tested architectures.

Static size has some importance (Table 2.6), but it is less significant than dynamic size—the instruction bandwidth required for memory. The relative dynamic instruction count is seen in Table 2.7, and the instruction bandwidth required is presented in Table 2.8.

As can be seen from Huck's results, compilers play a big role in machine performance. A reduction of instruction traffic (I-bandwidth) or instruction count of 2:1 can be observed, while the differences in architectures themselves seem to have slightly less effect on the ultimate results.

For data traffic, the HLL measures assume a machine or instruction set that has only a few registers (see Table 2.9). Temporary variables that are used in expression evaluation are assumed to be held in registers—a stack—and references to these variables are not counted in the measures. Variables or objects that are stored as the result of an expression evaluation are included in data memory activity. Consider the example:

$$A := B * (C + D) \tag{2.1}$$

$$E := B - C \tag{2.2}$$

Statement (2.1) requires three reads and one write in the "HLL" machine; the $C + D$ result is contained in an (implied) register. Statement (2.2) requires two reads and one write; B and C were not assumed to be allocated to registers.

Implied by the HLL is a stack-type machine that does not hold values from statement to statement, but rather can evaluate temporary variables or variables that are used to hold the results of a partial expression evaluation without referring back to memory. Thus, the HLL measures do not represent a bound for register set machines, and these measures consistently overestimate the amount of memory read and write activity required for

Table 2.7 Dynamic instruction count relative to HLL [136]: (a) simple compilation; (b) optimized compilation.

Arch.	Instruction Set		Result (relative to an HLL operation)
HLL	HLL		1.00
Stack	P-code	Pascal	5.46
R/M	S/370	Fortran Hopt1	3.10
R+M	VAX	UNIX Fortran	1.99

(a)

Arch.	Instruction Set		Result (relative to an HLL operation)
L/S	PA RISC	Fortran	1.98
R/M	S/370 Hopt3	Fortran H opt 3	1.78
R+M	VAX/VMS	VMS Fortran	1.14

(b)

Table 2.8 Instruction traffic (per HLL operation) [136]: (a) Instruction activities (per HLL operation)—optimized compilation; (b) Dynamic instruction bandwidth—optimized (average) I-bandwidth relative to instruction count.

Architecture	L/S PA RISC	R/M S/370	R+M VAX
Instructions Fetched	1.98	1.78	1.14
Instruction Bytes Fetched	7.92	6.3	–

(a)

		Bytes/I	inst/HLL op	I-bw rel. to HLL op count
R/M	S/370 Hopt3	3.54	1.78	6.30
L/S	PA RISC	4.0	1.98	7.92

(b)

Table 2.9 Memory object reads/writes per HLL read/write [136].

(a) Simple			Reads	Writes
R/M	S/370	Fortran Hopt1	0.53	0.89
R+M	VAX UNIX	Fortran	1.11	1.66

(b) Optimized			Reads	Writes
L/S	PA RISC	Fortran	0.29	0.83
R/M	S/370	Fortran Hopt3	0.38	0.84
R+M	VAX/VMS	Fortran	0.32	0.74

data values for such machines. Still, they represent a baseline for architectural comparison that is not sensitive to register allocation strategy.

The register allocator is a special part of the program optimization process, an issue that we discuss later.

VAX

VAX implementations have been widely distributed throughout the university and scientific user communities. The VAX instruction set is a product of the late 1970s, when designers gave considerably more thought to code density than to pipelined implementations. In fact, it could be argued that pipelined implementations were the furthest thing from their minds. In a major retrospective study by Bhandarkar and Clark [34], VAX implementations of the late '80s were compared with a contemporary, MIPS R2000. Their study indicated that VAX required between 1.8 and 3.7 times as many cycles to execute a program as the MIPS (L/S) or RISC-type implementation. Their term for this factor was "the RISC factor." We believe it is better viewed as "the VAX factor."

Instruction sets are the product of their times, but they often outlive their times and the technology constraints on their times. Another way of looking at the situation is that VAX implementations can match RISC implementations, but to do so requires an extraordinary amount of hardware. Consider the remark by Bhandarkar and Clark:

> ...So while VAX may "catch up" to *current* single-instruction-issue RISC performance, RISC designs will push on with earlier adoption of advanced implementation techniques, achieving still higher performance. The VAX architectural disadvantage might thus be viewed as a time lag of some number of years.

In reacting to VAX instruction set problems, some L/S instruction set designs make the opposite mistake of ignoring code density. Fortunately, this is usually somewhat of an easier problem to fix later (by adding additional complex instructions) than the VAX encoding problem.

2.6.3 Invariant Effects

The occurrence (per HLL operation) of certain types of instructions is relatively independent of the architecture used and the degree of compiler optimization employed (excluding only very naive compilers). They are already in 1:1 correspondence with dynamic high-level language actions. These instruction classes generally include:

1. Integer multiply and divide.

2. Floating-point operations.

3. Conditional branches.

The use of code optimization in a compiler can reduce superfluous load and store instructions, provide better register utilization, and reduce the number of unconditional branches, but does not affect source-code-specified actions.

The invariant operations include those that consume the most time on a per-instruction basis. These are the so-called run-on instructions that will be described in Chapter 4. They are also the most expensive operations to speed up. The overhead instructions can be minimized by compiler optimization, but unfortunately they are also the ones that execute most rapidly, especially in modern pipelined machines, thus eliminating exactly those instructions that can be made easiest to execute.

Recognizing this, designers have proposed the RISC architectural approach (L/S) that does not reduce the number of overhead instructions [228]. Their goal is to accept a relatively large occurrence of overhead instructions, but to simplify the overall structure of the machine so that cycle time can be reduced. Any additional available hardware can then be used to speed up the invariant instructions (e.g., faster floating-point operations or the use of register windows to improve call/return). As a consequence, the number of formats (the code density) is reduced; this increases the dynamic size of the program as it is interpreted by the machine. This simplifies the task of machine design *per se*, but increases the scope, size, and complexity of the (on- and off-chip) cache system, since large resulting program sizes require larger caches to maintain a reasonable cache "hit" rate.

2.6.4   Code Density

The instruction set has two general effects on processor design. It has a direct effect on the complexity of a processor implementation, and it partially determines the effectiveness of memory use through its corresponding code density (Figure 2.40).

Code density is simply a measure of the instruction traffic; it is the reciprocal of the number of (instruction) bits required to execute a program (the dynamic program size) normalized by the dynamic HLL operation count. Code density is not directly related to the amount of time it takes to execute any particular instruction. Code density cannot be ignored, as we shall see in Chapter 5. On the one hand, if one encodes the instruction stream so as to complicate the determination of the starting point of the next instruction, as in the VAX, the performance of the processor can decrease dramatically. On the other hand, low code density results in large dynamic program sizes, which require large instruction buffers and large caches to provide required instruction bandwidth.

The canonic HLL instructions are generally the same as the invariant instructions mentioned in the previous section. The instruction set and the level of compiler optimization determine the number of additional instructions that are required to execute a program. The way each instruction is encoded determines the average size of the instruction. The number of instructions that appear in the execution of a program is largely a function of the format set. The encoding of the instruction is a function of the number of formats and the particular type of code used to represent objects.

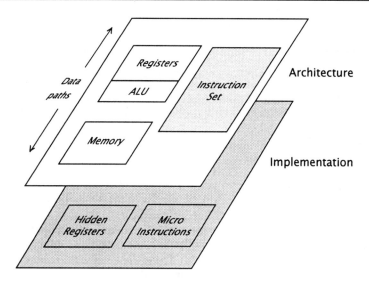

Figure 2.40   Computer architecture and its implementation: the instruction set is a tradeoff between decoder complexity and code density.

As a general rule, instruction sets that have more formats and more variability in instruction size have fewer instructions to execute overall than instruction sets with less variability.

The Marginal Utility of Code Density

As mentioned earlier, there is a basic instruction set tradeoff between code density and the effect of code density on storage hierarchy, especially the instruction cache (I-cache). Well-encoded instruction sets such as the R/M or R+M instruction sets use more decoder area, but provide a better level of I-cache performance. A more densely encoded instruction set requires fewer bits to be fetched from memory to execute a program than a less well-encoded instruction set. Consider our three base architecture types— we assume for the moment that they all have the same ALU vocabulary. (This is basically true for the scientific environment.) If we add an I-cache (Figure 2.41), then all architectures improve because of improved average memory access time.

As we shall see in chapter 3, we expect to have the following relative instruction count for our three architectures:

Load/Store	1.0
Register/Memory	0.9
Register+Memory	0.6

Accounting for instruction size differences, the approximate relative dynamic instruction traffic would be:

Instruction Set Hype

The grander the descriptions of an instruction set, the more suspect the results. Nowhere is this more true than in an evaluation of instruction sets. Consider the following description of the Intel iAPX 432 system [145], a processor with an extremely complicated instruction set:

> The vacuum tube, the transistor, the microprocessor—at least once in a generation an electronic device arises to shock and strain designers' understanding. The latest such device is the iAPX 432 micromainframe processor, a processor as different from the current crop of μPs (and indeed, mainframes) as those devices are from the early electromechanical analog computers of the 1940's.
>
> —Hemingway and Grappel, *Electronic Design News*, Apr. 29, 1981

If truth be told, the comparative effect of instruction sets, given correspondingly good implementations, is rather limited—usually less than a factor of two and certainly less than a factor of three to one. It is, however, possible to define an instruction set processor that will "shock and strain designers' understanding," creating a bad mismatch between the instruction set and the implementation technology. The result is usually a big disappointment.

Contrast the preceding quote with the following remark:

> Since the development of the stored-program computer around 1950, there have been remarkably few true innovations in the areas of computer organization and architecture. One of the most interesting and potentially one of the most important innovations is the reduced-instruction-set computer (RISC). The RISC architecture is a dramatic departure from the historical trend in CPU architecture and challenges the conventional wisdom expressed in words and deeds by most computer architects ...
>
> —W. Stallings, "Reduced Instruction Set Computer Architecture," *Proc. IEEE*, Vol. 76, No. 1, January 1988

The real issue for processor designers is not so much the intrinsic differences among instruction sets, but rather the correspondence between a particular instruction set and the implementation technology at hand. In the world of microprocessors the question is a simple one: is there enough silicon available to fully implement the required processor functions and provide various support features such as buffers and cache?

Continued...

Instruction Set Hype *(continued)*

Formally defining instruction sets, especially in mainframe design, without strongly considering implementation considerations might not be a fatal error. After all, an ill-considered additional functional unit might require an additional several chips out of twenty or more in an implementation. In microprocessor design things are much different. Processors must fit on a single chip. If the functionality is overblown with respect to the chip area, implementations can be disastrously slow in executing the required instructions and functions.

RISC technology is the result of a realization in the early 1980s that chip area was quite limited and that efficient instruction execution could be achieved with minimum functionality instruction sets (operand vocabulary, formats, etc.).

Over time, RISC implementations have added features and functions. The IBM RS/6000 introduced a fused multiply and add instruction. RISC processor implementations have now almost universally adopted the IEEE standard, probably the most complex floating-point representation ever proposed. As most designers readily recognize, there is nothing "reduced" about it.

Implementation capacity changes rapidly; instruction sets change more slowly. The instruction set designer not only must recognize today's technology limitations, but also must be able to intelligently predict the evolution of future technology. Over the longer term, there is no single answer to instruction sets, just as there is no single fixed implementation technology.

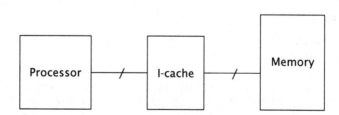

Figure 2.41 The processor register: I-cache model. The processor accesses cache in one cycle. The cache requires n cycles to access memory on a miss $(n > 1)$.

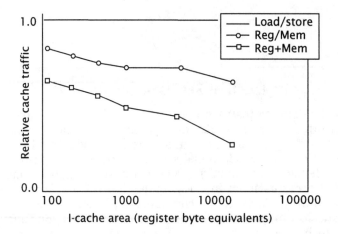

Figure 2.42   Relative I-cache traffic for three different code densities.

Load/Store	1.0
Register/Memory	0.8
Register + Memory	0.6

Using our cache area model, suppose the same area was available for I-cache to each of our three processor types. Figure 2.42 shows the relative I-cache traffic for our three different levels of code density corresponding to our three different architectures. Each architecture reduces its cache traffic (on-chip cache to memory) and improves its performance by having an I-cache—for this simple model, the larger the better, but across a reasonable amount of I-cache area—up to 10,000 **rbe**—the more densely encoded architectures continue to improve their relative cache advantage over the less densely encoded architectures. Of course, this data does not tell the whole story, since there are several other important considerations:

1. The more dense architectures require more instruction decoder area, so it is unfair to simply allocate the same amount of I-cache area to each of these three processors.

2. The relative effect on performance of the I-cache diminishes as the cache gets larger.

3. Large decoders may limit the cycle time of the processor, distorting the comparisons.

Suppose we now compare the marginal utility of extending the load/store architecture by either adding an I-cache or recoding the instruction set to either register/memory or register + memory and then adding an I-cache. An estimate of the additional area cost to go from a load/store machine to a register/memory machine is about 250 **rbe** [94]. This includes an additional 32-bit register and multiplexers for justifying 16-bit half-word instructions so that they may be properly decoded. A very rough estimate of the reg-ister+memory decoder area would be approximately 4,000 **rbe** (approximately 500 register byte equivalents) in decoder overhead to accommodate the additional formats and instruction sizes. Assuming a cache access time

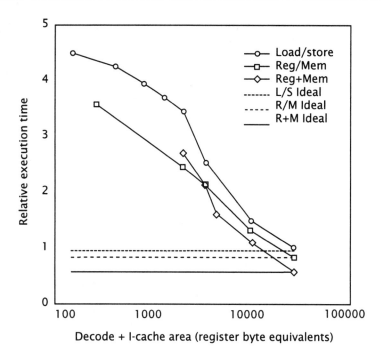

Figure 2.43   Execution time relative to L/S for three architectures with different code densities with the same allocation of area to decoder plus I-cache. Figure assumes all architectures ultimately achieve 1 cycle per instruction.

of one cycle and a cache miss time of five cycles, we can compare the relative execution time of our three architectures. Using an ideal cache for each, we can plot the relative execution time vs. the available area for decoder plus I-cache (Figure 2.43). Figure 2.43 then represents the relative execution time for the three architectures with different code densities, but with the same allocation of marginal area to the decoder plus the I-cache. When little or no additional area is available to the base processor, the best instruction set is the L/S instruction set, as it is the only instruction set that is realizable without significant implementation compromises. When a small additional area is available, the R/M instruction set prevails. Finally, assuming the cycle time remains constant, the R+M architecture provides the best performance by a small measure, as it executes the fewest instructions. If we model the base execution time as proportional to the number of instructions executed, then asymptotically the R+M machine would use only .6 of the execution time of the L/S machine, and the R/M machine would use only .9 of the execution time of the L/S machine.

The preceding argument is more generally applicable than just to the comparison among our prototypical instruction sets. Given a base L/S architecture (or any other), any instruction encoding improvement that provides a 20% bandwidth reduction (no cache) would achieve performance improvement similar to that outlined in Figure 2.43. The cost (i.e., area required) of any such encoding improvement must be added to the I-cache area.

From studies such as the preceding, the following observations can be made concerning code density and instruction sets:

1. As more area becomes available to a designer, denser architectures tend to outperform less dense architectures unless the processor is limited by the time through the I-decoder itself.

2. Once area is available for an I-cache, it is important to reexamine the instruction representation and the code density issue.

The Value of Code Density

The design of instruction format was straightforward since we religiously adhered to a maxim given in the first working document on MIPS-X. It stated: "The goal of any instruction format should be: (1) simple decode, (2) simple decode, and (3) simple decode." Any attempts at improved code density at the expense of CPU performance should be ridiculed at every opportunity.

—P. Chou and M. Horowitz, "Architectural Tradeoffs in the Design of the MIPS-X," *Proc. 14th Int'l. Symposium on Computer Architecture*, pages 300–308, 1987

It may be perfectly correct to religiously follow a principle within the context of a particular project, but it does not mean that that principle is universally applicable or even useful in another project.

Observers who discount the importance of code density fail to realize the cost of not having it. The demise of Intel x86-based microprocessors has not happened in anywhere near the schedule that was predicted by L/S or RISC instruction set advocates. Part of the reason is that the size of the instruction decoder and its complexity can be outweighed by resultant code density and improved cache performance.

Eventually, changes will come to the x86; but (it would seem) these changes will reflect the need for additional address capabilities (a "64-bit" address) and, particularly, for additional registers.

2.6.5   Role of Registers, Evaluation Stacks, and Data Buffers

In this section we look at the tradeoff between register set size and organization and required memory traffic (Figure 2.44).

The simplest form of data buffer is a first-in–last-out stack (evaluation stack). This has been commonly used in computer architecture [122] and, with three or four entries, can usually capture most temporaries that are evaluated within statements. For example, the statement

$$A := B + (C * D)$$

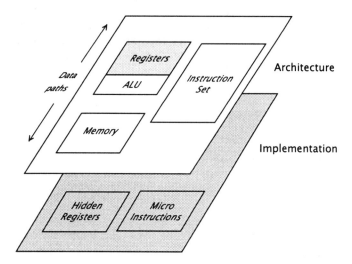

Figure 2.44 Computer architecture and its implementation: the register set represents a tradeoff between memory bandwidth and chip area.

could be implemented using a stack with the following code:

```
PUSH  C
PUSH  D
MPY
PUSH  B
ADD
POP   A
```

No value remains in the stack at the end of an expression evaluation, and two stack entries are used during evaluation. The simple evaluation stack has no facility for storing the data values from statement to statement for reuse. A simple register set can accomplish the same objective, managing temporary storage for expression evaluation, yet retain values for use from statement to statement within a procedure. At the end of a procedure, either a stack or a single register set can be used to store argument values for use by the called procedure. The greatest disadvantage of using registers to hold temporaries is that active data values in the register set must be saved (moved to memory) as control passes to new procedures. The called procedure may require use of registers that contain valid data belonging to the calling procedure. This data must also be restored after the return. With early register allocation software, the value of the register set was marginal compared to the value of a stack. The savings in data traffic by keeping results in registers was only marginally better than the save and restore data traffic required on procedure change. Modern register allocators more than overcome the save and restore traffic disadvantage and provide significant advantage for register sets [212]. This is best illustrated by Huck's data cited in Table 2.9. Since the HLL machine assumes a stack, the advantage (read and write ratios < 1) of the register set machines over the HLL demonstrates the effectiveness of modern allocators.

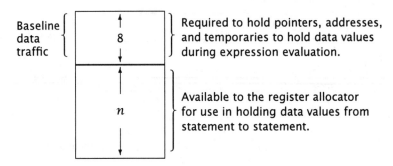

Figure 2.45   Register set architectures.

Registers may be organized in many different ways:

1. As a conventional single register set (SRS).

2. As multiple or windowed register sets (MRS).

3. As a stack cache buffer or a contour buffer.

Even a few registers, however organized, go a long way in reducing the memory traffic. For example, an all-memory three-address architecture has about twice the data traffic of a simple stack-based architecture. In fact, as few as three registers in a register set architecture can play the role of a stack in capturing temporary values that are used within expressions, resulting in about the same data traffic that would have been realized with the stack architecture. Of course, temporary storage is only part of the picture, as registers play valuable functions in maintaining addresses for indices and in maintaining pointers to various control and data functions.

Suppose that all architectures of interest consist of at least eight registers, whether explicitly available for programmer use or implicitly designated for various functions; this number is sufficient to capture most temporary values that are used within statements (Figure 2.45). Additional registers can be used to reduce data traffic from statement to statement. We define the eight-register processor as a *baseline processor* or as *unity data traffic* [206] (Figure 2.46). Additional registers improve the data traffic; however, it is not simply the *number* of registers but the kind of *organization* and *algorithms* surrounding the registers that make the difference in the resulting data traffic.

Registers (and data buffers) hold values that are usable within a cycle (Figure 2.47). They generally are multiported and allow the access of two source variables and the storage of the result in the same cycle. The "register-to-register ADD" or similar basic ALU operation is one of several paths critical to determining the cycle time. The larger the register set, the more difficult it is to maintain rapid access and hence fast cycle times. On the other hand, the larger the buffer available to the processor, the lower the memory traffic demand on the memory system. The number of buffer entries and the way they are used determine the data traffic to memory.

Before describing multiple register sets, consider the topic of buffering data. It is common practice in modern systems to assign data variables relative to a *run-time stack* in memory (Figure 2.48). Global variables (or

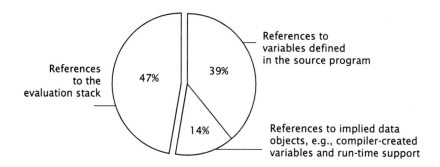

Figure 2.46   Unity data traffic.

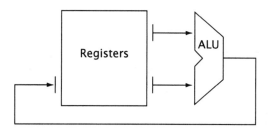

Figure 2.47   Multiported registers. Registers can access two values and return a result within a single cycle.

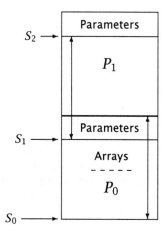

Figure 2.48   Run-time stack (in memory).

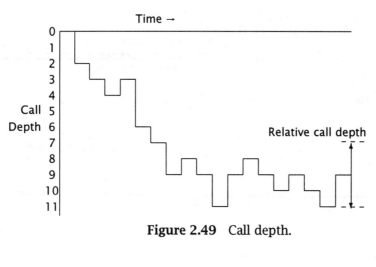

Figure 2.49   Call depth.

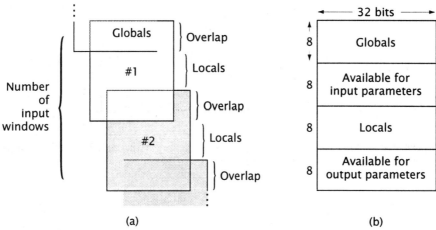

Figure 2.50   Register windows.

P_0 variables) are first assigned to space allocated by a stack organized in memory starting at S_0. Suppose variables are assigned to the stack by their complexity: first scalars and constants, then complex structures (arrays, etc.). Then the level P_0 routine calls another routine, and the called routine (P_1) is assigned space starting at the top of the stack address (S_1). Similarly, when a level-one routine calls a second level routine, space is allocated following the level-one routine. Parameters may be passed easily on this stack in memory as the calling routine stores arguments for the caller at the top of its space. This becomes the initialization point for the called routine. The number of call levels at which execution occurs is called a *call depth* of execution. The average departure from the mean call depth is called the *relative call depth*. The call depth varies dynamically, and the overall call depth may vary considerably over several programs. However, it appears that most of the program execution occurs with a relative call depth of four or five routines [275] as shown in Figure 2.49.

Multiple register sets can be organized as *register windows* with a degree of overlap between register sets, an analog to the *run-time stack* organization. The overlap allows space for arguments to be passed from one routine to another, and the multiplicity of sets avoids the necessity of having to save and restore registers upon entering or exiting a routine (Figure 2.50 a). The net effect of multiple register sets (assuming sufficient size) is twofold:

1. Reduction of data memory traffic.

2. Depending on the architecture, it may reduce the required instruction traffic by eliminating load and store instructions associated with item 1.

Of course, multiple register sets (MRS) have a limited capacity; they consist of a fixed number of register sets. MRS can be parameterized by the number of registers privately available (the locals), by the number of register words shared among procedures (the overlap), and finally by the number of windows in the multiple register set. Figure 2.50(b) shows the arrangement used in several SPARC implementations; each window has eight local registers. The processor addresses 32 registers at any one time, eight of which are reserved for global variables and eight of which are shared, each with input and output procedures. Thus, 16 new registers are added for each additional window in the MRS ensemble. A SPARC-type window can be designated as $(8, 8, n)$ with notation (number of local registers, number of overlap registers, and n, the number of windows present in a particular implementation). In a particular program, a sequence of calls may exceed the number of windows implemented. MRSs are usually arranged as a circular buffer so that when the set size is exceeded, the entry furthest back is stored in memory, allowing the called routine proper register space (*overflow*). After a routine has overflowed, when the program sequence later returns to a level that is not in the MRS, an *underflow* occurs, causing the register set most removed to be saved in memory, and the underflowed register space to be restored for the current routine.

Data buffers can be arranged as an even closer mapping of the run-time stack. Such buffers can be organized in at least two ways:

1. As a transparent buffer for the run-time stack (stack cache buffer [73]).

2. As a programmer-addressed buffer that is used in conjunction with the run-time stack in memory (contour buffer [92]).

As only the MRS approach is in common use and all these techniques perform roughly the same function, we discuss only this approach here.

All data buffers profit from register allocation. In evaluating the effectiveness of various kinds of data buffers, a fundamental difference is the kind of register allocation scheme used. Simple allocation, called *one-one allocation*, assigns commonly used variables to the available registers, but does not attempt to reuse those registers after they are no longer needed in a procedure. More sophisticated allocators analyze the flow of the data throughout the procedure to determine when a particular register is available for reuse; that register is then reassigned. These allocators are called *many-one allocators* or *global allocators*, since they act globally over a single procedure. Even more advanced allocators can do *interprocedural allocation*, that is, allocate registers on a many-one basis across procedures

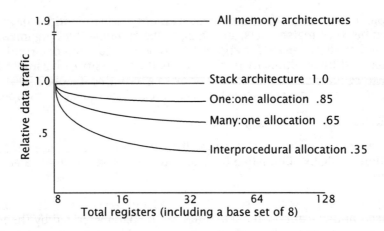

Figure 2.51   The effect of register allocation on register traffic [206].

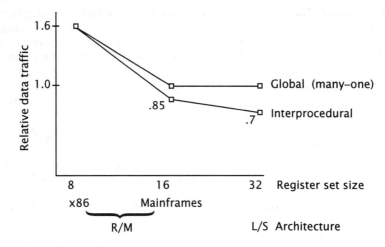

Figure 2.52   Expected data traffic relative to a 16-register R/M processor with global allocation for several architectures [206].

(Figure 2.51). Clearly, the best allocation serves to make the best use of available resources.

It is in the area of register set size and the resulting effectiveness of register allocation that the behavior of contemporary computer architecture is changing.

The Intel x86 series has few registers (8), with perhaps 3 or 4 available for use by the allocator. While allocation for the x86 is very important, since registers are a scarce resource, there is a limit to what can be done. Mainframes have 16 registers, with 8 or so available to the allocator. Global allocation is very helpful, and interprocedural allocation helps even more, but L/S architectures with 32 registers profit the most from advanced allocation techniques. Therefore, it is no surprise that these processors have led the way in introducing interprocedural allocation. These trends are shown in Figure 2.52.

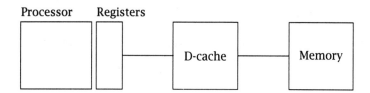

Figure 2.53   The processor register: D-cache model.

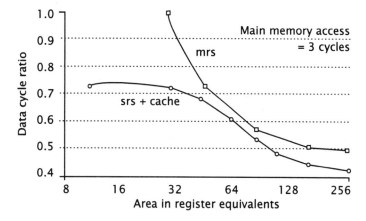

Figure 2.54   Execution time for register windows or multiple register sets (MRS) compared with a single (16-entry) register set (SRS) plus a data cache, each occupying area measured in dual ported register word (32^b) equivalents. Data cycle ratio is defined as the execution time for an ideal pipelined processor (SRS) with cache or with MRS compared to the same processor with zero cache (misses each reference).

We can use another simple D-cache model to evaluate the value of register windows, organized as $(8, 8, n)$. Consider Figure 2.53.

We assume that the processor may read two registers and write one register within a cycle. The D-cache access requires one cycle. Memory access (from either registers or D-cache) is three cycles, and a total of seven cycles is required to process a cache miss.

Suppose again that we use the area model to evaluate the advantages of register windows compared to a single register set plus cache occupying the same area. Register windows clearly perform a valuable function by reducing the cost of procedure call and return; but suppose we took a single register set (SRS) of 16 registers and added a data cache occupying the same area as a register window (MRS) implementation. Again calling on our **rbe** model, and assuming a three-cycle memory access time, we can compare the area effectiveness of the two approaches, as in Figure 2.54. We assume that both architectures are L/S, with the area in addition to the base processor allocated either to register windows or to a single register set with data cache. Register windows improve performance on call and return, but caches are able to capture localities containing dynamically allocated data structures that cannot be assigned to registers. Thus, over the long run, caches appear to be a more effective use of area, although for certain values of area there is little to distinguish one approach from the other.

Some observations:

1. For a three-cycle memory, a single register set of about 16 registers plus a data cache seems to be more area-effective than multiple register windows.

2. As the memory access time increases beyond three cycles, data indicate that the single register set approach plus the data cache is even more effective than the register window approach.

3. Since register windows require a significant amount of chip area and increased control complexity compared to the single register set plus cache approach, MRS (windows) may cause a deterioration in the cycle time due to increased register select logic.

4. If a significant amount of area is available for data cache and a data cache is added to an MRS implementation, then ultimately this combination will use fewer cycles than a single register set implementation with data cache using the same area. The MRS approach saves additional time at procedure call.

Basic Optimization Design Rules:

1. Within instruction set (compatibility, etc.) constraints, determine effect of instruction set enhancements on code density and I-cache size and decoder area. For purposes of this optimization assume separate I- and D-caches split about evenly.

2. Within constraints outlined in (1), determine the effects of register set enhancements on memory traffic and memory access delay. Optimize D-cache/register area allocation.

3. Based on any changes made in (1) and (2), reevaluate cycle time and any adverse effect on performance.

2.7   Conclusions

Cycle time is of paramount importance in microprocessor design. It is largely determined by technology, but is significantly influenced by secondary considerations such as clocking philosophy and pipeline segmentation.

Once cycle time has been determined, the designer's next challenge is to optimize the cost–performance of a design by making maximum use of chip area—using chip area to the best possible advantage of performance. A technology-independent measure of area called the *register bit equivalent*—the **rbe**—provides the basis for storage hierarchy tradeoffs among a number of important architectural considerations.

The instruction set is the glue that brings together implementation and technology and forms the specification of the "user-visible logical machine."

The dynamic character of the high-level language source program is represented by HLL measures of the program. The number of HLL instructions executed corresponds to the dynamic count of high-level language operations that are expected to be executed during the course of a program. Architectures can then be compared relative to a hundred HLL instructions, and distribution of types of instructions and instruction profiles can be developed.

An instruction set affects the performance of any processor implementation by determining the amount of dynamic activity that the processor must complete in order to execute a program. A more robust instruction set with a large set of formats decreases the number of instructions that must be executed for a particular program. More complete encoding of individual instructions (using register modes, etc.) reduces the size of individual instructions and may secondarily affect the dynamic instruction count. A reduced dynamic instruction count, together with smaller-sized instructions, reduces the instruction bandwidth requirements for memory for a processor to execute a program. All of these contribute positively to processor performance. Offsetting this is the increased number of cycles for instruction execution and the increased decoder complexity required to decode multiple format types and highly encoded portions of the instruction. Such decoder complexity may in fact affect the processor cycle.

With advances in register allocation technology, general-purpose register set architectures have become the dominant instruction set. Registers provide faster access than cache or main memory. Registers reduce the data traffic to both cache (where present) and memory. While even a few registers provide a significant value to the processor, increasing register size beyond a certain point provides only a marginal increase in performance. In fact, in certain situations, large register sets may actually decrease performance. This could arise either because the register set access increases cycle time or because frequently occurring interrupts require the transfer and restoration of register contents to and from memory.

2.8   Some Areas for Further Research

The *wave pipelining* concepts have only recently been applied to microprocessors and on-chip technology as a method of speeding up cycle time. A good deal of work remains to be done, especially in developing circuits that better support the concepts of wave pipelining—with stable and predictable delay. Predictable delay is especially a problem with CMOS technology, and the applicability and use of wave pipelining in large implementations remains a challenge.

The categorization of area on a functional (**rbe**) rather than a geometric basis currently exists only for storage elements. Units such as decoders, ALUs, etc., have received little attention in area modeling, yet it is impossible to do performance optimization without similar functional area models. Indeed, an understanding of minimum cycle time and functional modeling of area are basic ingredients that must be present in any formalized model of microprocessor optimization.

With the abundant literature on instruction set analysis, it might seem that this is a time-worn area that is well-understood; but when the field can move from the breakthrough of a highly encoded Intel iAPX 432 in 1981 to a breakthrough of a very loosely encoded RISC-1 in 1985, it is clear that a comprehensive analytic basis for instruction set design is not at hand. A lack of area models mentioned earlier inhibits a good deal of sensible instruction set tradeoff, but comprehensive well-correlated instruction set analysis (accounting for compiler, systems, I/O, etc., effects) remains a precious commodity.

2.9   Data Notes

Data Note 1   (Tables 2.6–2.9).

The data in these tables are taken from Huck [135]. They are based on a study of five scientific programs. Compiler effects were carefully normalized so as to be comparable to other studies. The notion of an HLL operation is more completely defined in Huck where it is referred to as a *canonic measure* or CI measure.

Reliability.   The data seem generally consistent with other published results where compiler effects have been similarly normalized.

Stability.   Dynamic instruction count should be relatively stable as a fraction of the HLL operation count. The instruction count, however, is a strong function of compiler optimization. Similarly, memory object read-writes (Table 2.9) are a direct function of the type of source program used, and a strong function of the register allocator available in producing the final object code.

Data Note 2   (Figures 2.51 and 2.54).

The data presented here are from Alpert [13] and Mulder [206], based upon a series of medium-sized Pascal benchmarks generally characterized as representing a workstation environment.

Reliability.   While the general trends and conclusions ought to be unaffected by most problem environments, different applications and source languages will display different overall behavior. Data traffic is generally not a function of architecture, but simply a function of the number of registers available for allocation and the type of register allocator used. The *relative* results are expected to be reliable.

Stability.   The reduction of relative data traffic with a relatively small number of registers seems to be a stable result. The actual achieved relative data traffic is, however, quite dependent on the program studied. One should expect significant variations in the actual achieved relative data traffic as a function of application.

2.10   Annotated Bibliography

The determination of cycle time in modern processors is closely associated with the design of synchronous, hazard-free logic implementations. Much of the basic work on hazard-free sequential circuits was done in the 1950s and 1960s. (See, for example, E. J. McCluskey, *Introduction to the Theory of Switching Circuits*, McGraw-Hill, New York, 1965.) Since the late 1950s there has been a good deal of interest in alternative approaches to clocking, such as asynchronous clocking—the use of logic with completion signals to allow the entry of new data. Early work at the University of Illinois under Muller and Bartky [208, 209] basically outlined how such a logical schema would work. General considerations are outlined in Ungar [293] and Miller [197].

For a general discussion on clocking schemes for high-speed systems, [294] and [297] are particularly useful. Our treatment of some of the aspects of partitioning of time and cycle time determination follows the work of Dubey [77] and Kunkel and Smith [175], using some of the formulations of Hallin [118].

Work on very fast cycle times that employ storage in the form of guaranteed minimum delay was first published in [18]. Although the discussion there is limited, it was generalized by [60]. Recent attention to the so-called *wave pipelining* method generally references the work of Wong [310, 311] and Klass [164].

Optimum use of area is a standard concern in microprocessor design and is treated in various ways by works in that subfield. The earliest comprehensive reference is Mead and Conway [194]. Area optimization is generally focused on particular functions such as in the work of Marple and El Gamal [190].

Area optimization with respect to cache function is discussed in Chapter 5. Also, see Flynn et al. [94] for a more complete discussion of I-cache instruction code density issues. The general area model we follow was initially developed by Mulder [206, 207]; see also the work of Mudge and his colleagues [214, 295] which uses the **rbe** model for processor tradeoffs.

There is an enormous body of literature on instruction sets, but significantly less on instruction set evaluation. A good deal of interesting data is presented in several works [156, 277, 52, 304, 127]. Our data presented in this chapter and in the next is based upon the work of Huck [135, 136], as it both normalized compilers and did a comparative analysis on instruction sets.

For discussion of the instruction set measures as a basis of high-level language defined measures of program and machine behavior, see Flynn and Hoevel [93]. There have been numerous machine-specific studies of either individual instruction sets or comparative treatments of several instruction sets; particularly noteworthy is the work of Clark [52], Wiecek [304], Lunde [187], and Huck [135]. The analysis of code density or the marginal utility of code density register windows is taken from Flynn et al. [94].

Additional Reading

Basic Issues in Clocking and Pipelining

S. Ungar. *Asynchronous Sequential Switching Circuits.* Interscience. Wiley, New York, 1969.

K. Wagner. A survey of clock distribution techniques on high speed computer systems. Technical Note CSL-TN-86-309, Stanford University, December 1986.

P. Kogge. *The Architecture of Pipelined Computers.* McGraw-Hill, New York, 1981.

S. Kunkel and J. Smith. Optimal pipelining in supercomputers. *Proc. 13th Annual Symposium on Computer Architecture*, pages 404–411, 1986.

Area Modeling

D. Marple and A. El Gamal. Area-delay optimization of programmable logic arrays. *Proc. 4th MIT Conference on Advanced Research in VLSI*, pages 171–194, April 1986.

C. Mead and L. Conway. *Introduction to VLSI Systems* (Series in Computer Science). Addison-Wesley, 1980.

J. Mulder, N. Quach, and M. Flynn. An area model for on-chip memories and its application. *Journal of Solid State Circuits*, 26(2), February 1991.

Economics of Processor Development

J. Hennessy and D. Patterson. *Computer Architecture: A Quantitative Approach.* Morgan Kaufmann, San Mateo, CA, 1990.

Instruction Set Optimization

S. Fuller and W. Burr. Measurement and evaluation of alternative computer architectures. *Computer*, 10(10):24–35, October 1977.

A. Tanenbaum. *Structured Computer Organization* (Series in Automatic Computation). Prentice-Hall, Englewood Cliffs, NJ, 1976.

J. Huck and M. Flynn. *Analyzing Computer Architectures.* IEEE Computer Society Press, New York, 1989 (2nd edition).

W. Stallings. *Reduced Instruction Set Computers.* Tutorial. IEEE Computer Society Press, Los Alamitos, CA, 1990.

2.11   Problem Set

1. A four-segment pipeline implements a function and has the following delays for each segment ($b = 0.2$):

Segment #	Maximum delay*
1	17 ns
2	15 ns
3	19 ns
4	14 ns

*Excludes fixed clock overhead of 2 ns ($k = 0$).

(a) What is the cycle time that maximizes performance without allo-cating multiple cycles to a segment?

(b) What is the total time to execute the function (through all stages)?

(c) What is the cycle time that maximizes performance if each seg-ment can be partitioned into sub-segments?

2. Repeat problem 1 if there is a 1 ns clock skew (uncertainty of ±1 ns) in the arrival of each clock pulse.

3. A four-segment pipeline to execute a function has the following pa-rameters:

Segment #	P_{max}	P_{min}
1	14	7 ns
2	12	9 ns
3	16	10 ns
4	11	5 ns

The clock overhead, C, for each register stage is 3 ns.

(a) If no controlled clock skew is allowed, what is the latency of exe-cution (through all stages) for the function? What is the minimum cycle time?

(b) If we now allow controlled clock skew to take advantage of P_{min}, what is the latency, minimum cycle time, and clock skew required at each stage?

4. Repeat problem 3 if there is an additional 1 ns of uncertainty in the arrival of the clock at each segment.

5. Plot S_{opt} with respect to clock skew factor (k) for $k = 0.05$ to $k = 0.20$. Assume $T = 120$ ns, $C = 5$ ns, and $b = 0.2$.

6. We can generalize the equation for S_{opt} by allowing for pipeline inter-ruption delay of $S - a$ cycles (rather than $S - 1$), where $S > a \geq 1$. Find the new expression for S_{opt}.

7. (a) Show that the effect of uncontrolled clock skew ($\pm\delta$) in a regular pipeline is to increase C, and hence cycle time, by 2δ.

(b) Show that the effect of uncontrolled clock skew ($\pm\delta$) in a wave pipeline is to increase C, and hence cycle time, by 4δ.

8. Repeat Study 2.1, with the delay in R→ALU→R = 16 ns and instruction and data cache data access = 8 ns.

9. A certain pipeline has the following functions and functional unit de-lays (without clocking overhead):

Function	Delay
A	6
B	8
C	3
D	7
E	9
F	5

Function units B, D, and E can be subdivided into two equal delay stages. If the expected occurrence of pipeline breaks is $b = 0.25$ and clocking overhead is 2 ns ($k = 0$):

   (a) Ignoring quantization, what is the optimum number of pipeline segments (round down to integer value)?

   (b) What cycle time (with quantization) does this give?

   (c) Compute the pipeline performance with this cycle time.

   (d) Can you find a better cycle time?

   (e) If there is an additional ± 1 ns uncontrolled clock skew in (b), what is the adjusted cycle time?

10. Compute the area in **rbe** with and without aspect-mismatch adjustment of a 32^{KB} direct-mapped cache with 256-bit lines and a 20-bit tag.

11. A processor die (1.4 cm $\times$ 1.4 cm) will be produced for five years. Over this period, defect densities are expected to drop linearly from 1.5 defects/cm^2 to 0.8 defects/cm^2. The cost of 6-inch wafer production will fall linearly from \$5,000 to \$3,500, and the cost of 8-inch wafer production will fall linearly from \$10,000 to \$6,500. Assume production of good devices is constant in each year. Which production process should be chosen?

12. DRAM chip design is a specialized art where extensive optimizations are made to reduce cell size and data storage overhead. For a cell size of $135\lambda^2$, find the capacity of a DRAM chip. Process parameters are: yield = 10%, $\rho_D = 1$ defect/cm^2, feature size = 1μ, overhead consists of 10% for drivers and sense amps. Overhead for pads, drivers, guard ring, etc., is 20%. There are no busses or latches.

Since memory must be sized as an even power of 2, find the capacity and *actual gross area* (eliminating wasted space) and find the corresponding yield.

13. Compute the cost of a $1^M \times 1^b$ die, using the assumptions of (12). Assume a 21 cm diameter wafer costs \$5,000.

14. Suppose a 2.3 cm^2 die can be fabricated on a 15 cm wafer at a cost of \$5,000, or on a 20 cm wafer at a cost of \$8,000. Compare the effective cost per die for defect densities of 0.5 defects/cm^2 and 1 defect/cm^2.

15. The net area required for a processor is 280 mm^2. The processor can be implemented using one, two, four, or eight chips. Assume that the design is partitioned equally among all chips. Model the cost per chip as \$50 per good device for packaging and testing plus the effective cost of the die. Devices are produced with 15-cm wafers costing \$4,000, and the defect rate is 1 defect/cm^2. Assume that a defect anywhere on the die renders the device inoperable. Tabulate the cost of the processor for each of the four possible partitions. The area overhead for pads, etc., is 20% on each chip.

16. In Cragon [61], several architectures are compared, including:

3M — three address memory to memory; | OP | A | B | C |

2M — two address memory to memory; | OP | A | B |

ACC — single accumulator; | OP | A |

R/M — register set (16 registers); | OP | R | R$_B$ | A |

(R plus R$_B$, base register, occupies one byte)

S — stack. | OP | or | OP | A |

Assume one byte is allowed for opcode and from one to three bytes are allocated for an address.

Plot the expected static code size for each architecture relative to S (stack) for address sizes of one, two, and three bytes. (Compute the size of a functional instruction, then add the size of the fraction of overhead instructions defined by the M-ratio.) Assume:

- No procedural instructions.
- M-ratio of zero for 3M.
- M-ratio of 0.1 for 2M.
- M-ratio of R/M is 2.0.
- M-ratio for stack is the same as ACC, 2.5.

17. Continue Cragon's analysis of problem 16. Plot the expected execution time for each architecture relative to stack for 2-, 3-, and 5-cycle memory access with a three-byte address only. Each memory access fetches a single instruction or data operand regardless of size. Assume a well-mapped host with one cycle for Decode (D), one cycle for Address Generate (AG), and one cycle for Execute (EX). Note that no EX cycles are required with M-type instructions.

18. For each machine model defined in problem 17, find the CFA measures (Section 2.6.2) of M and R. Be sure to include the effects of referencing IC, IR, and SR registers (each 32 bits).

19. For a routine (procedure) to find the roots of the quadratic equation (assume a square root instruction), find the HLL measures of:

(a) Instruction count.

(b) Memory reads and writes.

Assume the three arguments are in memory and the results must also be written to memory.

20. Repeat problem 19, assuming a hardware square root instruction for:

    (a) Stack machine (all instructions 32 bits).

    (b) VAX-type machine (i.e., select proper register modes to go with each instruction).

21. Refer to Table 2.9. The data write ratios are consistently higher than the data read ratios. Explain.

22. For each architecture shown in Table 2.4(b) and Table 2.6(b), the relative static program size is significantly smaller than the relative I-bandwidth. Explain.

Chapter 3

Data: How Programs (and Machines) Behave

3.1 Introduction

The data in this chapter represents the way our three prototypical architectures are expected to behave. There is great variability in the data that is used to model computer performance. This occurs because of variations in architecture, compiler optimization, operating systems environment, and most importantly the applications themselves. While it is useful to note historical data observed by a particular experimenter, the problem is consistency. Our goal is to measure processors, to evaluate various tradeoffs among features to be included in one of several different types of architectures and their implementations. The problem with most reported literature results is that they do not have a common basis. It does no good to know that researcher X has determined that the frequency of procedure calls for an L/S architecture is 10% for a particular programming environment and application, while researcher Y finds a frequency of 3% for an R/M architecture on a completely different set of applications or programming environments. In fact, we know from Huck [136] that the frequency of occurrence or the absolute number of procedure calls for both architectures should be the same for the same application.[1] The goal of this chapter is to present a consistent set of data across our three prototypical architectures. The data presented are subject to wide variability, but we have made every attempt to keep it consistent within the guidelines outlined in this chapter. It is our best attempt at getting an architectural signal out of the applications/compiler/etc. noise that surrounds all measurements.

We first examine dynamic instruction count, the basic measure of activity. Later, we look at secondary effects of program behavior that affect the performance of pipelined processors. With this data, we are able to evaluate the effectiveness of techniques for speeding up processor execution (discussed in later chapters).

---

[1]Assuming the same operating system and generally the same compiler optimization strategy.

3.2   Instruction Usage

Before beginning any design, we must have an idea as to the type of applications that are to be supported by the design. This involves the formulation of a workload model, usually at the instruction level, based on projected user environments [189]. Workload characterization is itself a fine art, but a good characterization of the environment is also essential to good design. Workload characterization is derived from studies of "typical" applications. When representative user applications have been determined, each are weighted by the expected frequency of appearance in an environment. Behavior can then be traced to give the designer a database to be used in design studies. A primary aspect of the data is the instruction distribution or the distribution of instruction usage. Format distribution, data dependency distribution, etc., are also aspects important to the understanding of instruction set behavior, and hence are important ingredients in the design of the processor. The data derived from tracing representative applications can be used to generate the design target instruction mix.

3.2.1   Data Categories

The data presented in the following sections are categorized by three types of environment:

1. The scientific environment, which has been derived largely from Fortran object code but includes both compiler traces and Pascal programs.

2. The "classical" commercial environment (payroll, report generation, etc.), which is largely derived from Cobol object and compiler code.

3. The systems environment, which is largely derived from data based on the DEC Ultrix® and Unix operating systems. (This data also generally corresponds to online transaction processing.)

This data has been developed using a variety of sources (Huck and Flynn [136], Rossmann [248], MacDougall [189], Clark [52]) and necessarily involves a considerable variety of source programs, applications, and compilers. Three types of instruction set architectures are distinguished for the scientific environment and two types for the commercial environment. In the scientific environment, we distinguish between the L/S, R/M, and R+M types of machines. For the commercial environment, we treat R/M and R+M as being the same, since the R/M prototype (S/390) has MM formats for character and decimal operations.

Typically, many load/store architectures have arithmetic coprocessors or floating point support within the instruction set. Therefore, it is assumed that the L/S instruction set has direct support for floating point operations in the scientific environment. However, these instruction sets usually do not support decimal and character strings. These operands may be supported one byte or digit at a time, but rarely is the support more extensive than that. Hence, for the commercial environment we have basically two types of instruction set architectures to consider:

1. The baseline load/store architecture. Here, it is assumed that the load/store architecture supports byte-at-a-time character string movement through registers and supports decimal on a digit-by-digit basis, again through movement of operands through registers.

2. The general register–memory architectures. Here, R/M (as well as R+M) generally includes memory-to-memory operations (e.g., on IBM mainframes) in support of commercial data types. Thus, for this class of application, the register/memory and the register plus memory architectures are the same.

In the following data, we generalized the published statistical information. Since the variance across some of the data is high, we have simplified the data groups and conservatively estimated the expected value of key aspects of the data. For example, as a generalization we might lump together a variety of instructions that all have similar execution properties and similar expected timing, such as ALU-based operations including shift, compare, and logical operations. In distinguishing among various types of operands, if floating-point data indicate an occurrence of 80–85% floating-point adds, with the bulk of the remainder being floating-point multiply, we use 80% distribution of adds. Since floating-point multiplies are a more difficult (and slower) operation than adds, a larger number of multiplies provides a more conservative performance estimate. The data is from a combination of sources on a variety of different architectures, adjusted for these differences. Where alternate data are available, the statistics are based upon the best compiler and global register allocator technology available at the time of this writing. As the compiler art advances, we expect an evolution of statistical data towards distributions representing increasing levels of compiler optimization.

Since the variance is large, the designer must use caution lest the resultant design become too sensitive to a particular aspect of program behavior. These data should be used only as a starting point for a design—further analysis including simulations should be done for the final selection and fine-tuning of the design.

Architectural Changes

The L/S architecture continues to evolve. Our baseline L/S corresponds to a simple architecture with an instruction vocabulary of perhaps 100 instructions, including minimum support (byte LD/ST) for character string operations. The various L/S approaches in the marketplace have been changing in several ways in recent years:

1. Increased size of instruction vocabulary.

2. Increased sophistication of compiler technology.

The first trend should, in time (at least for some L/S architectures), minimize the difference in the commercial environment between the L/S and the R/M approaches.

The second trend should allow L/S processors to more effectively use their 32 registers (see Figure 2.51). Over the next few years, we expect the difference in dynamic instruction count to largely disappear. The optimized register allocation for the L/S will cancel out the advantage of the main-frame's RM format. Table 3.1 illustrates the L/S instruction set evolution.

3.2.2   Format Distribution

Instruction size and the relative frequency of instructions determine in-struction bandwidth. Instruction bandwidth is measured as the number of bits required from memory to support the execution of the program with-out the presence of a cache.

The required instruction bandwidth is a product of the number of instruc-tions (dynamic count) that are required to be executed and the average size of each instruction. Architectures that allow only one instruction size (the L/S architectures) are the simplest. Slightly more complex are the R/M architectures, which have two or three different size instructions. R+M in-struction sets, especially as typified by VAX, provide the most variation in instruction sizing. Note that the expected instruction size in R+M is greater than in R/M (scientific). This accounts for the use of longer memory-to-memory formats in R+M, also allowing significantly fewer instructions exe-cuted per 100 HLL operations (Table 3.3). The design target data are shown in Table 3.2.

3.2.3   Operation Set Distribution

Table 3.3 shows the expected number of instructions executed (scientific environment) per 100 HLL operations executed using a common source workload. Tables 3.4–3.6 show the expected opcode distribution for the various architecture families for scientific applications (Table 3.4), com-mercial environments (Table 3.5), and systems (workstation) environments (Table 3.6). The tables are broken down by a classification scheme originally developed a number of years ago by Gibson [103, 105]. The breakdown of operations within each of these classes is described later. A primary concern is to understand the reasons for differences that occur among ar-chitectures given the same source program and level of compilation, and to understand the expected performance differences that arise because of these architectural differences.

The commercial application environment is a very important segment of the processor marketplace and is generally overlooked by those primarily in-terested in the scientific environment. This area has long been the mainstay for mainframe processors managing large "farms" of disks for centralized database inventory control and transactions management. We break the data into two classes: (i) the "classical" commercial (Cobol) such as payroll, report generation, etc., and (ii) the online transaction processing (written in C). This latter class generally behaves similar to a systems environment and many nonscientific workstation applications. The first class (Table 3.5) we generally refer to as "commercial," and the second class (Table 3.6) we refer to as "systems" environments.

We provide the L/S data in Table 3.5 merely for completeness. This is what we would expect to happen *if* the L/S compilers, etc., executed the work-load of our R/M architecture in the same way, simply mapping over R/M (or R+M) constructs into an L/S format. The result is an increase in dynamic

Table 3.1   Evolution of the MIPS instruction set.

Original MIPS R2000/R2010 Instruction Opcodes	
Load/Store:	LB, LBU, LH, LHU, LUI, LW, LWCz, LWL, LWR, SB, SH, SW, SWCz, SWL, SWR
Computational:	ADD, ADDI, ADDIU, ADDU, AND, ANDI, DIV, DIVU, MULT, MULTU, NOR, OR, ORI, SLL, SLLV, SLT, SLTI, SLTIU, SLTU, SRA, SRAV, SRL, SRLV, SUB, SUBU, XOR, XORI MFHI, MFLO, MTHI, MTLO
Jump and Branch:	BCzF, BCzT, BEQ, BGEZ, BGEZAL, BGTZ, BLEZ, BLTZ, BLTZAL, BNE, J, JAL, JALR, JR, RFE,
Coprocessor:	CFCz, COPz, CTCz, MFCz, MTCz
Special:	BREAK, SYSCALL TLBP, TLBR, TLBWI, TLBWR
Floating-point:	ABS, ADD, C, CVT, DIV, MOV, MUL, NEG, SUB
MIPS R4000 Extensions	
Branch likely:	BCzFL, BCzTL, BEQL, BGEZL, BGEZALL, BGTZL, BLEZL, BLTZL, BLTZALL, BNEL
Load/Store doubleword:	LDCz, SDCz
Floating-point:	ROUND, TRUNC, CEIL, FLOOR, SQRT
Conditional trap:	TEQ, TEQI, TGE, TGEI, TGEIU, TGEU, TLT, TLTI, TLTIU, TLTU, TNE, TNEI
Special:	CACHE, LL, SC, SYNC, ERET

Comments: The R2000 and the R3000 [153] have the same instruction sets and the same basic architecture. The R4000 [154] was enhanced to include a floating-point unit and instruction and data caches on board. Also, the pipeline in the R4000 was increased from 5 stages to 8, to improve the clock rate.

The onchip caches are direct-mapped and virtually indexed. The data cache is write-back. New instructions were added to deal with these changes and to allow multiprocessor configurations:

1. Due to the longer pipeline, "branch likely" instructions were added to reduce the branch penalty using statically predicted branches.

2. Load and store double word were added to coprocessor instructions to boost their floating performance. The R4000 has the floating point onchip, but it still uses the coprocessor instructions.

3. Floating point was enhanced to do square root.

4. Cache control instructions were added so that cache lines could be invalidated or flushed under software control.

5. Conditional trap instructions were added.

6. Multiprocessor synchronization instructions (Load linked, Store conditional, and Sync) were added.

Table 3.2   Instruction size distribution by program category.

	2-byte Reg–Reg Avg.%	4-byte Mem–Reg Avg.%	6-byte Mem–Mem Avg.%	Composite Average
Design Target: L/S	0%	100%	0%	4^B
Design Target: R/M				
Sci./Sys. Environments	40%	60%	–	3.2^B
Commercial Environment	30%	50%	20%	3.8^B
Design Target: R+M*				
Sci./Sys. Environments	25%	50%	25%	4^B
Commercial Environment	30%	50%	20%	3.8^B

* In current practice, R+M instruction sizes are byte-variable. The data presented here simply approximate the expected distribution. Thus, the entry "2 bytes" represents instruction sizes of 1 and 2 bytes; "4 bytes" represents instruction sizes 3 through 5 bytes; and "6 bytes" represents instruction sizes of 6 bytes and longer.

Table 3.3   Expected instructions executed per 100 HLL operations (scientific application).

Architecture	Instructions per 100 HLL Operations
L/S	200
R/M	180
R+M	120

Table 3.4   Expected Gibson classification profile for scientific applications by architecture. Expected instructions executed per 100 HLL operations. (For a breakdown of operations *within* a class, see indicated table.)

Scientific	L/S	R/M	R+M	See Table
Move (integer, floating point)	107 (54%)	87 (48%)	27 (23%)	3.15
Branch	26 (13%)	26 (15%)	26 (22%)	3.10
Floating Point	24 (12%)	24 (13%)	24 (20%)	3.14
Fixed Point	16 (8%)	16 (9%)	16 (13%)	3.14
Shift, Compare, Logical (word)	27 (13%)	27 (15%)	27 (22%)	—
	200	180	120	

The Role of Formats in Dynamic Instruction Count

More formats in an instruction set generally result in fewer instructions executed; fewer formats result in more instructions required to execute a program. The ratio 100:90:60 illustrated in Table 3.3 for relative instruction count across the L/S-R/M-R+M instruction sets seems to be well validated across many scientific environments. Whether additional instructions necessarily imply additional execution time is a much more problematic and debatable issue. For example, the additional instructions in a L/S program required because of its limited format are generally load and store instructions, which can be quickly executed. The instruction count using the R+M instruction set has been reduced by eliminating the need for load and store instructions. The instructions remaining are more formidable functional instructions—add, multiply, etc.—that consume a good deal of program execution time.

While execution time does not necessarily scale with dynamic instruction count (at least directly), there are secondary issues relating to code density such as cache efficiency which must be taken into consideration. We saw some of these effects in Chapter 2 and will again see these effects arise in Chapter 5.

Notice that the trend in L/S architectures is to increase instruction set vocabulary and improve register allocation. Both can significantly improve L/S dynamic instruction behavior.

Table 3.5 Expected Gibson classification profile for commercial (Cobol) applications by architecture type; see text for L/S assumptions. Character includes byte and variable length operands. Expected instructions executed per 100 HLL operations.

Commercial	L/S	R/M and R+M	See Table
Move (integer)	75 (11%)	28 (15%)	3.16
Move (character)	364 (53%)	16 (9%)	3.16
Branch	138 (20%)	72 (40%)	3.10
Decimal	46 (7%)	13 (7%)	3.14
Fixed Point	15 (2%)	15 (8%)	3.14
Shift, Compare, Logical (word)	15 (2%)	15 (8%)	—
Test, Compare, Logical (character)	35 (5%)	22 (12%)	—
	688	181 99%	

Table 3.6   Expected Gibson classification profile for transactions processing and systems applications by architecture. Expected instructions executed per 100 HLL operations.

Systems	L/S	R/M	R+M	See Table
Move (integer, floating point)	107 (54%)	87 (48%)	27 (23%)	3.17
Branch	47 (23%)	47 (26%)	47 (39%)	3.10
Fixed Point	19 (10%)	19 (11%)	19 (16%)	3.14
Shift, Compare, Logical (word)	27 (13%)	27 (15%)	27 (22%)	—
	200	180	120	

code size of more than three times. We expect that as L/S machines achieve
significant impact in this commercial environment, the distribution shown
in Table 3.5 will be significantly different, presumably somewhat reducing
the overall dynamic instruction count and difference between these architectures. As L/S processors move into the commercial arena, they are being
extended to include the supporting data types and operations required by
such programs. This has the effect of significantly diminishing the difference, making it somewhat more akin to the differences cited in Table 3.3.

Tables 3.3–3.6 are referenced to the HLL measures mentioned in Chapter 2.
For 100 HLL operations executed, we expect the L/S-type architecture to require 200 instructions to be executed, the R/M to require 180 instructions,
and the R+M to require 120 instructions to be executed. This assumes optimized compilation and full floating point support across all architectures.
The reason for the difference between instruction counts for R/M and L/S
is that the R/M architecture possesses a format the L/S does not. It allows
the R/M format, which combines two L/S instructions:

```
LD.W     R2, ADDR
ADD.W    R1, R1, R2
```

into a single instruction:

```
ADD.W    R1, ADDR.
```

The R+M-type machine takes this one step further by allowing all memory
formats, as illustrated next.

Suppose we have the isolated statement:

A := B + C.

In the L/S architecture, we would have:

```
LD.W     R1, B
LD.W     R2, C
ADD.W    R3, R2, R1
ST.W     A, R3,
```

while in R/M we might have:

```
LD.W    R1, B
ADD.W   R1, C
ST.W    A, R1.
```

Finally, for R+M, we could have:

```
ADD.W   A, B, C.
```

The data presented in Table 3.4 are presented as the occurrence per 100 HLL operations and as a percentage of all instructions for that particular architecture. Thus, in the R/M architecture, we expect 87 move-type instructions to be executed per 100 HLL operations, and these 87 operations represent 48% of a total of 180 instructions executed per 100 HLL source operations.

Certain Gibson classes of instructions (branch and floating point) are invariant across architectures and appear to be invariant across compilers also. Fixed-point add, shift, compare, and logical are presented here as being invariant, but in practice they are heavily influenced by the compiler, especially when the compiler does machine-dependent optimizations such as replacing $2 * x$ with a left shift of x. Fortunately, from a performance evaluation point of view, these instructions are largely interchangeable—they all require use of an ALU and usually take about the same amount of ALU time to execute. They have similar instruction timing and similar access requirements to memory.

Since R/M and R+M both include memory-to-memory operations for commercial data types, they are largely indistinguishable in commercial applications. Differences that arise due to address arithmetic are ignored here. One should note the relatively high occurrence of the branch classification in these commercial applications (R/M and R+M).

Most currently available L/S architectures (as well as some R/M microprocessors) do not have direct support for moving character strings or for operating on variable-length decimal operands. However, there may be support for loading a character into a register or single-digit decimal arithmetic operations. Since data on such machines in commercial applications is not generally available, the information presented in Table 3.5 for L/S is synthetic. It represents a straightforward mapping of the available commercial environment data for other architectures to the L/S, assuming interpretive code to execute string and decimal operations. The high incidence of move (characters) is a reflection of the occurrence of move characters in commercial-type applications and the expectation that this instruction moves a field of about 32 characters. In this interpretive model, the branch occurrence is not commensurately affected. Thus, the commercial L/S data provided here is not measured data; it is a simple projection on the L/S architecture of available data for other architectures and should be used with care.

Consistency of Empirical Data

The great problem with reported instruction set data is the problem of consistency. Unless the source programs, compilers, operating systems, and input data sets are standardized, little meaning can be inferred from reported instructional set distributional data. There have been only a few attempts at normalizing most of these variables and studying the resultant sensitivities. The best study to date is by Loboz [186], who looks at all of the previously cited factors. Our work has relied primarily on consistent data, even at the expense of a greater corpus of program material. We do not believe that a larger corpus of uncorrelated and inconsistent material would provide more reliable data than a smaller, but consistently used, set of data.

3.3   Process Management

An important aspect of processor performance is the behavior of applications during a process switch. Particular architecture features that are present in the processor significantly affect the number of instructions required to execute the switch and the time to manage the memory system. We review process switch data and resulting tradeoffs in this section.

Control passes from one procedure to its successor, requiring housekeeping. There are three types of control transfer:

1. Passing control to another user procedure.

2. Passing control to a supervisor or other privileged procedure.

3. Passing control through an interrupt.

All require at least the equivalent of a procedure call.

3.3.1   Procedure Calls: User State

Procedure call is one of the more difficult and controversial areas of program behavior. Calls are subject to significant variability across applications, data inputs, and operating systems. Even in the area of user programs only, the average number of instructions between a call varies significantly by application and programming language. Consider the following three sets of data [186] for the number of instructions between calls and/or returns:

- C programs (10 applications)
  maximum = 333, average = 100.

- Pascal programs (13 programs)
  maximum = 71.4, average = 52.6.

- Algol (2 programs)
  maximum = 40, average = 27.

The preceding dynamic instruction count represents the number of instructions between a procedure call instruction and a procedure return instruction. It is not the same as procedure size, since often procedures call other procedures before a return.

Calls are expensive. For a simple load/store machine, the following instructions (`call` and corresponding `return`) are typically associated with each procedure entered:

Call/return	2.0	instructions
Local stack adjustment	2.0	instructions
Parameter passing	1.5	instructions
Register saves/restores	4.8	instructions
Return value	0.6	instructions
Total cost per call/return pair	10.9	instructions

Thus, each time a call and return is invoked, about ten additional instructions are required to support it. These instructions are usually of the load/store/increment/register move type. The use of load multiple/store multiple instructions reduces the number of instructions for save and restore (but not necessarily the amount of time involved with this activity). It would, for example, reduce the 4.8 instructions to 2 instructions. Similarly, the use of register windows eliminates the register save and restore cycles as well as some time associated with parameter passing. The elimination of the time associated with register save and restore does not eliminate the time associated with the call activity, as the local stack adjustment must be done as before. Also as pointed out by Loboz [186], the use of techniques such as in-line expansion of procedures can significantly change the call frequency and resulting call overhead. He reports changes of about 40% in the mean number of instructions between procedure calls by using such techniques.

The depth of procedure nesting can be important if the architecture includes register windows or a version of a stack cache buffer. Unfortunately, the degree of nesting is widely variable from program to program and even for different runs of the same program [186]. Additionally, operating system structure may have a significant impact on this depth as well. For one cited program Loboz found that the minimum nesting depth was 3 and the maximum depth was 1,004, with a dynamic profile depending strongly on the input. Fortunately, it appears that the relative call depth seems to be not nearly as volatile as the absolute depth [275], and this is the principle upon which register windows and similar techniques rest. (However, the success of register windows still depends on aspects of the operating system.)

The net effect of all this on performance models can be summarized as follows:

1. Call frequency generally is relatively low—1 to 3% of HLL actions (i.e., about $\frac{1}{2}$% to 1% of machine instructions).

2. The variance, however, in frequency of calls is large, and thus some programs may exhibit frequencies as high as 10 or 12%, while others have frequencies of much less than 1%.

3. Calls are important because of the activity they represent. They cause between 5 and 10 additional instructions to be executed. These instructions, such as load/store, increment, etc., are generally independent of architecture type except where the architecture includes special provision for managing calls.

4. Among the provisions that reduce the number of instructions required to support a call is the use of load multiple/store multiple and the use of a generalized call instruction that saves/restores a number of registers. Both of these approaches reduce instruction count, but do not affect the total time it takes to manage the call, since the various load and store activities must still be accomplished.

5. Use of register windows reduces but does not eliminate the cost of the call.

6. One should expect about 60% of total execution time to be spent in the user state and 40% in the system state (including libraries), although individual programs will vary widely from this. For systems that regard library functions as part of the user state the ratio is 70% user state and 30% systems state.

Most modeling aspects of the call as it affects performance are included in Tables 3.4 and 3.5; for example, the number of load and store instructions, etc., have already been included in these tables.

One must use some discretion before drawing conclusions about the behavior of load multiple and store multiple instructions. The LDM and STM are not used exclusively with call/return, and calls involving only one or no parameters will not use these instructions. Even if we know the distribution of the number of registers involved with the load multiple and store multiple, we do not know the number of registers saved and restored in the call. The load multiple/store multiple is frequently used by the user in applications programs. The load multiple, for example, is used to load long operands into the registers or to store double-sized operands back in memory. A study by Rossmann [248] measuring an older move register allocation environment gives a conservative estimate for a 16 general-purpose register file of the mean number of operands used for load and store multiples as:

Move register allocation	LDM	5.989 registers
	STM	13.231 registers

As we have seen in Chapter 2, interprocedural register allocators can significantly reduce register traffic. We project that these allocators would both slightly reduce the number of LDM and STM instructions and significantly reduce the mean number of registers moved by LDM and STM. Thus, our projection for sophisticated register allocation for the mean number of registers moved is:

LDM	3.0 registers
STM	4.0 registers

As in everything else associated with the call, it should be understood that the preceding values are subject to wide variance. The preceding data [248]

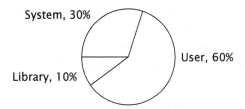

Figure 3.1   Expected percent of time in various machine states (UNIX workstation environment).

include *all* uses of load and store multiples, not just calls. The Rossmann data is older than other data cited, perhaps from a time when software took a more brute-force approach to save and restore by conservatively saving more registers than required.

The LDM/STM behavior is important, since the number of registers involved in the transfer directly determine the number of cycles or the amount of time involved in accomplishing the operation.

3.3.2   Calls to the System

During the execution of any user program, the operating system must usually be invoked to provide services. Inspection of 20 workstation-type programs under UNIX has shown that programs spend less than one percent of the time in systems execution for some applications, while others spend as much as 95% of the time in systems execution. The average time that UNIX applications were in the system state was 28.6% (exclusive of virtual memory swapping time). Figure 3.1 shows a rough user-to-system allocation and, within the user allocation, the execution time spent in user procedures vs. library procedures. A 60–10–30 breakdown for user procedures, library procedures, and systems execution seems a reasonable expectation, although the variability from application to application is huge.

Systems calls typically differ from user procedure calls by requiring additional activity (instructions) to complete their execution. This additional "work" depends on the type of system call invoked. Much system activity can be classified as falling into one of four categories:

1. System call.

2. Trap/interrupt.

3. Page table entry change (not in TLB).

4. Context switch.

A system call/return differs from a procedure call/return by usually requiring that all of the general-purpose registers (rather than just those required for parameters) be saved and later restored. Additionally, some bookkeeping is involved for managing the process id number.

A trap or an interrupt requires additional work, as the floating point registers need to be saved and restored and the processor must examine the

Table 3.7 Instructions executed per operating system function [20].

Operation	VAX	MIPS R2000	SPARC	i860
System call/return	12	84	128	86
Trap/interrupt	14	103	145	155
Page table entry change	11	36	15	559
Context switch	9	135	326	618

interrupt or trap vector to determine which specific systems routine is to be called.

The activity required to change a page table entry has been implied in our earlier discussion of the *not-in-TLB* operation (see section 1.7), and it depends on the TLB structure. It differs from other systems calls as it is not necessary to save and restore more than a relatively small number of registers to do the required address arithmetic.

A *context switch* requires that new values be brought in for all registers. For a straightforward register set, context switch ought to require somewhat less work to process than a trap or interrupt, since the analysis of exceptional conditions is not required. However, for a system with multiple register sets (register windows), a context switch may require that all sets be saved and new values loaded for all of the multiple register sets. Table 3.7 shows a number of instructions executed for various operating system primitive functions [20].

Moreover, there are a number of trends in operating systems. A simple R+M machine such as the VAX executes between 9 and 14 instructions per systems call, while L/S machines execute many more (Table 3.7). Even though time does not scale with instruction count, this result is a source of concern. The reason for this is twofold:

1. The VAX has a relatively simple register state.

2. The VAX supports robust save and restore instructions.

Our modern load/store machines have larger register spaces (Table 3.8), which must be saved and restored and generally support only simple call mechanisms, requiring software to manage the details of directing the system call to the correct system handler routine. Adding registers and/or multiple register sets may improve user state performance, but doing so may come at the expense of system performance.

Moreover, modern operating systems are moving along interesting lines. Two particular developments are certain to affect processor performance in the future. These are:

1. The client/server model.

2. Partitioning the operating system into multiple threads.

The client/server model is a form of distributed operating system particularly well suited for multiple processors on a network system. It basically

Table 3.8   User state to be changed in a context switch.

	R+M	R/M	L/S		
	VAX	S/390	R2000	SPARC	i860
G. P. Registers	16	16	32	136	32
F. P. Registers	0	8	32	32	32
Other (PSW, etc.)	1	2	5	6	9

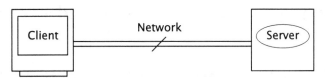

1. Call to system.	4. Link stub.	6. Network
2. Link stub.	5. Service.	transmission.
3. Network transmission.		7. Return from system.

Figure 3.2   Actions in a remote procedure call.

partitions the functions of the operating system into various services, which may be local (within the same processor or workstation) or remote (accessible via a network). A distributed operating system has obvious advantages, as not all services need be present on all systems on the network and various services can be located with appropriate files that need be accessed to provide a particular service. Remote services are accessed via a remote procedure call (Figure 3.2). This remote procedure call (RPC) communicates messages between address spaces. The client (the caller processor) makes a call to the system, and the system automatically generates a link via a message to the server process on the network. This link is referred to as a *stub*, which packages up the procedure's parameters into a message. At the server, another stub receives the parameters and makes the call to the designated server resource. After executing the service routine, the server returns a result, again via the network, to the requestor. Table 3.9 (from Anderson [20]) shows the various functions involved in the RPC and the percentage of time observed in these functions. Notice that network transfer time is a relatively small amount of the entire RPC processing time.

Table 3.9   Profile of remote procedure call processing time [20].

Function	% Time
Network transfer time	17%
Interrupt processing	30%
Receiving thread	17%
Stub processing	29%
Check sums (message validation)	7%

Threads are special sub-processes that share the address space of a process. They promote the parallel execution of various functions of the operating system, and allow the system to support finer-grain parallel processing. The use of threads in parallelizing the operating system creates many small processes. These processes must communicate via some type of context switch. The additional cost of the context switch in the modern large register systems defeats the operating system designer's attempts to improve performance through parallel execution of the operating system.

3.4   Breaks in Pipelined and Overlapped Machine Execution

Certain aspects of program behavior disrupt the execution of an overlapped or pipelined host. *Breaks* or delays in execution occur, and instruction processing must be suspended until these events are resolved. These delays are usually caused by one of the following phenomena:

1. Branching and similar control delays.

2. Data dependencies.

3. Run-on instructions.

4. Memory hierarchy delays.

Branching may cause significant delays, since a delay is usually associated with the fetching of the target instruction; thus, a successor instruction is delayed by the fetch time of the targeted instruction. Many operations depend on a preceding operation for completion. These data dependencies add further delay to program execution. Some instructions (e.g., floating point divide) take many more cycles than the bulk of instructions executed. These instructions, by their nature, require multiple EX cycles (or accesses to memory, etc.) before a result is available. This delay frequently cannot be masked by execution of other instructions, and adds to the delay in program execution. Figure 3.3 represents a possible allocation of delay for program execution. We model pipeline performance as the sum of the decode time or the minimum time allocated for the execution of any instruction, independent of dependencies or resource conflicts, plus the accumulation of delays due to these various sources. The sources of delay are assumed to be independent of one another; that is, a delay from one source cannot be masked by a simultaneous occurrence with delay from another source. This is generally true, but may be only approximate in certain cases. The model, assuming a *linear independent composition* of delays, provides a conservative estimate of performance. In order to evaluate the effects of the various delays, we must first determine the frequency of various program events that cause delays [170, 256].

3.4.1   Instruction Run Length

The number of instructions between taken branches defines the *instruction run length*. This run length is an important parameter in selecting a pipeline organization and an instruction buffer strategy. Figure 3.4 shows that the

Back to the Future

Modern processor designers have been rapidly moving in ways to speed up processor performance. Unfortunately, these methods are largely based upon user state benchmarks and program behavior. At the same time, operating system designers have been moving toward speeding up their programs by creating distributed operating systems partitioned into fine grains of control called threads. Such systems require much more frequent context switching than earlier systems. The added processor state that the designers have included to improve user state performance serves to degenerate systems state performance. All of this has been observed best in a paper by Anderson et al. [20]. They conclude:

- Operating systems are being decomposed into kernelized structures with independent servers executing in separate address spaces. These separate address spaces communicate with users and with each other using RPC. At the same time, architectures have made message-based communication (relatively) more expensive because system calls, interrupt handling, and byte copying are (relatively) more expensive.

- Operating systems are requiring more use of memory management, at a time when handling memory management events has become more difficult.

- Operating systems are moving towards support of fine-grained, multithreaded application programs. At the same time, architectures are adding more processor state, which makes fine-grained threads more expensive.

The net effect of all this can be summarized as follows:

1. Very large register sets such as register windows may limit the performance of a modern operating system (e.g., SPARC).

2. Ideas such as virtual caches, which must be flushed or whose contents are declared invalid on a context switch, can also have a negative effect on overall systems performance (e.g., SPARC implemented in SUN 4).

3. Other hardware ideas such as user-visible out-of-order instruction execution (imprecise interrupts) or software-managed pipeline control are probably equally bad ideas, since they significantly complicate the task of managing traps and context switches (e.g., early MIPS or Intel i860).

In an effort to move away from the slower, cumbersome, and complex instruction set baggage of systems such as VAX and Intel 432, some designers may have lost sight of the value that these instruction sets provided for at least some of the systems support constructs. As the operating system becomes increasingly important in modern systems, and time spent in the system increases as a fraction of total time, these designers may find that they have "thrown the baby out with the bath water"—the performance gained in the user state has been lost in the system state.

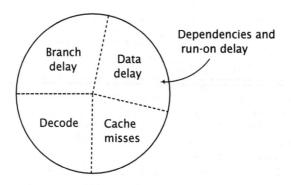

Figure 3.3   Possible delay allocation in program execution.

Pipeline Breaks

Multiple instructions can be concurrently executed and still produce the correct sequential answer so long as there are no "surprises" in the instruction sequence. For a high-speed processor with instruction execution concurrency, a "surprise" is some sort of dependency where one instruction uses the result of a previous one, or a particular instruction in the sequence is a branch instruction directing execution of a target instruction out of the sequence line. The effect of such "surprises" is to "break" the flow of information in a pipeline processor.

Terms such as "pipeline breaks" and "dependencies" generally are used synonymously.

---

mean instruction sequence length is 7.5 instructions (all environments), but note that 70% of the sequences are seven instructions or fewer. The variance over user environments was not significant; the mean varied from 5.18 to 8.33. Sequences of one instruction (8%) represent a taken branch followed by a taken branch. With many short runs, it is easy to understand the importance of a short branch resolution delay.

3.4.2   Branches

Branch instructions are a very important consideration in the design of a pipelined processor. They tend to disrupt the natural flow of instructions through the pipeline by reducing the processor's ability to prefetch the instructions that it needs. There is no easy way to avoid these effects, since, as Tables 3.4–3.6 illustrate, they represent a significant fraction of the instructions executed no matter what the workload.

While the overall occurrence of branches varies from one application in an environment to another, the profile of branches remains generally constant. Between 70 and 80% of all branches are branch-on-condition, and about 10% are loop control (Table 3.10a). The remaining instructions are procedure call. Among these classes, the most variable is procedure call.

Table 3.10   Branch profiles summarized.

(a) **Occurrence of Branch Classes**

Type 1. Branch (BC, BR, BCR, and BRR)	72.5%
Type 2. Loop Control (BCT, ...)	9.8%
Type 3. Procedure Call, Return (BAL, BALR)	17.7%

(b) **Type 1 Branch: What it uses**

Target address in register (BCR and BRR)	17.4%
Target address formed by AG (BC and BR)	82.6%

(c) **Type 1 Branch: Where it goes**
and, within BC class, taken and non-taken (%)

	Scientific	Commercial	Systems
Unconditional (BR and BRR)—100% go to target	20%	40%	35%
Conditional—went to target (BC)	43.2% (54%)	24.3% (41%)	32.5% (50%)
Conditional—went in-line (BC)	36.8% (46%)	35.7% (59%)	32.5% (50%)

(d) **Type 2: Loop constructs** (All environments)

That go to target	91%
That go in-line	9%
	100%

(e) **Type 3: Call/return** (All environments)

100% go to target

BAL	(80%)
BALR	(20%)
	100%

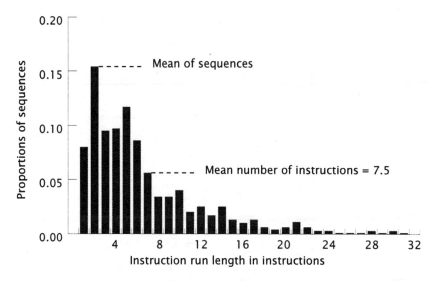

Figure 3.4 Distribution of basic blocks (number of instructions between branches), from MacDougall [189] (R/M architecture). Note that while the mean distance between branches is 7.5 instructions, about 66% of the basic blocks are shorter than this. A few very large basic blocks significantly affect the mean sequence length.

Procedure call is less frequent in Fortran-based scientific code, and much more frequent in commercial and systems type applications. Many architectures allow the target address to be either available in a register (BCR) or computed by an address generation (AG) action (BC). Architectures that allow 2-byte register-to-register operations would include BCR as a 2-byte instruction, while BC occupies four bytes (Table 3.10b).

Within the branch-on-condition category, about 20% of the BC instructions are expected to be unconditional, and of the true conditional branch instructions, we expect 54% to go to the target and 46% to go in-line. This latter statistic is highly sensitive to both the application and the compiler. Available data in the commercial environment indicates a much higher frequency of unconditional branches and also a higher frequency of branches that go to the in-line path. Most loop-type branches go to the target as expected (Table 3.10d), and (statistically) almost all call and return instructions also go to target (Table 3.10e). As we shall see, knowledge concerning the direction selected by a branch is important in selecting a branch strategy to improve the performance of pipelined systems.

In interpreting Table 3.10, recall that the conditional branch instruction includes a mask field (Chapter 1) which specifies the condition code state that is being tested. An all-1's mask field implies that the branch must be taken, since the machine must be in one of the tested states. We designate these as BR instructions. Similarly, all 0's implies a no-op instruction. The remaining branch instructions are "true" conditional branches and are designated as BC.

Table 3.13 shows the results of the BC test on the condition code established by an earlier instruction of various types. (For most architectures, *not all* instructions set the CC.)

To get an idea of the distribution of the number of instructions between branches, consider Figure 3.4. The mean of 7.5 instructions would correspond to a branch frequency of about 13%, akin to our L/S scientific environment model, although the actual data (MacDougall [189]) are from a somewhat different environment. Figure 3.4 illustrates the wide variance of basic block lengths.

EXAMPLE 3.1   USING BRANCH DATA

Find the fraction of all branches that go to the target:

(a) For a scientific environment.

Refer to Table 3.10. From 3.10(a) we have:

BC, BR, BCR, and BRR	72.5%
Loop control	9.8%
Procedure call	17.7%

Now, using 3.10(c) and (d), and noting that all procedure calls go to the target, we have:

BC, BR, BCR, and BRR	$7.25[.2 + .432]$	(Table 3.10c)
+ Loop control	$.098[.91]$	(Table 3.10d)
+ Procedure call	$.177$	
Total	*0.724*	

(b) Repeat for a systems environment.

Now only the type 1 branch is changed, so:

BC, BR, BCR, and BRR	$.725[.35 + .325]$
+ Loop control	$.098[.91]$
+ Procedure call	$.177$
Total	*0.756*

(c) What fraction of branches use an AG stage? Assume that all loop control branches use an AG.

Now we have (Table 3.10):

BC, BR	$.725[.826]$	(Table 3.10b)
Loop control	$.098$	
Procedure call (BAL)	$.177[.8]$	(Table 3.10d)
Total	*0.729*	

◆

3.4.3   Branch Target Distribution

One approach to minimizing the problem of branch instructions is to provide a small, high-speed buffer managed by the instruction fetch stage of a pipelined processor (Figure 3.5) that would contain a set of sequential

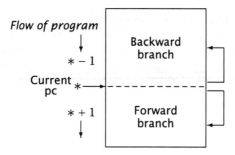

Figure 3.5   Branch target table (or buffer).

Table 3.11   Percent of branch target references found in a branch table with two different strategies (R/M). (A branch table is a single-block I-cache with prefetch.)

Size (bytes)	Backward Branch	Forward Branch
16	1	32
32	5	32
64	11	35
128	16	39
256	19	42
512	22	46
1024	24	49
2K	26	53
4K	28	55
8K	30	57
16K	33	60
32K	36	63
Unlimited	36.5	63.5

instructions (dynamic). The buffer functions in two ways. First, it contains instructions sequentially ahead of the current instruction fetch address; thus, instructions fetched in sequence are available without the usual memory access time. Second, it keeps previously executed instructions and it recognizes when the target of a branch falls within its contents (backward branches). In either case, the buffers deliver those branch target instructions without accessing memory.

How successful it is depends on the distribution of branch distances for successful branches. Figure 3.5 and Tables 3.11–3.12 illustrate this relationship, where table size defines an instruction region starting at the address of the instruction following the branch instruction (in bytes). This region extends either to addresses less than the current address (backward) or greater than this address (forward). The centered region is for a buffer that both prefetches instructions and retains previously executed instructions.

While retaining history (previously executed branches) involves only storage, prefetching in anticipation of forward branches places an added bur-

Table 3.12   Centered branch table in bytes.

Size (bytes)	Configuration	Percent
16	± 8	13%
32	± 16	33%
64	± 32	37%
128	± 64	46%
256	± 128	55%
512	± 256	61%
1k	± 512	68%
2k	± 1k	73%
4k	± 2k	79%
8k	± 4k	83%
16k	± 8k	87%
32k	± 16k	93%
64k	± 32k	99%

den on the memory system. Many of these prefetched instructions represent wasted fetches even if the target is correctly captured, as they are "skipped over."

In the next chapter, we study branch table buffers in more detail, but from Figure 3.5, Tables 3.11 and 3.12, and obvious implementation considerations, only relatively small tables ought to be considered practical.

3.4.4   Condition Code Testing

In many architectures, the conditional branch instructions test the state of a condition code in order to determine whether or not a branch should be taken. Since not all instructions modify the condition code, it is possible for the code to be set many instructions prior to the execution of a branch and not be altered in the interim. (Instructions such as LD usually do not affect the CC.) A processor can make use of early knowledge of the condition code to reduce the amount of work that the processor must perform. (See study 5.3.) If the condition code is already known at the time that a conditional branch instruction is decoded, the processor may be able to resolve the branch at decode time rather than at execution time. This allows the processor to treat the branch as either unconditionally taken or not taken. There is no need to prefetch instructions from both paths, and there is no chance that a wrong branch guess will require excess prefetching of instructions. Table 3.13 shows the length of this interval of condition code setting for various mixes.

The relatively small intervals available indicate that early condition code setting (and similar techniques discussed in this chapter) have limited effectiveness and that effectiveness is probably in the scientific environment.

Table 3.13   Mean interval* between condition code set and test (instructions) for a variety of programs. General data are for both compiler and object code for commercial and scientific environments. The second part of the table is for scientific environment only (object and compiler code).

	General	Scientific Only
Program with max. interval	1.58	1.58
Program with min. interval	0.05	0.95
Arithmetic mean	0.68	1.27
Geometric mean	0.33	1.24

*An interval of 0 means that the conditional branch instruction is immediately preceded by an instruction capable of modifying the condition code.

Branches

Few areas of pipelined processor design have received as much attention as the effect of branches on program execution. Branches are frequent and can be disruptive. Avoiding branches by unraveling code may be counterproductive by increasing code size and hence decreasing cache performance.

A number of misleading claims are sometimes made describing particular actions that have been incorporated into high-speed processors to mitigate the effect of branches. A claim such as "zero branch penalty" generally means that the implementation uses a rather shallow pipeline—there is not much concurrency going on, and/or the cycle has been elongated to ensure that the outcome is known before the next instruction is executed. As processors go faster and pipelines deeper [199], branches become more of a problem. Additional hardware can only go partway in providing a solution. For example, hardware to correctly predict the outcome of a branch succeeds only in making a conditional branch appear as an unconditional branch, which itself may represent a significant "break" in the pipeline.

3.4.5   Move and Arithmetic Class Operations

Understanding the composition of the various instruction classes may be vital in accurately predicting performance. Certain instructions generally take considerably longer to execute than others. Instructions such as fixed point add/subtract, load or store register, shift, compare, and logical operation usually have a minimum execution time. On the other hand, floating and fixed point divide and certain character string move and decimal instructions have long execution times, well in excess of the minimal allocation. These instructions are called *run-on instructions*, meaning that they occupy the execution unit for significantly longer than the minimum period. Run-on instructions, while infrequent, can dominate program execution. For example, an instruction that occurs only 2% in dynamic frequency but requires an additional 33 cycles of execution increases overall instruction execution by .66 cycles per instruction. Since most machines do not allow

Table 3.14   Expected distribution of arithmetic operations.

Floating Point (Scientific)	
Add/Subtract	54%
Multiply	43%
Divide	3%
Fixed Point (All applications)	
Add/Subtract	80%
Multiply	15%
Divide	5%
Decimal (Commercial)	
Move decimal[a]	
(includes Pack/Unpack and Clear-and-Add)	54%
Add/Subtract	39%
Multiply	4%
Divide	3%

[a]For the L/S architecture we assume that this is implemented by 17 LD and 8 ST per 100 HLL operations. Also see Tables 3.5 and 3.16.

instructions to execute out of order, the run-on delay (that is, the delay attributable to a particular instruction in excess of a minimum allocation in a timing template) directly contributes to overall processor delay.

For the two most important Gibson classes, arithmetic and move, the expected distribution of operations is shown in Tables 3.14, 3.15, and 3.16. For fixed point operations, simple add/subtract represents about 80% of the fixed point arithmetic class. Floating point, in the scientific environment, shows a more equal distribution between add/subtract and multiply. Divide is an infrequent operation across all environments. Commercial environments generally use decimal arithmetic, which, without decimal arithmetic hardware support, becomes fixed point arithmetic with conversion routines.

Within the decimal category (where supported), the most frequently occurring instruction pair is PACK/UNPACK. These instructions take a decimal string represented in 8-bit type ASCII format, and translate (PACK) the string into a 4-bit decimal format of half the size. Most decimal processing is done in packed format. UNPACK reverses the procedure. Another frequently occurring decimal operation is clear-and-move or zero-and-add (ZMOVE). This operation moves a second operand into a first operand location which has been zeroed out. The operation then is the equivalent of addition to zero. This operation, as well as the basic decimal arithmetic operations, is done in a packed format. All of the decimal arithmetic operations take two source operands of perhaps unequal length and produce the resultant decimal string.

The move class of instructions is broken out by application environment because of the significant differences that arise between the two application environments. Tables 3.15–3.17 present two entries, one being the number of occurrences of this type of operation and the second (in parentheses)

Table 3.15 Expected distribution (per 100 HLL operations) within Move class of instructions (scientific applications) by architecture type.

	L/S		R/M		R+M	
Integer Load (LD)	36	(34%)	24	(28%)	11	(41%)
Integer Store (ST)	16	(15%)	13	(15%)	6	(22%)
Floating Point Load (LD.F)	23	(21%)	17	(20%)	2	(7%)
Floating Point Store (ST.F)	18	(17%)	16	(18%)	1	(4%)
Integer Register Move (MOVE)	10	(9%)	12	(14%)	3	(11%)
Floating Pt. Register Move (MOVE.F)	2	(2%)	3	(3%)	2	(7%)
Load Multiple Registers (LDM)	1	(1%)	1	(1%)	1	(4%)
Store Multiple Registers (STM)	1	(1%)	1	(1%)	1	(4%)
Total	107	(100%)	87	(100%)	27	(100%)

Table 3.16 Expected distribution (per 100 HLL operations) within Move class of instructions (commercial applications) by architecture type.

	L/S		R/M and R+M	
Integer Load (LD)	54	(12%)	18	(41%)
Integer Store (ST)	16	(4%)	5	(11%)
Memory-to-memory Move (MOVE.C)	364	(83%)[a]	16	(36%)
Move decimal (see decimal arithmetic)	–		–	
Load Multiple Registers (LDM)	4	(1%)	4	(9%)
Store Multiple Registers (STM)	1	(0%)	1	(3%)
Total	439	(100%)	44	(100%)

[a]We assume that this is implemented as 243 LD and 121 ST.

Table 3.17 Expected distribution (per 100 HLL operations) within Move class of instructions (systems applications) by architecture type.

	L/S		R/M		R+M	
Integer Load (LD)	65	(61%)	50	(57%)	14	(52%)
Integer Store (ST)	23	(21%)	18	(21%)	5	(19%)
Integer Register Move (MOVE)	13	(12%)	13	(15%)	2	(7%)
Load Multiple Registers (LDM)	4	(4%)	4	(5%)	4	(15%)
Store Multiple Registers (STM)	2	(2%)	2	(2%)	2	(7%)
Total	107	(100%)	87	(100%)	27	(100%)

being the frequency of occurrence of this type of instruction, where the move as a class is 100%.

For the scientific environment, the higher occurrence of load and store for the L/S architecture is the result of the lack of a register-to-memory format. This occurs for both general-purpose and floating-point registers. This data *does not* assume use of interprocedural register allocation, hence the advantage of more registers in L/S (32 vs. 16 in R/M or R+M) is not significant. If interprocedural allocation were used, the additional registers in L/S would then reduce the required number of move instructions. In this case, we estimate that the L/S and R/M counts would be roughly equivalent. We suggest that the designer simply use the R/M data for this situation.

The R+M architecture with full memory-to-memory support goes a long way towards eliminating load and store instructions, since floating point and integer operations can be performed on a memory-to-memory basis. Register MOVE instructions simply move values from register to register. They can be used to zero out registers, or to protect a register value from being overwritten. Finally, load and store multiple registers are operations that are often associated with procedure calls. For our data, a load multiple occurs about three times more frequently than a store multiple. However, both are low-frequency operations. Usually the load and store multiple instructions are run-on instructions. Generally, their execution time is closely related to the number of registers transferred.

For commercial applications (Table 3.16), we lump the R/M and the R+M architectures. This architectural equivalence is only approximate, as the R/M architecture has some additional integer load and store activity to manage address computations that well-compiled code for an R+M might avoid. A major member of the move class for this environment is memory-to-memory character string move (or move characters, MOVE.C). As mentioned earlier, this table shows an unusually high number of move character instructions for the L/S architecture, since it is assumed that four bytes are moved into a register at a time. Notice that an L/S architecture may use no more execution cycles than the R+M with full support for character moves, depending on how the R+M architecture has been designed. For example, it may treat the occurrence of a MOVE.C as a run-on instruction and allocate one execution cycle per byte to its execution.

3.4.6 Register-Based Addressing

One of the most important stages in the pipeline is the address generation (AG) stage. In a typical R/M architecture, the result of address generation is the sum of a base register, an index register, and a displacement. Table 3.18 from Peuto and Shustek [231] shows the frequency of use of the address components.

In more than 75% of the cases only one register is actually used (usually the base register).

Recall that the R/M format has the following components:

```
OP R1,DISP [RX,RB],
```

Table 3.18   Register use for effective address calculation in various programs.

Range	No Registers	One Register	Two Registers
		(either base or index)	(base and index)
Max.†	4%	99%	22%*
Min.†	.01%	77%	1.1%
Avg.	1.4%	90%	9%*

† Max/min refers to the program that makes maximum/minimum use of registers in address calculation.
*Excluding scientific object code, the usage would be max = 8% and average = 4.3%.

where R1, RX, and RB designate three general-purpose registers. Now suppose we have the sequence:

```
LD   R4, ...
ADD  R7, DISP [R5, R4]
```

We are unable to generate the operand address for the ADD until the LD is completed, as the value in R4 is unknown until then. The destination of the LD instruction may be either the index register or base register, creating an address generation dependency. If the destination were a source operand (in the ADD R7,) then we would have an execution dependency. Address and execution dependencies occur in L/S architectures in similar ways; e.g.,

```
LD   R4, ...
LD   R7, DISP [R5, R4]
```

The second LD instruction must await the completion of the first instruction before it can complete its address generation.

Address Generation Dependencies

An *address generation dependency* occurs when the result register of one instruction is used as an index or base register by a following instruction. Address generation delay is determined by the distance (number of instructions) between instructions that set a particular register and the instruction that uses it in generating addresses. The distance is weighted by the corresponding delay, e.g., a distance of one could cause a corresponding delay of two, while a distance of two would have a delay of one; distances beyond two would have no delay. The greater the distance the less the effect. Table 3.19 shows the address interlock distances for a scientific environment.

Execution Dependencies

An *execution dependency* occurs when the result register of one instruction is an operand register of a following instruction. The effective execute interlock delay is also determined by the distance between the instruction

Table 3.19 Composite address interlock distance.

Percent	Cum.%	Distance
9.901	9.901	The previous instruction
8.397	18.299	2 instructions back
2.801	21.100	3 "
2.201	23.301	4 "
0.258	23.560	5 "
0.661	24.221	6 "
0.046	24.268	7 "
0.360	24.628	8 "
0.612	25.240	9 "
0.499	25.740	10 "
0.666	26.407	11 "
0.209	26.617	12 "
0.466	27.083	13 "
0.303	27.386	14 "
72.613	100.000	15 or more instructions back

Table 3.20 Composite execute interlock distance—number of instructions between dependent instructions.

Percent	Cum.%	Distance
40.297	40.297	The previous instruction
14.700	54.998	2 instructions back
3.559	58.557	3 "
4.898	63.456	4 "
6.650	70.107	5 "
1.706	71.813	6 "
3.217	75.030	7 "
2.518	77.549	8 "
2.776	80.325	9 "
2.215	82.541	10 "
3.473	86.014	11 "
1.548	87.562	12 "
1.225	88.787	13 "
1.557	90.345	14 "
9.654	100.00	15 or more instructions back

that set a particular register and the instruction that uses it as an operand. Table 3.20 shows the execute interlock distances for the same scientific mix used to determine address interlock distances.

Assume we have a delay of three cycles (if interlocked by the preceding instruction) on an address interlock and a delay of one cycle (1 ~) on an execution interlock (if dependent on the preceding instruction). The effect of these dependencies can be computed for addresses using Table 3.19 as follows:

$$
\begin{aligned}
\text{Address:} \quad & 3 \text{ cycles} \times 0.099 \\
+ & 2 \text{ cycles} \times 0.084 \\
+ & 1 \text{ cycles} \times 0.028 \\
\hline
& 0.493 \text{ cycles}
\end{aligned}
$$

This delay of 0.49 cycles occurs with frequency of $1 - .40 = 0.60$ (excluding RR formats, in Table 3.2) for the R/M architecture. For the L/S architecture, it would occur with frequency 0.54 (from Table 3.4); in L/S only Move class instructions can have an address interlock. Thus, the effective delay due to the address interlock is $0.60 \times 0.49 = 0.30$ cycles in R/M and $0.54 \times 0.49 = 0.26$ cycles in L/S.

The execute interlock occurs only on instructions that have an execute phase; i.e., excluding Gibson classes Move and Branch. From Table 3.4, this occurs with frequency 37% (R/M) and 33% (L/S). Thus, the effective delay due to the execution interlock (Table 3.20) is

$$
\begin{aligned}
.37 \times .403 &= 0.15 \text{ cycles for R/M} \\
.33 \times .403 &= 0.13 \text{ cycles for L/S.}
\end{aligned}
$$

The designer must keep in mind the variance in workload data and project performance on a conservative workload (and hope for better!).

3.4.7   Decimal and Character Operand Length

Decimal and character operations are memory-to-memory instructions in which the lengths of the operands are not implied by the opcode, but are defined in other fields of the instruction or are data-dependent. Even in a commercial environment these instructions tend to be infrequent, but their execution times can be very long and they can account for a substantial part of the execution time. Consequently, their implementation is often given careful attention. For our purposes, we divide the variable operand length instructions into two classes:

1. The character manipulation instructions: Move Character(s) (MOVE.C) and Compare Character (CMP.C).

2. The decimal arithmetic instructions such as Add Decimal (ADD.P).

Data are for the commercial environment only, as this environment makes the predominant use of these instructions.

The Compare Logical Characters instruction (CMP.C) is an MM instruction that compares the bytes of the first operand (length-specified instruction)

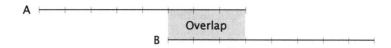

Figure 3.6   Overlapping character strings. If A is to be moved to B (starting within A), then the *overlap* must be detected lest the overlapped portion of the two be stored into before it is accessed.

with the bytes of a second operand (length is assumed to be the same as first operand). The comparison is logical (no sign recognized), and a condition code is set after execution.

The Move Characters (MOVE.C)—also MM—copies data from the second operand into the first operand using the length specified by the instruction.

Character Manipulation Instructions   This group of instructions specifies a source and destination starting location for a character string and a length in the range 1–256. One of the characteristics of these instructions that makes their implementation very difficult is that overlapped operands may occur and must be treated a byte at a time (Figure 3.6). This allows, for example, a single byte to be propagated throughout a string by a move instruction whose destination address is one greater than the source address, since the fields are processed left to right.

Peuto and Shustek [231] report that in two of the programs (a PL/1 compilation and a Cobol compilation) the nonoverlapped case occurred about 50 times more frequently than the overlapped case. However, the average number of bytes moved was less than 8 for the nonoverlapped move and greater than 50 for the overlapped move.

There are also instructions in this class for which the number of bytes processed may be much smaller than indicated in the instruction, such as CMP.C For these instructions, the distribution of the length specified in the instructions is a poor indicator of the length actually used. Peuto cites a typical example from one of his programs (a Cobol compilation), when the average CMP.C instruction specifies 4.53 bytes, but an average of only 1.744 bytes is examined by the hardware.

Table 3.21 indicates operand length from the character manipulation instructions.

The MOVE.C has a frequency of about 9% for this mix—with almost all of these being for unoverlapped operands. For two-thirds of the instructions, the operand length is eight or fewer bytes. However, most of the data moved by MOVE.C instructions is done with large operand lengths. Thus, the designer faces the dilemma of providing rapid execution of the more frequently occurring short operand MOVE.C instructions without slowing down the MOVE.C instructions that move the bulk of the character-oriented data.

Decimal Arithmetic Instructions   This group of instructions specifies two operands of length 1 to 16 bytes that either do not overlap or have co-

Table 3.21   Length (by class).

		Commercial
I (a)	Move characters	32.6^B
(b)	Move decimal	
	operand 1	4.2^B
	operand 2	3.3^B
II	Test, compare, logical	
	(as specified)	3.5^B
	(as executed)	2.0^B
III	Decimal arithmetic	
	Operand 1	4.2^B
	Operand 2	2.5^B

Table 3.22   Frequency of variable operand length instructions in R/M or R+M.

	Commercial	# per 100 HLL ops	
I (a)	Move character	16	9%
(b)	Move decimal	7	4%
II	Test, compare, logical (character)	22	12%
III	Decimal arithmetic	6	3%

incident rightmost bytes. Table 3.21 indicates operand lengths from the decimal instructions in a Cobol object mix.

There are basically six generic decimal instructions (all MM format): Pack (PACK), Unpack (UNPK), Add (ADD.P), Subtract (SUB.P), Multiply (MPY.P), and Divide (DIV.P). The Pack instruction takes the second operand and translates it from character or digit-per-byte representation to the packed two-digit-per-byte representation used in arithmetic processing. Unpack is the complementary operation. The four basic arithmetic operations follow expected conventions by using the format *first operand OP second operand → first operand*, and by keeping all operands in memory with length not exceeding 16 bytes.

Length of String Operands   Character and decimal operands have variable length (up to 256 bytes for character operands). Since execution time is almost always a function of operand length, the distribution of these operands is important. For execution purposes, character and decimal operations fall into one of three distinct types:

1. One source operand (of variable size) and a separate result operand (of variable size). Included here is MOVE.C. Certain decimal instructions form a separate sub-class (ZMOVE.P, PACK, and UNPK).

2. One or two source operands (of variable size) that are processed (executed) only up to the first occurrence of a particular byte. Usually, the result is the setting of a condition code. Instructions include CMP.C and CMP.P (decimal compare).

3. Operations with two source operands (of variable size) and a result operand that assumes the location and size of one of the operands—primarily decimal arithmetic instructions.

The distribution of the first type of character operation (excluding decimal) is dominated by the MOVE.C (move character instruction), which copies one operand into a result operand. For a commercial mix, the operand distribution is:

Occurrence of these instructions	9%*
Operand length	32.6 bytes

* 16 out of 181 instr per 100 HLL operations; R/M architecture, Tables 3.16 and 3.5.

Some decimal support operations also have a single source, single result format. These include PACK and UNPK (changing from/to packed decimal format) and ZMOVE.P.

The second type of operation includes several instructions led by the CMP.C (compare logical characters) which compares two character strings and sets a condition code.

Operand length (specified in instruction)	3.5^B
Operand bytes processed until instruction completion	2.0^B

The frequency and length data are summarized in Tables 3.21 and 3.22.

As execution time is frequently limited by operand length, a simple improvement is to treat MOVE.C with special word (4- or 8-byte) oriented hardware—i.e., move four or eight bytes at a time. Other operations, because of their complexity, are processed serially.

Using the longer operand as the determinate of execution time, we compute the following estimates of operation length for the commercial environment:

(a) All MM operands 12.2^B

(b) Excluding move character (type Ia in Table 3.22) 2.8^B

Program behavior design rules summary

1. Determine application design environment.

2. Choose instruction set class most appropriate.

Note the discussion in the text, i.e., an L/S machine that uses interprocedural register allocation uses the R/M data in the scientific environment. An L/S machine with full support for character and decimal operations may also resemble R/M behavior.

3. From preliminary machine target data, find delays for each of the "run-on" instructions and determine its frequency in number per 100 HLL operations.

4. If "run-on" delay depends on operand length, determine the various lengths.

5. Find applicable branch data from this chapter. Find dependency data.

6. Now on to Chapter 4!

3.5   Conclusions

The role of an instruction set in processor design depends on the expected program behavior of that instruction set. The architectural families L/S, R/M, and R+M can be compared relative to the number of high-level language operations executed by a program. This distributional data provides the basic design information required by a designer to optimize a design.

Although the obvious instruction set measures (dynamic instruction count, etc.) have a primary effect on performance, there are other aspects of the instruction set that are particularly important to pipeline processor implementation. These include the frequency and behavior of branch instructions. How often does the branch go to the target, and how far away is the target instruction? These issues can directly influence the design of the processor. Similarly, the investment of hardware and execution resources is determined by the expected occurrence of various types of functional instructions. Good data (valid and reliable) is a scarce commodity, yet it is a necessary ingredient in creating a good overall processor design.

3.6   Some Areas for Further Research

> *Data, data, everywhere,*
> *And all the results perused;*
> *Data, data, everywhere,*
> *Nor any bit to use.*[2]

This might well be the theme of this chapter. Despite enormous amounts of published instruction set material, it is very difficult to access data that has been validated in a consistent way across a number of different instruction sets. There never seems to be enough data on instruction set usage or machine behavior! Despite the notable work of Huck [135] and Loboz [186], a true understanding of the performance of different instruction sets across varying compiler optimizations and within varying operating systems environments is still poorly understood.

---

[2]With apologies to Samuel Taylor Coleridge and *The Rime of the Ancient Mariner.*

3.7 Data Notes

Data Note 1. The data in Tables 3.2, 3.3, 3.4, and 3.5 are primarily from Huck and Flynn [136] and Rossmann [248, 247], although other published sources have been considered. The Rossmann data are generally based on extensive studies of IBM mainframes. This seems to be one of the few architectures that provide a reasonable body of available data for the commercial environment. The systems data were taken from studies at DEC Western Research Lab [245] and from OLTP data from HP labs. The studies target L/S and (in the DEC case) R+M architectures; our R/M data is interpolated.

Reliability. There is a significant variability in the distribution of operations by application. The data presented assume an optimizing compiler (when such data are available). These data are an attempt to create a conservative representation of the operation profiles by emphasizing the expected occurrence of more difficult operations, such as floating point and decimal. The data provided for the L/S architecture in the commercial environment is completely synthetic—simply mapped-over data from R/M and R+M studies. The L/S data also make assumptions concerning the availability of certain instructions to interpret operations that occur in R/M architectures. The overall reliability for the scientific environment and for the R/M and R+M commercial environment should be reasonably good if somewhat conservative. The reliability of the L/S commercial data is low.

Variance. The variance in Tables 3.2 and 3.3 is expected to be relatively low, while the variance in Table 3.4 within each architecture is much higher. The occurrence of floating point, e.g., in scientific applications, has been variously reported between 4 and 20 percent. Similarly, the occurrence of branch can be much higher than that indicated here. There is less data available for the classification profile of commercial and systems applications (Tables 3.5 and 3.6). Similarly, the variance across classes is expected to be relatively high.

Data Note 2. The data in Tables 3.10 and 3.11 are taken from Rossmann [248, 247] and Huck and Flynn [136] (for Table 3.10) and Peuto and Shustek [231] (for Table 3.11), based upon monitor and trace studies done largely for the System/370 architecture.

Reliability. The data presented in these tables should be interpreted as typical data.

Stability. Significant differences may arise from program to program, especially in areas such as branch distances (Table 3.11).

Data Note 3. The data in Tables 3.14, 3.15, and 3.16 are derived from Huck and Flynn [136] and Rossmann [248, 247].

Reliability. The data are generally consistent with other reported results in the area.

Variance. As the categorization is refined in these tables, the variance for individual classes is expected to increase (compared to, e.g., Tables 3.4 and 3.5).

Data Note 4. The data in Tables 3.19 and 3.20 are taken from Rossmann [248, 247], again based upon a series of monitor and trace studies for the R/M architecture.

Reliability. The data presented are for a reasonably comprehensive study of various benchmark and trace materials; however, no software has been used to reorganize code to reduce the interlock effects. Further, one would expect that the interlock effects for the L/S architecture would be somewhat diminished because of the occurrence of additional instructions in the dynamic instruction stream. Similarly, one would expect that the R+M architecture would show an even greater effect from these interlocks. No direct data is available for either of these architectures.

Stability. Interlock distance is a strong function of application and of the availability of optimizing software.

Data Note 5. The data presented in Tables 3.22 and 3.21 are also from Rossmann [248, 247].

Reliability. The reliability of the use of variable and operand instruction is a strong function of the application and the compiler.

Stability. Significant differences are expected as a function of a particular application.

3.8   Annotated Bibliography

Among the earliest papers published on program and machine behavior is the work of Knuth [167] and Gibson [103]. System/360 has been thoroughly studied by Connors, among others [55]. Clark [52] has a particularly useful analysis of the VAX architecture. Lunde [187] and Tanenbaum [277] are particularly noteworthy earlier references on high-level machine behavior. The design target data presented in this chapter is largely the work of Huck [136]. This data has been validated against other data based on Pascal and C programs using simulation tools developed at Stanford. (See Mitchell and Flynn [201].)

Additional Reading

Machine and Program Behavior

D. Knuth. *An Empirical Study of Fortran Programs.* Technical Report STAN-CS-70-186, Computer Science Department, Stanford University, Stanford, CA, 1970.

J. C. Gibson. *The Gibson Mix.* Technical Report TR 00.2043, IBM Systems Development Division, Poughkeepsie, NY, 1970.

D. W. Clark. Measurement and analysis of instruction use in the VAX 11/780. *Proceedings of the 9th Annual Symposium on Computer Architecture*, pages 9–17, IEEE Computer Society Press, Washington, DC, April 1982.

A. Lunde. Empirical valuation of some features of instruction set processor architectures. *Communications of the ACM*, 20(3):141–200, 1977.

A. S. Tanenbaum. Implications of structured programming for machine architecture. *Communications of the ACM*, 21(3):237–246, 1978.

Design Target Data and Tools Used in This Chapter

J. C. Huck. *Comparative Analysis of Computer Architectures.* PhD thesis, Stanford University, May 1983.

J. C. Huck and M. J. Flynn. *Analyzing Computer Architectures.* IEEE Computer Society Press, 1989.

C. L. Mitchell and M. J. Flynn. A workbench for computer architects. *IEEE Design & Test*, 5(1):19–29, February 1988.

Systems Effects

C. Z. Loboz. *An Analysis of Program Execution: Issues for Computer Architecture.* PhD thesis, The Australian National University, July 1990.

T. E. Anderson, H. M. Levy, B. N. Bershad, and E. D. Lazowska. The interaction of architecture and operating system design. *ASPLOS-IV Proceedings*, pages 108–120, Santa Clara, CA, April 1991.

Compiler Effects

A. V. Aho and J. D. Ullman. *Principles of Compiler Design.* Addison-Wesley, Reading, MA, 1977.

C. Z. Loboz. *An Analysis of Program Execution: Issues for Computer Architecture.* PhD thesis, The Australian National University, July 1990.

3.9   Problem Set

1. Based on the data in Tables 3.2 and 3.3, compute the expected instruction bandwidth for R/M and R+M architectures relative to L/S. The instruction bandwidth is the number of instruction bits required to execute a program (e.g., suppose a program consists of 100 HLL operations).

2. For an R/M machine, suppose all instructions but the LDM and STM execute in unit time. If the LDM and STM require a number of time units equal to the number of registers moved less one (i.e., the excess over a simple LD or ST), compute the effect of LDM and STM on performance. Use mean LDM/STM data from section 3.3.1 and Table 3.15.

3. What percentage of branch instructions have generally predictable outcomes (greater than 90%)? For both scientific and commercial environments, make a table of branch instruction types. Specify the probable outcome and whether the outcome is predictable to greater than 90%.

4. In a L/S architecture with a branch target table, suppose that forward branches are four times "more expensive" (due to the cost of prefetching, etc.) than backward branches. For a 256- and 512-byte buffer, create a cost-effective branch table. The cost can be approximated as the number of entries for backwards-directed branches plus four times the number of prefetched entries. Use Table 3.11 and interpolate data for intermediate (non-power of 2) buffer sizes, as needed. Compare the percent of found references and the cost to the centered branch table of the same sizes.

5. What is the effect of floating-point operations that add the following extra cycles to execution:

Add/subtract	2 cycles
Multiply	6 cycles
Divide	12 cycles

Assume a scientific environment and L/S architecture where all non-floating-point instructions execute in one cycle and floating-point extra cycles cannot be overlapped. Compute the effect of the preceding floating-point execution on *per-instruction* execution time (in cycles per instruction).

6. Suppose now that the floating point extra cycles in the previous problem can be overlapped *except* for dependency effects noted in Table 3.20. Compute the effects of dependency [i.e., given floating point operation, compute the effect of a preceding (a) add, (b) multiply, and (c) divide].

7. The execution time of variable operand length instructions is usually determined by the operand length. For a commercial environment and R/M machine, suppose all instructions (except variable operand length instructions) execute in one cycle. Suppose for the variable operand length instructions their execution is the same as the number of bytes (or digits, for decimal) of the length of the source operands. Assuming these cycles cannot be overlapped, what is the resultant performance in cycles per instruction? Use Table 3.22.

8. For an R/M machine, if integer multiply and divide each take 32 cycles and floating point multiply and divide each take 48 cycles, and character and decimal instructions take execution time (in cycles) equal to the length of the longest operand (in bytes or digits) and multiple register moves take an execution cycle per register moved, compute the run-on delay for:

   (a) Scientific environment.

   (b) Commercial environment.

   (c) Systems environment.

Execution occurs in order and all other instructions have been allocated one execution cycle.

9. Assume all instructions execute in a single cycle. By adding a new feature, the number of Shift, Compare, and Logical (word) instructions can be reduced by 50%. This feature increases the cycle time by 10%. What performance impact will this feature have on the R+M architecture for (a) scientific applications, and (b) commercial applications?

10. The fixed-point multiplies for the L/S architecture are to be implemented with sequences of integer shifts and adds. Assume that per fixed-point multiply, the mean additional number of shifts is 13, adds is 5, and branches is 22. Recompute the expected instructions per HLL in Table 3.4 for the L/S architecture.

11. A superscalar architecture is capable of concurrently executing one branch instruction and nine non-branch instructions. For the workload characterized by Figure 3.4 and assuming single-cycle execution of all instructions, what is the expected maximum utilization of the processor? Ignore data dependencies.

12. What does the difference between the branch target reference capture rates of a small forward branch table and a small backward branch table tell us about the nature of conditional branches? What high-level language instructions would produce these distributions?

13. A branch table of 512 bytes can be configured asymmetrically. For the following combinations of *backward bytes/forward bytes*, compute the branch target capture percentages using the linear interpolation of data given in Table 3.11: (a) 256/256, (b) 384/128, (c) 448/64, (d) 480/32, (e) 496/16.

14. Assume for the R/M architecture that a conditional branch takes one cycle if the condition code was set prior to the preceding instruction, and two cycles otherwise. Assume all other instructions take a single cycle. What is the range of cycles per 100 HLL instructions for the scientific workload? What is the expected number of cycles?

15. Assume a delay of four cycles for an address interlock, and a delay of two cycles on an execution interlock. For the following sequence of code, identify all dependencies and compute the total delay:

```
ADD.W   R7, R7, 4
LD.W    R1, 0(R7)
MUL.W   R2, R1, R1
ADD.W   R3, R3, R2
LD.W    R4, 2(R7)
SUB.W   R5, R2, R3
ADD.W   R5, R5, R4
```

16. Suppose two character move instructions are implemented (MOVD.C and MOVO.C), which move disjoint and overlapped character strings, respectively. MOVD.C moves up to 8 characters in at most three cycles. MOVO.C moves up to 128 characters between overlapping source and destination addresses at the rate of 4 characters per cycle, with a fixed initial delay of 2 cycles. Does this solve the dilemma of character moves? Why, or why not?

Chapter 4

Pipelined Processor Design

4.1 Introduction

This chapter discusses the design of pipelined processors. A processor is designed as several different levels, each with increasing design detail. In this chapter we discuss *high level* or the architectural level. This serves as the specification for the logic design and implementation levels. Even at this high level a large number of decisions need to be made, each of which involves evaluating the relative cost and performance of a set of design alternatives. Here, we present such alternatives as they apply to the central processor, or CPU. Memory performance enhancements such as caching and interleaving are discussed in later chapters, and therefore are considered here only insofar as they directly affect CPU design.

Of course, every processor design begins with a set of market objectives. Commercial manufacturers usually envision a range of products: from those with low performance and low cost to those targeted for very high performance where cost is a secondary consideration. An entry product might have a target of 10 MIPS (million instructions per second). Other products could have targets of several hundred MIPS, with a price perhaps 10-20 times that of the entry system. This range of products necessitates a whole series of different design decisions to meet the market objectives. Two fundamental elements of the decision process are the characteristics of the technology to be used and the organization of the machine. The technology choices often seem overwhelming: BiCMOS, CMOS, CML, ECL; each implemented in gate array, standard cell, or custom parts and packaged in a single-chip package or on multichip carriers. We assume that the "right" technology choices for the product have been made, and that an efficient (in some cost-performance sense) fundamental cycle time for the machine has been determined, based on the number of levels of logic in critical paths, the speed of each level of logic, and the time required for signals to propagate between levels. Now a machine organization must be designed that is appropriate to the technology and achieves the cost-performance goals.

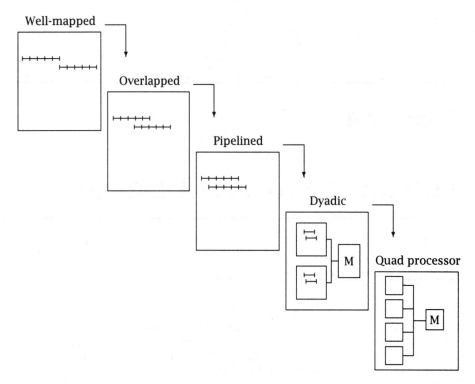

Figure 4.1   Evolution of a computer processor family.

4.1.1   Evolution of a Computer Processor Family

As an example of the family development process, consider the product line of the IBM 370 series as it emerged over the period 1970–1983 (Figure 4.1). The relationship between certain variables in a machine design—cycle time, machine organization, and effective access time of the memory—and the key performance metric, MIPS, is presented in Table 4.1. The first five products range in performance from 0.25 MIPS to 4.9 MIPS, and show the variations one can achieve as the nature of the design space changes. The first two machines, which were TTL designs, had very long cycle times, strictly serial organizations (well-mapped—that is, they serially performed decode, address generation, operand fetch, and execute), and memory access times that were significant compared to the internal cycle times. These products had MIPS rates in the range of 250–500 KIPS (thousand instructions per second). The next product, the 158, had a cycle time of 115 nanoseconds, had a cache so that its effective memory access time was on the order of 200 ns, and had a simple overlap design; that is, the 158 attempted to overlap the fetching of instructions with the execution of those instructions. The next two designs, the 168 and 3033, which came out of the same basic organizational definition, were pipelined ECL machines that in addition used many other techniques to enhance performance.

IBM replaced the 168 and 3033 products with new high-end products in the early 1980s: the 3083s, which are uniprocessor products, and the 3081s, which are dyadic multiprocessor products—two processors sharing a common main memory. In this generation, the cycle time is fixed across the

Table 4.1   Elements of the IBM 370 family (1970–1983).

Machine	Cycle Time (ns)	Eff. Access Time (ns)	Organization	MIPS
370/138	275–1430	715–935	Serial	0.25
370/148	180–225	540	Serial	0.50
370/158	115	207	Overlapped	1.00
370/168	80	192	Pipelined	2.50
3033	57	135	Pipelined	4.90
3083B	26	86	Uni-overlapped	5.60
3083J	26	86	Uni-pipelined	7.50
3081D	26	86	Dyadic-serial	10.20
3081K	26	86	Dyadic-pipelined	14.40
3081Q	26	86	Quadratic-pipelined	27.00

product line because the same circuit and packaging technology is used. The memory system is basically the same across the line, although there was some variation in cache sizes for individual processors.

A family of computer systems is developed by altering the organization of the machine, going from well-mapped to pipelined machine organization, and accelerating different operations. Another strategy emerges; in addition to altering machine organization, IBM used multiprocessor structures for speedup.

During the mid-1980s, IBM replaced the 3081X series with a 3090X series and correspondingly replaced the smaller family members with other offerings. For the high end, the cycle time was decreased to under 20 ns, and *vector facilities* (VF) were introduced. Vector arithmetic facilities, discussed later in the text, provide the potential for a 2–3-times speedup on scientific and other suitable applications.

For the '90s, IBM, through its S/390 series, offers both multiprocessing and vector facilities, plus faster cycle time and very large memory configurations (Table 4.2). In the early '80s, memory configurations were generally limited to 16–64 MB; by the '90s, over 9 GB (1 GB control store and 8 GB expanded (slower) storage) were available. Finally, significantly expanded I/O capability was made available through the use of fiberoptic communication for I/O channel interconnection (ESCON, in IBM terms). The resulting S/390 family ranges in price from $70,000 to $22 million, weighs from 60 pounds to over a ton, and offers performance from under 10 MIPS to perhaps over 500 MIPS.

In 1993, IBM once again revised the S/390 offerings, generally expanding functional capacity, improving performance, and improving price/performance. At the time of writing, the top-performing water-cooled model is the 982, and the top-performing air-cooled model is the 742. There are eight air-cooled models and ten water-cooled models; see Table 4.3. Notice the relatively predictable evolution of the processor capabilities and performance.

Table 4.2   The IBM S/390 family models (1991).

Model	Type[a]	Max Total Storage	Max. ESCON & Parallel Channels	Max. Vector Facilities	Cycle Time (ns)
Water Cooled					
900	6-way MP	9 GB	256	6	9.5
820	4-way MP	9 GB	256	4	9.5
720	6-way MP	4.5 GB	128	6	9.5
620	4-way MP	4.5 GB	128	4	9.5
580	3-way MP	2.25 GB	64	3	9.5
500	2-way MP	2.25 GB	64	2	9.5
340	Uniproc.	2.25 GB	64	1	9.5
330	Uniproc.	1152 MB	64	1	9.5
Air Cooled					
480	2-way MP	1024 MB	48	2	15
440	2-way MP	1024 MB	48	2	15
320	Uniproc.	1024 MB	48	1	15
260	Uniproc.	1024 MB	48	1	15
210	Uniproc.	1024 MB	48	1	15
190	Uniproc.	512 MB	32	1	15
Rack Mounted					
170	Uniproc.	256 MB	24	0	30
150	Uniproc.	256 MB	12	0	35
130	Uniproc.	256 MB	12	0	38
120	Uniproc.	256 MB	12	0	38

[a]MP indicates maximum number of multiprocessors in a system.

Table 4.3   IBM S/390 models (1994).

Model	Type	Max. Total Storage	Max. ESCON	Max. Vector	Estimated Cycle Time
Water cooled					
9X2	10-way MP	10GB	256	10	6.0 ns
(plus 9 other models)					
Air cooled					
421	4-way MP	2GB	96	4	10.0 ns
(plus 7 other models)					

Similar evolution of product lines can be seen in the Intel 80X86 family of microprocessors, or the Motorola 680X0 family.

4.1.2   Processor Design

Two key elements in the design of a processor are the definition of processor performance and some notion of what type of work is to be performed. The design and performance evaluation process involves two interlocking hierarchical models: a model of the design and a model of the workload.

Analysis is usually based on an instruction-level workload model. This requires instruction distribution data describing the operational characteristics of a machine when it is executing a program. If a manufacturer is concerned with a product that uses the same architecture as previous machines, like IBM with the S/390 architecture, we ought to be able to obtain data that characterizes the nature of programs when they are in execution. How do branches behave? How do the decimal operations behave? How do the string operations behave? What is the average length of an instruction? What is the frequency of use of various instruction formats? A stable architecture provides a significant advantage, providing behavioral available data that allows well-informed design decisions. A new architecture requires more guesswork unless it has certain similarities to the architectures that have preceded it. The only possibility is to use or extrapolate from data obtained from another product. Many early microprocessor designs were predicated on PDP-11 and S/370 data. Cache models were based on models of existing machines and then extrapolated to proposed microprocessor designs.

4.1.3   Organization of the Chapter

In Chapter 1, we saw serial machines that execute with little or no overlap of actions. While serial machines include many well-known older machines (Intel 80286, VAX 780, etc.) and thus may have historic interest, there is no current design in such machines (Table 4.4). Today's designs are usually of the pipelined processor type with an assortment of functional improvements to improve performance. The performance limit of these machines is one cycle per instruction (CPI) although, as we shall see, this is not realizable in practice. This chapter covers processor design and evolution techniques that correspond to the general microprocessor state of the art (Table 4.4). Chapter 7 discusses more advanced approaches.

To begin our discussion, we look at types of pipelined processors (section 4.2), observing how the pipeline can be represented and the timing variability of various pipelined processor implementations.

The next section (4.3) develops a methodology for evaluating the performance of a pipelined processor given certain instruction timings and the frequency of occurrence of certain pipeline disruptions.

Section 4.4 looks at implementation issues for pipeline processors: the number and extent of buffers required in certain areas of the processor, methods of improving the flow of instructions to the decoder to minimize pipeline disruptions, and other issues.

Table 4.4 Types of processors.

Performance	Machine Type	Comments
5–6 CPI (typ.)	Serial or well-mapped	See chapter 1.
3 CPI	Serial processor with some overlapped functions	
1.5–2 CPI	Simple pipelined processor with static pipeline	See this chapter (4).
1.2–1.5 CPI	Pipelined processors with dynamic pipeline, instruction buffering, branch prediction, etc.	See this chapter (esp. 4.4–4.8).
Below 1.0 CPI	Multiple instruction issue	See chapter 7.

Section 4.6 treats a specialized area of pipelined processor implementation called *instruction interlocks.* These interlocks detect dependencies among instructions that are being processed by the pipelined processor.

Section 4.8 considers other miscellaneous effects in pipelined processor design and evaluation.

For this chapter, the pipelined processor is assumed to operate under the following constraints:

1. At most, one instruction is decoded each cycle.

2. Instructions are decoded in the sequence they appear in the program representation.

3. Instructions are completed in the sequence they are decoded, i.e., the original program sequence.

Chapter 7 removes these constraints and examines the consequences on machine performance and machine behavior and implementation.

4.2   Approaching Pipelined Processors

In this section, we look at the various stages of instruction execution used by a typical pipeline processor. As we noted in Chapter 2, all processors do not define the partitioning of instruction execution events in the same way. In one case, a designer might combine events, creating a so-called *shallow pipeline* consisting of just a few events or stages in the pipeline. On the other hand, a more aggressive designer might partition instruction execution into a *deep pipeline* consisting of many stages of instruction execution. In this section, we look at various possibilities—ways that have been used to partition instruction execution into pipelineable events.

In the design of a pipelined processor, a *processor framework* is needed—a picture of the functional units that compose the processor—so that trade-offs can be made among these functional units to provide an overall optimum cost–performance design. Before beginning, we must know the timing

---

Mainframes, Microprocessors, and the Future

Either consciously or unconsciously, microprocessors have followed the path of large mainframe processors, generally lagging behind the top-of-the-line mainframe computers in cycle time, features, and performance by about five to ten years. The lag has evaporated in recent years as microprocessor designers have become increasingly aggressive in the use of technology and the technology itself enables more complex functional realizations.

It is sometimes amusing to read in microprocessor development literature about the rediscovery of older mainframe techniques. One such concept is *superpipelining*, the ability of a pipelined processor to have multiple instructions in various stages of operand execution (for example, EX). Most large top-of-the-line mainframes over the past two decades have done exactly this.

It is still interesting to contemplate that within the next few years, microprocessors will be able to support the type of high-end processing capabilities outlined in Tables 4.2 and 4.3—microprocessor ensembles supporting 10 gigabytes of storage, each with a cycle time of 6.0 nanoseconds or less,[1] full vector arithmetic facilities, and perhaps 256 fiberoptic I/O channels. It is in this last area, I/O connectivity, that the mainframes have made their last stand, providing access to huge database ensembles and storage access systems.

The best "mainframe" cycle time is currently 2 ns (Hitachi 3800).

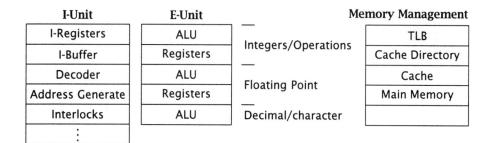

Figure 4.2   View of a processor.

---

template or execution sequence of an instruction and the allocation of cycles to functional actions that execute the instruction. Generally, the action that occurs within any functional unit requires one or more cycles.

The general view of the processor (Figure 4.2) has a memory system, execution unit (data paths), and instruction unit. The more efficient the memory system (the larger and faster the cache, etc.), the smaller the number of cycles required for fetching instructions and data (IF and DF). The more extensive the execution unit, the smaller the number of execution cycles (EX) that an average instruction requires. The management of the cache and execution unit is the responsibility of the instruction unit. The better it is designed, the fewer the delays in the pipeline.

The design of the processor begins with a tentative definition of a typical instruction timing (the timing template). This also serves to give some additional information on the partitioning of the processor into stages. The *execution unit* consists of data paths, registers, and ALU or execution resources. The registers are defined by the instruction set to hold data values; the execution resources transform the data as specified in the instruction vocabulary. There may be multiple execution resources, perhaps one for each data type (floating point, integer, character, decimal, etc.), since it is more efficient (results in faster execution time) to execute each data type with a specialized unit. The *data paths* are the transmission or communication paths that connect registers with the execution units and with the memory system.

An *instruction unit* consists of the state registers as defined by the instruction set—the PSW and the instruction register—plus the instruction buffer, decoder, and an interlock unit. The instruction buffer's function is to fetch instructions into registers so that instructions can be rapidly brought into a position to be decoded. The complexity of the instruction buffer depends on the instruction set. If instructions all have a common length, the buffer may be easier to design and manage than in architectures with multiple size instructions. The decoder has the responsibility for controlling cache, ALU, registers, etc. Frequently in pipelined machines, the instruction unit sequencing is managed strictly by hardware, but the execution unit may be microprogrammed so that each instruction that enters the execution phase will have its own microinstruction associated with it. The interlock unit frequently is regarded as part of the decoder, although for purposes of our studies we separate the functions of the two. The interlock unit's responsibility is to ensure that the execution of multiple instructions has the same result as if the instructions were executed completely serially—one after another, as in a well-mapped machine.

Suppose we have an R/M pipelined processor with the following instruction timimg template:

```
   IA   DF    D   AG    DF   EX    PA
  |----+----+----+----+----+----+----|
```

Ideally, instructions follow through the pipeline; one entering each cycle.

Instruction N
```
       IA    IF    D    AG    DF    EX    PA
      |----+----+----+----+----+----+----|
```
Instruction $N + 1$
```
         IA    IF    D    AG    DF    EX    PA
        |----+----+----+----+----+----+----|
```
Instruction $N + 2$
```
           IA    IF    D    AG    DF    EX    PA
          |----+----+----+----+----+----+----|
```
Instruction $N + 3$
```
             IA    IF    D    AG    DF    EX    PA
            |----+----+----+----+----+----+----|
```

Each instruction takes just as long to complete as in a simple, well-mapped processor; but, ideally, the rate at which instructions are completed is one per cycle.

The rigid sequencing of events as just shown may or may not be required in particular pipeline processor implementations. The most restrictive form of a pipeline, sometimes called the *static pipeline*, requires the processor to go through all stages of the pipeline whether required by a particular instruction or not. Thus, instruction $N + 1$ in the preceding would go through

Table 4.5   Types of pipelined processors.

Type	Max # of Instr Decoded per Cycle	Comment
Static pipeline	1	All actions in order
Dynamic pipeline Type 1*	1	All D and all PA in order
Dynamic pipeline Type 2	1	All D in order PA unordered
Dynamic pipeline Type 3	1	No order restriction**
Multiple-issue pipeline	n	No order restriction**

* If the timing template omits PA, then EX must be in order.
** Ordered only by dependencies.

the AG and DF phases even if it used only registers for its operands. *Dynamic pipelines* allow the bypassing of one or more of the stages of the pipeline, depending on the requirements of the instruction with the specifications of the instruction. Even within the category of dynamic pipelined processors, there are at least three levels of pipeline sophistication (Table 4.5):

Type 1: Dynamic pipelines that require instructions to be decoded in sequence and results to be executed—put away (PA)—in sequence. For these types of simpler dynamic pipeline processors, the advantage over a static pipeline is relatively modest, as we shall see. In-order execution requires that the actual change of state—the storage of the data result for sequential instructions—must occur in the order that the data were specified in the instruction sequence. Thus, for instructions with a putaway cycle, the execution may complete but the putaway must not be done until all previous instructions have put away their own respective results. All actions are conditional on the successful completion of all prior instructions.

Type 1-Extended: A popular extension to the Type 1 pipeline is to require decode to be in order, as well as references that affect the memory state. The execution stage of ALU operations need not be in order. In these organizations, the AG (address generate) and T (translate) stages of LD/ST instructions must be completed *before* any subsequent ALU instruction does a PA (putaway). The reason for this is that the translate operation may reveal that the referenced page is not now in (real) storage, and require a task swap while the page is brought in. Such a swap cannot easily proceed with an altered state subsequent to the interrupting instruction.

Because of these restrictions and the overall frequency of LD/ST instructions, the Type 1-Extended pipeline behaves much as the basic Type 1 pipeline. In this chapter, we treat basic Type 1 pipelines with the understanding that Type 1-Extended pipelines will behave in (almost) exactly the same manner.

Type 2: Dynamic pipelined machines that can be configured to allow out-of-order execution, yet retain in-order instruction decode. (Decode is also sometimes called *instruction issue*.) For this type of pipelined processor, the execution and putaway of all instructions (including LD/ST) is a function only of dependencies on prior instructions. If a particular instruction is independent of all preceding instructions, its execution can be completed independently of the successful completion of prior instructions.

Type 3: The third type of dynamic pipeline allows instructions to be issued out of order as well as completed out of order. A group of instructions is analyzed together, and the first instruction that is found to be independent of prior (uncompleted) instructions is decoded.

For our purposes, we assume a simple dynamic pipelined processor (Type 1) for this chapter. In Chapter 7, we look at more sophisticated dynamic pipelined processors of the second and third types.

4.2.1 Examples of Pipeline Implementations

The examples in this section illustrate some of the different ways in which the conceptual steps in the processing of an instruction can be mapped into a pipelined hardware structure. These examples assume no dependencies or delays among instructions.

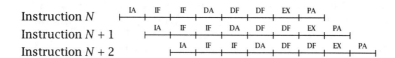

Figure 4.3 The IBM 3033 processor (cycle time = 57 ns).

Older Mainframes: the IBM 3033 and Amdahl 470 V/8 Processors (both R/M machines)

In the IBM 3033 processor, instructions and data are normally fetched from a cache memory that has a pipelined access time of two cycles. Consequently, the instruction fetch (IF) and operand fetch (DF) steps are each two cycles long.

The 3033 overlaps the instruction decode step (D) with the operand address generation step (AG). Both are performed in a single cycle called a decode/address cycle (DA). Figure 4.3 illustrates the timing of the 3033 pipeline.

Note the IA (instruction address generation) stage in this and other (Amdahl and MIPS) machines. This represents the incrementing of the instruction counter and subsequent address translation. In evaluating performance we usually ignore this stage, as its outcome can normally be anticipated.

Instruction *N*

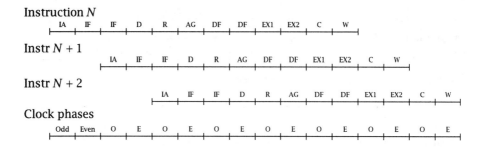

Figure 4.4   The Amdahl 470 V/8 processor (cycle time = 26 ns).

The 3033 processor was IBM's top-of-the-line flagship pipeline processor of the early 1980s. Compared with a contemporary machine, the Amdahl 470 V/8, the 3033 used a longer cycle time (57 ns) and fewer stages. While the 3033 uses a putaway cycle, results from the execution unit, if required by the address generation unit, can bypass the putaway cycle and forward results directly to the address generator. As with most large mainframe processors, the 3033 uses a dynamic pipeline with in-order execution. The Amdahl 470 V/8 processor represents an alternate machine design to the 3033, although it executes exactly the same instruction set. In order to understand the timing on the V8 the reader should recall the Chapter 2 discussion of two-phased clocking systems. In Figure 4.4, clocks are designated as odd or even. Actions indicated for a particular phase must occur on that phase. Similarly, the address generation step has been decomposed into two steps, the register access (R) and the address generation (AG). The execution step now requires two cycles, EX1 and EX2, and the putaway step takes two cycles, error check (C) and write (W). A new instruction can be initiated (i.e., decoded) only every other cycle. Within the limitations of the two-phased clock, the result of one instruction can be forwarded, bypassing the putaway cycle, to an address generation unit.

Some Microprocessors: the MIPS R2000

The R2000 is a statically pipelined L/S machine with a template bearing some similarity to the Amdahl 470 V/8. Since the R2000 uses a two-phase clock (as in other microprocessors), a separate action can be performed in each phase. As with the Amdahl 470, the granularity of an action is the phase time (or one-half the "clock"). For purposes of our evaluation, we consider this phase time the same as the logical clock, which is the unit for our timing template.

Here, for an ALU instruction, we have:

$$\text{IA} \quad \text{IF} \quad \text{IF} \quad \text{D} \quad \text{EX} \quad \text{EX} \quad \cdots \quad | \quad \cdots \quad \text{PA}$$

For an LD instruction, we have:

$$\text{IA} \quad \text{IF} \quad \text{IF} \quad \text{D} \quad \text{AG} \quad \text{AG} \quad \text{DF} \quad \text{DF} \quad \text{PA}$$

The PA for the functional instructions is delayed to occur at the same relative sequence time as for the LD. Instructions are offset by two phase times

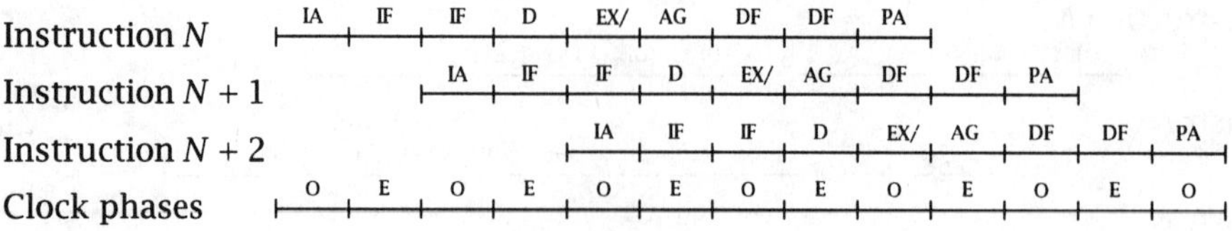

Instruction N IA   IF   IF   D   EX/   AG   DF   DF   PA

Instruction $N + 1$ IA   IF   IF   D   EX/   AG   DF   DF   PA

Instruction $N + 2$ IA   IF   IF   D   EX/   AG   DF   DF   PA

Clock phases   O   E   O   E   O   E   O   E   O   E   O   E   O

Figure 4.5   The MIPS R2000 microprocessor.

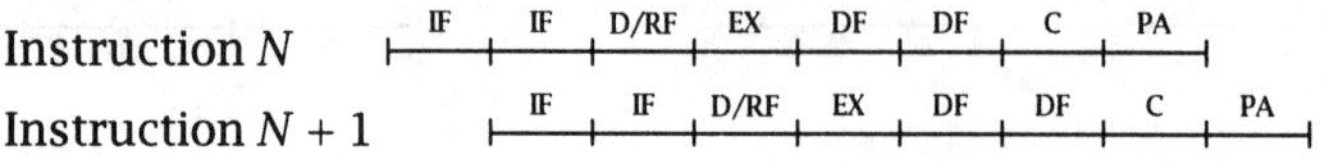

Instruction N IF   IF   D/RF   EX   DF   DF   C   PA

Instruction $N + 1$ IF   IF   D/RF   EX   DF   DF   C   PA

Figure 4.6   The MIPS R4000 microprocessor.

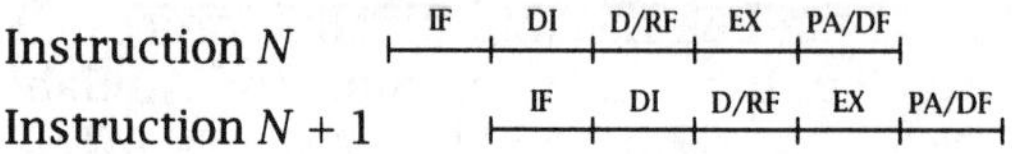

Instruction N IF   DI   D/RF   EX   PA/DF

Instruction $N + 1$ IF   DI   D/RF   EX   PA/DF

Figure 4.7   The IBM RS 6000 microprocessor.

(one "cycle" in R2000 terms; two cycles or actions in our terms); see Figure 4.5.

The MIPS R4000 processor also uses a two-phase clock, only here a new instruction is issued each clock phase. On a LD/ST the EX is replaced by AG. On an ALU instruction the template allows four EX (half) cycles before PA is delayed. The C (half) cycle is for a cache tag check (Figure 4.6).

The IBM RS 6000

This machine can, under certain conditions, issue multiple instructions in a single cycle, and is discussed further in Chapter 7. The determination of which instructions are to be issued is made in the DI (dispatch) stage. In an LD/ST, the EX is replaced with AG and PA with DF. If only one instruction were issued in each cycle, we would have the timing template shown in Figure 4.7.

The HP PA-RISC

The HP PA-RISC has a conventional L/S timing template, but is known for aggressive technology implementations with high clock rates. In the LD/ST instructions, the first EX is replaced with AG and the second does the D-cache read (Figure 4.8). Most ALU operations use only the first EX.

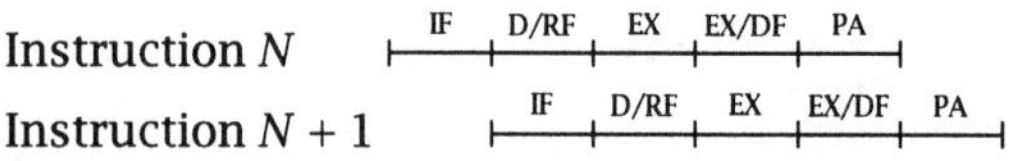

Instruction N IF   D/RF   EX   EX/DF   PA

Instruction $N + 1$ IF   D/RF   EX   EX/DF   PA

Figure 4.8   The HP PA-RISC 1.1 microprocessor.

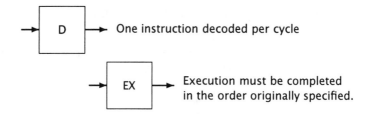

Figure 4.9   Some key modeling assumptions.

4.3   Evaluating Pipelined Processor Performance

In order to evaluate the execution (or interpretation) of a pipelined instruction, we assemble the various execution steps into the actions (cycles) required by a particular machine to execute a typical in-line instruction, forming the instruction timing template—for example,

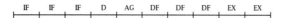

This template describes the complete execution of a single instruction without dependencies. A simple (ALU-based) instruction is usually one that requires all of the steps of execution with a minimum number of cycles devoted to each execution step.

The ideal relationship between successive instructions is determined by their relative decode cycles. Until the decode is complete, dependencies and the remaining instruction template cannot be established. The maximum instruction decode rate determines the peak instruction execution rate (in MIPS).

In evaluating the effect of dependencies, the instruction causing a dependency is designated by its hypothetical memory location ($*$). Occasionally, multiple dependencies exist. For example, in the case of a conditional branch, the outcome and the relative timing depend both on the branch ($*$) and a preceding instruction that sets the tested condition. Since all instructions must be decoded, the time to decode plus the minimum time between successive decodes is the reciprocal of the maximum decode rate (assuming a maximum of one instruction decoded per cycle). This time may be measured in time (seconds) or in cycles. To this sum we simply accumulate delays for the various instruction dependencies to determine the actual time used by each of the instructions. In assessing these penalties, we usually make several assumptions (Figure 4.9).

Pipelined Processor Design Assumptions

1. We decode at most one instruction at a time.

2. We do not allow out-of-order instruction execution and putaway. If the timing template has a PA cycle, then execution (EX) may complete but not PA. If the template incorporates PA into EX and shows only EX cycles, then the EX may not complete out of order. Note that instruction $* + 1$ does not execute before $*$ *even if* $* + 1$ has no dependency

on $*$. Out-of-order execution significantly complicates performance evaluation and is treated in chapter 7.

3. As a result of (2), "time lost is lost forever." It is impossible to regain time lost by delays later in program execution. Delays add linearly to compose the overall program execution time. In practice, occasionally delays are overlapped; for simplicity, we ignore this. Dubey [76] has a more complete model which includes the effects of overlapped delays.

4. We assume sufficient processing resources to execute a single sequence of instructions. Thus, "going both ways on a branch" is not allowed.

5. For our evaluation purposes, we assume that most (by frequency) functional-type instructions set a condition code (CC). We assume that this is always available at the end of the last EX cycle, even if other cycles such as a PA cycle follow, so that

$$\overset{\downarrow CC}{\underset{\text{EX}\quad\text{EX}\quad\text{PA}}{\vdash\!\!\!+\!\!\!+\!\!\!+\!\!\!\dashv}}$$

Thus, the process of timing evaluation consists of the following steps.

Pipelined Processor Design Evaluation Rules

1. Form the timing template for the basic instructions. Suppose each instruction consists of five actions (IF, D, AG, DF, EX) and each action consists of a single cycle. We would have:

$$\underset{\text{IF}\quad\text{D}\quad\text{AG}\quad\text{DF}\quad\text{EX}}{\vdash\!\!+\!\!+\!\!+\!\!+\!\!+\!\!\dashv}$$

as the timing template.

2. Create the relative templates for two successive (non-dependent) instructions—e.g., for a fully pipelined processor, we might have (for two successive instructions located at $*$ and $* + 1$):

$$*\qquad \underset{\text{IF}\quad\text{D}\quad\text{AG}\quad\text{DF}\quad\text{EX}}{\vdash\!\!+\!\!+\!\!+\!\!+\!\!\dashv}$$
$$* + 1\qquad\quad \underset{\text{IF}\quad\text{D}\quad\text{AG}\quad\text{DF}\quad\text{EX}}{\vdash\!\!+\!\!+\!\!+\!\!+\!\!\dashv}$$

3. Assess the time for instruction execution (at the maximum decode rate). In the preceding example, the ideal execution rate is one instruction each cycle.

4. For each delay type, find the scheduled occurrence of an action (D', AG', etc.) in $* + 1$, and the actual time that $* + 1$ was able to perform the action (D, AG, etc.) due to the dependency on $*$. The *delay* is the number of cycles by which effective execution was deferred. For most functional instructions, this will be the time by which the completion of execution (EX) is delayed. For example, suppose an unconditional branch instruction (BR) located at $*$ is decoded. The next instruction (the target instruction, TI) is then delayed by two cycles:

```
             IF    D    AG    TIF
   *       ├─────┼────┼────┼────┤
                        D'         D    AG    DF    EX
   TI                 ├────┤     ├────┼────┼────┼────┤
```

5. The weighted occurrence of this delay is added to the minimum execution time found in (3).

6. Continue until the major delay classes have been assessed.

Dependencies or *breaks* generally arise from one of three causes:

1. Procedural dependencies or branches. The pipeline is delayed because in-line fetching of instructions is disrupted. The branch target must first be fetched before the pipeline can resume execution.

2. Data conflicts—unavailability of a source operand. This can occur for several reasons; typically, the current instruction requires an operand that is the result of a preceding uncompleted instruction.

3. Resource contention or run-on effects—multiple successive instructions using the same resource or an instruction with a long execution time that delays a successor instruction to preserve *in-order* execution.

We now summarize these for a simple pipelined processor.

Simple Pipelined Processor Break Evaluation Rules

1. Branch

   (a) BC (in-line) instruction.
   For the next instruction ($*$ + 1), the decode (D) waits until the cycle following the CC set.

   (b) BC (target).
   Decode of target instruction waits until target is fetched (TIF) and CC is set.

   (c) BR.
   Decode of target waits for TIF of the BR.

2. Data

   (a) Address dependency.
   The AG stage of the pipeline of the dependent instruction waits for the execution of a prior instruction.

   (b) Execution (PA).
   The EX stage of the dependent instruction waits for completion (PA) of a prior instruction.

3. Run-on

   On a run-on, the instruction following the run-on waits before entering execution (EX) for a time sufficient to ensure that its PA (final EX) occurs *after* the PA (or final EX) of the run-on instruction.

4. Resource

Only one instruction can occupy a single resource (D, AG, and cache access) at a time. As described in the following, segmented resources (EX, cache) allow only one instruction in any one segment at a time.

In the following study, we evaluate the dependency effects in a simple pipelined processor with a typical R/M mainframe timing template.

Study 4.1   Evaluating Dependency Effects

In this study, assume an R/M architecture with a pipelined layout vaguely similar to the Amdahl V/8 mentioned earlier, but without alternate cycle decode and with a more simplified timing template. We assume that the memory access is a three-cycle pipelined (segmented) access to a cache memory, and that execution similarly has a two-cycle pipelined execution through the ALU. Pipelined or segmented access or execution means that the process is segmented into several stages so that three accesses to the cache can be going on simultaneously; but they are segmented so that they are in different phases of access. Thus, a three-cycle access to a cache might represent the following pipelined actions:

1. Access to a cache directory.

2. Access to a data array.

3. Transmission of result to processor ALU.

Each of these actions is segmented by registers that can independently hold intermediate results. Most processors that we see throughout the remainder of the text have segmented or pipelined accessing and/or execution units. It is important to realize that a three-cycle cache access does not mean that only one access can be made every three cycles. Rather, it means that one access can be made per cycle but a total of three cycles is required for any individual access to complete.

We now assume that the following time is required to execute the actions comprising the instruction execution:

Cache Access:	3 cycles
Execution Time:	2 cycles (average OP)
Address Generate:	1 cycle
Putaway:	0 cycles (included in EX)

Now for the ideal case, we create the timing template or the sequence of actions that must occur for the execution of an individual instruction, and then show two instructions (located at $*-1$ and $*$). This instruction sequence represents the maximum execution rate—limited by the resources (the decoder, the AG, etc.) of the system. The astute reader will notice that if in fact we had only the ideal case and we could make only one access to a cache per cycle, we would soon create a resource conflict at the cache, since each instruction requires both an IF and a DF. As we shall see later and in Chapter 5, not every instruction need require its own IF. It may be possible to fetch multiple instructions at a time, or to otherwise reduce conflicting use of a scarce resource. In the remainder of this study, we ignore apparent resource contention at the cache.

1. Ideal case:

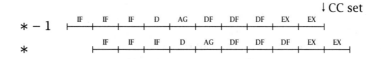

In case 1, the instruction interpretation *latency* is ten cycles; that is, the total time from the initiation of the instruction fetch (IF) to the execution of indicated operation (setting of the condition code) without dependencies is ten cycles. Under ideal conditions, on each cycle boundary an instruction is fetched, an instruction is decoded, an address is generated, an operand (data) is fetched, and an execution is begun. Two accesses are made to memory in each cycle (one for instruction and one for data), one decode is performed per cycle, and an address generation is performed while two operations are being executed in the two cycles allowed for execution. The pipelined processor designed to support this arrangement has been partitioned into autonomous functional units and each unit is coordinated on cycle boundaries to accommodate this maximum rate; the decoder is an independent unit that can decode one operation each cycle, the same being true for the address generation unit. The memory must be designed to accommodate two accesses per cycle if we are to sustain this maximum rate.

Note the influence the architecture has on these requirements. A simple single-accumulator machine requires two fetches (one for instruction, one for data) each cycle (maximum rate). In a L/S architecture, we might expect to see, on average, fewer than one data reference per cycle, since there are none for the register-to-register instructions. While the architecture influences the distribution of functional operations, total performance depends more on the behavior of the instruction set, i.e., the distribution of various types of dependencies that arise during program execution.

2. Branch dependencies:

(a) Unconditional Branch (BR) at ∗:

4 cycle penalty

(b) Conditional Branch (BC) at ∗:

e.g.,

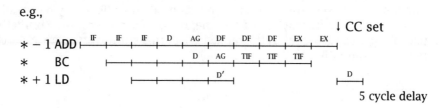

In case 2, if we designate D′ as the scheduled time for decoding the next instruction, there is a four-cycle delay attributable to the generation of the address for the next instruction and fetching that address into the instruction register. Thus, a four-cycle delay has been introduced, and the execution time for the unconditional branch is therefore five cycles. The conditional branch frequently represents an even worse case (case 2b). The instruction following the branch is not known (typically) until the execution of the instruction preceding the branch has set the condition code. On decoding the branch, the machine fetches the alternate instruction and then continues to fetch the in-line path (∗ + 1, ∗ + 2,...) begun earlier. Both paths are available once the condition code is known. Thus, as soon as ∗ − 1 is completely executed, the instruction following the ∗ can be decoded and the pipeline can resume operation. There is a five-cycle penalty time under the condition shown in case 2b.

Unconditional/conditional branches are statistically the biggest causes of pipeline breaks (see Chapter 3). The pipelined processor assumes that all instructions lie in a line and that the sequence of instructions can be prefetched—fetched ahead of the instruction that is currently being decoded. When a branch occurs, however, the prefetched instructions are of no value and a new sequence of instructions must be fetched based upon the target instruction. The fetching of the target instruction in a branch instruction occurs at the same time a data fetch would have occurred in an arithmetic instruction. In the case of a conditional branch, the prefetched in-line instructions may still be of value, depending on the outcome of the instruction that is determining the condition (i.e., setting the condition code). It is useful to save prefetched in-line instructions, as well as to take the opportunity to fetch the target instruction in the timing slots usually reserved for a data fetch. Thus, we have at least one instruction from both paths when the condition code is resolved. Simple pipelined processors do not attempt to decode instructions beyond the branch until the condition code is known. More complex processors guess at the outcome of the branch and proceed down one of the paths, thereby saving the branch delay time when the guess is correct.

3. Data dependencies:

Instructions frequently depend upon the result of predecessor instructions for an operand. The case that causes the most delay in a pipelined processor is when instruction ∗ depends upon the immediately preceding instruction (∗ − 1) for an operand such as an index value that is used during an address generation operation in instruction ∗. The effect of this is illustrated next.

Address dependency:

```
* - 1 ADD R1, D1[R2,R3]
        IF    IF    IF    D    AG    DF    DF    DF    EX    EX
      ├─────┼─────┼─────┼────┼─────┼─────┼─────┼─────┼─────┤

*        ADD R7, D2[R1,R4]
                  IF    IF    IF    D    AG'                    AG    DF    DF    DF    EX    EX
                ├─────┼─────┼─────┼────┼─────┤              ├─────┼─────┼─────┼─────┼─────┤
```

The AG of * is delayed by five cycles.

4. Store dependencies:

The store instruction is another instruction that may slow down program execution. It is relatively common in code (especially unoptimized code) for a store instruction that puts away a particular register to immediately precede a load instruction that puts a new value in that same register.

The store (*) cannot be completed until the preceding instruction (* − 1) has completed execution and determined the final value for the same register, R1. The load (* + 1) cannot be executed until R1 is freed by the execution of the store instruction. Sequences such as those shown below (case 4) are common enough that *store buffers* are frequently used. Here R1 is freed one cycle after a final value is established, after the data in R1 has been transmitted to the store buffer (SB). The problem described in this case is actually one of naming. Instructions starting with * + 1, the load, are independent of the instructions preceding it, at least insofar as their usage of R1 is concerned. The problem is simply that instructions * and * + 1 use the same name (R1). We consider this issue in Chapter 7.

Without store buffers, we have:

```
* - 1 ADD R1, D[...]
                D    AG    DF    DF    DF    EX    EX
              ├────┼─────┼─────┼─────┼─────┼─────┤

*        ST A, R1...
                     D    AG                         DS
                   ├────┼─────┤              ├──────┼──────┤  R1 is free

* + 1         LD R1,...                                   ↓
                          D    AG    DF'                      DF    DF    DF
                        ├────┼─────┼─────┤              ├─────┼─────┼─────┤
```

The * + 1 execution is delayed six cycles. To avoid this, special store buffers are used to hold pending stores.

With store buffers, we have:

```
        ADD  ├────┼─────┼─────┼────┼─────┼─────┼─────┼─────┼─────┤
             IF   IF    IF    D    AG    DF    DF    DF    EX    EX

*       ST                         D    AG            R1→SB  DS    DS    DS
                 ├────┼─────┼─────┼────┼─────┤       ├──────┼─────┼─────┤
                                                       ↓ R1 is free
* + 1   LD                              D    AG                DF    DF    DF
                 ├────┼─────┼─────┼────┼─────┤ ...         ├─────┼─────┼─────┤
```

As a further optimization, R1's availability could be anticipated so that the DF in * + 1 could begin three cycles before R1 is available.

Certain instruction pairs, such as LD/ST, ST/ST, and ST/LD may also create dependencies as a resource conflict. The LD and ST do not always use the cache pipeline segments in the same order. For example, the ST may update the cache directory in the cycle following its initial access to an entry. This could be the same cycle required for a fetch by the next instruction, requiring a one-cycle delay.

5. Run-on:

Suppose that in the previous example, the divide execution took six cycles, and each division had to be serially executed (i.e., no pipelining *within* the divider). Then, if we had the following sequence:

$$\text{DIV R1, ALPHA[...]}$$
$$\text{DIV R2, R3}$$

the following penalty might ensue:

DIV R1, ALPHA

| D | AG | DF | DF | DF | ← | Divide | → |

DIV R2, R3

| D | | | | | ← | Divide | → |

A similar situation arises with the "run-on" delays; the instruction following the divide must be delayed, even if it does not depend in any other way on the divide. This ensures in-order execution. Thus,

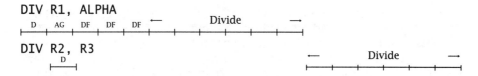

DIV R1, ALPHA

ADD R2, R3

While divide itself is infrequent in typical code, clustered arithmetic operations using the same function are not unusual. Thus, processor resources must be carefully designed to accommodate peak rates.

Data dependencies (case 3) and resource dependencies (case 5) create obvious pipeline breaks or delays with no out-of-order execution, and even if out-of-order execution were allowed, they significantly aggravate delays due to conditional branch. Case 3 is a good example; suppose $*-2$ is an add instruction whose result is to be placed in R1. Now, instruction $*-1$ is a multiply instruction (with 6-cycle execution), one of the components of which lies in R1; thus, the operand for the multiplier cannot be determined until $*-2$ is completely executed. If a BC instruction lies at $*$, then $*+1$ is delayed by 10 cycles over its scheduled decode time. Similar situations arise with resource dependencies.

The next three studies concern a hypothetical R/M machine that uses a single 32-bit instruction format. This is a hybrid machine between our L/S and R/M machines. In the first study, we look at dependencies that arise in a sequence of five instructions. We look at both the individual dependencies as they arise and their cumulative effect on the execution of these instructions. Study 4.3 uses the same machine, but now analyzes performance on a statistical basis, computing the ideal performance plus the effects of the presumed dependency types. The effects of conditional branch on performance are quite noticeable in both studies 4.2 and 4.3. Study 4.4 looks at ways of potentially lessening the effect of branches on performance by studying two possibilities: early condition code setting and delayed branches.

Study 4.2   Dependencies in Sequences of Code

Assumptions:

This study assumes a single instruction template for all instructions, and a single instruction size—32 bits—for each instruction. This timing template represents a simple dynamic pipeline with in-order execution of instructions. Register-to-register instructions (RR format) require a 32-bit instruction but do not use AG or DF cycles. Still, their execution must be delayed to preserve in-order execution.

A new R/M 32-bit machine has been designed (Figure 4.10). All instructions are 32 bits, but otherwise it is similar to our R/M prototype processor described in Chapter 2. Each R/M instruction has one data reference except for branch, which takes a target instruction fetch (TIF). The execution pattern is:

```
  IF    IF    D    AG    AG    DF    DF    EX    EX
|-----|-----|-----|-----|-----|-----|-----|-----|-----|
```

with one instruction decode per cycle (pipelined). The problem is to assess all code dependency and cycle penalties assuming all references are in the cache. Assess the penalty both with and without considering branches taken.

```
1.   LD    R4, 1000[R5,R6]
2.   LD    R3, 1002[R4,R6]
3.   ADD   R3,R4
4.   ST    1004[R5,R6], R3
5.   BC CC 1004[R5,R6]
```

Discussion: In instruction 1, the Load takes no EX cycles. This is generally true for most timing template configurations. Templates that include putaway cycles (PA) usually include these cycles for loads.

In instruction 2, address generation (AG) cannot begin until instruction 1 completes, since R4 is used and its value is determined by instruction 1. Similarly, instruction 3 depends on 2 for an operand (R3). Once a dependency is detected (e.g., instruction 2), that instruction remains in the stage where the dependency was detected and a new instruction does not enter

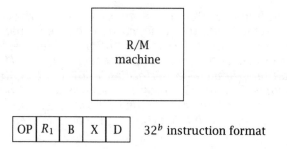

$$OP \mid R_1 \mid B \mid X \mid D \qquad 32^b \text{ instruction format}$$

Figure 4.10   R/M machine. All instructions follow $R_1 \leftarrow R_1$ OP Mem[D + $[R_B] + [R_X]$] or $R_1 \leftarrow R_2$ OP R_3 (where R_2 and R_3 replace R_B and R_X).

that stage until the dependency is removed. Thus, the decode of instruction 3 and all subsequent instructions is delayed by three cycles.

The D for instruction 4 is delayed so as to preserve the in-order decoding of instructions. In resolving the issue of additional total delay or marginal delay for sequences of code, we use the first instruction as a reference. Its total allocated latency is nine cycles. Instruction 2 is nominally scheduled to complete at the end of cycle 8, but is delayed by three cycles. Instruction 3 is an RR instruction that needs no AG or DF. It completes (despite its dependency) by the end of cycle 13 (the sum of its scheduled time plus already incurred delay), so no *further* overall delay is encountered. The same is true for instruction 4 decode, but its DS is additionally delayed. The target of the branch incurs further delay, as the target address is the same as the store address in instruction 4. This is detected as a store dependency and the TIF does not occur until the DS is complete. Since the CC is set by instruction 3, the in-line path, if selected, is not delayed by this interlock.

Instructions 2 through 5 could be queued up in the decoder while dependencies are being resolved. What actually happens is that instruction fetch ceases when a prior instruction is held in the decoder. The dependency analysis remains the same (Table 4.6).

Study 4.3   Internal Performance

This study evaluates processor performance of the processor in study 4.2, now taking into account the following effects:

1. Branches.

2. Data dependencies.

3. Run-on instructions (instructions with long execution times).

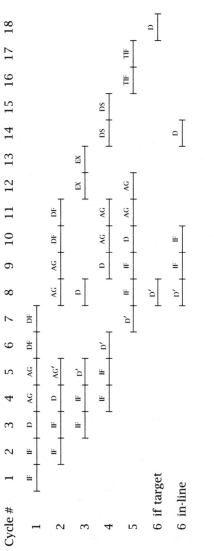

Figure 4.11 Target vs. in-line cycles.

Table 4.6   Dependencies and delays.

Instr Number	Instr Dep.	Dependency	Marginal Delay	Total Delay[1]
2	1 → 2	address[2]	3	3
3	2 → 3	data[3]	0	3
4	3 → 4	data[4]	0	3
5	4 → 5		0	3
	Branch			
6	5 → TI	procedural	7	10
	No branch			
6	5 → 6	procedural	3	6

[1] Marginal delay is the delay between the currently scheduled cycle for an action and the actual occurrence of that action and following instruction. Total delay is the sum of the marginal delays, and is related to the pipeline's overall efficiency. We compute the total delay with respect to the originally scheduled (instruction 1) actions and the marginal delay with respect to the current instruction's scheduled actions (where they differ).

[2] An address dependency exists because register 4 must be loaded before it is used in an address calculation. This causes instruction 2 to delay until register 4 is loaded.

[3] A data dependency exists because register 3 must be loaded before it is executed upon. This causes instruction 3 to delay its EX until register 3 is loaded.

[4] A data dependency exists because register 3 must be calculated before it is stored. This causes instruction 4 to delay its DS until the previous instruction's calculation has been stored in register 3.

Assumptions:

1. *The primary sources of delay are the branch, data dependencies, and run-on instructions.*

2. *The memory system is ideal. The performance we compute ignores cache access contention, cache miss effects, and memory access delay due to interference.*

Moreover, for this study, we assume a *simple* pipelined processor, i.e.:

1. *There is a simple in-line instruction buffer. Each in-line instruction has its own instruction fetch (IF) from cache. There is a one-entry target instruction buffer for use with branch instructions.*

2. *There is no branch prediction mechanism. On the occurrence of a conditional branch (whose outcome is unknown), decoding of subsequent instructions ceases until the condition code (CC) is set.*

Later studies in the chapter examine more complex processors with additional features.

The overall effect of dependencies on performance is to raise the CPI from an ideal of 1 cycle per instruction to:

$$CPI = 1.0 + \sum w_i d_i,$$

where w_i is the weight or frequency of the ith delay and d_i is the corresponding delay in cycles. Note that this is a simplifying (linear) assumption. Dubey [76] has developed a more accurate model, that is, corresponding more to complex models of overlapping delays (d_i).

We now compute each delay.

(i) Evaluate the conditional branch (BC) penalty:

The conditional branch instruction tests the condition code (CC) set by a preceding instruction. While some instructions set the CC, some do not— and the CC setting instruction could occur several instructions before the branch that tests the CC. The most frequent case is that the instruction that immediately precedes the branch sets the CC. For evaluation purposes, we assume that this is the case and, at $* - 1$, there is an arithmetic instruction with a basic timing template that sets the CC. If the condition specified in the branch on condition matches the CC, the branch is taken (or the branch *succeeds*). In this case, the next instruction following the branch is the target instruction (TI) whose location is determined by the branch instruction and is fetched by the branch instruction during TIF. Of course, if the condition specified by the BC is not met, instruction sequencing continues in-line. What should the processor do while awaiting the outcome of the branch? There may be a number of cycles available between the decoding of the branch and the setting of the condition code (in $* - 1$). The simplest strategy is for the processor to do nothing; simply await the outcome of the CC set and defer the decoding of the instruction following the BC until the CC is known. Both in-line and target paths can and normally would be fetched; the target path is fetched during the time allocated to a data fetch in an arithmetic instruction. This policy is simple to implement and minimizes the amount of excess memory traffic created by branch instructions. More complicated strategies that attempt to guess a particular path will occasionally be wrong and cause additional or excess instruction fetches from memory.

In the preceding, the actual decode is 5 cycles late (i.e., a 5-cycle branch penalty). This is not the whole effect, however. Consider the timing of $* + 2$. If the path selected is in-line, and the branch fetch policy is to continue fetching in-line until the CC is set (one word of target is fetched at TIF), then the $* + 2$ penalty is 5 cycles; but if the target path is taken, then:

"$* + 1$" is actually "TI"

"$* + 2$" is actually "TI + 1"

and

In this case, $TI + 1$ decode is delayed 6 cycles. If the branch is equally likely to go in-line as it is to take the target (TI), then the effective penalty is 5.5 cycles.

(ii) The effects of the unconditional branch (BR) can be similarly evaluated:

```
                  IF    IF    D    AG    AG    TIF   TIF
* (BR)       ├────┼────┼────┼────┼────┼────┼────┤
                              D'                  D
TI                       ├────┤              ├────┤
```

For this case, the penalty is 4 cycles.

Now, assuming the frequency of conditional branch is 15% and unconditional branch is 5%, we can compute the effect of branches on processor performance.

$$\begin{aligned} CPI &= 1 \text{ (decode)} + .15(5.5) + .05(4), \\ &= 1 + 0.825 + 0.20 = 2.025. \end{aligned}$$

(iii) Consider the effect of address dependencies:

Cases such as:

```
    LD R5, ALPHA[R6,R7]
    LD R6, BETA[R5,R7]
```

are evaluated as:

```
                                    D    AG    AG    DF    DF
LD R5, ...              *      ├────┼────┼────┼────┼────┤
                                    D    AG'                   AG
LD R6, BETA[R5,R7]    * + 1    ├────┼────┤ ··· | ··· ├────┤
```

This results in a 3-cycle penalty. Similarly,

```
    ADD R5, ALPHA[R6,R7]
    LD  R6, BETA[R5,R7]
```

is evaluated as:

```
                                  D    AG    AG    DF    DF    EX    EX
ADD R5, ALPHA[R6,R7] *       ├────┼────┼────┼────┼────┼────┼────┤
                                  D    AG'                         AG
LD  R6, BETA[R5,R7] * + 1    ├────┼────┤                      ├────┤
```

or a 5-cycle penalty.

Assume a 3-cycle penalty occurs in 4% of the instruction executions and a 5-cycle penalty occurs 1.5% of the time. We now have performance:

$$\begin{aligned} CPI &= 2.025 + 0.04(3) + 0.015(5), \\ &= 2.025 + 0.12 + 0.075, \\ &= 2.22. \end{aligned}$$

(iv) Evaluate run-on instructions.

These usually consist of a myriad of instruction types that are infrequently executed and expensive to implement within minimum cycle constraints. Divide, character operations, and load multiple (registers) are examples. When strict order of execution is to be maintained, the penalty assessment is straightforward. In our example, all instructions are allocated two cycles for execution. Load multiple (LDM) and store multiple (STM) are typical of a class of run-on instructions whose execution time is dependent upon operand size. Typically, in the case of LDM, a cycle is required for each register that is loaded. A single load instruction (LD) would complete after the second DF and use no EX cycles—it completes two cycles earlier than the expected "average" instruction—but LDM continues using data fetch cycles, moving one word into a register each cycle. Thus, if the LDM calls for a movement of seven integers from memory into registers, eight cycles are required—a combination of two DF cycles plus an addition of six EX cycles that are now actually DF cycles. Suppose a run-on (e.g., LDM—load multiple registers) takes 8 cycles for combined DF/EX. Then the LDM appears to have a penalty of 4 cycles, as shown:

Actually, this is somewhat deceptive. Six cycles of DF have been lost to subsequent instructions. If these instructions required a DF, the actual penalty is six cycles. If they did not (as in the case of an RR instruction), then we may approach a four-cycle penalty, mentioned earlier. The type of linear modeling we follow here represents a conservative estimate on performance. Normally, the designer bases performance estimates on the more conservative estimate (e.g., the six-cycle penalty), which is simply the additional time (over that allocated in the timing template) required to complete an action.

Instruction $*+1$ must not alter a register state until the cycle after $*$ completes execution. This assumes that $*+1$ did not depend on a result from $*$'s execution—the delay is caused solely by the need to preserve the order of execution, so that this overlapped machine behaves (on interruptions, etc.) exactly the same as a well-mapped machine. While order of execution might be preserved if both $*$ and $*+1$ completed execution simultaneously, implementation considerations usually prevent this. There are simply insufficient paths to a common register set.

The effects of run-on instructions on performance can be assessed simply by summing the weighted occurrence of those instructions whose execute (or data fetch, etc.) phase exceeds E_0. E_0 is the number of EX (or other outcome) cycles allocated in the template—in this case, two cycles:

$$\sum_i w_i (E_i - E_0).$$

When $E_i - E_0$ is negative, the ith delay is zero.

While run-on delays are relatively infrequent for many instruction sets, the delay-weighted effect of run-on instructions (even without data dependencies) may be a principal delay contributor because of the associated large delay and the requirement to preserve order during execution.

Drowning in a Lake That's Six Inches Deep

It is easy to ignore secondary performance effects during the course of the design. Apparently infrequent events such as overflowing a store buffer, context switches, execution time for character movement instructions, etc., can easily become primary problems in certain applications environments. These applications "drown in a lake that's (on the average) only six inches deep," since the weighted average of their frequency times their delay can dominate the total execution time of a program. The designer strives for high performance in, for example, a scientific user state. The fact that the system behaves significantly differently from this, or that a new release of the operating system behaves differently from the last, can present unfortunate surprises. There are numerous episodes where designers have ignored one or two presumably infrequent events, only to find—sadly, too late—that the events were not quite as infrequent as they had assumed. Such cases include:

- Store buffer overflow. In a particular processor, a store buffer was designed so that, statistically, it would rarely overflow. (See also Chapter 6 on the statistical design of store buffers.) However, on calls to the operating system, all of the registers are stored by the system. This event was not anticipated to be frequent, so that the delay on a buffer overflow was significant and the delay on storing 32 registers was truly formidable— significantly degrading the overall processor performance when applications made frequent calls to the operating system.

- The small I-cache. In another processor design, a small I-cache was added to enhance performance. Early releases of the processor worked well. Unfortunately, a later version of the operating system had a primary service loop that exceeded the cache size by several bytes, causing almost every reference to the I-cache to cause a cache miss. The operating system had been tested on an older, but compatible, version of the processor, and the problem was not uncovered until outcries from the marketplace reached the development team.

Processor design consists of a series of complex tradeoffs. The designer must be vigilant that all aspects of current program usage and future possible usage are covered; maximizing the minimum performance is an important goal. Coupled with that is a thorough understanding of what the minimum performance could be.

(v) Data dependencies play a role similar to run-on instructions. Consider:

$$* \qquad \text{ADD R5, ALPHA}$$
$$*+1 \quad \text{ADD R5, BETA}$$

The second ADD instruction uses as an argument the result of the first instruction.

*

*+1

Thus, $*+1$ is delayed a cycle by the dependency. Note that in this case, as is a common occurrence, the delay required by in-order EX masked part of the data dependency. For machines that require in-order EX we'll ignore data dependency effects since they are largely accounted for as a run-on effect.

Let us assume that the sum of run-on effects and dependency effects adds another 0.6 cycles per instruction. For a more complete analysis, we could use the statistics of Chapter 3 and evaluate each of the run-on dependencies using a list of the run-on delays. Depending on the environment and the machine parameters, run-on effects either may be limited or may dominate performance considerations. The 0.6 CPI assumed here is a low estimate as to the run-on effects in a simple pipelined processor. It might correspond to a simple processor in an application environment dominated by systems code, where the frequency of run-on arithmetic instructions is low.

In summary, we are now at

$$2.22 + 0.6 = 2.82 \text{ CPI}$$

without including the effects of cache miss or other memory-related penalties.

Study 4.4   Improving Branch Performance

Assumptions:
In this study, we again use the timing template of study 4.2, and the simple nonpredictive, nonbuffered branch type strategy of study 4.3.

From study 4.3, we see that the performance cost of branches can be high. We now evaluate the effects of two strategies for minimizing the branch penalty: *early CC setting* and *delayed branch*. We use the processor timing outlined in studies 4.2 and 4.3.

(i) Early CC (condition) setting:

Here, the compiler rearranges code to find (and place) useful non-CC setting instructions (e.g., load, store) between the instruction that sets the CC and the branch that tests it. We evaluate the effect of $n = 1, 2,$ and 3 intervening instructions. If the CC (condition code) is set in $* - 1$ (the immediately preceding instruction), $n = 0$ (n being the number of instructions between the CC setting instruction and the branch).

For $n = 0$, the BC penalty is 5.5 cycles as determined in study 4.3. The effect of n intervening instructions is simply to delay the *scheduled* decode time (D'). When the branch is taken this reduces the BC penalty to the greater of $6.0 - n$ or the unconditional branch penalty. The BC penalizes $5.0 - n$ if the branch is untaken. There is no effect on the unconditional branch. Thus,

		$n = 0$	$n = 1$	$n = 2$	$n = 3$	$n = 5*$
BC penalty	– taken	6.0	5.0	4.0	4.0	4.0
	– untaken	5.0	4.0	3.0	2.0	0
BC delay	(cycles)	2.03	1.88	1.73	1.65	1.5

  * n is the number of instructions between the CC setting instruction and the branch.

The performance includes only the effects of branch—conditional and unconditional.

(ii) Delayed branch.

The delayed branch (DB) has an effect similar to the early setting of the CC. The delayed branch (at $*$) may immediately follow the instruction setting the CC, but the resulting instruction (target or in-line) is not decoded until $* + n + 1$. Other useful instructions (if available) are placed in-line and the delayed branch instruction is to be executed n instructions later (n is usually fixed at 1 or 2 but may be a parameter of the DB).

The following illustrates the delayed branch ($n = 1$). Assume the delayed branch (DB) is unconditional:

```
              DB       ALPHA
              LD
      ALPHA   INSTR
```

With proper implementation support, the DB can reduce penalties for all branch types. Again assume that we prefetch in-line, and fetch only one target instruction:

		For $n = 0$	$n = 1$	$n = 2$	$n = 3$	$n = 5$
DB unconditional		4.0	3.0	2.0	1.0	0
DB conditional	– taken	6.0	5.0	4.0	3.0	1.0
	– untaken	5.0	4.0	3.0	2.0	0
DB delay	(cycles)	2.03	1.83	1.63	1.43	1.08

The performance includes only the effects of branch. The taken conditional DB case for $n = 3$ is shown as follows:

$* - 1$

$\quad\quad\quad\quad$ D $\quad$ AG $\quad$ AG $\quad$ DF $\quad$ DF $\quad$ EX $\quad$ EX

$\quad\quad\quad\quad\quad\quad\quad\quad\quad\quad\quad\quad\quad\quad\quad\quad\quad\quad$ ↓CC set

$* \quad$ (DB, $\ n = 3$) $\quad$ D $\quad$ AG $\quad$ AG $\quad$ TIF $\quad$ TIF

$* + 1 \quad\quad\quad\quad\quad\quad$ D1

$* + 2 \quad\quad\quad\quad\quad\quad\quad\quad$ D2

$* + 3 \quad\quad\quad\quad\quad\quad\quad\quad\quad$ D3

TI $\quad\quad\quad\quad\quad\quad\quad\quad\quad\quad$ D′ $\quad\quad\quad$ D

TI+1 $\quad\quad\quad\quad\quad\quad\quad\quad\quad\quad\quad$ D′ $\quad$ IF $\quad$ IF $\quad$ D

There is a 3-cycle decode delay in TI + 1.

The effectiveness of either approach depends on finding useful instructions that can be done in the *delay slots*. Current implementation data suggest that $n > 1$ [192] (i.e., more than one delay slot) may be of only marginal value.

No Panacea for Branches

There is no easy way around the branch delay penalty. The designer may avoid the penalty completely by creating a very simple processor with a long cycle and limited performance in the first place.

In modern microprocessors, the processor cycle time is decreasing at a faster rate than the memory cycle time, creating multiple cycle accesses to external storage, either cache or main memory. These trends tend to increase the number of cycles involved in instruction execution, and also increase the relative size of the branch penalty.

Even for microprocessors with on-chip cache, the relative size of these processors and size of their caches create a need for multiple cycle access to the cache, again promoting the long-term trend toward increased branch penalty.

Study 4.5   Static and Dynamic Pipelines

Assumptions:

In this study, we assume a L/S architecture with a simple basic timing allocation. A fast access to memory (IF or DF) of one cycle is assumed. This reduces branch penalties. We further assume that the processor guesses the in-line path on a conditional branch.

Simple pipelined processors use a *static* pipeline, where an instruction must go through all stages of pipeline whether required or not. In a *dynamic* pipeline (as assumed throughout this chapter), the instruction goes through just those stages required for completion. Using a dynamic pipeline may or may not affect the various pipeline delays, since in-order decode and especially in-order execute (or putaway) restrict any advantage.

We compare these two approaches for a L/S processor with decode on successive cycles. First, assume a **static** pipelined processor with the following timing templates:

LD/ST $\vdash$IF$\dashv$D$\dashv$AG$\dashv$AG$\dashv$DF$\dashv$PA$\dashv$

ALU type $\vdash$IF$\dashv$D$\dashv$EX$\dashv$EX$\dashv$$\varnothing$$\dashv$PA$\dashv$

$\uparrow$ CC set

Here, an ALU operation takes two EX cycles, then a dummy cycle ($\varnothing$), and finally a PA (CC is set at the end of the last EX cycle). The load/store instruction uses the ALU for two AG cycles instead of EX. For a static pipeline, we would have the following branch delays:

$\downarrow$CC set

$*-1$ $\vdash$D$\dashv$EX$\dashv$EX$\dashv$$\varnothing$$\dashv$PA$\dashv$

$*$ BR $\vdash$D$\dashv$AG$\dashv$AG$\dashv$TIF$\dashv$

Target $\vdash$D'$\dashv$ $\vdash$D$\dashv$

Thus, the delay is three cycles on unconditional branch (BR). The PA in $*-1$ is delayed to ensure ordering of events within the timing template ($\varnothing$ represents no action). Note that $*-1$ and $*$ end at the same time, but there is no out-of-order problem, since only the PA must be in order and only $*-1$ uses PA.

For BC, the situation is the same, but since the CC is set early, the in-line path can proceed with only one cycle of delay. Assume that 50% of the BC instructions go to the in-line and 50% go to the target instruction path (roughly following the Chapter 3 data). Then the BC delay is $0.5 * 3.0$ cycles (for the target path—see BR) plus $0.5 * 1.0$ (for the in-line path decode, which occurs immediately after CC set), for a total of 2.0 cycles.

For address dependency (assuming no bypassing), we might have:

ADD R1, R2, R3 $\vdash$D$\dashv$EX$\dashv$EX$\dashv$$\varnothing$$\dashv$PA$\dashv$

LD R4, A[R1] $\vdash$D$\dashv$AG'$\dashv$ $\vdash$AG$\dashv$AG$\dashv$DF$\dashv$PA$\dashv$

This has a 3-cycle delay.

For the **dynamic** pipeline, we might have timing templates such as:

LD/ST $\vdash$IF$\dashv$D$\dashv$AG$\dashv$AG$\dashv$DF$\dashv$PA$\dashv$

ALU-type $\vdash$IF$\dashv$D$\dashv$EX$\dashv$EX$\dashv$PA$\dashv$

Despite the more flexible pipeline, the BR and BC delays remain the same, since the CC is set at the same time in both pipelines and the target fetch time is the same. The situation with an address dependency is different, however:

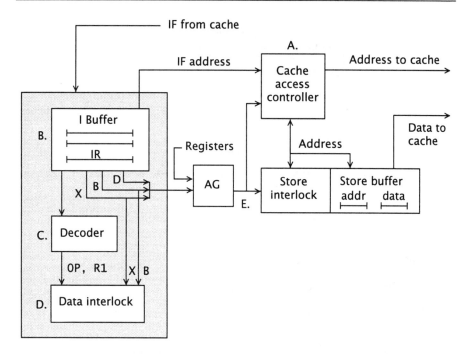

Figure 4.12   Processor control unit.

ADD R1, R2, R3
LD R4, A[R1]

Now the AG is delayed only one cycle, assuming the ALU result is "bypassed" to the AG stage (discussed later).

For most processor arrangements, there is not a significant performance difference between static and dynamic pipelines, as long as both must meet the in-order execution requirement. The primary difference is the use of additional dummy cycles in the pipeline.

We assume dynamic pipelines for most of this chapter and text. They are basic to out-of-order implementations, and simpler, static pipeline applications can be developed directly from techniques studied in the context of dynamic pipelines.

4.4   Design of a Pipelined Processor

With multiple instructions in various stages of execution, there are many design considerations and tradeoffs in pipelined processors. After the functional partitioning of the processor is complete, the timing template is determined, and initial performance estimates are made, the design of the control unit (or *I-unit*) can be begun and performance estimates refined.

Figure 4.12 shows the processor control unit and some basic interactions with the rest of the system. For our purposes, there are five separate subunits in the control unit:

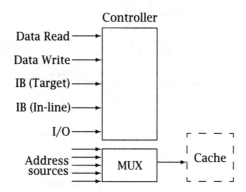

Figure 4.13   Cache access controller.

A. Cache access controller.

B. I-buffer (including the I-register).

C. Instruction decoder (including branch and run-on instruction manager).

D. Data interlocks (including address interlock manager).

E. Store interlocks and store buffers.

Sub-units B, C, and D are closely related, with relatively more information flow among these units than external to them. Similarly, sub-units A and E control access to the storage system and are closely related to one another. Still, the decoder, for example, must be aware of actions taken by the cache access controller.

We look at each of these sub-units and their effect on system performance.

4.4.1   Cache Access Controller

Requests to the cache may come from one of five sources (Figure 4.13):

1. Data read (from AG).

2. Data write (from AG and store buffer).

3. I-buffer: target I-fetch.

4. I-buffer: in-line I-fetch.

5. External access (I/O, etc.).

If, as usual, the rate of external accesses is low, these can be given highest priority to avoid problems such as I/O run-out or overrun (I/O buffer overflow).

Ignoring external accesses, cache access priority is usually arranged (highest to lowest):

1. Data access (read).

2. I-buffer (target fetch).

3. I-buffer (in-line fetch).

4. Data write (unless the store buffer is full).

Data reads are given priority, assuming that an ample I-buffer is part of the design. (See section 4.4.2.) For data writes, priority is given to stores if the store buffer is full; otherwise, priority is given to reads (of all types).

Contention for cache access is frequently a concern for processor designers, and split cache designs (I and D, see chapter 5) are a popular method to double the available cache accessing bandwidth. For many register set architectures with a well-designed I-buffer and 8-byte access paths, cache contention at a single integrated cache should not be a serious source of contention, so long as the cache can accommodate a request each cycle. (See study 5.4.)

4.4.2   Accounting for the Effect of Buffers in a Pipelined System

Buffers, however they are organized, change the way our instruction timing templates are used. The buffer decouples the time at which an event occurs from the time at which the input data is used.

For example, so far we have shown processors without explicit I-buffers. Thus, actions proceed:

```
           IF    IF    D
*        |-----+-----+-----|
               IF    IF    D
* + 1        |-----+-----+-----|
```

Suppose now that * is a branch (BC) and * + 1 has its decode delayed by three cycles:

```
           IF    IF    D
*        |-----+-----+-----|
               IF    IF    D'              D
* + 1        |-----+-----+-----|        |-----|
```

The IF for * + 1 occurs before * is known to be a branch. Presumably, there is someplace to keep the result of the IF (a minimal one-entry buffer) so that the decode of * + 1 can proceed when the branch decision is determined (assuming the in-line path is selected). Note that in this case the IF completed three cycles before its decode began.

Larger buffers generalize the preceding situation. A single IF may fetch two instructions (*A* and *B*) into the instruction buffer to be used several cycles later, and we might have:

```
              IF    IF
IF → IB     |-----+-----|
                                    D
I_A                               |-----|
                                       D
I_B                                  |-----|
```

The instruction buffer ought to be transparent to instruction execution. If an instruction is in the I-buffer, we assume that it can be accessed and decoded in one decode cycle (D). Depending on the type of analysis we are doing, we may show a buffered instruction execution sequence as:

```
                  D      AG
*                 |———+———| . . .
                         D      AG
* + 1                    |———+———|
                                D
* + 2                           |——| . . .
```

without indicating the IF, or we may show it as:

```
            IF     IF     D
*           |———+———+———|
                   IF     IF     D
* + 1              |———+———+———|
                          IF     IF     D
* + 2                     |———+———+———|
```

to indicate that the IF occurred at some time prior to the corresponding decode (D). The reader should note that in the presence of a buffer, the IF may have occurred several cycles earlier than indicated. Also, while it appears that a single IF occurs per instruction, the IF may actually fetch several instructions at once. We consider these possibilities later in this chapter.

4.4.3   Buffer Design

Buffers may be designed for a *mean* request rate or for a *maximum* request rate. In the former case, we estimate the expected number of requests and then trade off buffer size against the probability of an overflow. Overflows *per se* (where an action is lost) do not happen in internal CPU buffers, but an "overflow" condition—full buffer and a new request—will force the processor to slow down to bring the buffer entries down below buffer capacity. Thus, each time an "overflow" condition occurs, the processor pipeline stalls to allow the overflowed buffer to access memory (or other resource). The store buffer is usually designed for a mean request rate.

For request sources that dominate performance, such as in-line instruction requests, we design for the maximum request rate. We ensure that the buffer size is sufficient to match the processor request rate with the cache service rate. A properly sized buffer allows the processor to continue accessing instructions at its maximum rate without the instruction buffer running out of instructions.

4.4.4   Designing a Buffer for a Mean Request Rate

Suppose we have determined the mean request rate for a particular source. How large should we make the buffer to hold these requests? Assume we know Q, the mean number of requests present in a cycle. For internal processor buffers, each source can make a maximum of one request per cycle, but these requests can cluster and appear to a buffer accessing a slower memory as multiple concurrent requests. Now we can use the well-known Chebyshev's Inequality or a variation thereof.

The modeling asumption is that the number of items that appear at a particular pipeline stage can be defined as a random variable (q) with mean (Q) and standard deviation (σ). Notice that our modeling approach does not recognize the "history" or sequential nature of items collecting at a pipeline stage. In chapter 6, we will see another modeling approach using queueing theory. Generally, the results of the two modeling approaches are consistent.

We assume that q is a random variable describing the actual request size and Q is the mean this distribution, the buffer is of size BF, and the probability of buffer full or overflowed is p.

Bound 1 (Chebyshev's Inequality)

The probability of buffer full or overflowed (p) is:

$$Prob\{q \geq BF\} = p \leq \frac{Q}{BF}.$$

That is, the probability of a buffer overflow is less than the mean number of requests divided by the buffer size.

Bound 2 (Chebyshev's Inequality Corollary)

The probability of buffer full or overflowed (p) is:

$$Prob\{q \geq BF\} = p \leq \frac{\sigma^2}{(BF - Q)^2}.$$

This corollary is a direct result of Chebyshev's Inequality and the definition of variance, since

$$\text{Prob}\{|q - Q| \geq B\} \leq \frac{\sigma^2}{B^2}$$

is simply restating the inequality in terms of variance. (B is an arbitrary number.) We rearrange the above and let $B = BF - Q$ to get the corollary.

This corollary can be rewritten and solved for BF:

$$\sqrt{p} \leq \frac{\sigma}{BF - Q}$$
$$BF \leq Q + \frac{\sigma}{\sqrt{p}}$$

We now can use the most favorable BF size:

$$BF = \min\left(\frac{Q}{p}, Q + \frac{\sigma}{\sqrt{p}}\right).$$

Alternatively, we may know the BF size and wish to determine p:

$$p = \min\left(\frac{Q}{BF}, \frac{\sigma^2}{(BF - Q)^2}\right).$$

Modeling notes and assumptions:

We associate a trial (or q) with a short sequence of events that affect the number of requests made to a buffer. We ignore the fact that in most situations the trials $\{q\}$ are not independent (a full buffer at one time increases the probability that it will be full on the next trial). Actual buffer occupancy is determined by both the request arrival distribution and the departure distribution. In most buffer situations, the departure distribution that describes an exit from the buffer is extremely complex. For example, the acceptance of a request from the store buffer to the cache depends on the state of all higher priority requestors. For simplicity, we use only the arrival distribution and simply assume that entries depart the buffer after a few cycles (corresponding to the expected time required to service a request).

It is also important to correctly interpret the meaning of p. The (unstated) modeling assumption is that p is the probability of a full or overflow *given* that a trial occurs. A "trial" does not necessarily occur every cycle, so the effect of the overflow must be corrected by the frequency of trials per cycle.

Finally, the event $q \geq BF$ involves the meaning of the buffer, BF. If a certain value q arises, the buffer will no longer accept new entries and the requestor must halt, slowing down the entire pipeline. The size (BF) is determined by the point (q) at which the slowdown occurs, which is not necessarily the apparent buffer size. For example, assume a store buffer of size = 1, but slowdown occurs only when the AG produces another request and the store buffer is full. This second request is held in the AG. From a modeling point of view, $BF = 2$, since it is at that point ($q \geq 2$) that the processor slows down.

EXAMPLE 4.1

Suppose we wish to determine the effectiveness of a two-entry write buffer. Assume the write request rate is 0.15 per cycle, and that the expected number of cycles to do the store is 2. The mean of the arrivals is $2 \times 0.15 = 0.3$. The variance (σ^2) on this mean is 0.3.

So, $BF = 2$, $Q = 0.3$, $\sigma^2 = 0.3$, and

$$
\begin{aligned}
p &= \min\left(\frac{Q}{BF}, \frac{\sigma^2}{(BF - Q)^2} \right) \\
  &= \min\left(0.15, \frac{0.3}{(2 - 0.3)^2} \right) \\
  &= 0.10.
\end{aligned}
$$

Thus, the probability that a given write request finds a full buffer is at most 0.10. Since writes occurred at a rate of 0.15 per cycle, we would expect that a "write buffer full" event would occur in only about 1.5% of all machine cycles.

◆

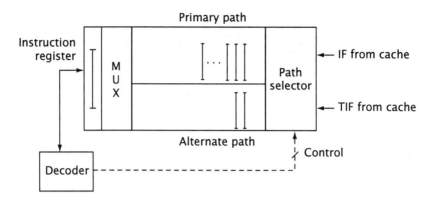

Figure 4.14   I-buffer components.

4.4.5   Buffers Designed for Maximum Request Rates: The I-Buffer

The I-buffer (sub-unit B in Figure 4.12, page 213) contains the following features (Figure 4.14):

1. An instruction register. This register holds the instruction being decoded.

2. An alternate path buffer (or target buffer). When a branch is encountered and its outcome is unknown, the "DF" cycle is used to access the target path. If the branch is known (or guessed) to go to the target path, this buffer holds the previous requested in-line instructions.

3. A primary path buffer. This is the buffer that accesses in-line instruction words. On a branch, this buffer continues to fetch in-line instructions unless the outcome is known (or guessed) to go to the target path. Then branch target instruction words are retrieved into this buffer.

Each entry in the buffer holds an IF. The alternate path buffer usually holds only one or two "words" or IF accesses, while the primary path buffer should be large enough to avoid run-out (discussed next).

The selection of a branch direction is done by the decoder (sub-unit C). For each branch type (and mask combination if appropriate), the decoder may have a predetermined strategy—either to fetch the in-line or target path. We will see more of this in a subsequent section.

The first problem in designing a pipeline is to ensure a steady flow of instructions to the initial stage of the pipeline. Even when the memory bandwidth is sufficient to sustain the instruction flow, the memory access time requires multiple cycles. For this reason, we introduce an intermediate buffer in order to maintain the pipeline rate. This intermediate buffer is referred to as a *prefetch register*, or simply an instruction buffer or I-buffer.

If the I-buffer is of insufficient size, it is unable to mask out the accessing delay of sequential IFs. This results in an additional delay (in addition to the IF itself) in performing the fetch. This delay is called *runout*.

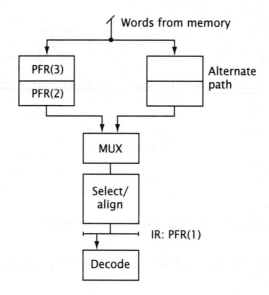

Figure 4.15   Instruction buffer.

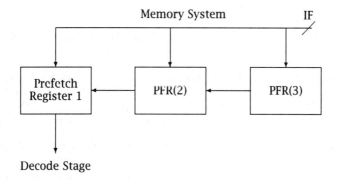

Figure 4.16   Instruction prefetch mechanisms.

An I-buffer is designed to take advantage of the sequentiality of instruction fetch references between taken branch instructions. The instruction buffer consists of one or more prefetch registers (PFR), as shown in Figure 4.15. The width of each register is normally some multiple of the unit of access (word, doubleword) from the memory system. The first PFR, PFR(1), is the instruction register (Figure 4.16) and contains the instruction word that is currently being decoded. The prefetch unit attempts to keep the remaining PFRs filled with the instructions that follow the one being decoded. When the instructions in PFR(1) have been used, the contents of the remaining PFRs are transferred to the immediately preceding PFR, and a memory fetch is initiated to fill the last PFR, which is now empty. (In practice, a circular buffer with a pointer to the next available PFR is used.) When a successful branch occurs, all of the prefetch registers in the unsuccessful path become useless and memory fetches must be initiated to refill them. Instruction decoding resumes as soon as PFR(1) is loaded and continues as long as it is not empty.

Number of prefetch registers = 3
Memory access time = 6 cycles
Width of a prefetch register = 2 instructions

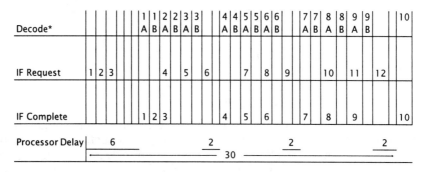

*Entries indicate the two instructions (A and B) contained in each of the designated IFs.

Figure 4.17   Instruction prefetch. Three IF requests are made to fill the I-buffer (PFR1 through PFR3). The first completes at the end of cycle 6 and contains two instructions, 1A and 1B, which are decoded in cycles 7 and 8, respectively. After cycle 8, when instruction 1B is decoded, a PFR is available and IF 4 begins.

The important operational parameters of the instruction prefetch unit are: the instruction length distribution (Table 3.2), the width of the memory interface that supplies the unit, the width and number of PFRs, and the distribution of instruction execution sequence lengths (Figure 3.4 and Table 3.11).

The operation of a prefetch unit is illustrated in Figure 4.17. This example assumes a memory access time of six processor cycles and three prefetch registers, each capable of holding two instructions. The processor is pipelined, and is capable of decoding one instruction per processor cycle while the prefetch buffer (PFB) is not empty. Memory interference is ignored and the memory is assumed to be capable of one request per processor cycle.

The first instruction word fetched corresponds to the target of a branch that was taken. Since all three registers are invalid, three instruction fetches (two instructions per instruction word) are initiated on successive cycles. The instruction words begin arriving six cycles later and decoding begins as soon as the first word arrives. Since the words arrive faster than the instruction unit can decode them, after the delay of six cycles in decoding the first instruction the next five instructions are processed without delay. However, since there are only three registers, the request for the fourth instruction word cannot be initiated until the first instruction word has been processed, i.e., its two instructions have been decoded. Consequently, the seventh instruction sees a delay of two cycles, since four of the six cycles of the memory access time are masked by the decode of the second and third instruction words. This, of course, is the purpose of the PFB. Had the number of prefetch registers been four or more, the memory access time would have been completely masked for all but the first instruction.

In order to avoid I-buffer runout, the primary path buffers (or buffer registers) must be sufficient to cover the IF access time. The width of the IB for either path is equal to to the IF width. If we decode one instruction per cycle, the number of in-line buffer words (BF) is:

$$BF = 1 + \left\lceil \frac{\text{IF access time (cycles)}}{\text{instructions/IF}} \right\rceil .$$

If we have s instructions decoded each cycle, then:

$$BF = 1 + \left\lceil s \cdot \frac{\text{IF access time (cycles)}}{\text{instructions/IF}} \right\rceil .$$

Here, the IF access time (cycles) is simply the number of cycles required for an IF, and instructions/IF is the average number of instructions accessed by an IF. These BF registers should be viewed as a minimum; in many cases, it is useful to have a larger buffer. This would allow for normal processing in case of a delayed IF due to cache access contention. The alternate path buffer should be the same size as the primary path if target branch prediction is used. If we use strictly "guess in line" then we need only one entry (for TIF) for the alternate path buffer.

The average instruction decode delay is less if the average execution sequence length is greater, for the unmaskable delay experienced on the fetch of the first word is amortized over more instruction decodes. The average instruction decode delay is also reduced by increasing the degree of prefetch. However, the traffic to the memory is increased, since more unnecessary words are fetched when the degree of prefetch is increased. The two criteria by which instruction prefetch techniques can be evaluated are: (1) the average delay per instruction decoded and (2) the average number of words fetched from memory per instruction decoded. In our simple example, 18 instructions were decoded in 30 cycles. Thus, there is an instruction buffer runout delay of 0.667 cycles per instruction decoded. Since the example does not contain any taken branches, we do not experience any wasted fetches from memory, and thus the number of instruction words fetched equals the number of instructions decoded. When taken branches are present, this is obviously not the case.

By using a sufficiently high degree of instruction prefetch, it is possible to mask the memory access time for all instruction fetches except for the first one of an instruction execution sequence (although this could be at the expense of a substantial increase in the memory traffic). Any further reduction in the average instruction access time must concentrate upon the first instruction, which contains the target of the branch instruction.

4.5   Branches

As we have seen, branches can be a major limitation to pipeline processor performance [72, 264]. There are four major approaches to the branch problem:

1. Branch elimination. For certain code sequences, we can replace the branch with another conditional operation.

2. Branch speedup. Reducing the time required for target instruction fetch and CC determination (Figure 4.18).

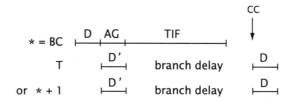

Figure 4.18   Basic branch delays.

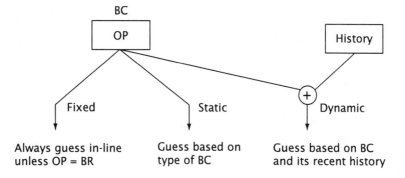

Figure 4.19   Branch prediction.

3. Branch prediction. Using available information about the branch one can predict the branch outcome and begin processing on the predicted program path. If the strategy is simple or trivial—e.g., always fetch in-line on true conditional branches—it is called a *fixed strategy*. If the strategy varies by opcode type but is predetermined, it is called a *static strategy*. Finally, if the strategy varies according to current program behavior, it is called a *dynamic strategy* (see Figure 4.19).

4. Branch target capture. After a branch has been executed we can keep its target instruction in a table for later use (Figure 4.20).

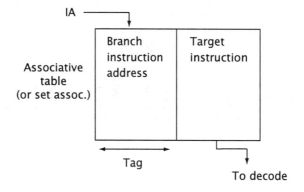

Figure 4.20   Branch table buffer.

Table 4.7   Branch management techniques.

Approach	What It Does	Cost	Effect on Branch Delay (Taken Branch)	Effect on Branch Prediction
Speedup				
Early CC set	Determine outcome of tested condition early	Nil	Can save up to a cycle	None
Delayed branch	"	Small	"	None
Branch adder	Determine target address early	Small	Generally saves a cycle	None
Prediction				
Static:	Use branch opcode or test to predict outcome	Small	None	60–70% accurate
Dynamic:				
History	Records outcome of each branch	Some increase in I-cache size	None	70–90+% accurate
Branch table buffer	Stores last target inst for each branch in a special associative table	Can be significant for large tables	Can reduce to zero	70–90+% accuracy; depends on size and application

Table 4.7 summarizes the major aspects of each of these approaches. In the following sections we will look at the details of each approach.

4.5.1 Branch Elimination

Sequences of code that include small basic blocks (i.e., one or two instructions between branches) can be very disruptive to pipelined instruction execution. Referring back to chapter 3 (Figure 3.4), we can see that about 8% of all basic blocks consist of a single instruction. In these cases we frequently can eliminate the initial branch and make the execution (or PA) of the subsequent instruction conditional on a certain condition code.

For example, suppose we had:

```
OP  ...
BC  CC = Z,  * + 2
ADD R3,R2,R1
BC  CC,  ALPHA
```

This could be replaced by:

```
OP  ...
ADD R3,R2,R1,NZ
BC  CC,  ALPHA
```

That is, if the CC = Z (zero), the ADD instruction is not executed.

This elimination of the first BC requires that other operations such as the ADD carry a condition code specifier. The result of the ADD is actually stored (PA) only if the machine CC corresponds to the CC in the instruction. Such instructions are called *conditional instructions.*

In the preceding example, presumably almost all instructions could be conditional. The number of instructions that can be conditional is usually limited. One alternative is to have a single select instruction which chooses between two register values depending on the Conditional instruction approaches have also been referred to as *guarding* the instruction [134].

Since all of these approaches require knowledge of the CC before instruction PA, they are still subject to delay, depending on the timing template. Indeed, for machines that require the PA to be in order, these techniques have limited value. For machines that allow our-of-order execution, however, these techniques can be helpful.

4.5.2 Branch Speedup

For a simple processor, the branch delay (Figure 4.18) is:

Branch delay = max {time for TIF, time for CC set}.

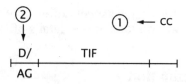

Figure 4.21 Branch speedup: the two basic techniques consist of (1) advancing the relative time of the CC set and (2) concurrently decoding and computing the branch target address.

The most obvious approach to improving branch delay is to simply speed up:

1. TIF time, and

2. The relative time at which CC is set.

Depending on the instruction set, the TIF time can be reduced by using a separate branch adder. This adder operates on each instruction *at the same time* it is being decoded to form (AG) a target instruction address (D/AG). The branch adder *assumes* each instruction is a branch; if it is not a branch, the result of the addition is discarded. Thus, if the instruction is a branch, the AG is completed at the same time the branch is decoded. Indeed, if the target instruction address lies in the same virtual page (has the same upper bits), then even the translate (T) step can be stripped and the TIF can begin immediately after the decode (D) cycle (Figure 4.21). Data from Chapter 3 (on centered branches) indicates that for 4KB pages, about 79% of target addresses lie in the same page.

Knowing the state of the condition code early is always helpful in branch delay reduction. Two strategies for providing early data outcomes (study 4.4) are:

1. Early condition code setting.

2. Delayed branch.

The first approach places the instruction whose result is to be tested early in the code sequence, so that the CC is set by the time the conditional branch needs it. Instructions that do not affect the CC are used as intervening instructions. The second approach is similar, except the action of the branch is delayed by a designated number of instructions, as discussed in study 4.4. The delayed branch (DB) uses other instructions that are placed after the DB to minimize the branch delay by getting useful work done while the CC is being resolved.

4.5.3   Branch Prediction Strategies

Target fetch delay represents the pipeline "delay" that may occur between a taken branch instruction and its target. This change in the executed sequence of instructions causes the contents of part of the pipeline to be discarded, and the pipeline to be reloaded. This "branch problem" is closely

Table 4.8   A static branch prediction strategy.

Instruction Class	Instruction	Guessed Successful (S)	Guessed Unsuccessful (U)
Unconditional branch	BR	Always*	Never
Branch on Condition	BC	Never	Always
	BCR	Never	Always
Loop Control	BCT	Always	Never
Call/	BAL	Always*	Never
Return	BALR	Always*	Never

*These are called "known successful" branches. We ignore the case when the target is specified as the successor in-line instruction.

Table 4.9   Static branch prediction success rates (scientific environment).

Instruction Class	Branch Instr %	Guess	% Correct Guess
BR unconditional	(72.5)(.20)=14.5	S	14.5
BC conditional	(72.5)(.80)=58	U	(58)(.46)=27
Loop	(9.8)	S	9.8×.91=9
Call/Return	(17.7)	S	17.7
			68.2%

related to the timely fetch of instructions, since the delay for a taken branch depends on the time required to fetch the branch target.

Beyond the trivial fixed prediction, there are two classes of strategies for guessing whether or not a branch will be taken: a static strategy, which is based upon the type of branch instruction, and a dynamic strategy, which is based upon the recent history of branch activity.

Even perfect prediction does not eliminate branch delay. Perfect prediction simply converts the delay for conditional branch into that for unconditional branch (branch taken).

One static strategy is to make an early prediction of the outcome of the branch based on the particular branch opcode. When a branch is decoded, a guess is made on the outcome of the branch, and if it is determined that the branch will be successful, the pipeline fetches the target instruction stream and begins decoding from it. A simple approach using R/M instructions is shown in Table 4.8.

The general effectiveness of a strategy described in Table 4.8 can be determined using R/M data from Tables 3.4–3.10.

For a scientific environment, 26 out of 100 HLL operations are branches (Table 3.4). The branch frequency varies by architecture from 13% to 22%. In Table 4.9 we compute the success rate of the Table 4.8 static prediction strategy using Table 3.10.

If we had used the Table 3.10 data to guess the most likely outcome, we would guess that conditional branches went to target (i.e., S). This "all S" strategy would have improved our prediction rate to about 72%. However,

Table 4.10 Static branch prediction success rates (commercial environment).

Instruction Class		Branch Instr %	Guess	% Correct Guess
BR	unconditional	(72.5)(.40)=29	S	29
BC	conditional	(72.5)(.60)=43.5	U	(43.5)(.59)=25.6
Loop		(9.8)	S	(9.8)(.91)=9
Call/Return		(17.7)	S	17.7
				81.3%

the goal of branch prediction is not simply accuracy but rather processor speedup, and up to a certain point more performance is gained by guessing in-line rather than target.

In a conditional branch, more is gained by guessing and going in-line than to target. One should select a strategy that minimizes the expected branch delay, not simply maximizes the prediction accuracy. This is more fully described in study 4.6. Any successful strategy must be coupled to an appropriately designed I-buffer (both in-line and target) to avoid run-out.

For a commercial environment (Tables 3.5–3.10), we can achieve even better prediction rates (Table 4.10). For this environment, a simple static strategy gives over 80% correct prediction rates.

One dynamic strategy is to make predictions of the outcomes of branch instructions based on past history; that is, use the sequence of past actions of a branch—was it or was it not taken?—to predict what will happen the next time it is encountered. Table 4.11 from Lee and Smith [181] shows the effectiveness of a branch prediction when prediction is based on exactly the n preceding executions of the branch in question, and whether that branch was taken or not taken. The prediction algorithm is quite simple. For example, with $n = 3$, if in two (or three) of the previous branch outcomes the branch was taken, it is now predicted to be taken; otherwise, it is predicted as not taken. In implementing this scheme, a small up/down counter can be associated with a cache line. The organization of such a cache is shown in Figure 4.22. If the branch is taken, the counter is incremented up to a maximum value (n). An unsuccessful branch decrements the counter. A count of zero is the same as $n = 0$. Of course, as mentioned earlier, prediction should be based not only on accuracy of outcome, but on minimization of expected branch delay.

The counters are referred to as *saturating counters*, since they remain at a maximum value on repeated increment.

If the line size is small then usually only one branch is present per line and only one counter is needed. When two branches are present, their results can be merged in the counter. This limits the effectiveness, but only in the (presumably) unlikely event of multiple branch instructions in the same line. As larger lines are used, multiple history counters can be implemented.

A number of interesting observations can be made from Table 4.11. First, the predictive accuracy very closely approaches its maximum with one or two preceding branches used for prediction. Second, the predictive accuracy for as few as two preceding branches is from 83.4 to 96.5%, which is

Table 4.11   Percentage correct guess using history of past n branches [181].

	Mix Definition			
n	Compiler	Business	Scientific	Supervisor
0	64.1	64.4	70.4	54.0
1	91.9	95.2	86.6	79.7
2	93.3	96.5	90.8	83.4
3	93.7	96.6	91.0	83.5
4	94.5	96.8	91.8	83.7
5	94.7	97.0	92.0	83.9

much higher than the accuracy using only the branch opcode prediction strategy of Table 4.8. Third, the effectiveness of prediction varies significantly among the workloads.

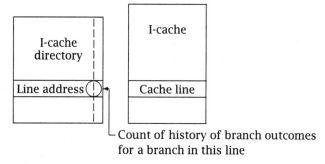

Figure 4.22   Dynamic branch prediction using branch history.

In the following study (4.6), we look at a static branch prediction strategy coupled with a simple I-buffer.

Study 4.6   Simple I-Buffers and Static Branch Prediction

Assumptions:
   In this study (and in some of the following studies), we slightly alter the template of study 4.2 to include a two-cycle AG—perhaps one cycle for effective address generation and one for translate. Otherwise, we follow the general architecture of the R/M machine as used in studies such as 4.2. The significant new assumptions made in this study include:

   1. *We now introduce an I-buffer of sufficient size to avoid run-out. Thus, we generally ignore the IF cycles for in-line instructions. Of course, any unpredictable delay such as TIF that directly affects machine timing must be evaluated.*

   2. *In conjunction with the I-buffer, the decoder now predicts the outcome of a branch and issues instructions in anticipation*

of the outcome of the branch. Any such instructions must be issued conditionally subject to the outcome of the setting of the condition code. Thus, such instructions may generate addresses and fetch data, but must not enter execution (or at least certainly not putaway) to prevent altering established data in the case of a mispredicted outcome of the condition code. For the simple type of machines considered here, this is not a severe restriction and does not cause any additional delay. It becomes a more serious concern with more sophisticated instruction-issuing mechanisms considered later.

3. *The decoder is assumed to use a static prediction mechanism. It predicts the outcome of a conditional branch based upon the particular type of branch encountered, using data presented in Chapter 3.*

Unlike simple branch processing used in previous studies, it is possible to predict a path following a branch and proceed with D, AG, and DF (but not PA or EX if it includes PA). Since a bigger savings occurs when the in-line path is successfully predicted, that path is guessed even if the target path actually occurs more frequently. Thus, up to a point it is better to guess in-line, even though it is frequently wrong.

There are secondary issues, however. Branch prediction carries the penalty of increasing I-references. These extra I references might cause a cache or TLB miss. A miss causes suspension of processing while code or a virtual address (which might not have been needed) is readied.

Ignoring secondary issues, for an R/M architecture with the following template, we want to find the minimum probability of target path selection for which it is better to predict the target path.

$$\text{IF} \quad \text{IF} \quad \text{D} \quad \text{AG} \quad \text{AG} \quad \text{DF} \quad \text{DF} \quad \text{EX} \quad \text{EX}$$

The first issue to be considered is the I-buffer (IB) configuration. From the earlier discussion, we can avoid a run-out delay if the in-line path has the following number of IB entries:

$$1 + \left\lceil \frac{2 \text{ cycle/I} - \text{fetch}}{\# \text{ of Instr/I-fetch}} \right\rceil.$$

Since (from Table 3.2) the typical R/M instruction length is less than 4^B, there are more than two instructions in an 8-byte IF. Only two 8^B buffers are required. We assume one double word (8^B) of target is also available.

At issue is determining the strategy (guess in-line or guess target) to minimize the expected branch penalty.

Now compute the four penalties:

(a) Guess in-line and the code goes in-line.

(b) Guess in-line and the code goes to the target.

(c) Guess target and the code goes to the target.

(d) Guess target and the code goes in-line.

(a) Guess in-line and go in-line.

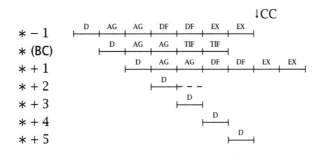

The CC is set before ∗ + 1 enters EX and therefore no penalty is incurred.

(b) Guess in-line and go to target.

Unless the TIF captures both the target and its successor completely (the target is aligned on a double word boundary), we need a 6-cycle delay (shown) to restore processing.

Guessing on Branches

It is easy for designers and researchers to become preoccupied with the correct prediction of branch outcome. Correct prediction of a conditional branch outcome merely changes the branch penalty from that of a conditional branch to that of an unconditional branch—the unconditional branch penalty remains.

Since the delays for a branch going in line and to the target are not symmetric, it is *not* the best strategy simply to guess the most probable outcome for the branch. This is clearly demonstrated in the preceding study.

In general, the much simpler strategy of guessing in-line on a conditional branch is a very cost-effective strategy. This can be made especially effective if the compiler recognizes this and rearranges the code so that the in-line path is preferred.

(c) Guess target and go to target.

$\downarrow$CC

```
* − 1       D   AG   AG   DF   DF   EX   EX
            ├───┼────┼────┼────┼────┼────┼───┤
* (BC)          D   AG   AG   TIF  TIF
                ├───┼────┼────┼────┼───┤
T                        D'             D
                         ├──┤           ├──┤
T + 1           IF'  IF'  D'        IF  IF   D
                ├───┼────┼───┤      ├───┼───┼───┤
```

The four-cycle delay here is the same as that seen in an unconditional branch. By guessing the target path, we have made sure that the primary path and both words of the IB are filled before $T + 1$ decodes, so further delays are avoided.

(d) Guess target and go in-line.

$\downarrow$CC

```
* − 1       D   AG   AG   DF   DF   EX   EX
            ├───┼────┼────┼────┼────┼────┼───┤
* (BC)          D   AG   AG   TIF  TIF
                ├───┼────┼────┼────┼───┤
T                                       D
                                        ├──┤
* + 1                    D'             D
                         ├──┤           ├──┤
* + 2           IF   IF   D'                 D
                ├───┼────┼───┤               ├──┤
```

The target strategy is not invoked until the end of $*$ decode. By this time, both instructions $* + 1$ and $* + 2$ have begun to be fetched from the cache. Either we discard the $* + 2$ I-fetch or we use an additional word of alternate path IB to hold this information, since it has already begun IF. Assuming the latter situation, the penalty is 5 cycles.

Let P = probability that the branch is taken.

Guess target: Delay $= 4P + 5(1 − P)$.

Guess in-line: Delay $= 6P + 0(1 − P)$.

We should guess target if $6P \geq 4P + 5(1 − P); P \geq 5/7 = .71$

Study 4.7   More on Static Branch Prediction

Assumptions:
   This study uses the same assumptions as study 4.6, only here we complete the analysis begun there using the actual data from Chapter 3 to determine the advantage of static prediction over a simple in-line strategy, at least for this particular machine with its particular constructs.

Using the data on branch opcode distribution in Tables 3.4, 3.5, 3.10, and the timing template of study 4.2, we now evaluate the effect of selectively guessing target vs. in-line paths on branch. The guessed path proceeds up to EX (but no out-of-order execution) until the CC is set. Assuming a scientific environment and an R/M processor, we want to create a guess strategy based on opcode type and CC mode tested (i.e., identify unconditional BCs). We then compute the actual (weighted) branch penalty (CPI) based on the created strategy, and compare it to a simple "choose in-line" strategy. An in-line strategy means if there is a choice, choose in-line. There is no choice on unconditional branches.

The BCR and BALR (Table 1.14) with target address already in a register take the equivalent of only one cycle of AG (actually a general-purpose register to PSW transfer cycle).

In order to find the fraction of each branch instruction that uses an AG as a percent of all instructions, we compute a frequency for each instruction class. For example, BRs and BCs are computed as 72.5% (Table 3.10) times 82.6% (branches that use AG, Table 3.10) times 15% (Table 3.4)—this is split into two categories by the data in Table 3.10.

	Opcode	% of Instr	% Taken
BRR	uncond	0.4	100%
BCR	cond	1.5	54%
		1.9	
BR	uncond	1.8	100%
BC	cond	7.2	54%
		9.0	
BALR		0.5	100%
BAL		2.1	100%
Loop Control		1.5	91%

(a) For BRR (unconditional) or for BALR (one-cycle AG, address is in register):

Target penalty = 3 cycles

(b) For BCR (true conditional):

If we guess in-line and go in-line, we have:

that is, zero penalty.

If we guess in-line and go to the target, we have:

```
                                            D
TI                  |—D'—|               |———|
TI+1                    |—D'—|        |——+——+——|
                                       IF   IF   D
                                       (assuming TI+1 is not in IB)
```

In-line penalty = 0 cycles
Target penalty = 6 cycles

If we guess the target and go in-line we have:

```
                                            D
∗ + 1               |—D'—|               |———|
```

If we guess the target and go to the target, we have:

```
                            D'           D
TI                  |—D'—|            |———|
TI+1                        |——+——+——|
                              IF   IF   D
```

In-line penalty = 5 cycles
Target penalty = 3 cycles

Let P = the probability of branch going to target. Then expected in-line delay is $6P + 0(1 - P)$; expected target delay is $3P + 5(1 - P)$. Then we should guess the target path if

$$3P + 5(1 - P) < 6P \rightarrow P > 5/8.$$

(c) For BR (unconditional) or for BAL:

```
          D    AG   AG   TIF   TIF
∗ = BR   |——+——+——+——+——|
                                    D
TI             |—D'—|            |———|· · ·
TI+1                      |——+——+——|· · ·
                            IF   IF   D
```

Target penalty = 4 cycles

(d) For BC (conditional branch):
```
          D    AG   AG   DF    DF    EX    EX
∗ − 1    |——+——+——+——+——+——|
          D    AG   AG   TIF   TIF
∗ = BC   |——+——+——+——+——|
```

If we guess in-line and go in-line:
```
                          D
∗ + 1                   |———|
```
that is, zero penalty.

If we guess in-line and go to target:
```
                                        D
TI                                    |———|
TI+1                                |——+——+——|
                                     IF   IF   D
```
In-line penalty = 0 cycles
Target penalty = 6 cycles

If we guess target and go in-line:∗
```
                                        D
∗ + 1                                 |———|
```
∗ Assumes in-line instructions already fetched are kept in IB.

If we guess target and go to target:
```
                                    D
TI                                |———|
TI+1                           |——+——+——|
                                IF   IF   D
```

In-line penalty = 5 cycles
Target penalty = 4 cycles

Then we should guess the target path if
$$4P + 5(1 - P) < 6P \rightarrow P > 5/7.$$

(e) For loop control:

∗   D   AG   AG   TIF   TIF   EX   EX

* Note: we assume that the target is fetched *before* the loop arithmetic is completed (EX) to avoid EX conflict with other instructions.

If we guess in-line and go in-line, we have (remember, no conditional EX):

∗ + 1   D   AG   AG   DF   DF   EX   EX

If we guess in-line and go to target, we have:

TI   D'   D
TI+1   D'   IF   IF   D

In-line penalty = 1 cycle
Target penalty = 7 cycles

If we guess target and go in line:

∗ + 1   D

If we guess target and go to target:

TI   D
TI+1   IF   IF   D

In-line penalty = 6 cycles
Target penalty = 4 cycles

Then we should guess the target path if:
$$4P + 6(1 - P) < 7P + 1(1 - P) \rightarrow P > 5/8.$$

P = probability of branching.

Penalty = (taken penalty ∗ P + in-line penalty ∗ $(1 - P)$) ∗ frequency of instruction.

Remember, the in-line strategy means if there is a choice, choose in-line. (There is no choice on an unconditional branch.)

Once we have computed the "best" static strategy, we compute the penalty based on that strategy. For example, for BCR, our analysis shows that we should guess in-line. The penalty for guessing in-line on BCR is the frequency of BCR times the sum of the expected in-line penalty (frequency × penalty) and the expected target penalty = (0 cycles × 0.46 + 6 cycles × 0.54) 0.015 = .049 cycles.

The in-line strategy is simply to fetch in-line on branch, except when the branch is unconditional. The only difference in strategy is for the loop control instructions, but the net change was only 0.04 CPI, or about 5%.

Table 4.12   Choosing strategies.

Opcode +Mode	Best Static Strategy	Cycles Penalty	In-line Strategy	Cycles Penalty
BRR uncond	target	0.01	target	0.01
BCR	in-line	0.05	in-line	0.05
BR	target	0.07	target	0.07
BC	in-line	0.23	in-line	0.23
BALR	target	0.02	target	0.02
BAL	target	0.08	target	0.08
Loop control	target	0.06	in-line	0.10
		0.52 CPI		0.56 CPI

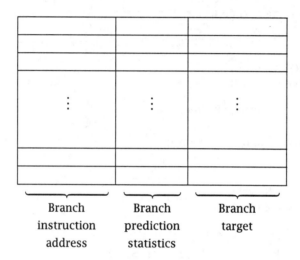

Branch instruction address	Branch prediction statistics	Branch target

Figure 4.23   Branch target buffer (BTB) organization.

4.5.4   Branch Target Capture: Branch Target Buffers

The branch target buffer (Figure 4.23) captures the target instruction (or at least the target instruction address after a taken branch). Each branch target buffer (BTB) entry has three fields: the address of a previously executed branch instruction, branch prediction information, and the most recent target instruction or target address for that branch. (The target address is not necessary for predictive purposes, but is valuable because it enables the initiation of the target fetch earlier in the pipeline, since it is not necessary to wait for the address generation to complete.) The BTB functions as follows: the instruction fetch stage compares the instruction address to the instruction addresses in the BTB. If there is a match, then a prediction is made as to whether the branch is likely to be taken. If the prediction is that the branch will occur, then the target instruction is used as the next instruction. When the branch is actually resolved, at the execute stage, the BTB can be updated with the corrected prediction information and target,

Table 4.13 Fraction of branch targets found to have changed from previous execution of that branch.

Workload	Probability of Target Change
Compiler	4.2%
Business	2.1%
Scientific	4.4%
Supervisor state	1.4%

Table 4.14 Branch target address buffer hit ratio (organized as a LRU stack).

n Entries	Mix Definition			
	Compiler	Business	Scientific	Supervisor State
1	0.031	0.121	0.158	0.012
2	0.075	0.150	0.223	0.066
4	0.185	0.212	0.272	0.154
8	0.298	0.247	0.402	0.259
16	0.369	0.315	0.636	0.275
32	0.514	0.412	0.693	0.301
64	0.634	0.624	0.812	0.435
128	0.769	0.832	0.953	0.545
256	0.888	0.929	0.970	0.615
512	0.967	0.968	0.993	0.672

and, if necessary, the pipeline can be flushed if the actual target differs from the stored target (an infrequent event; see Table 4.13).

The effectiveness of such a branch target buffer depends on its *hit ratio*—the probability that a branch is found in the BTB at the time it is fetched. Table 4.14 shows the hit ratios for various sizes of branch target buffers, where an entry is created whenever a branch is recognized and a global LRU replacement algorithm is used to remove the least recently used (executed) branch in the BTB in order to place a new entry into the BTB.

The BTBs described previously that contain the target instruction(s) [129] are sometimes called *target instruction buffers* (TIB). TIBs have been used in implementations such as the AMD 29000.

BTBs (or TIBs) can be used quite well in conjunction with the I-cache. Suppose we have a configuration as shown in Figure 4.24. The IF is made to both BTB and I-cache. If the IF "hits" in the BTB, the target instruction that was previously stored in the BTB is now fetched and forwarded to the processor at its regularly scheduled time. The processor will begin the execution of the target instruction.

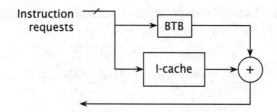

Figure 4.24   Typical BTB structure. If "hit" in BTB, then BTB returns target instruction to processor; CPU guesses target. If "miss" in BTB, then cache returns branch and in-line path; CPU guesses in-line.

Consider the following timing sequence:

```
         IF    IF    D    AG    DF    DF    EX    EX
* – 1    ├──┼──┼──┼──┼──┼──┼──┼──┤
               IF    IF    D    AG    TIF   TIF
* = BC         ├──┼──┼──┼──┼──┼──┤
                ↓

BTB hit        ├──┤
                                  D
Next                        ├──┼──┤
                      IF    IF    D
Next + 1              ├──┼──┼──┤
```

The BTB provides both the target instruction and the new PC (usually the latter is unnecessary when a branch adder is available). There is now no delay on a taken branch *so long as the branch prediction is correct.* Note that the branch itself must still be fetched from the I-cache and be fully executed. If either the AG outcome or the CC outcome is not as expected, all instructions in the target fetch path must be aborted. Clearly, no conditionally executed (target path) instruction can do a PA, as this would make it impossible to recover on a misprediction.

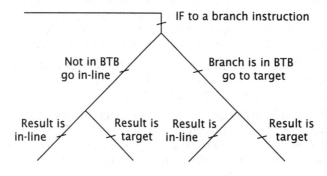

Figure 4.25   BTB outcome tree.

Consider now what happens when the BTB contains target addresses only:

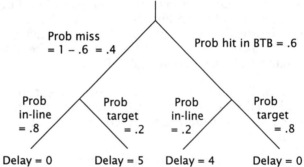

Again, there is no branch delay on correctly guessed branches. With the above template, it is only necessary to have addresses in the BTB. Of course, this depends on the particular timing template.

Figure 4.25 shows the tree of possible outcomes. The expected delay for branches can be computed as shown in the following study.

Study 4.8 Branch Target Buffer

What is the delay due to a branch instruction?

First, we represent the outcome tree:

```
                                        |
                                       / \
              Prob miss              /     \      Prob hit in BTB = .6
              = 1 – .6 = .4        /         \
                                  /             \
         Prob        Prob         Prob        Prob
         in-line     target       in-line     target
         = .8        = .2         = .2        = .8

       Delay = 0   Delay = 5    Delay = 4   Delay = 0
```

Next, we sum up the expected outcome delay:

$$(.6)(.8)(0) + (.6)(.2)(4) + (.4)(.2)(5) + (.4)(.8)(0) = 0.88 \text{ cycles.}$$

Note that without the BTB, if we had simply guessed in-line, we would have a significantly larger penalty.

$$\begin{aligned}
\text{Prob (go in line)} &= (.4)(.8) + (.6)(.2) \\
&= .44 \\
\text{Prob (go to target)} &= .56.
\end{aligned}$$

Assume that the in-line delay is 0, while the target delay is 5 cycles:

$$\text{Expected delay} = .44(0) + .56(5) = 2.8 \text{ cycles.}$$

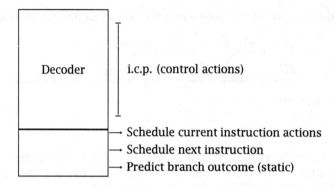

Figure 4.26   Decoder for a pipelined processor.

4.6   Interlocks

4.6.1   Decoder and Interlocks

In a well-mapped machine, the decoder is simply the sum of the micro-programmed routines and support hardware (or logic equations) that realize each of the operations in the machine vocabulary (See chapter 1.) In pipelined machines, several instructions are in execution during each cycle. In these machines, when an instruction is decoded, it is insufficient for the decoder to provide only control point and sequencing information. Proper execution *depends* on the other instructions in the pipeline. Thus, the decoder (Figure 4.26) must additionally determine:

1. Scheduling of the current instruction. The current instruction may be delayed if a data dependency (AG) is recognized or if an exception arises—e.g., *not in TLB* notification, cache miss, etc., from a preceding instruction.

2. Scheduling of subsequent instructions. Later instructions may be delayed if, for example, the current instruction is in the "run-on" class so as to preserve order of execution.

3. Strategic path selection on branch instruction.

In mainframes, in order to speed instruction execution, only the execution unit is microprogrammed—the rest of the processor has fixed control. Thus, a single microinstruction can contain necessary controls and state information.

The data interlocks (sub-unit D in Figure 4.12) may also be part of the decoder. This sub-unit determines *register* dependencies and schedules the entry of the decoded instruction into the AG and EX units so as to ensure proper action. (See study 4.9.) The interlocks must ensure that the current instruction does not *use* (depend on) a result of a previous instruction until that result is available.

The "run-on" controller performs a similar function on *subsequent* instructions—ensuring that they do not enter the pipeline until the execution unit is scheduled to complete the current "run-on" instruction, thus preserving the execution order.

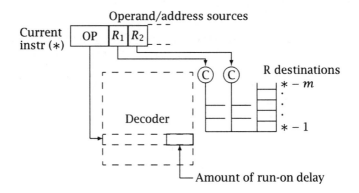

Figure 4.27   Interlocks.

The effect of the interlocks (Figure 4.27) is that for each instruction as it is decoded, its source registers (for operands or addresses) must be compared against the destination registers of previously issued but uncompleted instructions to determine dependencies. The opcode itself usually establishes the number of EX cycles required. If this exceeds that number specified by the timing template, subsequent instructions must be delayed by that amount to preserve in-order execution.

The store interlocks (E) perform the same function as the data interlocks for storage addresses rather than registers. On store instructions, the address generated must be sent to the store interlocks so that subsequent reads either from the AG (data reads) or the IB (instruction reads) can be compared with pending stores and dependencies detected.

4.6.2   Bypassing

Bypassing (sometimes called *forwarding*) is accomplished by a data path that routes a value from a source (usually an ALU) to a user (perhaps also the ALU), bypassing a designated destination register. Especially for static pipelines, this allows the value produced to be used at an earlier stage in the pipeline than would otherwise be possible. Bypassing can also be used at the instruction level, where instruction dependencies arise from the use of a designated register rather than the value in that register. Instruction level bypassing is discussed later in this chapter.

At the pipeline level, the bypass data path routes results from ALU (EX) or from storage (as in an LD instruction, DF) to either the address generate (AG) unit or to the ALU (EX). Thus, in a timing template such as:

$$\begin{array}{ccccc} D & AG & DF & EX & PA \\ \vdash & + & + & + & \dashv \end{array}$$

↓result available

a subsequent instruction can only use the register after PA without bypassing. With bypassing, the result could be available after the EX (or after the DF in case of an LD instruction, as shown in examples 4.2 and 4.3).

EXAMPLE 4.2   ALU BYPASS

Suppose we have the following sequence of two ADD instructions, in which (2) depends on (1). We look at the effect of ALU bypass on instruction (2).

          1. ADD R3, ALPHA

Without ALU bypassing:

          2. ADD R3, BETA

With ALU bypassing:

          2. ADD R3, BETA

◆

EXAMPLE 4.3   AG BYPASS

Now we look at the effect of AG bypass on instruction (2).

          1.LD R3, ALPHA

Without AG bypass:

          2.ADD R4, BETA[R3]

With AG bypass:

          2.ADD R4, BETA[R3]

◆

4.6.3   Address Generation Interlocks

An *address generation interlock* (AGI) condition exists whenever an instruction requires a register for its operand address calculation but the register is unavailable because it will be written by some preceding, uncompleted instruction. (See previous examples.)

A pipeline designer can reduce, and in some cases eliminate, address generation delays by incorporating bypasses at appropriate points in the pipeline. As in the example, an address generate bypass routes an ALU value (EX) or a DF value directly to the address generator (without PA). We may estimate this effect by using the data in Table 3.19. For example, if there were three stages between address generation (AG) and putaway (PA), then the performance degradation experienced without bypassing (as seen in Chapter 3) would be:

$$\text{Distance } 1 = \text{3-cycle loss} \times 0.099 = .297$$

$$\text{Distance } 2 = \text{2-cycle loss} \times 0.084 = .168$$

$$\text{Distance } 3 = \text{1-cycle loss} \times 0.028 = .028$$

$$\text{Distance 4 or more} = \underline{\text{0-cycle loss}}$$

$$\text{Total delay} = 0.493 \text{ cycles/instruction.}$$

Bypassing a result from DF to AG results in only a one-cycle loss, i.e.:

Distance 1 = 1-cycle loss $\times$ 0.099 = 0.099 cycles/instruction
Distance > 1 = 0-cycle loss.

4.6.4 Execution Interlocks and Interlock Tables

An *execution interlock* condition exists where the result register of one instruction is an operand register of a following instruction. This type of interlock can also be dealt with by incorporating bypasses at appropriate points in the pipeline.

For very simple instruction sets and a single execution unit, it is easy to organize the execution facilities of the processor in the form of a bypassed pipeline. Then the execution facilities can accept a new instruction on every cycle.

For most instruction sets, there are complex instructions whose execution requires a substantial process of iteration. (Examples might include floating-point multiplication and division instructions.) Such instructions may not be easily pipelined to accept new operands every cycle without cost increase, since pipelining amounts to the unraveling of the iterations onto a hardware assembly line. Instead, most implementations allow the execution facilities to become busy and hold up the pipeline while the execution proceeds iteratively.

To minimize the performance loss due to execution run-ons, multiple execution resources can be provided; i.e., one or more add/logical units, a multiply unit, a decimal or character string manipulation unit, etc. These units can now be independently scheduled so that execution run-ons are reduced. However, since the units are likely to have different latencies, it is possible that instructions will complete out of order; i.e., an instruction with a relatively short execution time such as an add may be completed before a multiply instruction that preceded the add is completed. This means that a new stage in the pipeline must be defined, one that holds the results of completed instructions until their effects can be propagated in the proper order.

Analysis of the performance impact of such interlocks is based on data such as that shown in Table 3.20.

Cache Access and Priority Interlock Delays

Cache access delays are associated with priority interlocks that are the result of limited bandwidth at various levels in the storage hierarchy. For example, an instruction fetch can be delayed because an operand fetch or store initiated by a preceding instruction takes priority. Also an operand can be delayed when a preceding instruction is storing an operand; the store is given priority when the store buffer is full, and the fetch is delayed. Analysis of such delay is discussed in the next chapter.

Table 4.15   Store/fetch interlock.

Occurrence by Number of Instr between Store and Fetch	Occurrence within This Type of Interlock
0	56%
1	6%
2	4%
3	4%
4	2%
5	1%
6	5%
7	1%
8 or more	21%
Total occurrence of this interlock	7%

Store–Fetch Interlock Delays

A *store-fetch interlock* condition exists whenever an instruction requires an operand from storage but the operand is unavailable because it will be modified by some preceding, uncompleted instruction. Consider the following example, which was found in a major control program by Rymarczyk [250]. The move character instruction (MOVE.C) stores into its operand (workarea) during the last step of its execution, and the subsequent compare character instruction needs to fetch from the modified storage area. Consequently, the compare character instruction is unable to perform its operand fetch step (DF) until after the MOVE.C instruction completes its putaway step (PA), resulting in a substantial pipeline disruption.

```
MOVE.C    WORKAREA, USER
CMP.C     #C, WORKAREA+7
```

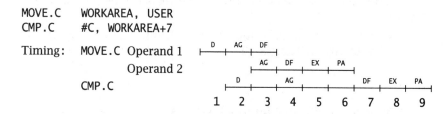

To determine the potential for a store-fetch interlock delay, one needs to know the distribution of distances between instructions that store a result into a particular storage location and those that use this location as an operand source.

This dependency occurs in 7% of the executed instructions; of these, 56% require a fetch based on the preceding instruction's store. Table 4.15 shows a distribution for the general environment.

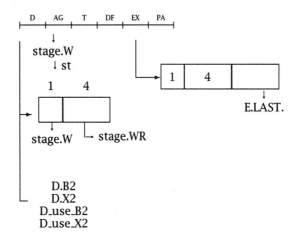

Figure 4.28   Interlock logic.

Study 4.9   Pipeline Interlock and Bypasses

Assumptions:
For this study, we assume a simple timing template with an R/M: S/390-type instruction format.

In this study, we examine the control logic required to interlock a pipelined processor, as well as the extra logic needed to allow for a bypass of the needed data, which reduces the delay. The problem is to design the logic for the address generation interlock, and then to add the bypass logic.

We assume a design typical of a pipelined R/M architecture with a pipeline structure as shown in Figures 4.28 and 4.29. The stages operate as follows:

D — Decode instruction and read registers for address generation. There are 16 GPRs, each 32 bits wide. Depending on the type of instruction, address generation may or may not be required; if it is, it may require one or two registers.

AG — Generate the logical operand address (3-input adder).

T — TLB to translate to a real address.

DF — Fetch operand from cache and align as needed.

EX — Execute the function. Execution may take one or many cycles; on "run-on" (EX of more than one cycle), the E-unit interlocks other operations until it is done. The E-unit always "knows" when it is in the last cycle of execution at the beginning of that cycle.

PA — Write results to register file or store buffer.

Recall the R/M instruction (S/390) layout is as follows:

OP	R1	B2	X2	D2

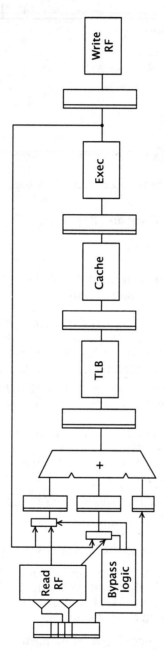

Figure 4.29   Data paths.

Table 4.16   Signals.

Signal	Size	Produced by	Meaning
D.B2	4^b	IR	Base register field from instruction.
D.X2	4^b	IR	Index register field from instruction.
D_use_B2	1^b	Decoder	Is B2 register used by this instruction? Y=1, N=0.
D_use_X2	1^b	Decoder	Is X2 register used by this instruction? Y = 1, N = 0.
Stage.W	1^b	Decoder	Does decoded instruction write into the register set (GPR)? Y=1, N=0.
Stage.WR	4^b	Decoder	GPR number to be written.

with action:

$$R1 \leftarrow R1 \text{ OP Mem} [[B2] + [X2] + D2]$$

and where R1, B2, and X2 each point to one of 16 general-purpose registers (GPRs).

We assume that the register file includes bypass logic. Specifically, if a particular register is being written and read in the same cycle, the register file automatically detects this and bypasses the new value as the result of the read. In the copy of the register used for address generation, we assume that reading register 0 always results in a value of zero. A typical address generation dependency (without the bypass) has the following timing:

```
ADD   R1, D[R2,R3]   |—D—|—AG—|—T—|—DF—|—EX—|—PA—|
LD    R4, D[R1]          |—D—|—AG'—|              |—AG—|—T—|—DF—|—EX—|—PA—|
```

As shown, the load instruction can successfully read R1 for address generation in the same cycle as the PA for the add, resulting in a three-cycle delay. The decoder uses or produces the signals shown in Table 4.16.

This pipeline may have hard-wired control or microcode. In either case, during decode, the logic determines whether the instruction (or microinstruction) writes a GPR in the PA cycle. This information is carried along to each stage of pipeline in two fields of information. In each stage other than D, there is a field named Stage.W that indicates whether the instruction in the stage writes a GPR, and another field named Stage.WR that provides the four-bit identifier of that GPR.

Stage.W and Stage.WR (Table 4.17) are generic labels for register use designators produced by the decoder for each instruction in the pipeline. An instruction in the decoder produces:

Stage.W

Stage.WR

Table 4.17   Stages.

Stage.W	Stage.WR	Register to be Written by Instr
A.W	A.WR	in AG stage
T.W	T.WR	in T stage
F.W	F.WR	in DF stage
E.W	E.WR	in EX stage

When this instruction passes to the AG stage, it becomes A.W and A.WR.

If a pipeline stage is empty, the W bit is false (=0). In the EX cycle, there is another field, E.LAST, which indicates whether this is the last cycle of execution for the current instruction; this information is needed to control the bypass.

Thus, suppose the instruction

    ADD R1, D[R2, R3]

enters the decoder. It generates a one- and a four-bit field:

         .W   .WR

1	0001

As this instruction passes into different pipeline segments (assume only one instruction in a segment at a time), this information is transferred to the stage interlock controller for that segment. Since there are four segments involved, we need four 5-bit registers to hold this information:

                        ↓ in (from decode)

                1   4

	1	4	
AG	A.W	A.WR	↓
T	T.W	T.WR	↓
DF	F.W	F.WR	
EX	E.W	E.WR	

                     ↓ complete

As the preceding ADD instruction passes from stage to stage, its stage interlock information is shifted down one position until execution is complete.

In the D stage, the following signals are also available:

D.B2	Base register field from the instruction.
D.X2	Index register field from the instruction.
D_use_B2	Signal indicating whether B2 register is needed for address.
D_use_X2	Signal indicating whether X2 register is needed for address.

Note that D_use_B2 and D_use_X2 are false if the respective register field in the instruction is zero, since register 0 is never used for address generation.

Now we can formulate the logic to determine whether the current instruction should interlock (and remain) in the D stage due to an address generation dependency. To do so, we need to determine whether any of the stages AG, T, DF, or EX contains an instruction that writes a result into a register needed for address generation by the instruction in D. We need not consider any instruction in the PA stage, since the register file logic automatically provides the right value. In this part of the study, we do not attempt to use the bypass path. We use the following logic:

A_G_Interlock = A.W [D_use_B2 (A.WR = D.B2) + D_use_X2 (A.WR = D.X2)]
+ T.W [D_use_B2 (T.WR = D.B2) + D_use_X2 (T.WR = D.X2)]
+ F.W [D_use_B2 (F.WR = D.B2) + D_use_X2 (F.WR = D.X2)]
+ E.W [D_use_B2 (E.WR = D.B2) + D_use_X2 (E.WR = D.X2)]

The interpretation is straightforward. If the current instruction uses a base or index register (D_use_B2 or D_use_X2), then the register it uses should be checked against registers that are yet to be written. Thus, if the instruction in the AG stage were the ADD R1, D[R2,R3] instruction, A.W would be valid and A.WR = 0001. If the current instruction uses a base register but no indexing, then D_use_B2 = 1 (valid). The A.WR compare against D.B2 then determines whether an interlock is placed on the instruction being decoded. The instruction must be checked for an interlock for all stages. If an interlock is found, the instruction remains in the decoder until the interlock is removed (when the instruction causing the interlock completes execution).

Number of Gates Required   If we assume that all the fields and signals used in the preceding logic equation had to be available even without interlock detection, we can determine the number of additional gates needed to implement the interlock logic. A four-bit comparator can be built with five gates (four XOR and one NOR). There are eight comparisons needed, requiring 40 gates. The rest of the logic requires 12 two-input AND gates, 4 two-input OR gates, and 1 four-input OR. The grand total is 57 gates.

Using the Bypass   Figure 4.29 shows a 32-bit data path from the output of the execution logic to a pair of 2:1 multiplexers in the D stage. With appropriate control logic, the result of an operation in the E stage can be selected in place of the DF outputs and used for address generation a cycle earlier than before. To take advantage of this bypass capability, we need slightly different logic for the A_G_Interlock signal (to avoid the interlock when the bypass becomes available), and we also need two new bypass control signals to control the multiplexors. The following logic equations do the job:

A_G_Interlock = A.W [D_use_B2 (A.WR = D.B2) + D_use_X2 (A.WR = D.X2)]
        + T.W [D_use_B2 (T.WR = D.B2) + D_use_X2 (T.WR = D.X2)]
        + F.W [D_use_B2 (F.WR = D.B2) + D_use_X2 (F.WR = D.X2)]
        + E.W [D_use_B2 (E.WR = D.B2) + D_use_X2 (E.WR = D.X2)] $\overline{\text{E.LAST}}$

Bypass_B2 = E.W D_use_B2 (E.WR = D.B2)
Bypass_X2 = E.W D_use_X2 (E.WR = D.X2)

The interlock logic is identical except for including $\overline{E.LAST}$. This means a register dependency caused by an instruction in the E stage ceases to cause the interlock in its last EX cycle.

The bypass controls can be very simple, since they only have to work if the D cycle is not interlocked. In particular, the bypass controls need not consider E.LAST. If the causing instruction is in the EX stage but not yet in its last cycle, the instruction in D is interlocked, so it makes no difference which way the MUX controls are set.

It is interesting how little extra control logic is needed to allow this bypass. The logic for the interlock signal still takes the same number of gates, but one of the two-input AND gates changes to a three-input AND. Each of the two bypass signals requires only a single three-input AND. Clearly, the control logic for such a bypass is trivial. Most of the logic needed is in the multiplexors in the data paths, where the bypass requires 64 2:1 multiplexors. In actual designs, whether to implement such a bypass or not depends on details of the data path implementation and timing.

The Cost of Interlocks

The preceding example may tend to give the impression that interlocks are not overly significant in the design of a processor. That would certainly be a wrong assumption. Even if, in a simple, static pipelined processor, they do not add greatly to the hardware gate count, the design effort to fully ensure correct operation can be considerable. Issues such as the integrity of state and buffer information on interrupt, the restoration of such data after interrupt, instruction retry after an error has been detected—all must be managed (in part) through the interlock control circuits. Dynamic pipelines with timing templates of unequal length further increase design complexity.

In an effort to present essential elements of processor control and optimization, we skip over much of the detailed elements of the interlock/control design. As any pipelined processor designer knows, a great deal of engineering effort is required to efficiently realize a fully functional set of interlocks!

4.7   Run-On Delay

As we saw in study 4.3, we can compute the effect of long EX instructions by finding the difference between the total execution latency and the number of EX cycles that an instruction may use *before* causing a delay in the scheduled time for PA. We referred to the number of EX cycles the instruction may use before affecting PA as E_0. This is usually one or two cycles, but can be larger, as in the case of L/S processors with relatively fast ALU instructions and slower LD/ST instructions. The MIPS R4000 described earlier has $E_0 = 4$ (half) cycles.

Table 4.18 illustrates the execution delays for some recent microprocessors.

Table 4.18   Estimated arithmetic delays (EX) in some current microprocessors.

E_i	IBM RS/6000	HP PA-RISC 1.1	MIPS R4000*
E_0	1	1	4
ADD/SUB	1	1	1
MPY	5	3	12
DIV	20	10	76
ADD.F	2	3	4
MPY.F	2	3	6
DIV.F	19	12	22

* in half cycles. Run-on delay = $E_i - E_0$. If $E_i - E_0 < 0$, then the run-on delay is 0.

The total run-on effect is simply:

$$\text{Run-on delay} = \sum (E_i - E_0) w_i,$$

where w_i is the fraction of occurrence of instruction type i and E_i is its number of EX cycles. If $(E_i - E_0)$ is negative, then it is treated as a zero entry in the run-on delay summation.

4.8   Miscellaneous Effects

The following study illustrates what can happen to machine performance when stores occur into locations that are close to the current area of instruction execution. Machines tend to make the worst possible assumptions (to err on the side of safety) about the behavior of instructions in execution.

4.8.1   Store in Instruction Stream Delay

This delay occurs when a store address falls within the address range of the instructions already in the pipeline and instruction fetch buffer; these instructions are discarded, and instruction fetching is reinitiated when the store is completed. study 4.10 illustrates the resulting problem.

Fortunately, self-modifying programs have been recognized as being undesirable for other reasons and are relatively rare; but even if the instruction *code* is not self-modifying, it may appear to be so if it is intermixed with data variables.

Study 4.10   Delays Due to Apparent Stores into the Instruction Stream

Assumptions:
This study uses a simple timing template similar to the ones used earlier in the chapter. Since only load, store, and branch

instructions are used in the example, the architecture could be R/M or L/S. This study also assumes an I-buffer with a primary path consisting of two 8-byte-wide entries and a target path of one 8-byte buffer entry. This study is taken from Rymarczyk [250].

Some coding practices (e.g., storing parameters in the instruction stream) degrade the performance of fully pipelined processors by forcing interlock mechanisms into serializing non-dependent code [250]. Many machines do not allow such practices by forbidding writes to code segments. Assuming such writes are allowed, we evaluate the effect of each (apparent) dependency in the following code:

```
          LD   R5, 0[R6,R7]
          ST   ARGLIST, R5
          LD   R5, 4[R6,R7]
          ST   ARGLIST+4, R5
          BAL R2, SUBROUTINE
ARGLIST: X
          X
```

For IF → IB ⊢──IF──┼──IF──┤

The timing templates, excluding IF, are:

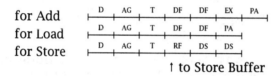

↑ to Store Buffer

For I-fetch, an I-buffer is used consisting of two 8-byte memory word buffers (double word aligned) for in-line buffering, and one 8-byte buffer for TIF. The in-line IB is managed "round robin"—as soon as the last byte from an IB word is transmitted to the 4-byte IR, the fetch of the next eight bytes in the in-line path begins. (This will be two double words ahead, as the next double word ahead is in the other IB word.) The transmission of four bytes of IB to IR occurs while the current instruction is being decoded. Thus, at the beginning of the decode of ∗, an instruction that exhausted an IB word, a new fetch begins. (LD, ST, BAL are RM instructions, and are four bytes each.)

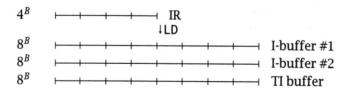

The first load brings four bytes into IB #1, and IB #2 has just been loaded. Assume that either a store into one of the I-buffers or the anticipated next IF invalidates the contents of both IB #1 and #2. Also assume that an IF is checked against any addresses pending in the store buffer. Figure 4.30 shows the contents of the two I-buffers at various times.

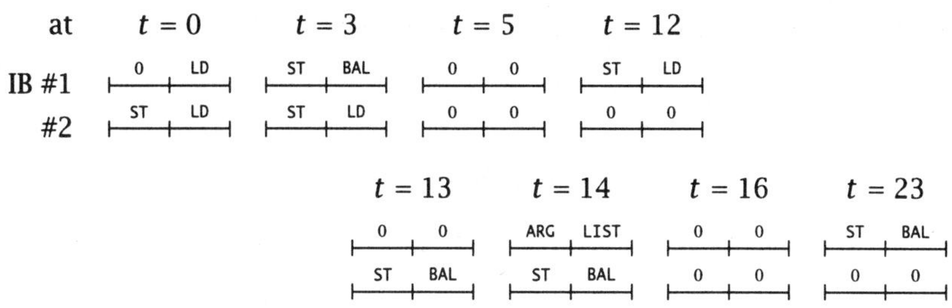

Figure 4.30 Contents of the I-buffers.

A plausible timing for the study code is shown in Figure 4.31. At $t = 0$, we assume that the first three instructions are already in the two IB words, as shown. At $t = 1$ the (first) LD instruction passes into the decoder and an IF begins to fetch the next eight bytes of instruction into IB #1. This completes at $t = 3$, when instructions 4 and 5 are now in IB #1. When the address generate (AG) and translate (T) completes for instruction 2 (ST), it is found that the destination is within a few bytes of the current instruction. Since this is an unusual occurrence, further checking is not done; rather, the current contents of the IB (#1 and #2) are declared invalid and are to be refetched when the store has completed (at the end of $t = 9$). The IF → IB1 refetches the ST and LD instructions during cycles 10 and 11. Another IF brings the ST and BAL into IB2. The LD is decoded in cycle 12, freeing IB1 (and fetching the contents of ARGLIST into IB1 by cycle 14). Again, at the end of cycle 15, a potential store into the instruction buffer is detected and the IB is invalidated. The store completes in cycle 20, and again (cycles 21 and 22) a final fetch into the IB allows the BAL to be decoded.

Study 4.11   Evaluating the Performance of the Baseline Microprocessor

In this study, we look at the performance of the processor outlined in study 2.3. Our baseline microprocessor is a straightforward design using an L/S instruction set. We assume for the moment that, as is current practice, we have a short pipeline. For the moment, we do not use branch enhancement techniques such as I-buffers, etc. We have the following timing templates:

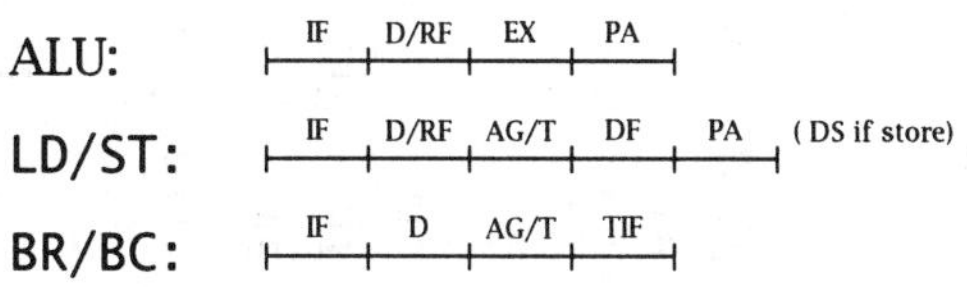

We assume that the register file is accessed during the decode cycle and hence the values are available for either address generation or execution in the cycle following the decode cycle. We also assume that address generation and translation can be done in a single cycle. This is common practice in less aggressive L/S microprocessor designs. More aggressive designs will increase the total number of execution cycles and achieve significantly

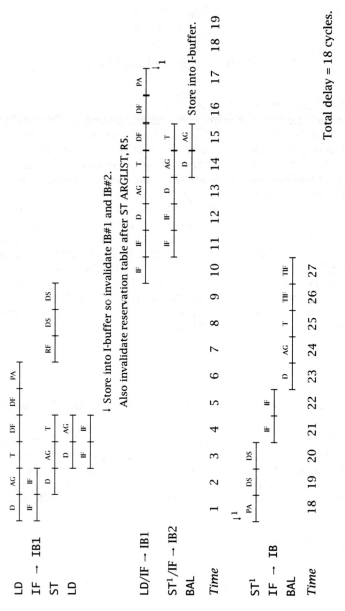

Figure 4.31   Timing for code with apparent stores into the instruction stream.

Software Practices and Benchmarking

Designers try to understand their environment by sampling benchmarks that they believe to be representative of their environment and, at the same time, somewhat control the future usage of the machines by controlling software practices. Depending upon the breadth of benchmarks used in preparing the design, the resultant processor may be very sensitive to particular aspects of new benchmarks [185]. A large and robust sample set of user programs is invaluable in assessing many issues in processor design. This suite of test programs forms the basis of the design process, the basic data and information upon which the design will be based.

In the marketplace, however, users choose their own benchmarks that may or may not have already been considered in the design process. Almost every design team will consider all of the well-known widely available benchmarks in making design decisions. Until the advent of SPEC marks, these better-known benchmarks did not come in a single standardized version, nor were they maintained by some independent agency. They frequently underwent change, modification, and extension.

Yes, Gentle Reader. It has not been unknown for vendors to modify a well-known benchmark and quietly introduce it into the user community. The purpose of the modification may not be particularly to show one's own product at great advantage, but rather to demonstrate a particular "killing flaw" in a rival's product offering.

---

higher clock rates. For the moment, we assume the processor uses a guess in-line branch prediction.

From Chapter 3, the relevant instruction frequency profile derived from Tables 3.4 and 3.14–3.15 is as shown in Table 4.19.

The branch profile is: BR = 2.6%, BC = 10.4%, BC that go to target 54%.

We evaluate the BR penalty as:

BR |—IF—|—D/RF—|—AG/T—|—TIF—|
Target |—D′—| ⋯ |—D—|

or a two-cycle penalty.

The delay due to BC can be determined:

∗ − 1 ALU |—D—|—EX—|—PA—|
∗   BC |—D—|—AG—|—TIF—|
     Target |—D′—| ⋯ |—D—|

Since the CC is set by the end of EX, there is no penalty when the BC goes in line. If the BC goes to the target, the situation is the same as the BR case—a 2-cycle penalty.

Table 4.19   Instruction profiles.

Instruction Profiles	
BR	2.6%
BC	10.4%
IALU[a]	25.8%
IMult	1.2%
IDiv	0.4%
FPAdd	6.5%
FPMult	5.2%
FPDiv	0.4%
Load	30.0%
Store	17.5%
Total	100.0%

[a]This category includes Iadd, shift, compare, etc., and those moves that do not reference memory (i.e., register to register).

$$
\begin{aligned}
\text{BC penalty} \quad &= \quad (0.54 \text{ BC's that go to target})(\text{BC\%})(\text{BC delay}) \\
&= \quad 0.54 \times .104 \times (2.0) = .11 \\
\text{BR penalty} \quad &= \quad (\text{BR\%})(\text{BR delay}) \\
&= \quad 0.026 \times 2 = 0.052 \\
\text{Total branch delay} \quad &= \quad 0.11 + 0.05 = 0.16 \text{ CPI delay}
\end{aligned}
$$

We can now compute the data dependency effects (using Tables 3.19 and 3.20). Because of bypassing, there is no ALU dependency for our baseline processor.

```
        IF   D    EX   PA
*       ├────┼────┼────┤
             IF   D    EX   PA
* + 1        ├────┼────┼────┤
```

However, there is a load-ALU dependency required to keep the PA in order:

```
        IF   D/RF  AG/T   DF   PA
*       ├────┼─────┼──────┼────┤
             IF    D/RF  EX'   EX   PA
* + 1        ├─────┼─────┼────┼────┤
```

There are actually two effects:

1. Since the PA must be done in order (the register store bandwidth is usually limited to one PA per cycle), the ALU PA is delayed one cycle.

2. When the ALU instruction uses the result of the LD, the EX of the ALU is delayed one cycle.

For simplicity, we combine these two effects and assume that both EX (and PA) are delayed one cycle. This is shown above and is manifested as a delay in the ALU instruction that sets the CC immediately before a BC. If the BC goes to the target no additional delay is encountered, but if the BC goes in-line, the CC is set at the end of the cycle in which $* + 1$ should have been decoded. In this simple processor, we assume that decode is not performed until CC is set. This results in a delay of one cycle each time a BC fails (goes in line). This adds a delay of

$$\text{Prob ((BC) and in line) (one cycle)} = .104 \times .46 \times 1 = 0.05 \text{ CPI.}$$

Thus, address dependencies can be caused by any of the following:

$$\text{LD--LD,}$$
$$\text{LD--ST,}$$
$$\text{LD--BR,}$$
$$\text{LD--BC.}$$

We can estimate the occurrence of these events by making the assumption that these instructions occur with independent probability; then:

$$
\begin{aligned}
\text{Prob of dependency event} \quad &= \quad \text{Occurrence of LD preceded by LD/ST/B} \\
&= \quad (\text{Prob LD})(\text{Prob LD/ST/B/}) \\
&= \quad .3 \, (.605) = .18
\end{aligned}
$$

However, simply the occurrence of a potential address dependency does not mean that there is an actual dependency. In a LD–LD instruction pair, not every leading LD references a register used in the subsequent LD address computation. In fact, we know from Table 3.19 that the actual dependency occurs with frequency 0.099. So, the net frequency of an address dependency is:

$$\text{Prob of address dependency} = 0.18 \times 0.099 \doteq 0.02$$

and

$$
\begin{aligned}
\text{Delay due to address dependency} \quad &= \quad 0.02 \, (1.0) \text{ cycle delay} \\
&= \quad 0.02 \text{ CPI delay}
\end{aligned}
$$

For run-on instructions, we simply sum up the execution times of each of the run-on instructions and weight that execution time by their frequency of execution. The run-on instructions that we consider for the baseline processor are:

Instruction	Execution time	Run-on time
MPY.W	3 cycles	2 cycles
DIV.W	15 cycles	14 cycles
ADD.F	3 cycles	2 cycles
MPY.F	3 cycles	2 cycles
DIV.F	15 cycles	14 cycles

$$\text{Run-on delay} = \sum_i w_i (\text{Run-on delay})_i,$$

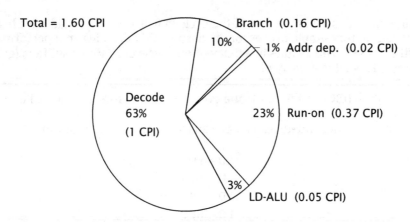

Figure 4.32   Baseline processor performance (without cache).

where w_i is the probability of a particular run-on instruction, corresponding to its frequency of occurrence. For our instruction profile:

Run-on delay = 0.37 CPI delay.

Our processor performance is now determined as:

$$CPI = 1(\text{decoder}) + 0.16(\text{branch delay}) + 0.05(\text{LD–ALU})$$
$$+0.02(\text{addr dep. delay}) + 0.37(\text{run-on delay})$$
$$= 1.60$$

Suppose we are now pressured by our marketing organization to show better performance. What can we (easily) do? Overall, our baseline processor without modification has .67 excess CPI per instruction. Of these, 0.16 are due to branches that can be reduced with a minimum of additional area:

1. We can overlap the branch address generation with branch decode by using a separate branch address adder. So long as the branch target lies within the current page, it requires no translation. This has the effect of changing the branch timing templates to the following:

   BR/BC   ├──IF──┼──D/AG──┼──TIF──┤

   This halves the branch penalty from two cycles to one, and reduces the overall effects of branch from .16 excess CPI to about 0.08.

2. We can also use a small instruction buffer. Suppose we have a 64-bit path from high cache to the instruction buffer. This will not affect the overall timing or delays due to branches, but it will later reduce the possibility of contention at the cache, which at this moment we are not considering.

While there is not much to be (easily) done about data dependencies, we can improve run-on delay simply by changing the application (benchmark) base. Of the run-on delay (.37 cycles per instruction), 0.29 excess CPI is due

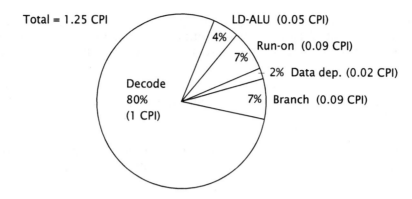

Figure 4.33 Improved baseline processor with branch adder running "integer" benchmarks (no cache misses).

to floating-point instructions when running non-floating point programs. Suppose that in these workstation (or benchmark) applications the instruction profile remains unchanged, except that floating-point instructions are absent. This eliminates 12% of the instructions (we assume floating-point LD and ST are replaced with integer LD and STs). The remaining branch, run-on, and data dependencies are now slightly more frequent. We estimate this effect as amplifying these non-floating delays by $1/(1 - .12) = 1.136$, so that now we have:

$$
\begin{aligned}
\text{Run-on delay} \quad &= \quad \text{Integer run-on delay} \times 1.136 \\
&= \quad (14 \times 0.004 + 2 \times 0.012) \times 1.136 \\
&= \quad 0.09 \text{ excess CPI} \\
\text{Data dependency} \quad &= \quad 0.02 \times 1.136 \approx 0.02 \\
\text{Branch delay} \quad &= \quad 0.08 \times 1.136 = 0.09
\end{aligned}
$$

The new performance is 1.32 CPI. This is shown in Figure 4.33.

Of course, all of this ignores delays in the memory hierarchy, which we discuss in the next chapter.

4.9   Conclusions

Pipelined processors have become the implementation of choice for almost all machines from mainframes to microprocessors. High-density VLSI logic technology, coupled with high-density memory, has made possible this movement to increasingly complex processor implementations.

In modeling the performance of pipelined processors, we generally allocate a basic quantum of time for each instruction and then add to that the expected delays due to dependencies that arise in code execution. These dependencies usually arise from branches, dependent data, or limited execution resources. For each type of dependency, there are implementation strategies that mitigate the effect of the dependency. Implementing branch prediction strategies, for example, mitigates the effect of branch delays.

Dependency detection comes at the expense of interlocks, however. The interlocks consist of logic associated with the decoder to detect dependencies and ensure proper logical operation of the machine in executing code sequences.

Complete analysis requires multiple models with multiple simulators and a well-developed and representative workload, but a good estimate of performance for a representative workload can be found with the linear additive delay model outlined in this chapter.

We will study more complex processors in Chapter 7, after we better understand the role of cache (Chapter 5) and memory (Chapter 6).

4.10   Some Areas for Further Research

Analysis of pipelined processor designs, new algorithms for improving performance, and the organization and analysis of multiple-instruction-issue pipelined machines have become hot topics in computer hardware research. Even a cursory review of any of the recent computer architecture conference proceedings will illustrate the scope of activity and the depth of interest in these areas.

Despite being well studied, pipelined processor design still remains a fruitful research area, since many tradeoffs and optimizations are possible. The basic tradeoff between cycle time and the action completed with the cycle (hence, the number of cycles for instruction execution) remains a key issue. Techniques that improve branch performance, execution run-on, or dependency delay can be important secondary factors in the cycle-time issue. Design techniques that maintain good pipeline performance with a large latency (number of cycles) of instruction execution allow the use of shorter cycles and, potentially, realize higher overall performance.

4.11   Data Notes

Data Note 1:   The Linear Performance Model.

The model of pipeline performance presented here is based on a linear accumulation of various delays. The implicit assumption is that these are delays that occur independently and that their effects on performance are linearly accumulated—that is, they are not overlapped. While generally true, there are exceptions. For example, a divide operation (run-on) may continue despite the fact that a subsequent instruction causes a cache miss. The net effect of this is that the linear accumulation of delays ought to be a conservative estimate of performance. (Dubey [76] presents a more accurate model.)

The difficulty for the designer is in accurately anticipating all of the events that cause delay and properly attributing the frequency of occurrence of these events. The biggest flaw in modeling pipeline processor design is to overlook the occurrence of a generally infrequent event that has a large performance penalty. If crucial applications incur a disproportionately high ratio of the overlooked dependency, the performance objectives will not be met.

Data Note 2:   Branch Prediction.

Tables 4.11 and 4.14 are based upon the work of Lee and Smith [181] and are generally consistent with other work in this field. They are based upon a workload of reasonable diversity and size.

Reliability. The data seem consistent across reported studies.

Stability. The data vary significantly by environment and application. Probably the largest problem facing the designer of a branch enhancement unit is the variance across applications in the occurrence of and profile of the branches in programs.

4.12   Annotated Bibliography

The earliest and best documented efforts at pipelined machine design include the IBM 7030 [46], the CDC 6600 [281], and the IBM 360 Model 91 [17]. Many of the techniques described here are used in older large mainframe processors. These techniques are now being introduced into microprocessor implementations. See also [198, 124] for a discussion of deeply pipelined RISC machines.

Our discussion of branches follows the work of Lee and Smith [181].

Additional Reading

C. Z. Loboz. Measuring transfers of control in program execution–input sensitivity. *Proceedings of the 13th Australian Computer Science Conference*, 1990.

M. Kobayashi. Dynamic characteristics of loops. *IEEE Transactions on Computers*, C-33(2):125–132, 1984.

L. J. Shustek. *Analysis and performance of computer instruction sets.* Ph.D. thesis, Stanford University, May 1978.

Computer Family Evolution

D. P. Siewiorek, C. Gordon Bell, and A. Newell. *Computer Structures: Principles and Examples.* Computer Science Series. McGraw-Hill, New York, 1982.

C. G. Bell, J. C. Mudge, and J. E. McNamara. *Computer Engineering*, Chapter 17: VAX-11/780, W. D. Strecker. Digital Press, Bedford, MA, 1978.

W. Stallings. *Reduced Instruction Set Computers*, 2nd edition. Tutorial Series. IEEE Computer Society Press, Los Alamitos, CA, 1990.

Pipelined Processors

P. M. Kogge. *The Architecture of Pipelined Computers.* McGraw-Hill, New York, 1981.

H. S. Stone. *High-Performance Computer Architecture*, 2nd edition. Electrical and Computer Engineering. Addison-Wesley, Reading, MA, 1990.

Branch Performance

J. A. DeRosa and H. M. Levy. An evaluation of branch architectures. *Proceedings of the 14th Annual Symposium on Computer Architecture*, pages 10–16, June 1987.

J. E. Smith. A study of branch prediction strategies. *Proceedings of the 8th Annual Symposium on Computer Architecture*, pages 135–148, May 1981.

4.13   Problem Set

1. Evaluate the performance (cycles per instruction) of processors based on each of the three templates (IBM 3033, Amdahl V-8, and MIPS R2000, assuming the same ALU operations) described earlier in the chapter. Assume all have the same (unit) cycle time, with the relative decode rate as shown in Section 4.2.1. Treat the "half-cycles" as full cycles. Also assume that the CC is set at the end of the last EX cycle. Follow the assumptions of study 4.3.

2. Repeat study 4.2 for the R/M machine used in that study, but with the following code sequence:

   ```
   LD      R3,          1000[R1,R2]
   ADD     R3,          1008[R1,R2]
   MPY     R4,          2000[R1,R3]
   ST      3000[R1,R3], R4
   BC.NE*  TARGET[R1,R3]
   ```

   *Assume the ADD is the only instruction in this sequence that sets the CC.

   Follow all other assumptions made in study 4.2.

3. Now repeat study 4.3, ignoring "run-on" effects, using design target data (scientific environment) from Chapter 3 for branch and address dependencies for the timing templates for:

   (a) The IBM 3033.
   (b) The Amdahl V-8.
   (c) The MIPS R2000.

   Treat "half-cycles" as full cycles.

4. Repeat study 4.3 using design target data (scientific environment) from Chapter 3. Assume that the only run-on instructions are the variable field length instructions (plus LDM and STM). The R/M architecture described includes these MM instructions. Calculate run-on effects as one EX cycle for each byte in the larger of the source operands. Note that the MM instructions necessarily have an extended timing template (for multiple AG, DF, etc.) and this must be included.

5. Following study 4.4 and the assumptions of problem 1, compare delayed branch and early condition code setting for each of the timing templates. (Note: TIF takes the same number of cycles as a DF.)

   (a) IBM 3033.
   (b) Amdahl V-8.
   (c) MIPS R2000.

   Treat "half-cycles" as full cycles.

6. For the statement $C := A + B$ and the assumptions of study 4.9, find the code and timing for our R/M machine with the IBM 3033 timing template. Again use the assumptions of problem 1.

7. Describe I-buffer arrangements (number of in-line and target registers) suitable to each of the IBM 3033, Amdahl V-8, and MIPS R2000 timing templates and for w (the size of the IF path) = 4 and 8 bytes. Assume branch prediction is used.

8. A certain store buffer has a size of 4 entries. The mean number used is 2 entries.

   (a) Without knowing the variance, what is the probability of a "buffer full or overflow" delay?
   (b) Now suppose the variance is known to be $\sigma^2 = 0.5$; what is the probability of such a delay?

9. Determine an effective static branch prediction strategy for the following timing templates:

   (a) The Amdahl V-8.
   (b) The MIPS R2000.

   Treat "half-cycles" as full cycles. Follow study 4.6, then use data in study 4.7.

10. Modify the interlock of study 4.9 for an L/S architecture and MIPS R2000-type timing template.

11. Suppose the processor timing in study 4.10 was based on a machine with split I- and D-cache (cache miss of 6 cycles). Assume that all the code is initially present as a block in the I-cache, but that a store into a block in the I-cache invalidates that entry. Show the effect on the timing.

12. (a) Suppose a certain processor has the following BC behavior: A three-cycle penalty on correct guess of target, and a six-cycle penalty when it incorrectly guesses target and the code actually goes in-line. Similarly, it has a zero-cycle penalty on correct in-line guess, but a six-cycle penalty when it incorrectly guesses in-line and the target path is taken. The target path should be guessed when the probability of going to the target is known to exceed what percent?

    (b) For an L/S machine that has a 3-cycle cache access and an 8-byte physical word, how many words (each 8 bytes) are required for the in-line (primary) path of an I-buffer to avoid runout?

13. (a) A branch table buffer (BTB) can be accessed while the branch is decoded so that the target address (only) is available at the end of the branch decode cycle.

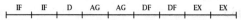

IF   IF   D   AG   AG   DF   DF   EX   EX

For an R/M machine with BTB and timing template as shown in the preceding (one decode each cycle), what is the BR penalty and the BC penalty in cycles? (Assume that all of the BRs and 50% of the BCs hit in the BTB, that 80% of those BC's that hit are actually taken, and that 20% of those BC's that did not hit were actually taken.)

(b) If target instructions are placed directly in the BTB, what is the penalty for BR and for BC in cycles (same assumptions as (a))?

14. Estimate the value (in CPI) of a small BTB for our baseline processor (without branch adder).

Assume a 64-entry BTB (containing target instructions) and a scientific environment (use Table 4.14). Assume a BTB hit actually goes to target 80% of the time and a BTB miss goes in-line 80% of the time.

15. A BTB can be used together with history bits to determine when to place a target in the BTB. This might make small BTB's more effective. Below what size BTB would a 2-bit branch history approach be attractive (for the scientific environment)?

Chapter 5

Cache Memory

5.1 Introduction

As mentioned in chapter 1, the memory system consists of a hierarchy of storage elements (Figure 5.1). Excluding the register set, the cache has the shortest access time, or *latency*, of all the levels of the storage system, and the highest bandwidth. The goal of an effective memory system is that the effective access time that the processor sees is very close to t_0, the access time of the cache. Most accesses that the processor makes to the cache are contained within this level. The achievement of this goal depends on many factors: the architecture of the processor, the behavioral properties of the programs being executed, and the size and organization of the cache.

Caches work on the basis of the locality of program behavior [117]. There are three principles involved (Figure 5.2):

1. **Spatial Locality** — Given an access to a particular location in memory, there is a high probability that other accesses will be made to either that or neighboring locations within the lifetime of the program.

2. **Temporal Locality** — This is complementary to spatial locality. Given a sequence of references to n locations, there is a high probability that references following this sequence will be made into the sequence. Elements of the sequence will again be referenced during the lifetime of the program.

3. **Sequentiality** — Given that a reference has been made to a particular location s it is likely that within the next several references a reference to the location of $s + 1$ will be made. Sequentiality is a restricted type of spatial locality and can be regarded as a subset of it.

Locality is a characteristic of most programs, but it is significantly influenced by the program representation—the architecture. The cache designer must deal with the processor's architecture and accessing requirements on the one hand, and the memory system's requirements on the other. Effective cache designs balance these two factors within the cost constraints of the cache design itself.

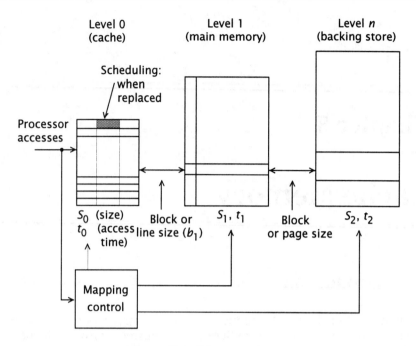

Figure 5.1   Memory space.

5.2   Basic Notions

Processor references that are found in the cache are called *cache hits*. References not found in the cache are called *cache misses*. On a cache miss, the cache control mechanism must fetch the missing data from memory and place it in the cache. Usually the cache fetches a spatial locality called the *line* from memory. The line consists of one or more physical words accessed from main memory. The physical word is the basic unit of access in the memory.

The processor–cache interface can be characterized by a number of parameters. Those that directly affect processor performance (Figure 5.3) include:

1. Access time for a reference found in the cache (a hit) — property of the cache size and organization.

2. Access time for a reference not found in the cache (a miss) — property of the memory organization.

3. Time to initially compute a real address given a virtual address (*not-in-TLB time*) — property of the address translation facility, which, though strictly speaking, is not part of the cache, resembles the cache in most aspects and is discussed in this chapter.

From the cache's point of view, the processor behavior is integral to an effective design. This includes such issues as:

1. The number of requests per cycle—property of the instruction set and the CPU organization.

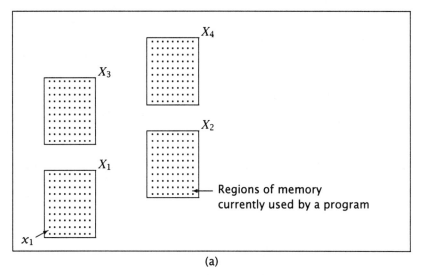

(a)

Spatial locality: If a reference has been made to item x_1, then it is likely that a reference will occur somewhere in region X_1.
Temporal locality: If a sequence of references x_1, x_2, x_3, x_4 have recently been made, then it is likely that the next reference will be one of x_1, x_2, x_3, or x_4.

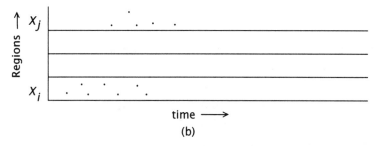

(b)

Spatial locality: References (shown as $\cdot$) tend to cluster into distinct regions. The regions around x_i and x_j contain the recent references (or the working set).

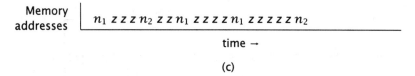

(c)

Temporal locality: References tend to repeat. Memory addresses n_1 and n_2 tend to be repeated in a sequence of references (z indicates any other reference).

Figure 5.2   Localities. (a) General locality. (b) Spatial locality. (c) Temporal locality.

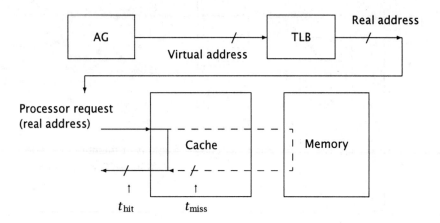

Figure 5.3   Parameters affecting processor performance.

1. Physical word: unit of transfer between CPU–cache.
   Typical physical word sizes:

   > 4 bytes – minimum.
   > 8 bytes – most cases.
   > 16 bytes – maximum.

2. Line size (sometimes called *block* or *page size*):
   Usually the basic unit of transfer between cache and memory. Usually consists of n physical words transferred from main memory as physical words (this is the usual bus size) from n memory modules in n cycles.

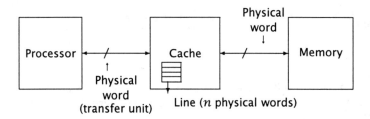

Figure 5.4   Line and physical word.

2. The physical word size (Figure 5.4), or the transfer unit between CPU and the cache.

The primary measure of cache performance is the miss rate. This is the probability of a reference made to the cache that is not found in the cache. The miss rate times the miss time measures the delay penalty due to the cache miss. In most processor designs, the processor ceases activity when a cache miss is encountered. Thus, a cache miss behaves in much the same way as a pipeline break.

Cache Operation and Information Theory

An alternative view of the operation of cache memory is that caches work because of redundancy in the sequence of address requests made to memory by the processor. It is this redundancy that allows the simple demand fetch hardware algorithm to accurately predict the future reference requirements of the processor. In a now well-known study on the subject, Hammerstrom [120]showed that there was generally no more than about 1% information content in an address trace. Given knowledge of past references, 99 bits out of every 100 bits of address reference made by the processor to the memory system are predictable. The remaining bit of information represents the occurrence of references to new localities undeterminable until the time of program execution.

5.3 Cache Organization

A cache may be organized to *fetch on demand* or to *prefetch* data. The former organization, usually referred to as *demand fetch* organization, is the most commonly used and the one that is the focus of this chapter. As the name implies, a demand fetch cache brings a new memory locality into the cache only when a processor reference is not found in the current cache contents (a miss occurs). The prefetch cache attempts to anticipate the locality about to be requested by the processor and thus *prefetches* it into the cache. The prefetch cache has only marginal advantage over a demand fetch cache [259]. Its use is usually restricted to certain I-cache applications.

Within the cache, there are three basic types of organization: (fully) associative mapped (Figure 5.5), direct-mapped (Figure 5.6), and set associative mapped (Figure 5.7, which is really a combination of the other two). In fully associative mapping, when a request is made to the cache, the requested address is compared in a directory against all entries in the directory. If the requested address is found (a *directory hit*), the corresponding location in the cache is fetched and returned to the processor; otherwise, a *miss* occurs.

In a direct-mapped cache, lower order line address bits are used to access the directory (*index bits* in Figure 5.8). Since multiple line addresses map

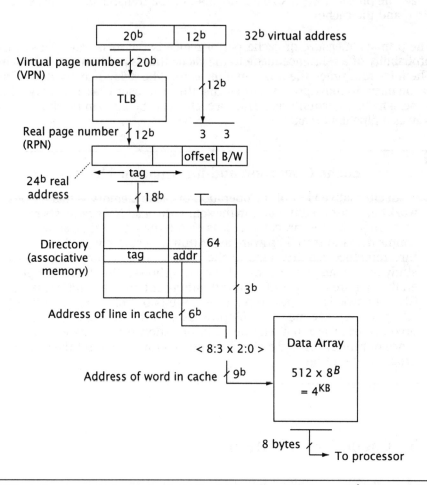

CPU produces a virtual address from the AG function. The lower 12^b (4K pages)
of the virtual address are the same as the real address.

Example:

24^b	real address (real memory size 16^{MB})	
8^B	physical word	
4^{KB}	cache	
64^B	line	
$\therefore$ 64	lines (4K/64) in cache	

Steps of operation:

1. Translate VPN to RPN with TLB.

2. Access the cache directory, then the cache.

3. Access cache with addr from the directory index and offset 9^b bits.

4. If compare valid, enable data to go to processor.

Figure 5.5   Fully associative mapping.

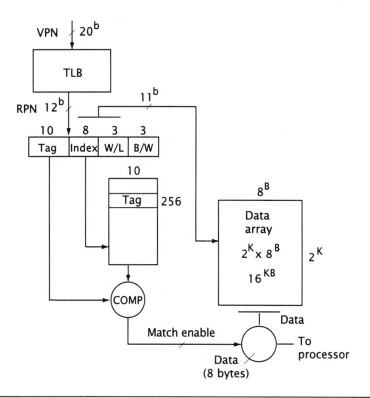

Figure 5.6 Direct mapping.

Example:

24^b	real address
8^B	physical word
16^{KB}	cache
64^B	line
$\therefore$ 256	lines (16K/64) in cache

Advantage— Cache directory and cache are simultaneously accessed.
Disadvantage— Line in memory location maps into only one line in cache.
Steps of operation:

1. Translate VPN to RPN with TLB.

2. Access cache array and directory simultaneously and compare tag with directory entry to ensure correct line is accessed.

3. Access cache array with index and offset (11^b) bits.

4. If compare valid, enable data to go to processor.

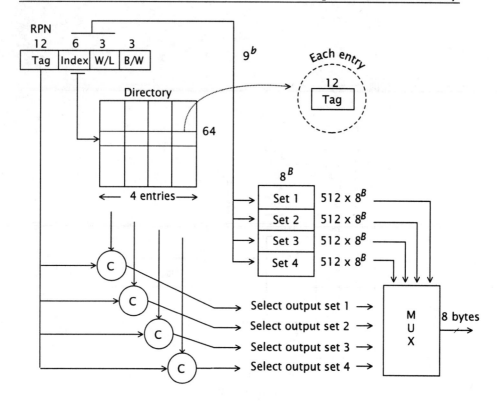

Example:	24^b	real address
	8^B	physical word
	16^{KB}	cache
	64^B	line
$\therefore$	256	lines

Simultaneous access to TLB, directory, and array.

Advantages:

- Has simultaneous access of directory and array.

- Improves locality (hit rate), since now line may lie in one of four locations.

- Fewer higher-order bits involved in directory access. (If only lowest 12^b are involved, the TLB access can occur simultaneously with cache access, since lower bits are unaffected by TLB.)

Disadvantages:

- Uses smaller RAM sizes.

- Additional compares/multiplexing may increase cycle time.

Steps of operation:

1. Translate VPN to RPN with TLB (not shown).

2. Access cache array sets and cache directory entries to ensure correct line is in cache.

3. Compare tags from directory (12^b) with tag address bits.

4. If compare valid, select corresponding set and MUX data to processor.

Figure 5.7   Set associative (multiple direct-mapped caches).

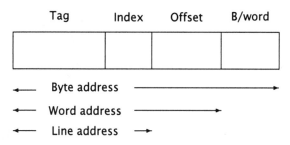

Figure 5.8 Address partitioned by cache usage.

into the same location in the cache directory, the upper line address bits (tag bits) must be compared with the directory address to ensure a hit. If a comparison is not valid, the result is a cache miss, or simply a miss. The advantage of the direct mapped cache is that a reference to the cache array itself can be made *simultaneously with the access of the directory*, with minimum control overhead.

The address given to the cache by the processor actually is subdivided into several pieces, each of which has a different role in accessing data.

Suppose we have a processor address partitioned as in Figure 5.8. The most significant bits that are used for comparison (with the upper portion of a line address contained in the directory) are called the *tag*.

The next field of the address is called the *index* and it represents the bits used to address a line entry in the cache directory. The *tag* plus the *index* represent the line address in memory.

The next field is the *offset* and it represents the address of a physical word within a line.

Finally, the least significant address field specifies a *byte in a word*. These bits are usually of no interest to the cache, since the cache always references a word. (An exception arises in the case of a *write* that modifies only a part of a word.)

The set associative cache operates in a fashion somewhat similar to the direct-mapped cache. Bits from the line address are used to address a cache directory. However, now there are multiple choices: two, four, or more complete line addresses may be present in the directory. Each of these line addresses corresponds to a location in a sub-cache. The collection of these sub-caches forms the total cache array. In a set associative cache, as in the direct-mapped cache, all of these sub-arrays can be accessed simultaneously, together with the cache directory. If any of the entries in the cache directory match the reference address, and there is a hit, that particular sub-cache array is selected and outgated back to the processor. While selection in the outgating process adds somewhat to the cache access time, the set associative cache access time is generally better than that of the associative mapped cache. Still, from an access time consideration alone, the direct-mapped cache provides the fastest processor access to cache data for any given size cache.

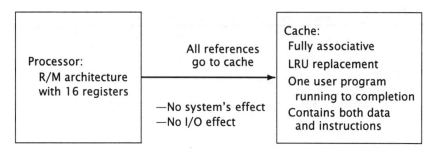

Figure 5.9   Design target miss rate (DTMR).

5.4   Cache Data

Cache size is the primary determinant of cache performance (miss rate). The larger the cache, the lower the miss rate. Almost all cache miss rate data is empirical, and as such has certain limitations. Data based upon older machines, where the memory size was fixed and small, shows the working set being captured by relatively small size caches, since these caches are significant in size relative to the original memory size for these programs. Thus, there is a tendency for the reported miss rate of a particular cache size to increase over reporting time. This is simply the result of measurements made on programs of increasing size. Notwithstanding the difficulty in producing stable design data, Smith [260] has developed a series of design target miss rates (DTMR) that represent a conservative estimate of what a designer should expect from an integrated (instruction and data) cache. These data are presented in Figure 5.10, which covers cache sizes to 256 KB. The data points in this figure represent design target miss rates per reference to memory. They are based upon demand fetch, copyback cache with LRU (least recently used) replacement. Except for 4- and 8-byte line sizes, the data is for a fully associative cache. In the case of 4- and 8-byte line sizes, four-way set associative cache is assumed. The figures show that for large caches, large block sizes or line sizes perform best, the crossover point being about 4–8KB. Large line sizes have better spatial locality and hence reduce the miss rate. Smaller caches have better performance with smaller line sizes. Since there simply are not enough localities captured in the cache with large line sizes, there are not enough temporal localities in the small cache with a large line size. Large line sizes have an added disadvantage not reflected in these figures: increased memory traffic. For example, 4KB both at 64- and 128-byte line sizes give approximately the same miss rate, but the 128-byte line size creates twice as much memory traffic per miss—requiring twice as many bytes to be transferred from memory to cache—to support its operation.

Figures 5.11 and 5.12 show the design target miss rates in light of other studies. In all cases, the design target miss rates represent conservative expectations of cache performance. Some of the studies (e.g., S/360 and CDC 64000) were based on address traces of older machines that did not have cache. As expected, systems code represents the largest overall body of

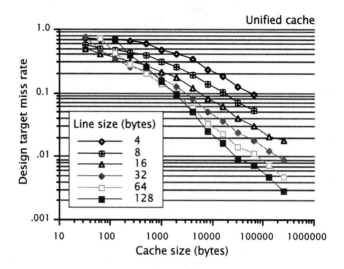

Figure 5.10   A design target miss rate per reference to memory (fully associative, demand fetch, fetch (allocate) on write, copyback with LRU replacement). See appendix A for detailed tables.

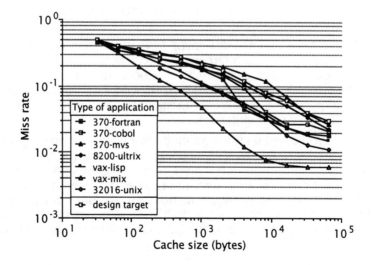

Figure 5.11   Effect of different application environments (fully associative, 16-byte lines).

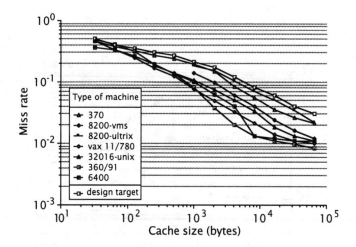

Figure 5.12   Effect of different machine traces.

code and also has the poorest locality. As such only (S/370—MVS) actually exceeds the miss rate projections of the design target miss rate. Overall, however, the DTMR represents a reasonable assessment of expected performance for modern processors.

The processor architecture and its organization play important roles in determining overall cache effectiveness. Better-encoded instruction sets have smaller-sized working sets, and hence they require smaller instruction caches to capture that working set and minimize the miss rate. The instruction working set is most affected by differences in architecture.

The data working set, on the other hand, is not directly affected by instruction set encoding, but is affected more by register set organization and register allocation policy.

Most of the data presented in this chapter is with respect to a reference architecture (Figure 5.9). This reference architecture is our R/M architecture, with 16 registers using a global register allocation. It is the architecture characterized by the chapter 3 design target R/M data. Architectures that do not correspond to the reference architecture (L/S or R+M) require an adjustment of the design target data.

The DTMR data is based on traces of individual programs running through to completion. These relatively large programs present the cache with the opportunity to capture the working set of the program and minimize the miss rate. If the same program were run in an environment that was interrupted (a multiprogrammed environment, or an environment that required a good deal of system services such as I/O), the miss rate would be higher. In an effort to distinguish environments, Smith [259] introduces a Q factor, where:

Q = average number of instructions executed between task switches.

The DTMR data then represent Q exceeding 100,000; the user program is run to completion. We discuss the effect of lower Q's and the presence of the system in later sections.

Table 5.1   DTMR adjustments (detailed tables are found in Appendix A).

Effect	DTMR assumes	Adjust for	Section
Associativity	Fully assoc.	Direct mapped, set assoc.	5.5
Line replacement	LRU	FIFO/random	5.7
Writes	Copyback	Write through (exclude write reference traffic)	5.6
Systems	One user, no systems effect	System, multi-programming transactions	5.8
Instruction set	R/M	L/S	5.10
Type	Integrated	I-cache, D-cache, other	5.9–5.12

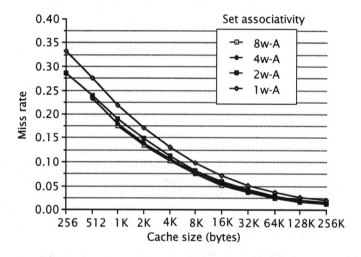

Figure 5.13   Miss rate for different set associativities (16-byte lines).

5.5   Adjusting the Data for Cache Organization

The DTMR data assumes a fully associative cache with LRU replacement. For caches of other design, adjustments must be made to the DTMR data (Table 5.1). Figure 5.13 shows the effect on miss rate of varying degrees of set associativity (16-byte lines). The lower the associativity (i.e., the closer to direct mapped), the poorer the miss rate. This can be expressed as a correction factor for the DTMR. Thus, in Figure 5.14, the relative miss rate data for various cache line sizes and combinations is expressed relative to the corresponding DTMR caches. For a 16-byte line, direct mapped 32-kbyte cache, we would multiply our DTMR miss rate from Figure 5.10 by a factor of 1.45 (given by Figure 5.14).

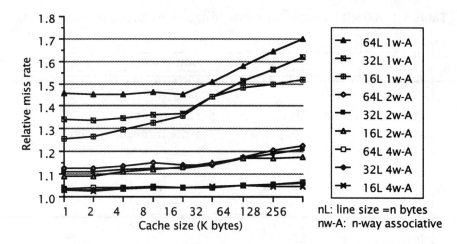

Figure 5.14 Relative miss rate with respect to a fully associative cache. We assume that 8w and higher degrees of associativity behave the same as a fully associative cache.

Table 5.2 Associativity adjustment for DTMR.

Unadjusted MR	< 1%	1–2%	2–6%	6-12%	12-25%
Direct	1.65	1.52	1.38	1.37	1.33
2-way	1.21	1.17	1.14	1.13	1.11
4-way	1.06	1.05	1.04	1.03	1.03

Table 5.2 is an alternative form of the adjustment. Here we find the DTMR rate and use it directly to find the adjustment factor. Table 5.2 basically provides the same overall adjustment as Figure 5.14, but with slightly less resolution and slightly more flexibility. We will use Figure 5.14 when adjusting direct DTMR data, and Table 5.2 when we adjust derived cache data—split caches, caches with systems effects, etc.

For architectures other than the R/M architecture, adjustments can be made for code density of the referenced architecture. We treat these issues in more detail later in this chapter.

A Note on Anomalous Results

The adjusted DTMR may give obviously anomalous or impossible results, such as miss rates over 1.0. These situations may develop for small direct mapped caches. Clearly, the miss rate cannot exceed 1.0. Actually, such caches may still be of practical value, but our data indicate that for some applications, the miss rate will be very poor. The designer cannot prudently rely on such caches unless users and applications developers are made aware of the design limitations.

Cache Data—Should It Be Conservative or Optimistic?

A good deal of confusion arises in comparing cache miss data rate reports from various manufacturers or designers in new product announcements. There are at least four types of literature describing processor/cache performance:

1. Technical descriptions of new processors which frequently cite performance data for the "all in cache" or 100% hit rate environment. This is an attempt to recognize the variability of miss rate across environments, and to give the reader an idea as to the performance of the processor alone, so that the reader may factor in an appropriate cache miss rate.

2. Marketing performance data. Product announcements, especially those prepared by marketing and sales organizations, are notorious for overstating performance. Data cited are usually the best possible that could ever be experienced (and oftentimes well beyond that).

3. Benchmark data. This is commonly cited both by users and designers to typify performance experience; but benchmarks are usually small, and rarely invoke significant systems services. Whatever their value in measuring processor performance, benchmark results applied to cache data are usually suspect. Gee et al. [98] report the miss rate for the well-known SPEC benchmark [74]. While the SPEC floating-point results are generally consistent with the DTMR, the SPEC integer benchmarks had a miss rate significantly lower than the DTMR. (See Appendix C.)

4. Designers' data. If the designer is to make intelligent tradeoffs, conservative and comprehensive data is needed. Certainly, the scope should be well beyond that of benchmark data.

The purpose of this chapter is to provide designer data. The reader will find other sources that indicate a more optimistic expectation for cache performance for a given size. Of course, in any design situation, before completing the design, the designer wishes to understand the response of the system to stressful environments. If the actual user environment is more benign, so much the better. Moreover, there are several factors that one must carefully consider in using empirical cache data. Each of these factors argues for a conservative approach.

1. Historically, as memory prices have decreased, memory capacities have increased. This has promoted the use of applications of increasing size. As program size increases, so does its working set. Figure 5.15 indicates the trend over time of reported cache miss rates.

2. Systems effects, including the effect of the operating system, multiprogramming, and I/O, are rarely adequately accounted for in cache miss projections. Moreover, just as application programs increase in size over time, so also do operating system size and functionality. As the computing environment becomes more sophisticated, its cache miss rate deteriorates.

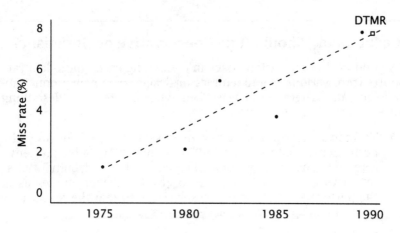

Figure 5.15 Some selected reported miss rates for 8-kbyte caches using 16-byte lines. (Data from machines cited in Figure 5.12 and [240] for 1989.)

5.6   Write Policies

How is memory updated on a write? One could write to both cache and memory (write-through), or write only to the cache (copyback), updating memory when the line is replaced. These two strategies are the basic cache write policies (Figure 5.16).

The write-through cache (Figure 5.16a) stores into both cache and main memory on each CPU store.

> Advantage: this retains a consistent (up-to-date) image of program activity in memory.

> Disadvantage: memory bandwidth may be high—dominated by write traffic.

In the copyback cache (Figure 5.16b), the entire line is stored in main memory on replacement if a write has occurred to that line (a dirty line).

1. Dirty bit is set if a write occurs anywhere in line.

2. From various traces [259], the probability that a line to be replaced is dirty is 47% on average (ranging from 22% to 80%).

3. Rule of thumb: half of the data lines replaced are dirty. So, for a data cache assume 50% are dirty lines and for an integrated cache assume 30% are dirty lines.

1. **Write-through** — In a write-through policy, a write is directed at both the cache and the main memory for every CPU store. This has the advantage of maintaining a consistent (up-to-date) image of program activity in main memory. It has the disadvantage of increasing memory traffic for large caches, as those caches with low read-miss rates may now find the memory traffic to be dominated by the write traffic.

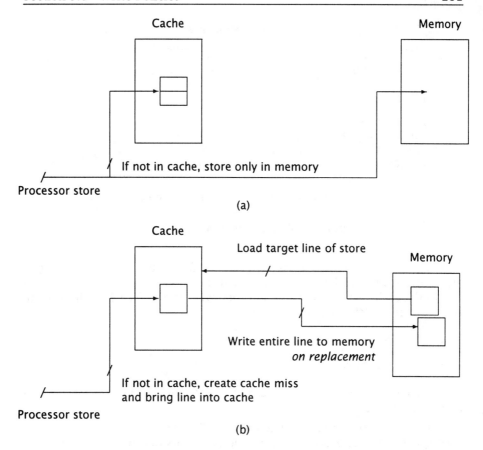

Figure 5.16   Write policies. (a) Write-through cache (no allocate on write);
(b) Copyback cache (allocate on write).

2. **Copyback** — In a copyback policy, the entire line is replaced in main
   memory if a write has occurred into that line. A line which has been
   unaltered when replaced is simply discarded, as the main memory
   continues to retain the correct contents of that line. In copyback,
   the selection of the line to be replaced is usually unaffected by the
   write policy (allocate or non-allocate on write), since that line is usually
   determined by the line replacement strategy (dictated only by reads).
   Thus, when a read miss occurs in copyback, either the new line is
   accessed from main memory and placed in the cache (if the replaced
   line was clean) or the replaced line is first written out and then the
   new line is accessed and put into the cache. Copyback caches require
   an additional bit associated with each line in the cache directory. This
   "dirty bit" is set *on* if a write occurs anywhere in the line. The presence
   of the dirty bit indicates that the line must be written out completely
   to main memory on replacement. For various traces consisting of
   S/370, VAX, and CDC 6400 data [259], the probability of a line being
   dirty is 47% on average, ranging from 22% to 80%. As a rule of thumb,
   we assume for our studies that 50% of the lines replaced from a data
   cache are dirty, and 30% of the lines from an integrated cache are
   dirty.

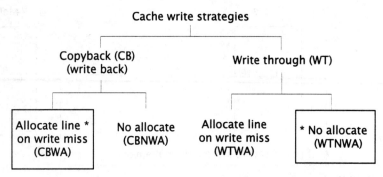

* These strategies are the most commonly used.

Figure 5.17 Possible write strategies.

Suppose the store reference is initially not found in the cache. We can either bypass the cache and store only in memory, or we can *allocate* the line to the cache—cause a miss—and then write into the cache. These write replacement policies are designated:

- "No allocate on write" or

- "Write allocate,"

respectively. Neither policy has a distinct advantage over the other with respect to miss rate.

Usually, write-through caches use the "no allocate" policy, while copyback caches use "write allocate" based on memory considerations (Figure 5.17).

An important consideration in write policy selection is the effect of the decision on memory traffic. Selecting a write-through cache results lower memory traffic with small caches, while selecting a copyback cache results in lower memory traffic with large caches (Figure 5.18). Memory traffic usually is measured by the *memory traffic ratio*, which is simply the ratio of actual memory references (cache + processor) to processor memory references (assuming there was no cache present).

The following example shows a crossover point between two write policies.

EXAMPLE 5.1   EFFECTS OF WRITES ON MEMORY TRAFFIC

Assume the following:

An integrated cache with two references per instruction (one I reference, one D reference). The data (D) references are divided: 68% reads, 32% writes.

30%	dirty lines
8B	physical word
64B	line
5%	read miss rate

Compute the memory traffic for a 5% miss rate for each:

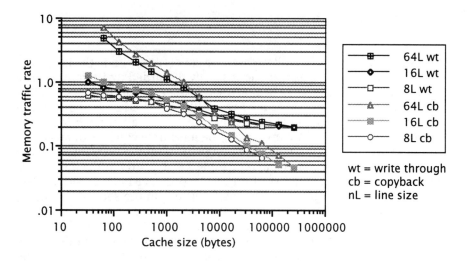

Figure 5.18   Effect of write policy on memory traffic.

1. WTNWA: Write-through (no write allocate), at 5% miss rate.

   100 instructions create 200 references (168 read references and 32 writes). This creates 8.4 read misses or traffic of 8.4 × 8 physical words plus 32 write references. (Assume each takes a physical word.)

   Write-through total: 67.2 + 32 = 99.2 actual references.

   Memory traffic = 99.2/200 = 0.50.

2. CBWA: Copyback (write allocate), at 5% miss rate.

   100 instructions now create 200 cache references and thus 10 misses, but 3 of these require a line write (since this is an integrated cache, we assume that 30% of all lines are dirty). Thus, 13 × 8 = 104 actual references.

$$\frac{104 \text{ references}}{200 \text{ processor references}} = 0.52 \text{ refr/I.}$$

   Memory traffic = 0.52 refr/I.

Conclusion: A 5% miss rate is nearly the crossover point. (See Figure 5.18.) For lower miss rates, copyback reduces memory traffic, while for higher miss rates, write-through reduces memory traffic.

◆

5.7   Strategies for Line Replacement at Miss Time

What happens on a cache miss? If the reference address is not found in the directory, a *cache miss* occurs. Two actions must promptly be taken: (1) the missed line must be fetched from main memory; (2) one of the current cache lines must be designated for replacement by the currently accessed line (the missed line).

5.7.1   Fetching a Line

With a write-through policy, all we need be concerned with is the accessing of the missed line. The replaced line is simply discarded (written over). The access of the missed line may begin either at the start of the line (on a line address boundary) or at the faulted word (the word address that created the read-miss). This second approach is sometimes called *fetch bypass* or *wraparound load.* In the first approach, the miss time consists of an access time to the first word and then (presuming sufficient memory interleaving) the time required to transmit the remaining $L - 1$ words in the line across the memory bus (L, the number of physical words per line). Processing resumes when the entire line has been transmitted. In the second approach, processing resumes as soon as the first word has been accessed and forwarded to the processor. The remaining words of the line are stored in the cache while the processor has resumed processing based upon the initial returned word. This can result in contention for the cache, as both the processor and the memory may simultaneously wish to access the cache. (In this case the memory usually gets priority.) If another miss arises while the first miss is being processed, the first miss must complete before the second miss can begin its access.

For a copyback policy, the situation is slightly more complicated. We must first determine whether the line to be replaced is *dirty* (has been written to) or not. If the line is clean, then we have the same choices as we had with the write-through cache. However, if the line is dirty, we must make provision for the replaced line to be written back to memory. The simplest strategy here would be to first select the line to be replaced, then, if it is dirty, write the line back to memory, and finally bring the missed line into the cache, resuming processing when that line has been completely written to the cache. In order to speed up this process, a write buffer can be introduced that allows the replaced line to be written into the buffer during the time that the fetched line is being accessed from main memory. This frees up space in the cache to store the fetched line. Of course, one can include fetch bypass with the write buffer in order to minimize the miss time penalty.

Potentially, the fastest approach is the *nonblocking* cache or *prefetching* cache. This approach is applicable in both write-through and copyback caches. In this approach, the cache has additional control hardware to allow the cache miss to be handled (or bypassed) while the processor continues to execute. Clearly, this strategy only works when the miss is accessing cache data that is not currently required by the processor—the processor is not immediately dependent on the line to be accessed. Thus, nonblocking caches should be used with compilers that provide adequate prefetching of lines in anticipation of processor use. The value or effectiveness of nonblocking caches depends on two factors:

1. The effectiveness of the prefetch and the adequateness of the buffers to hold the prefetch information. The longer the prefetch is made before expected use, the less the miss delay; but this also means that the buffers or registers are not more occupied with anticipated data and hence less available for (possible) current requirements.

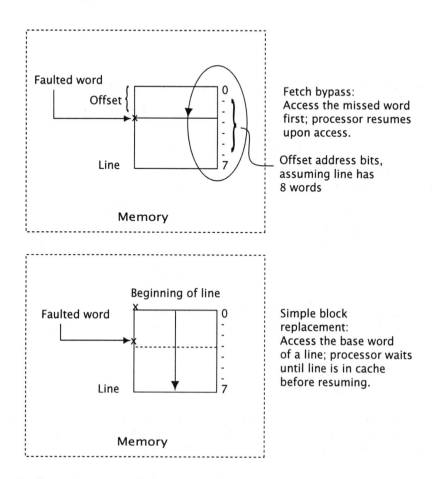

1. Slow, minimizes cache control (*access and fill*):
   Reference to a line always starts on a line boundary in memory. CPU does not resume until entire line is placed in cache.

2. Fast, or minimum miss time (*fetch bypass*):
   First reference to memory is to the faulted (missed) word. This is forwarded directly to the CPU (and simultaneously to the cache) and processing resumes. The remainder of the line is loaded into the cache as the CPU activity allows.

3. Various intermediate strategies are possible.

4. Nonblocking caches wherein the processor continues execution so long as the execution does not directly depend on or use the cache data to be fetched.

Figure 5.19   Line access strategies.

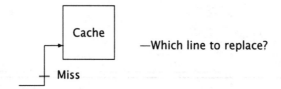

The replacement policy determines which line to replace when cache is full.
Policies:

LRU	(Least Recently Used)
FIFO	(First In-First Out)
RAND	(Random Replacement)

LRU is generally regarded as the best and most expensive to implement.
RAND is least expensive, but amplifies the miss rate by 12% (average).

- For various S/370 traces, the FIFO to LRU ratio varies from 0.96 to 1.38.
- RAND appears to perform about the same as FIFO (with respect to LRU).

Figure 5.20 Replacement policies.

2. The number of misses that can be bypassed (or controlled by the cache) while the processor executes. Current implementations do not exceed one bypassed miss.

5.7.2   Line Replacement

The replacement policy determines which line to replace when a miss occurs and the cache is full (Figure 5.20). There are three replacement policies that have been widely discussed and used; these include:

1. Least Recently Used (LRU) — Under this policy, the line that was least recently accessed (by a read or write) would be the candidate for replacement.

2. First In-First Out (FIFO) — Under this policy, the line that had been in the cache the longest is designated the line to be replaced.

3. Random Replacement (RAND) — Under this policy, replacement is determined randomly.

The LRU policy is generally regarded as an ideal policy, since it most closely corresponds to the concept of temporal locality. It is also the most complex to implement, as a counter must be associated with each line and modified on a read (or write) activity. It is possible to create reasonable approximations to the true LRU with small counters.

Generally, for most cache sizes, LRU performs better than either FIFO or RAND. For various traces, RAND appears to perform about the same as FIFO and with a range of between 0.96 and 1.38 relative performance with respect to LRU. An overall average of traces studied indicates that RAND or

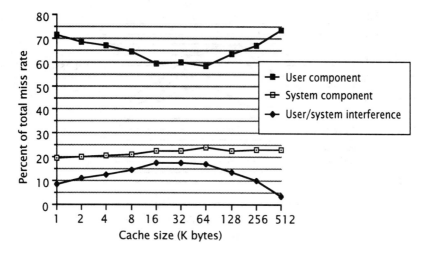

Figure 5.21 Interference of system references.

FIFO amplifies the LRU miss rate (DTMR) by 1.12 (i.e., 12%) on the average [259].

While LRU is the best-performing replacement algorithm, it does involve additional hardware control and complexity. For two-way set associativity, only one extra directory bit is required for directory entry. This bit is then toggled to indicate which of the entries was last accessed. As the degree of associativity increases, the number of "history" bits also increases [259]. For an m-way set associative memory, $(m - 1) \log_2 m$ bits are required per directory entry. This represents not only directory cost (in bits) but significant additional control to manage the update process. This cost can be reduced by various mechanisms that approximate LRU performance.

5.8 Cache Environment: Effects of System, Transactions and Multiprogramming

Most available cache data is based upon trace studies of user applications. It is from this environment that our DTMR figures have been derived. Actual applications are run in the context of the system. The operating system tends to slightly increase the miss rate experienced by a user program; Agarwal [4] has studied this for the VMS operating system. Figure 5.21 shows the results of his study. The system itself contributes 20% of the miss rate over a broad spectrum of cache sizes. Another 10%–20%, roughly, is attributable to system-user interference. The data in this figure is derived from the assumption that the user program runs through to completion, and calls upon the system only for those services required for its execution. We can adjust the DTMR from Figure 5.10 by including the effect of the system for a single user process running through to completion, which can be seen in Figure 5.22.

Multiprogramming environments (especially extended multiprogramming transaction environments) create special demands on a cache. Caches in

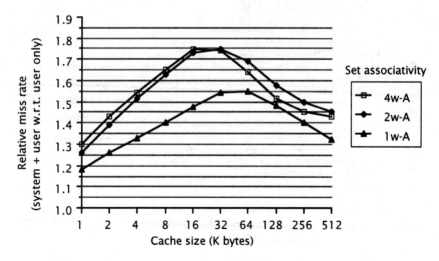

Figure 5.22   Effect of system activities on miss rate (16-byte line cache). Data were based on an integrated cache. We assume that indicated data are applicable to integrated, instruction, and data caches. (See text.) We also assume that caches with set associativity greater than 4 behave as 4w set associative.

such environments must be analyzed in a separate framework. For our purposes, we distinguish two environments:

1. A multiprogrammed environment. In this environment, a system together with several programs is resident in memory. Control is passed from program to program, in round-robin fashion, after a number of instructions have been executed, and eventually returns to the first program.

2. Transaction processing. Here, the system is resident in memory together with a number of support programs. Very short applications (transactions) are run through to completion. These programs are brought in on demand.

Both of the preceding environments are characterized by passing control from one program to another after executing instructions. Both the transaction environment and the multiprogrammed environment share these common features:

- An operating system resident in memory and its working set, presumed resident in the cache.

- A possibly low number of instructions between task switches — a relatively low Q factor.

This low Q factor causes a higher-than-average miss rate, since misses tend to cluster at the beginning of a task switch as a working set is loaded for a particular task (Figure 5.23). If that task is then not run through to completion, the initial misses caused by loading of the cache working set cannot be amortized over the complete task. The working set must be reloaded

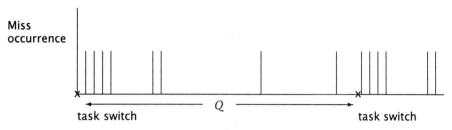

Time (measured in number of instructions executed)

Figure 5.23   Miss occurrence and task switches.

the next time control is passed to a particular task. It is here that these two environments differ.

Requests for I/O involve transmission of blocks of data to and from main memory to an external device. When an I/O device is read, its data cannot simply be placed in memory without checking the cache. Otherwise, the cache would have a stale copy of those lines written in memory by the I/O device. Similarly, on an I/O write with a copyback cache, the cache directory must be checked to ensure that memory has an updated image of the lines to be transmitted to the I/O device. In a write-through cache, memory writes to I/O devices need not be checked with the cache. I/O creates additional memory traffic and cache traffic, amplifying the cache miss rate. The effect of I/O on the cache read miss rate is dependent largely on the I/O rate:

$$\text{I/O rate} = \frac{\text{I/O memory and cache references}}{\text{CPU references to cache}}.$$

Historically, it has been assumed that I/O rates for typical scientific and batch processing environments vary from about 0.03 to 0.05, rising to perhaps as much as 0.10 for commercial transaction processing environments. Data from Smith [259] on the effects of I/O rates on cache indicate that I/O amplifies the role of the miss rate from about 1.1 to almost two times the unity reference rate.

We regard I/O as part of the systems activity already incorporated into the earlier discussion on systems effects. This ought to be accurate for most environments, especially scientific single-user environments. I/O simply acts as an additional process in the system. If this process is not large with respect to the system, it can be considered to be nearly an extension of system activity. This would be the expected outcome for a scientific and single-user environment. On the other hand, for multi-user environments, the I/O represents simply one additional process. For large-scale multiple process or multiprogrammed (multitransaction) commercial systems, the addition of one more process in a system that already has perhaps 10 processes (MP = 10) should not alter the performance predicted by Figure 5.24. For the special case of a commercial user with a single process and a large expected I/O rate, a designer may treat this as an additional user process (MP = 2) and use appropriate data such as in Figure 5.25.

In the multiprogrammed environment, control passes back to a task that has already once resided in the cache. If the cache is big enough and there are few enough tasks, the cache may still contain a portion of the working set of a newly reactivated task. In a multiprogram environment, if tasks

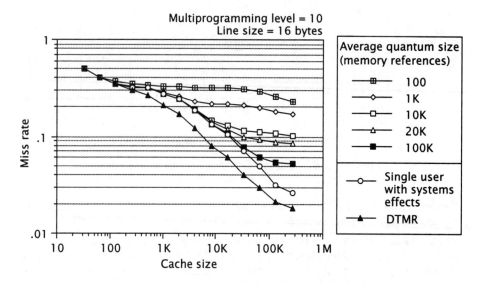

Figure 5.24   Warm cache, $MP = 10$.

retain a significant portion of their working set from a previous execution, this cache is said to be a *warm cache.* Caches that have no history from prior executions are said to be *cold caches.* Clearly, the individual transactions are dealing with a cold cache for their working set. In a multiprogrammed cnvironment, the cache may be either warm or cold depending upon the cache size, the degree of multiprogramming involved, and the average working set requirement of each task. With low degrees of multiprogramming and reasonable Q factors, a warm cache approximates the single user (DTMR) in the presence of the system (Figures 5.10 and 5.22 ad-

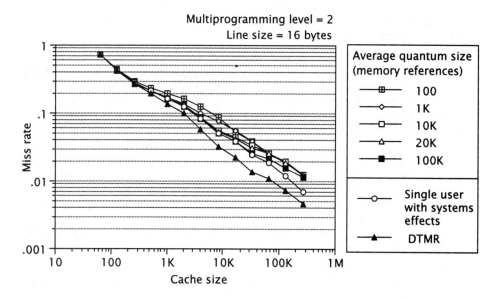

Figure 5.25   Warm cache, $MP = 2$.

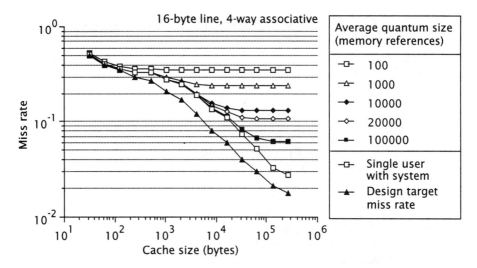

Figure 5.26   Miss rate on cold-start cache including system activities (16-byte lines, 4-way set associative).

justed for line size, etc.). Cold cache environments resemble the adjusted DTMR for small cache sizes. If Q is small enough, the cache never captures the working set or has relatively few instructions to amortize the effect of cache misses. As shown in Figure 5.26 (see Appendix A for other line sizes and associativity), increasing cache size beyond a certain critical point has only marginal advantage in these environments, since it is only the system working set that can be completely captured in the enlarged cache. For example (Figure 5.26), in a transaction environment where $Q = 1,000$, the use of a cache any larger than 4 KB produces no noticeable improvement in miss rate. It is important that the designer carefully distinguish among the types of environments that the system is designed for. Clearly, it is a poor use of resources to design very large caches for a transaction environment, as the performance gain is minimal.

For low degrees of multiprogramming (two users: $MP = 2$), as in Figure 5.25, the system behaves similarly to a single-user program with the system effects included. Principal portions of the working sets of both applications remain in the cache and are present when control passes back to the previous task. As the number of users (the MP level) increases, it becomes increasingly likely that when control returns to a task, all of its working set will have been removed. The system then resembles the cold cache case. (See Figure 5.22.) System effects on miss rate are summarized in Table 5.3. (See Appendix C for a discussion of how these results were derived.)

5.9   Other Types of Cache

So far we have considered only the simple integrated cache (also called a "unified" cache) which contains both data and instructions. In the next several sections we consider various other types of cache. The list we present

Table 5.3   System environment effects on miss rate.

Environments	Miss Rate
User program only	DTMR
User program plus operating system, I/O	MR adjusted by Figure 5.22 or Appendix A.
MP: Multiple user programs and system. Control passes round-robin among programs ("warm" cache).	MR adjusted by Q and MP in Figures 5.25–5.24 or Appendix A.
T: Transactions or multiple short user (Q instructions) programs plus system. Control always passes to a new user program ("cold" cache).	MR adjusted by Q in Figure 5.26 or Appendix A.

A Note on Warm Caches

A cache that contains several processes among which control passes from time to time is said to be a *warm* cache. For all but very small caches, each process finds some of its working set present when it is restarted.

A user program together with its required system support is also a *warm* cache. Available data for caches with low degrees of multiprogramming seem consistent with data for user plus system environment. Even a *cold* cache, where each user task is new to the system, has some system support working set.

Systems and I/O Effects

The effects of the operating system and the degree of multiprogramming on cache performance have not been widely studied. The studies available [4, 54] indicate that operating systems behave rather differently from applications.

Operating system policy can have a significant effect on cache performance. The working set of the run-time systems kernel will obviously affect the cache miss rate. The cold and warm effects outlined here are direct functions of the degree of multiprogramming. Environments of many short transactions that run through to completion approximate a cold cache with a high degree of multiprogramming. For such environments, increasing the cache size beyond a relatively modest capacity has little or no effect on performance. Such applications truly tax the memory system designer.

Table 5.4 Common types of cache.

Type	Where Usually Used
Integrated (or "unified")	The DTMR cache/common processor cache
Split cache I and D	Provides additional cache access bandwidth at some loss of MR. Commonly used as an on-chip L/S processor cache.
Sectored cache	Improves area effectiveness (MR for given area) for on-chip cache.
Two (multiple) level cache	First level is usually on-chip, second level is usually much larger than first and reduces time delay in a first-level miss.
Write assembly cache	Specialized; reduces write traffic; usually used with a WT on-chip first-level cache.

Table 5.5 Some microprocessor cache configurations.

(All use split caches)	DEC Alpha	IBM RS/6000	MIPS R4000	H-P PA7100	Intel Pentium
1st level I-cache					
On/off-chip	On	Multichip	On	Off	On
Size	8KB	8KB	8KB	128KB	8KB
Virtual/Real	R	R	V	V	R
Organization	DM	2W	DM	DM	4W
Line size	32B	64B	64B	32B	32B
1st level D-cache					
On/off chip	On	Multichip	On	Off	On
Size	8KB	64KB	8KB	256KB	8KB
Virtual/Real	R	R	V	V	R
Organization	DM	4W	DM	DM	4W
Line size	32B	128B	64B	32B	32B

(Table 5.4) is hardly exhaustive, but it illustrates some of the variety of cache designs possible for special or even commonplace applications.

Many currently available microprocessors use split I/D caches, described in the next section. Table 5.5 outlines the characteristics of some currently available processor caches.

5.10   Split I- and D-Caches and the Effect of Code Density

Multiple caches can be incorporated into a single processor design, each cache serving a designated process or use. Over the years, special caches for systems code and user code or even special I/O caches have been considered. The most popular configuration of partitioned caches is the use of separate caches for instructions and data.

A Note on Split Caches

Certain older programming environments, especially Fortran, apparently intermixed data and instructions rather frequently—enough to degrade performance significantly when duplicate lines were not allowed to appear in both data and instruction cache [259]. Usually, however, the designer can safely adopt a "no duplicate policy," where lines are contained in either the instruction or the data cache but not allowed to be present in both caches at the same time. This avoids some implementation complexity. In any event, the instruction cache as well as data cache should be interrogated on all stores; if an entry is found in the instruction cache, this line should be made invalid in order to preserve the consistency of the memory system.

5.10.1   I- and D-Caches

Separate instruction and data caches offer the designer the possibility of significantly increased cache bandwidth, potentially doubling the access capability of the cache ensemble. Split (I/D) caches have become especially useful in L/S microprocessors whose instruction set increases I-bandwidth requirements. Split caches come at some expense, however; a unified cache with the same size as the sum of a split data and instruction cache gives a lower effective miss rate. Figure 5.27 illustrates this. In the unified cache, the ratio of instruction to data working set elements changes during the execution of the program and is adapted to by the replacement strategy. No such adaptation is possible in the split cache.

Split caches offer some implementation advantages. Since the caches need not be split equally, there may be certain environments where a 75–25 or other split may prove more effective. Also, the I-cache is not required to manage a processor store. If a store into the instruction cache is detected, the line is simply invalidated, as this is presumably an unlikely occurrence (i.e., contrary to modern programming practice).

The DTMR for the instruction cache is presented in Figure 5.28, and for the data cache in Figure 5.29. In comparing these figures, note the difference in spatial locality between the instruction cache and the data cache. Larger lines are more effective in small instruction caches than in data caches. The DTMR is for a fully associative LRU cache for our reference R/M architec-

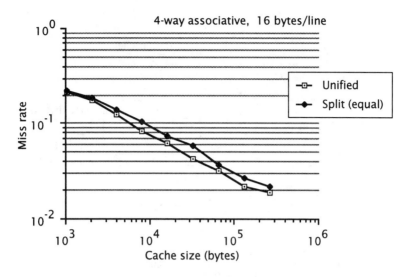

Figure 5.27   Split cache vs. unified cache.

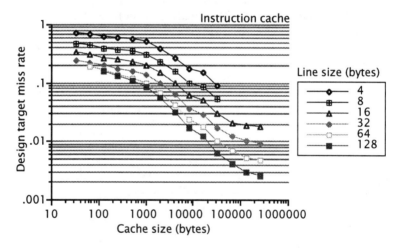

Figure 5.28   Design target miss rate of instruction cache (fully associative, demand fetch, copyback with LRU replacement).

ture. The associativity should be adjusted for other caches using the data presented earlier.

In certain older program environments, data parameters are frequently placed directly in the program so that when a particular program location is fetched into the I-cache, the same line might also bring data into the I-cache. When the operand parameter is fetched into the D-cache, a duplicate line entry occurs. This appears to happen especially in Fortran programs. Two split-cache policies are possible for dealing with duplicate lines. (See Figure 5.30.) Duplicate lines may be either supported or prohibited. The designer must decide whether enough older programs are expected to be run to warrant the support of duplicate lines. It has been shown that in these older environments, cache performance significantly degrades when a "no-duplicate-line" policy is adopted. In more modern programming envi-

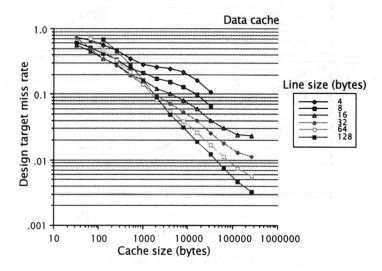

Figure 5.29 Design target miss rate of data cache (fully associative, demand fetch, fetch on write, copyback with LRU replacement).

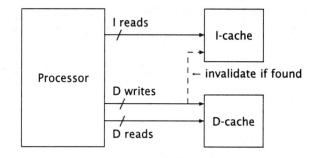

1. Duplicate lines: If miss on I-reference, memory line goes to I-cache.

                       If miss on D-reference, memory line goes to D-cache.

                       On CPU store reference check both directories:
                       — Use write policy in D-cache;
                       — Invalidate line in I-cache.

2. No duplicate lines: If miss on I reference, memory line goes to I-cache
                       and check D-cache directory; invalidate if present.

                       If miss on D reference, memory line goes to D-cache
                       and check I-cache directory; invalidate if found.

                       On CPU store difference check both directories.

Figure 5.30 Split cache management.

ronments, a designer can safely adopt a no-duplicate policy and not allow a line to be present in both caches at the same time. The no-duplicate policy somewhat simplifies implementation complexity.

Of course, the instruction cache as well as the data cache must be interrogated on all stores, as noted in Figure 5.30. In the event an entry is found in the instruction cache on a data access (or vice versa), this line must be made invalid in order to preserve the consistency of the memory system.

5.10.2   Code Density Effects

Instruction set architecture can have a significant effect on cache performance. More densely encoded architectures capture their program working set (most of the localities used in program execution) in fewer lines than a less densely encoded instruction set. This code density difference directly affects the cache miss rate of two instruction sets. Differences are naturally most dramatic for caches that contain only instructions (I-caches). Caches that contain only data (D-caches) are generally unaffected by instruction encoding and instruction set code density, since all instruction sets need basically the same data sets for program execution.

For our three prototype architectures, we compute a code density relative to R/M (the DTMR reference), which can be determined by data in chapter 3 (Tables 3.2 and 3.3). For the scientific environment, we have the following relative code densities:

$$\text{Relative Code Density} = \frac{\text{Instr Size} \times \text{Number of Instr per 100 HLL Instr}}{\text{R/M Instr Size} \times \text{R/M Instr per 100 HLL Instr}},$$

$$\text{L/S Code Density} = \frac{4 \times 200}{3.2 \times 180} = 1.39,$$

and

$$\text{R+M Code Density} = \frac{4 \times 120}{3.2 \times 180} = 0.83.$$

Mitchell [202] has shown that for small and very large caches, the relative miss rate of I-caches for two different instruction sets is directly related to the relative code densities:

$$\frac{\text{Miss Rate for Architecture 1}}{\text{Miss Rate for Architecture 2}} \doteq \frac{\text{Code Density for Architecture 1}}{\text{Code Density for Architecture 2}}.$$

The preceding relationship is not true for intermediate size caches. For certain cache sizes, the relative *performance spike* occurs when the more dense architecture begins to capture its instruction working set, while the less dense architecture has not done so. Figure 5.31 illustrates this phenomenon for a particular program and several architectures of different code density. The spike produces a *relative performance* difference of about 3.0 when, at around 16KB, the reference instruction set captures its working set. Spikes as high as 20.0 have been noted for programs with well-defined working sets. All architectures profit from increasing cache

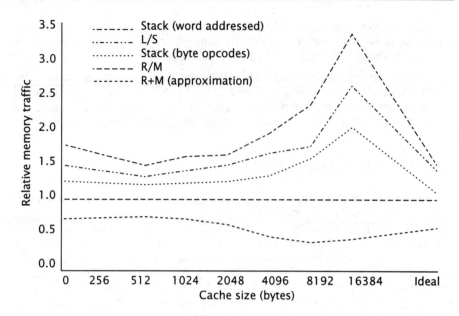

Figure 5.31 Instruction traffic (relative to R/M) for a compiler application, from Mitchell [200]. "Ideal" represents the cache size that contains the whole program.

size and spikes are measured in terms of *relative* performance only. For certain cache sizes, the more dense architecture captures most of its program localities and as a result has a very low miss rate.

Aside from the instruction set, compilers, and register allocators in particular, can have a significant effect on cache performance by affecting code density. Some compiler optimizations improve code density (and hence cache performance), and some reduce it. Optimizations that eliminate redundant instructions improve code density. Optimizations such as loop unrolling that are targeted at reducing branch frequency have the side effect of reducing code density. Because of the variance in compiler optimizations, there is no easy way to adjust our cache data for instruction set differences. The data presented is for the R/M architecture with optimized compilation. Presumably, a well-designed L/S instruction set architecture with advanced register allocation (taking advantage of the 32 registers) would achieve a relative code density significantly better than the factor of 1.39 mentioned earlier.

In predicting an L/S miss rate from (adjusted) DTMR data, the user should consider the robustness of the instruction set and the kind of compiler optimizations that are anticipated. Overall, it is likely that L/S I-cache performance will be worse than DTMR, probably by 20% to 40%. Integrated caches for L/S machines show fewer differences, probably no more than a 10% to 20% miss rate increase.

Since register allocation is an improving art, in the longer term the 32 registers in the L/S architecture should largely cancel the R/M architecture (with 16 registers) instruction size advantage. In the analyses in this book, we will not adjust L/S architecture over the R/M-based DTMR data. In particular cases, the designer may wish to make adjustments as suggested above.

Split Instructions and Data (I/D Split)

Advantage:

- Twice the access bandwidth available to the CPU, i.e., simultaneous instruction and data access.

Disadvantage:

- Poorer hit rate than same amount of integrated cache.

- More hardware for control.

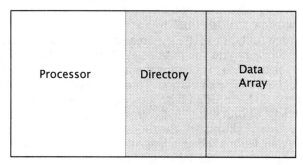

Fixed area available for cache

Figure 5.32   On-chip cache: how to organize the cache so as to maximize the data area (and minimize the directory).

5.11   On-Chip Caches

On-chip caches behave like any other type of cache with two notable exceptional considerations:

1. Because of pin limitations, the transfer path to and from memory is usually limited, frequently to four bytes and generally to a maximum of eight bytes.

2. The cache organization must be optimized to make the best use of the allocated area.

This latter consideration drives the designer to keep the cost of the directory small so that the bulk of the area available for the cache is available for the data array. This favors caches that require fewer directory entries, caches that are simply organized (e.g., direct mapped), and caches with large block sizes. On the other hand, these cache limitations may increase the cache miss rate, and large block sizes certainly increase the time that the processor is idle handling the cache miss. A relatively narrow transfer path also restricts the designer's flexibility in arranging or managing large blocks.

In order to optimize the design of an on-chip cache, consider the area model introduced in chapter 2 based on the register bit equivalent (the **rbe**). Since presumably both the cache directory and the cache array are made from the same technology, we are not concerned (as we were in chapter 2) with normalizing the per-bit area costs over the two different technologies: registers and caches. Here, we assume that the cost of a directory bit v is the same as the cost of a data bit:

$$\text{Area for cache data bit} \quad = \quad \text{area for cache directory bit}$$
$$= \quad \text{bit area unit} = 0.6 \text{ \textbf{rbe}}$$

The area used by the directory represents overhead to the overall cache design, since the directory holds no cache data. Associated with each line in the cache or data array is an entry in the directory. Suppose we designate the amount of area occupied by a directory entry as the bit area units. In Table 5.6, we assume that the total area available for a cache in the directory is 1,024 byte area units, or 8,192 bit area units. This area must accommodate both the directory and the data array. Table 5.6 shows the amount of area available for the data array after the bits of directory overhead per line have been allocated to the directory. Thus, if there were no line overhead, i.e., $v = 0$, we would have 1,024 byte area equivalents available for the data array independent of block size. Of course, $v = 0$ is an unrealizable cache configuration, since it eliminates the directory completely. A simple direct-mapped cache may have a rather small overhead per line, sufficient only to contain the tag portion of the address. Suppose such an overhead was 32 bits. For very small line sizes—say, 16 bits or 2 bytes—the directory still occupies approximately twice as much area as the data array, since each line has 32 bits of directory area and only 16 bits of data area and, as shown in Table 5.6, only 341 data bytes are available for storing data. Increasing line size decreases the number of entries in the directory and decreases the line or directory overhead, so that using a 64-byte line and the same 32-bit ($v = 32$ bit) overhead allows the data array to have effectively 964 bytes out of the total 1,024 bytes available.

The directory overhead (or the line overhead) is inversely proportional to the line size and the number of bits contained in the entry. A typical entry includes an address tag, valid bits, and replacement information. If the number of data bytes per line is represented by b, then the cache utilization factor is:

$$\text{Cache utilization} = \frac{b}{b + v/8}.$$

Cache utilization is a rough estimate of the fraction of area available for data storage compared to the total area. Thus, a line size of 2 bytes with a block line overhead of 32 bits has a cache utilization of $2 \div (2 + 32 \div 8) = 1/3$, hence $1,024 \times .33 = 341$. Larger line sizes make more of the area available for the data array and require less to hold the directory.

A single line of b bytes has an area of $8b$ area units and has an overhead of:

$$\text{Overhead} = v \text{ bit area equivalents.}$$

Table 5.6   Quantity of data storage (bytes) available in a cache with various line overhead values and a total available area of 1,024 byte- or 8,192 bit-area equivalents (from Mulder [207]).

Line Size	Line Overhead = v			
(Bytes)	0	32	64	128
2	1024	341	205	114
4	1024	512	341	205
8	1024	683	512	341
16	1024	819	683	512
32	1024	910	819	683
64	1024	964	910	819

One can estimate the number of overhead bits directly from the structure of the cache directory with one exception. If a fully associative cache memory is used, using a content address memory (CAM), the CAM bit occupies approximately twice the area of a data bit. This factor of two can then be used in determining the overhead. Table 5.6 shows the effect of line size on area utilization for various directory overheads. The table assumes that there is a table bit area equivalent for the cache of 8,192 data bits (1,024 data bytes) if there were no directory overhead. The table shows that the amount of space in the cache available for data storage varies dramatically with a line overhead, especially for line sizes less than 16. It varies less for larger line sizes. From this, we can see the usefulness of large blocks to the on-chip cache designer. Unfortunately, the use of large lines, especially for small caches, causes an increase in the miss rate and especially increases the total miss time. This makes some sort of a compromise a necessity. One compromise is a *sectored cache.*

In a sectored cache (Figure 5.33), each line is broken into transfer units (a type of sub-line that represents one access from the cache to the memory). The directory is organized around the line size insofar as the address tags, etc., are concerned. When a miss occurs in a cache, the missed line is entered into the directory, but only the transfer unit that is required by the

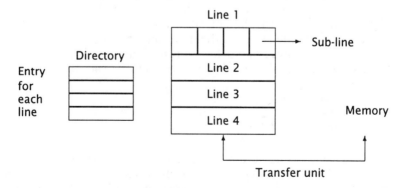

Figure 5.33   Sectored cache. A bit in each sub-line indicates validity of that sub-line.

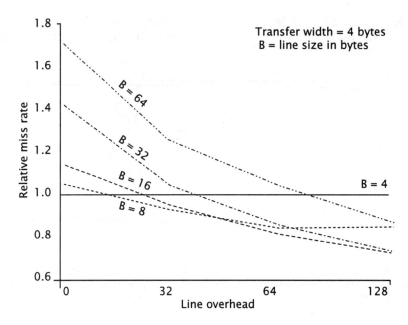

Figure 5.34   Miss rate relative to an unsectored cache with line and transfer width (physical word size) of 4 bytes. Line overhead is the number of bits associated with each line entry in the cache directory (except for case of fully associative cache with CAM: see text).

processor is brought into the data array. A valid/invalid bit (not shown in Figure 5.33) indicates the status of the sub-lines. If a subsequent access is made to another sub-line in this newly loaded line, that sub-line is then brought into the cache. The effect of the sectored cache is to diminish somewhat the value of spatial locality, but to retain the temporal locality of the cache, and to greatly diminish the size of the directory.

The overall effect of this can be seen in Figures 5.34 and 5.35. Both of these figures show the miss rate of sectored caches relative to an unsectored cache for various line sizes and transfer widths of four bytes (Figure 5.34) and eight bytes (Figure 5.35). For the commonly used transfer width of four bytes, if the directory entry overhead exceeds 32 bits per line (line overhead), then the sectored caches provide better overall performance for most configurations except for the line size of 64. Notice that Figures 5.34 and 5.35 do not include the effect of the miss penalty itself. They describe the miss ratio only. Measuring actual miss rates and including the effects of the actual miss penalty itself further favors sectored caches.

5.12   Two-Level Caches

Frequently the designer encounters a situation where, for one reason or another, the first-level cache has been specified and designed (as in the case of an on-chip first-level cache) and a larger second-level cache must be added to the system to improve overall performance. This situation occurs frequently in multiprocessor configurations whose special considerations

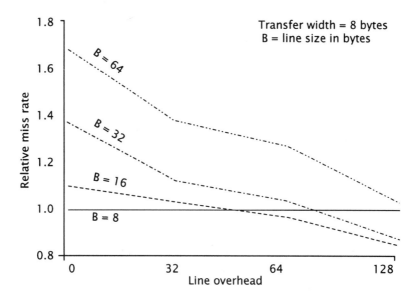

Figure 5.35   Miss rate relative to an unsectored cache with line and transfer width (physical word size) of 8 bytes. Line overhead is the number of bits associated with each line entry in the cache directory.

Microprocessor Caches

For reasons outlined in this chapter, modern microprocessor systems are moving in the following directions:

1. Split I- and D-caches. This ensures (especially for L/S processors) adequate cache–processor bandwidth. Some processors have implemented an I-cache only. This is probably not a good idea, since data access time to memory tends to dominate execution time. Except in extraordinary cases, some cache area should be allocated for both I and D functions.

2. The use of sectored caches. To optimize the area available for storing data, the sectored cache minimizes the directory size and affords an overall best marginal use of area.

3. Two-level cache, where the on-chip cache is supported by a larger, off-chip or even on-chip second-level cache. The two-level cache improves performance by effectively lowering the first-level cache access time and miss penalty.

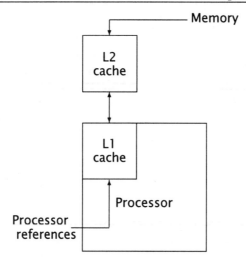

Figure 5.36   A two-level cache.

will be addressed later. For now, we look at the problem of analyzing the second-level cache given the presence of a first-level cache. A two-level cache system is termed *inclusive* if all the contents of the lower-level cache (L1) are also contained in the higher-level cache (L2).

Second-level cache analysis is done using the *principle of inclusion*—i.e., a large second-level cache includes everything in the first-level cache. Thus (at least statistically and for purposes of evaluating performance of the second-level cache), the first-level cache can be presumed not to exist. The total number of misses that occur in a second-level cache can be determined by assuming that the processor made all of its requests to the second-level cache without the intermediary first-level cache.

There are also more or less obvious design considerations in accommodating a second-level cache to existing first-level cache. Clearly, the line size of the second-level cache should be the same as or larger than the first-level cache. Otherwise, if the line size in the second-level cache were smaller, loading the line in the first-level cache would simply cause two misses in the second-level cache. Further, it would be of almost no value to have a second-level cache whose overall size was not at least as large as the first-level cache; it should usually be significantly larger.

Suppose we have a two-level system as shown in Figure 5.36. The first-level cache, designated L1, is associated with the base machine. The second-level cache, designated L2, is intermediate between the first-level cache and main memory. Following the terminology of Przybylski et al. [237], we define the following miss rates:

1. A *local miss rate* for a cache is simply the number of misses experienced by the cache divided by the number of incoming references. This is our ordinary understanding of *miss rate*. The difficulty arises in evaluating the L2 cache performance, since we may not know the number of references made to it from L1.

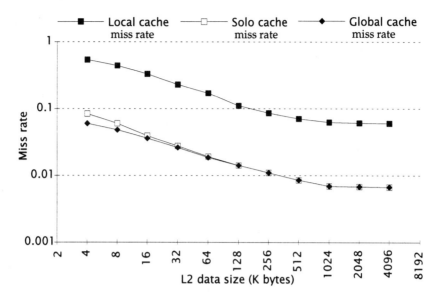

Figure 5.37   L2 miss rates with a 4KB L1 cache (data from Przybylski [237]).

2. The *global miss rate* of a cache is the number of L2 misses divided by the number of references made by the processor. This is our primary measure of the L2 cache.

3. The *solo miss rate* is the miss rate the cache would have if it were the only cache in the system. It is the miss rate defined by the principle of inclusion. *If* L2 contains *all* of L1 then we can find the number of L2 misses from our DTMR and the processor reference rate, ignoring the presence of the L1 cache. The principle of inclusion specifies that the global miss rate will be essentially the same as the solo miss rate, allowing us to use the solo miss rate to evaluate our design.

The principle of inclusion for a pair of two-level caches can be assessed in Figures 5.37 and 5.38. Figure 5.37 shows the miss rates for a L2 cache with a 4KB level-one cache, while Figure 5.38 shows the L2 miss rate with a 32KB level-one cache.

If the second-level cache is truly inclusive of the first-level cache, the global and solo cache miss ratios would be coincident in Figure 5.38 so long as L2 was equal to or greater than the L1 cache size. A discrepancy illustrated in these figures arises because the L2 cache did not have the same degree of set associativity as the L1 cache. It was "inclusive" only on a statistical basis, not on a complete logical basis.

The preceding data (read misses only) illustrate some salient points in multilevel cache analysis and design:

1. The local miss rate of a second-level cache is quite dependent upon the behavior of the level-one cache.

2. So long as the level-two cache is the same as or larger than the level-one cache, analysis by the principle of inclusion provides an excellent estimate of the behavior of the level-two cache.

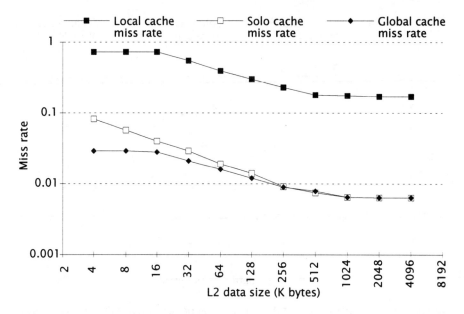

Figure 5.38 L2 miss rates with a 32KB L1 cache (data from Przybylski [237]).

3. The level-two cache, so long as it is significantly larger than the level-one cache, is completely independent of the level-one cache's parameters; its miss rate corresponds to a solo miss rate. Thus, the memory hierarchy problem can be decomposed into the design of individual levels.

EXAMPLE 5.2

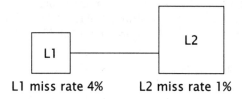

L1 miss rate 4%   L2 miss rate 1%

Miss penalties:

Miss in L1, hit in L2:	2 cycles
Miss in L1, miss in L2:	7 cycles

Suppose we have a two-level cache with miss rates of 4% (L1) and 1% (L2). Suppose the miss in L1 and hit in L2 penalty is 2 cycles, and the miss penalty in both caches is 7 cycles (5 cycles more than a hit in L2). If a processor makes 1.5 references per instruction, we can compute the excess CPI due to cache misses as follows:

Excess CPI due to L1 misses

=   1.5 refr/inst × 0.04 misses/refr × 2 cycles/miss

=   0.12 CPI

Excess CPI due to L2 misses

=   1.5 refr/inst × 0.01 misses/refr × 5 cycles/miss

=   0.075 CPI

Note: the L2 miss penalty is 5 cycles, not 7 cycles, since the 1% L2 misses have already been "charged" 2 cycles in the excess L1 CPI.

Total effect   =   excess L1 CPI + excess L2 CPI

=   0.12 + 0.075

=   0.195 CPI

◆

True or logical inclusion, where *all* the contents of L1 reside also in L2, should not be confused with statistical inclusion, where *usually* L2 contains the L1 data. There are a number of requirements for logical inclusion. Clearly, the L1 cache must be write-through. (The L2 need not be.) If L1 were copyback, then a write to a line in L1 would not go immediately to L2, so L1 and L2 would differ in contents. The following example shows that inclusion fails in many cases.

EXAMPLE 5.3

Consider a 2-line direct mapped L1 cache with a 4-line fully associative L2 cache (both with the same line sizes):

$$\text{L1 set size} = \frac{2}{1} = 2.$$
$$\text{L2 set size} = \frac{4}{4} = 1.$$

Consider the following reference pattern:

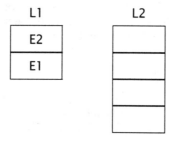

Designate a reference to line E1 in L1 as an R1 reference, and a reference to line E2 as an R2 reference, then associate a sequence number $R1 - 1$ as the first line to go into E1 and $R1 - n$ as the nth line. Consider the sequence:

$$R2 - 1, R1 - 1, R1 - 2, R1 - 3;$$

i.e., a reference to E2, then three references to (new) lines in E1. The cache contents would be:

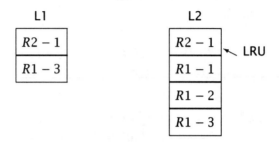

Now a miss to E1 creates a reference $R1 - 4$, which will make the caches inconsistent, as the new line will replace $R2 - 1$ in L2 and $R1 - 3$ in L1.

♦

5.12.1   Logical Inclusion

Assuming LRU replacement in both levels, logical inclusion will be violated if and only if we do not provide L2 entries for all L1 entries. Obviously, L2 must be at least as large as L1. Let us define the following:

$$\text{Cache size} \;=\; \text{set size} * \text{number of sets}$$
$$=\; (\text{line size} * \text{assoc}) * \text{number of sets},$$

where set size = (line size $*$ assoc).

The crucial requirement for logical inclusion is that *the number of L2 sets has to be greater than or equal to the number of L1 sets*, irrespective of L2 associativity. (Assume that the L2 line size is at least as large as L1.) If this were not true, multiple L1 sets would depend on a single L2 set for backing store. Hence, references to a given L1 set can affect the backing store for another L1 set.

Another requirement is that *the L2 associativity be no less than that of L1*, irrespective of the number of sets. For a L1 associativiy greater than L2's, there will be many L2 entries backing for a given L1 set. Each L2 entry can hold many lines that can go into the L1 set. Therefore, it is possible to have many references to an L1 set such that each would hit in the same L2 entry. Since the L2 associativity is lower, it will have to replace valid L1 lines before L1 starts to replace.

Let us formalize these constraints: If

$$\text{Cache size} \;=\; \text{line size} * \text{assoc} * \text{number of sets},$$
$$\text{Number of sets} \;=\; \frac{\text{cache size}}{(\text{assoc} * \text{line size})}$$

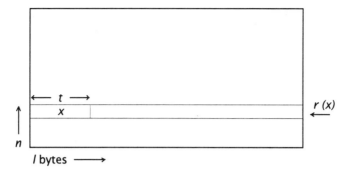

Figure 5.39   Write assembly cache with line size l bytes, n lines, and transfer unit (physical word size) t bytes.

Then

1. Number of L2 sets ≥ number of L1 sets.

   L2 size/(L2 assoc * L2 line size) ≥ L1 size/(L1 assoc * L1 line size).

   L2 size/L2 assoc ≥ L1 size/L1 assoc * (L2 line size/L1 line size).

2. L2 assoc ≥ L1 assoc.

We have assumed that all L1 references are passed to L2 so that it can update its LRU. If this were not true, we could never have logical inclusion. For example, say L1 and L2 have the same associativity (2) and number of sets. Let L2 currently include L1, with E1-2 being the last referenced, implying that E1-1 is the next to be replaced in L2. The CPU can reference E1-1 in L1, making E1-2 the next to be replaced. A reference to E1-3 would replace E1-2 in L1 and E1-1 in L2, and ruin inclusion. Alternatively, other replacements such as a FIFO scheme offer simpler consistency. Even RAND might be consistent if L1 and L2 use a similar algorithm.

5.13   Write Assembly Cache

Certain types of "write only" caches can be very valuable to the designer in reducing traffic to the memory system [43, 96].

Suppose we have a processor with a write-through cache. From our earlier discussions on memory traffic in copyback and write-through caches, beyond a certain cache size write-through traffic is dominated by writes, and this residual write traffic defines a lower limit to the memory traffic required for write-through cache. Write-through caches have advantages over copyback caches by generally requiring less software management to support memory consistency as used in multiprocessor configurations. The write assembly cache (WAC) offers an intermediate strategy, centralizing pending memory writes in a single buffer, which reduces resulting bus traffic, but accomplishing this at some sacrifice in consistency (since writes can now be delayed).

Consider Figure 5.39. A buffer of n entries consists of a number of transfer units that compose a line of l bytes. The transfer unit or physical word size

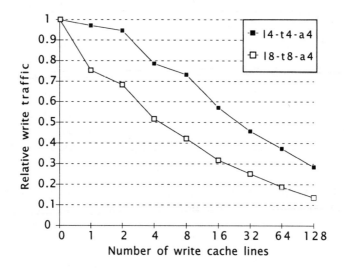

Figure 5.40   Write assembly cache, relative write traffic (line size of 4 and 8 bytes, transfer unit of 4 and 8 bytes, four-way set associative) (data from Bray [43]).

is also measured in bytes. Assume for the moment that the write assembly cache (WAC) is fully associative and fully bypassed. If a reference $r(x)$ occurs, and x is in the WAC, then x is returned to the processor without otherwise affecting the memory system or the WAC.

The goal of the write assembly cache is to assemble writes so that they can be transmitted in an orderly way to the memory system, minimizing the use of the bus for memory traffic. If a synchronizing event occurs as in the case of multiple shared memory processors, the entire WAC should be transferred to memory to ensure memory consistency.

Suppose we organize the WAC such that $l = t$, creating a WAC of multiple small entries. Figure 5.40 shows the temporal localities of writes and the efficiency of such a buffer. Now write traffic can be reduced to about one-quarter of the null buffer case, providing a significant performance improvement in those cases where write traffic dominates the memory traffic.

Figure 5.40 shows the resultant write traffic (from the write assembly cache to memory) relative to a null buffer (i.e., the write traffic to memory without a WAC). The data presented are generally independent of set associativity. For most programs (such as the ones included in the benchmarks used for Figure 5.40), temporal locality seems to play a more important role in write traffic than spatial locality. Thus, it is advantageous to have more smaller lines rather than fewer larger lines to reduce resultant write traffic. An exception occurs in the case of large scientific programs accessing data arrays, where spatial locality (fewer large lines) dominates the reduction in write traffic. A suggested general solution for implementing a WAC [43] would be the following strategy:

- Number of lines—minimum of 4.

- Line size—8 bytes (equal to the transfer size).

- Associativity—direct mapped.

Single-line WACs have been used in the VAX 8800 [96], while NCR has used multiline WACs in its workstations.

Generally temporal locality seems to play a more important role in write traffic than spatial locality—an issue that the designer must carefully consider in developing a write strategy and an overall integrated design of a hierarchical memory system.

5.14   Cache References per Instruction

Instructions create three types of cache traffic:

1. Instruction traffic.

2. Data read traffic.

3. Data write traffic.

The cache–memory traffic depends on whether the cache has an "allocate on write" policy or not. The processor-cache traffic is the sum of these types of traffic, since writes must be checked in the cache directory regardless of allocation strategy.

5.14.1   Instruction Traffic

In determining the amount of traffic that a typical instruction creates, there are a number of factors that must be considered:

1. The size of the I-fetch data path and the use of an I-buffer.

2. The branch strategy.

3. The distribution of data reads and writes.

4. The use of instructions that create multiple data accesses to memory (such as load multiple, etc.).

Statistically, each instruction requires I/P fetches, where I is the average instruction size in bytes, and P is the data path width (physical word size) from cache to I buffer. We assume that $P \geq I$ as this is the usual case. Branch instructions add additional instruction traffic depending upon the branch policy followed. Usually, the branch instruction policy creates an additional fetch to the target instruction, even if untaken. Depending upon the branch strategy, the branch may create further traffic by fetching instructions in anticipation of a predicted branch path outcome. Each of these additional instructions requires I/P fetches. Total instruction traffic per instruction is the sum of I/P and the excess of instructions fetched on branches:

$$\frac{I}{P} + [\text{Excess I traffic on BR}] + [\text{Excess I traffic on BC}].$$

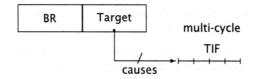

Figure 5.41   BR traffic.

A branch (BR) and its target instruction requires the BR I-traffic (I/P fetches) plus the fetch for the target instruction. Thus, the total I-traffic caused by the BR-target pair of instructions is $2I/P$; but in our computation, we have already allocated I/P fetches for each instruction, including both the branch and its target. Thus, *assuming that branch target references are aligned* (they start at the beginning of the reference), there is no *excess* traffic caused by the BR except for the extra in-line fetches. So:

$$\text{Excess I-traffic on BR} = \text{Prob (BR) } [N_1 \frac{I}{P}],$$

where Prob(BR) is the probability (frequency) of an unconditional branch and N_1 ($N_1 \geq 0$)is the allocated or maximum number of in-line instructions fetched before the branch is decoded (usually equal to the number of cycles in an IF).

The excess traffic given a conditional branch (BC) is:

$$\text{Excess I-traffic on BC}$$
$$= \text{Prob}(BC) \left[\text{Prob (c.p.)}[N_2 \frac{I}{P}] + (1 - \text{Prob (c.p.)})[N_3 \frac{I}{P}] \right],$$

where Prob(c.p) is the probability of a correct prediction given a BC, N_2 ($N_2 \geq 0$) is the allocated number of unused instructions fetched given a correct prediction (c.p.), and N_3 ($N_3 \geq 0$) is the allocated number of unused instructions fetched given an incorrect prediction. Usually the minimum value for N_2 or N_3 is P/I—the number of instructions corresponding to a single IF or TIF.

Study 5.1   Instruction Traffic

Compute the instruction reference traffic for the processor in study 4.3.

This R/M processor has a timing template of:

$$\text{IF} \quad \text{IF} \quad \text{D} \quad \text{AG} \quad \text{AG} \quad \text{DF} \quad \text{DF} \quad \text{EX} \quad \text{EX}$$

The processor decodes one instruction per cycle and guesses in-line on conditional branch, proceeding up to EX. There is a sufficiently large IB to hold prefetched instructions. We use an 8^B physical word size.

Each instruction identifies or fetches a successor. In the case of branch, two successors may be fetched (in-line and target). "Identification" may or may not create a reference, however. Assuming the path between cache and processor is 8^B, the average instruction is considerably smaller, and multiple instructions may be brought into an instruction buffer by a single reference.

In our case, with an 8^B data path between cache and processor, we can estimate the average instruction size from Table 3.2, assuming the scientific environment average size is 3.2^B.

Thus, each instruction creates $3.2^B/8 = 0.40$ I references/instruction. To the preceding we must add the extra traffic created by branch instructions, which depends on the branch prediction strategy.

As in study 4.3, we fetch one word of target, otherwise fetch in-line, and conditional branches are taken 50% of the time.

Unconditional branch ($*$) excess traffic (the frequency of unconditional branch is 0.05, from study 4.3):

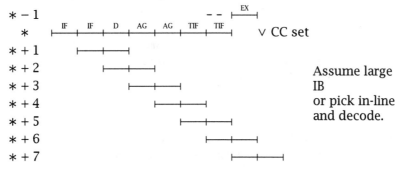

Before the IF for $*+3$, the branch at $*$ has been decoded and in-line fetching ceases, $N_1 = 2$. So, the excess traffic for unconditional branches is:

$$.05\,[2I/P] = 0.05(0.8) = 0.04 \text{ excess references.}$$

Conditional branch ($*$) with target taken (from study 4.3, the frequency of conditional branch is 15%):

$*-1$ `-- EX`

$*$ IF IF D AG AG TIF TIF $\vee$ CC set

$*+1$

$*+2$ Assume large

$*+3$ IB

$*+4$ or pick in-line

$*+5$ and decode.

$*+6$

$*+7$

Here, seven in-line instructions are fetched, so $N_3 = 7$ and for the conditional branch ($*$) with in-line taken:

$$N_2 = 1 \text{ reference (the target fetch)/conditional branch untaken}$$
$$\text{(this corresponds to } P/I \text{ instructions),}$$
$$N_2 = \frac{1}{.4} = 2.5,$$

since only the target fetch is in excess of instructions used.

Now we can compute the excess BC traffic:

$$0.15\,[.5(7)(.4) + .5(2.5)(.4)] = 0.285,$$

and the total I-traffic per I is

$$
\begin{aligned}
&= \quad I/P + \text{ excess traffic}\\
&= \quad 0.4 + 0.285 + 0.04 = 0.725 \doteq 0.73.
\end{aligned}
$$

The 0.73 I-reference per I was computed without regard to the I-cache design. Note that it appears that two references must be simultaneously handled by the I-cache during TIF fetch. If, as is common, the cache is limited to one access per cycle, the fetch of $* + 5$ and subsequent words are delayed by one cycle—thus, only six excess references are made. However, only 3.0 references are actually made to the cache to fetch the additional instructions, so this accessing is completed before the TIF is initiated.

5.14.2   Data Traffic

Computation of data traffic is relatively straightforward. First, we determine the number of instructions that use a data operand from memory and then distinguish between reads and writes. In the scientific environment for L/S architectures, we can use Tables 3.4 and 3.15. Note that there are no memory to memory instructions; thus:

(Data Reads + Data Writes)/I

$$
= \frac{(\text{Move instr}/100 \text{ HLL ops} + \text{Excess LDM and STM traffic per } 100 \text{ HLL ops})}{(\text{Total L/S instructions per } 100 \text{ HLL operations})}
$$

We find the LD and ST instructions breakdown per 100 HLL ops in Table 3.15 and the number (200) of L/S instructions per 100 HLL ops in Table 3.4.

Some instructions take more than one operand (load multiple, store multiple, and the memory to memory instructions). For the load and store multiple instructions we need to know the average number of registers that are involved in the operation (section 3.3.1).

(Data reads)/I

$$
\begin{aligned}
&= \quad (\text{Integer loads} + \text{floating-point reads} + \text{LDM})/I\\
&= \quad \frac{\text{LDs}/100 \text{ HLL ops} + \text{LD.Fs}/100 \text{ HLL ops} + \text{LDM}/100 \text{ HLL ops}}{\text{L/S instr}/100 \text{ HLL ops}}\\
&= \quad \frac{36 + 23 + 1(3)}{200} = 0.31.
\end{aligned}
$$

for (Data writes)/I only

$$
\begin{aligned}
&= \quad (\text{Integer writes} + \text{floating-point writes} + \text{STM})/I\\
&= \quad \frac{\text{STs}/100 \text{ HLL ops} + \text{ST.Fs}/100 \text{ HLL ops} + \text{STM}/100 \text{ HLL ops}}{\text{L/S instr}/100 \text{ HLL ops}}\\
&= \quad \frac{16 + 18 + 1(4)}{200}\\
&= \quad \frac{38}{200} = .19 \text{ refr/I.}
\end{aligned}
$$

Table 5.7   Expected Processor Data Traffic per Instruction

Architecture	Scientific		Commercial			
			P = 4		*P* = 8	
	Read	Write	Read	Write	Read	Write
L/S	0.31	0.19	0.47	0.22	0.47	0.22
R/M	0.34	0.21	1.35	1.19	0.92	0.76
R+M	0.52	0.32	1.35	1.19	0.92	0.76

Table 5.8   Expected data traffic (R/M and R+M) created by variable-length operations instructions (commercial environment).

			P = 4		*P* = 8	
Type	Freq. per 100 HLL ops	Length (bytes)	Reads	Writes	Reads	Writes
Move Character	16	33	9	9	5	5
Move Decimal	7	4	1.75	1.75	1.38	1.38
Compare,[a] etc.	22	4	1.75	1.75	1.38	1.38
Decimal arith[b]	6	4/3	3.25	1.75	2.63	1.38
Total per 100 HLL ops	—	—	214	205	136	128

[a] as specified (assuming prefetch).

[b] write goes to longer operand (4B).

For the R/M architecture, we would expect the same number of reads or writes from memory per HLL operation. This increases the data traffic by the decrease in R/M instructions per 100 HLL operations:

200/180, or for R/M traffic, we have:

$$\text{Data reads/I} = 0.34$$
$$\text{Data writes/I} = 0.21$$

For a scientific environment, the data traffic per instruction is summarized in Table 5.7. To evaluate data traffic for a commercial environment, we need to assess the traffic created by MM operations.

The memory-to-memory (MM) operations require a bit more analysis, since usually such operations are only byte-aligned, not aligned with respect to the data paths of the processor. Also, there are two types of MM instructions: two-source operand and one-source operand. The one-source operand (such as in MOVE.C) takes (reads) an operand in memory, then writes it back into memory. Each memory access takes:

$$\left\lceil \frac{d}{P} \right\rceil + \frac{(d-1) \bmod P}{P} \text{ references,}$$

where d is the operand size in bytes and P is the data width (bytes). The operand access takes $\lceil d/P \rceil$ references as a minimum, but on $(d-1) \bmod P$ address sites (out of P), an extra fetch is required.

EXAMPLE 5.4

Suppose for MOVE.Cl, the operand length l is 32 bytes and $P = 4$.
We require:

$$\left\lceil \frac{32}{4} \right\rceil + \frac{31 \bmod 4}{4} \text{ references} = 8.75,$$

since only when the operand is word-aligned will we need only eight references. The other times (3/4 of the time), we require an extra fetch. This instruction requires 8.75 read references and 8.75 write references.

$\blacklozenge$

EXAMPLE 5.5

Suppose for ADD.Pl, the operand length l is 3 bytes and $P = 4$.
Now we have:

$$\left\lceil \frac{3}{4} \right\rceil + \frac{2 \bmod 4}{4} = 1.5 \text{ references.}$$

This instruction creates 2×1.5 read references (two operands) and 1.5 write references.

$\blacklozenge$

For the L/S data traffic in the commercial environment, all move class operations take a single reference (assuming some operand prefetching into registers), with the LDM and STM exceptions. We also need to account for some LD/ST to support decimal operations. Thus, from Table 3.16, we compute the traffic:

$$\text{Total reads per 100 HLL ops} \; = \; \text{Integer reads + Byte reads + LDM,}$$

$$\text{Read traffic} \; = \; \frac{\text{Total reads per 100 HLL ops}}{\text{Instructions per 100 HLL ops}}.$$

For L/S,

$$\text{Read traffic} \; = \; \frac{54 + 243 + 17 + 4(3)}{688} = 0.47;$$

similarly,

$$\text{Write traffic} \; = \; \frac{16 + 121 + 8 + 1(4)}{688} = 0.22.$$

Now to compute R/M or R+M data traffic for the commercial environment, we first consider the references created by the variable operand length instruction (Tables 3.22 and 3.21). By rounding operand length to the nearest integer, we compute traffic for each instruction type (only decimal arithmetic takes two source operands). This is tabulated in Table 5.8.

Combining this with frequency data, we can compute the read and write traffic per instruction ($P = 4$, see Table 5.7):

Total reads per 100 HLL ops

= Integer reads (Table 3.16) + Byte reads (Table 5.8) + LDM's,

and then continue as above:

$$\text{Read traffic} = \frac{18 + 214 + 4(3)}{181} = 1.35,$$

$$\text{Write traffic} = \frac{5 + 205 + 4}{181} = 1.19.$$

Similarly, for $P = 8$:

$$\text{Read traffic} = \frac{18 + 136 + 4(3)}{181} = .92,$$

$$\text{Write traffic} = \frac{5 + 128 + 4}{181} = 0.76.$$

As with the scientific environment, we treat the number of integer fetches and stores as invariant across architectures. (Assume all architectures have the same register set design.) These numbers (54 fetches/100 HLL ops and 16 stores/100 HLL ops) are more readily available from L/S data, as that architecture does not allow a data fetch as part of an arithmetic operation. The LDM and STM activity is also the same for all architectures.

5.15 Technology-Dependent Cache Design Considerations

There are several other effects that the cache may have on the overall effectiveness of the processor design. For example:

1. The cache may determine the CPU cycle time; the cycle time is then a function of cache size.

2. The cache determines the memory access time.

3. The cache determines the bus busy time, and through this the effective memory access time.

All of these may directly affect processor performance.

So far, our model of CPU performance is:

CPU time per instruction =

$$t_{\text{cycle}} * \left[\text{CPI} + \frac{\text{references}}{\text{instruction}} * (\text{miss rate}) * (\text{miss penalty}) \right],$$

where t_{cycle} is the processor cycle time. CPI is the computed cycles per instruction for the processor, including pipeline breaks. Miss penalty is the cache miss penalty in cycles; in other words, the number of cycles the processor is idled by a miss awaiting data from memory.

In our performance model, suppose the CPU cycle is determined by cache access time. Large cache sizes or higher degrees of associativity give smaller miss rates but may result in larger CPU cycle times. For large cache sizes, more performance improvement can be achieved by decreasing CPU cycle time than by doubling the cache size. For small caches, the opposite is true [220].

Consider this in the context of the processor used in study 4.1.

Study 5.2   A Cache Study

This study demonstrates how our data (i.e., DTMR, etc.) can be incorporated with system parameters to evaluate the overall performance. We show part of the design space and illustrate some performance tradeoffs possibly encountered in cache design [237, 130].

Assumptions:

- Unified cache.

- Line size: 32 bytes.

- Set associativity: two-way associative.

- System activities included.

- System parameters:

CPI	2.82
memory ref/instr.	2
T_{access}	250 ns
$T_{bus\ cycle}$	50 ns
W_{bus}	8 bytes (width of bus in bytes).

In this study, we are interested in machine speed (i.e., MIPS rate). The performance measure is *CPU time per instruction* (CTPI), defined earlier.

We use the following equations to compute CTPI:

$$T_{c.miss} = T_{access} + (L - 1) * T_{bus\ cycle},$$

$$\text{miss penalty} = \left\lceil \frac{T_{c.miss}}{T_{cycle}} \right\rceil,$$

where L is the number of physical words in a line ($\lceil$ line size, bytes $/ W_{bus} \rceil$), $T_{bus\ cycle}$ is the bus transfer time for a physical word, and W_{bus} is the size of the physical word fetched on each bus cycle (in bytes). We assume that $T_{bus\ cycle}$ is the same as the processor cycle (T_{cycle}). T_{access} is the access time for a word in memory.

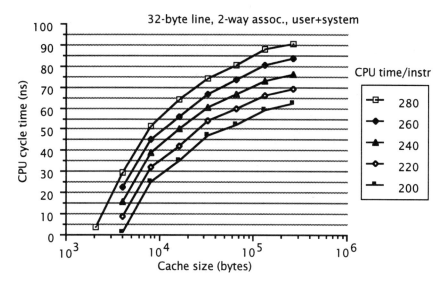

Figure 5.42   CPU time per instruction as a function of CPU cycle time and cache size.

We now consider CPU cycle time vs. cache size.

Suppose our initial choice is set at 50 ns cycle time and 16 KB cache. Figure 5.42 shows the design space around the initial choice. From this figure, CTPI is 240 ns at the chosen point. This means a 4.17 MIPS machine.

When resource constraints are also considered, we may want to select a new design point:

- If we are running out of resources, we need to free up resources by sacrificing speed. For example, we may reduce the cache size from 16KB to 8KB, or, alternatively, increase the CPU cycle time from 50 ns to 65 ns. In either case, the machine slows down from 4.17 MIPS to about 3.6 MIPS (CTPI of 280 ns) as we move to a higher contour in Figure 5.42.

- If we have extra resources, we may want to speed up the machine. The 200 ns CTPI contour in Figure 5.42 gives choices that lead to a 5 MIPS machine. We may increase the cache size from 16KB to 64KB, or decrease the cycle time from 50 ns to 35 ns (although the latter case may not always be possible).

In general, the gradient of the contour lines in Figure 5.42 gives the most effective direction to change machine speed. As cache size increases, the slope of the contours decreases from more than 20 ns per doubling of cache size to less than 5 ns per doubling of cache size. This suggests that for small caches, it is more effective to improve performance by doubling the cache size than by reducing CPU cycle time (if that is feasible). For large caches, the opposite is preferred.

In cases when CPU cycle time is determined by cache, the choice of cache size becomes less obvious. In this case, any increase in cache size may also increase CPU cycle time. There is a tradeoff between smaller miss ratio

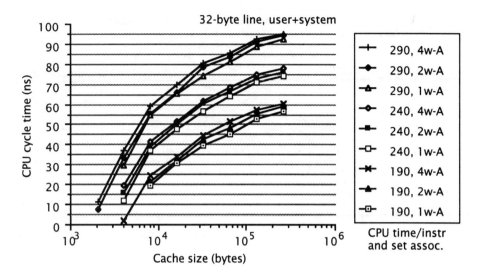

Figure 5.43   Effect of set associativity on CPU time per instruction.

and longer CPU cycle time. For example, if the cache size is doubled from 128KB to 256KB, the increase in CPU cycle time should be less than 3 ns in order to achieve higher machine speed. Otherwise, machine performance may actually be degraded.

Now consider the choice of set associativity.

Figure 5.43 shows three CTPI contours for different set associativities. The differences between set associativities vary quite a bit. (This is largely due to the fact that miss penalty is in terms of integral number of CPU cycles.) The choice of set associativity is not so straightforward as indicated by the miss rate figures. For example, when running at 55 ns CPU cycle time, an 8KB two-way associative cache is only marginally better than an 8KB direct-mapped cache. A direct-mapped cache is preferred for its lower implementation cost. When moved to a cache size of 32KB, a four-way associative cache is only marginally better than a two-way associative cache, which in turn is clearly better than a direct-mapped cache. A two-way associative cache becomes the preferred choice.

In cases when CPU cycle time is determined by cache, the effect of increase in cycle time should be examined. Figure 5.43 shows that if any change of set associativity from direct mapping to two-way associative mapping results in an increase in cycle time of more than 4 ns, machine performance can actually be degraded. If this is the case, the simplest direct-mapped cache should be used.

Now let us consider the change of instruction template.

In the previous discussion, the same instruction template is used for different values of CPU cycle time. When the CPU cycle time is shorter than the cache access time, there is no reason to use the same template. A template based on a shorter processor cycle time should be used, requiring multiple cycles for cache access.

Suppose the cache access time (T_{cache}) is 65 ns. When the CPU cycle time is greater than 65 ns, a shorter template is used and the CPI decreases from

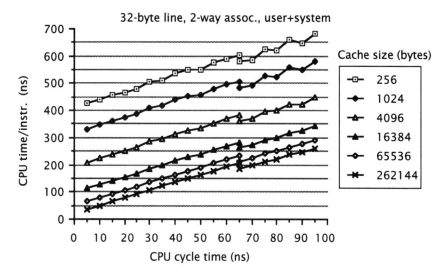

Figure 5.44   CPU time per instruction.

2.82 to 2.49. Figure 5.44 shows how CTPI changes with CPU cycle time for different cache sizes. Note the dips that occurred at the 65 ns boundary. When the cycle time is below 65 ns but larger than 58 ns, the machine actually performs poorer than when running at 65 ns. In this case, a CPU cycle time that matches the cache access time is preferred. The figure also shows that a change in cache size is more effective in small caches than in large caches.

To summarize the results of the preceding study, smaller cycle times require faster technology and more expensive implementations. Larger cycle times, however, require increased cache size, which also contributes significantly to cost. The data presented in Figure 5.42 assume that the processor timing template is invariant as cycle time changes. This generally is not the case, however, as the cache *per se* rarely determines the cycle time over any broad range of cycle time. Usually, the cache itself can be pipelined, that is, staged so that single access can be achieved in two or three stages. When the access time for the cache was fixed at 65 ns, the timing template was modified, i.e., simplified, to allow for one access to the cache for cycle times of 65 ns and above. Below this, the template remains at a two-cycle access.

Other Measures

An alternative approach to evaluating the effectiveness of cache is to measure the effective memory access time ($T_{\text{eff.mem.}}$):

$$T_{\text{eff.mem.}} = T_{\text{cache}} + \text{miss rate} * T_{\text{c.miss}},$$

Table 5.9   Virtual to real address translation.

Uses TLB that requires:

  (a) Translation (T) action with each memory reference.

  (b) "Not in TLB" cycles for a translation miss. Can be costly if TLB is too small.

In order to avoid translate (T) delay, we can use:

  (a) Virtual cache.

  (b) Set associativity (of sufficient depth).

  (c) Colored bits page assignment.

---

where $T_{c.miss}$ is:

$$T_{c.miss} = T_{access} + (L - 1)T_{bus\ cycle},$$

as described in the above case study. (Also, see the next chapter.)

This is a useful measure when there is no good model for CPU time. As before, the goal is to minimize the effective memory access time or provide the minimum effective memory access for a given cost.

For bus-based processors (especially multiprocessors), bus traffic can be an important limitation on performance. As bus saturation approaches, contention for the bus increases the waiting time for memory service and hence increases the $T_{eff.mem.}$ time significantly. When bus saturation occurs, it is necessary to consider the bus traffic caused by the memory system. Usually, this is not a simple process of reducing memory traffic, since a single-word transfer occupies significantly more bus time than a multiword transfer. The goal then in reducing bus traffic is primarily to reduce the number of separate bus requests, even if the number of words transferred increases.

5.16   Virtual-to-Real Translation

So far in this chapter, we have assumed that the cache is accessed with a real memory address: the address translated by the TLB (translation lookaside buffer) or similar mechanism into the address used by the physical memory. There are at least three important performance aspects that directly relate to virtual-to-real address translation:

1. Improperly organized or insufficiently sized TLBs may create excess not-in-TLB faults, adding time to program execution.

2. For a real cache, the TLB access time must occur before the cache access, effectively extending the cache access time.

3. Two-line addresses (for example, an I-line and a D-line address) may be independent of each other in the virtual address space yet collide

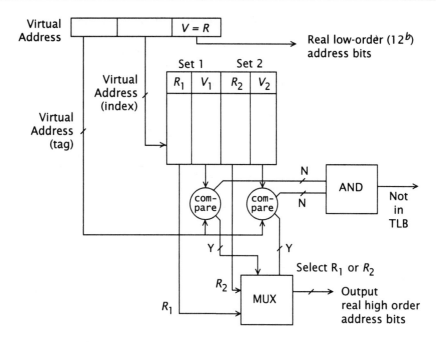

Figure 5.45   TLB with two-way set associativity.

in the real address space, when they draw pages whose lower page address bits (and upper cache address bits) are identical.

The organization of this section is summarized in Table 5.9.

Excess not-in-TLB translations can generally be controlled through the use of a well-designed TLB. The size and organization of the TLB depend on the desired performance.

5.16.1   Translation Lookaside Buffer (TLB)

The translation lookaside buffer (TLB), as described in chapter 1, is closely associated with the cache. It provides the real addresses used by the cache by translating the virtual addresses provided by the processor into real addresses.

Figure 5.45 shows a two-way set associative TLB. The page address (the upper bits of the virtual address) is composed of the bits that require translation (a byte within a page—the lower 12 bits for a 4KB page—is unaffected by translation). Several of the virtual address bits are used to directly address the TLB entries. These are usually not simply the lowest order except the virtual address, but rather selected (or *hashed*) from the bits of the virtual address. Hashing the bits of the virtual address is sometimes done to avoid too many address collisions, as might occur, for instance, when both address and data pages have the same, say, "000," low-order page addresses. The size of the virtual address index is equal to $\log_2 t$, where t is the number of entries in the TLB divided by the degree of set associativity. When a TLB entry is accessed, a virtual and real translation pair from each entry is accessed. The virtual addresses are compared to the virtual address

Table 5.10   Some TLB data (published/reported data).

For S/370 and 4^{KB} Pages:

Machine	TLB Organization	Entries	Not-in-TLB rate
Amdahl V/6	128×2	256	0.3–0.4%
Amdahl V/8	256×2	512	(not available)
IBM 3081	128×1	128	1%
IBM 3033	64×2	128	(not available)

For VAX and 512^B Pages:

VAX 11/780	64×2	128	4.5%

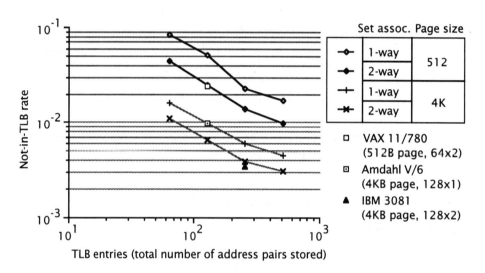

Figure 5.46   Not-in-TLB rate.

tag (the virtual address bits that were not used in the index). If a match is found, this match controls the MUXing of the corresponding translated real address to the output of the TLB.

The TLB access is integral with the cache access for fetching information into the processor. When a translation is not found in the TLB, the process described in chapter 1 must be repeated to create an accurate virtual-to-real address pair in the TLB. This may involve 15 to more than 30 cycles; TLB misses—called *not-in-TLB*—are costly to performance. TLB access in many ways resembles cache access. Fully associative organization of TLB is generally too slow, and therefore set associative TLB is generally preferred. Some TLB organizations and TLB miss rates are shown in Table 5.10.

We use general cache DTMR together with cited data (Table 5.10) to create a TLB design target miss rate (Figure 5.46).

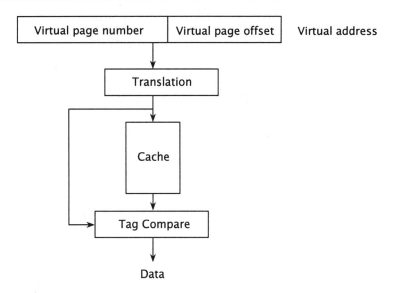

Figure 5.47   Sequential translation and access.

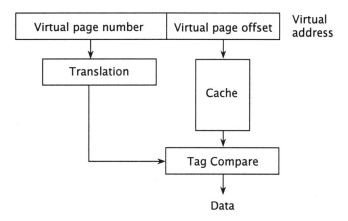

Figure 5.48   Parallel translation and access.

5.17   Overlapping the T cycle in $V \to R$ Translation

There are three general approaches to avoiding the serial translation step in cache access (as shown in Figure 5.47). In order to avoid the sequential translation, the translation must be arranged so that it can be performed simultaneously with data access in the cache array (Figure 5.48). This can be done by one of three means:

1. Using high degrees of set associativity, so that the directory index bits are not affected by the translation.

2. Using a virtual cache.

3. Using *perfectly colored pages.*

We consider each in the following subsections.

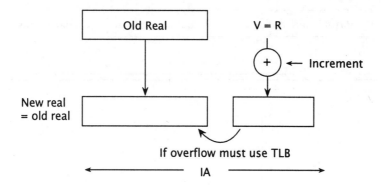

Figure 5.49   Instruction address translation.

5.17.1   Set Associative Caches

In simpler processors the instruction timing template allows for sequentially executing the events:

$$AG \rightarrow T \rightarrow DF \text{ (cache access)},$$

where T represents the $V \rightarrow R$ translation using the TLB. The IF usually is simpler:

$$IA \rightarrow IF,$$

where the T is implied as part of the IA. This is possible since the IA generates an address outside the current page only infrequently (even on most branch target addresses, 80% lie within a 4KB page). Thus, in IA the result need only be checked, perhaps during IF, to ensure that it lies within the same (previously translated) page (Figure 5.49).

The DF is a different case, as the result of the data AG frequently lies outside its previous page. Thus, for DF the ordinary process is:

$$AG \rightarrow T \rightarrow DF.$$

So long as the cache size is equal to or less than the page size, we have (set associative and direct mapped)

$$AG \rightarrow T/DF,$$

since the bits needed to address the cache line (index bits) are those (lower-order) bits that do not need translation. The tag bits require the TLB access but the cache data can be accessed at the same time as the TLB access.

For direct-mapped caches larger than the page size, translated bits are needed for the index and hence to address a line in the cache.

In some processors, set associative caches of high degree have been used to allow parallel access to cache and TLB. Figure 5.50 shows the virtual-to-real address translation process. The virtual page offset identifies a byte in a page and, as mentioned earlier, is unaffected by TLB and translation. In the

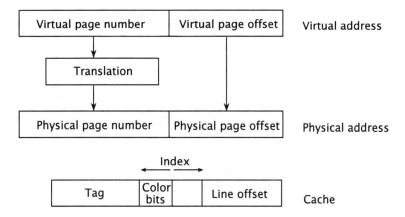

Figure 5.50 Virtual-to-physical address translation.

case of 4KB pages, the lower 12 bits are unaffected by translation; thus, for up to 4KB caches, the TLB and the cache may be accessed simultaneously, since the cache index bits are known. Of course, before the accessed cache word can be forwarded to the processor, the cache directory must be compared with the output of the TLB to validate that the correct word has been accessed. As caches get larger, one approach has been simply to increase the degree of set associativity. For example, an 8KB cache with two-way set associativity still uses only the lower 12 bits to reference cache information. For larger caches, this rapidly becomes impractical; a 64KB cache requires 16-way set associativity. Notice that there is little or no advantage in a miss rate above about four-way set associativity.

5.17.2 Virtual Caches

Most caches buffer information exactly as it has been stored in memory. A real address is computed before accessing the cache, and real addresses are used as tags in the cache directory. This requires the translation of virtual addresses into real addresses (via the TLB) prior to accessing the cache. In a virtual cache, when a miss occurs, that address is then translated into a real address and the line is accessed from main memory. This introduces additional complexity, however. Now two processes may use different addresses to access the same real line, or the same address to access different real lines. For example, it is common for a process to be coded relative to address 0.0...0. These addresses will be assigned to different segments and different pages but their *virtual* addresses are the same. These addresses are referenced as *aliases*. Thus, it becomes important to distinguish among processes that might simultaneously reside in a single cache, or simply to prohibit multiple processes from occupying the virtual cache at the same time. There are two basic control strategies here:

1. To prohibit any process aside from the operating system to cohabit the cache at the same time as a user process.

2. To require a process ID number (PID) to be associated with each line in the cache directory. This uniquely determines the mapping from a virtual address to a real address.

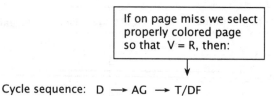

Cycle sequence: D $\longrightarrow$ AG $\longrightarrow$ T/DF

Figure 5.51   T/DF overlap with colored pages.

The first approach requires the cache to be purged when a new process is entered. This might be satisfactory for small caches, but is limited as the cache size increases. The second approach increases the size of the cache directory but otherwise gives reasonable performance.

Either approach requires special attention to I/O, since I/O addresses are usually referenced to the real memory address space. In order to manage the I/O problem, certain areas of memory may be defined for which the virtual and real address spaces are the same. In this case, the I/O would use this space exclusively.

5.17.3   Physically Addressed Caches Using Colored Pages

Only a few virtual bits need go through the TLB before the cache access is made. We call these bits the *color bits*. The operating system (memory manager) chooses the real page address from a list of available pages (the *free list*) when a page miss occurs. By maintaining several free lists, one for each color bit combination, we can force the address bits required for cache access to always be $V = R$, i.e., have the same real bit address as virtual address. The remaining (upper) virtual address bits still must go through the TLB and be checked, but, as in approach (a), the cache access can occur concurrently with this TLB access. (See Figure 5.51.)

When the real page address is a function of the virtual page address, it is referred to as a *colored page*. Instead of adding additional hardware to maintain high degrees of set associativity, we accomplish the same effect in software by maintaining multiple free lists for page assignment.

Using colored pages has an added bonus: it reduces the cache performance variance caused by differing relative page assignments on different program runs when allocated off a (randomly assigned) single free list. Figure 5.52 illustrates the effective random assignments on an I-cache compared to a cache using colored pages. A colored physical cache gives the same relative performance as a virtual cache. I-caches are particularly sensitive to page relationships and assignments; hence, the random assignment usually produces a much poorer performance than the original address assignment (as in the virtual address), since the program is generally sequentially moving across its pages.

It seems nothing comes without a price, including page coloring. Main memory is now partitioned into 2^b sets, where b is the number of low-order page number bits that are colored. Page allocation must now be accomplished from multiple correctly colored free lists. Since memory is now partitioned into classes or bins by the free lists, there is a higher probability, especially

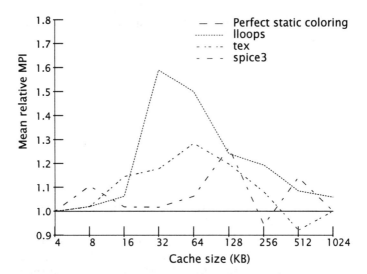

Figure 5.52   Mean misses per instruction (MPI) for a standard cache (4KB pages, single LRU free page list) *relative* to the MPI for a colored cache vs. cache size for three sample programs (16B lines, unified cache). Data from Lynch [188].

as memory becomes fully occupied, of thrashing in the memory. The net effect of this is to reduce the effective memory size somewhat. Based on a number of program simulations, Lynch [188] has shown that this effect is minimal—probably less than a 1% effective reduction in memory size.

Is the loss of (say) half a megabyte out of 64 megabytes reasonable, in light of the improved cache access time and relative miss performance? Here again, the designer must use careful judgement in selecting the strategies suitable for a particular environment.

5.18   Studies

Study 5.3   Cache Design

Design a cache for a 20 MIPS (peak) R/M-type CPU, used in study 4.3, with the following parameters.

Assume: $T_{internal} = 50\,ns$
               Cache miss = 300 ns (6 cycles)

Cost and memory considerations dictate a cache of 64KB with 32B lines and an 8B memory–cache transfer path (i.e., 8B is the physical memory word size).

For the cache data storage, assume $T_{access} = 50\,ns$, but that the total $T_{access} = 65\,ns$, including compare, multiplex, and transit delay to processor register.

Also assume a user plus system environment (where the system includes the effect of I/O).

The Design

The instruction timing layout is similar to study 4.3:

The total cache access requires two cycles (i.e., increasing it from 65 ns to 100 ns) in order to match cycle boundaries.

We know from study 4.3 that an average instruction takes 2.82 cycles, but the cache should be designed so as not to be limited by cache bandwidth. The processor activity is dominated by bursts of execution at the maximum rate separated by delays due to branches, etc. The design should be limited by the more expensive facilities. For this study, we assume that the cache is not such a limiting facility.

Since two requests (one instruction, one data) may simultaneously be directed at the cache, a fundamental consideration in cache design is whether to integrate data and instructions in a single cache, or to split references into separate caches. The split cache is simpler to implement and more readily accommodates two requests/cycle, but the integrated cache has a lower miss rate.

Assuming two-way set associativity, from Figure 5.10 we can estimate a worst-case miss rate of about 1.8% for an integrated 64^{KB} cache in a scientific environment, ignoring the details of the cache organization. This is increased by a factor of 1.70 due to systems effects (Figure 5.22), giving an overall miss rate of 3.1%.

Now, the simplest cache to implement would be a split I/D cache, each of 32^{KB} with no duplicate entries allowed. From Figures 5.28 and 5.29, this gives us:

$$I_{miss} = 1.7\%,$$
$$D_{miss} = 2.5\%.$$

Taking the system (and I/O) into account, we have:

$$I_{miss} \text{ effective} = 1.7 \times 1.75 = 3.0\%,$$
$$D_{miss} \text{ effective} = 2.5 \times 1.75 = 4.4\%.$$

Since the total references per instruction cannot exceed two (one for instruction and one for data), and the cache miss penalty is unlikely to exceed 6 cycles, we can estimate the performance degradation effect of an integrated design as miss rate × references per instruction × miss penalty:

$$0.031 \times 2 \times 6 = .37 \text{ CPI};$$

while split cache would degrade performance by:

$$.03 \times 1 \times 6 + .044 \times 1 \times 6 = .44 \text{ CPI.}$$

In the context of the study 4.3 result of 2.82 CPI (without cache miss), the difference between cache approaches is limited to less than 5% and we might well select the simpler split cache approach. While we assume a split I/D implementation for the rest of this study, we have simply made *estimates* at this point and these must be carefully checked later.

5.18.1   Actual Reference Traffic

Now we return our attention to computing the actual reference activity from the processor to the cache (memory system). We need to know the total traffic or references per instruction as well as the constituents of this traffic. This allows us to compute the exact cache miss rate and to make required design tradeoffs between cache and memory.

The processor traffic has three constituent parts:

1. Instruction references/instruction.

2. Data (read) references/instruction.

3. Data (write) references/instruction.

Given the parameters of the problem (R/M instruction set, 8-byte physical word size), we know the I-references/instruction to be 0.73 from the computation on page 313. Similarly, from the data in Table 5.7, we know the data (read) references/instruction to be 0.34 and data (write) references/instruction to be 0.21.

Cache Design

After the traffic evaluation, the design of the cache is rather straightforward. Notice that an actual traffic rate of 0.73 I references/instruction is similar to that used in the earlier evaluation of miss rate, while the D read references/instruction is significantly lower. The effect of actual traffic on performance is:

$$0.03 \times .73 \times 6 + 0.044 \times 0.34 \times 6 = .22 \text{ cycles,}$$

which is well under 10% of the estimated execution time per instruction. We select the conventional cache attributions, stressing low cost.

For I_{cache}, we select:

Size:	32^{KB}
Organization:	set associative degree 2
Replacement:	random
	No writes (I-cache)

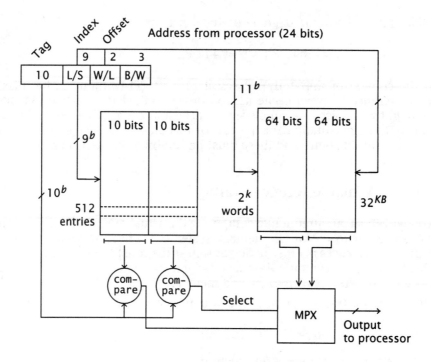

Figure 5.53   Cache configuration.

For the D-cache, we select:

Size:	32KB
Organization:	set associative degree 2
Replacement:	random
Writes:	no allocate on write
	Write-through

In selecting random replacement (RAND), we should adjust the miss rates upward by about 12%. Our evaluation is also affected by our degree of association. Miss rate is increased by 15% for two-way associative cache.

Thus, the effective miss rates are now:

$$(\text{Miss rate}) \times (\text{adjustment for RAND}) \times (\text{adjustment for associativity}).$$

$$\text{For instructions:}\quad 0.03 \times 1.12 \times 1.15 = 0.039.$$
$$\text{For data:}\quad .044 \times 1.12 \times 1.15 = 0.057.$$

Each cache is organized as in Figure 5.53.

Processor performance with cache and *six-cycle* miss penalty is:

$$2.82 + 0.73 \times .039 \times 6 + 0.34 \times .057 \times 6 = 2.82 + .29 = 3.11 \text{ CPI}.$$

Study 5.4 Assessing Contention in an Integrated (vs. Split) Cache

Suppose we had selected an integrated cache in study 5.3. Now let us compute the delay at the cache access controller due to this contention.

In solving this problem, we must first recognize that not all of the traffic per instruction determined in study 5.3 causes contention. In particular, contention can arise only when both the I-buffer and the Data AG are making requests to the cache access controller. Specifically, this does not happen when "run-on" instructions are making excess data requests (more than one) as the I-buffer goes idle, since there is a "run-on" interlock issued from the decoder.

Initial Analysis

Contention arises when *both* the I-buffer (IF) and the DF are active. The probability that the I-buffer makes a data request to cache in a given (non-interlocked) cycle is 0.80 (from study 5.3). The probability that the DF will make a request during a non-interlocked (or non-run-on) period is:

D-reads + D-writes − excess LM/STM traffic (the run-on traffic),

or, using Table 3.15:

$$\frac{36 + 16 + 23 + 18 + 1 + 1}{180} = 0.53.$$

Here we determine reads and writes from the L/S data (Table 3.15) but divide by the R/M instruction count. All register set architectures with about the same number of registers should create the same number of reads and writes per HLL operation. This is then adjusted by the instruction count per HLL operation.

The model assumes that all reads or writes create a reference to cache except the branch, and that the first LM or STM data reference occurs while the I-buffer is active.

Thus, *if all contention caused delay*, we would have contention of:

$$\text{Prob(IF)} * \text{Prob(DF or DS)} = (0.73) * (0.53) = 0.39.$$

We would thus add 39% additional cycles to manage this contention. Not all of these cycles need cause execution delay, since either the in-line I-buffer or the store buffer can be delayed a cycle without affecting performance. However, even with a well-buffered processor and well-managed cache access priority system, we still require:

$$0.73 + 0.53 \text{ cache access/instr} = 1.26 \text{ cache access cycles/instr.}$$

Improved Analysis

This "lower bound" on contention ignores an important factor—many of the I-requests arise from branches that occur during "extra" branch resolution cycles. From study 4.3, decoding and branch effects result in processor performance of 2.025 ~/instruction. In other words, for every 100 instructions, we have 202.5 cycles of expected execution (assuming that data dependencies will interlock, or "lock out," IF). Thus, there are ample cycles available to "fit in" the 126 requests (i.e., the 100×1.26 cache CPI developed earlier).

Which accesses cause delay? Since contention cannot arise between TIF and DF (TIF uses a DF slot), the primary source will be between *in-line* and *executed* instructions whose execution is delayed by a DF. (Delay cannot arise if a nonexecuted instruction is delayed.) Assume that each requestor source can make at most one access in a cycle and that the probability of an access corresponds to the expected number of accesses per cycle from that source.

We can then model contention by first computing:

$$\text{Prob (IF of an executed instr in any given cycle)} \quad = \quad \frac{0.4 \text{ IF/instr}}{2.025 \text{ cycles/I}}$$

$$= \quad 0.20$$

The probability of an *executed* instruction, eliminating the excess I-traffic, is just $I/P = 0.4$ (see study 5.1). The number of cycles/I as discussed previously is 2.025. Instructions that are fetched but not executed are those fetched in anticipation of a branch. If the branch takes the other path, any contention delay incurred in fetching these nonexecuted instructions cannot have a performance effect. We eliminate this excess instruction and target traffic, which (since they are not executed) cannot cause delay, and

Prob (DF or DS in any given cycle)
$$= \quad \text{(DF or DS/I) divided by CPI} = (0.34 + 0.20)/2.025 = 0.27.$$

Now assuming that IF and DF are independent events, the probability of a conflict in any cycle is:

$$\text{Prob (IF/cycle)} \cdot \text{Prob (DF/cycle)} = (0.20) \cdot (0.27) = 0.05.$$

This can be summarized as

$$\text{CPI loss due to cache access contention} = \frac{(\text{IF}/\text{I})(\text{DF} + \text{DS})/\text{I}}{\text{CPI}^2},$$

where IF/I is I/P (the expected number of in-line I-fetches per instruction), (DF + DS)/I is the expected number of data references per instruction, and CPI is computed without inclusion of any cache delays.

Actually, for many cases, a delay of an executed instruction fetch for a cycle may not cause delay, but a sequence of such delays (two or more) causes delay. However, we use the conservative estimate of 0.06 for cache contention. This gives a total delay estimate of $2.02 \text{ CPI} \times 0.05 = 0.10 \text{ CPI}$. This analysis apparently violates our chapter 4 timing rule: "always design for peak (here, one cycle per instruction) execution rates." The point of this analysis is to recognize the role of branches both in creating the contention problem *and* in (partially) relieving the problem.

The 1.26 cache CPI and execution rate of one CPI are inconsistent statements, since the first includes branch effects and the second does not. Once we have accepted a branch strategy frequency, we can use this information in a consistent way.

Integrated Cache Evaluation

Now we can complete the analysis of the integrated 64^{KB} cache (WTNWA). To make the comparison with the split cache as fair as possible, assume we use four-way set associative, 32^B line with RAND—random replacement of lines. We determine a miss rate of $1.8 \times 1.05 \times (1.7) = 3.2\%$ miss/reference (DTMR adjusted for 4w and system's effect). From our earlier split cache analysis, we have determined the read traffic per instruction of:

$$0.73 \text{ I-refr/I} + 0.34 \text{ D-reads/I} = 1.07 \text{ refr/I}.$$

Then the actual miss rate is:

$$3.2\% \times 1.12 \text{ (for RAND)} = 3.6\%,$$

and the delay due to cache misses per instruction is:

$$.036 \text{ misses/refr} \times 1.07 \text{ refr/I} \times 6 \text{ cycles/miss} = 0.23 \text{ CPI}.$$

This compares to the split cache delay of 0.29 CPI.

To the integrated cache delay, we add 0.10 CPI caused by cache access contention, or:

$$0.23 + 0.10 = 0.33 \text{ CPI}.$$

Thus, split cache is more effective in this example. Note that the 0.10 CPI is still a conservative estimate and, in all likelihood, both caches would perform about the same.

Study 5.5   The Cache for the Baseline Processor

From study 2.2, we know that we have 28,633 bytes (cache bytes) available for cache data arrays and directories.

Based on an I-traffic to D-traffic ratio of about 2:1, let us split the cache and assign 16KB (16,384 bytes) to the I-cache array and 8KB (8,192 bytes) to the D-cache. This leaves 4,057 bytes available for directories.

Suppose we have fully blocking caches with a 5-cycle memory access, a 4B physical word and bus, and a one-cycle time per (4B) word transferred. In order to keep the cache miss penalty down, let us select a 16B line (4 words).

Assuming a memory that supports fast sequential page mode (at least one word per processor cycle), this gives us a cache miss delay of:

$$\begin{aligned} T_{c.miss} &= T_{m.miss} = 5 + (L - 1) \text{ cycles} \\ &= 8 \text{ cycles} \end{aligned}$$

Now we can compute the size of the directories. Assume direct-mapped caches. The directory entry consists of a tag plus some control information. We can now compute the tag size. The real address size is 24 bits (study 2.3).

For the I-cache, we have $16K/16 = 1,024$ lines, and for the D-cache we have 512 lines. This means that the I-cache index is 10 bits and the D-cache index is 9 bits. Therefore (allowing 4 bits for B/line), the I-cache tag is

$$24 - 10 - 4 = 10^b$$

and the D-cache tag is

$$24 - 9 - 4 = 11^b.$$

Even if we allow 2 bytes for tag + control for each directory entry, we would use only 3,072 bytes of the 4,057 available.

Now consider the effect of cache misses on performance. Suppose we use CBWA policy—no LRU considerations are necessary, as the cache is direct mapped. We have 1 IF/I, 0.31 DF/I, and 0.20 DS/I (from section 5.14).

Now the miss rate (Appendix A) for the I-cache is $0.05 \times 1.35 = 0.068$ and the D-cache is $0.08 \times 1.32 = 0.106$. We can find the CPI loss due to cache misses by summing

$$\text{Refs/I} \times \text{misses/ref} \times \text{delay/miss}.$$

$$
\begin{aligned}
\text{CPI loss} \quad &= \quad \text{I-cache loss} + \text{D-cache loss} \\
&= \quad 1 \times 0.068 \times 8 + 0.50 \times 0.106 \times 8(1 + .5) \\
\text{CPI loss} \quad &= \quad .54 + .64 = 1.18.
\end{aligned}
$$

Now we must account for TLB misses. Suppose the "not in TLB" delay is 20 cycles. From Figure 5.46, we estimate that a TLB (4KB pages) with 128 entries (64×2) will have a miss rate of 0.006. There is one access to the I-TLB and 0.5 references to the D-TLB each instruction. The resulting delay estimate is:

$$\text{CPI delay} \quad = \quad 0.006 \times 20 \times 1.5 = 0.18.$$

From study 4.10, we have a CPI (without cache misses) of 1.60. So we now have in total:

$$\text{CPI} = 1.60 + 1.18 + 0.18 = 2.96.$$

How to improve this? Clearly, we need larger caches, more aggressive overlapping of misses with processor execution and (perhaps) increased associativity. All this requires area. We see more alternatives in chapter 7.

5.19   Design Summary

5.19.1   Cache Evaluation Design Rules

1. Find DTMR based on cache size and line size.

2. Adjust for set associativity and line replacement (if other than fully associative and LRU).

3. Select the most representative system environment and adjust miss rate.

5.19.2   Cache/TLB Excess CPI Design Rules

1. Find effective miss rate per reference (see cache evaluation design rules).

2. Compute IF/I.

3. Compute DF/I (with WTNWA) or (DF + DS)/I (with CBWA).

4. Find memory miss penalty (also see discussion in chapter 6).

5. Excess CPI due to cache is:

   (Miss rate)(references/I)(Miss penalty in cycles).

6. Find the "not in TLB" rate per instruction (Figure 5.46). Multiply by references per instruction. No further adjustments are needed.

7. Excess CPI due to TLB is:

   (Not in TLB rate)(TLB miss penalty)(references per instruction).

8. Excess CPI is sum of (5) and (7).

5.20   Conclusions

Caches operate on the principle of spatial and temporal locality. Regions and words of memory that have been recently accessed will probably be accessed again in the near future. The effect of the cache is to provide the processor with a memory access time equivalent to that of a high-speed buffer, and significantly faster than the memory access time would be without the cache. Without a cache, the processor instruction timing template would be significantly extended, and the effects of the memory system on pipeline breaks such as branches would become much more pronounced. Thus, the cache is an important constituent in the modern high-speed processor. The design target miss rate (DTMR) provides a basic objective for cache designers in achieving overall processor performance. The DTMR may be adjusted for various factors, such as the architecture, the operating system, the system's environment, and I/O effects, to give an overall effective or adjusted DTMR. Each environmental factor, such as the system or the processor architecture, requires an adjustment to the DTMR so that the effects of various working set differences are properly accounted for.

The processor architecture in particular affects not only the miss rate by affecting the working set size, but it directly affects the processor traffic to the cache (the number of references per instruction). These effects must be carefully incorporated into any performance model to correctly determine processor–cache interaction.

This chapter addresses only the effect of cache on a single processor. In a later chapter we will see more on cache and the role it plays in multiprocessor configurations.

5.21   Some Areas for Further Research

While it may appear that uniprocessor caches have been well-studied, data in certain areas, such as miss rate for very large caches, is still limited. The behavior and miss rate under various systems and I/O disciplines have really not been fully explored. The major research thrust for caches is supporting multiprocessor configurations. Here there are many additional issues, including the various protocols required to maintain consistent data images across multiple caches, as well as the associated bus traffic to support this consistent data image.

5.22   Data Notes

The first mention of the concept of a transparent buffer memory appears to be by Wilkes in 1965 [306]. The earliest reported data on the effectiveness of cache-type buffers is from Gibson [102]. Gibson, Pomerine, and Conti, all of IBM, provided the early basis for cache-type buffers. The System 360/Model 85 [56] was the first commercial processor to effectively incorporate cache memory. Much of the data in this chapter has been derived from the work of Smith, Clark, and Hill, in addition to earlier studies. When dealing with statistical adjustments, the derivation of comparable data can be quite difficult, as the data reported are based on incomparable work loads. Thus, in using the work of Agarwal or Mitchell, for example, we have had to normalize their data to the expected DTMR. This naturally involves some uncertainty. The adjustments, therefore, are always less reliable than the basic DTMR data.

Analytical models for cache have been proposed, which could in principle resolve a good deal of the uncertainties in dealing with empirical data. Unfortunately, these models largely rely on the availability of statistical parameters that are also quite difficult to obtain and are workload-dependent.

Data Note 1:   Design Target Miss Rate (Figures 5.10, 5.28, and 5.29).

Design target miss rate (DTMR) was first introduced by Smith [262, 260]. Based on extensive program traces from eight different workloads (mostly S/370 and VAX traces), Smith [262] gave DTMR for cache size ranges from 32 bytes to 32K bytes. In [260], Smith also listed DTMR for 16-byte line caches (for cache size up to 64K bytes). Following the methodology used in [262], DTMR in the higher range (128K and 256K) are determined from additional data (16-, 32-, and 64-byte line caches for cache size up to 256K bytes) given in Hill [129]. DTMR for 128-byte line cache in the 128–256K cache size range are extrapolated from existing data and should be used with caution.

Use of the data.   The data in Figure 5.10 should be used in conjunction with the adjustment data (Figures 5.13–5.14) to determine the effective miss rate for integrated caches. The adjustment process is described in the text.

Reliability.   As described previously, the data presented in Figure 5.10 has been based on many sources and should represent a good design basis. Data for large caches is based upon a smaller sample and is less reliable.

Stability. Data should represent a conservative estimate of miss rate. Small programs especially may perform significantly better than DTMR.

Data Note 2: Empirical Data for Different Application Environments and Machine Traces (Figures 5.11 and 5.12).

Extensive data for 370, VAX, 360/91, and 6400 traces are given in Smith [260]. Data for 32016-UNIX traces are taken from Alexander [11]. Data for 8200 traces are from Agarwal [4]. All these data are obtained by cache simulation on program traces.

Use of the data. This data is presented as a validation for the DTMR. The DTMR data shown are for two-way associativity and 16-byte lines. The other data were selected to be as comparable as the sources allow.

Data Note 3: Effect of Set Associativity (Figures 5.13 and 5.14).

Data for different set associativities are taken from Hill [129]. Relative miss rates are computed directly from miss rates and the curves shown here have been smoothed.

Use of the data. This data has been prepared for use with DTMR data in Figures 5.10, 5.28, and 5.29.

Reliability. The data presented seems consistent with other reported results. It should be useful for conservative design estimates.

Stability. Individual programs may vary as to the effect of set associativity. Variance is expected to be higher with direct-mapped and low degrees of association.

Data Note 4: Effect of System Activities (Figures 5.21 and 5.22).

Materials on effect of system activities are taken from Agarwal [4]. Since data on few program traces have been reported, the relative miss rates should be treated cautiously.

Use of the data. Data (Figure 5.22) should be used as an adjustment to basic DTMRs.

Reliability. Data presented is for a particular operating system running a relatively small number of benchmarks. While the data is certainly indicative of expected performance, the actual values may vary with environment.

Stability. One would expect a significant variation with operating systems. There are only limited data sources available for this data.

Data Note 5: Cold-Start Caches and Effect of Multiprogramming (Figure 5.26).

These curves are computed from DTMR using the Markovian cache model by Haikala [116]. The warm-start cache data include the effect of system activities. Due to the accuracy of the cache model used and the estimation of the input data, miss rates shown in these figures are pessimistic. (See Appendix C for a more complete discussion.)

Use of the data. This data should be used with care. Cold-start (transaction) data *should not be adjusted for I/O*, as these effects are included in the transaction model.

Reliability. Data seems consistent with earlier work of Smith [259]. but since it is not based upon direct measurements, reliability should be interpreted as low (best available data).

Stability. Variance may be high.

Data Note 6: Effect of Architecture Family (Figure 5.31).

Instruction cache data is taken from Mitchell [200]. Data caches vary little across different architecture families.

Data Note 7: Not-in-TLB Rate (Figure 5.46).

Amdahl V/6, IBM 3081 and VAX 11/780 data are published/reported measurement data [259, 54]. Data for 512-byte page size are simulation results taken from Clark and Emer [54]. Data for 4K-byte page size are projected from DTMR and are included for reference.

Use of the Data. Data can be used directly.

Reliability. Low. Data presented are based on limited reports. It appears consistent with manufacturers' projections.

Stability. Data are expected to be reasonably stable over various environments.

5.23   Bibliography

Additional Reading

Basic Cache Data

Alan J. Smith. Cache memories. *Computing Surveys*, 14(3):473–530, September 1982.

M. D. Hill. A case for direct-mapped cache. *IEEE Computer*, pages 25–40, December 1988.

J. E. Smith and J. R. Goodman. A study of instruction cache organizations and replacement policies. *IEEE Transactions on Software Engineering*, SE-9(3):132–137, 1983.

D. W. Clark. Cache performance in the VAX-11/780. *ACM Transactions on Computing Systems*, 1(1):24–37, February 1983.

Systems Effects

A. Agarwal, J. Hennessy, and M. Horowitz. Cache performance of operating system and multiprogramming workloads. *ACM Transactions on Computer Systems*, 6(4):393–431, November 1988.

D. W. Clark and J. S. Emer. Performance of the VAX-11/780 translation buffer: simulation and measurement. *ACM Transactions on Computing Systems*, 3(1):31–62, February 1985.

On-Chip Caches

J. M. Mulder, N. T. Quach, and M. J. Flynn. An area model for on-chip memories and its application. *Journal of Solid State Circuits*, 26(2), February 1991.

Multilevel Caches

S. Przybylski, M. Horowitz, and J. Hennessy. Characteristics of performance-optimal multi-level cache hierarchies. *Proceedings of the 16th Annual Symposium on Computer Architecture*, pages 114–121, June 1989.

Working Sets and Workload

L. Balady and C. Kuehner. Dynamic space sharing in computer systems. *Communications of the ACM* 12(5), May 1969.

P. Denning. The working set model for program behavior. *Communications of the ACM*, 11(5):323–333, 1968.

P. Denning. Working sets past and present. *IEEE Transactions on Software Engineering*, SE-6(1):64–84, 1980.

A. Smith. Cache evaluation and the impact of workload choice. *Proceedings of the 12th International Symposium on Computer Architecture*, pages 64–73, June 1985.

5.24   Problem Set

1. A 128^{KB} cache has 64^B lines, 8^B physical word, 4^Kbyte pages, and is four-way set associative. It uses copyback (allocate on write) and LRU replacement. The processor creates 30-bit (byte-addressed) virtual addresses that are translated into 24-bit (byte-addressed) real byte addresses (labeled A_0–A_{23}, from least to most significant).

   (a) Which address bits are unaffected by translation $(V = R)$?

   (b) Which address bits are used to address the cache directories?

   (c) Which address bits are compared to entries in the cache directory?

   (d) Which address bits are appended to address bits in (b) to address the cache array?

2. Show a complete layout of the cache in problem 1. Present the same detail as in Figures 5.5 through 5.7.

3. Compute the effective miss rate for the cache in problem 1, assuming a single user and R/M processor architecture without systems or I/O effects.

4. Plot traffic (in bytes) as a function of line size for a DTMR cache (CBWA, LRU, scientific environment, R/M architecture) for:

    (a) 4^{KB} cache.

    (b) 32^{KB} cache.

    (c) 256^{KB} cache.

5. Suppose we define the miss rate at which a copyback cache (CBWA) and a write-through cache (WTNWA) have equal traffic as the crossover point.

    (a) For the DTMR cache, find the crossover point (miss rate) for 16^B, 32^B, and 64^B lines. To what cache sizes do these correspond?

    (b) Plot line size against cache size for crossover.

6. The cache in problem 1 is now used with a 16^b line in a transaction environment ($Q = 20,000$).

    (a) Compute the effective miss rate.

    (b) Approximately what is the optimal cache size (the smallest cache size that produces the lowest achievable miss rate)?

7. In a two-level cache system, we have:

    • L1 size 8KB with 4w set assoc., 16B lines, and WTNWA and

    • L2 size 64KB direct mapping, 64B lines, and CBWA

  Suppose the miss in L1, hit in L2 delay is 3 cycles and the miss in L1, miss in L2 delay is 10 cycles. The processor makes 1.5 refr/I.

    (a) What are the L1 and L2 miss rates?

    (b) What is the expected CPI loss due to cache misses?

    (c) Will *all* lines in L1 always reside in L2? Why?

8. A certain processor has a two-level cache. $L1$ is 4KB direct-mapped, WTNWA. The $L2$ is 8KB direct-mapped, CBWA. Both have 16-byte lines with LRU replacement.

    (a) Is it always true that $L2$ includes all lines at $L1$?

    (b) If the $L2$ is now 8KB 4-way set associative (CBWA), does $L2$ include all lines at $L1$?

    (c) If $L1$ is 4-way set associative (CBWA) and $L2$ is direct-mapped, does $L2$ include all lines of $L1$?

9. Suppose we have the following parameters for an $L1$ cache with 4KB and an $L2$ cache with 64KB.

  The cache miss rate is:

4KB	0.10 misses per refr
64KB	0.02 misses per refr
1 refr/I	
3 cycles	$L1$ miss, $L2$ hit
10 cycles	total time $L1$ miss, $L2$ miss

What is the excess CPI due to cache misses?

10. Suppose that the cache outlined in problem 1 replaces the cache in study 5.3. Find the new effective performance (split cache and integrated cache).

11. A certain processor produces a 32-bit virtual address. Its address space is segmented (each segment is 1 megabyte maximum) and paged (512-byte pages). The physical word transferred to/from cache is 4 bytes.

    A TLB is to be used, organized set associative, 128×2. If the address bits are labeled V_0–V_{31} for virtual address and R_0–R_{31} for real address, least to most significant:

    (a) Which bits are unaffected by translation (i.e., $V_i = R_i$)?

    (b) If the TLB is addressed by the low-order bits of the portion of the address to be translated (i.e., no hashing), which bits are used to address the TLB?

    (c) Which virtual bits are compared to virtual entries in the TLB to determine whether a TLB hit has occurred?

    (d) As a minimum, which real address bits does the TLB provide?

12. The translated address is now used to access a unified 32^{KB} cache (CBWA) with 16-byte lines and four-way set associativity (L/S, user only, no system effects, LRU, no I/O).

    (a) What is the expected miss rate?

    (b) Suppose the cache described earlier was determined to have a (read) miss rate of 2% and an effective miss time of 5 cycles. Assume an L/S processor (scientific environment) with

    | IF | D | AG | DF | PA | or | IF | D | EX | EX | PA |

    as the basic timing templates and 4^B fetched per IF. An instruction is decoded each cycle. Assume neither delayed branch nor bypassing and that the CC is set at the end of the last EX cycle. Use BR=0.05 and BC = 0.15; always guess in-line on BC (BC actually goes to target 50% of the time). The processor creates how many I references/instruction?

    For the same processor, assume the data referencing causes 0.33 D-read refr/I and 0.235 D-write refr/I. How many cycles per instruction do cache misses add to the processor execution time?

13. Suppose the microprocessor on-chip area is sufficient for only a 12 KB (32B line) integrated cache.

    (a) Show how a 26-bit address would be partitioned in tag, index, and line address using a 3-way set associative cache. Show directory entry.

    (b) What is the effective miss rate for (a)?

    (c) Suppose we now want to create a 12 KB (32B line) direct-mapped cache. Show address partitioning and directory entry using assumptions of (a).

    (d) Find the miss rate for (c).

14. For an 8KB integrated level 1 cache (direct mapped, 16B lines) and a 128KB integrated level 2 cache (2W set associative, 16B lines) find the solo and local miss rate for the level 2 cache.

15. Show the directory layout of a 64 KB sectored cache (two-way set assoc., 128B line, 8B transfer unit, 8B sub-line). Assume the processor address is 30 bits. Compute the total number of directory bits and compare with a non-sectored cache with 16B lines (otherwise similar).

16. Compute the instruction traffic per instruction for a scientific environment based on the following instruction timing templates described in chapter 4 ($P = 64$ bits). Use chapter 3 branch data. Assume guess in-line on BC.

    (a) MIPS R2000 (L/S architecture).

    (b) MIPS R4000 (L/S architecture).

    (c) IBM 3033 (R/M architecture).

    Assume a condition code is set at the end of the EX cycle. Ignore effects of delayed branch.

17. Consider the effect of changing line size on study 5.2. For 40, 50, and 60 ns CPU cycle times and for 4KB, 16KB, and 64KB compare the effect of a 64B and a 16B line with that shown in Figure 5.44. Other study assumptions remain the same.

18. A certain chip has area sufficient for an 8KB I-cache and a 4KB D-cache, both direct mapped. The processor has a virtual address of 32b, real address of 26b, and uses 4KB pages. It makes 1.0 I-refr/I and 0.5 D-refr/I. The cache miss delay is 5 cycles plus 1 cycle for each 4B word transferred in a line. The processor is stalled until the entire line is brought into the cache. The D-cache is CBWA, use dirty line ratio $w = 0.5$. Both caches are user-only environment with R/M architecture and line size of 64B. Find:

    (a) The CPI lost due to I-misses and the CPI lost due to D-misses.

    (b) For the 64B line, find the number of I- and D-directory bits and corresponding **rbe** (area) for both directories.

    (c) Find the number of colored bits in the I-cache and D-cache. How many "free" page lists are required to ensure $V = R$?

Chapter 6

Memory System Design and Processor–Memory Models

6.1 Introduction

In many processor design situations, the main memory system is the principal design challenge. It can be the most costly part of the processor electronics; moreover, it may go a long way in determining the overall effective or realized performance of the system.

There are two basic parameters that, at least in a general sense, determine memory systems performance. The first is the *access time*. This is the time for a processor request to be transmitted to the memory system, access a datum, and return it back to the processor. Access time is largely a function of the physical parameters of the memory system—the physical distance between the processor and the memory system, or the bus delay, the chip delays, etc. The second parameter is *memory bandwidth*, the ability of the memory to respond to requests per unit of time. Bandwidth is primarily determined by the way the physical memory system is organized—the number of memory modules and the use of special sequential accessing modes within a module. As processor ensembles can be quite complex, the memory system that serves these processors is correspondingly complex.

Figure 6.1 illustrates a general form of computer systems. It consists of multiple processors, each with its own private cache, connected to a memory system through a processor–memory interconnect. The processors may be of various kinds: well-mapped processors, pipelined processors, or even vector processors.

The memory consists of multiple memory modules, where each memory module is capable of performing one memory access at a time and contains a subset of the total physical address space. The memory modules are organized into memory banks. Each memory bank consists of multiple modules that share the same input and output buses. Consequently, within a memory bank, only one memory module is able to begin or complete a memory operation during any given bus cycle. Therefore, the memory bank organization is meaningful only if the memory cycle time is greater than the bus cycle time.

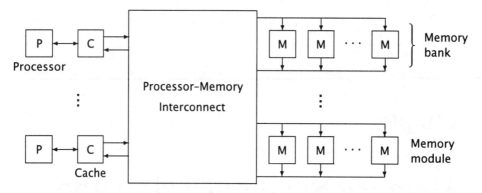

Figure 6.1 The canonical computer system, consisting of multiple processors, cache memories, and memory banks, connected by a processor-memory interconnect.

The Changing Role of Memory

In 1960, the cost for memory in a typical mainframe computer was about $1 per bit! Thirty years later, the cost has declined by a factor of a million, enabling memory sizes to increase by 1–10,000 and systems costs to decline by a factor of 100.

Access time and cycle time, however, have not changed nearly as dramatically—they have decreased by perhaps a factor of 10. Cache memory has been a key development in the interim allowing improved processor performance. Large memory, in turn, has significantly ameliorated serious limitations in the I/O storage system.

Looking ahead, one would expect memory costs to continue to decline and sizes to increase, although not at the same rates that we have seen in the past. The principal limitation to current memory technology is volatility (the loss of information when power is removed from the memory chips). As memory sizes increase, the I/O storage system increasingly plays the singular role of a nonvolatile data storage backup system.

In systems with multiple processors or with complex single processors, requests may cluster and congest the memory system. Either multiple requests may occur at the same time, providing bus or network congestion, or even within a single processor requests arising from different buffered sources may request access to the same memory module. Requests that cannot be immediately honored by the memory system result in memory systems contention. This contention degrades the bandwidth it is possible to achieve from the memory system.

The most obvious factor in determining memory bandwidth is the number of memory modules into which the memory space is divided. The maximum theoretical bandwidth of the memory system is given by the number of memory modules divided by the memory cycle time. One might reasonably expect that increasing the number of memory modules would reduce

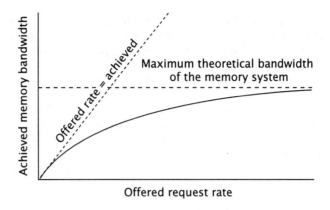

Figure 6.2   Achieved memory bandwidth as a function of the offered request rate.

the number of requests directed at each individual module and, correspondingly, the congestion and delay experienced at each module. Although this is generally true, certain highly structured reference patterns can result in anomalous behavior.

The *offered request rate* to the memory system is the rate at which the processor would be submitting memory requests if the memory had unbounded bandwidth and processed the requests without contention. The offered request rate establishes an upper bound on the *achieved* memory bandwidth. Another upper bound on the achieved bandwidth is the theoretical *maximum memory bandwidth*, which is determined by the cycle time of the memory and the number of memory modules. The achieved bandwidth, as a function of the offered request rate, initially is equal to the offered rate. As the offered rate increases further, the achieved bandwidth continues to increase, but not as fast, and it levels off asymptotically at the theoretical maximum bandwidth. (See Figure 6.2.) Aside from this overall behavior, the detailed dependence of the achieved bandwidth upon the offered request rate varies depending on a host of other factors.

The offered request rate is not influenced by the organization of the memory system. In the absence of cache, the factors that affect it are the instruction set architecture of the processor, including register set size and organization, the nature of the program currently executing on it, and the organization of the processor. As discussed in chapter 2, an instruction set architecture that provides a general-purpose register set can be expected to generate fewer memory requests per instruction executed than would a memory-to-memory architecture. Assuming an architecture of the former type, a program that made more effective use of the registers would offer a lower request rate to memory. The processor organization affects the offered request primarily through its speed, but factors such as prefetch of data and conditional execution of instructions following a branch increase the number of references per instruction and thus have an effect as well.

The modeling and analysis of memory contention is strongly dependent on the complexity of the processor making requests to memory and on the number of processors that request service from a common shared memory system.

In the simplest possible arrangement, a single simple processor makes a request to a single memory module. The processor ceases activity and waits for service from the module. When the module responds, the processor resumes activity. Under such an arrangement the results are completely predictable. There can be no contention of the memory system, since only one request is made at a time to the memory module. Now suppose we arrange to have n simple processors access m independent modules. This arrangement represents a classic study in computer systems analysis. Contention develops when multiple processors access the same module. Contention results in a reduced average bandwidth available to each of the processors. Asymptotically, a pipelined processor making n requests to the memory system during a memory cycle resembles the n processor m module memory system, at least from a modeling point of view. But in modern systems, processors are usually buffered from the memory system by cache. Whether or not a processor is slowed down by memory contention during cache access depends a great deal on the cache design and the number of processors that share the same memory system. To a first approximation, a single pipelined processor with a copyback cache is unaffected by bus or memory contention. The overall system is usually affected but slightly for a write-through cache.

As we shall see in the next chapter, the performance of vector processors can be significantly affected by bus or memory contention. Similarly, multiple cached pipelined processors are also directly affected by bus or memory contention.

Interleaving

Using multiple memory modules to provide sufficient memory bandwidth to the processor is a standard technique.

Most analyses of performance of interleaved memory systems assume that address requests are uniformly distributed across the modules. In many situations, address requests tend to be sequential; in fact, performance analyses of memory systems based upon a uniformly distributed address request pattern generally provide a conservative estimate of performance when the actual pattern is largely sequential.

References to vectored data structures—nonsequential systematic address references—are the nemesis of the memory system designer. If the vectors are long enough and the address distance between successive references is great enough, a data cache will be virtually useless; worse, it may create significant additional traffic, further slowing down the memory system. Yet techniques are available for organizing the memory system to provide reasonably robust performance for vector address references. The designer must anticipate such an application requirement during the design of the memory system.

Outline of this Chapter

In this chapter, we begin with the study of the basic memory module and its characteristics. Section 6.3.2 covers the solution of "classical" memory contention where n simple processors access m interleaved memory modules. Since modern processors are buffered and allow out of order accessing of data, the classical models are of limited value in systems analysis. We introduce queueing models in section 6.4 that are adequate for the solution of most simple design situations. Finally, we look at modern pipelined processors with various types of cache configuration and their effect on the memory system.

The memory models presented here are basic to understanding more advanced processor configurations. Thus, the queueing models presented in this chapter are the basis for understanding the performance of vector processors presented in chapter 7 and multiprocessors presented in chapter 8. Queueing models are also invaluable in the analysis of I/O systems as discussed in chapter 9.

The performance of almost any system is dependent on the performance of that part of the system with the least capacity. If the basic processor has the least capacity then our analysis of processor performance as discussed in the preceding chapters is sufficient to understand the performance of the entire system. This is usually not the case, however. Either the memory, or the network which accesses the I/O system, or the I/O processor, or the I/O devices themselves typically represent the capacity bottleneck in the system. Ultimately, it is this bottleneck that determines overall systems performance. Fortunately, the basic queueing models discussed in this chapter can give us a great deal of insight into the analysis of and effect of these capacity bottlenecks.

6.2   The Physical Memory

Each memory module has two important parameters: *module access time* and *module cycle time*. The module access time is simply the amount of time required to retrieve a word into the output memory buffer register of a particular memory module, given a valid address in its address register. Memory cycle time is the minimum time between requests directed at the same module. Various technologies present a significant range of relationships between the access time and the cycle time. The access time is the total time for the processor to access a word in memory. In a small, simple memory system (equivalent to a single module), this may be little more than chip access time plus some multiplexing and transit delays. The cycle time is approximately the same as the chip cycle time. In a large, interleaved memory system (Figure 6.3), the access time may be greatly increased, as it now includes the module access time plus transit time on the bus (two directions), bus accessing overhead, error detection and correction delay, etc. The cycle time (for the module) remains the same. In general, the designer should not be surprised to find system access times that are less than, equal to, or greater than the cycle time of a particular module, depending on the complexity of the system.

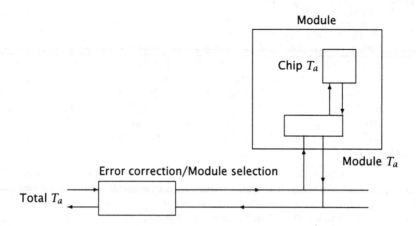

Figure 6.3 Accessing delay in a complex memory system. Access time includes chip accessing, module overhead, bus transit delays, etc.

6.2.1   The Memory Module

The memory module is the building block for the memory system. Throughout this chapter, we usually treat it as a unit. However, in this section we look inside a DRAM (*dynamic random access memory*) module to understand issues such as chip configuration, operation, and timing and their relationship to the overall operation of a module.

DRAM differs from SRAM (static random access memory) in the following ways:

1. The SRAM bit cell uses multiple transistors to hold information. It remains in a stable state as long as power is on. The DRAM cell usually consists of a single transistor and capacitor. The state of this cell must be refreshed at regular time intervals.

2. As a consequence of (1), these cell designs have evolved in significantly different ways. The SRAM is less dense than DRAM (usually less than one-hundredth the density), but has much faster access and cycle times (perhaps one-tenth the cycle time).

With the exception of certain supercomputers, almost all modern memory modules are composed of the DRAM chip. The DRAM chip is usually organized as $2^n \times 1$ bit, where n is an even number. Thus (in 1994) the one-megabit chip ($2^{20} \times 1$) and the four-megabit chip ($2^{22} \times 1$) are common commodity memory chips.

Why an even power of two? Internal to the chip is a two-dimensional array of memory cells consisting of rows and columns. Thus, half of the memory address is used to specify a row address, one of $2^{n/2}$ row lines, and the other half of the address is similarly used to specify one of $2^{n/2}$ column lines (Figure 6.4). The cell itself that holds the data is quite simple, consisting merely of an MOS transistor holding a charge (a capacitance). As this discharges over time, it must continually be refreshed (i.e., recharged) on a regular basis, approximately once every four milliseconds.

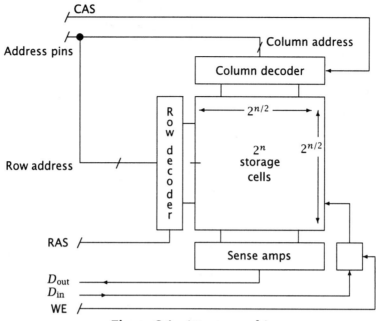

Figure 6.4   A memory chip.

With large-sized memories, the number of address lines dominates the pinout of the chip. In order to conserve these pins and provide a smaller package for better overall density, the row and column addresses are multiplexed onto the same lines (input pins) for entry onto the chip. Two additional lines are important here: RAS (row address strobe) and CAS (column address strobe). These gate first the row address, then the column address into the chip. The row and column addresses are then decoded to select one out of the $2^{n/2}$ possible lines. The intersection of the active row and column lines is the desired bit of information. The column line's signals are then amplified by a sense amplifier and transmitted to the output pin (data out, or D_{out}) during a read cycle. During a write cycle, the write-enable signal stores the data-in (D_{in}) signal to specify the contents of the selected bit address.

All of these actions happen in a sequence approximated in the timing diagram in Figure 6.5. At the beginning of a read from memory, the RAS line is activated. With the RAS active and the CAS inactive, the information on the address lines is interpreted as the row address and stored into the row address register. This activates the row decoder and the selected row line in the memory array. The CAS is then activated, which gates the column address lines into a column address register. Note that:

1. The two rise times on CAS represent the earliest and latest that this signal may rise with respect to the column address signals.

2. WE is write enable. This signal is inactive during read operations.

The column address decoder then selects a column line; at the intersection of the row and column line is the desired data bit. During a read cycle the write enable is inactive (low) and the output line (D_{out}) is at a high-

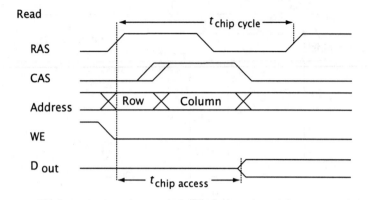

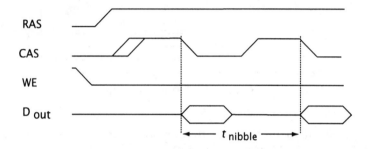

Figure 6.5   Memory chip timing.

impedance state until it is activated either high or low depending on the contents of the selected memory cell.

The time from the beginning of RAS until the data output line is activated is a very important parameter in the memory module design. This is called the chip access time or $t_{chip\ access}$. The other important chip timing parameter is the cycle time of the memory chip ($t_{chip\ cycle}$). This is not the same as the access time, as the selected row and column lines must recover before the next address can be entered and the read process repeated. Thus, the $t_{chip\ cycle}$ is determined by the amount of time that the RAS line is active and the minimum amount of time that the RAS must remain inactive to allow the chip and the sense amplifiers to fully recover in preparation for the next read.

The memory module does not simply consist of memory chips (Figure 6.6). In a memory system with p bits per physical word, and 2^n words in a module, the n address bits enter the module and are usually directed at a Dynamic Memory Controller chip. This chip in conjunction with a Memory Timing Controller provides the following functions:

1. Multiplex of the n address bits into a row and a column address for use by the memory chips.

2. The creation of the correct RAS and CAS signal lines at the appropriate time.

3. Provide timely refresh of the memory system.

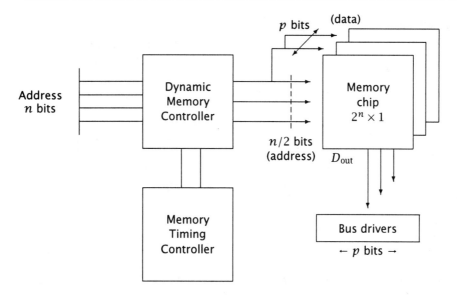

Figure 6.6 A memory module; some typical memory parameters are described in Appendix D.

Since the Dynamic Memory Controller output drives all p bits, and hence p chips, of the physical word, the controller output may also require buffering. As the memory read operation is completed, the data-out signals are directed at bus drivers which then interface to the memory bus, which is the interface for all of the memory modules.

The access and cycle time of the module differs from the chip access and cycle times. The module access time must now include the delay in multiplexing the address lines in the dynamic memory controller as well as the memory chip access time and any delay in transitioning through the output bus drivers. Since data access can be pipelined in a synchronous memory module, the cycle time is less affected by this peripheral circuitry than the access time. In larger memory systems, the cycle time for the module and the system remains relatively similar to the chip cycle time, while the access time is a direct function of the total size of the memory system.

Two important features found on a number of memory chips directly affect the design of the memory system. These features are called:

1. Nibble mode.

2. Page mode.

Both of these are techniques for improving the transfer rate of memory words. In nibble mode, a single address (row and column) is presented to the memory chip and the CAS line is toggled repeatedly. Internally, the chip interprets this CAS toggling as a *mod* 2^w progression of low-order column addresses. Thus, sequential words can be accessed at a higher rate from the memory chip. For example, for $w = 2$, we could access four consecutive low-order bit addresses, e.g.:

$$\overset{\raisebox{2pt}{$\ulcorner$}}{\underset{\raisebox{-2pt}{$\llcorner\hphantom{[00] \rightarrow [01] \rightarrow [10] \rightarrow [11]}\lrcorner$}}{[00] \rightarrow [01] \rightarrow [10] \rightarrow [11]}}$$

and then return to the original bit address.

In page mode, a single row is selected and nonsequential column addresses may be entered at a high rate by repeatedly activating the CAS line (similar to nibble mode, Figure 6.5).

While terminology varies, nibble mode usually refers to the access of (up to) four consecutive words (a nibble) starting on a quad word address boundary. Chips that feature the retrieval of more than four consecutive words sometimes identify this feature as *fast page mode*. To avoid confusion, we use the term *sequential page mode* for sequential addresses and simply *page mode* for chips that allow nonsequential accesses.

Since new addresses do not have to be entered in nibble mode, it gives somewhat faster access than page mode—however, page mode allows greater flexibility in addressing multiple words in a single address page. As an example of page mode, consider if we initially had row address 723 and column address 424; then entries with the same row and any other column address could be rapidly accessed in page mode.

Particular memory chips are equipped with nibble mode, with page mode, or with neither. (See Appendix D.) In the design of the memory module, the designer must consider the various available options in order to achieve the desired transfer rate. For the remaining discussion on non-cached processors, we treat the memory system as if it were a system composed of individual memory modules, usually without either nibble or page modes. In fact, nibble mode and page mode provide alternate ways of realizing multiple memory modules and the designer must take these into account in achieving overall design effectiveness.

Organizing the Memory Chip

As the capacity of memory chips becomes increasingly large, the conventional arrangement of organizing a chip $2^n \times 1$ bit becomes increasingly untenable. For a 16-megabit chip, organized $16 \text{ M} \times 1\text{b}$, a single module with a 64-bit physical word size would contain a gigabit (128 megabyte) of storage. Interleaving modules of such size becomes expensive, to say the least!

For memory bandwidth, the techniques are twofold: using chips organized $2^n \times p'$ bits, and using fast page mode (Appendix D). The first technique allows for a smaller memory module; for example, the 16-megabit chip could be organized 4 million $\times$ 4 bit, reducing the module size (64 bit physical word) to 32 megabytes. The second technique can, in many cases, eliminate the need for interleaving.

6.2.2   Error Detection and Correction

Most modern memory systems are implemented with high-density dynamic RAM cells. Each storage cell consists of a transistor that contains charge, representing the state of the cell. In an effort to improve density, these cells are shrunk in size to the limits permitted by lithography and reliable operation. Extremely small amounts of charge then determine whether or not the

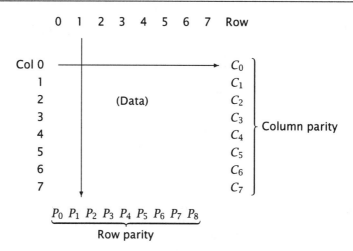

Figure 6.7   Two-dimensional ECC.

state of a cell is either one or zero. Small environmental perturbations—static electric discharge, alpha particles, etc.—may impinge on a cell, changing its state. Altered charge in a cell represents corrupted data—an error. Since these errors are a natural consequence of the type of technology used in memory design, they must be compensated for within the system design itself.

The simplest type of error detection is parity. To every physical memory word a bit is added (a check bit), which ensures that the sum of the number of 1's in the word is even (or odd, by predetermined convention). If a single error occurs to any bit in the word, the sum modulo two of the number of 1's in the word is inconsistent with the parity assumption, and the memory word is known to have been corrupted.

Knowing that there is an error in the retrieved word is valuable. Often, a simple reaccessing of the word may retrieve the correct contents. However, often the data in a particular memory cell has been lost and no amount of reaccessing can restore the true value of the data. Since such errors are likely to occur in a large memory system, most modern memories incorporate hardware to automatically correct single errors (ECC—error correcting codes).

The simplest code of this type might consist of a geometric block code. The message bits to be checked are arranged in a roughly square pattern, and the message is augmented by a parity bit for each row and for each column. If a row and a column indicate a flaw when the message is decoded at the receiver, the intersection is the damaged bit, which may be simply inverted for correction. If only a single row or a column or multiple rows or columns indicate a parity failure, a multiple-bit error is detected and a non-correctable state is entered.

For 64 message bits, we need to add 17 parity bits: eight for each of the rows and columns and one additional parity bit to compute parity on the parity row and column (Figure 6.7).

It is more efficient to consider the message bits as forming a hypercube, for each message combination forms a particular point in this hypercube. If the

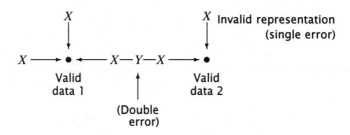

Figure 6.8   ECC code distance.

hypercube can be enlarged so that each valid data point is surrounded by associated invalid data points that are caused by a single-bit corruption in the message, the decoder will recognize that the invalid data point belongs to the valid point and be able to restore the message to its original intended form. This can be extended one more step by adding yet another invalid point between two valid data combinations (Figure 6.8). The minimum number of bits by which valid representations may differ is the code distance. This third point indicates that two errors have occurred. Hence, either of two valid code data points are equally likely and the message is detectably flawed but non-correctable. For a message of 64 bits, and for single-bit error correction, each of the 2^{64} combinations must be surrounded by, or must accommodate, a failure of any of the 64 constituent bits ($2^6 = 64$). Thus, we need 2^{64+6} total code combinations to be able to identify the invalid states associated with each valid state, or a total of 2^{64+6+1} total data states. We can express this in another way:

$$2^k \geq m + k + 1,$$

where m is the number of message bits and k is the number of correction bits that must be added to support single error correction.

Hamming codes represent a realization of ECC based on hypercubes. Just as in the block code before, a pair of parity failures address the location of a flawed bit. The k correction bits determine the address of a flawed bit in a Hamming code. The message bits must be arranged to provide an orthogonal basis for the code (as in the case of the columns and rows of the block code). Further, the correction bits must be included in this basis. An orthogonal basis for 16 message bits is shown in Example 6.1, together with the setting of the five correction bits. Adding another bit, a sixth bit, allows us to compute parity on the entire $m + k + 1$ bit message. Now if we get an indication of a correctable error from the k correct bits, and no indication of parity failure from this new d bit, we know that there is a double error and that any attempt at correction may be incorrect and should not be attempted. These codes are commonly called SECDED (single error correction, double error detection).

EXAMPLE 6.1   A HAMMING CODE EXAMPLE

Suppose we have a 16-bit message, $m = 16$.
$2^k \geq 16 + k + 1$; therefore, $k = 5$.

Thus, the message has $16 + 5 = 21$ bits. The five correction bits will be defined by parity on the following groups, defined by base 2 hypercubes:

k_5 bits $16 - 21$.
k_4 bits $8 - 15$.
k_3 bits $4 - 7$ and $12 - 15$ and $20 - 21$.
k_2 bits $2 - 3$ and $6 - 7$ and $10 - 11$ and $14 - 15$ and $18 - 19$.
k_1 bits $1, 3, 5, 7, 9 \ldots, 19, 21$.

In other words, the 21-bit formatted message bits f_1-f_{21} consist of original message bits m_1-m_{16} and correction bits k_1-k_5. Each correction bit is sited in a location within the group it checks.

Suppose the message consists of f_1-f_{21} and m_1-$m_{16} = 0101010101010101$. For simplicity of decoding, let us site the correction bits at locations that are covered only by the designated correction bit (e.g., only k_5 covers bit 16):

$k_1 = f_1$.
$k_2 = f_2$.
$k_3 = f_4$.
$k_4 = f_8$.
$k_5 = f_{16}$.

Now we have (m_1 is at f_3, m_2 at f_5, etc.):

$$f_1 f_2 f_3 f_4 f_5 f_6 f_7 f_8 f_9 f_{10} f_{11} f_{12} f_{13} f_{14} f_{15} f_{16} f_{17} f_{18} f_{19} f_{20} f_{21}$$
$$k_1 k_2\, 0\, k_3\, 1\, 0\, 1\, k_4\, 0\, 1\quad 0\quad 1\quad 0\quad 1\quad 0\ k_5\ 1\quad 0\quad 1\quad 0\ 1.$$

Thus, with even parity:

$k_5 = 1$.
$k_4 = 1$.
$k_3 = 1$.
$k_2 = 0$.
$k_1 = 1$.

Suppose this message is sent but received with $f_8 = 0$ (when it should be $f_8 = k_4 = 1$). When parity is recomputed at the receiver for each of the five correction groups, only one group covers f_8.

In recomputing parity across the groups, we get:

$k_5' = 0$ (i.e., there is no error in bits 16–21).
$k_4' = 1$.
$k_3' = 0$.
$k_2' = 0$.
$k_1' = 0$.

The failure pattern 01000 is the binary representation for the incorrect bit (bit 8), which must be changed to correct the message.

♦

6.2.3 Memory Buffers

The processor can sustain only a limited number of outstanding memory references before it suspends processing and the generation of further memory references. This can happen either as a result of logical dependencies in the program or because of an insufficient hardware buffering capability for outstanding requests. The significance of this is that the achievable memory bandwidth is decreased as a consequence of the pause in the processing, for the memory can service only as many requests as are made by the processor.

Examples of logical dependencies include branches and address interlocks. The program must suspend useful computation until an item has been retrieved from memory.

Associated with each outstanding memory request is certain information that specifies the nature of the request (e.g., a read or a write operation), the address of the memory location, and sufficient information to route requested data back to the requestor. All this information must be buffered either in the processor or in the memory system until the memory reference is complete. When the buffer is full, further requests cannot be accepted and the sources of these requests must be prevented from making any more requests. Eventually, this requires that the processor be temporarily frozen.

In interleaved memory, the modules usually are not all equally congested—indeed, some could even be idle while others are heavily congested. In such a situation, it is advantageous to maximize the number of requests made by the processor, in the hope that the additional references will be to relatively idle modules and will lead to a net increase in the achieved bandwidth.

The problems with logical dependencies between memory references are exacerbated when the processor is frozen due to memory request buffers filling up; the next request that would have been made had the buffer not been full might have been one on which all the subsequent memory references are logically dependent. If maximizing the bandwidth of a parallel memory organization is the primary objective, it is desirable to provide buffering for memory requests up to the point at which the logical dependencies in the program become the limiting factor.

6.2.4 Partitioning of the Address Space

Another factor that can have a substantial effect upon the achieved memory bandwidth is the manner in which the memory space is partitioned across the memory modules. The objective is to partition the memory space in such a manner that the references made by the processor are equally distributed across the memory modules, leading to fairly uniform (and preferably low) congestion at all the modules rather than heavy congestion at some modules with relatively low utilization of the remaining ones. The trouble with uneven congestion is that only a subset of the modules is being referenced. Thus, the memory system has an effective bandwidth corresponding to a much smaller number of modules than are physically present.

Most frequently, the partitioning strategy is based on the premise that successive references tend to be to successive memory locations. So, succes-

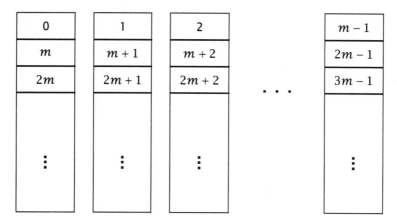

Figure 6.9 Assignment of address space to m memory modules in an interleaved memory system.

sive memory locations are assigned to distinct memory modules in the following manner: for m memory modules, labeled 0 through $(m-1)$, memory address x is assigned to module x mod m (Figure 6.9). A memory organization with a partitioning strategy of this kind is termed an *interleaved* memory system, and the number of memory modules is termed the *degree of interleaving*.

In general, the computation of x mod m involves a division operation, but when m is a power of two, it degenerates to a masking operation. In this case, the partitioning scheme is termed *low-order interleaving*, since the memory module to be referenced is determined by the low-order bits of the memory address. The address within the selected module is provided by the remaining higher-order bits of the memory address.

However, programs are often quite perverse in the manner in which they generate their references. Sequential reference patterns, when they do occur, are usually of short duration, and it is more common for successive references to hop back and forth in an apparently random manner; but matters can get worse yet! For instance, if the program is referencing equally spaced items of an array in a manner such that the difference in the addresses of successive references is a multiple of m, then every reference ends up being directed at the same memory module. This constitutes the worst possible degradation in memory bandwidth, for the achieved memory bandwidth will be that of a single module regardless of how large m is. The same thing happens, albeit to a lesser extent, if the program is stepping through an array with a step size that is not relatively prime with respect to m. Viewed in this light, a power of two would appear to be a poor choice for m, since it offers considerable opportunity for the step size not to be relatively prime. Selecting m to be prime would minimize the likelihood of experiencing such severe degradation, but would add the expense and complication of having to perform some operation to compute the module index. This is discussed more completely in chapter 7.

Memory addresses can also be mapped to individual memory modules by higher-order or quotient-class interleaving. The differences between high- and low-order interleaving are shown in Figure 6.10. In higher-order interleaving, the upper bits of the memory system address define a module and

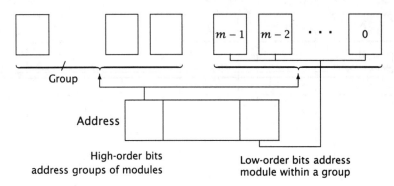

Figure 6.10   Module addressing.

the lower bits of the address define a word in that module.

In *lower-order interleaving*, the lowest bits are used to address a memory module within the memory system. Then the upper bits define an address for the word to be retrieved from the particular module and forwarded to the processor. In *higher-order interleaving*, most of the requests (by the locality principle) tend to remain in a particular module, at least over a short period of time, whereas in low-order interleaving the requests tend to be distributed across all of the modules. High-order interleaving is sometimes useful in memory systems design for increasing the reliability of the memory system. Given a failure in a low-order interleaved memory system, processing must cease, as it is very likely that a request will be shortly forthcoming directed at this damaged memory. On the other hand, with high-order interleaving the system can be reconfigured; that is, reconstituted to accommodate at least those applications that are small enough to fit in an undamaged part of memory. With additional control complexity a low-order interleaved memory system can also be reconfigured to a smaller memory size to allow continued processing.

6.3   Models of Simple Processor–Memory Interaction

The basic issue in modeling the memory system, given a collection of m modules each with cycle time T_c, access time T_a, and a certain processor request rate, is: how do we model the bandwidth available from these memory modules, and how do we compute the overall effective access time? Clearly, the modules in low-order interleave are the only ones that can contribute to the bandwidth, and hence they determine the factor m. From the memory system's point of view, it really does not matter whether the processor system consists of n processors, each making one request every memory cycle (i.e., one per T_c), or one processor with n requests per T_c, so long as the statistical distribution of the requests remains the same. Thus, to a first approximation, the analysis of the memory system is equally applicable to the multiprocessor system or the higher-speed pipelined processor. The request rate, defined as n requests per T_c, is called the *offered request rate*, and it represents the peak demand that the non-cached processor system has on the main memory system.

6.3.1   Memory Systems Design

The design of a high-performance memory system is an iterative process, where the bandwidth and partitioning of the system are determined by evaluation of cost, access time, and queueing requirements. As a general rule, more modules provide more low-order interleaving and more bandwidth, thus reducing queueing delays and improving access time. However, as interleaving increases, system costs are raised and the interconnection network becomes more complex, expensive, and potentially slower.

The basic steps in the design of the memory system consist of the following:

1. Determination of the number of memory modules and the partitioning of the memory system. The initial memory partition is determined by the relative cost of modules of various size, as well as the initial assessment of bandwidth required. Associated with this tradeoff is the choice of physical word size. Longer words provide enhanced sequential access, but create large memory module size when large-scale ($2^n \times 1^{bit}$) memory chips are used.

2. Determination of the offered bandwidth. As was mentioned before, the offered bandwidth is determined by the number of processors making requests on the memory system (or, equivalently, by the number of processor requests coming from one or more processors) per memory cycle. This rate is a function of the peak instruction processing rate that the processor(s) are designed for, times the number of expected references per instruction, times the number of processors in the processing ensemble. (See chapter 5 case study.) The memory system should be designed to accommodate the peak instruction execution rate, not the average rate, since the processor typically executes in bursts of high-performance execution interrupted by dead time for contention resolution.

3. The interconnection network. The interconnection network may provide an additional source of contention and bandwidth limitation, especially in the case where n processors are accessing m modules, $n \geq 2$. For simple designs with small numbers of processors, a high-performance time-multiplexed bus or a small crossbar switch is commonly used, providing access from the processors to the memory without contention. For these cases, it is merely necessary to assess the physical delay through the network, and adjust the overall access time accordingly. For complex memory systems with large numbers of processors, a crossbar switch becomes exceedingly expensive, and the contention network is commonly introduced. These networks reduce overall interconnection cost at the expense of a somewhat reduced bandwidth and somewhat increased access time due to network contention.

4. Referencing behavior. The important part of the evaluation process is an assessment of the probable program behavior in its sequence of requests to memory. Three cases are of particular interest:

   (a) Purely sequential—i.e., each request follows its predecessor.
   (b) Random—the addresses are uniformly distributed, at least across the low-order interleave partition of memory.

(c) Regular—this pattern arises from vector or array references and corresponds to an access pattern wherein each access is separated by a fixed number of addresses.

Purely sequential reference behavior arises from certain types of cache accessing main memory (copyback cache). The random request pattern is commonly used in memory systems evaluation for the design of general-purpose processors with or without cache, so long as copyback cache is not used. Regular reference pattern is used in the design of certain high-performance vector processors. For purposes of this chapter, we shall be concerned only with sequential and random address patterns.

5. Evaluation of the memory model. This step is the primary analytic evaluation of the proposed memory partition as measured against the processing requirements. The evaluation of the memory system model provides an assessment of the achieved bandwidth, the actual memory access time (including contention), and the queueing required in the memory system in order to support the achieved bandwidth.

6.3.2   Models of Multiple Simple Processors and Memory

In order to develop realistic memory models we need a more detailed model of the processor. Frequently, we model a single processor as an ensemble of multiple simple processors. Each simple processor issues a request as soon as its previous request has been satisfied. Under this model, we can vary the number of processors and the number of memory modules and maintain the address request/data supply equilibrium. While this is valuable from a modeling point of view, these configurations pose difficulties in interpretation to the designer of a single high-speed processor with known peak request rate. As a first approximation in order to convert the single processor model into an equivalent multiple processor, the designer must determine the number of requests to the memory module per module service time, $T_s = T_c$. If a certain processor has a peak request rate of 10 million accesses per second and the memory module has cycle time $T_c = 1$ μs, then the processor *acts* as if it were 10 processors, each requesting a single item of service from memory each memory cycle.

The nature of the processor is very important here. A *simple processor* makes a single request and waits for a response from memory. A *pipelined processor* makes multiple requests for various buffers before waiting for a memory response. Thus, the equivalence of n simple processors, each requesting once every T_s, and one pipelined processor making n requests every T_s (Figure 6.11) is only approximate. As we shall see, machines with buffering mechanisms and/or cache-organized memories have behavior different from multiple simple processors with equivalent memory traffic.

In the following discussion, we use two symbols to represent the bandwidth available from the memory system (the achieved bandwidth):

1. B: the number of requests that are serviced each T_s. Occasionally, we also specify the arguments that B takes on, e.g., $B(m, n)$ or $B(m)$.

2. Bw: the number of requests that are serviced per second: $Bw = B/T_s$.

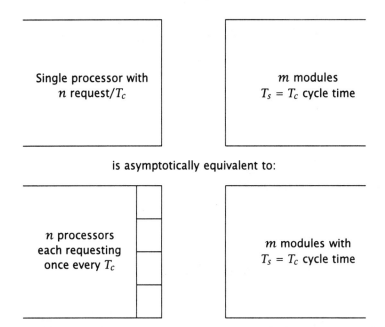

Figure 6.11   Processor equivalence.

6.3.3   Hellerman's Model

One of the best known memory models is that of Hellerman [125]. Hellerman assumes a single sequence of address. Addresses are examined until a match between two addresses occurs in the w low-order bit positions ($w = \log_2 m$; m = the number of memory modules). The average length of independent (unmatched) addresses (uniform access pattern) then determines the bandwidth. No referencing is allowed after a match is found, since the modeling assumption is that no address queue is present and no out-of-order requests are possible (Figure 6.12). Under these conditions, the maximum available bandwidth is found to be approximately:

$$B(m) = \sqrt{m}$$
$$\text{and } Bw = \sqrt{m}\,\frac{1}{T_s}.$$

The lack of queueing facilities limits the applicability of this model to simple unbuffered processors with strict in-order referencing to memory.

The achieved bandwidth is a function of the offered request rate, λ_s (Figure 6.13):

$$Bw = \min\left(\lambda_s, \frac{\sqrt{m}}{T_s}\right).$$

6.3.4   Strecker's Model

This model [273] (later developed independently by Ravi [243]) assumes that there are n simple processor requests made per memory cycle and

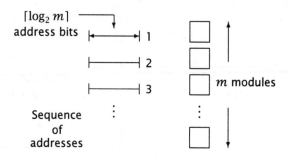

Figure 6.12 Hellerman's model. In this model, B is the average length of conflict-free sequences of addresses.

Figure 6.13   Bandwidth.

there are m memory modules. Further, we assume that there is no bus contention. The Strecker model assumes that the memory request pattern for the processors is uniform and the probability of any one request to a particular memory module is simply $1/m$. The key modeling assumption is that the state of the memory system at the beginning of the cycle is not dependent upon any previous action on the part of the memory—hence, not dependent upon contention in the past (i.e., Markovian). Unserved requests are discarded at the end of the memory cycle.

Modeling approximations:

1. A processor issues a request as soon as its previous request has been satisfied.

2. The memory request pattern from each processor is assumed to be uniformly distributed; i.e., the probability of any one request being made to a particular memory module is $1/m$.

Analytical approximation:

The state of the memory system at the beginning of each memory cycle (i.e., which processors are awaiting service at which modules) is ignored by assuming that all unserviced requests are discarded at the end of each memory cycle and that the corresponding processors randomly issue new requests.

Analysis:

Let the average number of memory requests serviced per memory cycle be represented by $B(m,n)$. This is also equal to the average number of memory modules busy during each memory cycle. Looking at events from any given module's point of view during each memory cycle, we have:

Prob [a given processor does not reference the module] $=$ $(1 - 1/m)$

$$\text{Prob [no processor references the module]} = \text{Prob [the module is idle]}$$
$$= (1 - 1/m)^n$$
$$\text{Prob [the module is busy]} = 1 - (1 - 1/m)^n$$
$$B(m, n) = \text{average number of busy modules} = m[1 - (1 - 1/m)^n]$$

The achieved memory bandwidth is less than the theoretical maximum due to contention. By neglecting the congestion that has carried over from previous cycles, this analysis results in an optimistic value for the bandwidth. Also, as in the previous example, the two modeling assumptions cause the calculated bandwidth to be higher still.

It has been shown by Bhandarkar [35] that $B(m, n)$ is almost perfectly symmetrical in m and n. He exploited this fact to develop a more accurate expression for $B(m, n)$, which is

$$B(m, n) = K \left[1 - (1 - 1/K)^l \right],$$

where $K = \max(m, n)$ and $l = \min(m, n)$.

6.3.5   Rau's Model

The most accurate closed-form solution for $B(m, n)$ for multiple simple processors is based upon the work of Rau [241], and is based upon the following analytic approximation.

All processors not awaiting service at a given memory module are queued at the remaining $m - 1$ modules with precisely the same distribution that would occur in a system consisting of the same number of processors and $m - 1$ memory modules.

The result of an analysis based on this approximation is that

Closed form:

$$B(m, n) = \frac{\sum_{i=0}^{l-1} 2^i * C(m - 1, i) * C(n - 1, i)}{\sum_{i=0}^{l-1} 2^i * C(m - 1, i) * (C(n - 1, i)/(i + 1))},$$

where $C(x, y)$ is the number of ways of choosing y objects out of a set of x objects, and $l = \min(m, n)$. When compared with the exact results from a Markov chain analysis [35] (see shortly), the preceding expression is never more than 0.25% in error, attesting to the accuracy of the analytical approximation.

These results are compared in Tables 6.1 and 6.2.

6.4   Processor–Memory Modeling Using Queueing Theory

Simple processors are unbuffered; when a response is delayed due to a conflict this delay directly affects processor performance by the same amount.

Table 6.1   Model comparisons for bandwidth B for *simple* processor-memory configurations.

$m = n$	1	2	3	4	5	6	7	8
Exact	1.0000	1.5000	2.0476	2.6210	3.1996	3.7809	4.3636	4.9471
Closed form	1.0000	1.5000	2.0526	2.6250	3.2056	3.7849	4.3675	4.9510
Strecker	1.0000	1.5000	2.1111	2.7344	3.3616	3.9906	4.6206	5.2511
Hellerman	1.0000	1.4142	1.7321	2.0000	2.2361	2.4495	2.6458	2.8284

Table 6.2   Comparison of percentage errors for $n = m$ for *simple* processor memories.

$m = n$	1	2	3	4	5	6	7	8
Closed form	0	0	0.2442	0.1526	0.1248	0.1047	0.0901	0.0841
Strecker	0	0	5.1012	4.3266	5.0631	5.5463	5.2866	6.1450
Hellerman	0	−5.72	−15.4083	−23.6932	−30.113	−35.2138	−39.3666	−42.8271

Note: All solutions, except the asymptotic solution, are exact for $n = 1$ or for $m = 1$.

More sophisticated processors—including certainly almost all pipelined processors—make buffered requests to memory, unless a cache is used. Even with pipelined processors that use cache, some of the requests (such as writes) may be buffered. Whenever requests are buffered, the effect of contention and the resulting delay are reduced. The simple models fail to accurately represent the processor–memory relationship. More powerful tools that incorporate buffered requests are needed. For these tools, we turn to queueing theory.

Open- and closed-queue models are frequently used in the evaluation of computer system designs. In this section, we review and present the main results for simple queueing systems without derivation of the underlying basic queue equations. While queueing models are useful in understanding memory behavior, they also provide a robust basis to study various computer system interactions, such as multiple processors and I/O. The reader is referred to Kleinrock [166] and Kobayashi [169] for a more general treatment of queueing theory.

Suppose requestors desire service from a common server. These requestors are assumed to be independent from one another, except that they make a request on the basis of a probability distribution function called the *request distribution function*. Similarly, the server is able to process requests one at a time, each independently of the others, except that the service time is distributed according to the server probability distribution function. The mean of the arrival or request rate is measured in items per unit of time and is called λ, and the mean of the service rate distribution is μ. The ratio of arrival rate to service rate (ρ) defines a very important parameter in queueing systems called the *utilization* or the *occupancy*.

The higher the occupancy ratio, the more likely it is that requestors will be waiting (in a buffer or queue) for service and the longer the expected queue length for items awaiting service. In open queueing systems, if the arrival rate equals or exceeds the service rate, an infinitely long queue develops in front of the server, as requests are arriving faster than or at the same rate at which they can be served. For open-queue systems, arrivals are truly independent of the server or the queue length. For closed-queue systems, the rate of arrival of requests is in some way limited or governed by the performance of the server.

The simplest queueing models are open-queueing models, where the arrival and service distribution are known.

Queueing Theory

As processors have become increasingly complex, their performance can be predicted only statistically. Indeed, oftentimes running the same job on the same processor on two different occasions may create significantly different execution times (based perhaps on the initial state of the list of available pages maintained by the operating system). Queueing theory has been a powerful tool in evaluating the performance of not only memory systems, but also I/O systems, networks, and multiprocessor systems.

6.4.1   Performance Models of Processor Memory Interactions

Review of Stochastic Models:

$$\lambda \longrightarrow \;\boxed{|\;|\;|}\; \longrightarrow \mu \longrightarrow \text{Departures}$$

Arrivals   Queue   Server

Arrival Process: Requests are made to a system. The interarrival times are random variables with arrival time probability distribution.

Server: Service is provided by the system; service times are random variables with service time probability distribution.

Certain distributions are very important in modeling complex systems. In the general case, the state of a complex system depends on the probability distribution of arrivals, the service distribution, *and* the previous state of the system (i.e., the usage history). For Markovian distributions, statistically the current (and future) state of the system does not depend on the previous state, but only on the request and service distributions. They are said to have a *memoryless distribution.*

One important such distribution is the *binomial distribution.* Suppose there are n items that enter a system in time interval T. Of these, k items request service each with probability p. For purposes of memory system analysis and interpretation, assume that n requests are made to m memory modules and each request occurs with probability $p = 1/m$ each memory cycle T. We want to know the number k of these requests that are directed to a particular module (since requests > 1 will queue up waiting for service). The probability that exactly k out of n requests are made to the designated server is:

$$P_n(k) = C\left(\begin{array}{c} n \\ k \end{array}\right)(p)^k(1-p)^{n-k}.$$

This is the binomial distribution.

We can derive the Strecker model discussed in the preceding section directly from the binomial distribution. We compute the probability that exactly 0 out of n requests are made to a designated module (i.e., the module is idle). This is referred to as the *null binomial* and

$$\text{Prob (0 out of } n \text{ requests go to module)} = C\left(\begin{array}{c} n \\ 0 \end{array}\right)(p)^0(1-p)^n,$$

where $p = 1/m$. This becomes simply

$$(1 - 1/m)^n = P_{\text{idle}}.$$

The probability that this module is busy is

$$P_{\text{busy}} = 1 - P_{\text{idle}} = 1 - (1 - 1/m)^n.$$

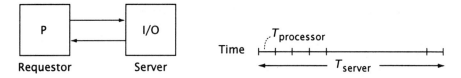

Figure 6.14   Processor and I/O time horizon.

Thus, the number of busy modules in an ensemble of m modules is

$$B(m, n) = m \left(1 - (1 - 1/m)^n\right).$$

The well-known Poisson distribution is a limiting case of the binomial distribution. Suppose we let n grow very large as p approaches zero (m very large) for a finite T. Now $n \cdot p$ is simply the expected number of arrivals at the designated server during T (n is the number of arrivals):

$$\lambda = \frac{n}{T} \cdot p$$

and

$$p = \frac{\lambda T}{n}.$$

Substituting and taking limits, we get the Poisson distribution:

$$P(k) = \frac{(\lambda T)^k}{k!} \epsilon^{-\lambda T},$$

where $P(k)$ is the probability that exactly k requests for service will be made during time T.

It may appear that the Binomial distribution is a more natural (accurate) description of memory behavior, as one rarely encounters memory systems with $m \to \infty$ memory modules (i.e., $p = 1/m \to 0$). Indeed, this is true as we shall see. The Poisson distribution provides somewhat simpler expression and provides a more accurate description of I/O behavior, especially for disk access models.

6.4.2   Arrival Distribution

To better understand the variety and selection of an arrival distribution such as arises in memory and I/O modeling, consider an I/O storage device attached to a high-speed processor (Figure 6.14). The I/O service time is much longer than the time it takes to initiate a request. From a modeling point of view, we can treat the system as consisting of a single server with multiple requestors with (about) the same time basis. Let

$$\frac{T_{\text{server}}}{T_{\text{processor}}} = n,$$

and model the processor as n requestors each making a single request during T_{server}. If n is large and the probability of a request in any particular processor cycle is small (i.e., $p \approx 0$), we use the Poisson arrival distribution.

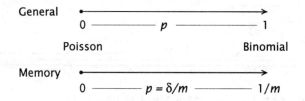

Figure 6.15   Characterizing request distributions with p. For the memory model, n items enter the system (or request), each with probability δ.

There is still another modeling possibility. Suppose we have the relationship described in Figure 6.14, but the probability of a request in any particular processor cycle is nonzero, say $p = \delta$. In the context of m interleaved memory modules, this means that the probability of a request to a particular module is $p = \frac{\delta}{m}$. In memory systems, we will refer to the case wherein the request sources (or items that enter the system) request or enter with probability δ as the δ-*binomial distribution*. (See Figure 6.15.)

6.4.3   Service Distribution

From a service point of view, there are three Markovian (i.e., memoryless) distributions of particular interest.

Constant Distribution:

All requests take time T for service, $\mu = \dfrac{1}{T}$.

Exponential Service-Time Distribution

The probability that service is completed by time t (μ is average service rate) is

$$P(t) = 1 - e^{-\mu t}.$$

The distribution for the time (t) between arrivals in a Poisson distribution is the exponential distribution. This can be seen by assuming the time of last arrival at a server is 0 and the time of a current arrival is a random variable t. Then the distribution of Poisson arrival times is

Prob (time between arrivals is $\leq t$)

$\quad = \quad 1 - \text{Prob (time between arrivals is} > t).$

This latter probability is simply the probability of no arrivals between 0 and t (i.e., $k = 0$ in the Poisson distribution). Thus,

Prob (time between arrivals is $\leq t$) $= 1 - e^{-\lambda t}$,

where $1/\lambda$ is the mean of the interarrival time distribution. So if $1/\mu$ is the mean inter*service* time, then the interservice probability is

$$P(t) = 1 - e^{-\mu t}.$$

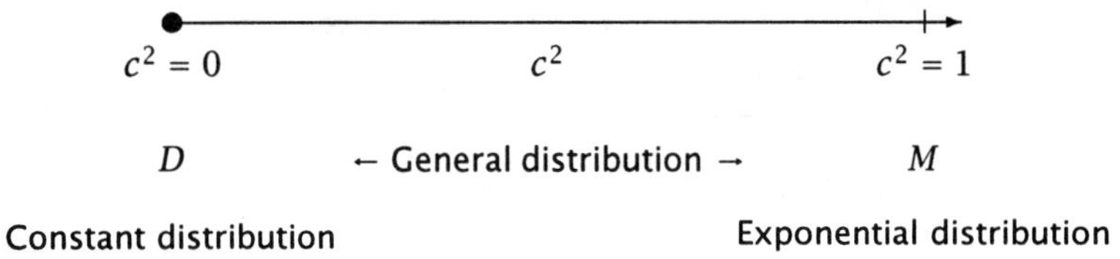

Figure 6.16 The coefficient of variance (c^2) is the key parameter in describing the service distribution.

General Service-Time Distribution

Service time may be constant or variable. Distributions can be categorized by the behavior of c, the coefficient of variation for the service time. Now c^2 is the squared coefficient of service time variance, or

$$c^2 = \frac{\text{Variance of service time}}{\text{Mean service time}^2}$$

$$= \frac{\sigma^2}{(\frac{1}{\mu})^2} = \sigma^2 \mu^2.$$

For constant service time, $c^2 = 0$, while for the exponential service time distribution, $c^2 = 1$. The factor c^2 is the primary parameter used in describing the distribution of service times (Figure 6.16).

6.4.4   Terminology

We indicate the use of a particular probability distribution by the following abbreviations:

Coefficient of variance:	$c = \frac{\sigma}{(1/\mu)} = \sigma\mu$	
M:	Poisson/Exponential	$c = 1$
M_B:	Binomial	$c = 1$
G:	General	$c = $ arbitrary, defined by coef. of variance
D:	Constant	$c = 0$
E:	Erlangian	$c < 1$
H:	Hyperexponential ..	$c > 1$,

where σ is the standard deviation of the service time (T_s) distribution and $1/\mu$ is the mean service time, T_s. The occupancy ρ is defined as the ratio of the request rate to the service rate, $\rho = \lambda/\mu$.

Queue models are categorized by the triple:

Arrival Distribution/Service Distribution/Number of Servers.

Thus, $M/M/1$ is a single-server queue with Poisson arrival and exponential service distributions.

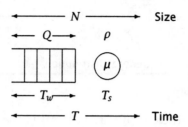

Figure 6.17   Time and queue size.

6.4.5   Queue Properties

For all of the previous distributions, the average time spent in the system (T) consists of an average service time T_s, plus a waiting time (due to contention) T_w:

$$T = T_s + T_w.$$

If N is the average queue length (including request being serviced) and T is the average time (including service time) for completion of service:

$$N = \lambda T \qquad \text{(Little's result)}.$$

Since N consists of items in the queue and an item in service (Figure 6.17), then

$$N = Q + \rho.$$

Recall that the server is occupied ρ part of the time. Hence the average number of items *in service* is ρ. Since

$$N = \lambda T,$$

then (see also Figure 6.17)

$$
\begin{aligned}
Q + \rho &= \lambda(T_s + T_w), \\
Q + \rho &= \lambda(1/\mu + T_w), \\
Q + \rho &= \rho + \lambda T_w, \\
Q &= \lambda T_w.
\end{aligned}
$$

Note that $Q = N - \rho$ or $N = Q + \rho$.

Queues that result from the buffering of requests that do not affect the request rate λ are called *open queues*, Q_o. Again, for these queues:

$$Q_o = \lambda T_w.$$

For $M/G/1$,

$$T_w = \frac{1}{\lambda}\left[\frac{\rho^2(1 + c^2)}{2(1 - \rho)}\right].$$

This is commonly referred to as the Pollaczek-Khinchine (or P-K) mean-value result. (See Appendix E for a derivation of this equation.) We can select c^2 for several cases of interest. In the first case, the service time is exponentially distributed ($\sigma = \frac{1}{\mu}$) and $c^2 = 1$. This might correspond to a model of an I/O server.

For $M/M/1$: $c^2 = 1$

$$\text{Waiting time:}\quad T_w = \frac{1}{\lambda}\left(\frac{\rho^2}{(1-\rho)}\right)$$

$$\text{\# of queued items:}\quad Q_o = \frac{\rho^2}{(1-\rho)}$$

In the second case, as in memory, the service time is constant and $C^2 = 0$. For this case, we have:

For $M/D/1$: $c^2 = 0$

$$\text{Waiting time:}\quad T_w = \frac{1}{\lambda}\left(\frac{\rho^2}{2(1-\rho)}\right)$$

$$\text{\# of queued items:}\quad Q_o = \frac{\rho^2}{2(1-\rho)}$$

For $M_B/D/1$:   (Binomial arrival, constant service)

$$c^2 \;=\; 0.$$

For $\rho \geq p$:

$$\text{\# of queued items } Q_o \;=\; \frac{\rho^2 - p\rho}{2(1-\rho)}$$

$$\text{Waiting time } T_w \;=\; \frac{1}{\lambda}\left(\frac{\rho^2 - p\rho}{2(1-\rho)}\right)$$

$$\;=\; \frac{1}{\lambda}\left(\frac{\lambda}{\mu}\right)\left(\frac{\rho - p}{2(1-\rho)}\right)$$

$$\;=\; \frac{1}{\mu}\left(\frac{\rho - p}{2(1-\rho)}\right) = \left(\frac{\rho - p}{2(1-\rho)}\right)T_s.$$

If $\rho < p$, then $T_w \approx 0$; $Q_o \approx 0$. (In simple memory-processor models, the case $\rho < p$ should not arise, since at least one processor request is assumed each memory cycle; a more general model, discussed later, is usually more appropriate to statistically distributed processor requests that accommodate $\rho < p$.)

For $M/G/1$, multiple (independent, Poisson) sources generate requests. A different service time can be assigned to the requests of each source. (Note there is still a single server.) This model allows us to split the request stream into smaller streams, capturing more detail. The M/G/1 model has a simple solution wherein *effective* request and service rates are calculated. The M/G/1 formulation for two sources, (λ_1,T_1) and (λ_2,T_2), is given next (multiple sources are calculated in a similar manner):

$$\lambda_s \;=\; \lambda_1 + \lambda_2$$

$$1/\mu \;=\; T_s = \frac{\lambda_1}{\lambda_s}T_1 + \frac{\lambda_2}{\lambda_s}T_2 \tag{6.1}$$

$$\rho = \frac{\lambda}{\mu} = \lambda T_s = (\lambda_1 T_1 + \lambda_2 T_2)$$

and

$$\sigma^2 = \frac{\lambda_1}{\lambda_s}(T_1 - T_s)^2 + \frac{\lambda_2}{\lambda_s}(T_2 - T_s)^2$$

$$c^2 = \frac{\sigma^2}{T_s^2} = \frac{\lambda_1}{\lambda_s}\left(\frac{T_1}{T_s} - 1\right)^2 + \frac{\lambda_2}{\lambda_s}\left(\frac{T_2}{T_s} - 1\right)^2 \tag{6.2}$$

Queue behavior of the various common queue model types is summarized in Table 6.3.

6.5   Open-, Closed-, and Mixed-Queue Models

Open-queue models are the simplest queueing form. These models (at least as used here) assume:

1. Arrival rate independent of service rate.

2. As a consequence of (1), a queue of unbounded length as well as a (potentially) unbounded waiting time.

Many will recognize the suitability of open-queue models to contain highway congestion or bridge access situations, but will also recognize the unsuitability to computer systems. In a processor–memory interaction, the processor's request rate decreases as memory congestion increases. The arrival rate is a function of the total service time (including waiting time). This latter type of situation can be modeled by a queue with feedback. The system is initially offered a request rate (λ_o), but certain requests cannot immediately enter the server and are held in a queue. The requestor slows down to accommodate this and the arrival rate is now λ_a (the achieved arrival rate—see Figure 6.18).

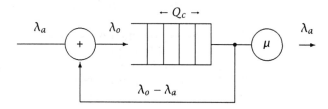

Figure 6.18   Capacity queues.

We call such systems *closed queue* (or a *capacity queue*) and designate them Q_c. These queues usually have a bounded size and waiting time.

It is also possible for systems to behave as open-queueing systems up to a certain queue size, then they behave as closed queues. We call such systems *mixed-queue* systems. The assumptions made in developing the open-queue model might make it seem an unlikely candidate for memory systems modeling, yet its simplicity is attractive and it remains a useful first approximation to memory systems behavior.

Table 6.3   Open queue behavior.

Queue Type	M/M/1	M/D/1	M/G/1	$M_B/D/1$
Arrival parameter, p (probability that an item entering system requests service during unit service time).	$p = 0^a$	$p = 0$	$p = 0$	$p = \frac{\delta}{m}$
Service parameter, c^2 (coefficient of variance of service distribution).	$c^2 = 1$	$c^2 = 0$	$c^2 \geq 0$	$c^2 = 0$
Waiting time (T_w).	$\frac{1}{\lambda}\left(\frac{\rho^2}{(1-\rho)}\right)$	$\frac{1}{\lambda}\left(\frac{\rho^2}{2(1-\rho)}\right)$	$\frac{1}{\lambda}\left(\frac{\rho^2(1+c^2)}{2(1-\rho)}\right)$	$\frac{1}{\lambda}\left(\frac{\rho^2-p\rho}{2(1-\rho)}\right)$
Mean queue size.	$\frac{\rho^2}{(1-\rho)}$	$\frac{\rho^2}{2(1-\rho)}$	$\frac{\rho^2(1+c^2)}{2(1-\rho)}$	$\frac{\rho^2-p\rho}{2(1-\rho)}$
Variance of queue size (σ^2).	$\frac{\rho}{(1-\rho)^2}$	$\frac{\rho(12-18\rho+10\rho^2-\rho^3)}{12(1-\rho)^2}$	—	$\frac{\rho[12-(\rho+p)(18-8p-10\rho+5p\rho+\rho^2)]}{12(1-\rho)^2}$

[a] $p = 0$ implies Poisson arrival distribution.

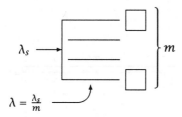

Figure 6.19   Splitting requests.

6.5.1   The Open-Queue (Flores) Memory Model

We can use open-queueing theory as an approximation to interleaved memory behavior by assuming a request rate independent of the service behavior. This allows us to find an initial partition of memory modules. This model was originally proposed by Flores [90] using the $M/D/1$ queue. We use the more appropriate $M_B/D/1$ queue model.

Let λ_s be the total request rate (processor and I/O) in requests/second.

Assume that λ_s splits m ways uniformly over the m modules. Then, at the module:

$$\lambda = \frac{\lambda_s}{m},$$

$$\mu = \frac{1}{T_c},$$

and

$$\rho = (\frac{\lambda_s}{m}) \cdot T_c,$$

and we now can use the $M_B/D/1$ model to determine T_w and Q_o (the *per module* buffer size).

Design with the Flores Model

1. Find peak processor (design) instruction execution rate measured in MIPS (million instructions per second). Again, we use *peak rates* so that the memory system is designed to support such execution rates. The memory system lowers processor performance in any event, when offered the peak rate due to contention.

2. MIPS * (references/instruction) + MIPS *(I/O references/instruction) = MAPS (million accesses per second).

3. As a balance between cost or interleaving factor and performance, choose m so that $\rho \approx 0.5$ and also so that $m = 2^k$ (k an integer).

4. $T_w + T_a$ = total memory access time.

5. Note that this model predicts the total average open-queue size as $Q_{o-t} = m \cdot Q_o$.

The selection of $\rho \approx 0.5$ is an empirical initial guess—a conventional "rule of thumb." It implicitly assumes that the processor cost and memory cost are balanced. If, for example, the memory cost is much greater than the processor cost and increasing its bandwidth to achieve $\rho \approx 0.5$ significantly contributed to this cost, it would be better to let ρ rise, even to the point where $\rho \approx 1$. At this point the Flores model (open-queue $M_B/D/1$) is no longer a useful model and other modeling techniques must be used to determine bandwidth.

EXAMPLE 6.2

Suppose we wish to design a memory system for a processor with peak performance of 50 MIPS and one instruction decoded per cycle.

1. Assume the memory module has

$$T_a = 200\,\text{nsec and } T_c = 100\,\text{nsec,}$$

and assume a total of 1.5 references per instruction = 1.5 references per processor cycle (1.5 references each 20 ns).

2. Compute MAPS = $1.5 \times 50 = 75$ MAPS (ignoring I/O traffic).

3. Find ρ.

$$
\begin{aligned}
\rho &= \frac{\lambda_s}{m} \cdot T_c \\
&= 75 \times 10^6 \times \frac{1}{m} \times 0.1 \times 10^{-6} \\
&= \frac{7.5}{m}.
\end{aligned}
$$

If we use $m = 16$, then

$$
\begin{aligned}
\rho &= 0.47 \\
T_w &= \frac{1}{\lambda} \cdot \frac{(\rho^2 - \rho p)}{2(1 - \rho)}
\end{aligned}
$$

$$\text{and} \quad p = \frac{1}{m}.$$

Or, for this case, we can simplify to:

$$
\begin{aligned}
T_w &= \frac{\rho}{\lambda} \cdot \frac{(\rho - p)}{2(1 - \rho)} = \frac{1}{\mu} \frac{(\rho - p)}{2(1 - \rho)} = T_c \cdot \frac{\rho - 1/m}{2(1 - \rho)} \\
T_w &= 38\,\text{ns,}
\end{aligned}
$$

$$
\begin{aligned}
\text{Total memory access time} &= T_a + T_w \\
&= 200 + 38 = 238\,\text{ns.}
\end{aligned}
$$

4. $Q_o = \dfrac{\rho^2 - p\rho}{2(1 - \rho)} = 0.18$, and total mean queue size $Q_{o-t} = 16 \times .18 \approx 3$.

◆

Clearly, the open-queueing model is limited in its applicability to inter-leaved memory. Memory systems are not open queues. When too many requests are made on a memory system, the overall system simply slows down. The processor cannot and does not keep making demands at a peak rate on the memory system, since its buffers are finite. Yet the simple queueing model has its appeal; it is very easy to use and compute, and it provides an initial guess to the low-order interleave partition. Also, it is a conservative estimate of expected performance for relatively low values of occupancy ratio ($\rho \leq .5$).

6.5.2   Closed Queues

Baskett [29] makes the following observation: Suppose we have an n, m system in overall stability, with n and m very large (i.e., $n, m \rightarrow \infty$); the number of busy servers becomes a constant fraction of the total equal to ρ. The distribution of arrivals becomes Poisson in the limit [87]. Then the average queue size (including the item in service) is known to be simply

$$N = \frac{n}{m}$$

and

$$Q_c = \frac{n}{m} - \rho_a = \rho - \rho_a$$

where ρ_a is the achieved occupancy (as contrasted with ρ, the offered oc-cupancy).

Recall from our discussion on open queues that

$$N = Q_o + \rho.$$

That is, the number of items in the system is equal to the number waiting for service, plus the (average) number of items in service; all under the constraint that the arrival rate is unaffected by queue size (Q_o) or resulting service time (T_w).

The closed-queue model assumes that the arrival rate is immediately af-fected by service contention. We may offer λ as an arrival rate, but we achieve only λ_a—this corresponds to occupancy ρ and ρ_a. Now the differ-ence, $\rho - \rho_a$, is the number of items denied service. They are held (queued in Q_c) for service at the next time interval, but the arrival rate immediately slows down so that only λ_a items/sec now arrive.

If we know the queue size, then we can use the $M/D/1$ model to find the achieved occupancy (ρ_a), which now gives us the overall effective band-width per module. Thus, a queueing model of an n processor, m memory module system can be reduced to an approximate $M/D/1$ model as shown in Figure 6.20. This solution to the bandwidth is called the *asymptotic so-lution*, and it exactly corresponds to the closed-form solution where n and m are large.

Then

$$N = \frac{n}{m} = \rho_a + \frac{\rho_a^2}{2(1 - \rho_a)}$$

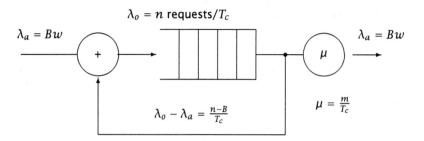

Figure 6.20   Asymptotic solution.

Notice that $N = n/m$ is the same as our open queue occupancy ρ, since $\lambda = \frac{1}{m}(\frac{n}{T_c})$, $\mu = 1/T_c$. Solving for ρ_a, we have the

Asymptotic solution:

$$\rho_a = (1 + n/m) - \sqrt{(n/m)^2 + 1}$$

or, if $\rho_a = \lambda_a/\mu$ and λ_a is the achieved request rate,

$$\rho_a = (1 + \rho) - \sqrt{\rho^2 + 1} \quad \text{and}$$
$$\lambda_a = \mu[1 + \rho - \sqrt{\rho^2 + 1}],$$

where $\rho = N = n/m$ is the open queue occupancy and

$$B(m, n) = m \cdot \rho_a = m + n - \sqrt{n^2 + m^2}.$$

This solution for $B(m, n)$ is called the asymptotic solution and it corresponds to the exact closed form solution when n and m are large.
Similarly, for the M/G/1 model, we have:

$$N = \frac{n}{m} = \rho = \rho_a + \frac{\rho_a^2(1 + c^2)}{2(1 - \rho_a)}.$$

Solving for ρ_a,

$$\rho_a = \frac{1 + \rho - \sqrt{1 + 2c^2\rho + \rho^2}}{1 - c^2}$$

and

$$\lambda_a = \mu \left[\frac{1 + \rho - \sqrt{1 + 2c^2\rho + \rho^2}}{1 - c^2} \right],$$

where $c^2 < 1$.

Simple Binomial Approximation

Suppose n is equal to 1. For a simple processor-memory configuration, there is no memory contention and the achieved bandwidth is $B(m, 1) = 1$. Now if $m = 1$ and $n > 1$, there is contention but the achieved bandwidth is the same, $B(1, n) = 1$. *Simple* processor configurations do not randomly generate requests each cycle, and hence the queueing models do not accurately describe behavior for low values of n and m. For small n or m (since any solution is symmetric), the binomial rather than the Poisson is a better characterization of the request distribution.

Suppose we now substitute the queue size for the $M_B/D/1$ (binomial arrivals) for the $M/D/1$ as used in the development of the asymptotic solution.

Now

$$N = \frac{n}{m} = \rho_a + \frac{\rho_a^2 - p\rho_a}{2(1 - \rho_a)}$$

and for this the processor always (Prob = 1) makes one request each T_c. As seen from a given module:

$$p = \frac{1}{m}$$

$$n/m = \rho = \rho_a + \frac{\rho_a^2 - \rho_a/m}{2(1 - \rho_a)}.$$

Solving for ρ_a,

$$\rho_a = 1 + \frac{n}{m} - \frac{1}{2m} - \sqrt{(1 + n/m - 1/2m)^2 - 2n/m}$$

and $B(m, n) = m\rho_a$

$$B(m, n) = m + n - 1/2 - \sqrt{(m + n - 1/2)^2 - 2nm}.$$

Note now that if either n or $m = 1$, $B(m, n) = 1$, since

$$
\begin{aligned}
B(x, 1) &= x + 1 - \frac{1}{2} - \sqrt{(x + 1 - \frac{1}{2})^2 - 2x} \\
&= x + \frac{1}{2} - \sqrt{x^2 - x + 1/4} \\
&= x + \frac{1}{2} - x + \frac{1}{2} = 1.
\end{aligned}
$$

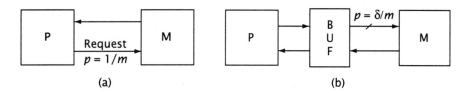

Figure 6.21 Pipelined processors: (a) binomial model (simple processor); (b) typical pipelined processor.

Thus, the binomial approximation is useful whenever we have:

1. Simple processor memory configuration (a binomial arrival distribution).

2. $n \geq 1$ and $m \geq 1$.

3. Request–response behavior between processor and memory, where the processor makes exactly n requests per T_c.

The Delta (δ)-Binomial Model

If we replace the simple processor (making a request each T_c) with a pipelined processor, the binomial model may fail. The binomial model assumes that the processor requests one memory access each T_c; n processors make n requests. Suppose that a processor has a buffer (e.g., I-buffer, register set, cache) that supplies many of the processor requests, so that the processor-requestor makes a request with probability δ. This simple binomial model cannot be used as it cannot distinguish between a single simple processor ($n = 1$) making a request each T_c with probability = 1 and, e.g., two processors each making (on the average) 0.5 requests per T_c ($n = 1$ but $\delta = 0.5$). The former case has no contention, but the latter case has memory contention, as both sources will occasionally make simultaneous requests to the same memory module. Worse still is the case where each of two sources makes requests with Prob = 0.25. Now n (requests per T_c) = 0.5 and the simple binomial model fails.

To correct this, we introduce the *δ-binomial model.*

Suppose the processor makes a request each T_c with probability p ($p \neq 1$). This can occur even in relatively simple processors with register sets (DF used primarily on loads) or with very simple I-buffers (IF fetches perhaps two instructions).

Since we still assume a relatively simple processor, when a request is made to the memory any resulting contention directly affects performance. The $M_B/D/1$ closed-queue model is still appropriate, but δ, the probability of a processor access during T_c, does not equal one (in fact, $p = \delta/m$). In the simple binomial model, the restriction on n ($n \geq 1$) is a direct consequence of $\delta = 1$. Thus, we have a more general definition of p:

$$\frac{n}{m} = \rho_a + \frac{\rho_a^2 - p\rho_a}{2(1 - \rho_a)}.$$

Solving

$$\rho_a = \frac{1}{m}\left[m + n - \frac{mp}{2} - \sqrt{(m + n - mp/2)^2 - 2nm}\right],$$

since $p = \delta/m$, we replace mp with δ:

$$B(m, n, \delta) = m + n - \frac{\delta}{2} - \sqrt{(m + n - \delta/2)^2 - 2nm}.$$

This is our basic processor–memory performance model. It assumes there are no source buffers for request sources. Processors with buffered request sources will perform better than predicted by this simple model.

Recall that the open queue model discussed in the previous section is not a system in equilibrium. Based on service time (T_s), and a peak request rate λ, we compute ρ and then T_w. We could then use this T_w to modify the effective service time to become T_w and T_s, which changes the request rate. If the processor could make requests at its peak rate unaffected by T_w, the processor would achieve the offered request rate. The memory system contention would not affect performance. The need to represent processor–memory models that recognize that processors are immediately affected by delayed memory responses and that the resulting model must have a meaningful equilibrium state is another motivation for closed-queue models.

The δ-binomial approximation is summarized as follows:

- Processor makes n requests each T_c.

- Each processor request source makes a request with probability δ.

Offered bandwidth each T_c

$$
\begin{aligned}
Bw \text{ offered} &= n/T_c = m\lambda, \\
\text{Achieved bandwidth} &= B(m, n, \delta), \\
B(m, n, \delta) &= m + n - \delta/2 - \sqrt{(m + n - \delta/2)^2 - 2nm}, \\
Bw &= \frac{B(m, n, \delta)}{T_c} = m\lambda_a, \\
\text{Achieved performance} &= \frac{\lambda_a}{\lambda} \times (\text{Offered performance}).
\end{aligned}
$$

6.5.3   Mixed Queues

Suppose we now consider a processor that makes requests from buffered sources. Further suppose its request rate is unaffected by server performance until its buffer is full. With a low request rate, this system will behave as an open queue, but once it reaches a critical occupancy it behaves as a closed-queue system. We call such systems *buffered closed queues*, and generally model them by simply recognizing the added queue in the system.

Consider the simple case of the $M/D/1$ queue. For a buffered closed-queue system,

---

Analyzing Interleaved Memory Systems

At first glance, it may seem that analyzing a processor (without cache) connected to an interleaved memory system is something of an anachronism. Yet the processor interleaved memory model is the building block for the analysis of any complex memory system. In the remaining sections, we extend this model to include processors with cache and eventually to multiple processors in various shared memory arrangements. Moreover, as processors get faster, and caches get larger, there will be a need to improve the cache–processor bandwidth. This need can be satisfied most simply by interleaved caches, whose performance analysis follows interleaved memory.

$$N = \frac{n}{m} + \overline{B} = \rho_a + \frac{\rho_a^2}{2(1 - \rho_a)},$$

where $\overline{B}$ is the achieved queue size in the buffer (per module). Now, since $n/m = \rho$, the offered occupancy is the same as the achieved occupancy (ρ_a) so long as $\overline{B}$ is less than the actual buffer size, (BF), $\rho = \rho_a$, since

$$\rho + \frac{\rho^2}{2(1 - \rho)} = \rho_a + \frac{\rho_a^2}{2(1 - \rho_a)}.$$

There is a critical occupancy (ρ_c) at which the mean buffer size approaches the physical buffer size. Suppose

$$\overline{B} = BF.$$

Here,

$$BF = \frac{\rho_c^2}{2(1 - \rho_c)},$$

or, solving for ρ_c:

$$\rho_c = \sqrt{BF^2 + 2BF} - BF.$$

To a first approximation, the system acts as an open-queue system so long as $\rho_c > \rho$, then as $\rho_c < \rho$ the queue saturates and behaves as a closed-queue system.

While the above is generally descriptive of buffered closed queues, it is analytically simplistic and inappropriate for general use. The problem is that a queue of mean size $\overline{B}$ ($\overline{B} < BF$) may momentarily have queue $> BF$. This slows the system down well before $\rho = \rho_c$.

We call systems that are tolerant of some system delay (waiting time) or have some buffering of requests *mixed queueing systems*. We will look at appropriate models for such systems in chapters 7 and 9.

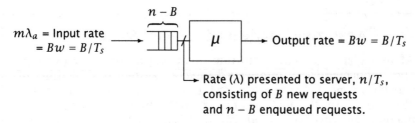

Figure 6.22   Waiting time.

6.6   Determining the Waiting Time, Relative Performance, and Buffer Size

Assume that from one of the previous models we have determined an effective memory bandwidth. We must determine the effective waiting time, to which must be added our fixed access time through the memory system to determine the overall effective memory access time. Assume first we have a purely closed queue without an open-queue buffer. If n requests are made to m modules each cycle, and only B of these requests are honored each cycle, then $n - B$ requests are delayed. As a simple model, the waiting time of the B accepted requests is zero, while the remaining $n - B$ requests are T_s, the service time (Figure 6.22). Thus, the waiting time per request is:

$$T_w = \frac{(n - B)}{B} T_s,$$

since the expected closed-queue size per module (Q_c) is

$$Q_c = n/m - \rho_a = \frac{n}{m} - \frac{B}{m} = \rho - \rho_a$$
$$Q_c = \frac{n - B}{m}$$

and the total closed queue

$$Q_{c-t} = mQ_c = n - B$$
and
$$m\lambda_a = B/T_s,$$

where T_s is the memory service time and λ_a is the achieved request rate. Recall that

$$\rho_a = \frac{m\lambda_a}{m\mu}$$
and
$$m\lambda_a = \frac{B(m, n)}{T_s} = Bw.$$

Since λ is the arrival rate of requests to memory *without* interference and λ_a represents the achieved rate, the relative performance of the processor–memory system compared to the processor with an ideal memory is:

$$\text{Perf}_{\text{rel}} = \frac{\rho_a}{\rho}.$$

The preceding assumes that the processor performance consistently depends on memory performance and scales accordingly. There may be cases when this is not true. Caches, for example, decouple processors and memory to some degree. If the processor is unaffected by memory for some fraction of requests (λ_u out of λ_p), then the resulting performance would be:

$$\text{Perf}_{\text{rel}} = \frac{\lambda_u}{\lambda_p}(1) + (1 - \frac{\lambda_u}{\lambda_p})\frac{\lambda_a}{\lambda}.$$

We can also rewrite T_w as:

$$
\begin{aligned}
T_w &= \left(\frac{n-B}{m}\right)\frac{m}{B}T_s \\
&= (\rho - \rho_a)m\frac{T_s}{B} = Q_{c-t} \cdot \frac{T_s}{B} = \frac{Q_{c-t}}{\lambda_a},
\end{aligned}
$$

or

$$T_w = \frac{(\rho - \rho_a)}{\rho_a}T_s \quad \text{(closed-queue waiting time)}.$$

The closed-queue model assumes that the processor is directly affected by the response of the memory system. The waiting time directly affects processor performance:

$$
\begin{aligned}
\text{Total service time} &= T_w + T_s \\
&= \frac{\rho - \rho_a}{\rho_a}T_s + T_s \\
&= \frac{\rho}{\rho_a}T_s.
\end{aligned}
$$

A processor requires a number of accesses to memory to complete a job. This corresponds to n requests per T_s, but it only achieves B services per T_s. Thus, the processor time horizon must be extended to accommodate the $n - B$ requests that are now processed at the rate of B/T_s requests/second. This extra time is $(n - B)\, T_s/B$, the waiting time.

Since the λ_a request rate must match the output rate, the processor must be slowed down by a factor of:

$$\lambda_a = \frac{\rho_a}{\rho}\lambda.$$

This is the offered processor rate, and $\frac{\rho_a}{\rho} = \frac{\lambda_a}{\lambda}$ is the relative performance.

6.6.1 Pipelined Processors

In order to apply the δ-binomial model to pipelined processors, we must determine δ, the probability that a processor source makes a request where each of the requesting sources is distinct. The nature of δ (as in the earlier example) is clear. It is not so clear in the case of the pipelined processor, which has many request sources.

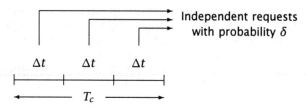

Figure 6.23   The pipelined processor.

To simplify the analysis, we assume that (1) the pipelined processor consists of multiple independent request sources (IF, DF, etc.). Only one request can be made by a source each cycle, and if multiple requests are made the processor randomly selects one and rejects the others. (2) the probability of a request in any cycle is independent of actions in the previous cycles (Figure 6.23). This second assumption certainly introduces some error into our analysis, as requests delayed in one cycle affect the requests in the next cycle. Still, for many processor design situations these are reasonable assumptions, since δ is usually not a strong determinant of performance.

Now we can compute δ, the probability that any given source makes a request.

First, the number of sources (z) is:

$$z = c_p \times \frac{T_c}{\Delta t},$$

where c_p is the number of processor sources making requests each processor cycle (Δt). Typically, c_p consists of a DF (data fetch), IF (instruction fetch), and DS (data store buffer). If a "source" makes more than one request per processor cycle (e.g., IF can be an in-line request plus a TIF), then it is treated as multiple sources. Each source can make only one request per processor cycle (Δt).

The δ is then:

$$\delta = \frac{n}{z}.$$

where n is the previously discussed mean number of requests per T_c (or, more generally, service time).

EXAMPLE 6.3

Suppose a pipelined processor has three request sources that contend for access to memory each machine cycle (Δt). These sources have discrete probabilities of:

IF:	Instruction fetch:	0.6
DF:	Data fetch:	0.4
DS:	Data store:	0.2

Suppose there are three processor cycles per memory cycle; then

$$z \quad = \quad 3 \times 3 = 9$$

$$\text{and} \quad n = 3 \times (.6 + .4 + .2) = 3.6$$

$$\delta = \frac{3.6}{9} = 0.4.$$

Note that n and m are unaffected and are computed as before.

$\blacklozenge$

Study 6.1   Using the δ-Binomial Performance Model

Assume we have a processor with cycle time 40 ns. It makes a memory request each cycle according to the following probabilities:

$$\text{Prob (IF in any cycle)} = 0.6$$
$$\text{Prob (DF in any cycle)} = 0.4$$
$$\text{Prob (DS in any cycle)} = 0.2$$

(The design execution rate is 1 CPI.)

Assume for each memory module $T_a = 120$ ns, $T_c = 120$ ns. In this study, we look at two different processor–memory modeling situations:

(a) Processor with interleaved memory.

Assume we use four-way interleaving, $m = 4$. Compute n:

$$n = \text{requests/cycle} \times \text{cycles per } T_c$$
$$n = (0.6 + 0.4 + 0.2) \times \frac{120}{40}$$
$$= 3.6 \text{ requests}/T_c.$$

Compute δ:

$$\delta = 0.4$$
$$B(m, n, \delta) = m + n - \delta/2 - \sqrt{(m + n - \delta/2)^2 - 2nm}$$
$$B(4, 3.6, 0.4) = 2.3 \text{ requests}/T_c.$$

The processor offers the memory system 3.6 requests each T_c, but the memory system can deliver only 2.3. This has a direct effect on processor performance, since only 2.3 new requests are being honored each T_c. Since

$$\frac{B(m, n, \delta)}{n} = \frac{(Bw)_a}{(Bw)_{\text{offered}}} = \frac{\lambda_a}{\lambda},$$
$$(\text{Perf})_{\text{achieved}} = \frac{2.3}{3.6}(25 \text{ MIPS}) = 16 \text{ MIPS}.$$

The offered performance (1 CPI at 40 ns/cycle) is 25 MIPS, while only 16 MIPS is achieved due to memory contention.

(b) Simple processor with ideal (write-through) cache.

Assume we have the same processor as in (a), but now we have an ideal—no misses at all—write-through cache. Only writes go to the memory system. We assume that the writes have only limited buffering and that processor performance is directly affected by memory write contention. (We will consider more complete cache models later in this chapter.)

Assume $m = 2$.

Compute n:

$$\begin{aligned} n &= \text{DS/cycle} \times \text{cycles per } T_c \\ n &= (0.2)3.0 \\ &= 0.6. \end{aligned}$$

Compute δ:

$$\begin{aligned} z &= 3, \text{ with one write source in each of three cycles.} \\ \delta &= \frac{n}{z} = \frac{0.6}{3.0} = 0.2. \end{aligned}$$

Compute $B(m, n, \delta)$:

$$B(2, 0.6, 0.2) = 0.54,$$

so that write traffic is affected by

$$\frac{B(2, 0.6, 0.2)}{n} = \frac{.54}{.60} = .90$$

and write traffic is slowed down by 10%. Of course, overall processor performance is affected by a lesser amount. For IF and DF, there is no performance slowdown. Thus, the overall performance estimate is:

$$\begin{aligned} \text{Perf}_{\text{rel}} &= \left(\frac{0.6 + 0.4}{1.2}\right)(1) + \left(\frac{0.2}{1.2}\right)(.90) \\ &= (.83) + (.17)(.90) \\ &= .983 \end{aligned}$$

and

$$\text{Perf}_{\text{achieved}} = .983(25) = 24.6 \text{ MIPS}.$$

Notes: Part (a) illustrates that for many situations there may not be a great difference between the simple binomial model $B(4, 3.6, \delta = 1) = 2.45$, and the δ-binomial model (a 6% error). Part (b) of this study illustrates the case where $n < 1$ and δ is small. Using the simple binomial model under such conditions produces significant error (> 20%).

6.6.2   Designing a $M/M/1$ Buffer Given a Mean Queue Size

In chapter 4, we discussed two bounds on a queue (Q) exceeding a fixed buffer size (BF).

For open queueing systems with a single server, we can introduce a third bound based on the M/M/1 model. Since the binomial request rate and the constant service rate have smaller variances than M/M/1, this bound should be safe for many memory and I/O design situations (i.e., so long as $c^2 \leq 1$). Here:

Prob (0 items in server) = $(1 - \rho)$.

Now, intuitively, we compute the probability of exactly *one* item in the queue by computing the probability of an item arriving given an empty queue; i.e.,

Prob (exactly 1 item in queue or server) = $\rho(1 - \rho)$.

Again (intuitively) extending this, we get:

Prob (exactly k items in queue or server)   = $(1 - \rho)\rho^k$.

Now we can compute the probability that there are k or fewer items in the queue or server:

Prob ($\leq k$ items in queue or server)   = $\sum_{j=0}^{k} (1 - \rho)\rho^j$.

This can be rewritten as:

$(1 - \rho)(1 + \rho + \ldots + \rho^k)$,

or, simplifying,

$1 - \rho^{k+1}$,

so that the probability that there are *more than* k items in the queue or servers is:

Prob ($> k$ items in queue awaiting service) = ρ^{k+1}.

Finally, since a buffer of size BF represents $BF + 1 = k$ items in the queue (BF) or in the server:

Prob (buffer of size BF overflows) = ρ^{BF+2}

or

Prob ($Q > $ BF items awaiting service) = ρ^{BF+2}.

Our Chebyshev bound (section 4.4.4) used the concept of "buffer full or overflowed" as the point of system slowdown. This corresponds to:

Prob ($Q \geq $ BF) = ρ^{BF+1}.

The essential issue in determining BF is that for us, BF is the value at which the system slows down. If we have a buffer of size 3 but the system does not slow down unless there are 4 items, then we are looking for the probability that $Q > 3$ or $Q \geq 4$, which in either case is ρ^5.

In our modeling assumptions for using Chebyshev's bound, we used the mean arrival rate as an estimate of the queue size. Assuming unit departures ($\mu = 1$), this is a safe estimate so long as $\rho \leq 0.5$ (i.e., so long as $\lambda \leq 0.5$).

For most cases, we will find that the $M/M/1$ buffer "full or overflowed" estimate is superior to the Chebyshev bound.

For closed queues, we replace ρ with ρ_a.

EXAMPLE 6.4   BUFFER OVERFLOW 1

Suppose we wish to ensure that the probability of buffer overflow ($Q > $ BF) is less than 7% for queue occupancy of $\rho = 0.5$:

$$\text{Prob} (Q > \text{BF} = 2) = (.5)^4 = 0.0625.$$

Note that the above bound is derived for a buffer plus a server, so that $BF = 0$ means that there is still a server in the system. If an item must enter, say, a pipelined buffer stage before it can proceed, one storage element is regarded as the server, while additional storage elements compose the buffer.

Using this bound in memory systems is limited by the single server requirement; after all, the case of $m = 1$ memory module is uninteresting!

If, indeed, we had a separate buffer for each module, then we could determine the probability of overflow in *any* module as:

$$\begin{aligned} \text{Prob} (Q > \text{BF in any of } m \text{ buffers}) &= 1 - [1 - \text{Prob} (Q > \text{BF})]^m \\ &= 1 - \left[1 - \rho^{\text{BF}+2}\right]^m. \end{aligned}$$

◆

EXAMPLE 6.5   BUFFER OVERFLOW 2

Let us consider the preceding example for $m = 2$. Again $\rho = 0.5$ and we wish to ensure Prob $(Q > \text{BF}) \leq 0.07$. Instead of BF = 2, let us try BF = 3 (buffer of three entries for each module):

$$\rho^{\text{BF}+2} = \rho^5 = (0.5)^5 = 0.03125$$

$$\text{Prob} (Q > \text{BF in either module}) = 1 - \left[1 - \rho^5\right]^2 = 0.062.$$

The obvious alternative is to pool the buffers into a larger buffer, BFP, that holds requests for all modules, so that:

$$\text{BFP} = m \cdot \text{BF}.$$

Table 6.4   Models and their assumptions.

Model	Model Assumptions	Comments
Hellerman	No out-of-sequence requests, no queues.	Simplest type of processor.
Strecker	No queues.	Maybe a useful model for unbuffered bus, etc.
$M/D/1$ open (Flores)	Unbounded queue, $Bw = \lambda_p$.	Useful for initial estimates or in mixed queue models.
$M_B/D/1$ closed (Simple binomial)	Processor memory in stability, queue per module $N = n/m$.	n simple processors making n requests per T_c (n a constant).
$M_B/D/1$ closed (δ-binomial)	Processor memory in stability, queue per module $N = n/m$.	n requests per T_c, each made with prob δ.

As a "rule of thumb" only, we can bound

$$\mathrm{Prob}\,(m \cdot Q > \mathrm{BFP}) \leq \rho^{\frac{\mathrm{BFP}}{m}+2}$$

for $m > 1$. For m large, this bound may be of limited value.

◆

6.6.3   Comparison of Memory Models

The issue of when to use a particular model depends a great deal on the structure of the processor and memory and the interaction between them. Each model discussed is valid for a particular type of processor–memory interaction; the question is when to use a particular model.

Table 6.4 presents the various models with their assumptions. Hellerman's model represents the simplest type of processor. This processor does not allow out-of-sequence requests to the memory and provides no queue for addresses or requests to memory. Since the processor cannot skip over conflicting requests and has no buffer (either in memory or core processor), naturally it achieves the lowest bandwidth. Strecker's model anticipates out-of-order requests; however, it does not explicitly model queues of requests. It might indeed be applicable to multiple simple unbuffered processors. Alternatively, it can be used to model multiple processors accessing an unbuffered bus.

The M/D/1 open model, with its assumptions of unbounded queue length and achieved bandwidth always equal to the offered bandwidth, has limited accuracy in typical processor memory situations. Still, it is useful in many situations as an initial estimate for occupancy, and can provide a reasonable estimate when the offered occupancy is low (for instance, $\rho < 0.25$).

The closed-queue models based upon $M_B/D/1$ represent a processor memory in equilibrium, where the queue length including the item in service (n) equals n/m on a per-module basis. The simple binomial model is useful only for processors making n requests per T_c, where n is the mean of the request distribution that is made to the memory system. For simple pipelined processors (limited buffer), the δ-binomial model seems most suitable.

As n and m become large (≥ 4), most of the models give a reasonably close estimate of performance. With the exception of the Hellerman and Flores models (both of which represent modeling extremes), the models should give a reasonably good estimate of processor–memory interactions across a reasonably broad range of multiple (or simple pipelined) processor/multiple memory module combinations. By the same token, when n and m are small (< 4) or the processor model is unusual (i.e., particularly constrained or simple), then special care must be taken in choosing the analytic model and properly parameterizing it in order to achieve reasonable accuracy.

The following example illustrates how the models compare numerically, without examining the underlying details of the processor–memory interaction.

EXAMPLE 6.6   MODEL COMPARISON

Suppose $n = m = 4$; assume the memory has $T_c = 100\,$ns. The processor offers the memory system four requests, each $100\,$ns(T_c) or 40 MAPS. The predicted bandwidth is:

(a) Hellerman:

$$
\begin{aligned}
B(m) &= \sqrt{m} = \sqrt{4} = 2, \\
Bw &= \frac{B}{T_c} = \frac{2}{.100} = 20 \text{ MAPS.}
\end{aligned}
$$

(b) Strecker:

$$
\begin{aligned}
B(m,n) &= m\left[1 - (1 - \frac{1}{m})^n\right] \\
&= 4\left[1 - (1 - \frac{1}{4})^4\right], \\
B(m,n) &= 2.734, \\
Bw &= 27.34 \text{ MAPS.}
\end{aligned}
$$

(c) Asymptotic:

$$
\begin{aligned}
B(m,n) &= m \cdot \rho_a, \\
\rho_a &= (1 + \frac{n}{m}) - \sqrt{(n/m)^2 + 1} \\
&= 2 - \sqrt{(1)^2 + 1} \\
&= 2 - \sqrt{2} = 0.586,
\end{aligned}
$$

$$B(m,n) = 2.34,$$

$$Bw = \frac{2.34}{.100} = 23.43 \text{ MAPS.}$$

(d) Simple binomial:

$$B(m,n) = m + n - \frac{1}{2} - \sqrt{(m+n-1/2)^2 - 2mn}$$

$$= 7.5 - \sqrt{(7.5)^2 - 32},$$

$$B(m,n) = 2.576,$$

$$Bw = 25.76 \text{ MAPS.}$$

◆

Design Summary:

- For an initial estimate of the module partitioning, use the open-queue model setting $\rho \approx .5$. This is subject to large errors, so it is useful as an initial partitioning estimate only.

- Find $B(m,n,\delta)$.

- In general, use the δ-binomial model for pipelined processor–memory configurations.

- Find T_w and access time.

Study 6.2   Interleaved Memory Systems Evaluation

Consider a 50 MIPS processor ($\Delta t = 20$ ns), requiring 75 MAPS, using $m = 16$ and $n = \lambda_s \cdot T_c = 75 \times 10^6 \times 0.1 \times 10^{-6} = 7.5$. Assume IF/cycle = 0.8, DF/cycle= 0.5, DS/cycle= 0.2.

This is a simple pipelined processor. We use the δ-binomial approximation for performance estimates. Compute δ:

$$z = 3 \times \frac{T_c}{\Delta t} = 3 \times \frac{100}{20} = 15,$$

$$\delta = \frac{n}{z} = \frac{7.5}{15} = 0.5,$$

$$\rho = \frac{n}{m} = \frac{7.5}{16} = 0.47,$$

$$B(m,n,\delta) = B(16, 7.5, 0.5)$$

$$= m + n - \frac{\delta}{2} - \sqrt{(m+n-1/2)^2 - 2mn}$$

$$B(16, 7.5, 0.5) = 5.9,$$

$$Bw = \frac{5.9}{T_c} = \frac{5.9}{.1 \times 10^{-6}} = 59 \text{ MAPS.}$$

Now the achieved occupancy *per module* is:

$$\rho_a = \frac{B(m, n, \delta)}{m}$$
$$= 0.37.$$

Thus, the processor is unable to achieve its requested 75 MAPS request rate, λ, and achieves only

$$\lambda_a = 59 \text{ MAPS}.$$

The processor slows down by the same rate:

$$(\text{MIPS})_{\text{achieved}} = 50 \left(\frac{59}{75}\right)$$
$$= 39.3 \text{ MIPS}.$$

We could have arrived at the same conclusion based on module occupancy:

$$\lambda_a = \frac{\rho_a}{\rho} \lambda.$$

Now that we know the effect of memory interference on performance, let us determine the memory waiting time (T_w):

$$T_w = \frac{n - B}{B} T_s$$
$$= \frac{7.5 - 5.9}{5.9} (100) \text{ ns}$$
$$= 27 \text{ ns}.$$

The average number of requests buffered by the memory system is:

$$Q_{c-t} = 7.5 - 5.9 = 1.6.$$

6.7   Review and Selection of Queueing Models

Throughout the remainder of this text, we shall from time to time use one or more of the variations of simple queueing models. In selecting an appropriate variation, the reader should recall that there are basically three dimensions to simple (single) server queueing models. These three dimensions represent the statistical characterization of the arrival rate, the service rate, and the amount of buffering that is present in the system before the system saturates.

For arrivals, the issue is δ, the probability that a given source requests service during a particular service interval. If the source always requests (with probability = 1) service during a service interval, we use the M_B, or simple

---

Approximations and Estimates

The modeling of any system is only as good as the assumptions that underlie that model. In our memory models, we may assume at various times Poisson arrivals or uniform address distributions—assumptions which are only approximately accurate. Under such conditions, it makes little sense to create more complex and precise models when the underlying assumptions are only approximate themselves. Still, the analysis must be performed carefully. Interference that is negligible in one case may be quite significant with different modeling parameters. Each component of delay or contention must be carefully analyzed based upon the environment under consideration. If, based upon that analysis, one can show that a particular source of contention is not significant, so much the better; but we know this only after the analysis is done.

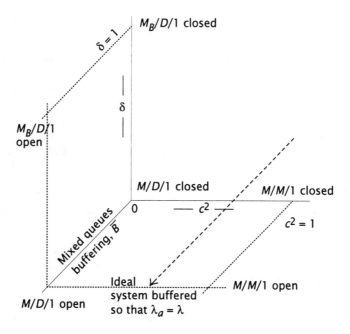

Figure 6.24   The three basic parameters of simple queues.

binomial model. If the particular requestor has a diminishingly small probability of making a request during a particular service interval (as in the case of, say, I/O) we use the Poisson arrival model.

The second dimension is the variance on the service distribution, measured by the coefficient of variance (c^2). In cases where the service time is fixed and unvariant, we use a constant service distribution (D), since the coefficient of variance c^2 equals zero. Frequently, the service time is known to vary, but the variance is unknown. For ease of analysis frequently one chooses $c^2 = 1$, which represents an exponential service time. Of course, if the actual variance is known, the c^2 can be computed and we can use the $M/G/1$ queueing model or a variation of it.

The third parameter determining the simple queueing model is the amount of buffering available to the requestor to hold pending requests (allowing bypassing if there are no requests while any pending requests are delayed). This bypassing, or buffering, factor is dealt with when we take up more complex processor models in chapter 7, or when we deal with complex I/O storage arrangements in chapter 9.

6.8   Processors with Cache

Almost all modern processors use caches to access both instructions and data. The only notable exceptions to this are the vector processors, which access data directly from memory. We will discuss vector processors further in the next chapter.

Conventional processors that access all of their instructions and data from cache require some discussion. Generally, processors that access noninterleaved caches ought to have either no or limited performance degradation due to memory systems contention. This does not mean that the memory system delay does not affect performance; indeed, the simpler the cache and the longer the cache miss penalty, the poorer the overall performance. However, in these cases the performance is quite predictable. The processor stops and waits until the memory system returns an entire line to the processor, then the processor resumes. Requests do not cause contention to memory, so only the predictable memory accessing delay remains. As discussed in chapter 5, there are three types of cache memory interactions:

1. Fully blocked. When the cache misses, the processor completely stops processing until the entire line is returned to the cache, then processing resumes.

2. Partially blocked. The processor resumes processing after some portion of the line is returned; thus, there is a period when both processor and memory are busy.

3. Nonblocked. A nonblocking cache allows multiple pending misses. Thus, the processor does not stop when the miss occurs unless required by a data dependency. Nonblocking caches that allow up to d misses before blocking are called nonblocking caches of degree d [267]. Prefetching of lines is associated with nonblocking caches, as it improves their anticipation of use. Some processors support prefetching with special instructions, e.g., touch.

In the remainder of this chapter, we look at (1) single or split caches with either fully blocked, partially blocked, or nonblocking interactions with memory, and (2) interleaved caches.

As we will see, simple caches with either fully or partially blocked memory interactions can easily be modeled without using queueing theory. We model nonblocking caches in a manner similar to the treatment of multiprogrammed processor-I/O systems. Finally, we model interleaved caches in much the same way we modeled interleaved memory systems.

6.8.1 Fully and Partially Blocking Caches

The addition of a cache to a memory system complicates the performance evaluation and design. For copyback systems with write allocate (CBWA), the requests to memory consist of line-read requests and line-write requests. For write-through systems without fetch-on-write (WTNWA), the requests consist of line-read requests and *word-write* requests.

In order to develop models of memory systems with cache, two basic parameters must be evaluated:

1. $T_{\text{line access}}$, the time it takes a cache to access a line in memory.

2. T_{busy}, the potential contention time during which the memory is busy *and* the processor/cache is available to make requests to memory.

In the following sections, we discuss these parameters and then apply them to the evaluation of various caches.

6.8.2 Accessing a Line ($T_{\text{line access}}$)

We consider pipelined single processor systems. The usual memory arrangement for supporting fast line access involves the use of:

1. Interleaving.

2. Fast sequential page mode.

3. A combination of the two.

We consider each of these arrangements in this section.

For our interleaved memory module analysis, we assume that the cache has a line size of L physical words. (The physical word is defined by the bus word size.) The memory is low-order interleaved to degree m, where $m \geq L$. The total time to move a line is given by:

$$T_{\text{line}} = T_{\text{line access}} = T_{\text{line-read}} = T_{\text{line-write}} = T_a + (L - 1)\, T_{\text{bus}},$$

where T_a is the word-access time, and T_{bus} is the shared bus cycle time. (Usually T_{bus} is the same as the internal processor cycle time.) The memory system, while interleaved, does not begin to process a request until it is completely free.

T_c plays a role for $L > m$, since the first accessed memory module may not be available when requested at the T_{bus} rate.

If $T_c \le (m)\, T_{\text{bus}}$, even if $L > m$, the memory cycle is faster than the bus usage and the initial memory module has recovered before it is to be used again. Thus, we have:

$$T_{\text{line access}} = T_a + (L - 1)\, T_{\text{bus}}.$$

Now for $L > m$ and $T_c > (m)T_{\text{bus}}$, the memory cycle time dominates the bus transfer. The result depends on the relationship between T_a and T_c, so a timing diagram is useful; but as an estimate, we can use

$$T_{\text{line access}} = T_a + T_c \cdot \left(\left\lceil \frac{L}{m} \right\rceil - 1 \right) + T_{\text{bus}} \left((L - 1) \bmod m \right).$$

Assume that we have $T_a = 300$ nsec, $T_c = 200$ nsec, $m = 2$, $T_{\text{bus}} = 50$ nsec, and $L = 8$. We would have the following timing relationship:

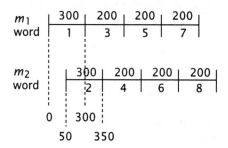

The first word in the line is available in T_a, but that module is not available again until T_c. A total of $\lceil L/m \rceil$ accesses must be made to the first used module, with the first access accounted for by T_a (assuming $T_a > T_c$). Thus, an additional $\lceil L/m \rceil - 1$ cycles are required. Finally, $(L - 1) \bmod m$ bus cycles are required for the other modules to complete the line transfer.

Now we assume a single module memory system ($m = 1$) with sequential page mode. We assume the memory has the following characteristics:

- T_a, the access time to the first retrieved item.

- v, the maximum number of *fast* sequential accesses that can be made to the module before a memory refresh time is required.

- T_v, the minimum time between sequential accesses during page mode.

- T_c, the *cycle* time assumed to be the same as the memory refresh time between accesses of v items in page mode.

Thus, we have the following relationship:

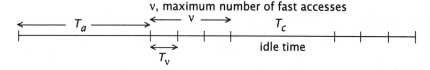

Assuming that T_{bus} is of the same order of magnitude as T_v, we would have:

$$T_{\text{line access}} = T_a + T_c \left(\left\lceil \frac{L}{v} \right\rceil - 1 \right) + (\max(T_{bus}, T_v)) \left(\left\lceil L - \frac{L}{v} \right\rceil \right). \quad (6.3)$$

This is generally similar in form to the interleaved case, with a minor adjustment for the T_{bus}, T_v distinction.

EXAMPLE 6.7   COMPUTING $T_{\text{LINE ACCESS}}$

Assume we have $T_a = 200\,\text{ns}$, $T_c = 150\,\text{ns}$, $T_v = 40\,\text{ns}$, $T_{bus} = 50\,\text{ns}$, $L = 8$, and $v = 4$.

We would have the following time relationship:

Time 0   50   100   150   200   300   400   500   600 650

Word retrieved   1   2   3   4   5   6   7   8

which we compute as:

$$
\begin{aligned}
T_{\text{line access}} &= 200 + 150 \left(\left\lceil \frac{8}{4} \right\rceil - 1 \right) + (50)(8 - \left\lceil \frac{8}{4} \right\rceil) \\
&= 200 + 150 + 300 \\
&= 650\,\text{ns.}
\end{aligned}
$$

The final case is an interleaved memory consisting of modules with fast sequential page mode. Assume

$$\frac{T_v}{m} = T_{bus}.$$

That is, that memory to processor transfers are determined by the bus time (T_{bus}), not the interleaved page time.

Here, the line access is approximately:

$$T_{\text{line access}} \le T_a + T_c \left(\left\lceil \frac{L}{m \cdot v} \right\rceil - 1 \right) + T_{bus} \left(\left\lceil L - \frac{L}{m \cdot v} - 1 \right\rceil \right).$$

◆

EXAMPLE 6.8   COMPUTING $T_{\text{LINE ACCESS}}$

Consider the case where:

$$
\begin{aligned}
L &= 16, \\
v &= 4, \\
m &= 2, \\
T_a &= 200\,\text{ns}, \\
T_c &= 150\,\text{ns}, \\
T_{bus} &= 25\,\text{ns}, \; T_v = 50\,\text{ns}.
\end{aligned}
$$

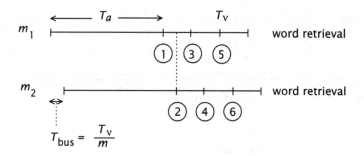

Figure 6.25   Computing line access time.

This is shown in Figure 6.25, and computed as:

$$T_{\text{line access}} = 200 + 150 \left(\left\lceil \frac{16}{8} \right\rceil - 1 \right) + 25(16 - 2)$$
$$= 700 \, \text{ns}.$$

◆

6.8.3   Contention Time (T_{busy}) and Copyback Caches

Consider a simple copyback cache (CBWA), where on a miss the processor does not resume until a dirty line (w = probability of a dirty line) is written back to memory and the new line is fully written in the cache. The miss penalty (T_{miss}) or delay is:

$$T_{\text{miss}} = (1 + w) \, T_{\text{line access}}.$$

If we ignore the effects of I/O, however, there is no possibility of memory contention for this simple cache! The processor ceases requests to memory when memory is busy and contention cannot develop.

Now, T_{miss}—the total "effect" of a miss—may be different for the cache than for the main memory. The processor may resume accessing the cache before the memory system completes processing the miss (e.g., writing back a dirty line). Let us distinguish between two miss times:

1. $T_{\text{c.miss}}$—the time the processor is idle due to a cache miss (without interference/contention).

2. $T_{\text{m.miss}}$—the total time the main memory system takes to process a miss (again ignoring contention).

We define the potential contention time (T_{busy}) as the time memory is busy *and* the time the processor is enabled to make requests to memory:

$$T_{\text{busy}} = T_{\text{m.miss}} - T_{\text{c.miss}}.$$

For copyback (CBWA) caches (ignoring I/O), we might have:

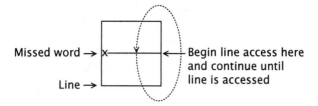

Figure 6.26   Wraparound load.

1. On miss, write a line (if dirty), then read the complete line before the processor resumes. This is the case discussed previously. Here, we first write the altered (dirty) line to the memory, then read the new line into the cache, then resume processing.

$$T_{\text{m.miss}} = (1 + w)\, T_{\text{line access}},$$
$$T_{\text{c.miss}} = (1 + w)\, T_{\text{line access}},$$
$$T_{\text{busy}} = T_{\text{m.miss}} - T_{\text{c.miss}} = 0.$$

2. On miss, write a dirty line to a write buffer while the new line is being accessed, then read in the new line. When the processor resumes, the dirty line is written back to memory. Now

$$T_{\text{m.miss}} = (1 + w)\, T_{\text{line access}},$$
$$T_{\text{c.miss}} = T_{\text{line access}},$$
$$T_{\text{busy}} = w \cdot T_{\text{line access}}.$$

More sophisticated caches access the faulted word first, then "wrap" around the accessing of the remaining words in the line. Processing resumes (as does referencing to the cache) as soon as the faulting word reaches the processor.

$T_{\text{c.miss}}$ is defined as the time the processor is idle awaiting its first word from memory. With demand fetching, fetch-bypass, and wraparound load, $T_{\text{c.miss}}$ is typically the same as T_a—the access time to the faulted word, assuming a typical cache configuration (Figure 6.26).

Fetch-bypass is used to accelerate a demand fetch: when a miss occurs, the desired bytes are passed directly from the main memory to the processor, bypassing the cache. Here, the load of the cache proceeds simultaneously with the fetch-bypass. A wraparound load means that the transfer begins with the bytes accessed and wraps around to the rest of the line.

Then

$$T_{\text{busy}} = T_{\text{m.miss}} - T_{\text{c.miss}}$$
$$= (1 + w)\, T_{\text{line access}} - T_a.$$

If the processor creates a miss during T_{busy}, it encounters delay in addition to $T_{\text{c.miss}}$. This is not, strictly speaking, a queueing delay; rather, it is simply interference by the processor with one of its own overlapped operations. Suppose we designate this time as $T_{\text{interference}}$. Then

$$T_{\text{interference}} = \text{Expected number of misses during } T_{\text{busy}} \cdot (\text{Delay per miss}).$$

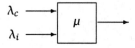

Figure 6.27   I/O contention.

Now

Expected number of misses during T_{busy}

= number of requests during T_{busy} · Prob (miss)

= $\lambda_p \cdot T_{\text{busy}} \cdot f$,

where λ_p is the processor read request rate and f is the miss rate per request.

The delay factor given a miss during T_{busy} is simply estimated as $T_{\text{busy}}/2$, assuming a uniform miss distribution. Then

$$T_{\text{interference}} = \lambda_p \cdot T_{\text{busy}} \cdot f \cdot T_{\text{busy}}/2$$
$$= \frac{\lambda_p \cdot f \cdot (T_{\text{busy}})^2}{2},$$

and the total miss time seen from the processor (excluding effects of I/O) is

$$T_{\text{miss}} = T_{\text{c.miss}} + T_{\text{interference}}.$$

For copyback cache (CBWA) and line buffered I/O, *all* references are to lines. If a cache miss immediately follows the beginning of an I/O line transfer,

$$T_{\text{busy}} = T_{\text{line access}}.$$

6.8.4   I/O Effects

Queueing delays (i.e., contention) arise whenever one of the following pairs of requests occurs (at the same memory module) within too short a time: CPU–I/O (CPU occupying channel, I/O requests service), I/O–CPU, CPU–CPU, or I/O–I/O. The CPU–CPU was previously handled by considering it as interference that the processor handles itself, and not as queueing contention/delay. Cases I/O–I/O and CPU–I/O cause queueing delays at memory, and delay the I/O unit, but do *not* delay the processor. The first case, I/O–CPU, causes queueing delays (visible to the processor) that can be calculated. For a CBWA cache with line-buffered I/O, the I/O (word) request rate λ_i is treated as if it were another processor, while $T_{\text{line access}}$ is the service time T_s. We model the effect of I/O by assuming that the processor is "blind" to its own accesses and that it can only "see" the I/O effect on memory as causing contention. The I/O–CPU contention delay (as seen by the CPU) can thus be calculated as $T_{w-\text{I/O}}$.

In computing this contention, we have two request sources λ_c from the processor–cache and λ_i from the I/O system, but only λ_i actually causes contention. The λ_c request stream, however, can secondarily affect the waiting time at the server as seen by the I/O system (Figure 6.27). We ignore this effect and compute an available service occupancy:

$$\rho_i = \frac{\lambda_i}{\mu}.$$

If the processor preempts the I/O from memory, then it only has to wait until any already started memory request is completed. This probability is ρ_i and we estimate the effective delay as $T_c/2$. Thus,

$$T_{w-I/O} = \rho_i \frac{T_c}{2}.$$

If the I/O is line buffered, it may have line priority use of memory—that is, it has priority use of memory while a line is being transferred; thereafter the processor has priority. Here we estimate:

$$T_{w-I/O} \doteq \rho_i \frac{T_{\text{line access}}}{2}.$$

Finally, the I/O may have priority over the processor in its use of memory. Now the processor must wait until any queued I/O requests are completed. We assume the I/O consists of several independent well-buffered sources, and thus T_w has no immediate effect on the I/O request rate (open queue), unlike the case of the processor. Here, T_w is the delay seen by the I/O due to memory contention. The typical I/O transaction occupies the memory (and memory bus, if appropriate) for

$$T_{I/O} = T_s + T_w,$$

where T_s is the memory service time (T_c or $T_{\text{line access}}$). Again, we estimate that the processor, when it sees I/O memory contention, observes:

$$T_{w-I/O} = \rho_i \left(\frac{T_s + T_w}{2} \right),$$

where T_w can be estimated from open-queue $M/D/1$ (low occupancy, I/O well buffered). The $M_B/D/1$ is inappropriate, since it models the source as making a request with Prob $= 1$ each memory cycle time.

In summary, the effect of I/O is to increase the access time for a line transaction by $T_{w\text{-I/O}}$, so that:

$$T_{\text{m.miss}} \text{ (I/O adjust)} = T_{\text{m.miss}} + T_{w\text{-I/O}}. \tag{6.4}$$

6.8.5 Performance Effects

Now suppose T_{cycle} is the processor cycle time (which is usually equal to T_{bus}). The number of cache misses per processor cycle is thus $f\lambda_p T_{\text{cycle}}$, while the number of cycles lost is $T_{\text{miss}}/T_{\text{cycle}}$. Therefore, the number of cycles lost per CPU cycle is:

$$c = f\lambda_p T_{\text{miss}} \tag{6.5}$$

Then the effective processor performance is:

Effective Performance (cycles per instr) = CPI $(1 + f\lambda_p T_{\text{miss}})$,

where CPI is the processor performance (cycles per instruction) without cache/memory delays.

The relative performance is

$$\text{Perf}_{\text{rel}} = \frac{\text{CPI}}{\text{CPI}(1 + f\lambda_p T_{\text{miss}})} = \frac{1}{1 + f\lambda_p T_{\text{miss}}}.$$

Other cache design parameters such as placement algorithm (e.g., degree of set-associative mapping), replacement algorithm, and prefetch strategy are less directly involved with the cache–memory interface. Their effects may be appropriately reflected through the miss ratio [259].

6.8.6   Copyback Cache Study

Assuming CBWA strategy and line-buffered I/O, all read and write cache misses result in line-read requests to the memory system, and the corresponding line-write requests if the lines are dirty and must be copied back. Ignoring I/O, there will be no queueing delay, as the processor will not make requests until memory is available. We consider the effects of I/O in study 6.3(d).

In considering I/O, the processor is blind to its own traffic ($T_{\text{busy}} = 0$) and thus can be affected only by the I/O traffic (λ_i). Once the I/O traffic (λ_i) is determined, T_w can be computed as discussed in the preceding section. All requests, I/O and processor–cache, are delayed by T_w, but only the processor–cache delays affect performance.

Study 6.3   Evaluating Copyback (CBWA) Caches

Assume a CBWA cache has a miss rate of 0.03 misses per reference with a dirty line ratio of 0.5. This cache is used with a processor that makes a reference every 40 ns (mean).

Assume the cache is configured with:

$$\begin{aligned}
\text{Cache line size} \quad &= \quad 16^{\text{B}}, \\
\text{Physical word size} \quad &= \quad 4^{\text{B}},
\end{aligned}$$

and the memory is configured as:

$T_a = 120\,\text{ns}, \; T_c = 100\,\text{ns}, \; T_{\text{bus}} = 40\,\text{ns}, \; m = 2.$

(a) Assume the cache writes a dirty line *before* reading lines (unbuffered) and that an *entire* line must be transferred to the processor before it resumes processing (these strategies are found in several microprocessor caches). What is the cache miss delay, ignoring I/O effects?

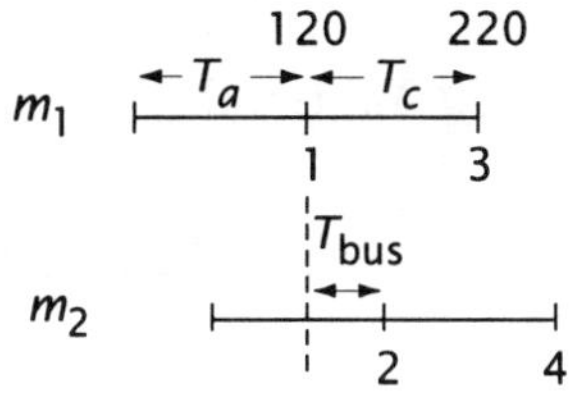

Figure 6.28   Accessing for $m = 2$, $L = 4$.

We begin by finding $T_{\text{line access}}$. Since

$$L = \frac{\text{line size}}{\text{word size}} = \frac{16^{\text{B}}}{4^{\text{B}}} = 4,$$

then $L > m$. Now

$$m \cdot T_{\text{bus}} = 2 \cdot 40 = 80\,\text{ns},$$

and therefore $T_c > m \cdot T_{\text{bus}}$.

Thus (Figure 6.28),

$$T_{\text{line access}} = T_a + T_c \cdot \left(\left\lceil \frac{L}{m} \right\rceil - 1 \right) + T_{\text{bus}} \left((L - 1) \bmod m \right),$$

$$T_{\text{line access}} = 120 + 100 \left(\left\lceil \frac{4}{2} \right\rceil - 1 \right) + 40 (3 \bmod 2)$$

$$= 120 + 100 + 40 = 260\,\text{ns}.$$

Thus, the average miss delay including the effects of writes is

$$T_{\text{m.miss}} = (1 + w)\, T_{\text{line access}} = 1.5(260) = 390\,\text{ns}.$$

For our example, $T_{\text{interference}}$ is zero—there is no contention for the memory. What has happened is that $T_{\text{busy}} = T_{\text{m.miss}} - T_{\text{c.miss}} = 0$.

The processor does not create any contention for memory, since it waits until memory is free before (potentially) making another request.

Now we can compute the effect of the cache on the processor in cycles/processor cycle. Assume the processor makes a reference to this cache every cycle (40 ns). The effect of this cache on processor performance is

$$\text{Perf}_{\text{rel}} = \frac{1}{1 + f \lambda_p T_{\text{miss}}} = \frac{1}{1 + 0.03(1/40\,\text{ns})(390\,\text{ns})} = \frac{1}{1.29} = 0.78.$$

(b) Assume now we have a CBWA cache with write (dirty line) buffer; again wraparound load is not used (ignore I/O). As before, $T_{\text{line access}} = 260$ nsec and $T_{\text{m.miss}} = 390$ nsec. Now $T_{\text{c.miss}} = 260$ nsec and $T_{\text{busy}} = T_{\text{m.miss}} - T_{\text{c.miss}} = 130$ nsec.

Then

$$T_{\text{interference}} = \frac{f\,\lambda_p(T_{\text{busy}})^2}{2}$$

$$= \frac{.03 \times (1/40\,\text{ns}) \times (130\,\text{ns})^2}{2}$$

$$= 6.3\,\text{ns},$$

$$T_{\text{miss}} = T_{\text{c.miss}} + T_{\text{interference}}$$

$$= 260 + 6.3 = 266.3\,\text{ns},$$

$$\text{Perf}_{\text{rel}} = \frac{1}{1 + 0.03 \times (1/40\,\text{ns})(266\,\text{ns})} = 0.83.$$

(c) Now we repeat the problem assuming both a dirty line buffer and wraparound load.

Here,

$$T_{\text{c.miss}} = T_a = 120\,\text{ns},$$

and

$$T_{\text{busy}} = T_{\text{m.miss}} - T_{\text{c.miss}}$$

$$= 390 - 120$$

$$= 270\,\text{ns}.$$

Then

$$T_{\text{interference}} = \frac{.03 \times (1/40\,\text{ns}) \times (270)^2}{2}$$

$$= 27.3\,\text{ns},$$

$$T_{\text{miss}} = 120 + 27.3,$$

$$= 147.3\,\text{ns}.$$

$$\text{Perf}_{\text{relative}} = \frac{1}{1 + 0.03 \times (1/40\,\text{ns})(147\,\text{ns})} = 0.90.$$

(d) Repeat (c), including the effects of line-oriented I/O without processor preemption of pending I/O request. Again, all requests are for lines. Suppose the I/O traffic is 0.05 of the processor traffic (i.e., I/O fraction $i = 0.05$).

$$\lambda_i = \frac{i\lambda_p}{L} = \frac{0.05(1/40\,\text{ns})}{4} = 0.3125\,\text{MLAPS},$$

$$\mu = \frac{1}{T_{\text{line access}}} = \frac{1}{260\,\text{ns}} = 3.85\,\text{MLAPS},$$

$$\rho_i = \frac{\lambda_i}{\mu} = 0.0812.$$

Since the ρ_i is low, we estimate $T_{w-I/O}$ using $M/D/1$ open queue:

$$T_{w-I/O} = \frac{\rho_i}{2}(T_s + T_w),$$

$$T_s = 260\,\text{ns},$$

$$T_w = \frac{\rho_i}{2(1-\rho_i)} T_s$$
$$= 11.5\,\text{ns},$$
$$T_{w-I/O} = 11\,\text{ns},$$
$$T_{\text{miss}} = T_{\text{c.miss}} + T_{\text{inf}} + T_{w-I/O}$$
$$= 147.3 + 11 = 158.3\,\text{ns},$$
$$\text{Perf}_{\text{relative}} = \frac{1}{1 + 0.03 \times (1/40\,\text{ns})(158\,\text{ns})} = 0.89.$$

6.8.7   Simple Write-Through Caches

The analysis of write-through caches largely follows that of copyback caches. There are two differences, however:

1. T_{busy} is simpler, since no dirty line writes need be considered.

2. Writes that immediately precede a miss can delay the line access until memory is available.

For a processor that waits until the cache line is filled before resuming:

$$T_{\text{busy}} = T_{\text{m.miss}} - T_{\text{c.miss}} = 0.$$

For the processors using fetch bypass, $T_{\text{c.miss}} = T_a$ and

$$T_{\text{busy}} = T_{\text{line access}} - T_a.$$

The modeling of memory and write-through cache interaction strongly depends on:

1. The existence of write buffers.

2. The policy of dealing with the write buffer contents on a read miss.

3. The amount of write traffic.

In the following, we consider some typical modeling cases:

1. No write buffer, low write traffic.

Here, we need only compute an interference time, since we assume that memory contention is generally negligible. $T_{\text{interference}}$ can then be computed, as in the case of copyback caches, but recall that the processor traffic (λ_p) now consists only of read traffic, since write cannot cause a miss. Writes that immediately (within T_c) precede a read miss occupy memory and delay the line access. For simplicity of discussion (and memory control), assume that all memory modules involved with a line access must be available before it can begin. Let us call the effect of these "writes before misses" $T_{\text{write interference}}$. As with read interference, we need to compute:

$$T_{\text{write interference}} = \text{Prob (write during } T_c \text{ given a read miss)} \cdot \text{delay factor}.$$

If Prob$_w$ is the probability of a write request in any processor cycle (Δt), then

Prob (write during T_c)

= Prob (write during any of the $T_c/\Delta t$ cycles preceding a miss).

Now

Prob (no write in any specified cycle) = $1 - $ Prob$_w$

and

Prob (no writes in a sequence of $T_c/\Delta t$ cycles) = $(1 - $ Prob$_w)^{T_c/\Delta t}$

and

Prob (a write in a sequence of $T_c/\Delta t$ cycles) = $1 - (1 - $ Prob$_w)^{T_c/\Delta t}$.

Finally, we (roughly) estimate the delay as $T_c/2$. So,

$$T_{\text{write interference}} = \frac{T_c}{2}\left[1 - (1 - \text{Prob}_w)^{T_c/\Delta t}\right].$$

The interference is independent of m, as the *entire* memory system must be available before the read miss can be handled.

When the total write traffic (perhaps from multiple processors with write-through cache) becomes significant with respect to the available memory bandwidth, additional contention analysis is required.

2. No write buffer, significant write traffic.

This case offers an extension to case 1, since now the write traffic is significant enough to affect processor performance. Thus, the principal modeling assumption is that when memory contention arises as a result of memory write traffic, it is immediately reflected in a lowered offered write request rate, which affects the overall processor request rate.

Imagine that processor requests are divided into two request streams: read and write. As seen by the processor, the read request rate is unaffected by memory contention. (The processor is blind to its idle time.) However, write requests are delayed by contention, so that if the total processor (offered) request rate is λ, then:

$$\lambda = \lambda_r + \lambda_w,$$

the sum of the offered read and write request rates.

The achieved rate is λ_a:

$$\lambda_a = \lambda_r + \lambda_{wa}.$$

The achieved rate λ_a differs from λ by the decrease in achieved write traffic (λ_{wa}). We can compute λ_{wa} by finding $B(m, n_w)$, where n_w is the effective mean number of write requests per memory cycle. Then

$$\lambda_{wa} = (B_w)_a = \frac{B(m, n_w)}{T_s}.$$

The processor request rate (MAPS) and its corresponding MIPS rate must decrease by a factor of:

$$\frac{\lambda_a}{\lambda} = \frac{\lambda_r + \lambda_{wa}}{\lambda}.$$

This decrease is not related to (and hence is in addition to) read cache misses and $T_{\text{interference}}$ referred to in case 1.

3. Write-through cache with write buffers.

We present a simple approximate analysis here (generally accurate for low write traffic, $\rho \approx 0.3$ or less).

There are two sub-cases in dealing with write buffers, depending on the type of buffer management protocol on a read miss:

  (a) On a read miss, the pending write buffer addresses are checked against the missed line address. If a match is found, the write is performed before the read. If no match is found, the read miss precedes (has priority over) all pending writes.

  (b) On a read miss, all pending writes in the write buffer are written to memory *before* the read miss is handled.

For both sub-cases, assume that the write buffer is relatively large (no overflows) and the traffic is relatively low—low mean queue size, hence insignificant read–write interlock delays (sub-case (a)). The write buffer allows write traffic to proceed at the offered rate, so there are no closed-queue slowdown effects.

Now the analysis of sub-case (a) is exactly the same as case 1, assuming the probability of a match is low. The only delay to the read miss occurs because of already initiated but currently incompleted writes.

Sub-case (b) introduces open-queue waiting time, as now the read request must wait in the queue until all pending writes are completed.

From the $M_B/D/1$ open model:

$$T_w = \left(\frac{\rho - p}{2(1 - \rho)}\right) T_s$$

or, for our memory system:

$$T_w = \left(\frac{\rho - \delta/m}{2(1 - \rho)}\right) T_c$$

where

$$\rho = \frac{\lambda_w}{\mu} = \frac{\lambda_w}{m}(T_c).$$

In this sub-case, the overall write miss time is (assuming no fetch bypass):

$$T_{\text{miss}} = T_{\text{write interference}} + T_w + T_{\text{c.miss}},$$

where $T_{\text{c.miss}} = T_{\text{line access}}$.

If fetch bypass is used, $T_{\text{c.miss}} = T_a$ and an additional $T_{\text{interference}}$ must be added to T_{miss} to account for read–read interference. This is the same as the $T_{\text{interference}}$ developed for the copyback cache.

6.8.8   Write-Through Cache Example

Assume WTNWA strategy and word-buffered I/O, so that only read misses access lines in memory. Queueing delays occur only when a write buffer is introduced or when I/O effects are taken into account. In the following study, we analyze some typical cases.

Study 6.4   Evaluating Write-Through (WTNWA) Caches

Assume we have determined that our processor traffic is 0.8 reads per cycle and 0.2 writes per cycle. Then, on the basis of read traffic, we determine that our cache has a miss rate of 0.024 misses per reference.

The cache is configured as:

$$\text{Line size} \quad = \quad 16^B$$
$$\text{Physical word size} \quad = \quad 4^B$$

and the memory is configured as:

$$T_a = 120\,\text{ns}, \ T_c = 100\,\text{ns}, \ T_\text{bus} = 40\,\text{ns}, \ m = 2.$$

We compute the cache miss delay for:

(a) No fetch bypass, no write buffer, no I/O effects, ignoring write traffic contention in effective processor performance.

   This is case 1 in our analysis.

$$
\begin{aligned}
T_\text{write interference} \quad &= \quad \frac{T_c}{2}\left[1 - (1 - \text{Prob}_w)^{T_c/\Delta t}\right] \\
&= \quad (\frac{100}{2})\left[1 - (1 - 0.2)^{100/40}\right] \\
&= \quad 21\,\text{ns},
\end{aligned}
$$

   and from study 6.3:

$$
\begin{aligned}
T_\text{line access} \quad &= \quad 260\,\text{ns} \\
T_\text{miss} \quad &= \quad T_\text{c.miss} + T_\text{write interference} \\
&= \quad 281\,\text{ns}.
\end{aligned}
$$

(b) Same as (a), but now including the effects of memory write contention.

   As with study 6.1(b),

$$
\begin{aligned}
m \quad &= \quad 2, \\
n \quad &= \quad 0.6, \\
\delta \quad &= \quad 0.2, \\
B(2, 0.5, 0.2) \quad &= \quad 0.54.
\end{aligned}
$$

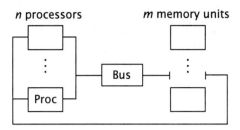

Figure 6.29   Shared bus.

and write performance is lowered by 8%, since:

$$\frac{B(2, 0.5, 0.2)}{n} = \frac{.54}{.60} = .90.$$

The effect on total performance can now be determined by combining the results from (a) of this study with study 6.1:

$$(\text{Perf})_{\text{achieved}} = \left(\frac{1}{.04 + (.024).281}\right).8 + \left(\frac{.90}{.04}\right).2$$

$$(\text{Perf})_{\text{achieved}} = 21.6 \text{ MIPS}.$$

6.8.9   Shared Bus

Multiple processors, or a single processor with multiple independent request sources, may encounter contention on a shared memory bus. (See Figure 6.29.)

Whether we need to analyze the bus as a source of contention depends on its offered bandwidth (or offered occupancy) relative to memory. As contention (and queues) develop at the "bottleneck" in the system, we treat the most limiting resource as causing contention as other parts of the system are simply delay centers. So buses must be analyzed for contention when they are more restrictive (have less available bandwidth) than memory.

Buses usually have no buffering (queues), and access delays cause immediate system slowdown. The analysis of the effects of bus congestion depends on the access circumstances.

Generally there are two types of access patterns:

1. Requests without immediate resubmissions. The denied request returns with the same arrival distribution as the original request. Once a request is denied, "something else" happens to delay the resubmission of the request.

2. Requests are immediately resubmitted. This is a more typical case, when multiple independent processors access a common bus. A denied request "sits on" the bus. It is immediately resubmitted. The processor is idled until the request is honored and serviced.

In the following, we assume that each request occupies the bus for the same service time (e.g., $T_{\text{line access}}$). Even if we have two different types of bus users (e.g., word request and line requests on a single line, or (dirty) double line requests), most cases are reasonably approximated by simple computation of the per-processor average (offered) bus occupancy.

So

$$\rho = \frac{\text{Bus transaction time}}{\text{Processor time} + \text{bus transaction time}}.$$

The processor time is the mean time the processor needs to compute before making a bus request. Of course, it is possible for the processor to overlap some of its compute time with the bus time. In this case, the processor time is the net unoverlapped time between bus requests. In any event, $\rho \leq 1$.

Bus Types

The nature of the bus transaction depends on the bus structure. Multiple bus users must arbitrate for access to the bus in any given cycle. Thus, arbitration can be part of the bus transaction (i.e., request cycle followed by ack cycle) or it can be performed by adding bus control lines and associated logic.

Buses may be *uni-* or *bidirectional,* or *split* (address + data). The unified bus is occupied with both address and data; the split has separate buses for each function.

Finally, the buses may be *tenured.* This refers to buses that are occupied only while delivering addresses or data. Such buses assume the receivers buffer the messages and create separate address and data transactions.

EXAMPLE 6.9   BUS EXAMPLES

Suppose we have a bus with transmission delay of one processor cycle and memory with 4 cycle access. Memory requires an additional 3 cycles to transmit a line. ($m = 1$ with page mode.)

(a) Simple bus. This might have the following bus transaction time:

(b) Bus with arbitration support:

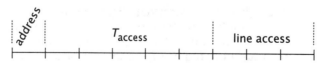

(c) Tenured split bus:

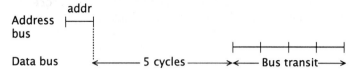

(d) Tenured split bus (width 16B):

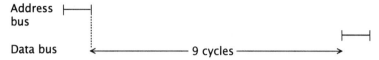

Bus transaction time: 1 cycle.

Cases (c) and (d) are interesting, since now the bus capacity exceeds the memory bandwidth. (4w in 8 cycles for memory, 4w in one cycle for the bus (case d).) In both of these cases, the "bus"-memory situation is better modeled as a shared memory and not as a shared bus, as that is where the contention will develop. In handling these cases, the analysis will simply add the bus time to the memory access time, and ignore bus contention.

The Models

The models for n processors accessing a bus are:

(1) The simplest model is the previously discussed null binomial:

$$
\begin{aligned}
\text{Prob (processor does not access bus)} &= 1 - \rho \\
\text{Prob (n processors do not access bus)} &= (1 - \rho)^n \\
\text{Prob (bus is busy)} &= 1 - (1 - \rho)^n \\
&= \text{Bus bandwidth} = \text{Bus } B(\rho, n)
\end{aligned}
$$

and

$$
Bw = \frac{\text{Bus } B(\rho, n)}{T_{\text{bus}}},
$$

and the achieved bandwidth per processor (ρ_a) is:

$$
\begin{aligned}
n\rho_a &= B(\rho, n) \\
\rho_a &= \frac{B(\rho, n)}{n}.
\end{aligned}
$$

(2) Bus model with request resubmission.

This is a more complex analysis, and requires an iterative solution. There are several solutions [139, 204, 205, 307, 316], each providing (roughly) the same result. We outline the solution provided by Hwang and Briggs [139].

This solution is based on a two-state (A, accepted—W, wait) request model. Requests are accepted with probability P_A.

A request in the waiting state leaves that state and is accepted with probability P_A (Figure 6.30). Once in the accepted state, A, the processor remains there either by making another request and having it accepted (ρP_A), or by not making a request ($1 - \rho$). If the processor makes a request and it is rejected ($\rho(1 - P_A)$), it returns to state W. A processor in W always resubmits a request; it remains in W if it is rejected ($1 - P_A$).

Now the probability of being in state A, q_A, is simply the ratio of the entry traffic (P_A) to the entry and exit traffic ($\rho(1 - P_A)$).

$$q_A = \frac{P_A}{P_A + \rho(1 - P_A)}$$

and

$$q_W = 1 - q_A.$$

The actual offered request rate, a, is:

$$a = \rho q_A + q_W.$$

That is, a request is generated with frequency ρ when in state A, and *always* when in state W.

So

$$
\begin{aligned}
a &= \frac{\rho P_A}{P_A + \rho(1 - P_A)} - 1 - \frac{P_A}{P_A + \rho(1 - P_A)} \\
&= \frac{\rho}{P_A + \rho - \rho P_A} = \frac{\rho}{\rho + P_A(1 - \rho)}.
\end{aligned}
$$

Now we also have from our earlier analysis:

$$n\rho_a = 1 - (1 - a)^n.$$

We recognize that P_A, the probability of having a request accepted, is

$$P_A = \frac{\rho_a}{\rho}$$

so that

$$a = \frac{\rho}{\rho + (\rho_a/\rho)(1 - \rho)}$$

and

$$n\rho_a = 1 - (1 - a)^n$$

are the two equations which we iterate to find a final ρ_a. Initially set $a = \rho$ to begin the iteration. Convergence usually occurs within four iterations.

◆

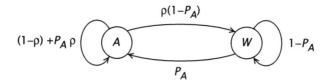

Figure 6.30 Resubmitted requests.

6.8.10 Nonblocking Caches

In a nonblocking cache, the processor prefetches a line in anticipation of its use. If all lines can be prefetched by an amount equal to the line access time, there will be no delays and no effect on processor performance. The problem is that it is generally impossible to predict which line is going to be required far enough in advance to always avoid delay.

There are two approaches to modeling the effects of nonblocking caches on memory contention. Both give generally similar results and (unfortunately) both are probably optimistic. Neither approach recognizes the dependencies that arise from being unable to prefetch a cache line far enough in advance of use to overlap the line access time.

The first approach is the direct extension of our partially blocked model. Now, since $T_{\text{busy}} = T_{\text{line access}}(1 + w)$,

$$T_{\text{interference}} = \frac{f\lambda_p \left[T_{\text{line access}}(1 + w)\right]^2}{2}.$$

The second approach is more sophisticated and uses an $M/M/1$ finite population model.

Here, we make a number of simplifying assumptions. We imagine that the program consists basically of two independent processes: when we fetch a line for one process, we turn to another process and hopefully before the second process makes its own line access, the first line is available. The fact that there are only two tasks in this system requires us to modify our Poisson arrival distribution and form a truncated Poisson distribution. We will describe this more fully when treating multiprogrammed I/O systems in chapter 9. We assume a modified Poisson arrival model, since the probability of an access in any given processor cycle is low. We assume further that the memory service time is not constant but rather has an exponential distribution ($c^2 = 1$). This is conservative, but it recognizes that the memory busy time has a variance associated with the fact that some lines are clean and some are dirty. Using the results of finite population queueing models in chapter 9, we can represent the achieved occupancy as:

$$\rho_a = \frac{1 + r}{1 + r + r^2/2},$$

where $r = t_s/t_p$; t_p being the time between cache misses, and t_s the mean time to process a cache miss. The above assumes that t_p is greater than t_s.

EXAMPLE 6.10

Assume that the processor and cache of study 6.3 are now nonblocking (CBWA). We will now access the processor–cache–memory performance using both methods outlined above.

$$T_{busy} = T_{line\,access}(1 + w) = T_s = 390\,ns;$$
$$\lambda_p = 1/40\,ns.$$

Approach 1:

$$\begin{aligned}
T_{interference} &= \frac{f\lambda p(T_s)^2}{2} \\
&= \frac{0.03(1/40\,ns)(390)^2}{2} \\
&= 57.0\,ns,
\end{aligned}$$

so that $T_{miss} = 57\,ns$ and relative performance is

$$T_p = \frac{1}{f}\left(\frac{1}{\lambda_p}\right) = \frac{1}{.03}\left(\frac{1}{40\,ns}\right) = 1333\,ns,$$

$$\frac{\lambda_a}{\lambda} = \frac{T_p}{T_p + T_{c.miss}},$$

$$Perf_{rel} = \frac{1333}{1333 + 57} = 0.96.$$

Approach 2:

$$r = \frac{T_s}{T_p} = \frac{390}{1333} = 0.29,$$

$$\rho_a = \frac{1 + r}{1 + r + r^2/2} = \frac{1.29}{1.33} = 0.97.$$

This is also the relative performance, since ρ_a is the achieved occupancy of the processor (not the memory).

◆

6.8.11   Interleaved Caches

Interleaved caches can be handled rather straightforwardly, and are almost completely analogous to interleaved memory. Generally, we use the δ-binomial to determine the realized performance from a system involving interleaved caches. This is especially effective and appropriate where we are modeling interleaved data caches which are dominated by read traffic. Generally, the reads appear unbuffered to the processor, and the processor slows down on a read conflict. If there is a mix of buffered and unbuffered references to the cache, we need a more powerful model of processor–cache interaction. We call this model the y-δ-binomial model, and we will introduce it in the next chapter when we cover superscalar machines. The following example illustrates the use of the delta binomial for interleaved caches.

EXAMPLE 6.11

Consider the Intel Pentium™ processor. This processor has 8-way inter-leaved data cache. It can make two references per processor cycle. The caches have the same cycle time as the processor. For the Intel instruction set, the

Prob (data references per instruction) = 0.6.

Note that the instruction issue mechanism is the source here (not some pipeline stage, as discussed earlier). This mechanism is modeled as having two independent requestors—one for each of the instructions that can be issued—so

Prob (data reference per instruction) = δ

and therefore

$\delta = 0.6$.

Since the Pentium tries to execute two instructions each cycle, we have

$$
\begin{aligned}
\delta &= 0.6 \\
n &= 1.2 \\
m &= 8.
\end{aligned}
$$

Using the δ-binomial model, we get:

$$B(m, n, \delta) = B(8, 1.2, 0.6).$$

The relative performance is

$$P_{\text{rel}} = \frac{B}{n} = \frac{1.15}{1.2} = 0.96,$$

i.e., the processor slows down by about 4% due to contention.

$\blacklozenge$

6.9 Conclusions

The primary objective of modern memory systems design is capacity (or size) at a low per-bit cost; but large memory capacity necessarily implies slow access time. Even if chip access is fast, the system's overhead, includ-ing bus signal transmission, error checking, and address distribution, add significant delay; and for most available technology, these overhead delays are likely to increase relative to decreasing machine cycle times.

Faced with multiple cycle memory access time, the designer can at least provide adequate memory bandwidth to match or exceed the offered band-width (request rate) from the processor. There are two ways of accomplish-ing this:

1. Low-order interleaving of multiple memory modules.

2. Fast sequential page mode within a module.

These two techniques can be combined as necessary to afford even higher memory bandwidth.

Accessing multiple memory modules can result in conflicts that reduce the available memory bandwidth to something less than that offered. The now-classic problem of modeling the conflicts that arise when n uniformly distributed address requests are made to m independent memory modules has been well-studied. Generally these modeling studies give the same result for $m, n \geq 4$. Moreover, any actual processor, and certainly all pipelined processors as outlined in this text, will not correspond to the ideal processor making exactly n uniformly distributed requests each memory cycle. Thus, an approximate solution is quite adequate for performance analysis purposes.

For purposes of this book, queue-based models are preferred for describing memory contention and processor memory interaction. While for large m, n they generally give the same result as other models, they have at least two advantages:

1. They are robust enough to describe complex processors that make references to memory under a probability distribution.

2. They are the basis for an analysis of many other computing systems issues, such as multiprocessor memory interaction and concurrent I/O.

For many cache-based processors, memory contention is eliminated, as the processor ceases action until the memory system handles the cache miss. For simple copyback caches, memory contention can be ignored unless the I/O traffic becomes significant. Processors with write-through caches may notice some performance degradation due to write memory traffic contention.

In the longer term, simple uniprocessors with cache are unlikely to be a primary focus of designers. Hence, robust memory models are a requirement for understanding complex processor–memory behavior. We shall see more of these in chapters 7 and 9.

6.10   Some Areas for Further Research

Memory systems design is broadly limited by technology, data integrity, and accurate multihierarchical models. While technological issues are generally beyond the research interests of most readers, issues such as the tradeoff between access time, capacity, and chip organization (e.g., $1^{MB} \times 4^B$ vs. $4^{MB} \times 1^B$) are generally not well understood. Increasingly, the problem with memory technology is not the memory chip itself, but rather the buses (data and address) that connect the processor to the multiple memory chips. The bandwidth and access time and latency on these buses frequently determine the basic performance limits of the memory system.

One of the great data integrity issues involving memory is the volatility of data in the current memory technology. As memory capacity increases, the DRAM technology gets ever closer to the cost per bit of disk, but the magnetic technology has the singular advantage of being nonvolatile. Volatile memory is easier to corrupt; hence, the need for and importance of a thoroughly checked high-integrity memory system. Breakthroughs in the area of volatility could significantly alter the whole nature of the computer system.

Processor–memory models are well understood insofar as a single (or even multiple) processor interacts with multiple memory modules. Much less well understood is the model of the virtual address space and its correspondence to real memory. Performance across the memory hierarchy is a function of the size of the real memory, as well as many systems attributes.

6.11   Data Notes

Binomial/Poisson arrivals are only an approximate description of the processor request stream to the memory system. The assumption of uniform address distribution is clearly erroneous given the sequential nature of instruction requests. The uniform address distribution assumption tends to predict a higher level of contention than actually exists in the system, i.e., provides a somewhat conservative estimate of performance.

6.12   Annotated Bibliography

The earliest memory contention modeling efforts were those of Flores [90] and Hellerman [125]. It is perhaps no surprise that their models represent extremes in contention modeling. With two such diametric views of processor modeling, it became obvious that the issue of contention lay in the definition of the processor-memory interaction. Thus, a good deal of attention focused on the solution of the problem of modeling n "ideal" processors, each making one request per memory cycle to m memory modules. There are many contributions to the solution of this problem, but the simplicity of the Strecker model [273], the queueing model of Baskett [29], and the comprehensive analysis of Rau [241] deserve special mention.

The work of Chang et al. [49] represents a particularly interesting treatment of the relationship among the models and how they correspond to processor reality.

Additional Reading

Memory Chip Technology

W. Stallings. *Computer Organization and Architecture: Principles of Structure and Function.* Macmillan, New York, 2nd edition, 1990.

Intel Corp. *Memory Components Handbook.* Intel, Santa Clara, CA.

Queueing Theory

L. Kleinrock. *Queueing Systems.* J. Wiley and Sons, 1975. Two volumes.

H. Kobayashi. *Modeling and Analysis: An Introduction to Systems Performance Evaluation Methodology.* Addison Wesley, Menlo Park, CA, 1978.

Modeling Memory

F. Baskett and A. J. Smith. Interference in multiprocessor computer systems with interleaved memory. *Communications of the ACM,* 19(6):327–334, June 1976.

B. R. Rau. *Program Behavior and the Performance of Memory Systems.* PhD thesis, Stanford University, July 1977.

D. Y. Chang, D. J. Kuck, and D. H. Lawrie. On the effective bandwidth of parallel memory. *IEEE Transactions on Computers,* C-26(5):480–489, May 1977.

6.13   Problem Set

1. A 32-megabyte memory module is implemented with a $4^M \times 1^b$ chip, with nibble mode. The memory module has the following specifications:

$$
\begin{aligned}
T_{access}/\text{module} &= 120\,\text{ns}, \\
T_c &= 120\,\text{ns}, \\
T_{nibble} &= 40\,\text{ns up to four accesses}, \\
\text{Physical word} &= 64 \text{ bits} + 8 \text{ bits ECC}.
\end{aligned}
$$

There are additional memory system delays of:

$$
\begin{aligned}
\text{Bus transit} &= 20\,\text{ns (one way)}, \\
\text{ECC} &= 40\,\text{ns}.
\end{aligned}
$$

   (a) What is the memory system access time?

   (b) What is the maximum memory data bandwidth (bytes per second) from four modules ($m = 4$, each module with nibble mode) with random address request? Assume that there are multiple buses and ECC units so that they do not limit.

   (c) Repeat (b) for sequential requests. Show how each module is accessed (i.e., which address bits are used for each function).

2. If the four module memory system of problem 1 were now implemented with page mode and $T_{page} = 40\,\text{ns}$:

   (a) How could this be used effectively in a memory design?

   (b) Describe in detail under what conditions this would perform better than an equivalent system using nibble mode.

3. Design a SECDED (Hamming type) coding scheme for a memory with data word size of 18 bits. Show placement of each check bit and give logic equations for its action.

4. A pipelined processor has a peak performance of 40 MIPS (decoding one instruction per cycle). It creates 0.90 instruction references/instr, 0.30 data reads, and 0.10 data writes per instruction. The memory system has:

$$
\begin{aligned}
T_a &= 200\,\text{ns},\\
T_c &= 100\,\text{ns}.
\end{aligned}
$$

Suppose it is possible to partition memory so that instruction references go to instruction memory and data references go to data memory. No cache is used.

Using the open-queue model, compute:

(a) The allocation of modules to instruction and data.

(b) Effective T_w per reference (overall).

(c) Queue size.

(d) Comparison to a single integrated (I and D) memory system (select m, a power of 2) using the same model.

5. Suppose two processors (in a multiprocessor system) make a total of exactly two references to memory every memory cycle ($T_c = 100\,\text{ns}$). The memory consists of eight low-order interleaved memory modules with $T_{access} = 120\,\text{ns}$. Find:

(a) Expected waiting time (T_w).

(b) Total access time.

(c) Mean total number of queued (waiting) requests.

(d) Offered memory bandwidth (references/sec).

(e) Achieved memory bandwidth (references/sec) according to above model.

(f) Achieved memory bandwidth using Strecker's model.

6. The processor defined in problem 4 now uses an integrated memory system of eight modules.

Compare performance (B, Bw, Q_t, and T_w) projections based on:

(a) Hellerman's model.

(b) Strecker's model.

(c) Open-queue model.

(d) Simple closed binomial model.

Compute achieved bandwidth, buffer size, and T_w for each; state all assumptions.

7. Evaluate the processor defined in problem 4 with single integrated memory and $m = 8$, using the δ-binomial model. Find the achieved processor performance.

8. For a copyback cache (CBWA) with memory system as specified:

   (a) Compute $T_{\text{line access}}$ for $T_a = 200\,\text{ns}$, $T_c = 100\,\text{ns}$, $m = 8$, $T_{\text{bus}} = 25$, and $L = 16$.

   (b) Repeat for $m = 2$ and $m = 4$.

   (c) Suppose nibble mode ($v = 4$) is now introduced, $T_v = 50\,\text{ns}$ and $m = 2$. Compute $T_{\text{line access}}$.

9. For a copyback cache (CBWA) and $w = 0.5$ using the memory system of 8(a), compute $T_{\text{m.miss}}$, $T_{\text{c.miss}}$, and T_{busy} for:

   (a) Unbuffered line transfers starting at line address.

   (b) Write buffer, line transfers starting at line address.

   (c) Buffered transfers with wraparound load.

10. In problems 9 and 8(a), if the cache miss rate (assume 1 reference per cycle) is 0.03 and processor peak performance is one instruction every 25 ns cycle, what is the effect on performance of each transfer strategy in problem 9? Ignore I/O.

11. Now the processor in problem 10 is to use a write-through cache (WT-NWA). The fraction of data writes is 0.16. Using the δ-binomial model, compute the overall processor performances.

12. When memory is implemented using DRAM organized as $2^k \times 4$, the failure of a single chip can result in errors of up to four bits. Devise an error correction scheme for device failure. Detail the scheme for $m = 16$. Hint: think of the memory as if it were four separate $2^k \times 1$ submemories.

13. A processor without a cache accesses every t-th element of a k-element vector. Each element is one physical word. Assuming $T_a = 200\,\text{ns}$, $T_c = 100\,\text{ns}$, and $T_{bus} = 25\,\text{ns}$, plot the average access time per element for an 8-way, low-order interleaved memory for $t = 1$ to 12 and $k = 100$.

14. A memory system must support an average of 75 MAPS. Using the open $M_B/D/1$ model, find an appropriate degree of interleaving and determine the mean queue size, given a memory service time of 100ns. To ensure the Prob {overflow} $\leq 1\%$, what should the total buffer size be if (a) the Chebyshev bound is used and (b) the $M/M/1$ bound is used.

15. You are to design the memory for a 50 MIPS processor (1 CPI) with one instruction and 0.5 data references per instruction (no cache). The memory system is to be 16MB. The physical word size is 4B. You are to use $1M \times 1b$ chips with $T_c = 40\,\text{ns}$. Draw a block diagram of your memory, including address, data, and control connections between the processor, DRAM controller, and the memory. Detail what each address bit does. If $T_a = 100\,\text{ns}$, what are the expected memory occupancy, waiting time, total access time, and total queue size? Discuss the applicability of the open-queue model in the analysis of this design.

16. A simple 1 MIPS processor (1 CPI, 2 refs/I) shares a memory with a simple DMA unit which transfers 1 data word to memory every 1 μsec. The memory cycle time is the same as the processor cycle time. The memory system is not interleaved and has an access time of 500 ns. Use the simple binomial approximation to find the achieved utilization (Bw) and the expected waiting time. What is the effective processor MIPS? Is the simple binomial appropriate for this system?

17. Repeat study 6.2 with IF/cycle = 0.5, DF/cycle = 0.3, DS/cycle = 0.1, and $m = 8$.

18. For study 6.3(a), assume that the miss rates of the CBWA cache for several possible line sizes are: 16B line = 0.03, 8B line = 0.07, 32B line = 0.02. Which line size would perform best?

19. For study 6.3(d), plot relative processor performance as a function of the I/O traffic rate for I/O rates from 0.01 to 0.20. Comment on the sensitivity of memory system performance to I/O traffic.

20. Repeat study 6.4 for $T_a = 180$ ns, $T_c = 150$ ns, and $T_{bus} = 40$ ns.

21. A 25 MIPS processor with 1 CPI makes two distinct types of requests to memory: word and block requests. If word requests occur at an expected rate of one per instruction, and block requests occur at an expected rate of 0.2 per instruction, find the effective request rate λ_s. Assume $T_a = 200$ ns, $T_c = 100$ ns, and $T_{bus} = 40$ ns, $m = 8$, and blocks are 8 words. Find the effective service time (T_s), the coefficient of variance, and the effective offered occupancy (ρ). Use the open-queue $M/G/1$ model to compute the expected waiting time and the expected number of requests in the queue. Should the open-queue model be used for this analysis?

Chapter 7

Concurrent Processors: Vector Processors and Multiple Instruction Issue Processors

7.1 Introduction

The processors we looked at in chapter 4 were generally limited to performance of greater than 1 CPI (cycle per instruction). To go beyond that requires an additional degree of concurrency over that found in simple pipeline processors. In one way or another, the processor must be able to execute multiple instructions at the same time. Concurrent processors must be able to make simultaneous accesses to memory and to simultaneously execute multiple operations. We refer to processors that achieve this higher degree of concurrency as *concurrent processors*, short for processors with instruction-level concurrency.

For this chapter, we restrict our attention to those processors that execute only from one program stream. They are *uniprocessors* in that they have a single instruction counter, but the instructions may have been significantly rearranged from original program order so that concurrent instruction execution can be achieved.

Concurrent processors are significantly more complex than simple pipelined processors. In pipelined processors, performance is largely a function of basic technology and timing, as well as program behavior (occurrence of branch and run-on events). In concurrent processors, performance depends in greater measure on compiler ability, execution resources, and memory system design.

Concurrent processors depend on sophisticated compilers to detect various types of instruction-level parallelism that exist within a program. Depending upon the type of concurrent processor, the compiler must restructure the code into a form that allows the processor to use the available concurrency. In vector processors, a single instruction replaces multiple (scalar) instructions. As we shall see, vector processors use vector instructions, which depend heavily on the ability of the compiler to vectorize the code to transform loops into sequences of vector operations. Similarly, multiple-issue machines require the compiler to detect sequences of instructions whose effects are independent from each another. (See study 7.2.) Without such code structuring, there is no concurrent instruction execution, and hence no use is made of the additional resources designed into the concurrent processor to achieve its potential speedup over a pipelined processor.

If programs are to execute multiple instructions concurrently, they require additional execution resources, such as adders and multipliers, to allow independent instructions to complete simultaneously. Associated with these resources is additional control to manage dispatching and scheduling of concurrent operations.

Finally, the concurrent processor depends heavily on the memory system to supply the operand and instruction bandwidth required to execute programs at the desired rate. In many ways, the memory system design is the key to achieving effective concurrent processor hardware [249, 301].

In this chapter, we look at two general approaches to realizing concurrent processors: the *vector processor* and the *multiple-issue processor*. Multiple-issue processors are further subdivided into *VLIW* (very long instruction word) and *superscalar* processors. The premise behind the concurrency in the vector processor differs somewhat from that of the multiple-issue processor. The premise underlying the vector processor is that the original program has either explicitly declared many of the data operands to be vectors or arrays or it implicitly uses loops whose data references can be expressed as references to a vector of operands.

The premise behind the multiple-issue machine is simply that instructions can be found whose effects are independent from one another. The search for independent instructions may be done at run time by the hardware or at compile time. The scope of the search is different, depending on which approach is chosen. At run time, the search for concurrent instructions is restricted to the localities of the last executing instruction, while at compile time the compiler may globally search the entire program for sets of concurrent (hence independent) instructions. Whether or not the hardware supports run-time concurrent instruction detection, it is always better to support the multiple-issue processor with the best possible compiler technology to provide the maximum program speedup.

The issue of program speedup as a result of concurrent processing is important to the understanding of the effectiveness of the concurrent processor. We introduce the notion of speedup here.

Speedup (S_p) is:

$$S_p = \frac{T_1}{T_p},$$

where T_1 is the time it takes a nonconcurrent, single-pipelined processor to execute a task, and T_p is the time it takes the concurrent processor to execute the same task. The subscript p is the maximum degree of instruction-level concurrency available in the concurrent processor. Since the minimum time it takes the concurrent processor to execute the program is $T_p = T_1/p$, the maximum speedup is p.

In the definition of S_p, it is assumed that the program representations for the simple pipelined processor (the T_1 time) and the concurrent processor (the T_p time) are optimized for their respective organizations. Several things are important to notice about the concept of speedup:

1. Speedup is referenced to the best pipelined processor algorithm (for T_1) and the best concurrent processor algorithm (for T_p). These are generally not the same algorithm.

2. Speedup is effectively determined by the harmonic mean of T_1/T_p, not the arithmetic mean. Suppose a certain concurrent processor executes half of its workload in the same manner as a uniprocessor ($S_p = 1$), but the other average workload is done in only 1/3 the time that the uniprocessor executes ($S_p = 3$). We have a speedup of:

$$S_p = \frac{T_1}{.5T_1 + .5T_1/3} = \frac{1}{.666} = 1.5.$$

Note that this is not the same as a speedup of $.5 + 1.5 = 2$.

7.2   Vector Processors

A classic method of speeding up processor performance in high-speed machines is to extend the instruction set and the architecture of the system to support the execution of commonly used vector operations in hardware. Directly supporting vector operations in hardware generally reduces or eliminates the overhead of loop control, which would otherwise be necessary in representing the vector operation as a loop construct. Thus, arithmetic operations of the form:

$$\vec{A} + \vec{B} = \vec{C}$$

are represented by a vector instruction of the type

| VOP | V3 | V1 | V2 |

,

where VOP represents a vector operation, and V1, V2, V3 indicate specific vector registers. The operation performed is:

$$V3 := V1\ VOP\ V2$$

for all register values within each vector register.

The individual element within a vector register is designated V1.X. Thus, the vector elements of a 64-element vector register V1 are indicated as V1.1 through V1.64.

Vector instructions are effective in several ways.

1. They significantly improve code density.

2. They reduce the number of instructions required to execute a program (they reduce the I-bandwidth).

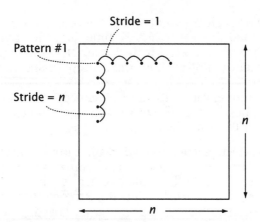

Figure 7.1   For an array in memory, different accessing patterns use different strides in accessing memory.

3. They organize the data argument into regular sequences that can be efficiently handled by the hardware.

4. They can represent a simple loop construct, thus removing the control overhead for loop execution.

Vector processing hardware does not come for free. It requires some obvious extensions to the instruction set, together with (for best performance) extensions to the functional units, the register sets, and particularly to the memory of the system. Early vector processors used primarily memory-to-memory instruction formats. Vectors, as they are usually derived from large arrays, are the one data structure that is not always well managed by a data cache. Accessing array elements, separated by an addressing distance (called the *stride*), may completely fill a smaller to intermediate-sized data cache with data of little or no temporal locality; hence there is no re-use of the localities before the items must be replaced (Figure 7.1).

To decouple arithmetic processing from memory, almost all modern vector processors include vector register hardware. The vector register set is the source and destination for all vector operands. Access from or to these registers to or from memory usually bypasses the cache. The cache then contains only scalar data objects—objects not used in the vector registers (Figure 7.2).

7.2.1   Vector Functional Units

The vector registers typically consist of eight or more register sets, each consisting of 16–64 vector elements. Each vector element is a floating-point word (Figure 7.3).

The vector registers access memory with special load and store instructions that will be described later. The vector execution units are usually arranged as an independent functional unit for each instruction class. Thus, as a

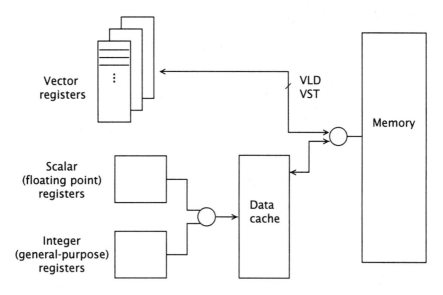

Figure 7.2 The primary storage facilities in a vector processor. Vector LD/ST usually bypasses the data cache.

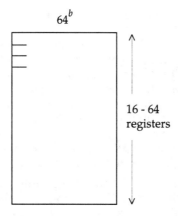

Figure 7.3 Typical vector register sizes.

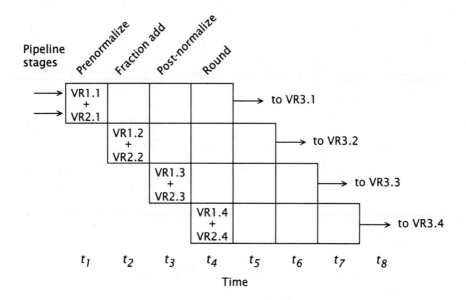

Figure 7.4 Approximate timing for a sample 4-stage functional pipeline.

minimum we would expect to see the following functional units for floating-point:

- Add/subtract.

- Multiplication.

- Division or reciprocal.

- Logical operations, including compare.

Usually there are separate and independent functional units to manage the load/store function. These functional units are also segmented (pipelined) to support the highest possible execution rate. Since the whole purpose of introducing the vector vocabulary is to manage operations over a vector of operands, it is assumed that there is a relatively large number of operands per operation. Thus, once the operation is begun, it can continue at the cycle rate of the system. Figures 7.4 and 7.5 show the approximate timing for a sample 4-stage functional pipeline. Figure 7.4 shows a vector add sequence of elements as vector elements pass through various stages in the adder. The sum of the first elements of VR1 and VR2 (labeled VR1.1 and VR2.1) are stored in VR3 (actually, VR3.1) after the fourth adder stage.

Segmentation, or pipelining, of the functional units is more important for vector functional units than for scalar functional units, where latency is of primary importance. If the ordinary scalar floating-point hardware can be pipelined at the clock rate of the system (the decode rate), then no further pipelining need be done. The advantage of vector processing is that fewer instructions are required to execute the vector operations. A single (overlapped) vector load places the information into the vector registers. The vector operation executes at the clock rate of the system (one cycle per executed operand), and an overlapped vector store operation completes the

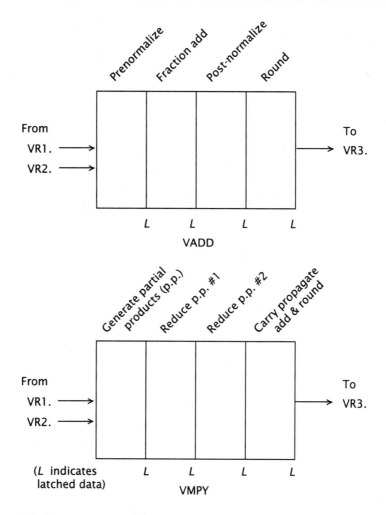

Figure 7.5   Two vector arithmetic units, each partitioned into four pipeline stages. Results are latched at each latch point (*L*).

vector transaction overlapped with subsequent instruction operations (see Figure 7.6), depending on data paths. Vector loads must complete before they can be used (Figure 7.7), since otherwise the processor would have to recognize when operands are delayed in the memory system.

The ability of the processor to concurrently execute multiple (independent) vector instructions is also limited by the number of vector register ports and vector execution units. Each concurrent vector load or store requires a vector register port; vector ALU operations require multiple ports. Notice that necessary loop control present in scalar code is absent in the vector code.

While it is not employed in the current generation of vector processors, it is possible to use a technique described in chapter 2—anticipatory cycle techniques—to further enhance the performance of the vector processor. It may be possible to execute operands using wave pipelining at two to three times the ordinary cycle rate of the system. Vector operations are rather

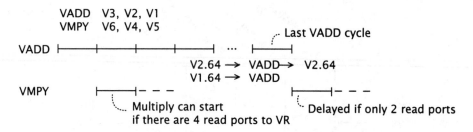

Figure 7.6 For logically independent vector instructions, the number of access paths to the vector register set and vector units may limit performance. If there are four read ports, the VMPY can start on the second cycle. Otherwise, with two ports, the VMPY must wait until the VADD completes use of the read ports.

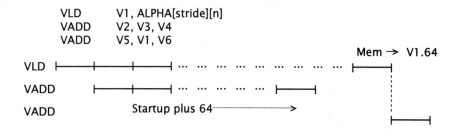

Figure 7.7 While independent VLD and VADD may proceed concurrently (with sufficient VR ports), operations that use the results of VLD do not begin until the VLD is fully complete.

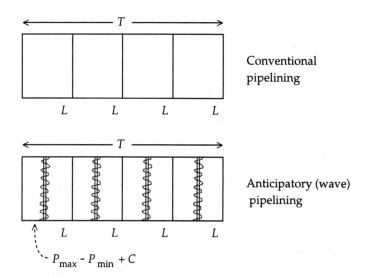

Figure 7.8 Anticipatory cycle functional unit.

well suited for anticipatory cycle timing because the sequence of actions in the pipeline is predefined. Figure 7.8 shows an anticipatory cycle functional unit for our previous example.

7.2.2   Vector Instructions/Operations

As most modern vector processors are organized about vector registers, we assume that the vector instruction set is an L/S type instruction set that executes functional operations from the registers, but with the result going to the registers. The vector load and vector store (also referred to as *scatter* and *gather* instructions) asynchronously access memory. Functional vector operations cannot use a vector register until any pending vector load from or vector store to that register is completed.

Generic vector operations include the obvious arithmetic operations: vector add, vector multiply, and vector divide. They also include a series of operations that either produce or use a logical vector as an argument. For example, the operation *vector compare* (Figure 7.9) may take two vector operands and produce a bit-vector result. The logical one indicates a match or that the compare was satisfied; a logical zero indicates otherwise. The result of this vector operation may be stored in a vector register or, in some machines, in a scalar register as a sequence of bits. This latter approach provides more efficient use of the relatively small number of vector registers that are usually available. The class of such instructions includes the following:

- Vector compare.

- Vector test.

Another type of vector operation also posts its result in a scalar register. This is called a *vector accumulate* operation, in which the sum of products is accumulated in a particular scalar register:

$$\sum_{i=1}^{n} V1.i * V2.i \rightarrow S.$$

This equation corresponds to an inner product of two vectors.

The class of logical vector instructions including compare is important in the vector processor. Generally, the vector instructions do not set the condition code in the program status word after each operation. The programmer does not wish to interrupt the flow of vector operations by specific tests for arithmetic conditions, which would disrupt the execution rate of the vector operations; rather, after the vector operation is complete, a *compare condition* instruction can be issued that compares the contents of each of the elements in the vector register to a particular condition and returns a logical vector indicating the elements in the vector that match the specified condition.

The results of the compare operation can be contained in a general scalar register or in a special vector mask register associated with each vector register.

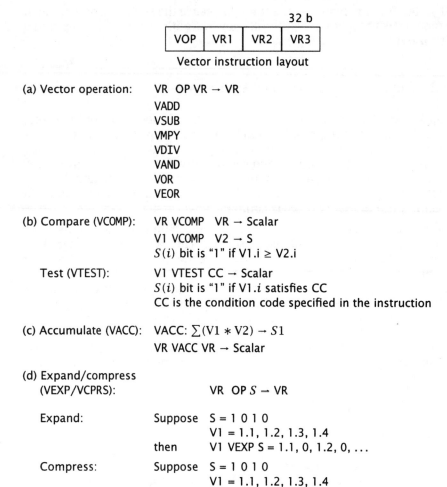

Figure 7.9   Types of vector operations and some examples.

Finally, there are vector *expand* and *compress* operations, which take logical vectors and apply them to elements in vector registers to create a new vector value (see Figure 7.9). The expand and compress operations are taken from the APL language [146], where they were originally introduced.

When a vector operation is done on two vector registers that contain contents of unequal length, some convention must be established for producing the result. The obvious convention is to specify a vector length in each vector instruction. An alternative specifies that the unused elements of the vector contain zero, the zero is applied to the other vector element, and the result is as defined. Another convention (Figure 7.10) is to establish the invalid contents symbol for all entries in a vector register that have not been explicitly stored into. This is akin to NAN in the IEEE floating-point standard, and the result is also NAN regardless of what the contents of the other register were.

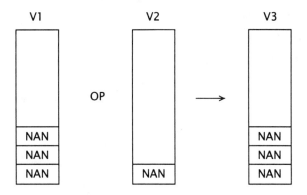

Figure 7.10 Padding out short vectors with NAN ("not a number") representation.

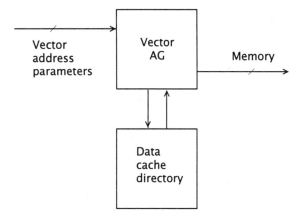

Figure 7.11   Vector address generator for VLD/VST.

7.2.3   Vector Processor Implementation

It is clear from the foregoing that the vector extension to a conventional processor requires a considerable amount of additional control and hardware. Figure 7.11 illustrates a vector address generate extension to a conventional processor. In many cases, as in the case shown, the vector register can bypass the data cache. The data cache is used solely to contain scalar values. Since particular values contained in a vector may be *aliased* as a scalar and stored in the data cache, all vector references to memory must be checked against the contents of the data cache. Hits invalidate the current value contained in the data cache and force memory update if required. Additional control, either in hardware or software, must be present to ensure that scalar references from the data cache to memory do not inadvertently reference a value contained in a vector register.

In earlier days, a number of vector processors were built that directly referenced main memory (i.e., without the use of vector registers). This had the advantage of accommodating vector operations of arbitrarily long vector length. However, the problem of accessing memory with addresses that differ by a fixed stride, or amount, may cause severe memory congestion

For these two instructions:

     VADD   VR3, VR1, VR2

     VMPY   VR5, VR3, VR4

the timing would be:

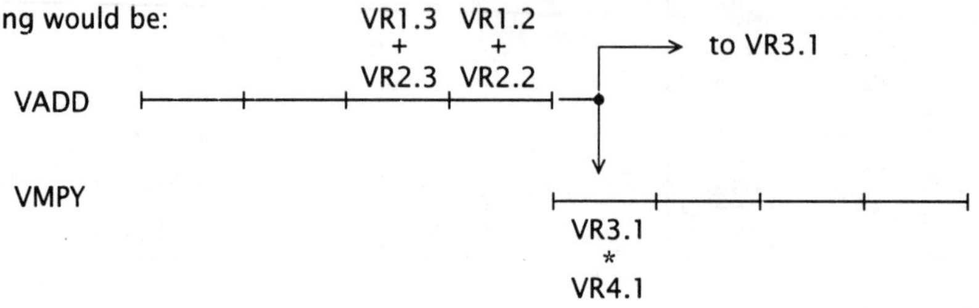

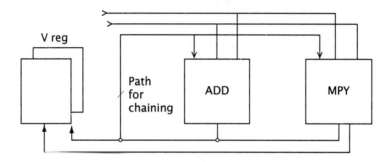

Figure 7.12   Effect of vector chaining.

Figure 7.13   Vector chaining path.

and contention. While memory can be designed to accommodate such reference patterns, the complexity for managing both scalar and vector accessing without excessive contention becomes prohibitive. Thus, most modern vector processors execute in the load/store fashion from local vector registers. The vector registers generally consist of a set of eight registers, each containing from 16 to 64 entries, and each entry generally accommodates a 64-bit floating-point word. The arithmetic pipeline or portion of the vector processor may be shared (at least in part) with the scalar or base portion of the processor. With current technology it is relatively straightforward to design floating-point add and floating-point multiply units to accommodate an operation-per-cycle execution rate and still maintain relatively low overall execution time (2–4 cycles). Divide is an exceptional case for which the vector processor may or may not provide a cycle-per-operation quotient. Cray machines use a multiplicative-based division or reciprocal operation that provides an approximation to the reciprocal of a number. This reciprocal can then be multiplied by a numerator to produce an approximation to the quotient. The Cray system's reciprocal operation is supported on an operation-per-cycle basis.

Under some conditions, it is possible to execute more than one vector arithmetic operation per cycle. The results of one vector arithmetic operation can be directly used as an operand in subsequent vector instructions without first passing into a vector register. Such an operation, shown in Figures

Table 7.1   Potential memory requirements (number of accesses/processor cycle).

	I	*D*
Scalar Unit	1.0^- [a]	1.0 [a]
Vector Unit	0.0^+ [b]	$2.-3.0$ [c]

[a]Nominally. Reduced by I-buffer, I-cache.
[b]Relatively small compared to other requirements.
[c]Minimum required is one VLD and one VST concurrently; preferably two VLD's and one VST, all concurrently.

7.12 and 7.13, is called *chaining*. It is illustrated in Figure 7.12 by a chained ADD–MPY with each functional unit having 4 stages. If the ADD–MPY were unchained, it would take 4 (startup) + 64 (elements/VR) = 68 cycles for each instruction—136 cycles total. With chaining, this is reduced to 4 (add startup) + 4 (multiply startup) + 64 (elements/VR) = 72 cycles.

One of the crucial aspects to achieving the performance potential of the vector processor is the management of references to memory. Since arithmetic operations complete one per cycle, a vector code makes repeated references to memory to introduce new vectors in the vector registers and to write out old results. Thus, on the average memory must have sufficient bandwidth to support at least a two-words-per-cycle execution rate (one read and one write), and preferably three references per cycle (two reads and one write). This bandwidth allows for two vector reads and one vector write to be initiated and executed concurrently with the execution of a vector arithmetic operation. If there is insufficient memory bandwidth from memory to the vector registers, the processor necessarily goes idle after the vector operation until the vector loads and stores are complete. It is a significant challenge to the designer of a processor not to simply graft a vector processing extension onto a scalar processor design, but rather to adapt the scalar design—especially the memory system—to accommodate the requirements of fast vector execution (Table 7.1). If the memory system bandwidth is insufficient, the designer will find that there is correspondingly less performance improvement from the vector processing hardware.

7.2.4   A Generic Vector Processor

We can now bring the major elements of the vector processor together (Figure 7.14). The functional units (add, multiply, etc.) and the two register sets (vector and scalar, or general) are connected by one or more bus sets. If chaining (Figure 7.13) is allowed, then three (or more) source operands are simultaneously accessed from the vector registers and a result is transmitted back to the vector registers. Another bus couples the vector registers and the memory buffer. The remaining parts of the system—I-cache, D-cache, general registers, etc.—are typical of pipelined processors.

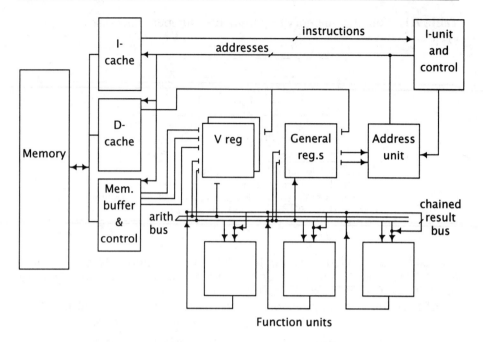

Figure 7.14   Major data paths in a generic vector processor.

7.3   Vector Memory

7.3.1   The Special Case of Vector Memory

Simple low-order interleaving is suitable for improving memory bandwidth for all reference patterns except the general vector category (in chapter 6), which is nonsequential but systematic. Such access patterns are typical of scientific applications involving matrix computations. In cases where access of elements by row is sequential and creates no interference, access by column can be disastrous if the array dimension is the same as the interleaving factor. Since the purpose of large scientific processors is to rapidly move vectors from memory into processing position, conventionally interleaved memory structures are inadequate.

In accessing a vector in memory, the address distance (in physical words) between adjacent elements is called the *stride* of the access pattern. It is common for these strides to be of the form 2^k, 10^k, or other even dimensions. For such applications it is very useful to consider designs that remap addresses (discussed later) and designs that use a prime number of memory modules (or at least a number that is relatively prime to most expected strides). The difficulty here is in translating mod 2^n addresses into addresses for the memory system.

Interleaving Using $2^k \pm 1$ Modules

Certain numbers have special properties, however, especially numbers of the form $2^k \pm 1$ [67]. First, consider interleaving by $2^k + 1$ modules. It is relatively straightforward to determine:

$$(\text{Address mod } 2^n) \bmod (2^k + 1).$$

This allows distribution of addresses across an odd number of modules (and in the case of $k = 2$ and 4, a prime number, 5 and 17).

This translation consists of initially decomposing the mod 2^n address into p digits, each of k bits. Thus,

$$X_{n-1}\dots X_0 \bmod 2^n = Y_{p-1}2^{(p-1)k} + \dots + Y_2 2^{2k} + Y_1 2^k + Y_0,$$

where each Y_i is a k-bit grouping of binary bits X.

Now observe that $Y_0 = X_{k-1}\dots X_0$, and

$$2^k \bmod (2^k + 1) = -1 \bmod (2^k + 1)$$

and

$$2^{2k} \bmod (2^k + 1) = +1 \bmod (2^k + 1),$$

since $2^{2k} = 2^k \cdot 2^k$, or $2^{2k} \bmod (2^k+1) = 2^k \bmod (2^k+1) \cdot 2^k \bmod (2^k+1) = (-1)(-1) = +1$.

Finally,

$$Y_i 2^{ik} \bmod (2^k + 1) = Y_i(\pm 1) \qquad (-1 \text{ if } i \text{ is odd}, +1 \text{ if } i \text{ is zero or even}).$$

Thus,

$$
\begin{aligned}
X_{n-1}\dots X_0 \bmod (2^k + 1) &= Y_{p-1}\cdots Y_0 \bmod (2^k + 1) \\
&= (\dots + Y_4 - Y_3 + Y_2 - Y_1 + Y_0) \bmod (2^k + 1).
\end{aligned}
$$

The pairwise differences can be computed using mod 2^k arithmetic with sign extension. The results are summed mod 2^k with end-around borrow, since if $(X_i + Y_j) < 2^k + 1$:

$$(X_i \bmod 2^k + Y_j \bmod 2^k) \bmod (2^k + 1) = (X_i + Y_j) \bmod (2^k + 1).$$

If $X_i + Y_j = 2^k$, then $X_i + Y_j = -1 \bmod (2^k + 1)$, since $100\dots00$ with end-around borrow is $00\dots00 - 1 = -1$.

If $X_i + Y_j = 2^k + 1$, then $X_i + Y_j = 0$, since $100\dots01$ with end-around borrow becomes $00\dots01 - 1 = 0$.

EXAMPLE 7.1

$$k = 4, \ 2^k + 1 = 17.$$

Consider a 24-bit mod 2^{24} address:

d_5	d_4	d_3	d_2	d_1	d_0

6 hex digits

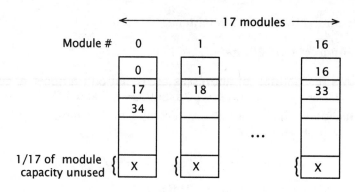

Figure 7.15   Address distribution.

Then the module address is:

$$[(d_4 - d_5) + (d_2 - d_3) + (d_0 - d_1)] \bmod 17.$$

Suppose we have (in hex):

$$
\begin{aligned}
d_5 &= F \\
d_4 &= 3 \\
d_3 &= 7 \\
d_2 &= A \\
d_1 &= 9 \\
d_0 &= 0,
\end{aligned}
$$

so that $3 - F = -12(-C)$, $A - 7 = 3$, $0 - 9 = -9$. For all negative results, we map the result to the resource (i.e., the least positive number that satisfies the congruence).

Then $[-C + 3 - 9] = -18 \equiv 16 \bmod 17 = 10,000$ (base 2), which becomes the module address. Note that the module addresses range from 0 through 16 (which is $-1 \bmod 17$).

Now the original address (X) must be decomposed into a module address and an index into the module (address of the word in a module). Even knowing $X \bmod (2^k + 1)$, it still may be difficult to find the address index ($\lfloor \frac{X}{2^k+1} \rfloor$). However, any divisor $d \leq 2^k + 1$ provides a unique index, and using $d = 2^k$ provides an index that simplifies the higher-order digits of X. Such a scheme wastes memory space, as $\frac{1}{2^k+1}$ of the memory space is now unused (Figure 7.15).

                                                             ◆

In the preceding example, the index is simply $d_5 d_4 d_3 d_2 d_1 = F37A9$. What we have done is to spread 16 "buckets" of data uniformly over 17 "buckets" of memory. Each memory "bucket" is addressed as before (using the "upper" address bits to specify a word in a module), but now each memory module has $\frac{1}{17}$ of its space permanently unused.

It is not too difficult to actually compute the quotient of the address divided by $2^k + 1$, thus saving otherwise wasted space at the expense of (perhaps) a cycle delay in the access path.

Note that any number that is $\beta + 1$ (β the radix) is represented as $1 \cdot \beta + 1$ (or 11, in decimal). We are trying to find:

$$Q = \frac{N - R}{2^k + 1},$$

where $R = N \bmod 2^k + 1$. Now we can write

$$(2^k + 1)Q = N - R = N_0.$$

Since $2^k + 1 = 11$ (base 2^k), we can write the digits $Q = q_{n-1} \ldots q_0$ and $N_0 = d_{n-1} \ldots d_0$ so $11Q = N_0$ can be written as

$$N_0 = \begin{array}{r} q_n \quad \ldots q_1 q_0 \\ q_{n-1} \ldots q_0 \\ \hline d_n \quad \ldots d_1 d_0. \end{array}$$

It is now clear that we can back-solve this for each of:

$$\begin{array}{ll} q_0 = d_0, & N_1 = N_0 - q_0 \\ q_1 = d_1, & N_2 = N_1 - q_1 \\ q_2 = d_2, & N_3 = N_2 - q_2 \\ \vdots \end{array}$$

where N_i is the most significant digit and q_{i-1} the least significant digit.

EXAMPLE 7.2   DECIMAL

Find the quotient Q and remainder r of 7394 (base 10) divided by 11.

$$\begin{array}{rcl} r & = & -7 + 3 - 9 + 4 = -9 \text{ or } +2 \\ N_0 & = & 7394 - 2 = 7392 \\ q_0 & = & 2 \\ N_1 & = & 739 - 2 = 737 \\ q_1 & = & 7 \\ N_2 & = & 73 - 7 = 66 \\ q_2 & = & 6 \\ Q & = & 672. \end{array}$$

Now consider interleave factors of the form $2^k - 1$. Here, the residue is even easier to compute, since

$$2^k \bmod (2^k - 1) = 1$$

and

$$2^{nk} \bmod (2^k - 1) = 1.$$

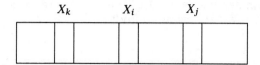

Figure 7.16 Hashing.

So, we merely need to sum up the digits of a number, i.e.,

$$N \bmod (2^k - 1) = \sum_{i-o}^{n-1} Y_i \quad (\bmod\ 2^k - 1).$$

◆

EXAMPLE 7.3

In decimal, the procedure for finding the mod residue is called "casting out nines." We find $732089 \bmod 9$ by:

$$7 + 3 + 2 + 0 + 8 + 0.$$

Note that the 9 is replaced ("cast out") by 0, since $9 \bmod 9 = 0$. Thus, $20 = 2 + 0 = 2$.

Now the problem of finding the quotient with divisor $= 2^k - 1$ is imperative, since we cannot take the naive strategy of wasting (half of) memory.

Finding the quotient is only slightly more complex with divisor $2^k - 1$ rather than $2^k + 1$. (See problem 7.)

◆

"Hashed" Addresses

A complementary technique for dispersing addresses is to "hash" the address bits (X). This "hashing" is a strict 1:1 mapping of the bits in X to form a new address X' based on simple manipulations of the bits in X. These manipulations usually consist of (Figure 7.16):

1. Rearrangement of bits.

2. Negation of bit values.

3. Exclusive OR of certain bit combinations.

For example, suppose three bits are selected from X: X_i, X_j, and X_k. (i, j, k are generally neither consecutive nor ordered.) Ordinarily, these bits would identify memory locations as indicated; mapping the addresses using exclusive-OR and negation provides a complete redistribution of addresses. No two conventional addresses map into the same mapped address. Note that if i, j and k were the standard low-order bits used for interleaving, there would be no advantage to hashing—we would still have mod 8 contention in this 3-bit example.

Table 7.2 Simple address mapping.

X_i	X_j	X_k	Conventional Address	$X_i \forall X_j$	$X_j \forall X_k$	$\overline{X_k}$	Mapped Address
0	0	0	0	0	0	1	1
0	0	1	1	0	1	0	2
0	1	0	2	1	1	1	7
0	1	1	3	1	0	0	4
1	0	0	4	1	0	1	5
1	0	1	5	1	1	0	6
1	1	0	6	0	1	1	3
1	1	1	7	0	0	0	0

Simple address mapping, as shown in Table 7.2, may be helpful in reducing contention in mod 2^k memories in mixed application environments. It reduces contention for simple array access patterns for some common strides. However, in applications involving significant matrix manipulations, the stride problem may resurface, since the same strides are likely to create recurrent patterns of bits (the same values of X_i, X_j, and X_k, in the example). Thus, while hashing is usually sufficient, the use of hashing in conjunction with mod $2^k + 1$ mapping provides the best address distribution across a variety of applications and strides.

A memory system for use in vector/matrix accessing would then consist of (Figure 7.17):

1. Address hasher.

2. $2^k + 1$ memory modules.

3. Module mapper.

The overhead associated with this vector memory should not be excessive—the hashing function takes one or two gate delays, while the module address determination requires about two serial bit "additions." This may add an extra cycle to the memory access, but since the purpose of the memory is to access vectors, this cycle can be overlapped in most cases.

7.3.2 Modeling Vector Memory Performance: The Gamma (γ)-Binomial Model

In a vector processor, we design for multiple simultaneous requests to memory. While access to memory (loading and storing the vector registers) can be overlapped with vector execution, a problem arises if the memory cannot keep up with the vector execution rate.

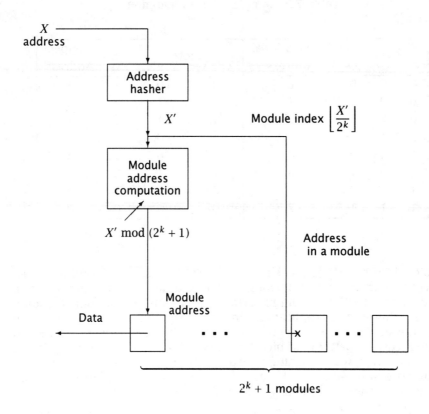

Figure 7.17   Vector memory.

An example of this design situation is:

```
LD.V   VR1, ·            loading VR1 for later use
LD.V   VR2, ·            loading VR2 for later use
ST.V   VR3, ·            clearing VR3 for later use
OP.V   VR4, VR5, VR6     using values previously fetched
LD.V   VR5, ·
LD.V   VR6, ·
ST.V   VR4, ·            using registers prepared above
OP.V   VR3, VR1, VR2.
```

The first four instructions are executed concurrently; then the next four instructions are executed.

We overlap the operand fetching and storing with vector execution. We fetch the operand for the next executable vector operation at the same time we execute the current operation.

Three concurrent operand accesses to memory are a common target for a vector processor, but they can significantly increase the cost of the memory system. Some systems limit concurrent access to two operations, hoping that it will suffice for most cases. Of course, chaining may require even more accesses, as shown in Figure 7.18.

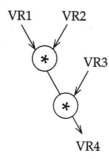

Figure 7.18 Vector memory requirements. In this illustration, 3 operands are read and 1 is written each cycle. Since the supply of operands from memory should balance their use, memory must keep up with this rate, or limit performance.

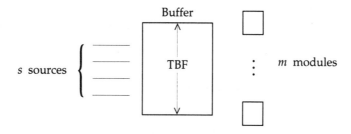

Figure 7.19 Bypassed vector requests held in a buffer of size TBF.

An associated issue is the degree of bypassing or out-of-order requests that a source can make to the memory system. Suppose a conflict arises: a request is directed to a busy module. How many subsequent requests can the source make before it must wait? Assume each of s access ports to memory has a buffer of size TBF/s (Figure 7.19). This buffer holds requests (element addresses) to memory that are being held due to a conflict. For each source, the degree of bypassing is defined as the allowable number of requests waiting before stalling of subsequent requests occurs.

From a modeling point of view, this is different from the simple binomial or the δ-binomial models. The basic difference is that the queue awaiting service from a module is larger by an amount y, where y is the mean queue size of bypassed requests awaiting service. Note that the average queue size (y) is always less than or equal to the buffer size:

$$y \leq TBF/s,$$

since y cannot exceed the size of the physically implemented buffer. (Although, depending on the organization of the TBF, one source buffer could "borrow" from another.)

With or without request bypassing, there is a buffer between the s request sources and the m memory modules (Figure 7.19). This must be large enough to accommodate denied requests (no bypassing), i.e.:

$$\text{Buffer} = TBF > mQ_c,$$

where Q_c is the expected number of denied requests per module, and m is the number of modules. Then $m \cdot Q_c = n - B$, as discussed in chapter 6.

If we allow bypassing, we will require additional buffer entries and additional control. Typically, an entry could include:

- Request source id.

- Request source tag (i.e., VR number).

- Module id.

- Address for request to a module.

- Scheduled cycle time indicating when module is free.

- Entry priority id (assuming more than one request can be bypassed).

While some optimization is possible, it is clear that large bypassed request buffers can be complex.

7.3.3   Gamma (γ)-Binomial Model

We now develop the γ-binomial model of bypassed vector memory behavior. Assume that each vector source issues a request each cycle ($\delta = 1$), and that each physical requestor in the vector processor has the same buffer capacity and characteristic. If the vector processor can make s requests per cycle, and there are t cycles per T_c, we have:

$$\text{Total requests per } T_c = t \cdot s = n. \tag{7.1}$$

This is the same as our n requests per T_c in the simple binomial model, but the situation in the vector processor is more complex. We assume that each of the sources s makes a request each cycle and *each of its γ-buffered requests* also makes a request.

Depending on the buffer control, these buffer requests are made only implicitly. The controller "knows" when a target module will be free and therefore schedules the actual request for that time. From a memory modeling point of view, this is equivalent to the buffer requesting service each cycle until the module is free.

Thus, we now have:

$$\begin{aligned}
\text{Total requests per } T_c &= t \cdot s + t \cdot s \cdot \gamma \\
&= t \cdot s(1 + \gamma) \\
&= n(1 + \gamma).
\end{aligned}$$

This can be substituted into the simple binomial equation:

$$\begin{aligned}
B(m, &n, \gamma) \\
&= m + n(1 + \gamma) - 1/2 - \sqrt{(m + n(1 + \gamma) - 1/2)^2 - 2nm(1 + \gamma)}.
\end{aligned} \tag{7.2}$$

Note that y is (usually) *not* the physical buffer size; rather, it is the mean expected bypassed request queue per source. Finding y allows us to properly implement the physical buffer.

Recall that:

$$\rho_a = \frac{B(m, n, y)}{m}$$

and the queue per module for the $M_B/D/1$ model is:

$$Q = \frac{\rho_a^2 - p\rho_a}{2(1 - \rho_a)} = \frac{n(1 + y) - B}{m}. \tag{7.3}$$

By increasing the number of bypass registers, we realize a larger effective y. We can continue this until there is no contention, so:

$$mQ = n(1 + y) - B = n - B + my. \tag{7.4}$$

Let us call this value of y, which eliminates contention, $y = y_{\text{opt}}$. We can find this by observing that "no contention" occurs when $B = n$, or:

$$\begin{aligned} B - n &= 0, \quad \text{so} \\ B(m, n, y) &= n. \end{aligned} \tag{7.5}$$

This occurs when (assuming $m > n$):

$$\rho_a = \rho = \frac{n}{m}. \tag{7.6}$$

Substituting Equation 7.6 into Equation 7.3 ($p = 1/m$), we get:

$$Q = \frac{n^2 - n}{2m^2 - 2nm}; \tag{7.7}$$

but rearranging Equation 7.4,

$$Q = \frac{n + ny - B}{m} = \frac{ny_{\text{opt}}}{m},$$

since $n = B$ at y_{opt}. Then:

$$y_{\text{opt}} = \frac{mQ}{n} = \frac{n - 1}{2m - 2n}. \tag{7.8}$$

At y_{opt}:

$$mQ = ny_{\text{opt}}.$$

Thus, the mean total buffer size (TBF) is ny_{opt}.

Recall that any physical buffer that avoids overflow must be considerably larger (chapter 4), e.g.:

$$\text{TBF} \geq \frac{ny_{\text{opt}}}{\text{Target prob. overflow}}$$

or, from $M/M/1$ (chapter 6),

$$\text{Prob. overflow (per module)} \doteq \rho^{\frac{\text{TBF}}{m}+2}.$$

Thus, by increasing the occupancy ρ and total queue size TBF, we need a physical buffer significantly larger to avoid pipeline stalls due to buffer overflow. Unless care is used in sizing the buffer, we simply exchange memory conflicts for buffer spills! Practically, it is difficult to get a good tight bound on the physical buffer.

Assuming a reconfigurable (TBF) buffer and $n < m$, we suggest that, as a very rough guideline, the designer:

1. Find y_{opt}.

2. Set $TBF = (n\, y_{\text{opt}}) \times 2$, rounded up to the nearest power of 2.

3. For performance evaluation purposes, assume the achieved y is $y \approx \min(y_{\text{opt}}/2, 1)$.

Consider the following example.

EXAMPLE 7.4

Assume we have a vector processor with the following parameters:

Processor cycle = 10 ns.
s, the number of simultaneous memory requests per cycle = 2.
T_c = 60 ns.
t, cycles per T_c = 6.
m, modules = 16.

Then $m = 16$, $n = 6 \times 2 = 12$. First, compute the worst-case performance, $y = 0$:

$$
\begin{aligned}
B(m, n, y = 0) &= 16 + 12 - 1/2 - \sqrt{(27.5)^2 - 2 \cdot 12 \cdot 16} \\
&= 8.2 \text{ requests}/T_c \\
\rho_a &= \frac{B}{m} = \frac{8.2}{16} = 0.51 \\
\text{Relative performance} &= \frac{B}{n} = 0.68 \\
mQ_c &= n - B = 12 - 8.2 = 3.8.
\end{aligned}
$$

Now the ideal y is:

$$y_{\text{opt}} = \frac{n-1}{2m - 2n} = 1.375.$$

This requires a much larger physical buffer to avoid overflows, as the mean buffer queue is:

$$mQ = n y_{\text{opt}} = 16.5,$$

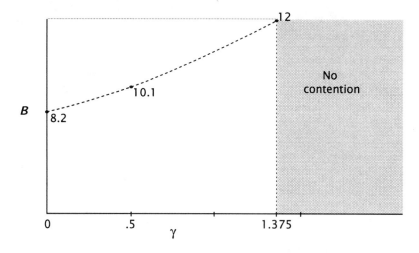

Figure 7.20   Bandwidth vs. the bypass factor (y).

with

$$\rho = \frac{n}{m} = 0.75.$$

As a design strategy, one could make the buffer two times the expected mQ, then realize that the effective y is significantly less than y_{opt} due to buffer overflows.

Conservatively assume that with a $TBF = 32$, we achieve $y = 0.5$; now:

$$B(m, n, y = 0.5) = 10.13$$

and

$$mQ_c = n + ny - B = 7.9$$

and

$$\text{Relative Performance} = \frac{B}{n} = 0.84.$$

Our buffer size now must be large enough to support $y = 0.5$. We have assumed that this could be accomplished with a total buffer (TBF) of, say:

$$2 \times ny_{opt} = 2 \times 12 \times 1.375 \doteq 33 \text{ entries,}$$

or about 32 entries, of which $ny + n - B$ or ($12 \times .5 + 12 - 10.13 \approx 8$) are occupied on the average. The achieved bandwidth and the expected number of requests in a buffer are plotted as a function of y in Figures 7.20 and 7.21.

$\blacklozenge$

7.3.4   Bypassing between Vector Instructions

Consider now the effect of all this in terms of a timeline. In order to load a vector register (64 entries), the following time steps are required:

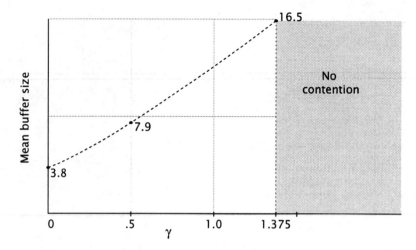

Figure 7.21 Expected buffer sizes required to achieve various bypass factors y. (Physical buffer must be significantly larger.)

1. Initial access (T_{access}).

2. Ideal memory access time (assume 64 cycles).

3. Time lost to memory contention.

4. Additional delay at the end of the load for the remaining (deferred) items in the buffer to be served.

It is the last step (step 4) that can have a significant effect on overall performance. Typically, vector processors complete each instruction before beginning the next vector instruction. This allows external events such as interrupts to be handled at the completion of an instruction without having disturbed the state of the machine for successor instructions. This delay in draining the pipeline at the conclusion of each instruction can have a significant effect. Assume in the foregoing example that one cycle is required to put away each pending memory request. This allows the load and the stores that have been concurrently executing with the vector ALU operations to all complete before the next cycle of ALU and vector load/store instructions begin. If we allowed the vector ALU instructions to begin before the previous cycle's vector load and store instructions completed, we would have the danger that the vector ALU instructions over a period of time would catch up with or overrun the vector load/store instructions using data that has not yet been loaded into the vector registers or writing registers that have not yet had their current value stored in memory.

Assume for the moment that the memory pipeline drains; that is to say, all vector instructions must be completed before a new set of vector instructions can begin. For example, we might have the following:

$$
\begin{array}{ccc}
6 \sim & & 8 \sim \\
\vdash\!\!-\!\!-\!\!-\!\!-\!\!+\!\!-\!\!-\!\!-\!\!-\!\!-\!\!\not\vdash \not\vdash\!\!-\!\!-\!\!-\!\!-\!\!+\!\!-\!\!-\!\!\dashv \\
T_{access} & 64+12=76 \sim^* & \text{buffer service (8 entries).}
\end{array}
$$

*The effect of memory contention is estimated as ideal time $\times n/B = 64/.84 = 76$.

Table 7.3   The effects of vector bypass on performance.

	No Bypass	Limited Bypass	Full Bypass
Buffer size and complexity	16 entries simple	32 entries complex	> 64 entries complex
y	0	0.5	1.375
Total cycles for single VLD (64 reg), $m = 16$ $n = 12$	104	90	86.5
Performance relative to ideal vector ALU with 6 cycles startup (70 cycles total)	0.68	.78	0.81

Suppose we increase the buffer size significantly so that we achieve $n = B$ (no contention). Then we have:

$$
\underset{T_{\text{access}}}{\underset{\longmapsto}{6 \sim}} \quad \underset{64 \sim}{\overset{\text{}}{\underset{\longmapsto}{}}} \quad \underset{\text{buffer service (16.5 entries} = n \times y_{\text{opt}})}{\underset{\longmapsto}{16.5 \sim}}
$$

Note that we reduced the total time for the load only from 90 cycles to 86.5 cycles! With no bypassing at all, we would have:

$$
\underset{T_{\text{access}}}{\underset{\longmapsto}{6 \sim}} \quad \underset{94 \sim^{*}}{\overset{\text{}}{\underset{\longmapsto}{}}} \quad \underset{\text{buffer service } (n - B = 3.8)}{\underset{\longmapsto}{4 \sim}}
$$

$^{*}n/B = 64/0.68 = 94 \sim$.

or a total time of 103 cycles.

The buffer to support this case is a simple one-entry-per-module (16 total) buffer merely holding the deferred address and source id.

From Table 7.3, it might appear that the "best" vector performance achievable would be in the range of 0.68–0.81 times maximum performance, based on memory system limitation.

Our analysis in this example is based on two simultaneous VLD or VST. Insofar as some applications may not require two simultaneous memory accesses, this is a pessimistic performance projection—e.g., for one access we would have (at $y = 0$):

$$B(6, 16, y = 0) = 5.06$$

and

$$\text{Rel. Perf.} = \frac{B}{n} = \frac{5.06}{6} = 0.84.$$

Here again, any request bypassing would improve performance. An obvious solution is to provide more vector registers, so that the VLDs would not be used in the next vector iteration. The problem here is the expense of (area occupied by) these additional registers.

The preceding discussion is based on the assumption that we are not bypassing memory operations between vector instructions. That is, while we allow bypassing to occur within a vector instruction, we assume that any ALU or other instruction that uses a vector register cannot begin until all previously designated operations that use that vector instruction have been completed.

Interinstruction bypassing can improve performance, as in the above example, but as mentioned earlier it can be accomplished only at significant expense. Some of the issues in dealing with interinstruction bypassing are similar to those discussed later in this chapter in the discussion on out-of-order execution for multiple instruction execution machines.

7.4   Vector Processor Speedup: Performance Relative to a Pipelined Processor

7.4.1   Basic Issues

Vector processor performance is determined by:

1. The amount of the program that can be expressed in a vectorizable form.

2. Vector startup costs. These correspond to the length of the pipeline for vector instructions.

3. The number of execution units and the support for the chaining of vector operands provided within the execution unit.

4. The number of operands that can be simultaneously accessed/stored from the memory system.

5. The number of vector registers.

A secondary element in the memory system design is the y factor, or the number of requests that can be bypassed before the memory accessing mechanism stalls waiting for a conflict-free reference. Suppose we compare the vector processor to a well-designed high-speed pipelined processor with the same cycle time. Depending upon the memory system design, the overall effect of speedup possible by the vector processor over the pipelined processor is generally limited to four. This assumes that the memory system supports the concurrent execution of two load instructions and a store instruction concurrently with the execution of an arithmetic operation. If chaining is allowed, the memory system must accommodate at least an additional concurrent load instruction, but the overall speedup is then limited (for most cases) at $S_{p\ max} < 6$ (3 LD's, 2 Arith, and 1 ST). In practice, such speedups are not achievable for a variety of reasons. In order to sustain high degrees of speedup, the program must consist of purely vector code. Since at least some address arithmetic and control operations are also required, some part of the program is not vectorizable. This limits the attainable speedup. Suppose a particular problem has a maximum speedup of four, and this was available for 75% of the operations to be executed by the processor. This would give an overall speedup of:

$$S_p = \frac{T_1}{T_p} = \frac{T_1}{\% \text{ vector} \cdot \frac{T_1}{4} + \% \text{ nonvector} \cdot T_1} = \frac{T_1}{.75(\frac{T_1}{4}) + .25T_1} = 2.3.$$

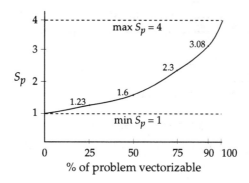

Figure 7.22   Speedup of an idealized vector processor vs. percentage of a program that is vectorizable. Assume that the maximum speedup over a pipelined processor is $S_p = 4$ and that the vector code is ideal (long vectors, no memory contention).

Figure 7.23   Timing templates for pipelined (scalar) processor and vector processor. The scalar processor accesses data (DF) from the data cache; the vector processor accesses data directly from memory (DF-M).

Figure 7.22 plots the speedup vs. the percent of vectorizable code for this illustration.

The depth of the pipeline itself also limits the effective speedup of the vector processor. A pipelined or scalar processor accesses its operands from data cache. Because of structured data accesses, the vector processor accesses directly from memory. This introduces extra cycles to the timing template of the vector processor (Figure 7.23). It may also be true (although it need not) that the vector processor's execution unit pipeline would be longer than the scalar processor's. Since predefined sequences of operations are expected in vector machines, there is a tendency on the part of the designers not to emphasize and minimize execution latency, whereas the scalar processor designer emphasizes latency even if the processor cannot match the execution bandwidth of the vector processor. For both these reasons, the scalar processor tends to have a shorter timing template than the vector processor. This has two effects:

1. It puts the vector processor at a performance disadvantage in processing branch instructions and similar code sequence interruptions.

2. It limits the speedup available to the vector processor on vector instructions that refer to short vectors.

Hockney and Jesshope [132] characterize the performance of vector processors with two parameters: R_∞, and $n_{1/2}$. $R_\infty = 1/\Delta t$, or one over the basic cycle time of the vector pipeline. This is a measure of the maximum vector arithmetic execution rate that the processor can sustain in the absence of

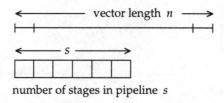

number of stages in pipeline s

Figure 7.24 The $n_{1/2}$ factor. If vector length $n \gg s$, then $S_p \approx S_{p \max}$, but if $n \approx s$ then $S_p \approx \frac{S_{p \max}}{2}$. This occurs when the vector length $n = n_{1/2}$.

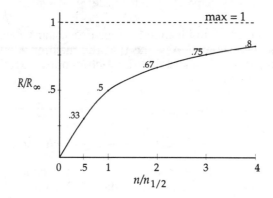

Figure 7.25 Relative vector performance vs. relative vector length (after Hockney and Jesshope [132]).

chaining. If c functional units can be chained, the maximum performance is simply $c * R_\infty$ (usually, $c = 2$).

Assume n is the vector size (number of elements in a vector register). The $n_{1/2}$ is a parameter that measures the depth of the pipeline, or the vector startup cost (in cycles). It is the length of the vector operand or vector that achieves exactly one-half of the maximum performance. Usually, vector processors cannot start a new vector instruction until a previous vector instruction is finished using the vector pipeline. This delay in the ability to begin a new instruction corresponds to the startup time of the pipeline (see Figure 7.24).

The Hockney and Jesshope vector efficiency is:

$$R/R_\infty = \frac{1}{1 + 1/(n/n_{1/2})}.$$

Figure 7.25 plots the efficiency or relative performance vs. the relative vector length ratio. For values of vector length n significantly less than $n_{1/2}$; not only is the vector efficiency low, but the processor performance (the speedup over a generic pipelined processor) is probably less than one.

For a simple vector processor, $n_{1/2}$ is approximately equal to the vector startup cost—the number of cycles required to produce the first result from the vector pipeline. In a vector processor with, say, a four-stage vector

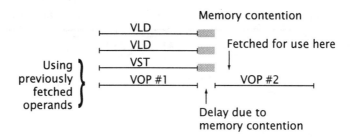

Figure 7.26   The effect of memory contention on vector performance.

arithmetic pipeline, the vector startup might be six cycles—four cycles for the operation plus two cycles for bus transit of data. So, in this case, the vector startup cost is 6~, and thus $n_{1/2} \approx 6$ ~.

Vector processors access data directly from memory, giving them a significant advantage in accessing complex or *large-stride* data arrays. However, the memory system necessarily experiences some contention under heavy referencing conditions. This contention causes the vector registers to be loaded and stored more slowly than vector instructions are executed through the vector ALU. The vector ALU in general, then, is waiting for the vector registers to be made available. The delay corresponds to the memory contention; see Figure 7.26.

For memory-limited processors, $n_{1/2}$ may be determined by the sum of memory access time, contention, and buffer putaway completion. Generally,

$$n_{1/2} \approx \max \left[\text{vector arithmetic startup cycles, vector memory overhead cycles} \right].$$

7.4.2   Measures

Since the vector processor is operating directly from memory, and it is assumed that the vector load and store traffic is being overlapped with vector arithmetic, we can asymptotically realize the vector speedup of perhaps 4 or 5. Delays in accessing memory due to memory conflicts accumulate during the course of vector arithmetic operations. This has the effect of slowing down the vector processor, making it impossible to achieve its asymptotic speedup performance.

All this may seem to paint a discouraging picture concerning vector processor performance, but this is somewhat deceptive. While the vector processor speedup is indeed limited to values significantly below the asymptotic maximum speedup of 4 or 5, speedups of 2–3 are achievable for applications that have significant vector content in their code. Moreover, the basis of the speedup that we have described is an idealized simple pipelined processor. This processor itself is, in general, unable to sustain its unit performance over a variety of large-stride vector code. Thus, the speedup, in practical situations, of a vector machine over a simple pipelined machine may be significantly greater than the factors of 2 or 3 anticipated here. We discuss this later in this chapter.

Fragment #1   Fragment #2   Fragment #3

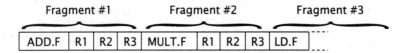

| ADD.F | R1 | R2 | R3 | MULT.F | R1 | R2 | R3 | LD.F |

Figure 7.27   A partial VLIW format. Each fragment concurrently accesses a single centralized register set.

7.5   Multiple-Issue Machines

The alternative to vector processors is multiple-issue machines. There are two broad classes of multiple-issue machines: statically scheduled and dynamically scheduled. In principle, these two classes are quite similar. Dependencies among groups of instructions are evaluated, and groups found to be independent are simultaneously dispatched to multiple execution units. For statically scheduled processors, this detection process is done by the compiler, and instructions are assembled into *instruction packets*, which are decoded and executed at run time. For dynamically scheduled processors, the detection of independent instructions may also be done at compile time and the code suitably arranged to optimize execution patterns, but the ultimate selection of instructions (to be executed or dispatched) is done by the hardware in the decoder at run time. In principle, the dynamically scheduled processor may have an instruction representation and form that is indistinguishable from slower pipeline processors. Statically scheduled processors must have some additional information either implicitly or explicitly indicating instruction packet boundaries.

Early static multiple-issue machines include the so-called VLIW (very long instruction word) machines [89], typified by processors from Multiflow and Cydrome. These machines use an instruction word that consists of 8 to 10 instruction fragments. Each fragment controls a designated execution unit; thus, the register set is extensively multiported to support simultaneous access to the multiplicity of execution units. In order to accommodate the multiple instruction fragments, the instruction word is typically over 200 bits long. (See Figure 7.27.) In order to avoid the obvious performance limitations imposed by the occurrence of branches, a novel compiler technology called *trace scheduling* was developed. By use of trace scheduling, the dynamic frequency of branching is greatly reduced. Branches are predicted where possible, and on the basis of the probable success rate the predicted path is incorporated into a larger basic block. This process continues until a suitably sized basic block can be efficiently scheduled. If an unanticipated (or unpredicted) branch occurs during the execution of the code, at the end of the basic block the proper result is fixed up for use by a target basic block.

More recent attempts at multiple-issue processors have been directed at rather lower amounts of concurrency. The potential speedup available from the Multiflow compiler using trace scheduling under ideal processor conditions is generally less than 3 [78]. Based upon this, it would seem that in the absence of significant compiler breakthroughs, available speedup is limited. Recent attempts at multiple-issue processor design have generally focused on more modest objectives (Table 7.4). Johnson [149] refers to this new generation of multiple-issue machines, whether concurrency is statically or dynamically determined, as *superscalar* machines.

Table 7.4   Some superscalar processors (based on a study by N. Ghazal).

(a) Chip Features of Processors

Characteristic	RS/6000	SuperSparc	DEC Alpha	Intel Pentium	Motorola/IBM Power PC	H-P PA RISC 7100
Chip configuration	3 (processing chips), 1 (mem control), and 1 (I/O control)	Single chip	Single chip	Single chip	Single chip	Single chip
Technology	CMOS, 1μm	BiCMOS, .8μm	CMOS, .75μm	0.6μm BiCMOS	0.6μm CMOS	0.8μm CMOS
Die size	161mm², largest chip	–	233.5mm²	163 mm²	120 mm²	202 mm²
No. of Transistors	3.5M	3.1M	1.7M	3.3M	2.8M	850K
Cycle Time	33–40 ns	20 ns	5 ns	10 ns	15 ns	10 ns

(b) Processor Organization Features

Feature	RS/6000	SuperSPARC	DEC Alpha	Intel	Motorola	H-P
Prefetch I Buffer Size	12-entry	12-entry	8-entry	–	8-entry	–
Issue Rate (max per cycle)	up to 4	up to 3	2	2	3	2
Instruction Window config.	Central	Central	Central (scoreboard)	Central	Central	Central
Data Dependency Resol.	Interlocks (renaming for FP ops)	Interlocks	Interlocks	Interlocking	Interlocking (some renaming)	Interlocking
Branch Policy Branch Technique	Static Predict in-line (early CC set)	Dynamic default: Predict in-line	Static/dyn. default: Predict in-line	Dynamic BTB with history bits	Static Backward branch predicted taken	Static Backward branch predicted taken
Exception Handling	Precise	Precise	Imprecise on arithmetic exc.			

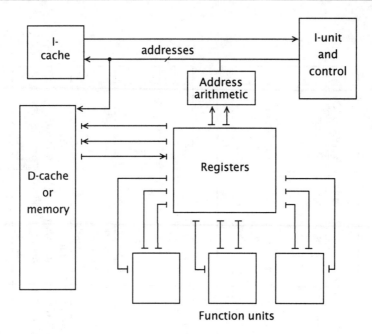

Figure 7.28   Major data paths in a generic multiple-issue processor (VLIW processor).

Figure 7.28 shows the data paths for a generic multiple-issue machine. The extensive use of register ports provides simultaneous access to data as required by a VLIW processor. This suggests the register set as a processor bottleneck. Dynamic multiple-issue processors can also be implemented as shown in Figure 7.28, but usually such processors use multiple buses connecting the register set and functional units, and each bus services multiple functional units. This may limit the maximum degree of concurrency, but it can also significantly reduce the required number of register ports.

The issue of detection of independence within or among instructions is theoretically the same regardless of whether the detection process is done statically or dynamically (although the realized effect is quite different). In the next sections, we review the theory of instruction independence and especially look at dynamically scheduled multiple-issue processors. Processors that decode but one instruction per cycle, yet allow instructions to execute simultaneously or out of order, must generally obey the same rules of instruction independence as multiple-issue machines; therefore, we treat these machines as a degenerate type of multiple-issue machine.

7.6   Out-of-Order and Multiple-Instruction Execution

In chapter 4, we looked at pipelined processors that are constrained to:

1. Decode at most one instruction per cycle.

2. Execute each instruction in the same sequential order that it appeared in the program representation.

Simple pipelined processors use an in-order pipeline organization; that is, the execution of each instruction (the PA or EX cycles) is performed in exactly the same order as it appeared in the dynamic sequence of instructions in the program. This rule is followed even though instructions may be independent of one another. The advantage of such a restricted pipeline organization is that anomalous events such as interrupts, etc., can be associated with particular instructions, and, further, no storage resource is affected subsequent to an interrupt. Consider the following example:

```
*       MPY   R1,   R2,   R3   · · · ⊢—EX—+—EX—+—EX—+—PA—⊣
* + 1   ADD   R4,   R5,   R6        · · · ⊢—EX—+—PA—⊣
```

If the second instruction completes its execution and alters the state of the registers before the first instruction completes execution, the instructions have executed out of sequential order. Now the first instruction creates an interrupt at the conclusion of its execution, and it is impossible to restore the machine—preserve its state as it was at the time of interruption—since the second instruction has already altered the contents of the processor registers.

It may be possible to detect an interrupt early enough to allow the concurrent execution of two instructions:

```
ADD.F   ⊢—D—+—EX—+—EX—+—EX—+—PA—⊣
ADD          ⊢—D—+—EX—+—EX—+—PA—⊣
```

In this case, the two instructions complete at exactly the same time, but if an interrupt is caused by instruction 1, it may still be possible to "kill the clock"—i.e., suppress the sampling of the final results into the registers and allow recovery of the machine as it would have been if only instruction 1 had executed. Multiple instruction execution, in practice, is usually limited by the number of ports to the registers, and resource limitations simply prevent the writing of multiple results simultaneously to a single register set. Multiple instruction execution, however, might still occur in situations where the architecture supports both general-purpose (integer) registers and floating-point registers as distinct storage entities. In such a case, even if the interrupt signal could not be generated soon enough to allow absolute sequential instruction execution, there is usually little damage done, since the sequential state of both the floating-point registers and the fixed-point registers is preserved.

7.6.1   Data Dependencies

Instructions can depend on preceding instructions for source operands. For purposes of this discussion, we adopt an instruction format notation that is similar to a three-address L/S type architecture: $OP\ D\ S_1, S_2$. Such an instruction has the following effect:

$$D := S_1 \text{ OP } S_2$$

and is represented as:

$$OP\ D, S_1, S_2.$$

S_1 indicates an address of a source operand (usually a register), S_2 is another source operand, and D is the address of the destination of the result. Of course, it is possible for S_1 to be the same as D, as in the R/M architecture, or for any of S_1, S_2, or D to be memory addresses, but for our examples we assume that these are registers; the general principles are the same.

With out-of-order execution, three types of dependencies are possible between two instructions I_i and I_j (i precedes j in execution sequence). The first, an *essential dependency*, arises when the destination of I_i is the same as the source of I_j:

$$D_i \;=\; S_{1j} \quad \text{or}$$
$$D_i \;=\; S_{2j}$$

This is the dependency seen in chapter 4 examples as a data or address dependency.

Another condition that causes a dependency occurs when the destination of instruction I_j is the same as the source of a preceding instruction I_i. This can be represented as:

$$D_j \;=\; S_{1i} \quad \text{or}$$
$$D_j \;=\; S_{2i}.$$

The second dependency arises when an instruction in sequence is delayed and a following instruction is allowed to precede in execution order and change the contents of one of the original instruction's source registers. Consider the following example (R3 is the destination):

$$
\begin{array}{lllll}
I_1 & \text{DIV} & \text{R3,} & \text{R1,} & \text{R2} \\
I_2 & \text{ADD} & \text{R5,} & \text{R3,} & \text{R4} \\
I_3 & \text{ADD} & \text{R3,} & \text{R6,} & \text{R7.}
\end{array}
$$

In this example, instruction 2 is delayed by a divide operation in instruction 1. Instruction 3, whose sources are independent of instructions 1 and 2, if allowed to execute as soon as its operands are available, would cause a change to a register (R3) used in the computation of instruction 2. A dependency of this type is called an *ordering dependency*, since it is created only when out-of-order execution is allowed.

The final type of dependency arises when the destination of instruction I_i is the same as the destination of instruction I_j, or

$$D_i = D_j.$$

In this case, it is possible that the instruction I_i would complete after instruction I_j, and the final destination contained in the register would be that of instruction I_i when it ought to have been that of I_j. This dependency, called an *output dependency*, is somewhat debatable as a true source of instruction conflict. If instruction I_i produces a result that is not used by an instruction that follows it until instruction I_j produces a new result for the same destination, then instruction I_i was unnecessary in the first place and should have been eliminated. Output dependencies thus occur

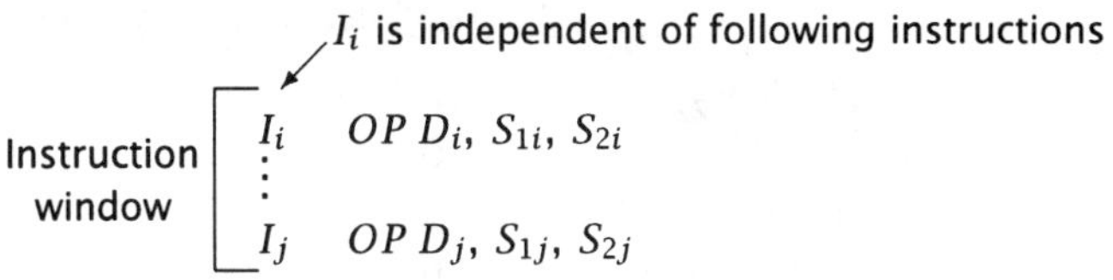

I_i is independent of following instructions

Instruction window

$$I_i \quad OP\ D_i,\ S_{1i},\ S_{2i}$$
$$\vdots$$
$$I_j \quad OP\ D_j,\ S_{1j},\ S_{2j}$$

Figure 7.29   Instruction window.

only in poorly represented code. Since this type of dependency is generally eliminated by any optimizing compiler, it can be largely ignored in our discussions and is not regarded by some as a true instruction dependency. Consider two examples:

Example #1

DIV	R3,	R1,	R2
ADD	R3,	R4,	R5.

Example #2

DIV	R3,	R1,	R2
ADD	R5,	R3,	R4
ADD	R3,	R6,	R7.

The first example is clearly a case of a redundant instruction (the DIV), whereas the second is a case that has an output dependency, but also has an essential dependency; since this essential dependency must be covered, the output dependency is also covered. It is important to realize that the fewer the dependencies that arise in the code, the more concurrency available in the code and the faster the overall program execution. Thus, if output dependencies cannot occur because of the compiler, we achieve a higher degree of concurrency than otherwise.

7.6.2   Representing Data Dependencies

Suppose we have a block of instructions as shown in Figure 7.29. Instruction i is by definition independent of all others, since it is the first one in sequence. From the previous discussion, subsequent instruction j is dependent and cannot be executed at this time if any of the following three conditions are satisfied (i precedes j):

1. **Essential**—$D_i = S_{1j}$ or $D_i = S_{2j}$
   (also called read after write dependency [171]).

2. **Ordering**—$D_j = S_{1i}$ or $D_j = S_{2i}$
   (also called write after read dependency [171]).

3. **Output**—$D_i = D_j$
   (also called write after write dependency [171]).

Instructions in the I-window

Dependency		$I_1{}^a$	I_2	I_3	I_4
Entry = 1	$I_1{}^a$	0	–	–	–
if I depends	I_2	1	0	–	–
on instructions	I_3	0	1	0	–
in window	I_4	0	0	1	0

^{a}Always independent.

Figure 7.30 The M^1 dependency matrix for sequentially dependent instructions.

	I_1	I_2	I_3	I_4			I_1	I_2	I_3	I_4
I_1	0					I_1	0			
I_2	0	0				I_2	0	0		
I_3	1	0	0			I_3	0	0	0	
I_4	0	1	0	0		I_4	1	0	0	0

(a)   (b)

Figure 7.31 (a) The M^2 dependency matrix ($M^1 * M^1$). (b) The M^3 dependency matrix.

These dependencies can be represented as an entry in a matrix, called a *precedence matrix*. The basic instruction-to-instruction dependencies are represented as a simple precedence matrix; together with secondary dependencies (if I_3 depends on I_2 and I_2 depends on I_1, then I_3 depends on I_1), they are represented in a higher-order matrix. In Figures 7.30 and 7.31, the N instructions in the instruction window are represented across the top of the matrix. The dependencies are represented as entries in the matrix; thus, if I_4 has a dependency on instruction 3, it has a 1 at m_{43}. The precedence matrix is a lower triangular matrix with a zero diagonal, since an instruction does not depend upon itself. Suppose a precedence matrix is created for a particular sequence of code. Since I_4 may depend upon I_3, and I_3 may depend upon I_2, I_4 also depends upon I_2, although it may not have an entry in the precedence matrix for entry m_{42}. This is not a concern for us, since instructions can only be executed when they are independent of all other instructions in the block. Independence is determined by having zeros for all elements in the row. Thus, the essential ordering is maintained despite the incompleteness of the dependency picture from the initial precedence matrix. This initial precedence matrix (M^1) is determined by applying the aforementioned dependency criteria to all preceding instructions in the block.

Simple precedence matrices cover the M^1 dependencies. We can get a complete picture of all the dependencies present simply by raising the precedence matrix to increasingly higher powers, up to $N - 1$ (there are N elements in the window), and summing (ORing) the resulting matrices:

$$\sum_{i=1}^{N-1} M^i = M^1 + M^2 + \cdots + M^{N-1}.$$

Here, $M^2 = M^1 * M^1$, etc. The M^2 matrix defines the second-order dependencies, e.g., if x depends on y, and y depends on z, then x has a second-order dependency on z. The multiply operation is the logical "AND," and the sum is the logical "OR," so that:

$$m_{ij}^2 = \sum_{k=1}^{N} m_{ik}' \cdot m_{kj}'.$$

This is shown in an example in Figure 7.31. The resultant matrix is called the *full precedence matrix.* If a structure such as a precedence matrix is used to control the dispatching and scheduling of instructions, the result is *control flow scheduling,* which is performed at decode time.

Regardless of how dependency is detected, it is important to maximize the available concurrency. This can be done by a number of different techniques:

1. Enlarging the block size.

2. Relieving the dependency constraints through hardware and compiler support.

3. Extending the range of the concurrency detection across basic blocks.

Simply increasing the instruction block size and attempting to detect additional concurrency within a single basic block has limited potential, as we shall see. Typically, the frequency of branch is high enough to limit the number of instructions that are available for simultaneous execution. Compiler support can, however, play an important role by loop unrolling and other techniques that minimize the occurrence of branches.

Detection of concurrently executable instructions across branch boundaries is a difficult problem. It is clearly better to minimize the occurrence of branches through static or compile time techniques. Still, successive iterations of the same loop can be executed largely independently from one another, offering significant concurrency potential.

Of the three conditions that determine dependencies among instructions, the first represents an essential dependency, where the sources of a particular instruction depend on the result of a previous instruction. Both ordering and output dependencies are resource problems for instructions using a common resource (register) to hold different values of variables. These two different values cannot occupy the same space (i.e., register) at the same time. If we can distinguish the two different values by renaming the second variable, we can avoid incurring this loss of concurrency. Schemes for accomplishing this are discussed shortly.

7.6.3   Other Types of Dependencies

In addition to data dependencies, two other types of dependencies can affect overall processor performance.

1. Procedural or Control Dependency. This is a dependency created by a branch instruction. The dynamic execution of a program consists

of the execution of a sequence of blocks of instructions that always execute together. The block is initiated by a target of a branch instruction and is concluded by a branch instruction. Since an unconditional branch is always executed without altering the sequence of instruction execution, i.e., the instructions that are its predecessors or successors, it is a member of such a block. These blocks of instructions are called *basic blocks*[1] (or *branch subsets* [302]). The last instruction in a basic block is always a branch instruction (conditional), called the *trailing branch*. Most algorithms for out-of-order instruction execution, or concurrent instruction execution, execute instructions only within a basic block. More complex algorithms have been developed to detect instruction concurrency between basic blocks [282, 302].

2. Resource Dependency. The last type of dependency that can occur among instructions is contention for a physical resource. For example:

        DIV   R3,   R1,   R2
        DIV   R6,   R4,   R5 .

While these instructions have no data dependencies or procedural dependencies, they both require the use of a divide unit. Since divide is a relatively infrequent operation, it is unlikely that a processor could accommodate two sequential divide operations without encountering a resource contention. Unfortunately, it is in the nature of code that resource requirements are not uniformly distributed across code segments. The probability of a relatively rare operation increases, given that there has already been a recent request for such an operation.

Some examples:

1. Floating-point resources. After a sequence of integer operations to get addresses' base and index values, there may be multiple (presumably independent) floating-point operations requesting respective resources. Contention is usually highest for ADD.F and MPY.F resources.

2. Load and store resources. Here, cache bandwidth is a limit as multiple instructions access (presumably independent) data operands. Contention occurs as a result of multiple DFs in the same cycle.

7.6.4   When and How to Detect Instruction Concurrency

There are three related issues here:

1. Detecting concurrency.

2. Dispatching concurrent instructions.

3. Scheduling execution of concurrent instructions.

---

[1] Sometimes compilers restrict the notion of basic block to instruction sequences that end in a branch of *any* type. For the run-time environment considered here, such restrictions are unnecessary.

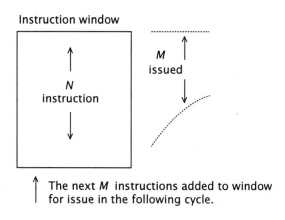

Instruction window

N
instruction

M
issued

↑ The next *M* instructions added to window
for issue in the following cycle.

Figure 7.32   Instruction window.

Detection of concurrent instructions may be done at compile time, at run time (by the hardware), or at both times. It is clearly advantageous to use both the compiler and the run-time hardware to support concurrent instruction execution. The compiler, for example, may be able to unroll loops and generally create larger basic block sizes, thus mitigating the effect of procedural dependencies. On the other hand, it is only at run time that the complete machine state—i.e., the state of the resources—is completely known. For example, an apparent resource dependency created by a sequence of `divide, load, divide` instructions may in fact not exist if, say, the intervening load instruction created a cache miss. The effect of this miss may be to insert a sufficient delay for the first divide to complete before the second divide is activated.

Wedig [302] treats compile time concurrency detection, while Wedig [302], Uht [292], and Kuck [174] provide an analysis of the complementary nature of compile and run-time instruction concurrency detection.

During decode, a number of instructions are examined to determine their independence. If an instruction is found to be independent of other, earlier instructions, and if there are available resources (reservation stations), the instruction is issued to the functional executional unit. The total number of instructions inspected (i.e, candidates for issue) determines the size of the *instruction window* (Figure 7.32). The instruction window has size *N* instructions, and at any given cycle *M* instructions are issued. In the next cycle, the successor *M* instructions are brought into the buffer and again *N* instructions are evaluated for their dependencies. Up to *M* instructions may be issued in a single cycle (although resource limitations may necessarily make this unobtainable.) Figure 7.33 illustrates the overall layout of an *M* pipelined processor inspecting *N* instructions and issuing *M* instructions.

When the window size is 1 (*N* = 1), we have a trivial case where only one instruction is issued per decode cycle. However, if out-of-order execution is allowed, the dependencies mentioned before apply. Both essential and ordering dependencies must also be allowed, to ensure current execution for out-of-order code. Table 7.5 illustrates some of the processor possibilities.

In the window model, any of up to *N* instructions are candidates for being issued, depending solely on whether they satisfy the independence proper-

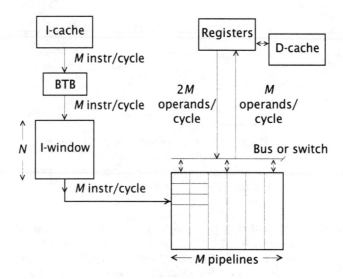

Figure 7.33   An M pipelined processor.

Table 7.5   Some types of concurrently executing processors.   (N is the number of instructions checked for concurrency; M, the maximum number of instructions issued per decode cycle.)

N	M	Restriction	Result	Dependency Conditions
1	1	In-order decode, in-order PA (or EX)	Simple dynamic pipeline	Only essential
1	1	In-order decode, out-of-order PA (or EX)	Dynamic pipeline with out-of-order results	All
N	1	Out-of-order PA/EX, out-of-order decode	Dynamic pipeline with out-of-order decode	All
N	M	Out-of-order PA/EX, out-of-order decode	Windowed (superscalar) dynamic pipeline	All

ties and whether or not there are sufficient execution resources available. As a practical matter, the second restriction more or less implies the use of an LIW (long instruction word) technique.

If the processor, for example, can only accommodate two load/store instructions, a floating-point instruction, and a fixed-point instruction, then the decoder in the instruction window must select exactly these classes of instructions for issue while also determining their independence, so that three load/store instructions could not be issued even if they were all independent from all other instructions in the instruction window.

Scheduling is the process of assigning specific instructions and their operand values to designated resources at designated times. Scheduling can be done either centrally at the time of decode, or in a distributed manner by the functional units themselves at execute time. The former approach is called *control flow scheduling*; the latter is called *data flow scheduling*. In control flow scheduling, data and resource dependencies are resolved during the decode cycle and the instructions are held (not issued) until the dependencies have been resolved. In a data flow scheduling system, the instructions leave decode stage when they are decoded and are held in buffers at the functional units until their operands and the functional unit are available. In data flow scheduling, instructions are, in a sense, self-scheduled.

Early machines used either control flow or data flow to ensure correct operation of out-of-order instructions. The IBM 7030 [46] and the CDC 6600 [281] used a control flow approach; in the CDC 6600, this was called the *scoreboard*. The IBM 360 Model 91 [288] was the first system to use data flow scheduling.

Superscalar Processors

The ability to issue multiple instructions in a single cycle is sometimes referred to as a *superscalar* implementation. Not all implementations are the same, however. Not only is the number of instructions that are issued per decode cycle different, but the constraints on the instructions may significantly differ. A processor with a concurrently operating floating-point coprocessor can be referred to as superscalar, but the performance advantage it offers over a simple dynamic pipeline may be marginal, because programs may not have the required integer and floating-point combination. It is especially important in these superscalar implementations for the user to understand the capabilities, restrictions, and limitations of the hardware in assessing any possible advantage it might offer in the execution of programs.

7.6.5 Two Scheduling Implementations

In this section, we look at two simple prototypical scheduling implementations. Both have $N = 1$ and $M = 1$, but allow out-of-order execution (PA).

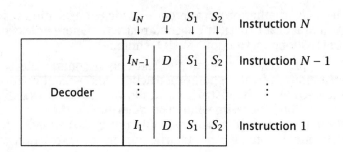

Figure 7.34 Dependencies and tagged register results in a control flow. The D, S_1, S_2 of instruction N are compared with source and destination of the preceding $N - 1$ instructions.

Consider a system with multiple functional units, each of whose executions may involve multiple cycles. Using the L/S architecture as our model, we assume that there is a centralized single set of registers that provide operands for the functional units.

Suppose there are up to N instructions already dispatched for execution, and we must determine how to issue an instruction currently at the decoder. The issuance of a single instruction in the presence of up to $N - 1$ unissued previous instructions is equivalent to the issuance of that instruction as the last of N instructions issued at one time.

Control Flow

A control flow approach to out-of-order instruction execution has been discussed for many years. Probably the best-known implementation is the *scoreboard* approach of the CDC 6600 [281]. While there are many scoreboard variations, we describe here a very simple one. Read and write tags are associated with each register. The tag associated with each register identifies the functional unit that produces a result destined for that particular register. A null tag indicates that the register has a valid (updated) result. A bit associated with the read and write tags indicates which of the read or write to that register must occur first (earliest in sequence order). A single reservation station is added for each functional unit, and a scoreboard, or concurrency control unit, is introduced. This allows dependencies to be detected and instructions to be issued, and it enables the results of the various functional units to be broadcast across a bus to designated destinations (Figure 7.34). When an instruction is decoded, it is issued to a particular functional unit based on its opcode. If that functional unit already has an instruction pending in the reservation station, the decoder cannot issue another instruction to it, and that instruction cannot be issued until it becomes available. All operand values for a particular instruction need not be available for the instruction to be issued to the reservation station; the tag of a particular register may be substituted for a value, in which case the reservation station remains in a pending state until the value is available.

On an essential dependency, the control unit may issue the instruction to the functional unit's reservation station, together with a tag for the unit that will provide the operand. Thus, for the instructions:

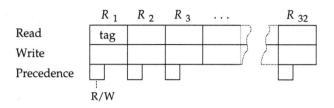

Figure 7.35 A scoreboard. (a) The tag identifies a functional unit that must read from, or write to, the register. (b) R/W indicates (if both read and write tags have entries) which action must occur first.

Functional unit

ADD | OP | D | S_1 | S_2 |

MPY | OP | D | S_1 | S_2 |

DIV | OP | D | S_1 | S_2 |

Figure 7.36 Reservation stations contain instructions pending entry into functional units.

```
ADD   R1, R2, R3
MPY   R4, R1, R3
```

the ADD instruction is issued to the adder on the first cycle, with an "adder" tag going to the write R1 scoreboard. The MPY instruction is issued on the next cycle to the multiply unit with an "adder" tag for its first source operand. On the cycle before the adder completes its operation, it broadcasts that a result will be produced on the next cycle. This allows both R1 and the multiplier unit to ingate the proper value.

For ordering and output dependencies, the control unit may issue the instruction but not allow the result to broadcast until the proper sequential use of the registers can be assured. Thus, for the instructions:

```
MPY   R1, R2, R3
ADD   R2, R5, R3
```

the result of the ADD instruction cannot be broadcast until the multiplier has begun using the R2 value. If the MPY were delayed in beginning execution, the scoreboard for R2 and R3 would contain MPY read tags.

The scoreboard keeps track of all instructions in execution, and it ensures that the three dependency requirements are honored by correctly scheduling instructions into the functional unit. Consider the following sequence (Figure 7.37):

```
DIV.F  R3,  R1,  R2
MPY.F  R5,  R3,  R4
ADD.F  R4,  R6,  R7.
```

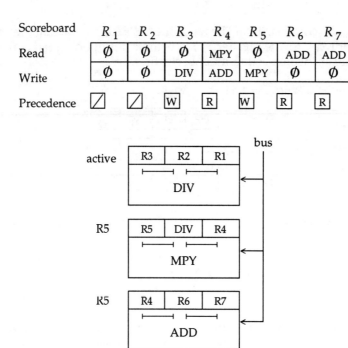

1. Issue I_1 to DIV
   [R1], [R2] → DIV
   Begin DIV

2. Issue I_2 to MPY (dependency) reservation station.
   TAG [DIV] (from R3) goes to MPY
   TAG [MPY] is placed in [R4] read scoreboard
   TAG [MPY] is placed in [R5] write scoreboard

3. Decode I_3 to ADD (dependency) reservation station.
   TAG [ADD] for [R6] read scoreboard
   TAG [ADD] for [R7] read scoreboard
   TAG [ADD] for [R4] write scoreboard

Figure 7.37   Example E-unit state after I_3 is decoded.

Initially, the DIV.F is issued to the divide unit, and the divide unit fetches the two source register values. Presumably, the divide takes a number of cycles for execution. In the cycle following the divide issue, the MPY.F is decoded and issued to the multiplier reservation station. The tag for R4 is placed in a reservation station for one source operand, while the divide unit tag is placed in the other operand identifier slot. When the divide unit completes, it will, with permission of the scoreboard, broadcast its result, and this result will be detected by both R3 and the multiplier reservation station. Since the multiplier gets its result directly from the divide unit, there is no need to put an "MPY" read tag in the R3 scoreboard. In the next cycle, the ADD.F is decoded and issued to the add reservation station. Since its source values are independent of other computations in process, the ADD.F can begin immediately; however, the scoreboard detects the ordering dependency mentioned earlier, based on R4, and the ADD.F will be delayed until after the R4 value is available to the multiplier unit. This insures that the ADD.F does not affect R4 before it is used by the multiplier. The scoreboard prevents the ADD.F from executing because of the MPY.F tag in the R4 read and the read (R) precedence scoreboard entry. When the MPY.F reads R4 (i.e., begins), its tag is removed (set to $\varnothing$) and the write (W) precedence is set. This causes the adder to be notified to begin operation. On the next cycle, it begins by reading R6 and R7, setting their scoreboard tags to empty ($\varnothing$). In the simple scoreboard shown, if the instructions following the ADD.F tried to read R4, it could not do so because of the pending write. In this case, the issuing stage "freezes," since there is no room in the scoreboard to enter another operation (at least, until the MPY.F read is complete).

A more complex scoreboard would schedule the ADD.F to begin a number of cycles earlier than the multiplier's use of R4. This early schedule corresponds to the delay in the adder itself.

Only one copy of the register value is kept, and that is in the register set. Since each unit must fetch its operands from a common register set and provide its results to the same register set, there is a possibility for contention. Multiple buses can be used to reduce the read-from-registers contention, and, since the results are broadcast to all units, contention for functional unit results must be arbitrated by a priority scheme to insure proper operation when multiple units compete for the same bus in the same cycle.

Dataflow

The dataflow approach is an alternative first suggested by Tomasulo [288]. Again, each register in the central register set is extended to include a tag that identifies the functional unit that produces a result to be placed in a particular register. Similarly, each of the multiple functional units has one or more reservation stations. The reservation station, however, can contain either a tag identifying another functional unit or register, *or it can contain the variable needed*. The centralized scoreboard is replaced with distributed control within the functional units. Each reservation station effectively defines its own functional unit; thus, two reservations for a floating point multiplier are two functional unit tags: multiplier 1 and multiplier 2 (Figure 7.38). If operands can go directly into the multiplier, then there is another tag: multiplier 3. Once a pair of operands have a designated functional unit tag, that tag remains with that operand pair until completion of

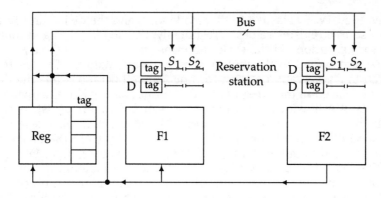

Figure 7.38 Dataflow. Each reservation station consists of registers to hold S_1 and S_2 values (if available), or tags to identify where the values come from.

the operation. Any unit (or register) that depends on that result has a copy of the functional unit tag and ingates the result that is broadcast on the bus. For the preceding example,

```
DIV.F   R3,  R1,  R2
MPY.F   R5,  R3,  R4
ADD.F   R4,  R6,  R7.
```

The DIV.F is initially issued to the divide unit with values from R1 and R2. (Assuming they are available, they are fetched from the common bus.) A *divide unit* tag is issued to R3, indicating that it does not currently contain a valid value. On the next cycle, the MPY.F is issued to the multiply unit, together with the value from R4 and a TAG [DIV] from R3. When the divide unit completes, it broadcasts its result; this is in-gated into the multiply unit reservation station, since it is holding a "divide unit" tag. In the meantime, the add unit has been issued values from R6 and R7 and commences addition. R4 gets the tag from the adder; no ordering dependency occurs, since the multiplier already has the old value of R4.

In the dataflow approach, the results to a targeted register may never actually go to that register; in fact, the computation based on the load of a particular register may be continually forwarded to various functional units, so that before the value is stored, a new value based upon a new computational sequence (a new load instruction) is able to use the targeted register. This approach partially avoids the use of a central register set, thereby avoiding the register ordering and output dependencies.

Whether the ordering and output dependencies are a serious problem or not is the subject of some debate [272]. With a larger register set, an optimizing compiler can distribute the usage of the registers across the set and avoid the register-resource dependencies. Of course, all schemes are left with the essential (type 1) dependency. Large register sets may have their own disadvantages, however, especially if save and restore traffic due to interrupts becomes a significant consideration.

Study 7.1   Control and Dataflow Timing

For the code sequence:

$$I_1 \quad \text{DIV.F} \quad \text{R3,} \quad \text{R1,} \quad \text{R2}$$
$$I_2 \quad \text{MPY.F} \quad \text{R5,} \quad \text{R3,} \quad \text{R4}$$
$$I_3 \quad \text{ADD.F} \quad \text{R4,} \quad \text{R6,} \quad \text{R7,}$$

assume three separate floating-point units with execution times:

Divide	8 cycles
Multiply	4 cycles
Add	3 cycles,

and show the timing for both control flow (scoreboard) and data flow.

For the scoreboard approach, we might have the following:

Cycle 1   Decoder issues $I_1 \rightarrow$ DIV unit
                               R1 $\rightarrow$ DIV unit
                               R2 $\rightarrow$ DIV unit
                               TAG_DIV $\rightarrow$ R3 write scoreboard
Cycle 2   Divide begins DIV.F
          Decoder $I_2 \rightarrow$ MPY unit
                               TAG_DIV (data not ready) $\rightarrow$ MPY unit
                               TAG_R4 (data ready) $\rightarrow$ MPY unit
                               TAG [MPY] $\rightarrow$ R4 read scoreboard
                               TAG_MPY $\rightarrow$ R5 write scoreboard
Cycle 3   Multiplier waits
          Decoder issues $I_3 \rightarrow$ ADD unit
                               TAG_R6 $\rightarrow$ ADD unit
                               TAG_R7 $\rightarrow$ ADD unit
                               TAG [ADD] $\rightarrow$ R6 read scoreboard
                               TAG [ADD] $\rightarrow$ R7 read scoreboard
                               TAG_ADD $\rightarrow$ R4 write scoreboard
Cycle 9   Data is ready, but scoreboard "holds" adder from execution.
          Divide completes in this cycle.
          Divide requests permission to broadcast result in next cycle (granted).
Cycle 10 Divide result $\rightarrow$ R3
          Divide result $\rightarrow$ MPY unit
          R4 $\rightarrow$ MPY unit
Cycle 11 Begin MPY.F
          Hold on adder removed (R4 is freed).
          R6 $\rightarrow$ ADD unit
          R7 $\rightarrow$ ADD unit
Cycle 12 Begin ADD.F
Cycle 14 MPY unit completes and requests data broadcast (granted).
          ADD unit completes and requests data broadcast (denied).
Cycle 15 MPY unit result $\rightarrow$ R5
          ADD unit requests data broadcast (granted).
Cycle 16 ADD unit result $\rightarrow$ R4 .

For the dataflow approach *with reservation stations that hold values*, we might have the following:

Cycle 1   Decoder issues I_1 → DIV unit
          R1 → DIV Res Stn
          R2 → DIV Res Stn
          TAG_DIV → R3
Cycle 2   Begin DIV.F
          Decoder issues I_2 → MPY unit
                         TAG_DIV → MPY unit
                         R4 → MPY Res Stn
                         TAG_MPY → R5
Cycle 3   Multiplier waits
          Decoder issues I_3 → ADD unit
                         R6 → ADD Res Stn
                         R7 → ADD Res Stn
                         TAG_ADD → R4
Cycle 4   Begin ADD.F
Cycle 6   ADD unit requests broadcast next cycle (granted).
          ADD unit completes this cycle.
Cycle 7   ADD unit result → R4
Cycle 9   DIV unit requests broadcast next cycle (granted).
          DIV unit completes this cycle.
Cycle 10 DIV unit → R3
          DIV unit → MPY unit
Cycle 11 Begin MPY.F
Cycle 14 Multiply completes and requests data broadcast (granted).
Cycle 15 MPY unit result → R5 .

In the preceding timings, the control details did not concern us; the timing difference arose from the use of *reservation stations that hold values* in the second implementation. This allowed the ADD.F instruction to proceed because the old value of R4 had already been transmitted to the multiplier.

While the savings of one cycle in this example may not appear very significant, the ADD.F instruction completed in cycle 7. Any instructions dependent on the ADD.F could then proceed—a speedup of more than twice for those instructions.

As far as implementation is concerned, the issue logic is now distributed in the reservation stations. If multiple instructions are to be issued in the same cycle, then there must be multiple separate buses to transmit the information: operation, tag/value #1, tag/value #2, and destination. With dataflow, we assume that the reservation stations are associated with the functional units. If we centralized the reservation stations for implementation convenience, the design would be generally similar to an improved control flow, or *scoreboard*, described in the next section.

Action Summary

We can summarize the basic rules for any processor (dataflow or improved scoreboard, discussed next) that has reservation stations that hold *values*:

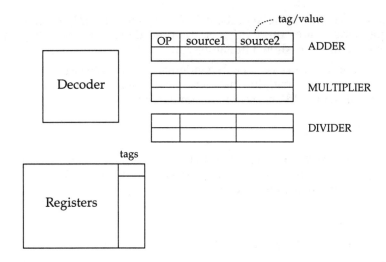

Figure 7.39   Improved control flow.

1. Decoder issues instruction to proper functional unit reservation station with values if available otherwise with register tag.

2. Destination register (specified by instruction) gets functional unit tag. A register tag can be overwritten in dataflow, but not in control flow (see following).

3. Continue issue until a type of reservation station is FULL. Unissued instructions are held PENDING.

4. By the basic sequencing mechanism (dataflow or otherwise), issued instructions observe essential dependencies (at least).

5. But any instruction that depends on an unissued or pending instruction (in any way: essential, ordinary, etc.) must also be held in a pending state.

7.6.6   An Improved Scoreboard

We can summarize the above by describing an improved scoreboard using value-holding reservation stations. Each register has a tag indicating the functional unit upon which it depends for a result. Each functional unit has one or more reservation stations (Figure 7.39). Each reservation station contains information about a pending instruction. If an instruction's source registers have valid data, then the instruction is issued to the functional unit (if it is available). In any event, the functional unit's tag is placed in the destination register. No entry need be made to the reservation station except to note when the functional unit is busy.

Since values are stored in reservation stations, no ordering or output dependency can occur with instructions that were previously issued. Output dependencies (if recognized) are detected by the presence of a tag at the destination register. The scoreboard is simplified as only (write) essential dependencies are entered. Thus, the precedence control and the read scoreboard entries as shown in Figure 7.37 are eliminated.

If an instruction has an essential dependency and accesses a source register with a functional unit tag, this instruction is placed in a reservation station together with any valid source value. For example, for

ADD.F R_1, R_2, R_3,

suppose R_2 depends on (has a tag for) the multiplier functional unit and R_3 has valid data. This instruction is then issued to the adder reservation station. After the instruction is issued:

- R_1 has ADD tag.

- R_2 is unaffected (still has MPY tag).

- R_3 is unaffected.

The adder reservation station has

$$\begin{aligned} \text{OP} &= \text{ADD.F} \\ \text{Source 1} &= \text{Tag of multiplier} \\ \text{Source 2} &= \text{Value from } R_3. \end{aligned}$$

When the multiplier has a result, it broadcasts it to the scoreboard (which is updated), the register set, and the adder reservation station. The reservation station activates the adder to ingate the multiplier result and begin the addition in the next cycle.

There are some notable items here:

1. The reservation stations and their control can be distributed to the functional units or centralized (say) with the decoder.

2. The copying of values into the reservation stations eliminates the need to check for ordering dependencies.

3. The tag associated with a register can be overwritten in dataflow, not in control flow.

4. The "improved" scheme is *not* equivalent to the dataflow approach, since all results still must go to their designated destination register, e.g.:

    MPY.F   R1, R2, R3
    ST.F   ALPHA, R1
    LD.F   R1, BETA.

In our improved scheme, the LD.F cannot execute until after the ST.F, since the result of the multiply must actually go through R1 to the store buffer.

In dataflow, the multiplier tag is passed to the store buffer unit when the ST.F instruction is issued. Now LD.F is free to proceed and is independent of the earlier instructions.

The difference between dataflow and improved scoreboard can be seen by some examples. Consider the following code sequences.

EXAMPLE 7.5

```
MPY.F  R1, R2, R3
ADD.F  R1, R6, R7
```

There is an output dependency. The dataflow approach will issue the ADD.F instruction, overwriting the tag for R1 so that the R1 tag will be ADD at the end of the second cycle. The result of the MPY.F will be broadcast, but will not be ingated by any unit.

The improved scoreboard will not issue the ADD.F until the MPY.F has entered R1 (and removed the MPY tag from R1).   ◆

EXAMPLE 7.6

```
MPY.F  R1, R2, R3
ADD.F  R4, R1, R6
DIV.F  R1, R9, R10
```

This is a similar example to 7.5, except that there is an essential dependency between the MPY.F and ADD.F using R1.

Both dataflow and improved scoreboard hardware will issue the ADD.F, placing the multiplier unit tag in R1 and the adder reservation station tag in R4. The adder reservation station holds a tag for the multiplier unit.

The DIV.F is issued in dataflow. The divider unit tag overwrites the multiplier tag in R1. The DIV.F is not issued in the improved scoreboard until the multiply is complete.   ◆

EXAMPLE 7.7

```
ADD.F  R1, R2, R3
ADD.F  R4, R5, R6
```

In this case, both strategies behave similarly. The first ADD.F is issued to the adder unit, the second to the adder reservation station. In both cases, there are separate identifiers for the adder unit and its reservation station, so that R1 will ingate the result of the adder unit and R4 will ingate the result of the adder reservation station after it completes the addition. Note that the tag for the reservation station remains with the operation even after it enters the adder unit.   ◆

It would seem that significant concurrency is lost by the improved scoreboard relative to dataflow. This may or may not be the case in practice. The real problem for the improved scoreboard is a lack of registers. With additional registers, each of the preceding differences can be overcome.

Techniques such as register renaming (to be discussed shortly) can provide these additional registers, largely eliminating the performance difference between the approaches.

Table 7.6 Tag id's in a dataflow.

Functional unit	TAG id
Register	R1
(R1–R32)	R2
Adder reservation station	ADD-1
Adder unit	ADD-0
Multiplier reservation station	MPY-1
Multiplier unit	MPY-0
First LD/ST	
LD/ST reservation station	LS-1
LD/ST unit	LS-0
Second LD/ST	
LD/ST reservation station	LS-3
LD/ST unit	LS-2

Study 7.2 Multiple-Issue Dataflow Machine

We are given a superscalar machine that can issue four instructions per cycle. The machine uses a dataflow approach to dependency control. A tag is associated with each register, functional unit, and each reservation station for a functional unit. We indicate these tags as, for example, TAG[R1], TAG[ADD-0], TAG[ADD-1] for the R1 tag, the adder tag, and the reservation station for the adder. There are four functional units. Each has a single-level reservation station, and each takes three cycles to complete execution. The tag ids and functional units are shown in Table 7.6.

Given the following code:

```
ADD   R1, R2, R3
ADD   R3, R4, R1
ST    ALPHA, R3
MPY   R6, R2, R3
ADD   R7, R2, R9
MPY   R1, R7, R8
LD    R3, BETA
LD    R4, GAMMA
```

show the values or the tags in the affected registers, reservation stations, and functional units.

1. We show the state of the registers after the first cycle (the first four instructions are compared and issued). V[Ri] indicates the value contained in Ri.

Table 7.7 Actions in a multiple-issue dataflow.

	After Cycle 1	After Cycle 2
Register	R6 has TAG [MPY−1]	Same
	R3 has TAG [ADD−1]	R3 has TAG [LS−3]
	R1 has TAG [ADD−0]	Same
		R4 has TAG [LS−2]
Adder RS	TAG [ADD−0], V [R4]	
Adder unit	V [R2], V [R3]	
Multiplier RS	V [R2], TAG [ADD−1]	
1st LD/ST RS	ADDR [ALPHA], TAG [ADD−1]	
2nd LD/ST unit		ADDR [GAMMA],
2nd LD/ST RS		ADDR [BETA],

The following registers now hold tags:

        R6 ← TAG [MPY − 1]
        R3 ← TAG [ADD − 1]
        R1 ← TAG [ADD − 0].

The adder has its operands (V[R2], V[R3]), and the adder reservation station has

    TAG[ADD − 0], V[R4].

Note that the adder unit *cannot* have operand tags, only values.

The first LD/ST reservation station has

    ADDR[ALPHA], TAG[ADD − 1].

The multiplier reservation station has

    V[R2], TAG[ADD − 1].

2. Now we present the state of the register after the second cycle. The next four instructions are compared in Table 7.7.

   The following two instructions remain unissued after the second cycle:

       ADD R7, R2, R9
       MPY R1, R7, R8.

   The ADD instruction cannot issue because the add unit and its reservation station are occupied. The MPY instruction cannot issue because it depends on the unissued ADD.

Study 7.3   Multiple-Issue Superscalar Machines Compared

Here we contrast the *decode issue* process (finding independent instructions) with the *scheduling* process.

A certain superscalar processor can inspect four instructions and issue three each cycle. Suppose we have current machine state as follows: each unit (ADD, MPY, and DIV) has one reservation station.

> R1 has MPY tag MPY-0 (unit).
>
> R3 has ADD tag ADD-0 (unit).
>
> R4 has ADD tag ADD-1 (unit).

That is, two ADDs and one MPY were previously issued. Assume that no state change occurs during the next (issue) cycle. The next four instructions are:

*	MPY	R1, R6, R7.
* + 1	ADD	R7, R8, R9.
* + 2	DIV	R8, R10, R3.
* + 3	MPY	R2, R11, R12.

(a) For dataflow, what is the state of the machine (which tags are associated with which registers) after these instructions are inspected? Which instructions are issued? Which instructions are held?

For a dataflow machine, the MPY R1, R6, R7 will be issued to the multiplier reservation station. Its TAG [MPY-1] will overwrite the tag for R1. the * + 1 instruction (the ADD) is held (not issued), since there is no unit or reservation station to accommodate it. The * + 2 instruction (the DIV) is an interesting case. It cannot be issued, and hence is held, because of an ordering dependency for R8. In dataflow, once an instruction is issued the scheduling stage ignores ordering dependencies, but they cannot be ignored at the issue stage. Suppose * + 2 were issued; then if * + 1 were seriously delayed, * + 2 would overwrite R8 before * + 1 had a chance to use it—i.e., get the old value in R8.

The * + 3 instruction (MPY) is now also held, since there is no available reservation station.

In summary,

- Only * (MPY R1,R6,R7) is issued.
- It causes the R1 tag to be replaced with TAG [MPY-1]; other tags are unchanged.
- The remaining three instructions are held in the issue stage. Only one new instruction will be inspected (together with the three instructions that are held). This new instruction (* + 4) will be at the bottom of the inspection list.

(b) Repeat for an improved scoreboard. What is the state of the machine (which tags are associated with which registers) after these instructions are inspected? Which instructions are issued? Which instructions are held?

For a control flow machine (improved scoreboard), the situation is somewhat different. Now *[MPY R1,R6,R7] cannot be issued, as the R1 tag cannot be overwritten. Only after the result of the multiply [MPY-0] is placed in R1 will the R1 tag be reset, enabling * to be issued. For instruction * + 1 [ADD] and * + 2 [DIV], the situation is exactly the same as with dataflow. Both instructions are held at the issue stage, but now * + 3 [MPY] can be issued (unlike dataflow), since the multiplier reservation station is available.

In summary,

- Only * + 3 MPY R2,R11,R12 is issued.

- It causes the R2 tag to be [MPY-1]; the other tags are unchanged.

- The first three (*, * + 1, * + 2) instructions are held in the issue stage.

Renaming and Shadow Effects

Using multiple value-holding reservation stations and labeling them separately allows the decoder to distinguish among the users of a resource. Consider the following example:

I_1	ADD	R1,	R7,	R8
I_2	MPY	R3,	R1,	R2
I_3	MPY	R6,	R4,	R5
I_4	ST	ALPHA,	R6.	

Assume a multiplier with two (sets of) value-holding reservation stations, MPY1 and MPY2. The decoder issues I_2 and I_3 on successive cycles to reservation stations MPY1 and MPY2, respectively. Since MPY1 has a tag for a value from the ADD (the R1 value), it cannot proceed, but MPY2 begins execution when I_3 is issued, because the multiplier and the operands are available. When I_4 is issued, R6 gets the TAG_MPY2, which is forwarded to the store buffer.

In the preceding example, the results of the two multiplies are distinguished by their unique tags; thus, the functional units that use the result of multiply 2 are distinguished from those using multiply 1, regardless of the order in which these multiplies are actually executed.

An analogous arrangement can be achieved by using shadow registers. Shadow registers are duplicate registers or sets of registers that allow the decoder to "rename" a sequence of code with new register values. Thus, suppose we have code in this sequence:

I_1	LD	R1,		ALPHA
I_2	MPY	R1,	R2,	R3
I_3	ST	BETA,		R1
I_4	LD	R1,		GAMMA
I_5	ADD	R4,	R1,	R5.

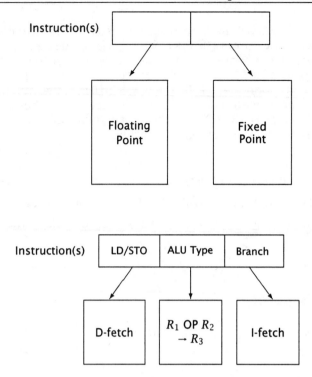

Figure 7.40   Multiple issuing schemes.

Instruction 4 depends upon instruction 3 only insofar as it uses R1. By assigning R1 in I_3 to a shadow register (or a second register set), we avoid the dependency. If there are sufficiently large register sets, there is little need for shadow registers, since the compiler can reduce the conflicting use of registers as shown in the preceding example. Similarly, the hardware can accomplish the same thing by using registers that are not visible to the instruction set; for example, if the instruction set had eight registers specified in the preceding example, the decoder could simply relabel the second use of register 1 as register 9.

Thus, shadow registers, extended register sets as used by the compiler, and reservation stations are alternate approaches for achieving a generally equivalent effect—eliminating ordering and output dependencies.

The Cost of Simultaneously Issuing Multiple Instructions—Simple Approaches

The simplest type of multiple-issuing scheme is a *partitioned* or *fragmentary occurrence* (Figure 7.40). In this type of scheme, concurrent execution occurs only if certain types of pairs or triples of instructions occur in a sequence:

1. **Fixed-Point/Floating-Point** — Here, any fixed-point instruction (i.e., one based upon the general-purpose registers) may be simultaneously executed with any instruction that is based only on the floating-point

registers. Clearly, there is no dependency between the two instructions, and therefore dependency analysis is avoided. Sequences such as:

```
ADD     R1,   R2,   R3
ADD.F   R1,   R3,   R4
```

can be handled easily, since the register sets and functional units involved are different. Of course, `convert instruction` (e.g., convert to floating-point), which uses both register sets, must be recognized as exceptional.

2. **Load/ALU/Branch** — Another type of concurrency can be achieved by allowing the issuance of a load or a store instruction simultaneously with a functional instruction, and/or perhaps even a branch instruction. A branch tests the results of a previous instruction, the ALU instruction (register-based) modifies the current register set state, and the load instruction prepares the register set for the next instruction. This type of concurrency is more common in highly microprogrammed machines, but has been useful in modern machine design [57]. It ensures the more regular use of resources. Note that with the floating/fixed-point operation, the two instructions may contend for memory resources, which is less likely to happen with the second type of partition concurrency.

3. **Composite Instructions** — Special instructions can be added to a processor repertoire to increase performance. A classic example is the combined `floating multiply` instruction, whose product is accumulated (added to) the content of a designated register. The accumulator add can be performed while the final product is being computed, reducing the add time. The occurrence of `MAD.F` opportunities seems high enough in certain benchmarks to consider its adoption for marketing purposes, if no other.

The Cost of Simultaneously Issuing Multiple Instructions—General Approaches

For more robust and generalized issue of multiple instructions, the equivalent of a dependency matrix is required. For control flow, this is accomplished by extending the interlock logic of study 4.9. Now each instruction in the issue window must compare its sources to the destinations of instructions that occur earlier in instruction sequence in the window *and* to the destinations of previously issued but uncompleted instructions.

Assume that we compare N instructions each cycle. In order to check for essential dependencies, each source operand specifier has to be compared with the destination of all instructions that occur earlier in the sequence in the window:

$$
\begin{array}{llll}
\text{Most recent} & 1 & D & S_1 \quad S_2 \\
& 2 & D \\
\vdots \quad & 3 & D \\
& \vdots & \vdots \\
\text{Least recent} & N & D
\end{array}
$$

There are a maximum of $N - 1$ compares per source operand. For the two source operands, we require:

$$2\,[1 + 2 + 3 + \cdots + (N - 1)]\quad \text{compares}$$

or

$$\text{Essential compares} = \frac{2(N - 1)N}{2}.$$

To evaluate ordering dependencies, we must compare the destination specifier with each pair of higher-precedence source instruction specifiers. Again, the maximum number of compares is $2 \times (N - 1)$, and the total is the same as before:

$$\text{Ordering compares} = (N - 1)N.$$

Suppose we ignore output dependencies, assuming they are detected at compile time. Thus, we have:

$$\text{Total compares} = 2(N - 1)N.$$

In addition to the preceding, there may be other instructions previously issued but incomplete. Here, we can use a scoreboard to reduce the comparison costs. Before each independent instruction is issued, its register scoreboard is checked. Issue is completed only if there are no conflicts. The scoreboard is updated when instructions are issued and when results are stored.

Dataflow control poses a different set of problems. All instructions in the instruction window can be issued if sufficient resources are available, but those with essential dependencies are issued to reservation stations. Thus, the basic limitations are on the number of buses, register ports, and reservation stations. The same amount of comparison hardware (essential dependencies) as with control flow is required so that tags can be properly determined.

For example:

```
ADD   R3,    R1,    R2
ADD   R4,    R3,    R2
MPY   R5,    R4,    R2
ST    ALPHA  R3
ST    BETA   R4
ST    GAMMA  R5
LD    R3,    DELTA
LD    R4,    EPSILON
```

might be configured as follows, after tags have been forwarded. The ∅ entry indicates that the destination tag has been forwarded to another unit:

```
ADD1      ∅        R1,     R2
ADD2      ∅        ADD1,   R2
MPY1      ∅        ADD2,   R2
ST-SB1    ALPHA,   ADD1
ST-SB2    BETA,    ADD2
ST-SB3    GAMMA,   MPY1
LD        R3,      DELTA
LD        R4,      EPSILON .
```

The ADD1, ADD2 refer either to independent adders or to a value-holding reservation station for the same adder. Similarly, three store buffers are assumed (SB1, SB2, SB3). The two LD instructions define new values for R3 and R4; it is their values, not the results of the two ADD instructions, that must take precedence.

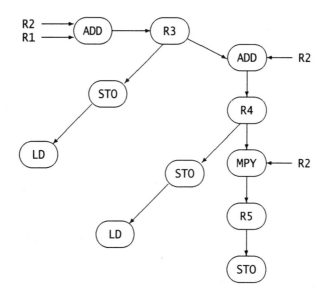

Figure 7.41   Original graph.

We compare the example program original graph (Figure 7.41), the dataflow graph (Figure 7.42), and the control flow graph with renaming (Figure 7.43). The latter two are quite close in their dependency graphs.

The complexity of the translation to dataflow graph form can be substantial, especially if performed at decode time. Each instruction may require a modification (or link) to any preceding instruction in the window (the second ST instruction links SB2 to ADD2, which is linked to ADD1).

The restructuring of code to create these dataflow graphs or (indeed) the renamed control flow sequences is best performed much earlier than at decode time. Compile time would be best, although a predecode translation (perhaps when code enters an I-cache) could also be considered.

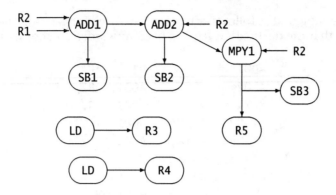

Figure 7.42   Dataflow graph.

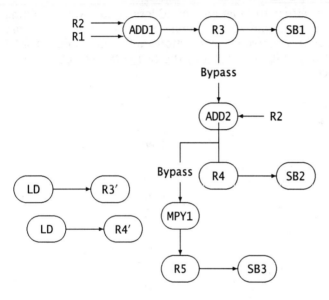

Figure 7.43   Control flow graph with renaming of R3 and R4.

7.6.7   Dealing with Out-of-Order Execution

Out-of-order execution, especially when coupled with out-of-order instruction issue and multiple instruction issue, leads to an apparently chaotic machine state, even when the code is correctly executing. If an interrupt arises or some sort of an exception is taken (perhaps even a misguessed branch outcome), there can be a general ambiguity as to the exact source of the exception or how the machine state should be saved and restored for further instruction processing. There are two basic approaches to solving this problem:

1. Live with it. This applies only to interrupts and involves the use of a device called an *imprecise interrupt*, which simply indicates that an exception has occurred someplace in some region of code without trying to isolate it further. This simple approach may be satisfactory

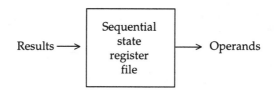

Figure 7.44   Simple register file organization.

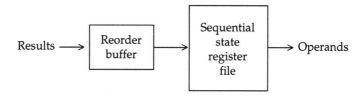

Figure 7.45   Centralized reorder buffer method.

for programs oriented toward the processing of large scientific code, but is generally unacceptable for other high-speed applications with significant interrupt frequency.

There is an important caveat here: A load instruction that accesses a page not currently in memory can have disastrous consequences if several instructions that followed it are already in execution. When control returns to the process after the missing page is loaded, the load can execute together with instructions that depended upon it, but other instructions that were previously executed should not be reexecuted. The control for all this can be formidable. The only acceptable alternative would be to require that all pages used by a particular process be resident in memory before execution begins. In programming environments where this is feasible and practical—such as in large scientific applications—this may be a solution.

2. Create an actual or a virtual putaway that preserves the ordered use of the register set or at least allows the reconstruction of such an ordered register set.

It is the second approach that we look at in this section, following the work of Smith [265].

In order to provide a sequential model of program execution, some mechanism must be provided that properly manages the register file state. The key to any successful scheme [260, 149] is the efficient management of the register set and its state. If instructions execute in order, as in most pipelined machines discussed in the earlier part of this chapter, then a simple register file can be used (Figure 7.44). Instructions that can complete early must be held pending the completion of previously issued but incomplete instructions. This sacrifices concurrency and performance.

Suppose we allow instructions to execute out of order and provide a *reorder buffer* (Figure 7.45). The results arrive at the reorder buffer out of program sequence, but they are put away to the sequential register file in program order, thus preserving the register file state. In order to avoid conflicts at the reorder buffer, we can distribute the buffer across the various

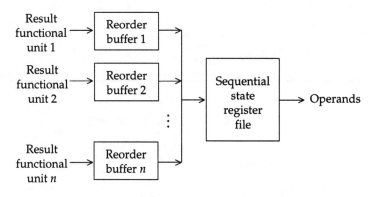

Figure 7.46   Distributed reorder buffer method.

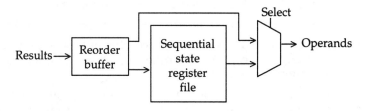

Figure 7.47   Centralized reorder buffer method with forwarding.

functional units as shown in Figure 7.46. Either of these techniques allows out-of-order instruction execution, but preserves in-order putaway to the register set.

Using the reorder buffer just described allows instructions to complete out of order, but the results are not available to the following instructions in other than program order; thus, instructions that depend upon a result must wait until all previous instructions are put away. This technique significantly reduces any advantage that the reorder buffer might have had in allowing out-of-order execution. One technique to eliminate this problem is to provide forwarding—bypassing the register file from the reorder buffer. (See Figures 7.47 and 7.48.) This allows values held in the reorder buffer (awaiting storage in the register file) to forward their contents to another functional unit while awaiting proper sequential putaway. The functional units and the reorder buffers execute instructions and put away results out of order, while the reorder buffer manages the correct in-order placement of results in the register set.

To get a sense of the level of complexity involved, consider the implementation of a 12-entry reorder buffer for a processor with a 2-instruction decoder with 32 general-purpose registers. Each reorder buffer must have the same access bandwidth as the register set (2 instr × 2 operands/instr for reads, plus 2 writes each cycle).

- Each reorder buffer requires four Read ports: two for each source operand (12 × 4 = 48 Read ports).

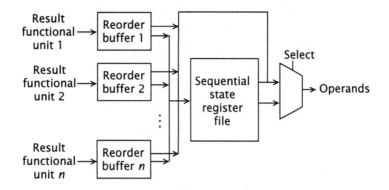

Figure 7.48   Distributed reorder buffer method with forwarding.

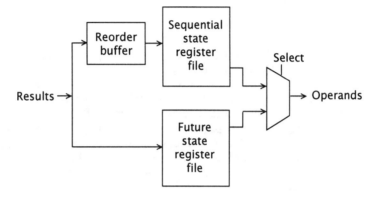

Figure 7.49   Reorder buffer method with future file.

- Each source operand requires two 5-bit comparators for its associative needs ($12 \times 4 = 48$ 5-bit comparators).

- Each writable entry requires two Write ports (24 Write ports).

- Each entry tag has to be compared to the result buses, with two buses assumed (24 4-bit comparators).

Altogether, this makes for a quite complex implementation.

To simplify the management of the reorder buffer, another technique can be used that adds a *future register file* to the reorder buffer method (Figure 7.49). This technique places functional unit results directly in the future register file. These results are available from the future file for dependent instructions. Upon receiving an exception, certain entries (those results beyond the point of the interrupt) in the future file may be invalidated, but the correct sequential register state is always available in the register file.

The cost of duplicating the register file, as in the future file method, may be too expensive for very large register sets, so a *history buffer* can be used (Figure 7.50). The history buffer contains only previously determined results overwritten by instructions whose predecessors have not completed. If an exception occurs, the appropriate values are restored into the future file. This restores the future file state to that of the sequential register

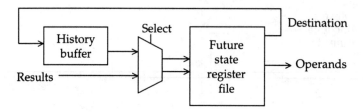

Figure 7.50   History buffer method.

set. Of course, since the restoration of the future file state to include the history file information may be somewhat time-consuming, the history file technique adds an overhead to exception handling.

7.6.8   Interleaved Caches

In order to handle multiple load/stores, adequate cache bandwidth must be available. This is especially true for the data cache. For instruction caches, bandwidth can be achieved by simply lengthening the access path, since instructions are accessed in-line and a wide instruction path generally provides adequate bandwidth. The effectiveness of such a wide access depends on the frequency and placement of branch instructions, as well as the relative frequency of taken branches. As in the rest of superscalar organization, compiler technology plays a key role in the achievement of efficient code execution, as can readily be seen in the effectiveness of a relatively large I-fetch.

Data caches generally require interleaved caches to provide adequate bandwidth since the number of accesses per cycle is generally relatively low, even to support high issue rates. It ought to be possible to support these issue rates with reasonable degrees of interleaving. In chapter 6, we saw that two load/store units were relatively conflict-free (only about 3% interference) with 8-way interleaving.

In principle, it ought to be possible to combine the bypassing techniques used with vector processors mentioned earlier in this chapter with the interleaving techniques described previously and in chapter 6. The bypassing of requests represents another way to avoid conflicts in data caches. If requests are bypassed, we can determine their effectiveness by combining the delta-binomial and gamma-binomial equations developed earlier into a generalized model of processor memory performance called the *gamma-delta* (γ, δ) *binomial model*:

$$B(m, n, \delta, \gamma)$$
$$= \ m + n(1 + \gamma) - \delta/2 - \sqrt{(m + n(1 + \gamma) - \delta/2)^2 - 2mn(1 + \gamma)}.$$

Following the discussion of chapter 6,

$$\delta = \frac{n}{z},$$

where z is the number of requestor sources that can occur in a processor cycle times the number of processor cycles per cache cycle.

By the same type of argument that we used earlier in this chapter, we can determine the optimal bypass factor (y_{opt}) as:

$$y_{opt} = \frac{n - \delta}{2m - 2n}.$$

Since n is generally small, in principle, even a rather small bypass buffer ought to provide effective conflict-free referencing of data caches. It should be emphasized, however, that conflict-free does not necessarily mean *dependence*-free; thus, even in situations where the cache can provide all the required bandwidth for the processor, delays in the accessing path may create dependencies that necessarily affect processor performance. These dependencies are not predicted or measured by our models.

The n requests may consist of buffered and unbuffered sources, as with buffered writes and unbuffered reads. In this case,

$$n = n_r + n_w,$$

that is, n consists of n_r read requests and n_w write requests per memory service time. So long as δ is small (at least with respect to either n components), we can treat the write buffer as linearly separate from the overall problem of optimal buffering. That is, we can find

$$y_{opt}^w = \frac{n_w - \delta_w}{2m - 2n_w},$$

where δ_w is n_w/write sources.

Then we can use this y_{opt}^w in our bandwidth estimate $B(m, n, y_{opt}^w, \delta)$. This assumes that the writes are perfectly buffered—no dependencies arise.

EXAMPLE 7.8

Suppose we have a superscalar processor with 4-way interleaved data cache. The processor has four LD/ST units, and each makes 0.3 reads per cycle and 0.2 writes per cycle. The cache has a unit cycle time. The writes are fully buffered; the reads are not. Find the expected performance.

Given

$$
\begin{aligned}
m &= 4 \\
n_r &= 4 \times 0.3 = 1.2 \\
n_w &= 4 \times 0.2 = 0.8 \\
n &= 1.2 + .8 = 2.0 \\
\delta &= \frac{n}{z}; \quad z = 4 \times 2 = 8 \qquad \text{(4 sources in each of 2 cycles)} \\
\delta &= \frac{2}{8} = 0.25 \\
\delta_w &= \frac{n_w}{\text{write sources}} = \frac{.8}{4} = .2 \\
y_{opt}^w &= \frac{n_w - \delta_w}{2m - 2n_w} \\
&= \frac{.8 - .2}{8 - 1.6} = 0.94.
\end{aligned}
$$

since there are 4 LD/ST units, each capable of issuing a LD and a buffered ST. So,

(a)

$$B(m, n, \gamma_{\text{opt}}^w, \delta) \quad = \quad B(4, 2, 0.94, .25)$$
$$= \quad 1.67.$$

The relative performance is

$$P_{\text{rel}} \quad = \quad \frac{B}{n} = \frac{1.67}{2.0} = 0.84.$$

(b) If we had no write buffer, we would have

$$B(4, 2, 0, 0.25) = 1.57,$$

and the relative performance would be

$$\frac{B}{n} = \frac{1.57}{2} = 0.78.$$

$\blacklozenge$

7.6.9   Branches and Speculative Execution

So far in our discussion, we have assumed that the instructions being tested for independence are non-branch instructions. The scope of the test for in-struction independence has been a branch subset or a basic block. If we restrict the scope of the search for instruction independence to instruc-tions that lie between conditional branches, we naturally limit the possible speedup. If branch frequency is 20% and we limit the scope of detection to branch subsets, then our maximum possible speedup is clearly less than 5.

In order to improve processor speedup, we may:

1. Minimize the frequency of branches, or

2. Predict the outcome of a branch and speculatively execute a predicted path.

Ideally, we would do both. In order to reduce the frequency of branch, we can use loop-unrolling techniques, which simply replicate multiple itera-tions of the same loop in line, eliminating the intervening branches. As this increases code size, however, it may have undesirable side effects. Trace scheduling, which was mentioned earlier in this chapter, is another tech-nique targeted at reducing the occurrence of branches.

Suppose that, using the techniques of chapter 4 (history bits, branch target buffers, etc.), we can be assured of a relatively high hit rate, say, greater than 90%. We might then choose to predict the outcome of a branch and conditionally or speculatively execute the chosen path. Of course, such speculative execution must be done in such a way that the results of specu-latively executed instructions cannot affect the final register state until the outcome of the conditional branch has been determined. Speculative exe-cution necessarily increases the required instruction bandwidth by at least an amount equal to the expected incorrect guess rate. As prediction rates may vary from environment to environment, it is useful to make speculative execution controllable by the programmer.

As we will see in the next section, speculative execution can provide significant additional program speedup, but the designer must be fully aware of the additional cost and complexity it introduces into the processor.

7.6.10   Adaptive Speculation

Since correct prediction in speculative execution is essential for performance, there have been a number of studies into improved branch predictions. As we saw in chapter 4, dynamic branch prediction, even through the use of history bits or branch table buffers or a combination of the two, is generally limited to prediction rates around 90% across multiple environments. Yeh and Patt [314, 315] and others have looked at adaptive branch prediction as a method of raising prediction rates to 95%. The basic method consists of associating a shift register with each branch in, for example, a branch table buffer. The shift register records branch history. A branch twice taken and twice not taken, for example, would be recorded as "1100." Each pattern acts as an address into an array of counters, such as the 2-bit saturating counters discussed in chapter 4. Each time the pattern 1100 was encountered, the outcome was recorded in the saturating counter. If the branch was taken, the counter was incremented; if the branch was not taken, it was decremented.

Adaptive techniques can require a good deal of support hardware. Not only must we have history bits associated with the possible branch entries, but we must have a table of counters to store outcomes. The larger the program, the more effective the large shift registers are. For small programs, it is unlikely that more than 12 history bits (i.e., an array of $2^{12} = 4096$ counters) offers any performance improvement. A number of large programs were run following the work of Yeh and Patt [315]. For these programs, the best that could be achieved for static branch prediction was 87.7%. This is termed *optimum static branch prediction* and is achievable only when a program is run multiple times. In this strategy, the dominant branch outcome (i.e., the complete history) is determined for each branch, and a "best guess" is determined. This can be biased (see chapter 4) by the unequal in-line and target branch penalties. Some results are shown in Figure 7.51.

An advanced adaptive strategy such as a 12-bit shift register (history bits, as shown in Figure 7.51) improves prediction rate to about 92%. The 2-bit saturating counter discussed in chapter 4 achieves 89.3% averaged over all programs. This corresponds to a history count of $n = 4$ in Table 4.11. While the data in Figure 7.51 is based on a different set of programs than those presented in Table 4.11, the results are generally consistent—equally weighting compiler, scientific, and supervisor codes predicts an expected hit rate of 90% ($n = 4$).

The adaptive results are shown in two curves. The upper curve is the prediction rate averaged over all programs. The lowest curve is the prediction rate achieved by the program with the poorest prediction rate. Differences between 86% and 92% may not seem significant, but if the delay in processor execution is represented primarily by miscast branches, the difference is

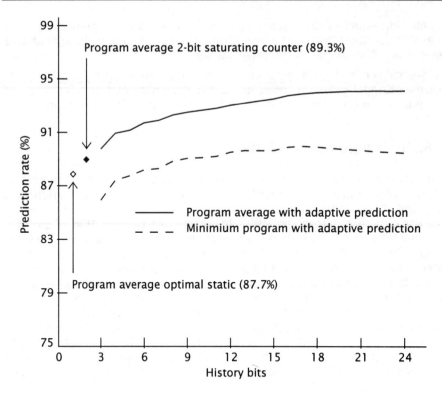

Figure 7.51   Branch prediction rates.

significant. It is the difference between 8% misses and 14% misses—almost a 2:1 difference in overall performance.

7.6.11   Results

There is a wide body of literature spanning many approaches to multiple instruction or concurrent instruction execution and concurrent instruction issue. Results of these studies can sometimes be confusing, since the premises can be quite different. Table 7.8 illustrates some of the better-known approaches reported in the literature, together with the reported speedup over a pipelined machine with in-order execution. The reported speedups may not be comparable, since the reference machine may be either idealized or realizable. The basic distinguishing characteristic of the studies is the scope over which the instruction dependency algorithm is applied. Studies that restrict the scope of detection to basic blocks—code between branches—clearly do poorer than more complex algorithms that apply beyond basic blocks or to multiple basic blocks.

Most studies cited issue or dispatch instructions out of order; that is, they examine N and issue M. Several of the earlier studies, however, issued only one, which of course was issued in order ($N = 1$, $M = 1$). Almost all of the studies allow out-of-order execution as discussed earlier. Scheduling strategy indicates whether a dataflow or a control flow approach is used, or whether scheduling is done statically—at compile time—and if done then,

Table 7.8   Comparison table (from Dubey [78]).

Reference Strategy	Branch Scope	Scheduling	Reported Speedup
Tomasulo [288]	within	dataflow	n/a
Thornton [281]	within	control flow	n/a
Tjaden/Flynn [283]	within	control flow	1.86
		static-stream	
Riseman/Foster [246]	unlimited	control flow	51.2
Tjaden [282]	within	control flow	1.96
Kuck [174]	1	sequential	8
Wedig [302]	1	control flow	3
Weiss/Smith [303]	within	dataflow	1.58
Nicolau/Fisher [218]	unlimited	sequential	90
		trace sched.	
HPSm [227]	> 1	dataflow	n/a
Uht [292]	1	control flow	2
Hsu/Davidson [134]	1	sequential	1.3–3.9
		decision tree	
Acosta et al. [2]	within	control flow	2.79
Sohi/Vajapeyam [267]	within	dataflow	1.8
iWARP [176]	> 1	sequential	3
		software pipe.	
CYDRA [242]	> 1	dataflow	n/a
Smith et al. [266]			
ideal fetch unit	1	control flow	2.3–4.1
nonideal fetch unit	1	control flow	1.9–2.3
Johnson [149]	1	control flow	2

Note: unless otherwise indicated, all control flow strategies are based on dynamic instruction stream. Branch scope refers to the limits that branch instructions place on instruction independence detection: "within" means that the scope cannot go beyond a conditional branch. The indicator "1" means that the hardware can detect independence beyond a single conditional branch, but not beyond two branches. In some cases, this was simply inferred by other processor limitations. "Unlimited" refers to analyses that assume a perfect prediction (an oracle) of the outcome of branches, or unlimited ability to proceed down all paths during execution.

Speedups given without a range are best-case speedups. Reported speedups should be taken with caution, as they are not relative to the same baseline processor.

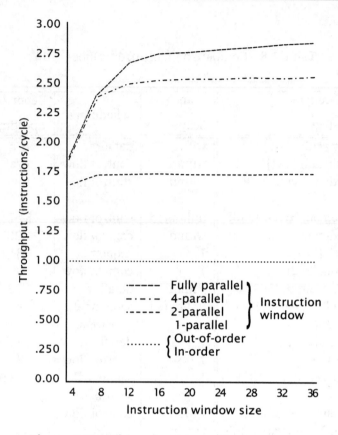

Figure 7.52   Throughput in an ideal processor.

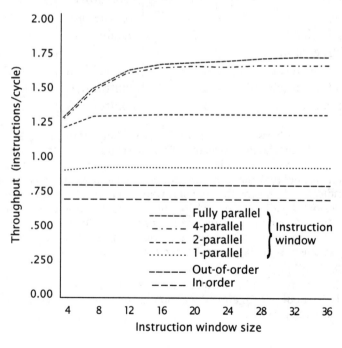

Figure 7.53   Throughput vs. DS size—duplexed execution units.

what technique is used. Looking at the reported speedups and excluding two studies that place no reasonable limits on hardware, there seems to be generally good agreement on the potential for multiple instruction issue in the range of 1.5–3.

Acosta's results [2] are useful for our evaluation, since he uses multiple execution unit models and compares several different approaches to speedup. Figure 7.52 shows the parallelism that is realizable for various control/dispatch strategies for an ideal processor. The ideal processor executes all operations in one cycle and is not limited in any way by branches. In the Acosta model, all parallelism detected is within basic blocks. Several processor combinations are studied; Figure 7.53 shows the speedup attainable for an ideal processor for varying amounts of instruction dispatch (instruction window size). The system is limited to about 2.75 instructions per issuing cycle when between 12 and 16 instructions are inspected (window size of 12–16). Any advantage beyond this is minimal. When a more realistic processor model is created (non unit time execution), various processor control strategies can be studied (Figure 7.53). In this processor model, there are two fixed-point adders, two fixed-point multipliers, two floating-point adders, and two floating-point multipliers. The fixed-point operations execute in one cycle; for the floating-point operations, the add executes in two cycles and the multiply executes in three cycles. Delays result primarily from data dependencies that arise among the operands. The following control models are considered:

1. Simple Control and In-Order Execution—This is the basic model on which many of our earlier pipelined processor examples are based.

2. Out-of-Order Execution—This control strategy, as the name implies, allows instructions to be dispatched so long as they do not have a dependency upon any instructions already in execution. Only one instruction is inspected per cycle, and it is either executed or delayed.

3. Windowed Out-of-Order Execution—Here, an instruction window of size N is examined, and at most M instructions are dispatched when found to be independent. These are labeled $M = 1$, $M = 2$, etc., for the number of instructions that can be dispatched per cycle. The case $M = 1$ corresponds to "out-of-order decode and out-of-order execute," limited to issuance of a single instruction each cycle. For the hardware model proposed, Figure 7.52 plots the throughput in instructions per cycle for the various control models plotted against window size, and Figure 7.53 evaluates the same control strategies for a processor with pipelined execution units [302]. This processor has only one integer adder and one integer multiplier, and one floating-point adder and one floating-point multiplier, but each of these units is capable of pipelining its operations at the rate of one pair per cycle. The execution times are increased so that the integer units execute in two cycles, a floating-point add in three cycles, and the floating-point multiply in four cycles.

A number of general conclusions can be developed:

1. Instruction concurrency can be potentially realized up to the point where two and one-half to three instructions can be issued per cycle.

2. Much of the available concurrency can be realized with relatively small window sizes (about eight).

3. When the execution pipeline is long (relatively slow floating-point execution, etc.), the advantage of multiple-instruction execution is greatly diminished.

4. Out-of-order execution, at least for most of the models studied, offers an improvement over in-order execution of about 20%.

5. Windowed out-of-order execution, dispatching one instruction per cycle ($M = 1$), affords an additional 20% performance advantage.

Which Machine Is Better?

It is becoming increasingly fashionable among computer marketing agents to cite the maximum number of instructions that can be simultaneously issued by a processor as a basic measure of processor performance. After all, a machine that can issue 5 instructions per cycle ought to be 5 times faster than a machine that issues only one instruction per cycle.

At least, it would seem that way. In assessing the performance potential, the careful observer will consider obvious resource limitations. For example, are there ports and busses enough to support four updates to the register set each cycle?

Ordering restrictions: is there support for out-of-order instruction execution? There is a fine point here, and essentially it is this: must load and store instructions execute in order? After all, these are the most common instructions by frequency. These are also the instructions most likely to create interrupts or faults due to memory management considerations. Regardless of what the marketing brochure says, if the processor does not have reordering hardware (history registers, etc.) and requires in-order execution of instructions that access memory, its overall behavior will resemble that of a machine that executes all instructions in order. There will be rather little advantage from the multiple-issue hardware.

Speculative execution: if the processor truly supports out-of-order instruction execution, does it support speculative execution (i.e., execution of code beyond the conditional branch)? Speculative execution can enhance processor speedup, possibly by up to 50%.

Typically, details on instruction ordering restrictions and speculative execution restrictions are not the kind of information generally provided when a processor is first introduced. The more complex the processor, the more certainly its effectiveness can be understood only by thorough understanding of its detailed organization and limitations.

7.7 Comparing Vector and Multiple-Issue Processors

Comparing two processor types that are based upon rather different design premises certainly resembles comparing apples to oranges. If the goal of any processor design is to provide cost-effective computation across a range of applications, then insofar as we can understand the relative strengths and weaknesses of two approaches, we may be able to succeed in combining obvious strengths and/or avoiding weaknesses in the resultant design.

7.7.1 Cost Comparison

In principle, the cost of the execution units for both the multiple-issue machine and the vector processor ought be about the same, given that they are targeted at achieving the same maximum performance. Historically, vector processors have not stressed short execution pipelines, since performance did not depend on it. The more recent multiple-issue designs recognize the importance of short execution pipelines, as well as result-per-cycle bandwidth within each execution unit, and have stressed both. In principle, however, there ought to be little difference between either the cost or the performance of the execution unit ensembles for either processor.

A major difference lies in the storage hierarchy. Both multiple-issue machines and vector processors rely heavily on multiported registers. These registers occupy a significant amount of area. Recall from chapter 2 that the area occupied by a "dual-ported" register expressed in **rbe** is:

$$\text{Area} = (\text{number of regs} + 6)(\text{bits per reg} + 6) \, \textbf{rbe}.$$

We can extend this model to accommodate more than two read ports and a shared write port. Let P be the number of ports (shared or nonshared). Then the area required is approximately:

$$\text{Area} = (\text{number of regs} + 3P)(\text{bits per reg} + 3P) \, \textbf{rbe}.$$

Most vector processors have eight sets of 64 registers, each having 64 bits. Clearly, each vector register must be "dual-ported"—implemented with a read port and a write port. Since the registers are sequentially accessed, each port can be shared by all elements in the register set.

This allows the vector registers to be serially switched among the P requesting sources. So, each vector register has area:

$$\text{Area} = (\text{number of element reg.} + 6)(\text{bits per reg.} + 6).$$

but there is an additional switching overhead required to switch each of n vector registers toeach of P external ports. We estimate this area (a switch point is about 2 **rbe**) as

$$\text{Switch area} = 2(\text{bits per reg.})P(\text{number of vector reg.}).$$

EXAMPLE 7.9   MULTIPORTED REGISTER AREA

Compute the area for the register sets.

1. A multi-issue processor with 32×64 register bits and 8 ports.

$$\text{Area} = (32 + 3(8))(64 + 3(8)) = 4928\mathbf{rbe}.$$

2. A vector processor with 8 registers, each of 64 elements, each element having 64 bits. The vector registers support 8 ports.

$$
\begin{aligned}
\text{Area (register only)} &= 8 \times [(64 + 6)(64 + 6)] \\
&= 39,200\mathbf{rbe} \\
\text{Area (switch)} &= 2(64)(8)(8) \\
&= 8,192\mathbf{rbe} \\
\text{Area total} &= 47,392\mathbf{rbe}.
\end{aligned}
$$

3. This results in an area difference of $47,392 - 4,928 = 42,464\mathbf{rbe}$ required to support the vector registers.

$\blacklozenge$

Note that from the preceding example, the difference (42,464 **rbe**), is a significant amount of processor area—as we recall from studies on our baseline processor, exceeding the probable area of the floating-point units themselves. Another way of viewing the additional vector register area is to compare it to an equivalent amount of data cache. The additional vector register area would correspond to about 70,800 cache bits (at 0.6 **rbe** per cache bit), or somewhat less than 8 KB of data cache. Recall that vector processors in general have a small data cache or buffer to contain scalar data values, but the multiple-issue machine will surely require a considerably

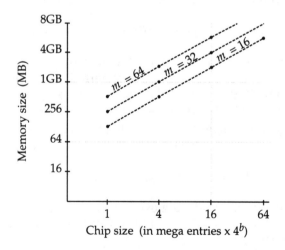

Figure 7.54 Memory size vs. entries per chip for various interleave factors (m), assuming memory word = 8 bytes. Chip size is number of memory words per chip (e.g., $4^M \times 4^b$ has chip size of 4^M entries).

Table 7.9 Estimated additional relative costs of vector processor and multiple-issue processor (assumptions: Same base processor and same execution units; changes (additions) measured in A units; $A = 1,481$ **rbe**).

	Vector Processor	Multiple-Issue Processor
Vector registers	28.7	—
Vector memory management and buffers ($m = 8$)	8.1	—
I-cache and I-fetch	—	4
Decoder	—	1
D-cache[a]	—	55–165 additional

[a]Assuming the vector processor has 16KB (scalars only); the multiple-issue processor has 32–64KB (i.e., 16–48KB additional).

larger data cache to ensure high performance. The vector processor also must have support hardware for managing access to the memory system, and the memory system itself is significantly complicated by the requirements for direct vector access. Even with processors with 64–256 MB of main storage, it is difficult to accommodate the high degrees of interleaving required to support processor bandwidth. Figure 7.54 illustrates memory size vs. chip size at various levels of interleaving.

Suppose we build a vector processor with a cycle time of 10 ns, using DRAM memory modules with a memory cycle time of 80 ns. If we allow two accesses to memory per processor cycle, then we have n, the total number of accesses per memory cycle, = 16. Assuming that $y = 1$ (recall that y is the bypass factor discussed earlier in this chapter) is achievable with sufficiently large buffer size, and reducing interleaving to the lowest practical limit ($m = n$), we have $B(16, 16, y = 1)$. This gives a vector processing slowdown of 0.78 due to memory contention. Instead of the speedup of S_p during vector processing, the processor achieves only 0.78 S_p. Of course, we could raise this by increased interleaving, say $m = 2n$, but this doubles the minimum memory configuration.

Multiple-issue machines do not achieve performance merely by including additional execution resources. The basic hardware register set (presumably 32 registers, each with 64 bits) must be arranged to support 4–6 reads and 2–3 writes per cycle. This also increases the area required for buses between the arithmetic units and the registers. The multiple-issue system must also have the ability to access and hold multiple instructions each cycle from the I-cache. This in general significantly increases the size of the I-fetch path between the I-cache and the instruction decoder/instruction register. Finally, at the instruction decoder, multiple instructions must be decoded simultaneously and detection for independence/instruction interlock must be performed. Table 7.9 summarizes the relative costs of the two approaches. The difference depends heavily on the size of the data cache required by the multiple issue processor to realize its performance potential and the relative cost of the memory interleaving required by the vector processor. We see more of this in the next section.

7.7.2   Performance Comparison

The performance of vector processors is primarily a function of two factors:

1. The percentage of the code that is vectorizable in a particular application.

2. The average length of the vector seen by the vector processor.

As we saw earlier, the $n_{1/2}$, or the vector size at which the vector processor achieves approximately half its asymptotic performance, is roughly the same as the length of the arithmetic-plus-memory access pipeline. Since the multiple-issue processors access data from the data cache, their equivalent $n_{1/2}$ is generally less than the vector processor, and so one would expect that for short vectors the multiple-issue processor would perform better than an equivalent vector processor. The actual advantage depends on the sophistication of the compiler for both vector and multiple-issue processors. It may be that the vectorizing compiler can recognize an occurrence of a short vector and treat that portion of the code as if it were scalar code using the scalar data cache. Usually, code corresponding to rather short vectors can be reassembled in such a way as to provide the type of instruction independence that is most suitable for the multiple-issue machine. As vectors get longer, the performance of the multiple-issue machine becomes much more dependent on the size of the data cache. When the vector (or underlying array) exceeds the size of the data cache, there is little reuse of data values stored in the cache and the performance of the processor suffers greatly.

Simmons and Wasserman [258] have done an interesting performance evaluation of the IBM RISC System/6000, a scalar processor capable of issuing up to four instructions with two vector processors (a Convex C240 and a Floating Point System, FPS-500). Figure 7.55 shows the results of their study for the particular version of the RISC System/6000 that was used, which contains a 32-KB cache and operates at a 50-ns cycle. The steep falloff in performance occurs after vector lengths of over 225. Ultimately, the processor is limited by the time required (about 15 clock periods) to load a cache line following a miss. The total cache capacity is exceeded at vector length 800, which accounts for the second dip in performance. It is interesting to note that neither a vector processor of similar capability (for instance, the Convex C240) nor an improved version of the IBM RISC System/6000 (with 40-ns cycle and 64-KB cache) suffered any performance degradation up to vector length 1,000. One would expect, of course, that at some point a similar performance degradation would be noticed on the larger cache version of the System/6000.

In addition to this simple example, Simmons and Wasserman compared the machines on applications programs. Across a broad range of applications, this 40-ns System RS/6000 performed quite well relative to the C240, with an execution time ratio of 0.4–2.3, and with most applications favoring the multiple-issue (RS/6000) machine by about 20–30%.

Another study conducted by Bennett [33] was restricted to the FFT algorithm, in which a high-speed pipelined processor was compared to a vector processor on a relative cycle count basis. The FFT problem consists of finding a functional approximation that fits a set of sample data of size N; in

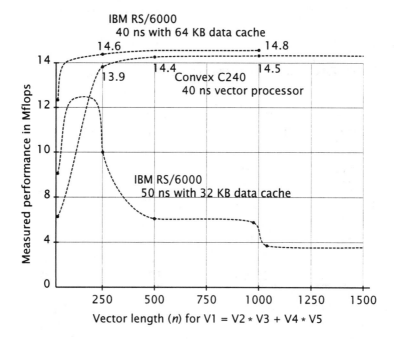

Figure 7.55 Performance of two 40 ns processors: the Convex 240 (a vector processor) and the IBM RS/6000 (a superscalar processor). A version of this processor was also measured with a 50 ns cycle and a (half-sized) 32 KB data cache. Data from Simmons and Wasserman [258].

other words, given an array of data of N sample points, where N is a power of 2, the sample array can be approximated as the sum of sines and cosines:

$$S[n] = \sum_{m=0}^{N-1} a_m \left(\cos(2\pi mn/N) + i \sin(2\pi mn/N) \right).$$

For fixed frequency m, n (the time) varies from 0 to $N - 1$; then the sine and cosine functions trace out exactly m complete cycles. We need to solve for the Fourier coefficients a_m.

This algorithm requires N complex multiplies for each coefficient and appears to be an N^2 algorithm. Because of the regularity of the matrix, the problem can be subdivided: the rows at the bottom half of the matrix are duplicates of the rows at the top half of the matrix, except for the signs in odd-numbered columns. Thus, the matrix may be reorganized and reduced by this reorganization to $N \log_N$ complex multiplies.

Table 7.10 indicates the performance, in cycles per iteration, for the MIPS R3000 33 MHz and a 64KB external cache for a variety of sample sizes. This can be compared with the performance as measured on a Cray-II, taken from Bailey [24]. This is plotted in Figure 7.56. Conventional processors, all of whose data accesses pass through a data cache, may experience significant performance degradation on large scientific problems. Vector processors avoid the problem by excluding vector data from entry into the data cache and forcing all such structured references to main memory.

Table 7.10   Some comparative results for FFT application.

Sample Size	N, number of Iterations	R3000 Cycles per Iteration	CRAY 2 Cycles per Iteration
256	1024	53	49
512	2304	53	45
1K	5120	53	40
2K	11,264	56	36
4K	24,576	92	34
8K	53,248	99	35
16K	114,688	120	34
32K	245,760	120	32

*CRAY 2 has $n_{1/2} \doteq 60$, $\Delta t = 4.1\,\text{ns}$, $R_\infty \doteq 244$ Mflop.

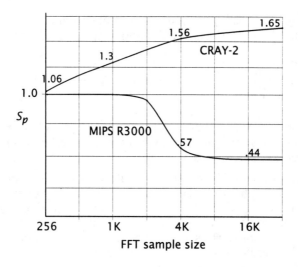

Figure 7.56 Vector processor and pipelined processor performance. *Based on cycle count* (not time). T_1 is the cycle count for the 256-point FFT for the MIPS R3000; T_p is the corresponding cycle count for various FFT sample sizes for either MIPS R3000 or the Cray-2. $S_p = T_1/T_p$.

7.7.3   Alternative Organizations

There are two obvious alternatives to overcoming the limitations of either processor type. If the memory implementations allow reasonably efficient, cost-effective direct access to memory, then the multiple-issue machine can profit significantly by simply having the ability to force the system to leave certain data structures (e.g., vectors and arrays) in memory and not allow those structures to be brought into the data cache. Of course, even if this is done, vector references directed at memory must still be checked in the cache directory to ensure that a data item was not accessed under a scalar alias. Another approach is to include a very large cache for all processors, either vector or scalar. According to a study by Gee and Smith [99], a cache of about 4 MB would be sufficient to capture most structured data. If this cache were designed to match required vector access bandwidth, it could provide an overall significant improvement in performance. It would have a double advantage; it would:

1. Reduce the $n_{1/2}$, or effective pipeline startup time, by providing a quicker access to the data structures, and

2. Provide a uniform access pattern between cache and main memory, so that main memory need not be accessed by both scalar cache and single word vector references.

7.8   Conclusions

Vector processors and multiple-instruction-issue processors are alternative approaches to realize performance in excess of one instruction per cycle (less than 1 CPI)—the usual limit for a pipelined processor. Historically, the evolution of microprocessors has closely followed that of mainframe computers. Microprocessors have increasingly adopted techniques pioneered in mainframes. It is in the area of highly concurrent processors targeted at under 1 CPI that we seem to see a cleavage in the mainframe and microprocessor approaches. Mainframes (and supercomputers) have adopted a vector processor approach to concurrent processing. This approach relies heavily on the availability of multiple large (vector) register sets, which are directly loaded from main store. In turn, these vector registers make rapid pipelined use of functional units. These processors depend on the ability of the compiler to detect and use large numeric data structures organized as vectors. They are generally limited by available memory bandwidth. As memory chips have increased in size, it has become increasingly difficult and/or expensive to design memory systems that can supply the very high data rates required by the vector processor.

Pipelined processors based on out-of-order execution and concurrent execution of multiple instructions are a natural extension to the pipelined processor. If instructions are allowed to complete their execution out of order, a speedup is realized in processor performance. Processor performance can be enhanced at three different levels of implementation, each requiring more complex implementation but affording an enhanced level of performance:

1. Out-of-order execution of instructions.

2. Out-of-order dispatching or issuance of instructions and out-of-order execution.

3. Issuance of multiple instructions, regardless of their order in the sequence of code.

Multiple-issue processors also have two classes: VLIW (very large instruction word) and superscalar. In the VLIW approach, multiple instructions are partitioned statically at compile time for concurrent execution. In the superscalar approach, a more conventional stream of instructions is partitioned dynamically by the action of an instruction window during execute time. Multiple-issue processors are also limited by memory; however, it is usually the data cache size rather than main memory bandwidth that forms the basic limitation. Data cache size can be a significant limitation, especially if the type of code being run references vector data structures. These structures may have a significant stride, which for smaller or intermediate-sized data cache and large vector sizes display little or no locality of execution. Effective execution of scientific code on multiple-instruction-issue processors requires software that effectively blocks large vector data structures into smaller pieces that will fit in the available data cache size.

7.9   Some Areas for Further Research

While vector processors represent a relatively mature organizational approach, there are still a large number of outstanding issues. The vector pipeline seems ideally suited to using wave pipelining, mentioned in chapter 2. These pipelined techniques require a relatively static pipeline. The possibility of extremely fast vector cycle times using wave pipelining may offer a significant advantage and compensate for the implementation difficulties.

Probably the most controversial (and hence most interesting) area is the efficiency of the multiple issue, or superscalar, pipelined processor. Since the performance of these processors is known to be relatively limited, can one justify the cost (area) that the implementations must occupy to deliver this performance? The issue returns to one mentioned in chapter 2: measuring the efficiency of an implementation as a function of the area it occupies. These questions cannot be answered in the isolation of a processor design, but they must include memory hierarchy considerations—cache and bandwidth requirements. In implementations of the future, it may be a more efficient use of area to include multiple processors on a single chip rather than to design extremely complex, but only marginally faster, single processors.

Both vector processors and multiple-issue machines require significant compiler support. "Vectorizing" compilers are generally available, but compilers that block vectors so that they fit in data caches suitable for either vector or multiple-issue processors are not yet available. Compiler optimization techniques certainly play a pivotal role in determining the ultimate evolution of concurrent processor architecture.

Finally, there is the issue of memory design for any of these organizations. Can large, second-level caches provide the appropriate bandwidth and operand supply for vector processors? Ultimately, the central question becomes one of optimizing performance for available silicon area for both the memory system and the processor design, given the best software technology. The multiplicity of technology and variables make the evolution of concurrent processors a particularly exciting area in computer design.

7.10 Data Notes

Data Note 1: The Vector Processor Model.

Vector processors have been well studied in the literature, and much of the data presented here uses models originally developed by Hockney and Jesshope [132] or Stone [272].

Data Note 2: Multiple Instruction Execution.

The data presented in Figures 7.52 and 7.53 are based on the work of Acosta. They represent a small program sample. No compiler assistance is provided.

Reliability. Because the results are based on a small number of benchmarks, they should be viewed with caution. Reported results seem consistent, but compilers may play a significant role in the future in altering the results.

Stability. The variance is expected to be high, although detailed statistical studies have yet to be done.

7.11 Annotated Bibliography

Vector Processors

One of the earliest vector processors was the Cray-1 from Cray Research. This was the first machine to make extensive use of vector registers. Most large scientific machines today are vector processors or, in the case of the mainframes, pipelined processors with optional vector processing adjuncts. Vector processors have been in production for close to twenty years. There is an extensive body of literature analyzing the advantages and limitations of these machines. The following three textbooks have extensive summaries of the literature on vector processors.

R. W. Hockney and C. R. Jesshope. *Parallel Computers 2.* Adam Hilger, Philadelphia, 1988.

H. S. Stone. *High-Performance Computer Architecture.* Electrical and Computer Engineering Series. Addison-Wesley, Reading, MA, 2nd edition, 1990.

P. M. Kogge. *The Architecture of Pipelined Computers.* McGraw-Hill, New York, 1981.

Multiple Instruction Execution

Multiple-issue processors were first studied by Tjaden [283] and later reviewed by Keller [159]. They have received a great deal of recent attention [149, 150, 227, 266]. Tjaden's result of 1970 is probably valid even today: without compiler support, multiple instruction execution is limited to about two instructions per cycle.

W. M. Johnson. *Superscalar Microprocessor Design*. Prentice-Hall, Englewood Cliffs, NJ, 1991.

Pradeep K. Dubey. *Exploiting Fine-Grain Concurrency: Analytical Insights in Superscalar Processor Design*. PhD thesis, Purdue University, August 1991.

B. R. Rau, J. A. Fisher. Instruction-level processing: History, overview and perspective. *Journal of Supercomputing*, Vol. 7, No. 1, January 1993.

This is an excellent survey of the field.

H. Dwyer, H. C. Torng. An out-of-order superscalar processor with speculative execution and fast, precise interrupts. *Proceedings of Micro 25*/SIGmicro Newsletter, December 1992.

A nice treatment of an implementation of multiple instruction execution with precise interrupts.

7.12   Problem Set

1. For the two-instruction example in Figure 7.12 (vector size = 64), find the total execution times assuming a chained and unchained vector ALU if the vector pipeline has eight stages:

   (a) What is the implied instruction memory bandwidth (bytes per cycle) for this computation?

   (b) Extend the code with the requisite VLD and VST. Now what is the implied data memory bandwidth (bytes per cycle) for this computation?

2. Suppose we want to use $m = 5$ memory modules. Find the module address and the address within the module for the following (hex) addresses:

   (a) F37B90.

   (b) AA3347.

3. Suppose the lower four bits of an address are designated m_3, m_2, m_1, and m_0. We hash the bits to specify the module as follows (m_3', m_2', m_1', m_0' are the new address bits):

$$
\begin{aligned}
m_3' &= m_3 \,\forall\, m_1 \\
m_2' &= m_2 \,\forall\, m_0 \\
m_1' &= \overline{m_1} \\
m_0' &= m_0
\end{aligned}
$$

(a) Will this scheme work?

(b) Find the new module address for each of the addresses in problem 2.

4. A certain vector processor has a cycle time of 8 ns and memory cycle of 64 ns. It uses eight modules and does not bypass requests in the memory buffer. For a sustained vector environment of two requests per processor cycle,

    (a) What is the requested (offered) memory bandwidth (in MBps)?

    (b) What is the achieved memory bandwidth (in MBps)?

    (c) What is the mean queue size of requests waiting for memory?

5. For problem 4, can you define a bypass buffer to improve performance? Explain carefully.

6. Suppose in problem 4 we now increase the interleaving to $m = 17$. Repeat problems 4 and 5.

7. Derive the rules for finding the quotient (section 7.3.1) after division by $2^k - 1$.

8. Suppose $y = 0.5$ can be realized with a certain buffer and $m = 17$. The processor parameters are the same as those in problem 4. What is the achieved memory bandwidth?

9. For concurrent code execution, what type of dependencies arise in the following code sequence?

```
DIV.F  R1,    R2,  R3
MPY.F  R1,    R4,  R5
ADD.F  R4,    R5,  R6
ADD.F  R5,    R4,  R7
ST.F   ALPHA, R5.
```

10. A vector processor has four ports to memory (i.e., it can make up to four memory requests per processor cycle). The processor cycle is 8 ns, while the memory cycle is 42 ns. What is the minimum amount of interleaving required to support a bypassed buffered system so that there will be no memory contention delay?

    If $m = 64$, what is y_{opt}?

    What will be the mean total buffer size?

    If the achieved $y = 0.2$, $m = 64$, then what is $B(m, n, y)$? What fraction of its maximum performance is the system able to achieve? (Ignore startup.)

11. A four-ported (three read, one write) memory system would support a vector processor with what maximum speedup over a uniprocessor? Explain.

12. (a) Show the precedence matrix, M^1, for the code in problem 9.

    (b) Find the full precedence matrix showing all dependencies.

13. If a set of shadow registers, RS1, RS2, RS3, RS4 were available, how could the code in problem 9 be restructured to minimize dependencies? Show the new M^1.

14. Using the assumptions of study 7.1, time out the code in problem 9 for

    (a) Control flow (improved).

    (b) Dataflow (with value-holding reservation stations).

    (c) Control flow with shadow registers.

15. How would the dataflow timing change in study 7.1 if all three instructions were issued in the same cycle?

16. Repeat problem 15 for the improved scoreboard, again using the functional unit timing of study 7.1.

17. A certain vector processor has a memory buffer that does not allow reconfiguration (each TBF/m is a separate buffer). How does this affect the overall overflow probability?

18. Using the baseline area assumptions of Chapters 2, 4, and this chapter, estimate the overall area ($f = 0.75$) of a dual-issue superscalar processor with 8KB I-cache and 8KB D-cache. Assume double-sized ALU to accommodate execution. State all assumptions and show functional area allocation.

Chapter 8

Shared Memory Multiprocessors

Beyond the instruction-level concurrency discussed in the last chapter, there are higher-level forms of concurrent program execution. Program sub-units, whether basic blocks, procedures, tasks, or threads of control, are the basic unit of concurrency for multiprocessors. A program consists of a collection of executable sub-program units. These units, which we refer to as *tasks*, are also sometimes called *programming grains*. They must be defined, scheduled, and coordinated by hardware and software before or during program execution.

There are many ways to arrange programs into executable grains to suit the needs of the processing ensemble that executes them. In this chapter, we consider only processing ensembles that consist of n (usually < 100) identical processors that share (at least) a common memory (or space of named objects). Recently there has been a great deal of work on machine configurations for massively parallel processors where the number of computing elements is greater than 1,000, and on processors that do not share a common memory but rather use a message-passing protocol among processors. While these are increasingly important forms of computing, we do not attempt to review them in this text, but rather consider the design of smaller-scale multiprocessors.

8.1 Basic Issues

Multiprocessors usually are designed for at least one of two reasons: fault tolerance and program speedup.

If we have n identical processors, we should reasonably expect that the failure of one processor ought not to affect the ability of the multiprocessor to continue program execution, although this execution may occur at a lower speed. For some multiprocessor configurations, this is not true. If the operating system is designated to run on a particular processor and that processor fails, the system fails. On the other hand, some multiprocessor ensembles have been built with the sole purpose of high-integrity, fault-tolerant computation. Generally, these systems may not provide any program speedup over a single processor. Systems that duplicate computations or that triplicate and vote on results (called *triple modular redundant*, or TMR, processors) are examples of designing for fault tolerance.

The objective of this chapter is to cover processor design for program speedup. We take as a premise that no reasonable design for speedup ought to come at the expense of fault tolerance. It is generally not acceptable for the whole multiprocessor system to fail if any one of its processors fail. Thus, the designer must be aware of a general need for fault tolerance in multiprocessor systems and do nothing to jeopardize this, while at the same time directing primary design attention to program execution speedup.

Since multiprocessors simply consist of multiple computing elements (multiple identical processors of a type such as described in chapters 4 and 7), each computing element is subject to the same basic design issues discussed in those chapters. These elements are slowed down by branch delays, cache misses, etc. The multiprocessor configuration, however, introduces speedup potential as well as additional sources of delay and performance degradation. The sources of performance bottlenecks in multiprocessors generally relate to the way the program was decomposed to allow concurrent execution on multiple processors.

These basic issues (see Figure 8.1) may be summarized as follows:

1. Partitioning. This is the process whereby the original program is decomposed into basic sub-program units or tasks, each of which can be assigned to a separate processor. Partitioning is performed either by programmer directives in the original source program or by the compiler at compile time.

2. Scheduling of tasks. Associated with each program is a flow of control among the sub-program units or tasks. Certain tasks must be completed before others can be initiated (i.e., one is *dependent* on the other). Other tasks represent functions that can be executed independently of the main program execution. The scheduler's run-time function is to arrange the task order of execution in such a way as to minimize overall program execution time.

3. Communication and synchronization. It does the system no good to merely schedule the initiation of various tasks in the proper order, unless the data that the tasks require is made available in an efficient way. Thus, communication time has to be minimized and the receiver task must be aware of the synchronization protocol being used. An issue associated with communications is memory *coherency*. This property ensures that the transmitting and receiving elements have the same, or a coherent, picture of the contents of memory, at least for data which is communicated between the two tasks.

Sarkar [252] provides a rather complete treatment of these three problems in the context of a single assignment language, SISAL.

Suppose a program *P* is converted into a parallel form, P_p. This conversion consists of partitioning P_p into a set of tasks, T_i.

P_p (as partitioned):

P_p consists of tasks, some of which can be executed concurrently. In actual execution, tasks are (usually) scheduled as processors become available.

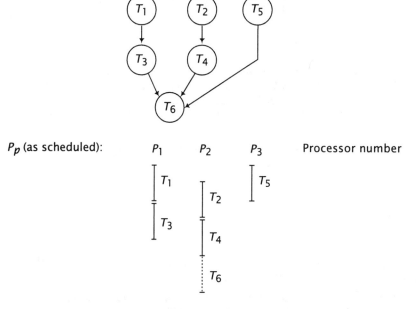

Figure 8.1   Partitioning and scheduling.

8.2   Partitioning

Partitioning is the process of dividing a program into tasks, each of which can be assigned to an individual processor for execution at run time. These tasks can be represented as nodes in a control graph. The arcs in the graph specify the order in which execution of the sub-tasks must occur. The partitioning process occurs at compile time, well before program execution. The goal of the partitioning process is to uncover the maximum amount of parallelism possible without going beyond certain obvious machine limitations. For example, searching for parallelism well in excess of *p*, the number of independent processors available in the system, is usually unprofitable.

The program partitioning is usually performed with some *a priori* notion of program overhead [252]. Program overhead (*o*) is the added time a task takes to be loaded into a processor prior to beginning execution. The larger the size of the minimum task defined by the partitioning program, the smaller the effect of program overhead. Table 8.1 gives an instruction count for some various program grain sizes. The essential difference between

Table 8.1   Grain size.

(Informal) Grain Description	Program Construct	Typical # Instr
Fine grain	Basic block ("instr-level parallelism")	5–10
.	Procedure	20–100
Medium grain	Small task ("process-level parallelism")	100–1,000
.	Intermediate task	1,000–100,000
Coarse grain	Large task	100,000 or more

multiprocessor concurrency and instruction-level concurrency (discussed in the previous chapter) is the amount of overhead expected to be associated with each task. Overhead affects speedup. If uniprocessor program P_1 does operation O_1, then the parallel version of P_1 does operations O_p, where $O_p \geq O_1$.

For each task T_i, there is an associated number of overhead operations o_i, so that if T_i takes O_i operations without overhead, then:

$$O_p^T = \sum_i^p (O_i + o_i) \geq O_1,$$

where O_p^T is the total work done by P_p, including overhead. Note that the task overhead grows with p.

In order to achieve speedup over a uniprocessor, a multiprocessor system must achieve the maximum degree of parallelism among executing subtasks or control nodes. On the other hand, if we increase the amount of parallelism by using finer- and finer-grain task sizes, we necessarily increase the amount of overhead. This defines the well known "U" shaped curve for grain size (Figure 8.2).

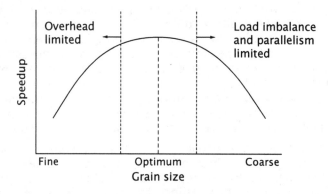

Figure 8.2   The effects of grain size.

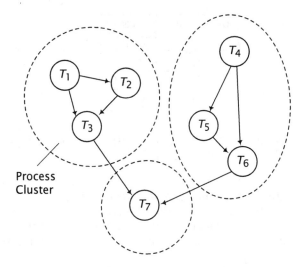

Figure 8.3   Grouping tasks into process clusters.

Moreover, the overhead time is:

1. Configuration dependent. Different shared memory multiprocessors may have significantly different task overheads associated with them, depending on cache size, organization, and the way caches are shared.

2. Overhead may be significantly different depending on how tasks are actually assigned (scheduled) at run time. A task returning to a processor whose cache already contains significant pieces of the task code or data set will have a significantly lower overhead than the same task assigned to an unrelated processor [268, 290].

Increased parallelism usually corresponds to finer task granularity and larger overhead. Consider the control graphs in Figure 8.3. *Clustering* is the grouping together of sub-tasks into a single assignable task. Clustering is usually performed both at partitioning time and during scheduling run time. The reasons for clustering during partition time might include:

1. The available parallelism exceeds the known number of processors that the program is being compiled for.

2. The placement of several shorter tasks that share the same instruction and/or data working set into a single task provides lower overhead.

The detection of parallelism itself in the program is achieved by one of three methods:

1. Explicit statement of concurrency in the higher-level language, as in the use of such languages as CSP (communicating sequential processes) [131] or Occam [75], which allow programmers to delineate the boundaries among tasks that can be executed in parallel, and to specify communications between such tasks.

2. The use of programmer's hints in the source statement, which the compiler may choose to use or ignore.

Dependency	Task List		
	T_1	T_2	T_3
T_1	0	–	–
T_2	1	0	–
T_3	0	1	0

Figure 8.4 Dependency matrix. A 'one' entry indicates a dependency; e.g., in this figure a T_2 depends on T_1 and T_3 depends on T_2.

3. Implicit parallelism, which can be detected via compilers such as Parafrase [235]. These compilers use sophisticated techniques to find the parallelism, such as data dependency tests to transform normal serial code into an efficient program form for execution on multiprocessors.

The techniques for partitioning programs into independent tasks suitable for concurrent execution use the same type of control graph to define task precedence as we used with instruction-level concurrency. This control graph can be represented as a dependency matrix (Figure 8.4). The same types of dependencies apply, and hence the same theory of task dependencies expresses the relationship among the concurrent tasks. The basic difference between instruction-level concurrency and task-level concurrency through compilation is the scope of the detection process. While instruction-level concurrency detection can be compiler-assisted, usually it is complemented by a run-time examination of the several instructions in the instruction window. The compiler sees the entire program, and, at least in principle, has a great deal more flexibility in determining and assigning independent events. A run-time concurrency detector sees the actual state of the machine and can optimize instruction issuance over a small scope of instructions.

EXAMPLE 8.1   FINDING PARALLELISM IN A PROGRAM

Section (a) of Figure 8.5 shows a small section of code that replaces an array, a[], of size $3n$ with a subsampled version of size n. Sections (b), (c), and (d) are attempts to improve the achievable execution concurrency. Section (e) shows the final subarray and the original array.

The loop in (a) cannot be split to run on multiple processors, due to the induction variable m and the forward dependency of the array a[]. On each iteration of the loop, the value of m is incremented by 3, using the previous value of m. We might write it this way in order to replace an expensive multiplication with an addition, on machines where multiplication takes more cycles than an addition.

The code can be rewritten as shown in (b) to eliminate m's dependence on its value in previous iterations of the loop. We hope that the increase in parallelization will offset any additional cycles lost by replacing the addition with a multiplication.

The code in (b) still has an essential or forward dependency with respect to array a[]. If all of the iterations were scheduled at once, it would be

a) /* Subsample with linear interpolation */

```
m = 0;
for(i=0; i < n; i++)
{
    m = m+3;                           /* Induction variable */
    a[i] = (a[m]+a[m+1]+a[m+2])/3;
}
```

b) /* Eliminating Dependency based on Induction variable */

```
for(i=0; i < n; i++)
{
    m = i*3;
    a[i] = (a[m]+a[m+1]+a[m+2])/3;   /* Forward Depen-
```
dency */
```
}
```

c) /* Eliminating Forward Dependency using double buffer */

```
for(i=0; i < n; i++)
{
    m = i*3
    aa[i] = (a[m]+a[m+1]+a[m+2])/3;
}
barrier();
for(i=0; i < n; i++)
{
    a[i] = aa[i];
}
```

d) /* Eliminating Forward Dependency using block scheduling */
```
schedule(0);
for(i=0; i < n; i++)
{
    waittillscheduled(i);
    m = i*3
    aa[i] = (a[m]+a[m+1]+a[m+2])/3;
    if(i != 0) schedule(3*i);
    schedule(3*i+1);
    schedule(3*i+2);
}
```

e) 0123456789
    0001112223334445556667778889999

Figure 8.5   Finding parallelism in a program.

possible for an element to be written before its value was read for use in computing the value for a lower-numbered element [27, 308]. For example, if element 9 were computed before it had been read, the array value for element 3 would have the wrong value.

To eliminate this problem, two solutions are shown. In (c), a temporary array is used to store the values until all of the original array has been read. Then, the values are copied from the temporary array to the original array. Since there are no dependencies between iterations of the loop, both loops can now be executed in parallel. The disadvantage to this solution is that roughly twice as much work must now be done.

Another solution is presented in (d). In this case, an array element is scheduled for execution as soon as the elements that use it for computation have read its values. The amount of parallelism varies through each iteration of the loop.

The choice of solutions is based on the configuration of the parallel machine. If the machine has a large number of processing elements, the double buffering solution might be best. For machines with a limited number of processors, the second solution is better.   ◆

The process of partitioning begins with the decomposition of the program into tasks. This process usually starts with the outermost loop of the program. Each iteration of the loop is a candidate for being designated a task. Once the various candidates have been defined, the process of dependency resolution can begin, as shown in Example 8.1. Techniques such as scalar renaming (similar to register renaming) can be used to reduce or eliminate apparent task dependency. Similarly, techniques such as forward substitution can have the same effect. Other techniques include loop normalization and subscript expansion. Clearly, the most effort must be spent in areas that have the most potential benefit. Stone [272] describes a recipe for, in his words, finding "easy parallelism" in a program:

Step 1. Find loop or recursion structures in the program.

Step 2. Determine the loops that account for the most time, i.e., those corresponding to the largest number of iterations.

Step 3. Assign instruction execution of these structures across the n processors, if this can be done in an independent manner.

Step 4. Add synchronization and communication instructions as required.

Step 3 collects sub-tasks into single tasks. In this clustering process, the compiler must be aware of the maximum number of resources that are likely to be available to it during the course of execution. Finding concurrency at any one point in excess of this is not profitable. Overhead considerations, then, can be used to assist in clustering tasks into units that afford the maximum potential speedup. This has been demonstrated by the Parafrase 2 compiler [235]. After the clustering process, the compiler may be used to determine potentially critical paths through the program. In order to do this, the amount of time required for task execution must be estimated. This corresponds to the probable number of instructions to be executed to complete the task. If determinable, this information is quite useful:

1. It indicates to the compiler those critical regions where a second pass at concurrency detection can perhaps best be used.

2. It provides an initial (or static) scheduling of tasks to processors.

As the overall goal is maximum speedup, the maximum degree of parallelism must be achieved, but with minimum overhead [252]. Data movement, whether of global or local data, must be minimized in order to maximize the overall processor utilization. Issues such as determination of the critical path structure and maximizing parallelism become very difficult problems in complex program structures.

8.3 Scheduling

Scheduling can be done either statically (at compile time) or dynamically (at run time). Usually, it is performed at both times. Static scheduling information can be derived on the basis of the probable critical paths. This alone is insufficient to ensure optimum speedup or even fault tolerance. Suppose, for example, one of the processors scheduled statically was unavailable at run time, having suffered a failure. If only static scheduling had been done, the program would be unable to execute if assignment to all n processors had been made. It is also oftentimes the case that program initiation does not begin with n predesignated idle processors. Rather, it begins with a smaller number as previously executing tasks complete their work. Thus, the processor availability is difficult to predict and may vary from run to run. While run-time scheduling has obvious advantages, handling changing systems environments, as well as highly variable program structures, it also has some disadvantages—primarily its run-time overhead. As Ngai [217] observes, all major issues in run-time scheduling center on "how to ensure performance gains and how to reduce overhead losses."

Run-time scheduling can be performed in a number of different ways. The scheduler itself may run on a particular processor, or it may run on any processor. It can be centralized (performed by only one processor) or distributed (performed by several processors). It is clearly desirable that the scheduling not be designated to a particular processor, but rather that it be initiated by any processor and then the scheduling process itself be distributed across all available processors. This is summarized in Table 8.2.

Typical run-time information includes information about the dynamic state of the program and the state of the system. The program state may include details provided by the compiler, such as information about the control structure and identification of critical paths or dependencies. Dynamic information includes information about resource availability and work load distribution. Program information must be generated by the program itself, and then gathered by a run-time routine to centralize this information.

The major run-time overheads in run-time scheduling include:

1. Information gathering.

2. Scheduling.

Table 8.2   Scheduling.

When: Scheduling can be performed at:

	(+) Advantage	(−) Disadvantage
Compile time	Less run time overhead	May not be fault tolerant Compiler lacks stall information
Run time	More efficient execution	Higher overhead

How: Scheduling can be performed by:

Arrangement	Comment
Designated single processor	Simplest, least effort
Any single processor	↓
Multiple processors	Most complex, potentially most difficult

3. Dynamic execution control.

4. Dynamic data management.

Dynamic execution control is a provision for dynamic clustering or process creation at run time. *Dynamic data management* provides for the assignment of tasks and processors in such a way as to minimize the required amount of memory overhead delay in accessing data.

The overhead during scheduling is primarily a function of two specific program characteristics:

1. *Program dynamicity* is a measure of how the program's concurrent behavior changes with respect to differing input data (Figure 8.6). On the one hand, a program may be fully static, where its behavior is the same across all data inputs. In this case, relevant scheduling information can be determined at compile time. On the other hand, we have a fully dynamic programming structure, where the behavior of the program with different data inputs differs significantly in both the time required to execute and the memory size required during execution. Most programs, of course, fall between these two extremes.

2. *Granularity* is the size of the basic program sub-task to be scheduled. Since additional run-time overhead in the scheduling process can be amortized over the execution of the entire scheduled task, large-grain concurrency affords less scheduling overhead than small-grain concurrency.

8.3.1   Run-Time Scheduling Techniques

Many techniques may be used for run-time scheduling, depending on the amount of available program information. The following techniques are generally arranged according to complexity. Each technique introduced also uses methods of its predecessors.

1. *System load balancing* uses only the number of available concurrent processors for task scheduling. The objective is to balance the systems load. The scheduling process consists merely of dispatching the

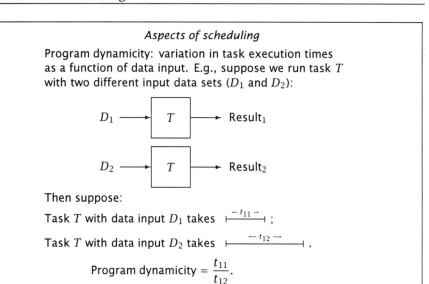

Figure 8.6   Program dynamicity.

number of ready tasks to each processor's execution queue. It has generally little run-time overhead, and since it requires little information, it is amenable to fully dynamic computations.

2. *Load balancing.* Scheduling using load balancing relies on estimates of the amount of computation needed within each concurrent subtask. This more evenly distributes the workload among available processors. The technique incurs only a little more run-time overhead than is used in systems load balancing.

3. *Clustering.* If we now assume that both a task's computational load and the amount of interprocess communication between process pairs is available, some tasks may be more optimally clustered together before assignment to available processors. The objective here is to both minimize interprocess communication and maintain load balance across the processors. Since pairwise communication process information must be developed, the run-time overhead with large numbers of tasks and processors can be quite high.

4. *Scheduling with compiler assistance.* Block-level dynamic program information is gathered at run-time, and used in conjunction with interprocess communication and information on the computational requirements of each task to determine the schedule of concurrent tasks.

5. *Static scheduling/custom scheduling.* If the program is relatively static, the exact interprocess communication and computational requirements can be determined at compile time, and an optimum schedule can be represented in a directed acyclic graph (DAG-type list structure).

Figures 8.7 and 8.8 from Ngai [217] indicate the speedup of several of these techniques for two scientific applications. Heuristic clustering

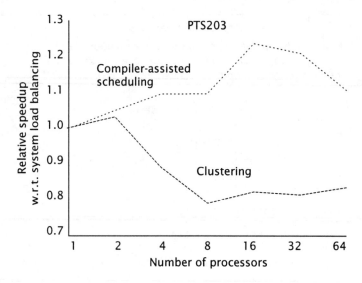

Figure 8.7   Processor allocation and speedup. This application (PTS203) is a parallel search tree with 203 nodes and four sub-trees.

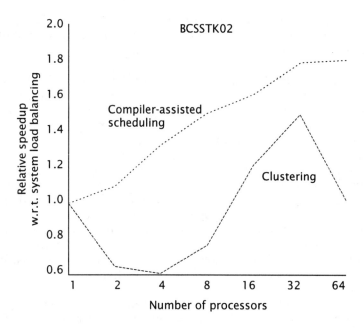

Figure 8.8   Processor allocation and speedup. This application (BCSSTK02) is a dynamic analysis problem in the structural engineering of an oil rig. It is a dense matrix problem.

and compiler-assisted run-time scheduling may offer 30–100% performance improvement, but only if the applications are of sufficient granularity.

8.4   Synchronization and Coherency

In a uniprocessor, instruction ordering is ensured during program execution. In providing out-of-order or concurrent instruction execution, the hardware provides the appearance of results executed in the order of the instructions as initially laid down in the program. For programs partitioned into a parallel form for execution on a multiprocessor, the notion of ordering changes. Order is defined by the sequence in which values are placed in memory. In a multiprocessor configuration, the objective is to achieve a high degree of task concurrency, but the tasks themselves must follow an explicit order as defined by the control structure and/or the scheduler. Also, communications between active tasks must be performed in an orderly way. If task 1 is to provide argument A for use by task 2, and task 2 is to return result B to task 1, the processor executing task 2 must have a mechanism to ensure that it receives the value A when it has been properly produced by task 1. The control of these values is performed by *synchronization primitives* or *semaphore*. Synchronization is the means to ensure that multiple processors have a coherent (similar) view of critical values in memory. *Memory* or *value coherence* is the property of memory that ensures that the value returned after a read is the same as the value stored by the latest write to the same address.

In complex systems of multiple processors, the memory may be physically remote from an individual processor. Thus, the order of *issue* (program order) of memory related operations (LD, ST, synchronize) may be different from the order in which the operations are actually *executed*. The extent to which the executed order of memory operations corresponds to the issued order is called the *consistency* of the ordering.

In multiprocessors, there are different degrees to which ordering may be enforced. The strongest type of order is referred to by Lamport [177] as *sequential consistency*. He defines this as follows:

> A system is sequentially consistent if the result of any execution is the same as if the operations of all of the processors were executed in some sequential order, and the operations of each individual processor appear in this sequence in the order specified by its program.

As pointed out by Adve and Hill [3], "operations" can, for practical purposes, be taken to mean memory reads or writes. As they observe, the effect of sequential consistency is to ensure that (1) all memory accesses execute atomically in some total order, and (2) that all memory accesses of a single process appear to execute (be performed) in program (issued) order. Sequential consistency defines a type of *strong ordering* [79, 254] of events in a multiprocessor (Figure 8.9a). It is sufficient for correct program execution, but may in practice create a great deal of overhead in multiprocessor program execution. For example, suppose two processors (P_1 and P_2) issue successive memory operations (M_{11} and M_{12}) for processor one, and M_{21} and M_{22} for processor two. Sequential consistency requires that these operations be performed in program order with respect to each processor, and in the same total order as seen by any other processor, so that if another processor saw the memory operations performed as M_{11}, M_{21}, M_{12}, M_{22}, then any other processor in the system would see the same ordering

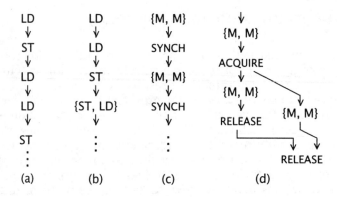

Figure 8.9 Illustrating four types of consistency [3]. (a) *Sequential consistency.* LD and ST follow program order. (b) *Processor consistency.* LD may precede buffered ST, other processors may see differing order of {ST,LD} access. (c) *Weak consistency.* synch operations are sequentially consistent; other memory operations {M,M} can occur in any order. (d) *Release consistency.* synch operations are split into acquire (lock) and release (unlock), and these operations are processor consistent.

of actions. Goodman [108] developed a less restrictive form of consistency called *processor consistency* (Figure 8.9b). The issuing processor sees sequences of loads or stores, or loads followed by a store to be performed in program order. But a store followed by a load is not necessarily performed in program order, nor is any sequence of memory operations as observed by another processor performed in program order. Allowing loads to precede stores as performed merely recognizes that many machines use store buffers. Allowing unpredictable sequences of memory operations requires observer processors to be explicitly synchronized by the programmer when using shared data.

Dubois et al. [79] introduced a notion of *weak ordering* or *weak consistency* that has been refined by Adve and Hill. Their definition was that a system is weakly ordered with respect to a synchronization model if and only if it appears sequentially consistent to all executions of a program that obey the synchronization model (Figure 8.9c). In practice, a program obeys the synchronization model if and only if:

1. All synchronization operations must be performed before any subsequent memory operation can be performed.

2. All pending memory operations are performed before any synchronization operation is performed.

3. Synchronization operations are sequentially consistent.

We now need to know that the various outstanding memory operations are complete. To do this, we introduce a new operation called a *fence* [42, 253]. This operation precedes a synchronization operation and ensures that the outstanding memory operations are performed.

An even weaker consistency model has been developed by Gharachorloo [101] called *release consistency* (Figure 8.9d). Here the synchronization primitives are categorized as either *acquire* (lock) or *release* (unlock). In release consistency, the third constraint of weak consistency is removed—the acquire and release operations need not be sequentially consistent. Accesses to synchronization primitives that require consistency are called *special accesses* and must be processor consistent.

The actual mechanism of synchronization includes as a basic element a *read-modify-write* function on a location in memory. The simplest type of synchronization is a single synchronization variable. Before access can be made to a shared variable, a particular location is referenced. If this location is (say) zero, then a write may be made to a shared variable, and the contents of the synchronization primitive is changed to one, indicating that the location containing the shared variable is *full*. Similarly, if an access is made to the synchronization primitive for a read, this is only allowed if the synchronization primitive is set at one, indicating that the shared variable is full and hence available.

For example, suppose process A is producing data to be used by process B (a consumer). They share a memory location (b) which they use to indicate the state of a separate data space in memory. Originally the bit is empty (say, $b = 0$), while the producer process creates and fills the data space. Any access by the consumer reveals that $b = 0$ and the data space is not yet ready. When the producer process A completes, it sets $b = 1$ (full). Now the consumer process B can access the data space, and, when finished, reset the bit to $b = 0$ (empty), indicating that the producer can resume storing into the data space. If there were multiple consumers, we would need additional bits to coordinate the consumers. Now we would designate certain bit combinations as giving exclusive rights to the producer or either one of the consumers; e.g., the following pattern might satisfy the requirements:

b_1 b_2

0	0	Producer working on data, consumers locked out.
0	1	Data available to any consumer, producer locked out.
1	1	A consumer has acquired data, producer and other consumers locked out.
1	0	Buffer empty, consumers locked out, buffer available to the producer.

Certain bit patterns *lock* and *unlock* access to this store region—these bits are referred to as *semaphores*.

A similar type of mechanism is the *test and set* instruction, which tests a bit in memory. The bit is tested as if it were a condition code. The test and set instruction tests a value in memory, and then sets that value to one. The processor acts on the original value of the tested bit. If a test-and-set instruction is executed and processing cannot proceed because the tested bit indicates that a shared variable is not yet available, then the accessing process could enter a loop in which it continues to access the primitive until it gets the indication that the shared variable is set. This process of looping on a shared variable with a test-and-set type of instruction is called a *spin lock*. The spin lock idea can be incorporated into a single instruction, or can simply be programmed using the *test and set* instruction.

Spin locks create significant additional memory traffic (at least, to cache memory) to the shared variables or to the synchronization primitives until access is granted [19]. In order to reduce this extra traffic, a *suspend lock* can be implemented. In the suspend lock, status can be recorded by the equivalent of a test-and-set instruction and then the requesting process can go idle, awaiting an interrupt from the producing process.

Finally, it is possible to combine synchronization primitives from multiple sources in an interconnection network. It is clear that in a fine-grain system we may have a good deal of synchronization traffic; since this traffic is typically directed at just a few synchronization cells, significant contention can arise at these particular designated cells. When such contention develops, it is referred to as a *hotspot* in memory [233]. In order to avoid such hotspots, the *fetch and add* primitive was developed [111], which is able to combine multiple test-and-set instructions into a single instruction that will access a synchronization variable and return the value. This combining is done in the network before access is made to the synchronization primitive in memory.

8.5   The Effects of Partitioning and Scheduling Overhead

When a program is partitioned into tasks, the maximum number of concurrent tasks can be determined. This is simply the maximum number of tasks that can be executed at any one time. It is sometimes called the *degree of parallelism* that exists in the program. Even if a program has a high degree of parallelism, a corresponding degree of speedup may not be achieved. Recall the definition of speedup:

$$S_p = \frac{T_1}{T_p}.$$

T_1 represents the time required for a uniprocessor to execute the program using the best uniprocessor algorithm. T_p is the time it takes for p processors to execute the program using an algorithm that corresponds to the best execution time for p processors. It may well happen that the uniprocessor algorithm is "significantly better" than the parallel processor algorithm, thus limiting the overall potential speedup even though the parallel processor algorithm used all of its p processors almost all of the time.

There is yet another reason that the parallel processor may fail to achieve high degrees of speedup with p processors. It may be that the maximum degree of parallelism that exists within the program may occur for a relatively small period of time, and that the rest of the program may indeed be serial. This is a problem related to the control structure or to the precedence defined within the program. For either of these reasons, or for other reasons, the overall efficiency of the parallel processor is usually less than the uniprocessor.

Efficiency has been defined by Kuck [173] as:

$$E_p = \frac{T_1}{p * T_p}.$$

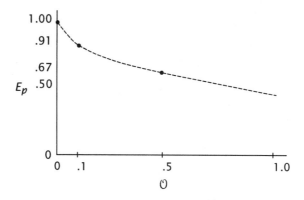

Figure 8.10   Efficiency (E_p) as a function of task overhead ($\mathcal{O}$), where $\mathcal{O}$ is a fraction of T_p, the task time.

E_p measures the effectiveness of the p-parallel multiprocessor ensemble, contrasted to a uniprocessor, which otherwise has the same capabilities as one of the parallel processors. In theory at least, $E_p \leq 1$. This is so since it ought to be possible for the single processor—in the worst uniprocessor case—to simply take the parallel processor algorithm and emulate it by executing p times. Cases where speedup is greater than p or efficiency is greater than 1 can arise in practice, however, and are referred to as *superlinear speedup*. These cases are usually the result of:

1. Failure to use the best uniprocessor algorithm in evaluating the uniprocessor case. In fact, most cases of superlinear speedup are the result of simply scaling the parallel processor algorithm down to $p = 1$.

2. More interesting examples of superlinear speedup arise from anomalies in the memory system. We can generally ensure that $E_p \leq 1$, and superlinear speedup does not occur if we insist that the memory system for both the uniprocessor and the parallel processor ensemble be the same.

If we allow the memory system to scale, that is, to be p times larger for the parallel processor system than for the uniprocessor system, then it is easy to imagine cases where the larger memory system captures working set information not available to the smaller-memoried uniprocessor. The larger memory then provides a considerable (i.e., $S_p > p$) overall performance advantage. For the rest of our discussion, we limit our attention to cases where $E_p \leq 1$.

In addition to partitioning and algorithmic limitations, synchronization represents an overhead which both limits speedup and decreases multiprocessor efficiency. For any particular system, if we regard the synchronization overhead as being relatively fixed per task, it is easy to see that the grain size or T_p is limited in order to achieve a given level of efficiency. Figure 8.10 illustrates the relationship between E_p and $\mathcal{O}$, the synchronization overhead in the absence of partitioning or other types of multiprocessor performance limitations.

Some time ago, Amdahl introduced the notion of serial time (T_s) in a parallel processor system [14]. T_s is simply the amount of time that only a single

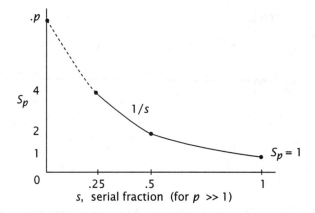

Figure 8.11 Speedup as a function of the serial fraction of program execution (Amdahl's Law).

processor is active in a multiprocessor system consisting of p processors. Each parallel processor system executing a single program must have, during the execution of that program, some T_s (i.e., $T_s > 0$). T_s represents initial and final program synchronization, if nothing else, since one processor must start the program and some other single processor must post the final result of the program. The relative size, cause and effect of T_s remains a controversial and important factor in determining overall multiprocessor performance. The effect of T_s is frequently referred to as *Amdahl's law* for multiprocessors [14]. We can perhaps see the effect of T_s best by using the model introduced by Karp and Flatt [155]. They introduce the notion of a *serial fraction* of program performance. Serial fraction is defined as:

$$s = \frac{T_s}{T_1}.$$

The serial fraction is the fraction of time the parallel processor has only a single active processor (T_s), compared to the uniprocessor execution time (T_1). Suppose the program is otherwise ideal (i.e., $0 = 0$ and the remainder of program execution ($T_1 - T_s$) is perfectly parallel). Then:

$$S_p = \frac{T_1}{T_p}.$$

$$T_p = T_s + \frac{T_1 - T_s}{p}.$$

$$S_p = \frac{T_1}{T_s + T_1/p - T_s/p} = \frac{1}{s(1 - 1/p) + 1/p}.$$

And, if $p \gg 1$:

$$S_p = \frac{p}{sp + 1} > \frac{p}{sp} = \frac{1}{s}.$$

Indeed, if p is large and s is large enough so that $sp \gg 1$, then $s_p = 1/s$.

Speedup as a function of the serial fraction s is plotted in Figure 8.11. It is easy to understand the strong limitation that s represents. If 10% of a

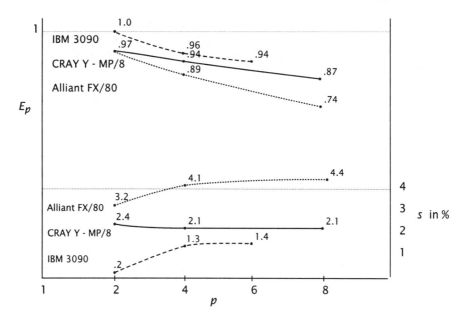

Figure 8.12 E_p and s for various processors vs. numbers of processors (p). Data from Karp and Flatt [155].

program is serial, then the maximum speedup is surely less than 10, since if the remaining 90% of the program executed in no time at all, we would still be limited to a speedup of $1/s$. As observed by Karp and Flatt, we would expect s to be an increasing function of p. As p increases, surely there will be additional memory contention, resource contention, and potential scheduling difficulties. Karp and Flatt provide data on measured efficiency and the serial fraction s for a series of machines on the Linpack problem (Figure 8.12). Linpack has significantly more logical parallelism available than configured in any of the tested multiprocessor configurations; hence, this example has no partitioning limitations. For rather large machines employing relatively small numbers of processors (such as the Cray), there is little change in the serial fraction as p is increased. The Alliant has a higher serial fraction, apparently because of larger task switching overhead; hence, it has a lower efficiency, and the serial fraction increases with p. If, as might be inferred from Figure 8.11, synchronization overhead increases with increasing numbers of processors and efficiency falls as s increases, then this puts a serious limitation on large multiprocessor configurations, since as we have seen earlier, speedup is generally limited to $1/s$.

Even if synchronization can be low, partitioning (especially control structure limitations) serves as another bound on multiprocessor speedup. Because of limitations in the control structure, a program that is amenable to execution by p processors may be able to use only a much smaller number of processors at various points during its program execution. The result is generally similar to the Amdahl Law effect that we saw in the previous discussion.

Suppose we designate the amount of time that a p processor system spends in the execution of a program using i processors $T_{i,p}$. Thus, $T_{1,p} = T_s$, the serial time that we introduced in our earlier discussion. R. B. Lee [182] has made an interesting observation about the character of control-flow-limited multiprocessors. She introduces an *equal-work hypothesis*. Under this hypothesis, let us assume that an equal amount of work is done while one processor is active, and that this is the same as the amount of work done by two processors, and finally as the amount of work done by i processors or p processors. The control flow limits the amount of work available so that it is equally distributed across each of the processor subsets from 1 to p. That is, $i \cdot T_{i,p}$ is the same for all i. Now assume that the amount of work required by the uniprocessor is the same as the amount of work required by the p processor ensemble. That is, if the number of operations for the uniprocessor execution is O_1 and the number of operations for parallel execution is O_p, then $O_1 = O_p$. If O_1 executes in T_1, then:

$$T_{i,p} = \frac{1}{p}\left[\frac{T_1}{i}\right],$$

since $1/p$th of the work is done by each of the i subsets, and the speedup for each subset is i. Thus:

$$T_p = \sum_i T_{i,p} = T_1/p \sum_{i=1}^{p} \frac{1}{i}$$

and

$$S_p = \frac{T_1}{T_p} = \frac{p}{\sum_{i=1}^{p} 1/i}.$$

The indicated series is simply the harmonic series. The sum of the harmonic series can be approximated as:

$$\sum_{i=1}^{p} \frac{1}{i} \doteq \ln p.$$

Thus, we can rewrite the speedup as:

$$S_p = \frac{p}{\ln p}.$$

Lee, in fact, goes on to show that the same bound is true, that the $p/\log p$ bound also holds not only when the amount of work is equal across all processor subsets, but so long as a much more general condition is satisfied, i.e.:

$$S_p \le p/\ln p,$$

so long as:

$$\sum_{i=1}^{p} \frac{\text{Prob}\,[i|p] - 1/p}{i} \ge 0,$$

where $\text{Prob}\,[i|p]$ is the probability that exactly i processors are used (out of p) at any given time.

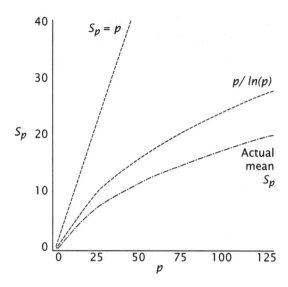

Figure 8.13   Realized mean speedup (S_p) for 24 Fortran programs vs. max number of processors used in a program execution (data from Lee [182]).

Thus, so long as there is sufficient work that occurs at relatively low degrees of parallelism, overall processor speedup will be limited to something less than $p/\ln p$. Lee compares the $p/\ln p$ bound to typical speedups for a variety of programs, as in Figure 8.13. Lee's bound and data might seem to represent a significant limitation for multiprocessor partitioning, but others such as Gustafson [114] generally argue that as machines get faster and larger, users scale up their program size so that the general lapsed time for any program remains constant. As program size grows, one would envision that the logical parallelism inherent in the program might greatly exceed the physical parallelism of the system, thus allowing significantly more time to be spent at maximum degrees of parallelism, and hence invalidating Lee's equal-work hypothesis.

While there may be little consensus on the long-term effect of partitioning on at least scientific programs, there is less controversy about the effect of synchronization and its subsequent effects on memory, bus, and cache traffic and its effects on system performance.

8.5.1   Grain Size and Overhead

The larger issue lurking here is how to pick an efficient grain size. The grain size is simply the number of instructions executed by an average size task on a single processor in a multiprocessor ensemble. If we make the grain size large, we reduce the amount of available parallelism. Even if we accept the argument that there is scaling of applications—as processing ensembles get larger, so do applications—it is still true that the larger the grain size, the less the parallelism. But as we reduce the grain size, the overhead becomes a significant factor in the computation. For effective computation, the grain size must be much larger than this overhead. Typically, the overhead consists of three items:

1. Communications delays. This includes the delays caused by messages that are passed among computational modes.

2. Context switching.

3. Cold-cache effects.

In order to make the grain size larger than this overhead effect, we must have

$$\frac{O_1}{p} \gg O;$$

$$O = [k_1(\text{communications delay/msg.})$$
$$+\text{context switch delay} + \text{cold cache delay}] \text{ MIPS}.$$

In this relationship, k_1 is the number of messages passed in a typical computational grain. This overhead delay, when multiplied by the MIPS available at the processing node, gives a measure of the equivalent number of overhead instructions present in the computation. The reader should recall that we are making the assumption that the program was perfectly partitionable without incurring algorithmic overhead; that is, the number of instructions to perform the computation with p processors (O_p), is the same as the number of operations required to perform that same computation on a single processor (O_1), ignoring overhead.

As networks of processors get larger, the network delay tends to increase, and as processor performance increases (MIPS), the effect of increased message delay and increased MIPS accelerates the overhead costs.

While one would expect that context switch time should scale with MIPS, it may or may not. As we have seen with advanced superscalar processors, there is a tendency to increase register set size or to increase the number of user-visible registers. Each of these tends to increase the context switch time.

Probably the most subtle effect of overhead is the cold-cache effect. Suppose we have a loop whose iterations are independent from one another. The first tendency would be to immediately recognize this as independent computational grains and distribute them across multiple processors. However, the single processor will load its instruction cache once with the loop, where the distributed version of the program now must incur the I-cache miss penalties n times. The same may be true with certain data, which may not even be shared among the processors (in the sense that it is communicating from processor to processor), but rather that it is simply used by the processors. Extra traffic created by cache initialization overhead both congests buses and slows down individual processing nodes.

Effective problem partitioning is a difficult problem that must be approached carefully—parallelism does not necessarily translate into speedup.

8.6   Types of Shared Memory Multiprocessors

Even within the seemingly limited class of processor architectures represented by shared memory multiprocessors, there is a great deal of variety.

Most of this variety results from the way the processors share memory. For example, processors may share at one of several levels:

1. Shared data cache–shared memory.

2. Separate data cache but shared bus–shared memory.

3. Separate data cache with separate buses leading to a shared memory.

4. Separate processors and separate memory modules interconnected with a multi-stage interconnection network.

We look at each of the representative designs from each of these classes throughout this chapter. Necessarily, our focus is on the simpler types of sharing arrangements.

The basic tradeoff in selecting a type of multiprocessor architecture is between resource limitations and synchronization/communications delay. Simple architectures are generally resource-limited and have rather low synchronization communications delay overhead. More robust processor-memory configurations may offer adequate resources for extensive communications among various processors in memory, but these configurations are limited by:

1. Delay through the communications network.

2. Multiple accessing of a single synchronization variable.

The simpler and more limited the multiprocessor configuration, the easier it is to provide synchronization communications and memory coherency. Each of these functions requires an access to memory. As long as memory bandwidth is adequate, these functions can be readily handled. As processor speed and the number of processors increase, eventually shared data caches and buses run out of bandwidth and become the bottleneck in the multiprocessor system. Replicating caches and/or buses to provide additional bandwidth requires management of not only the original traffic, but the coherency traffic also. From the system's point of view, one would expect to find an optimum level of sharing for each of the shared resources—data cache, bus, memory, etc.—fostering a hierarchical view of shared-memory multiprocessing systems [289].

8.7   Multithreaded or Shared Resource Multiprocessing

The simplest and most primitive type of multiprocessor system is what is sometimes called *multithreaded* or what we call here *shared resource multiprocessing* (SRMP) [5]. In the SRMP, each of the processors consists of basically only a register set—program counter, general registers, instruction counter, etc. The driving principle behind SRMP is to make the best use of processor silicon area. Area-intensive but perhaps infrequently used

NOW (Network of Workstations)

Or JPOW (Just a Pile of Workstations)—an alternative to shared memory multiprocessors?

As architects consider various ways of facilitating interprocessor communication in a shared memory multiprocessor, they must be constantly aware of the cost required to improve interprocessor communications. In a typical shared memory multiprocessor, the cost does not scale linearly—each additional processor requires additional network services and facilities. Depending on the type of interconnection, the cost for an additional processor may increase at a greater than linear rate. For those applications that require rapid communications and have a great deal of interprocessor communications traffic, this added cost is quite acceptable. It is readily justified on a cost-performance basis. However, many other applications, including many "naturally parallel" applications, may have limited interprocessor communications. In many simulation applications, the various cases to be simulated can be broken down and treated as independent tasks to be run on separate processors with minimum interprocessor communication. For these applications, simple networked systems of workstations provide perfectly adequate communications services. After all, typical networked message communication times are on the order of 1-3 milliseconds. For applications whose program execution time greatly exceeds its interprocessor communication time, this is a quite acceptable message passing time. Indeed, as they move to fiberoptics, networks will improve interprocessor communications delay.

The problem for the shared memory multiprocessor systems architect is to create a system that can generally satisfy a broad spectrum of applications. This requires a system whose costs scale linearly with the number of processors and whose overall cost effectively competes with the NOW—the simple network of workstations—on the one hand, and satisfies the more aggressive communications requirement for those applications that demand it on the other.

As with any systems design, it is impossible to satisfy the requirements of all applications. The designer simply must choose a broad enough set of applications and design a system robust enough to satisfy those applications.

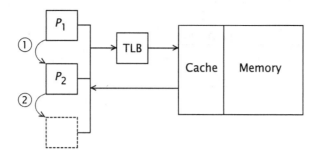

Figure 8.14   The SRMP. Only one processor issues instructions at any one time. Control passes (1, 2) from processor to processor on context switch or other event. Each processor has its own I-cache.

resources, such as floating-point hardware, can be shared by multiple processors together with a small high-bandwidth data cache which is used only for managing traffic to shared variables. The basic reason for SRMP is to facilitate context switches. With two processors, P_1 and P_2, control passes from P_1 to P_2 if there is a context switch in P_1 (Figure 8.14). The context switch then is handled in P_1 while P_2 is active. Since the switch from P_1 to P_2 can be done in no more than a processor cycle, the SRMP offers high performance to environments that consist of many small, "lightweight" processes (or *threads*, see chapter 3). All processors share the same data space and (usually) the same TLB(s).

There are two basic types of SRMP processor-switching protocols (Figure 8.15):

1. Each processor shares resources (floating point, data cache, etc.) in a time-multiplex fashion [263].

2. A processor has control to varying degrees over all resources, so long as it does not encounter a pipeline stall. As soon as it encounters a stall of any type—context switch, branch, run-on instruction, etc.— control passes to another processor, while its stall or pipeline break is resolved in the background [9].

Under either of these control scenarios, the maximum achievable performance is:

$$\text{Performance}_{maximum} = 1/\Delta t,$$

where Δt is the cycle time of either the shared resource or the maximum decode or maximum processing rate in the second case.

Figure 8.16 illustrates a generic SRMP layout. The number of (register set) processors is chosen to optimize the cost–performance.

SRMP makes reasonably good use of silicon, and could be a candidate arrangement for providing maximum processing power per unit of area on chip. This is illustrated in Study 8.1.

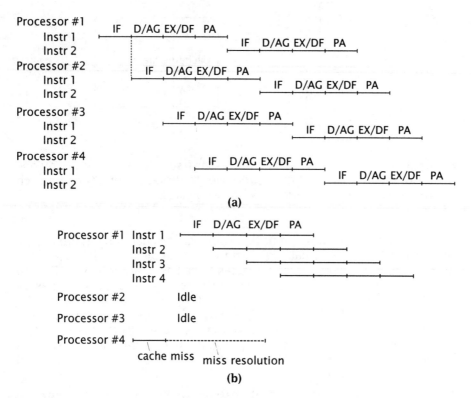

(a)

(b)

Figure 8.15 Two examples of SRMP: (a) with strict time multiplexing of resources. (b) with processor pipelined execution and task/processor switch on delay.

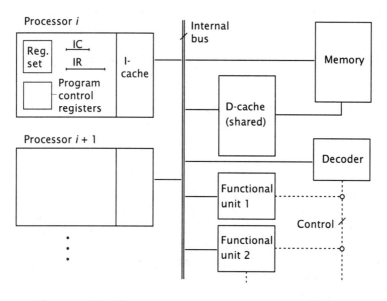

Figure 8.16 Shared resource multiprocessor (SRMP).

Study 8.1   SRMP vs. Pipelined Processor

In this study, we contrast a conventional pipelined processor (similar to our baseline) with a four-processor SRMP occupying (roughly) the same chip area.

Suppose an L/S pipelined processor has a 16KB I-cache and an 8KB D-cache, both set associative, CBWA and LRU replacement. The caches have a 16B line and miss delay of eight cycles. The processor makes one I-refr/I and 0.5 D-refr/I. The processor itself has performance of 1.5 CPI without cache misses (i.e., one CPI for decode and 0.5 CPI for branch, run-on, and other effects). We contrast the piplined processor with a four-processor SRMP. Each processor has its own register set and I-cache (4KB direct mapped). The SRMP shares D-cache, decoder, floating point ALU, etc. Once a processor is stalled (cache miss, etc.), it immediately switches on the next cycle—to the next available processor. The SRMP D-cache is designed to allow it to "non-block" on a miss; i.e., the miss is processed concurrently with accesses for another processor (unless, of course, it is to the missed line).

Pipelined Processor Analysis

The base CPI = 1.5.

The additional CPI lost due to cache misses (using chapter 4 data) is computed as follows:

$$
\begin{aligned}
\text{I-cache CPI loss} \;&=\; \text{I-cache miss rate} \times \text{I-refr/I} \times \text{miss penalty} \\
&=\; [0.05 \times 1.04] \times 1 \times 8 \text{ cycles} \\
&=\; 0.42 \text{ CPI.} \\
\text{D-cache CPI loss} \;&=\; \text{D-cache miss rate} \times \text{D-refr/I} \times \text{miss penalty} \\
&=\; [0.08 \times 1.04] \times 0.5 \times 8 \text{ cycles} \\
&=\; 0.33 \text{ CPI.}
\end{aligned}
$$

$$\text{Pipelined processor CPI total} \;=\; 2.25.$$

SRMP

Now each processor has its own I-cache: 4KB direct mapped. They share the D-cache. This ensures cache consistency and simplifies the I-cache design.

$$
\begin{aligned}
\text{I-cache CPI loss} \;&=\; [.095 \times 1.29] \times 1 \times 8 \text{ cycles} \\
&=\; 0.98 \text{ CPI}
\end{aligned}
$$

The D-cache has data for four processors resident. We approximate this situation by using MP = 3 (warm start) and $Q = 100$.

$$
\begin{aligned}
\text{D-cache CPI loss} \;&=\; [0.26 \times 1.04] \times 0.5 \times 8 \text{ cycles} \\
&=\; 1.08 \text{ CPI.}
\end{aligned}
$$

$$\text{Total CPI for single SRMP processor} = 3.56 \text{ CPI.}$$

A SRMP processor is busy for one cycle out of every 3.56 cycles of execution. It is idle for 2.56 cycles each instruction. Now we use our null-binomial model to predict performance. (Note: requests are *not* immediately resubmitted, as the stall must be resolved.)

$$\text{Prob of SRMP processor idle} = \frac{2.56}{3.56} = .72$$

$$\text{Prob of 4-processor SRMP idle} = .72^4 = .27$$

$$\text{Prob of SRMP busy} = 0.73$$

$$\text{SRMP CPI} = \frac{1}{0.73} = 1.37$$

Conclusion

Overall, the SRMP achieves 1.37 CPI while the pipelined processor achieves 2.25 CPI—a 1.64-times speedup. Of course, the SRMP requires some additional area (three register sets), partitioning and scheduling overhead, etc., so the net gain is less.

8.8   Memory Coherence in Shared Memory Multiprocessors

Probably no area of shared memory multiprocessor architecture has been more studied and discussed than memory coherence. Memory coherence is the essential ingredient in creating a *shared memory multiprocessor*. There are many methods or protocols for achieving a coherent memory picture, but the control of each protocol may be complex and the nomenclature is frequently confusing.

The fact that each node in a multiprocessor system possesses a local cache leads to the cache coherency problem. Since the address space of the processors overlaps, different processors can be holding (caching) the same memory segment at the same time, and possibly modifying the same physical memory location simultaneously. Therein lies the cache coherency problem—to ensure that all processors (caches) see the same, most updated copy of data. The protocol that maintains the consistency of data in all the local caches is called the *cache coherency protocol*.

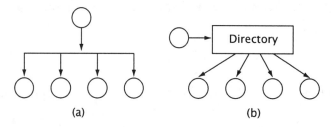

(a)   (b)

Figure 8.17 Snoopy and directory-based protocols. (a) Broadcast (snoopy) protocols: on a write to a shared line, all processors are notified. (b) Networked or directory-based protocols: on a write to a shared line, only processors that have a copy of the line are notified.

Protocols may be classified in a number of different ways. Probably the most important distinction among protocols is the way they distribute information about writes to memory to the other processors in this system. There are two basic approaches here (Figure 8.17):

- **Snoopy:** A write is broadcast to all processors in the system [21]. *Broadcast protocols* are usually reserved for shared bus multiprocessors. All the processors share memory through a common memory bus. The broadcast protocols are generally referred to as *snoopy* protocols, as all of the processors on the bus must monitor the bus for write transactions and take appropriate action if a monitored write is to a line contained in the processor's cache.

- **Directory-based:** The alternative to broadcast protocol is termed *networked* or *directory-based* protocols [48]. In these protocols, a write transaction is forwarded to only those processors that are known to possess a copy of the newly altered cache line.

These directory-based cache coherency protocols maintain the state information of the cache lines at a single (central or distributed) location called the *directory*. The requesting cache queries the directory for the owners and any caches who are sharing the same cache lines. Only the caches that are stated in the directory need to be sent the invalidate signal (or write updates). Because there is no need for buses to connect all caches, in contrast to snoopy protocols, directory-based cache coherency protocols can potentially scale better.

Clearly, snoopy protocols are simpler, in that information containing the ownership or use of lines does not have to be kept within the system. On the other hand, the snoopy protocols create a good deal of additional bus or network traffic, as the messages are broadcast to all processors regardless of whether or not the processors have a copy of the newly written line.

In directory-based protocols, information about the use of lines (the addresses of the users) is contained in a *directory*. As the number of cache lines in this system increases, and as the number of processor nodes in the system increase, the size of the systems directory for maintaining coherence and identifying users of cache lines becomes very large. So, optimization of the size of the directory is an important problem.

Regardless of whether we have a snoopy or a directory-based protocol, the local processor must take some action when an altered line is recognized. There are two types of actions: invalidate and update.

- **Invalidate:** This class of protocol invalidates all copies in other caches before making changes to the data in a particular cache line. For snoopy protocols, the initiating cache usually generates an invalidate signal on the bus. Other caches that possess the same cache line receive the invalidate signal from the bus and proceed to invalidate their copies.

- **Update:** The update class of protocol updates the lines in the caches sharing the line. For snoopy protocols, writes are broadcast on the bus, and caches sharing the same line snoop on the bus for the data and proceed to update the contents, and possibly the state, of their cache line.

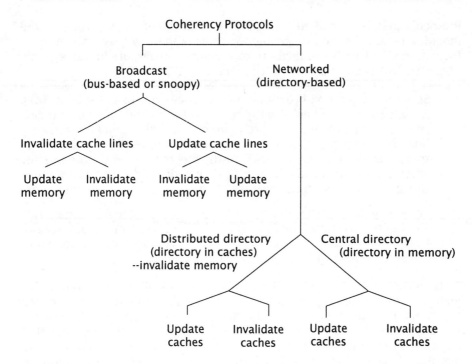

Figure 8.18 Possible coherency protocols. "Caches" refer to the action taken at remote processor caches when notified of a write to a shared line.

Even within the invalidate and update protocols, there is yet another set of distinctions possible. Is main memory updated when a write occurs, or are the only correct contents in the cache(s)?

There is a final important distinction among directory-based protocols, and this concerns the placement of the directory. The directory can be placed or associated with the memory system, in which case each line in memory has an entry defining the users of the line. Such a directory is referred to as a *memory-based* or *central directory*. The alternative is that memory and the individual users of the line are linked together in a list, and it is the responsibility of a pointer from memory to the head of the list to ensure that correct action is taken on a write to a line. Since in this case the cache-based directory is distributed across the processors, this directory is frequently called a *distributed directory* [147].

In the case of a distributed memory system, where a portion of global memory is associated with each processor in a network, the terminology is particularly confusing.

A portion of the central directory is associated with each portion of memory, and hence is distributed across the network. The term "central directory" is still used for such memory-based directories. The protocol alternatives are outlined in Figure 8.18.

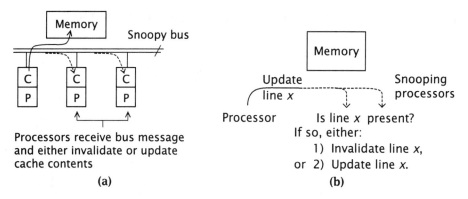

Figure 8.19 Snoopy protocols. (a) A shared bus multiprocessor. (b) Update and invalidate snoopy protocols.

8.9 Shared-Bus Multiprocessors

Possibly the most widely studied and most commonly used type of shared memory multiprocessor is the shared bus–shared memory multiprocessor. Consistency must be insured by a protocol which forces the respective processor caches to have a coherent picture of memory for any synchronized code passage. Since all processors share a bus, they can see all transactions. This ensures consistency by broadcasting the transaction. Bus-based protocols are also called *snoopy* protocols. Each protocol requires a different amount of bus and memory bandwidth and control complexity in managing coherence traffic. Our discussion of these protocols follows the work of Archibald and Baer [21]. There are two basic approaches to snoopy protocol consistency: *invalidate* and *update* (Figure 8.19a and b). Protocols assume that all of the processors are aware of, and receive, all bus transactions (they snoop on the bus). There are four well-known variations on the invalidate strategy. These are called:

1. Write-invalidate [107].

2. Synapse [95].

3. Illinois [225].

4. Berkeley [157].

The alternative protocols are called *update protocols.* If a write occurs to a line contained in any processor's cache, the write updates any cache that contains that line as well as memory. The two best-known approaches to update protocols are the *Firefly* [21] and the *Dragon* [191] approaches. We discuss all these protocols in this section.

8.9.1 Snoopy Protocols

Snoopy protocols can be categorized not only by whether they invalidate or update shared data lines in remote caches, but also by the source of the new data for a cache line. The data may be provided either by the main

Table 8.3   Bus-based or snoopy cache coherence protocols.

	Source of a new cache line	Number of States			
		3	4	4	5
		Invalid	Invalid	Invalid	Invalid
				Private–Clean	Private–Clean
		Shared–Clean	Shared–Clean	Shared–Clean	Shared–Clean
		Private–Dirty	Private–Dirty	Private–Dirty	Private–Dirty
			Shared–Dirty		Shared–Dirty
Invalidate	Memory	Write-Inval.		MESI	
Invalidate	Cache-to-cache data movement	Synapse Berkeley	Illinois		
Update	Cache-to-cache data movement			Firefly	Dragon

Table 8.4   Summary of snoopy protocols.

Name	Category	Memory Copy Policy	Unique Feature
Invalidate	Wr. invalid.	Copyback	Simplicity
Berkeley	Wr. invalid.	Copyback	Explicit memory ownership
Illinois	Wr. invalid.	Copyback	Clean private state; can supply data from any cache with a clean copy
Firefly	Wr. update[a]	Copyback for Private Write through for Shared	Memory updated on broadcast
Dragon	Wr. update	Copyback for Private Write through for Shared	Memory not updated on broadcast

[a] Or, Write broadcast in Eggers [83].

memory or by the cache that makes the most recent write to the shared data line (and now has an exclusive copy). Table 8.3 places seven widely discussed protocols into the various categories. Another important distinction among snoopy protocols is the complexity of the protocol itself. This is largely determined by the number of states that must be maintained by the individual cache lines for shared data. The simplest protocols use only three states to ensure coherency. More complex protocols use as many as five or more states for coherence. In general, the larger the number of states, the more complex the protocol, but the less traffic on the bus.

Examples of Snoopy Protocols

The following paragraphs describe some representative examples of the different classes of bus-based protocols. All caches are basically assumed to be CBWA, but requests to a shared line may force a line write. (See Table 8.4.) State tables of the protocol are provided in Appendix F, along with some descriptions.

Write-invalidate (or simply *Invalidate*)   This is one of the simplest protocols, and has only three states: *Invalid, Valid,* and *Dirty*. For a read hit, clearly there are no coherency problems. When there is a read miss, the CPU changes the state of the cache line to Valid. On a write hit, the bus notifies all users that the line is Invalid. This is similar to the action on a write miss. In either case, the write line is marked Dirty and all other users mark their lines Invalid (Figure 8.20).

When another processor tries to access a dirty line, a bus read for the line occurs. The processor holding the line supplies the data, updates memory, and marks the line *valid* if the remote process tries to write (i.e., a bus write occurs). The processor holding the line would respond similarly, but would mark the line *invalid* on completion.

The state diagram (Figure 8.20) is interpreted as follows. A line is initially *invalid* and not in any cache. A read miss causes the line to be transferred to the requesting cache and marked *valid*. Subsequent read misses to the same cache entry by conflicting memory line addresses also receive *valid* line copies. When a processor writes to a line in its cache, that line is marked *dirty* and the bus broadcasts an *invalid* signal for the line. This is repeated in any subsequent write to the dirty line. If a read miss to a dirty line (from another processor) is detected by the bus (*bus read miss*), the bus and cache update the line in memory. Then the requesting processor accesses the updated line now marked *valid*. The originating processor also marks the line *valid*.

Berkeley   The Berkeley (also called Berkeley–SPUR) cache coherency protocol [157] uses the idea of cache line ownership (see Figure 8.21). At any time, a cache line can only be owned by either one of the caches or, if no caches own the line, by memory. There are four states: *Invalid, Read Only, Shared Dirty,* and *Private Dirty*. When a line is shared, only the owner has the cache line in the Shared Dirty state; all others have the line in the Read Only state. Therefore, a cache line can be Shared Dirty or Private Dirty in only one cache (the owner).

When a **read miss** occurs, the requesting cache gets the data from the owner of the cache line, which can be memory (if the line is in the Invalid or Read Only states in other caches) or the other caches (where it is in the Shared Dirty or Private Dirty), and sets the state to Read Only. If the line requested is in the Read Only state in any other caches, it is main memory, the owner, which supplies the data. The state of the cache line then remains as Read Only. If the line requested is owned by another cache (i.e., in the Shared Dirty or Private Dirty state), then the cache (owner) that supplies the data sets the state of the cache line to Shared Dirty.

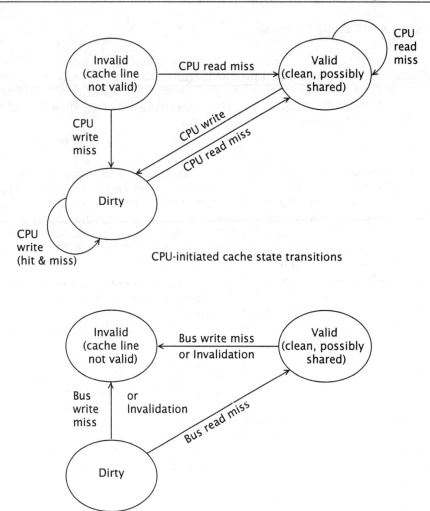

Figure 8.20 Cache state transitions for Write-invalidate cache coherency protocol. (Also see Appendix F.)

Similarly, for a `write miss`, the block comes directly from the owner (memory or other caches). All other caches with copies of the line invalidate their lines. The requesting cache sets the state of the cache line to Private Dirty and becomes the owner.

For a `write hit`, the requesting cache invalidates all other copies of the cache line and makes the write updates. The new state of the line is set to Private Dirty, regardless of the original state of the line. Note that if the line is already Private Dirty, there is no necessity for invalidation as it is only a copy of the cache line; therefore, the writing can proceed locally without waiting for invalidation.

Illinois   The Illinois model [225] has four states: *Invalid, Read Private* (also called *valid exclusive), Read Shared,* and *Private Dirty* (also called *modified*). A cache line which is owned by any cache is either in the Read Private or

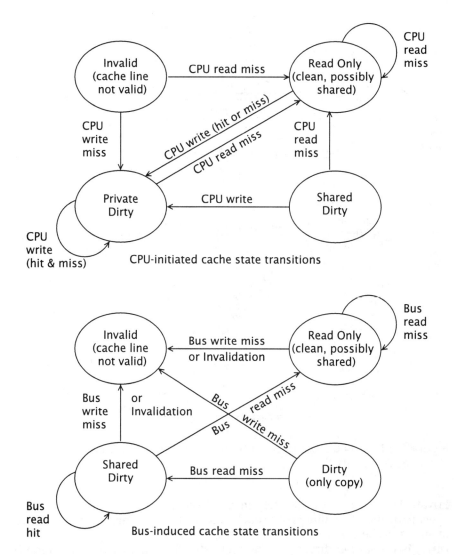

Figure 8.21   Cache state transitions for Berkeley cache coherency protocol. (Also see Appendix F.)

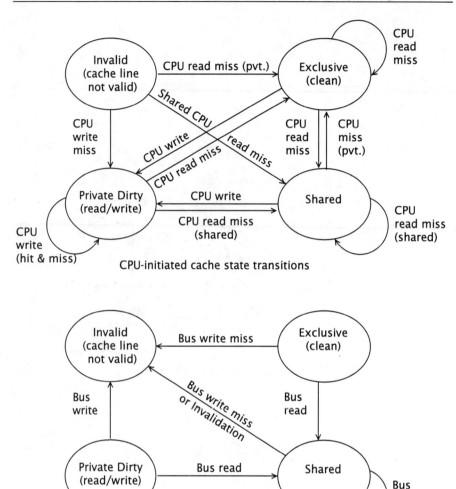

Figure 8.22 Cache state transitions for Illinois cache coherency protocol. (Also see Appendix F.)

Private Dirty state. Cache lines in the Read Shared state do not have a specific owner. The Illinois approach enables the determination of whether or not a cache line is shared when it is loaded. A modified line (Private Dirty) is forwarded directly to the requestor from the cache containing it. This eliminates the need to send out invalidations for cache lines which have not been shared. See Figure 8.22 for the state transition diagram.

The Illinois and similar four-state shared protocols are sometimes called MESI protocols, as per the states: modified, exclusive, shared, invalid.

When a read miss or write miss occurs, the missing line is first retrieved from other caches, and if none possesses it, from the main memory. If the line is dirty, it is also written back to memory at the same time. If the cache line is shared, the cache with the highest priority supplies the line. On read miss, if the line is supplied by another cache then it and all other caches

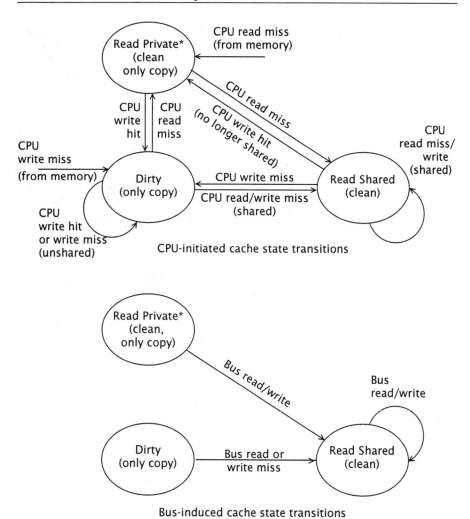

Figure 8.23   Cache state transitions for Firefly cache coherency protocol. (Also see Appendix F.) *Read Private is also referred to as Valid Exclusive.

change their state to Read Shared. However if the supplier is memory, the requesting cache sets the cache state to Read Private and becomes the owner. On write miss, the line is forwarded from memory or another cache and is updated and set to the Private Dirty state. All other caches invalidate their copies. Note that the Illinois approach only allows a single writer; a dirty cache line is present in only one cache.

For a write hit, if the requesting cache is the owner (cache state either Private Dirty or Read Private), the update proceeds without delay. If the line is shared by other caches (Read Shared), the update to the cache line by the requesting cache can only proceed after an invalidate signal is sent on the bus (for other caches to invalidate their copies). The state of the updated cache line is Private Dirty.

Firefly   The Firefly protocol [21] has four states, but uses only three: *Read Private, Read Shared,* and *Private Dirty,* in contrast to the previous examples (refer to Figure 8.23). The *invalid* state is used only to define an initial condition of a cache line. Firefly uses the update scheme instead of invalidation, i.e., writes to cache are broadcast and written to memory. All other caches sharing the line snoop on the bus and update their copies correspondingly. Therefore, no cache line will be invalid after being properly loaded. There is also a special bus line, the SharedLine, which is asserted to indicate that at least one other cache is sharing the line.

When a `read miss` occurs, if another cache has a copy of the line, it supplies it to the requesting cache by asserting the SharedLine. All sharing caches, including the requesting cache, set the state of the cache line to Read Shared. If the state of the cache line is previously Dirty, it is written to main memory. If no other cache has a copy of the requested line, it is supplied by the memory and is loaded in the Read Private state.

Similarly, for a `write miss`, the requested line is supplied either by other caches or by memory. When the line comes from other caches, the SharedLine is asserted and recognized by the requesting cache. Thus, the line is set to the Read Shared state and the ensuing write is broadcast to all caches and memory, which update their copies. If the line is supplied by memory, the cache line is loaded in the Dirty state and written to without broadcasting the new data.

For a `write hit`, if the line is Dirty or Read Private, it is written to immediately. For the latter case, the state is changed to Dirty. If it is in the Read Shared state, the requesting cache must write the new data to memory. All other caches sharing the line grab the data from the bus and update their copies. In addition, these caches assert the SharedLine. This is needed for the requesting cache to check whether the other caches are still sharing the line. If the line is no longer shared, the broadcast can be avoided (this can happen when other sharing caches have displaced the line from their caches), in which case it is loaded in the Read Private state. Otherwise, it is loaded in the Read Shared state.

Dragon   The Dragon approach [191] uses the update protocol (i.e., updates to a cache line are broadcast to the other caches sharing the cache line instead of invalidating the copies in the other caches). It makes use of a SharedLine, which is asserted to indicate that at least one other cache is sharing the same cache line. Dragon allows multiple writers, and a distinctive feature is that instead of also writing through to memory (whenever a cache writes to a shared line), the updates are only propagated to the other caches holding a copy of the same line. Memory is not updated until a line is replaced. This feature necessitates the addition of another state, so that the states of the Dragon are: *Read Private, Shared Clean, Shared Dirty,* and *Dirty Private.* The difference between the Shared Clean and Shared Dirty states is that the last cache, if any, to write to a Shared Clean line changes its state to Shared Dirty, while the other sharing cache retains the Shared Clean state. Thus, Shared Dirty (and also Private Dirty) imply ownership.

When a `read miss` occurs, if the cache line is supplied by other caches that also assert the SharedLine, the line is loaded in the Shared Clean state. For the supplying cache, the state is changed to Shared Dirty if it is previously in the Private Dirty state; or it remains in the Shared Dirty state if that is

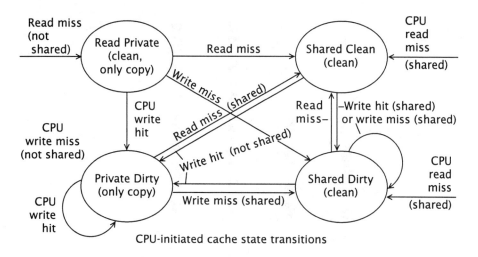

CPU-initiated cache state transitions

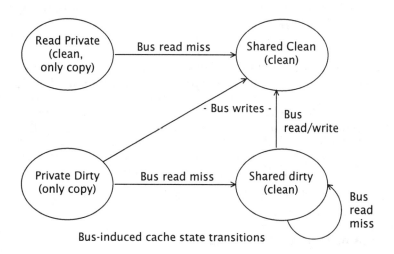

Bus-induced cache state transitions

Figure 8.24   Cache state transitions for Dragon cache coherency protocol. (Also see Appendix F.)

the previous state. Any cache with a Read Private or Shared Clean copy asserts the SharedLine and changes the copy to the Shared Clean state. The requesting line is then loaded in the Shared Clean state. However, if the line is supplied by memory (no other cache is sharing it), then the state of the cache line is set as Read Private.

The `write miss` case is similar. Upon loading the line, if the line is forwarded from the other caches, the requesting cache sets the state of the line of Shared Dirty and broadcasts the updates on the bus. All other caches with a copy of this line set the state to Shared Clean. If no other cache has a copy, the requesting cache makes the update locally without having to broadcast and the state is set to Private Dirty.

For a `write hit`, if the line is already Private Dirty or Read Private, the write can proceed immediately without the need for broadcasting. For the

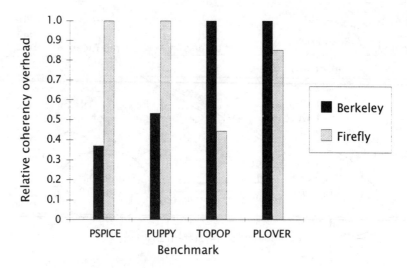

Figure 8.25   Relative traffic for Berkeley vs. Firefly on four applications. (Data taken from Eggers [84].)

Read Private case, the state is changed to Dirty Private. If the state of the line is either Shared Clean or Shared Dirty, the write must be broadcast to other caches. All other sharing caches snoop the bus for the write update, change the state of their copy to Shared Clean, and assert the SharedLine. If the SharedLine is not asserted, the requesting cache knows that no other cache is sharing the line and subsequent writes are not broadcast. So if the SharedLine is not asserted, the requesting cache sets the state of the cache line to Private Dirty; otherwise, it is set to Shared Dirty.

Table 8.4 summarizes the different snoopy cache coherency protocols [83].

Comparing Bus-Based Protocols

The relative performance of shared-bus consistency protocols is heavily dependent on program behavior. Eggers [84] has compared two of the most interesting protocols, Berkeley (a sophisticated invalidate protocol) and Firefly (an update protocol). Figure 8.25 shows that there is no consistent pattern in determining an optimal protocol. Moreover, studies of this sort focus on the shared traffic only. In many practical cases, the I-traffic, the shared read-only traffic, and private data traffic can easily dominate the traffic profile in an application. To make matters even more complex, selection of certain cache parameters such as line size to optimize shared data traffic may work to the detriment of other traffic. Generally, larger line sizes in large caches produce a lower miss rate and, for many read-only accesses, a lower traffic rate. Generally, however, for shared data, large line sizes can increase both miss rate and traffic rate. This occurs because of *false sharing* [289], when two processors write to two different words in the same line. Miss rate due to shared data traffic has been variously estimated at between 2–5% for a large cache (greater than 64 KB). The designer must ensure that in trying to minimize the shared miss rate one does not inadvertently increase the nonshared traffic.

8.9.2   Bus-Based Models

These are the simplest analytic models. While useful across a variety of applications (including memory), they are probably most appropriate for the analysis of bus contention when a bus is being accessed by multiple users (processors, etc.). We refer to a similar model of memory contention in chapter 6—Strecker's model [273].

For bus contention, assume there are n requestors each of which would occupy the bus for a fraction of time ρ. This factor ρ is akin to the queueing utilization factor ρ. It represents the offered amount of occupancy by a single source without contention. The model assumes that the bus has no memory. Its state at any time does not depend on previous history (number of requests denied, etc.), or on its immediate history in the case of resubmitted requests.

The bus utilization generally is:

$$\rho = \frac{\text{Bus transaction time}}{\text{Processor time + bus transaction time}},$$

where (in terms of 100 instructions):

Bus transaction time is the time spent on the bus (excluding waiting time) per 100 instructions executed, and

Processor time is the execution time per 100 instructions, excluding bus transactions. If processor execution and bus transaction time are overlapped, the processor time is the unoverlapped processor execution.

A simple CBWA cache-based processor might have:

$$\text{Bus transaction time} = 100f(1 + w)T_{\text{line access}},$$

where f is the miss rate per reference.

Once ρ has been determined, we have for n processors sharing the bus:

Prob   [a given processor does not reference bus] $= (1 - \rho)$
Prob   [no processor references bus] $= (1 - \rho)^n$
Prob   [bus is busy] $= 1 - (1 - \rho)^n$
$$= B(n)$$

where $B(n)$ is the achieved bandwidth as a fraction of the total available bus bandwidth.

Note that:

1. Offered bandwidth $= n\rho$.

2. Total available bus bandwidth $= 1.0$.

3. Achieved bus bandwidth $= B(n)$.

As mentioned in chapter 6, this ignores the obvious fact that a request to the bus that has been denied will be immediately resubmitted and wait until the bus is available. The net effect of this is to increase the actual realized bus bandwidth over that expected by the above analysis. As developed in chapter 6, we estimate the actual bus requests (a) per source [307] as:

$$a = \frac{\rho}{\rho + (\rho_a/\rho)(1 - \rho)},$$

and then

$$B(n) = n\rho_a = 1 - (1 - a)^n.$$

Initially estimate $a = \rho$, and then we can iteratively solve for a and ρ_a.

Processors slow down due to bus contention. They achieve only bus transaction rates (and hence performance) of λ_a when offered rates of λ. The expected delay due to bus contention for each transaction is:

$$T_w = \frac{n\rho - B(n)}{B(n)} T_s$$

so that the offered rate, λ, is:

$$\lambda = 1/\text{processor execution time} + \text{bus time},$$

while

$$\lambda_a = \frac{1}{\text{Processor execution time} + \text{bus time} + T_w}.$$

$$\frac{\lambda_a}{\lambda} = \frac{\text{Processor execution time} + \text{bus time}}{\text{Processor execution time} + \text{bus time} + T_w}.$$

This is the effective "slowdown" factor due to bus contention. Since we are primarily interested in the λ_a/λ ratio, we can compute the rates in terms of processor execution (MIPS) or bus transactions.

EXAMPLE 8.2

If a 10-MIPS processor has 9.75 misses per 100 instructions and each miss creates a 300-nsec bus transaction delay, then the offered rate is:

$$\lambda = \frac{1}{\text{Processor execution between bus transactions} + \text{bus transaction}}.$$

The processor execution time between bus transactions is 100/9.75 instructions:

$$10.26 \text{ instr} \times 100 \text{ ns/instr} = 1.03 \text{ } \mu\text{s between transactions.}$$

$$\lambda = \frac{1}{1.03 + .30} = .75 \text{ transactions per } \mu\text{s}$$

$$= 750\text{K transactions per sec.}$$

In terms of processor performance, the bus adds $300 \text{ ns}/10.26 \text{ instr} = 29.2 \text{ ns}$ to each instruction, or:

$$\lambda = \frac{1}{.100 + 0.029} = 7.75 \text{ MIPS.}$$

$\blacklozenge$

Study 8.2   Shared-Bus Multiprocessors

(a) Shared-bus multiprocessors with bus contention

Suppose four processors with CBWA caches share a common bus and memory system. Initially, we assume that there is no contention at the memory—only at the bus. Suppose we are given the following processor parameters:

Processor performance: 10 MIPS (all in cache).
References per instr: 1.3 (total from IF, DF and DS).
Cache miss rate: 0.05.
w, dirty line ratio: 0.5.
Bus transaction = $T_{\text{line access}}$ = 300 nsec.

We now look at the effects of bus contention on overall performance. First we compute:

Bus transaction time per 100 instr
$$= 100 \times (\text{miss rate}) \times \text{refr}/I \times (1 + w) \times T_{\text{line access}}$$
$$= 100 \times 0.05 \times 1.3 \times 1.5 \times 300\,\text{ns}$$
$$= 2.93 \text{ microseconds.}$$
Processor execution time per 100 instr
$$= \frac{100}{10\text{ MIPS}} = 10\mu s.$$

Total processor execution time including bus transactions = 12.93.

$$\rho = \frac{2.93}{12.93} = 0.23.$$
$$B\,(n = 4) = 1 - (1 - .23)^4$$
$$= 0.64$$

or, with resubmissions (after several iterations):

$$a = .273$$
$$\rho_a = .18$$
$$B\,(n = 4) = 0.72$$

We offered 0.92 of the total bus capacity, and achieved 0.72. The effect of this was to slow down each bus transaction by:

$$T_w = \frac{.92 - 0.72}{0.72}\,T_{\text{line access}}$$
$$= (.278)300\,\text{ns} = 83.3\,\text{ns.}$$

The effect of this delay on processor performance is to wait for 83.3 ns. Thus, there are:

$5 \times 1.3 \times 1.5 = 9.75$ transactions per 100 instructions

or

10.26 instructions per transaction.

So:

$$\frac{\lambda_a}{\lambda} = \frac{10.26 \times 100 + 300}{1026 + 300 + 83.3} = 0.94.$$

This slows down the processor from operating at 7.73 MIPS (no contention) to 7.27 MIPS.

(b) Shared-bus multiprocessors without bus contention and with memory contention

Now suppose each processor has its own bus (ideal bus), and the memory system has two independent modules each capable of a line access. They are interleaved on low-order line address, and any single module is busy for $T_{\text{line access}}$ for each line access (i.e., page mode).

We now use the δ-binomial model from chapter 6 to compute the memory performance:

$$B(m, n, \delta) = m + n - \delta/2 - \sqrt{(m + n - \delta/2)^2 - 2mn}.$$

Now $m = 2$ and we must find n and δ.

We compute n as the expected number of requests during $T_{\text{line access}}$. Each processor makes:

5.85 references $\times$ 0.05 misses/reference

$=$ 0.29 miss requests/line access.

Therefore, for four processors:

$n = 4 \times 0.29 = 1.16,$

$$\delta = \frac{n}{z}.$$

Since we have three request sources each cycle (IF, DF, DS) and three cycles per memory busy time (line access, in this case), we have $z = 3 \times 3 \times 4$ (processors) $= 36$. So

$$\delta = \frac{1.16}{36} = 0.03.$$

Now, using the δ-binomial equation, we compute:

$B(m = 2, \ n = 1.16, \ \delta = 0.03) = 0.85$

and

$$T_w = \frac{1.16 - 0.85}{.85} \times 300\,\text{ns} = 108\,\text{ns}.$$

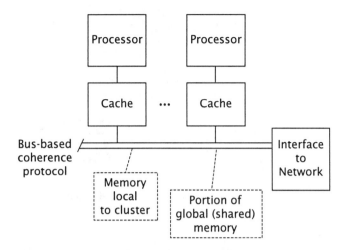

Figure 8.26   Typical processor–memory cluster.

The processor is slowed down due to this contention. There are $(1.5 \times 1.3 \times 5) = 9.75$ transactions each 100 instructions, so there are $100/9.75 = 10.26$ instructions between transactions, and each transaction takes 300 nsec.

So, the processor's effective execution rate is slowed down by:

$$\frac{\lambda_a}{\lambda} = \frac{(10.26) \times 100\,\text{ns} + 300\,\text{ns}}{(10.26) \times 100 + 300 + 108} = 0.93,$$

and the effective processor execution rate is:

$$0.93 \times 7.73\ \text{MIPS} = 7.19\ \text{MIPS}.$$

Note that in this case, the bus or the memory as defined would equally limit processor performance.

8.10   Scalable Multiprocessors

Shared bus configurations of multiprocessors are obviously limited by bus bandwidth. At some point, the traffic required by the processors to retain a coherent picture of the memory state saturates the bus and at that point adding additional processors into such a system provides no net improvement in performance. To extend performance beyond this point requires a high bandwidth network and some mechanism to ensure memory coherency across the network. Suppose we consider the shared bus multiprocessor as a processor *cluster* (Figure 8.26).

Figure 8.27 shows a system description of the scalable multiprocessor. Multiprocessor systems that consist of multiple clusters connected through a general interconnect network are the basis for implementing large-scale shared memory multiprocessors. If we can find a technique for facilitating a coherency protocol across an arbitrarily large number of clusters, we call that system a *scalable* shared memory multiprocessor. As the difficulty in

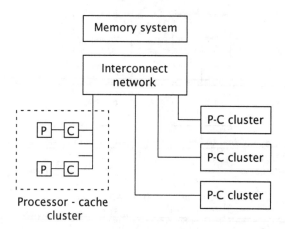

Figure 8.27   Scalable shared memory multiprocessor.

adding additional clusters to a system is not easily quantifiable, the notion of *scalability* is somewhat subjective. Many designers consider multiprocessor systems that contain more than a small number of clusters—perhaps, say, more than four—as a scalable system. Occasionally conference organizers and others have used the term *massively parallel* as synonymous with *scalable*, at least in the discussion of multiprocessor systems. It is left to the reader to determine what, indeed, is scalable or massive and what is not.

Since snoopy protocols cannot be used, there are two primary issues in dealing with large-scale multi-clustered multiprocessor systems: the first is memory coherence using directory-based protocols [48], and the second is the interconnect network. In the remainder of this chapter, we introduce some of the major issues and approaches in these areas.

8.11   Directory-Based Protocols

The following discussion is based on the work of D. Glasco [104]. From a coherency point of view, the processor cluster simply resembles a single processor with cache, since within the cluster a protocol has been selected to ensure that all the caches have a consistent picture of the memory state. In the discussion in this section, we assume that the processor cluster and the processor cache can be used synonymously, and thus, for simplicity of discussion, we consider a single processor cache in place of the cluster.

There are four general approaches to maintaining data consistency in a large shared memory multiprocessor system. Protocols are distinguished by what happens to memory and what happens to the caches when a line is written into them. Table 8.5 shows that either memory or the caches can be updated or invalidated on a write to a shared line. Writes to an exclusively owned line do not usually update memory in any case.

Directories specifying line ownership or usage can be kept with the memory (central) or with the processor–caches (distributed). Usually, if the memory is organized about a *central directory* (CD), memory will be updated on a

Table 8.5   Protocols based on memory hierarchy consistency.

Memory	Remote Caches	
	Invalidated	Updated
Not Updated	Invalidate (SCI/SDD)	Update (DD-UP)
Updated	Invalidate (CD-INV)	Update (CD-UP)

write update [10] (Figure 8.28). If the protocol uses a distributed directory to control the status of the shared information, the main memory is generally not updated and the true picture of the memory state is found only in the ensemble of caches. These protocols are called *distributed directory* (DD). The case of DD-INV is an important one, as a number of special protocols have been built for it, including the proposed IEEE standard protocol for large, shared multiprocessing systems. This protocol is called the SCI—the *scalable coherent interface* protocol [12, 148].

It is important to remember that the notion of *central* and *distributed* directory is somewhat misleading. If our system model has already partitioned memory into many pieces and associated each with a node (i.e., we have distributed memory), then the central directory is as distributed as the distributed directory. For example, if there are n nodes in the system and each node has a cache and portion of main memory ($1/n$ of main memory), then requests for directory information external to the node in both cases will be directed to another node. If accessing is random, in either case we

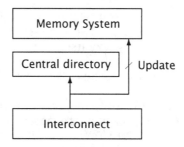

Figure 8.28   Central directory protocols (CD) can be used with memory update or invalidate.

are equally likely to access any other nodes. In the central directory case, we access a portion of a directory based upon a physical memory address. In the distributed directory case, a cache-based directory entry is based on accessed line ownership.

8.11.1   Directory Structure

A directory must contain a list of caches that have copies of a particular line so that that line can be either invalidated or updated [48]. In CD protocols,

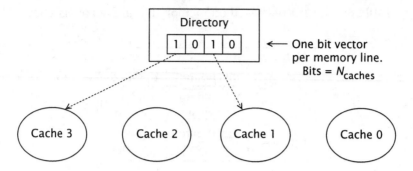

Figure 8.29　Centralized directory structure.

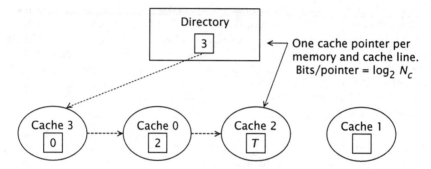

Figure 8.30　Singly linked distributed directory structure. N_c = number of caches.

the directory is associated with memory and contains information for each line in memory. Each line has a bit vector which contains a bit for each processor–cache in the system (Figure 8.29). The bit identifies a particular cache as having a copy of the line. These directories are known as *fully mapped directories*. The directory size itself consists of:

Directory size (bits) = Number of caches × Number of memory lines.

Clearly, if line ownership is low, fully mapped directories are spatially in-efficient. Other list-based approaches are possible for CD [10], and are spatially more efficient, although slower. To simplify the discussion, we present only fully mapped central directories.

The CD approach has been attractive because of its relatively straightfor-ward implementation. Clearly, its directory size and accessibility provide an ultimate limit on the usefulness of this protocol in large shared memory systems.

In a distributed directory (DD), the memory has only one pointer which identifies the cache that last requested it. Coherency is then based upon the use of a linked list. A subsequent request to that line is referred to the cache that received it last. The requestor then receives an updated copy of the line from that cache and the requestor's id is placed at the head of the linked list.

There are singly and doubly linked versions of the linked list called *scal-able distributed directory* (SDD) [280] and *scalable coherent interface* (SCI)

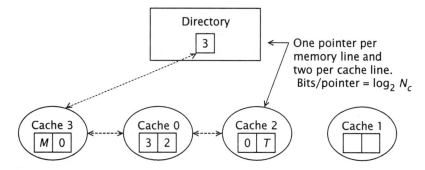

Figure 8.31   SCI distributed directory structure. N_c = number of caches.

[12, 148], respectively. In the singly-linked list (SDD), each processor–cache points only to its predecessor. Memory points to the head of the list (Figure 8.30).

The scalable coherence interface (the SCI) maintains this list as a doubly linked list, so that each cache entry points not only to its successor in the list, but also to its predecessor (Figure 8.31). In either scheme, a pointer occupies $\lceil \log_2 (\text{number of caches}) \rceil$ bits.

For a singly linked list, the overall number of bits required for the protocol is (approximately) determined by the number of bits required in memory to point to the possible "head of the list." The number of bits required for the memory directory is:

Directory size (bits) = Number of mem. lines $\times \lceil \log_2 (\text{number of caches}) \rceil$.

This does not include additional bits required in the local caches. For the doubly linked list (the SCI), the number of memory directory bits needed to maintain the protocol is, to a first approximation, the same as the singly linked case, but the local cache pointer bits are doubled.

8.11.2   Invalidate Protocols

The invalidate-based protocols maintain consistency by invalidating the entry for a shared line in all processors that are using the line except, of course, for the processor that is writing. The invalidate protocols use the directory to establish which processors have a copy of the line so that these invalidate requests can be forwarded to the appropriate processors. After the invalidate transaction, only the writing processor will have a cache with a copy of the line.

In the centralized directory invalidate protocol (CD-INV), the directory specifies each processor that has a copy of the line. Invalidate signals and a pointer to the requesting processor can be forwarded (in parallel, if the implementation allows) to all of the processors that have a copy of the line (processors 3 and 1 in Figure 8.32). Each invalidated cache acknowledges invalidation so that a completion of the write can be established. After the write and the subsequent invalidations, the directory indicates that the writing cache has an exclusive read–write copy of the line. Because of the

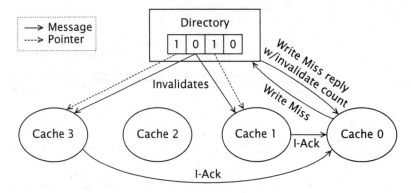

Figure 8.32 Centralized directory invalidations.

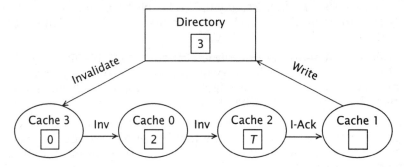

Figure 8.33 SDD actions in a distributed directory—invalidate prefetched. (*T* indicates tail of the list.)

central directory, the invalidate signals can be sent concurrently to other caches (Figure 8.32). This protocol is similar to that one used in DASH [184].

In the distributed directory protocols, the directory has a pointer to a linked list of caches. In the SDD protocol, or singly linked list protocol, the directory has a pointer to the last cache that has written this line. Invalidate requests are then sent to this cache, which invalidates its copy and forwards an invalidate signal to the next cache. The writing cache determines the head of the list by accessing the directory in memory. The directory then establishes the writing cache as the owner of the line and subsequent references to the line are referred to this cache.

In the singly linked list (as in Figure 8.33), processor 1 writes to the directory, which notifies the head of the list (processor 3) that this line has been made invalid by processor 1. The directory is then updated, pointing to processor 1. This information is then forwarded down the list until the last user of the list, in this case processor 2, invalidates its entry. At that point, processor 2 sends an invalidate acknowledgement to processor 1 and processor 1 then has the sole correct version of the line.

In the SCI or doubly linked list protocol, the directory also has a single pointer to the cache at the head of the list. The directory then sends the invalidate request down the list, purging the line and all current caches (Figure 8.34).

For example, assume the cache for processor 1 writes a particular line. If

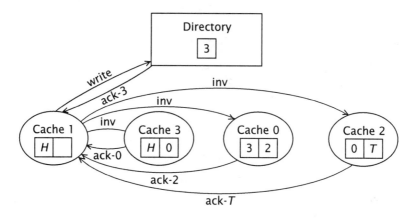

Figure 8.34   SCI actions in a distributed directory—invalidate protocol. (H, T indicate head, tail of list.)

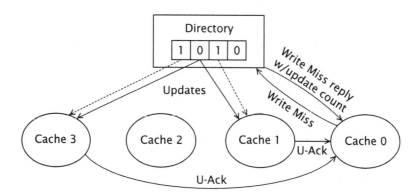

Figure 8.35   Centralized directory updates.

it is not already the head of the list, it removes itself from the list. It then references the directory with its write, placing itself at the head of the list. It now finds that cache 3 (i.e., processor 3) is at the head of the old linked list of users of the line. Cache 1 then sends an invalidate signal to processor 3 After receiving the invalidate signal, cache 3 acknowledges to cache 1 and identifies the next user of the line on the list. This process is repeated, invalidating all other users. When the last cache on the list receives the invalidate signal, it acknowledges to cache 1 and the write is complete.

The principal difference between invalidate protocols is the time it takes to maintain the consistency across the network of processors and the source of the miss data. With the central directory, the invalidate traffic can be forwarded in parallel to all using processors. In the distributed directory, this process must be done serially through use of the lists. Since studies show that the list depths are rarely more than a few entries, the central directory advantage is not as large as it might first appear.

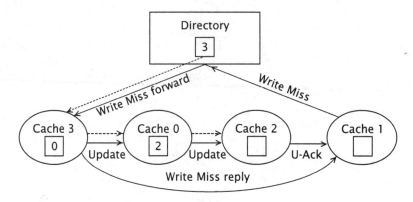

Figure 8.36 Distributed directory updates. At the end of the write transaction, the cache 1 pointer will be set to 3 and the directory will be set to 1.

8.11.3   Update Protocols

As expected, update protocols maintain consistency by updating, rather than invalidating, caches that share lines that are being written into. When the updates are complete, the caches are consistent. In the centralized directory (CD-UP), a write accesses the directory. The directory sends a count number to the writer, indicating the number of users of the line. Processors that already have copies of the line are notified that the line is being updated (processors 3 and 1 in Figure 8.35). This update signal is accompanied by the write data which has been forwarded now to the directory and the memory. When the processor updates its cache, an acknowledgement is sent to the writing cache. When acknowledgements match the count number, the update is complete.

For the distributed directory case (DD-UP), the new data must be forwarded to the directory and then the writing processor becomes the head of the list. As in the invalidate case, the update signal, together with the new data, is forwarded down the list. When the last cache receives the data, it updates its line and acknowledges this update to the cache that instigated the write (Figure 8.36). At this point, the write is complete and all processors have a consistent version of the line.

As with the invalidate case, the principal difference between the two update protocols is the amount of time required to create a consistent memory view. In the central directory case, the write may be forwarded in parallel to all using caches, as implementation allows. The situation is less attractive in the distributed directory update case (DD-UP), since the linked lists tend to be significantly longer than in the invalidate case. Invalidates necessarily shorten the length of the list; without invalidates, the length of shared data lists can be significant. The other side of that coin, however, is that the linked list has captured users of the line over a longer period; hence, requests for new copies of the line are reduced compared to invalidate protocols.

There is no clear winner among the protocol strategies. Each protocol has an advantage, either implementation-wise or traffic-wise, and various protocols appear attractive under differing implementation parameters.

Notice that in invalidate protocols, the processor–cache that last performed the write is the single owner of the line. Other processors may read the line and become owners of the line if they perform a write requiring the invalidation of all other users of the line. Invalidate protocols involve additional traffic to get updated copies of shared lines. Central directories, in general, are used with updated memories, as it is relatively easy to update memory with new data at the same time as the central directory is being updated. This can, of course, create additional congestion at memory, as the memory system itself may have less available bandwidth than the directory. In any event, the central directory and its memory (when updated) represent a significant limitation to the ultimate scalability of multiprocessor systems. For the distributed directory case, as systems and applications get large, so too do the lists; while traffic per se may not be as much of a problem, the length of the list increases the transaction time for each write. Ultimately, the write transaction time becomes the limit on the scalability of such systems.

8.12   Evaluating Some Systems Alternatives

Suppose we select an interconnect network based upon a grid. (The motivation for a grid interconnection will be clearer after our discussion on interconnection later in this chapter.) Now the question is how best to treat the design of the system. What coherency protocol should be selected to give minimum traffic? What parameters of an application will influence program behavior most strongly? What extra hardware ought be considered to improve performance?

In order to look at some alternatives, let us define a node (Figure 8.37) as containing a very high-speed processor with an infinite cache and in a network of n processors, $1/n$th of the memory. We assume a 64-byte line (16 4B physical words) for the cache, and a network link time (time to transmit a line between two nodes) of 16 cycles (i.e., $w = 32^b$, $l/w = 16$). Suppose we arrange a 64-node system as an 8×8 grid. We use this as a baseline system to evaluate some alternative protocols.

Applications vary in some important ways, even when there is ample parallelism in the program. From a network point of view, the number of distinct localities that are shared (or the number of shared data blocks) plays an important role. In our base system, we ignore nonshared traffic (infinite cache) so that we cannot have any misses due to the capacity of the cache. An important parameter is the size of the shared item. If the shared item is significantly less than a line, we have potential for poor line utilization and hence a great deal of excess traffic using protocols that move lines as a unit. An important parameter of an application is the number of consumers. Applications that have a great deal of consumers create different kinds of traffic patterns than those with just a few consumers. Finally, there is the issue of line utilization: how many words of a shared line are actually used by the consuming processor?

A producer of a shared data value has a timing relationship to the consumer of that value. The exact relationship is determined by the protocol. The producer of shared data information spends some time computing values which it then writes into a shared data line. Typically, these writes are

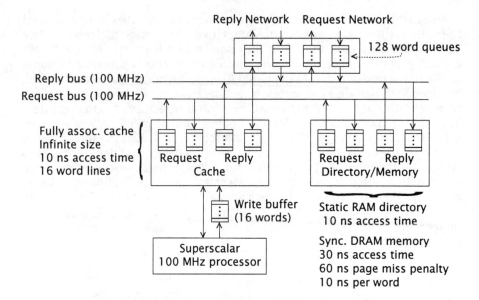

Figure 8.37   Node example [104].

fenced (or synchronized) at the end of the last write, so that all writes must complete before a flag can be set to allow consumers of the line to read the line. Consumers, on the other hand, attempt to read shared data potentially at some time earlier than the flag is set by the producer. The consumer will spin, that is, continue to access, a read flag in the cache until the producer, by setting the flag, changes its state either by declaring the current value of the flag invalid or by simply updating it, depending upon the protocol. After the read flag is changed to a valid state, the consumer reads the shared data. Protocols differ in at least three ways:

1. The time to complete the writes to the shared memory location.

2. The time to notify the consumer of the newly written data. This corresponds to the time required to either invalidate or update the read flag.

3. Protocols differ in the read latency—the time required for consumers to read the new data.

A number of design choices can significantly affect the relative performance of a coherence protocol. All protocols profit by line prefetching. Figure 8.38a illustrates the actions that a producer must take in producing a series of values. It performs its computation, writes its values to memory, then does a fence operation to ensure all of the writes are completed before the final operation, the setting of a semaphore, is completed. The consumer, on the other hand, must wait until the semaphore is set before it can consume, or use, the written values. Invalidate-based protocols (Figure 8.38b) can use a write prefetch effectively by providing early invalidation of a line that will be written into.

If this is performed at an auspicious time, it can overlap some of the delay in the fence latency. In the invalidate-based protocol, usually the reads should not be prefetched until the semaphore is set. Otherwise, fetched data will

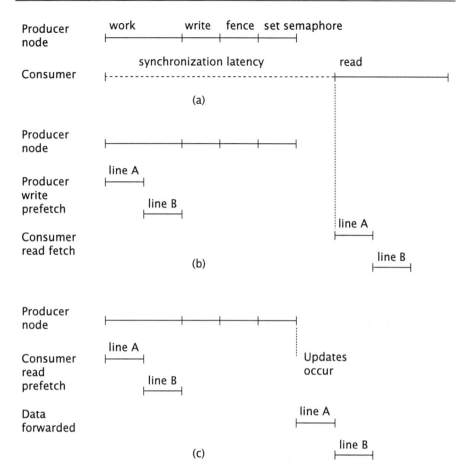

Figure 8.38   Producer–consumer timing. (a) Fetching without prefetch. (b) Invalidate protocols with write prefetch (early invalidate). (c) Update protocols with read prefetch. (Reads are forwarded to consumers when data is available.)

simply be invalidated again, creating extra network traffic. Prefetching gives update protocols (Figure 8.38c) a larger advantage. The consumer can read the unwritten line (i.e., the line before it is made available by the producer) and when it is available, the producer will automatically update or forward the value to the consumer. This enables the consumer to access the desired value as soon as it is available.

Two other techniques are available to update protocols which can enhance their performance. The first is *local combining*; the second is *word synchronization*. Local combining can be used effectively for update protocols. Suppose each node has a single line write buffer (Figure 8.39). When a write occurs, suppose we hold that value in the buffer for a fixed number of cycles (say, five cycles). If other values are produced to be written into the same line during that time, they are combined with the original write in that line buffer. As soon as five cycles elapse after the last write to the line buffer, the updated values are forwarded to all nodes in this system that have copies of that line. If a write to another line occurs while the

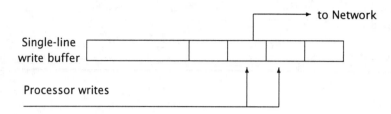

Figure 8.39 Local combining at node. Writes are not forwarded to the network until either a certain number of cycles elapse after last write to buffer, or a write occurs to a new line.

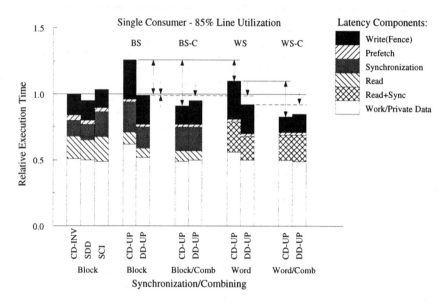

Figure 8.40   Relative execution time for MF application.

line buffer is waiting its five cycles, the original value is immediately forwarded to consumers. This simple local combining proves quite effective since writes tend to cluster—the producer produces a number of values for use by the consumers.

Local combining is especially useful under heavy traffic conditions. Under such conditions, when the network is busy, a properly buffered system with adequate write buffer size can combine write requests and then, when the network becomes available, make better use of the network bandwidth.

The second technique useful in update protocols is word synchronization. Rather than synchronize a block level, each update word carries its own synchronization or validity primitive with it. Thus, instead of waiting for all of the values to be delivered to the consumer by the producer, and then having a synchronization primitive forwarded so that the consumer can begin operation, the consumer can begin operation on a word-by-word basis as they are received.

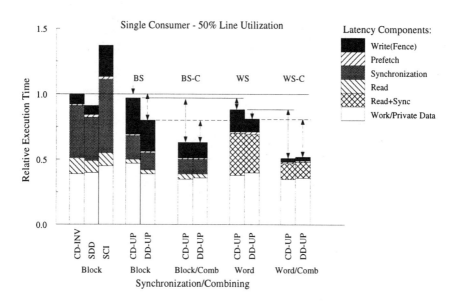

Figure 8.41   Relative execution time for PDE application.

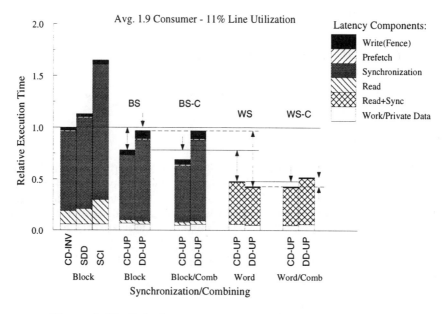

Figure 8.42   Relative execution time for SPCF application.

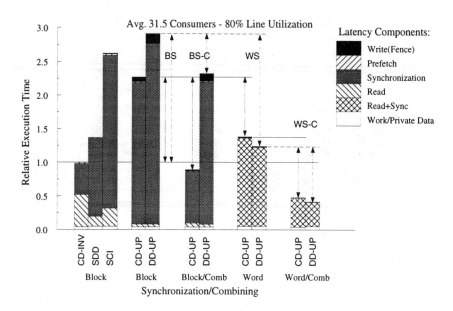

Figure 8.43   Relative execution time for LU application.

In Figures 8.40–8.43, we look at the performance of our five protocols (CD-INV, SDD, SCI, CD-UP, DD-UP) on a variety of application problems. Execution time is all relative to the central directory invalidate protocol (CD-INV).

The applications represented are:

1. (Figure 8.40) Multifrontal solver (M—$1^K \times 1^K$ array with 85% line utilization).

2. (Figure 8.41) Partial differential equation (PDE—32×32 array with 50% line utilization).

3. (Figure 8.42) Sparse Cholesky factorization (SPCF—1138×1138 array with 11.2% line utilization).

4. (Figure 8.43) LU.

The results (Figures 8.40–8.43) are clustered into groups for each figure. The first group shows the relative performance for the invalidate protocols (CD-INV, SDD, SCI). The second group shows the relative performance for the two update protocols (CD-UP, DD-UP) with block synchronization (BS). These two update protocols are then enhanced in the next three groups by:

1. Use of a one-line (64B) local combining buffer (BS-C).

2. Use of word synchronization (WS).

3. Use of both (1) and (2) (WS-C).

From the figures, we can draw some conclusions. Line utilization determines the efficiency of the update protocols. Low line utilization favors

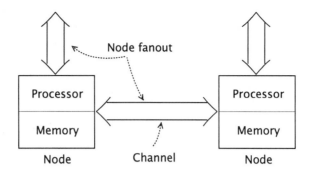

Figure 8.44   Node and channels.

update protocols, while high line utilization favors invalidate protocols. Combining is primarily applicable to update protocols and improves their efficiency. Overall, for these applications with comparable hardware, central directory update seems to be the best performing protocol. The worst performing protocol is the SCI. The SDD variation of the distributed invalidate protocol seems to perform better than either central directory invalidate or SCI.

8.13   Interconnections

Connections between multiple processor clusters must be structured in some orderly way in order to provide efficient intercluster communications. Informally, we can think of efficiency in terms of the cost–performance of the communications interconnection network. The overall topology or structure of the interconnection network determines its efficiency in three ways:

1. By determining the delay in connecting a requesting processor to its destination.

2. By determining the bandwidth or the number of connections that can be carried on concurrently.

3. By determining the cost of the network.

There are many different types of topologies [312] and switches that can be implemented at a node in the network, and different types of communication channels between nodes. There is a necessarily large and sometimes confusing set of nomenclatures used in describing different interconnect networks.

Consider a single processor or processor cluster. In a network, we refer to such a cluster or processor as a *node*. Nodes communicate with one another (Figure 8.44) via a channel (or in graph theoretic terminology, an edge of a graph). Channels may be either unidirectional or bidirectional. Channels are described by their capacity, or the number of bits per unit time that can be transmitted concurrently between nodes. Nodes can be characterized in two important ways:

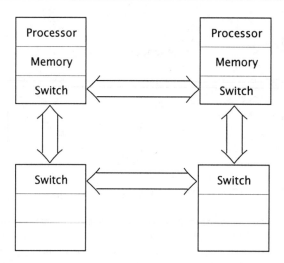

Figure 8.45   Direct network (switch resides at processor node).

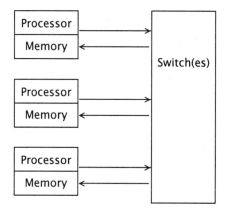

Figure 8.46   Indirect network (switches are separate from processor nodes).

1. Their fanout—the number of bidirectional channels that connect a particular node to neighboring nodes.

2. The location of the processor memory for a cluster with respect to the switching channels of the network (Figures 8.45 and 8.46).

Networks whose nodes contain a processor and a portion of global memory, as well as network switching in a cluster, are said to be *direct networks* (Figure 8.45). Networks where the switching is accomplished separately from the processor clusters are said to be *indirect networks* (Figure 8.46). Networks are also said to be static or dynamic. In a *static network*, the topology or the relationship between nodes in the network is fixed. The path or paths between two nodes does not change. In a *dynamic network*, the paths between nodes can be altered both to establish connectivity and also to improve network bandwidth.

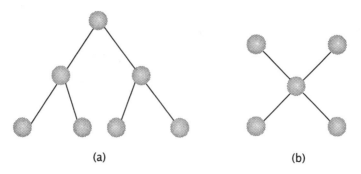

(a)   (b)

Figure 8.47   Examples of static networks with preferred sites (nodes).

8.14   Static Networks

Simple static networks are usually direct networks, and for purposes of this discussion we assume this. We also restrict our attention to simple, cubic forms of static networks where there is no preferred communications site or node. Figure 8.47a illustrates a tree topology where the root of the tree has a preferred accessibility to the rest of the nodes. A star network (Figure 8.47b) is another example. A linear network, on the other hand (Figure 8.48a), offers some advantage to interior nodes, but by converting the linear array into a ring, one removes site preference. In general, we consider a linear array with closure (a ring) as simply an enhanced case of the linear array (Figure 8.48b). The *distance* between two nodes is the smallest number of links or channels (or hops) that must be traversed in establishing communications between the two nodes. The *diameter* of the network is the largest distance (without backtracking) between any two nodes in the network.

Assume there are k nodes in a linear array, and we wish to interconnect several such linear arrays. Instead of simply increasing the number of linear elements, we can increase the dimensionality of the network, creating a grid network for two dimensions (Figure 8.48c). Figure 8.48(d) represents a torus, with the end-around enhancement discussed earlier, but we still refer to it as an *enhanced grid* or nearest-neighbor mesh. We can continue adding nodes to the network beyond the $k \times k$ specified in the grid by using a third dimension. Such an interconnection topology would be referred to as a *k-ary three-cube* [64]. When $k = 2$, we have the special case of the binary cube, or hypercube. In the binary hypercube, the dimensionality of the hypercube is determined by the fanout from each node. In general, the number of nodes (N) and the diameter can be determined as follows: for $(2, n)$, the binary n-cube with bidirectional channels has:

$$N = 2^n$$

and

$$\text{Diameter} = n.$$

For (k, n), the k-ary, n-cube with closure and bidirectional channels has

$$N = k^n$$

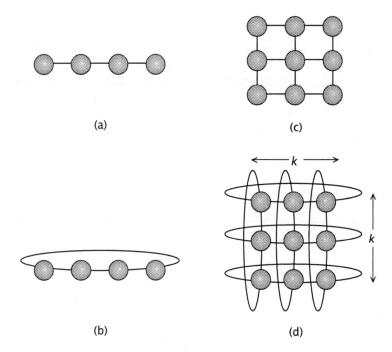

Figure 8.48 Example of static network without preferred sites. (a) Linear array. (b) Linear array with closure (a ring). (c) Grid (2D mesh). (d) $k \times k$ grid with closure (a 2D torus). These are also called (k, d) networks. In (a) and (b), we have $k = 4$, $d = 1$ (one-dimensional). In (c) and (d), we have $k = 3$, $d = 2$.

or

$$n = \log_k N.$$

In general, it is the dimension of the network and its maximum distance that are important in cost and performance, rather than exact details of its topology.

8.14.1   Links and Nodes

Links are characterized in three ways:

1. The cycle time of the link, T_{ch}. This corresponds to the time it requires to put a bit on a wire of a channel (or link) between neighboring nodes. $1/T_{ch}$ is the bandwidth of a wire in the link or channel.

2. The width of the channel, w. This determines the number of bits that may be concurrently transmitted between two nodes.

3. The directionality of the channel. Channels may be unidirectional or bidirectional. It is clearly preferable for channels to be bidirectional. Nodes with communication affinity may be placed together to reduce the distance (and therefore the time) of communications. Once channel A communicates with channel B, it is usually true that B communicates with A. This establishes a locality of interconnection which,

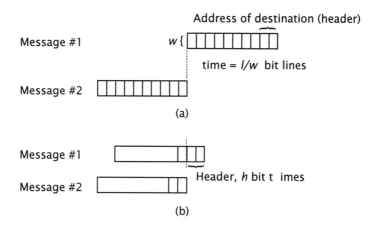

Figure 8.49 (a) Successive message transmission in a static network through an intermediate node with store and forward. (b) Relative message timing at a node with wormhole routing. Header contains address of destination path.

when recognized, can improve systems performance by placing communicating processors at adjacent nodes in the system. Note that there is little advantage to siting a node in a k-ary ($k > 2$) unidirectional system, as adjacent nodes for an A to B transmission (distance $= 1$) will require a distance $k - 1$ for the B to A transmission.

Associated with the link characterization is the length of the message in bits (l) plus H header bits. (The data portion of the message is frequently referred to as the "payload.") Thus, $T_{ch} \times (l+H)/w$ will be the time required to transmit a message between two adjacent nodes and, in general, the total message transmission time is:

$$
\begin{aligned}
T_{\text{store-and-forward}} &= T_{ch}\left[d \times (l + H)/w\right] \\
&= T_{ch}\left[d \times l/w + d \times h\right],
\end{aligned}
$$

where d is the distance between the two nodes and h is H/w, the header bit time. The preceding assumes that the node itself has a store and forward character. Suppose node A has a message for node C, which must be transmitted via node B. If node B is available, the message is transmitted from A to B and stored at B. After the message has been completely transmitted, node B accesses node C and transmits the message to C if C is available. An alternative to store-and-forward is *wormhole routing*. Under this scheme, as the message is received at B it is buffered only long enough to decode its header and determine its destination. As soon as this minimal amount of information can be determined, the message is retransmitted to C, assuming that C is available. The amount of buffering then required at B is significantly reduced and the overall time of transmission is decreased to:

$$
T_{\text{wormhole}} = T_{ch}[d \cdot h + l/w],
$$

where h is the number of header bit times.

There is a slight variation to wormhole routing called *virtual cut-through* [64], differing from wormhole routing in that only messages that are blocked are buffered at intermediate nodes, hence removing them from the network. With the wormhole routing, if the node C were busy, the message would be blocked at B and the channel between A and B would be occupied until the node C was free. With virtual cut-through, the channel between A and B is available as soon as the message is transmitted to and buffered at B.

While the above schemes govern the flow of packets in the network, the routing algorithm determines the actual path messages take. These can be deterministic (packets follow a fixed path, depending entirely on the source and destination addresses) or adaptive (the paths taken by packets are selected by intervening nodes, based on local network congestion as well as current and destination addresses).

The message to be transmitted between two nodes contains data and a header. The header is simply the address of the destination node. Once the header is decoded at an intermediate node, that node can determine whether the message is for it or for another node. The intermediate node selects a minimum distance path to the destination node. If multiple paths have the same distance, then this intermediate node will select the path that is currently unblocked or available to it. If multiple paths are unblocked, it can select a path either according to a schedule or randomly.

8.15   Dynamic Networks

Dynamic networks are usually indirect, which we assume in this discussion. The processor and presumably some local memory are separated from the switching mechanism which forms the interconnection network. The shared global memory may be located as separate nodes or may be included in processor–local memory nodes. In the latter case, each processor node includes its local memory and a fraction of the global memory. Thus, there can be three separate access times for the processor to access an item in memory:

1. The access time for local memory.

2. The access time for that portion of global memory which is located at the node (this could be rather similar to the access time for local memory).

3. Access time to global memory that is not part of the node.

The dynamic indirect network is shown in Figure 8.50a. For ease of representation, the network is usually shown as in Figure 8.50b. The access time to global memory that is not part of the processor node is generally uniform across all portions of the global memory (ignoring traffic-based contention).

Usually, the basic element in the dynamic network is a crossbar switch (Figure 8.51). The crossbar simply connects one of k points to any of another k points. Multiple messages can be concurrently executed across the crossbar switch, so long as two messages do not have the same destination. The cost of the crossbar switch increases as n^2, so that for larger networks, use of a crossbar switch only becomes prohibitively expensive. In order to contain the cost of the switch, we can use a small crossbar switch as the basis of a

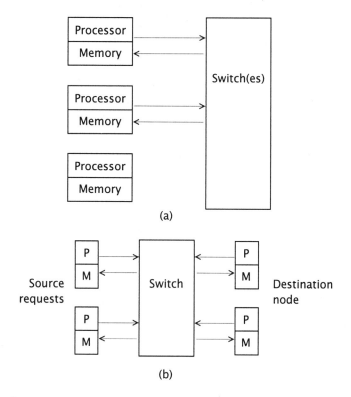

Figure 8.50   A basic dynamic, indirect switching network.

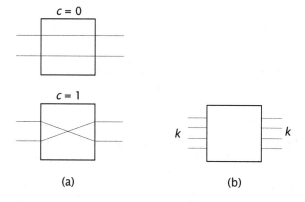

Figure 8.51   (a) A 2×2 crossbar with control c. (b) This can be generalized to a $k \times k$ crossbar switch.

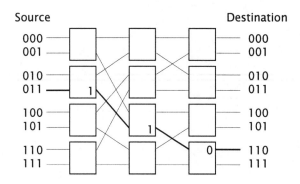

Figure 8.52   Baseline dynamic network topology.

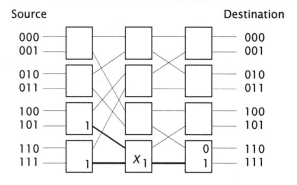

Figure 8.53   Network blocking.

multistage network, frequently referred to as a MIN—*multistage intercon-nection network* [312]. There are many types of such networks, including baseline, Benes, Clos, Omega [178], and Banyan. The baseline network is among the simplest, and is shown in Figure 8.52. The header causes suc-cessive stages of the switch to be set so that the proper connection path is established between two nodes. For example, consider a deterministic "obvious" routing algorithm for these M, N networks. Suppose node 010 sends a message to destination 110. The switch outputs labeled 1, 1, 0 cause the message to be routed to the 110 destination node by setting the control (c) so that either the upper output ("0") or the lower output ("1") of each switch is selected. Similarly, the return path is simply 010. The number of stages between two nodes is:

$$\text{Stages} = \lceil \log_k N \rceil,$$

where k is the number of inputs to the crossbar element ($k \times k$), and there-fore the total number of ($k \times k$) switches required for a one-bit wide path is:

$$\frac{N}{k} \times \lceil \log_k N \rceil.$$

The baseline network, such as shown in Figure 8.52, is subject to blocking. Blocking occurs between two messages at an intermediate point in the net-work, where the two messages share a common node output even though they do not share a common destination.

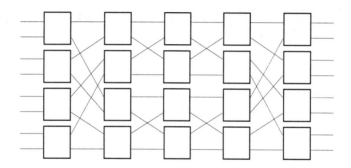

Figure 8.54   Benes dynamic network topology.

Table 8.6   Dynamic networks, switching N inputs $\times N$ outputs using $k \times k$ switches (each input is one bit).

Network	Other Equivalent Networks	Stages of Delay (in units of $k \times k$ switch delay)	Blocking	Approx. Cost ($k \times k$ switches)
Baseline	Delta, Omega SW Banyan	$\lceil \log_k N \rceil$	Yes	$\frac{N}{k} \lceil \log_k N \rceil$
Benes	—	$2 \lceil \log_k N \rceil - 1$	Nonblocking if reconfigured	$\frac{2N}{k} \lceil \log_k N \rceil$
Clos	—	$2 \lceil \log_k N \rceil - 1$	Strictly nonblocking	$\frac{4N}{k} \lceil \log_k N \rceil$

As an example of blocking, consider two source nodes: 110 and 101. Suppose they wish to simultaneously access destination nodes 110 and 111, respectively. The messages share a common channel (labeled X in Figure 8.53), and only one message can go through; the other is blocked.

The baseline network can be expanded into a nonblocking form as shown in Figure 8.54, but at the cost of extending the size of the network. The Benes nonblocking (reconfigurable) network now has distance (diameter) of:

$$\text{Diameter} = \# \text{ of stages} = 2 \lceil \log_k N \rceil - 1,$$

and the cost has increased to about:

$$2 \times (\text{Baseline cost}).$$

Other dynamic networks provide different tradeoffs on achievable message bandwidth, message delay, and fault tolerance. Table 8.6 summarizes some of the attributes of some common dynamic networks.

8.16   Evaluating Interconnect Networks

In recent years, there have been a number of important analyses on the comparative merits of various network configurations [226, 151, 172]. We report on two important developments here.

1. Direct networks are preferred over indirect networks, insofar as communication affinity or locality of interconnections can be established for a particular program. Indirect networks necessarily have a uniform interconnect time between nodes. This inability to preferentially site nodes with higher than average communications proves to be a limitation for dynamic and, indeed, all types of indirect networks. Since dynamic networks are generally more expensive than static networks, this is another reason for a preference for static direct network configurations.

2. Network topologies must be mapped onto a plane (certainly they must be contained or implemented within three dimensions). Because of this, it is not sufficient to simply count the number of hops required in a high dimensional network to establish a connection, but rather it is more important to look at the length of wire or the delay in transiting wire when that network is mapped onto two dimensions. When one analyzes networks based upon their maximum wire cross section, networks of low dimensionality are preferred. Thus, a two-dimensional mesh can produce significantly less message delay than a higher-order cubic static network.

Both of these results have generally pushed machine designers to develop interconnection networks of low dimensionality, statically configured.

8.16.1   Direct Static vs. Indirect Dynamic

In this section, we present the results and largely follow the analyses performed by Agarwal in his work on network performance [6].

Dynamic (Indirect)

Assume we have a dynamic indirect network made up of $k \times k$ switches with wormhole routing. Let us assume this network has n stages and channel width w with message length l. In the indirect network, we assume that the header network path address is transmitted in one cycle just before the message leaves the node (i.e., there is only one cycle of header overhead to set up the interconnect); see Figure 8.55.

Assuming the switches have unit delay (T_{ch} = one cycle), the total time for a message to transit the network without contention is:

$$T_c = n + \frac{l}{w} + 1 \text{ cycles.}$$

For all our subsequent analysis we assume that $n + l/w \gg 1$, so

$$T_c = n + \frac{l}{w} \text{ cycles.}$$

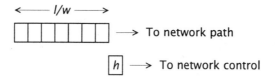

Figure 8.55   Message transmission from node to switch.

The network switches have no storage. If a block is detected, a queue develops at the processor node; so there are N queues, each with occupancy ρ, requesting service from the network. Since the number of connection lines at each network level is the same (N), then expected occupancy is ρ. Thus, as shown by Kruskal and Snir [172], the delay for an open-queue model (arrival traffic is not affected by waiting time) can be modeled by an $M_B/D/1$ open queueing model where $p = \delta/k$ and $\delta = \rho$ (the probability that a request is made during a service time), so that $p = \rho/k$. The binomial queueing model is appropriate here, since the output can be accessed by only one of k input ports with equal probability and the probability of a request from a source is simply $\delta = \rho$. The message time is $T_m = (l/w)T_{ch}$ and also corresponds to the time a switch (node) is occupied by a message. The channel occupancy is $\rho = m \times l/w$, where m is the probability that a particular node makes a request in any cycle. In the remaining discussion, we assume the $T_{ch} = 1$ cycle and express time in cycles.

$$T_w = \frac{\rho(l/w)(1 - 1/k)}{2(1 - \rho)}.$$

The total message transit time ($h = 1$), T_{dynamic}, is:

$$
\begin{aligned}
T_{\text{dynamic}} &= T_c + T_w \\
&= \left[n + \frac{l}{w} + \frac{\rho}{2(1 - \rho)}\left(\frac{l}{w}\right)(1 - 1/k) \right] T_{ch}.
\end{aligned}
$$

Static (Direct)

A similar analysis may be performed on a static (k, n) network; but now the analysis is a bit more complicated and requires the use of the $M/G/1$ open queueing model. Let k_d be the average number of hops required for a message to transit a single dimension. For a unidirectional network with closure $k_d = \frac{(k-1)}{2}$, and for a bidirectional network $k_d = \frac{k}{4}$ (k even), the total time for a message to pass from source to destination is:

$$T_c = [h \times n \times k_d + l/w] T_{ch}.$$

Again, we assume that $T_{ch} = 1$ cycle and perform the remaining computations on a cycle basis. Now the arrival rate on a channel is:

$$\lambda = m \cdot n \cdot k_d,$$

where m is the probability of a message request being initiated in any cycle, and $n \cdot k_d$ is the expected number of message hops (hence cycles) for the message to transit to a destination.

The service rate (μ) is:

$$\mu = \frac{2n}{T_m} = 2n\frac{w}{l},$$

since each node has $2n$ channels. T_m is the time it takes a node to process a message. Then the occupancy is

$$\rho = \frac{mnk_d}{2nw/l} = \frac{mk_d}{2}\frac{l}{w}.$$

As with the dynamic case, the intermediate node cannot store a blocked message, and the queue develops at the originating node only. Which open-queue model to choose? We could use $M_B/D/1$ as in the dynamic network; this would give

$$T_w = \frac{\rho - p}{2(1 - \rho)}\frac{l}{w},$$

where $p = \rho/2n$.

Since $n = 1$ is a special case, we are most interested in $n \geq 2$; thus, p will usually be small. Also (depending on the implementation), the service time is not necessarily constant. A blocked link may block predecessor nodes, creating a more complex service time determination. Using this rationale, for large k ($k \geq 4$), Agarwal [6] computes the waiting time ($M/G/1$) as:

$$T_w = \frac{\rho}{1 - \rho}\frac{l}{w}\frac{k_d - 1}{k_d^2}(1 + 1/n).$$

The $1/n$ term here is the self-contention arising when the message is directed at its own processing node. When k_d is much greater than 1, the contention delay is approximately:

$$T_w = \frac{\rho}{1 - \rho}\left(\frac{l}{wk_d}\right)(1 + 1/n).$$

Note that for a common network dimension, $k = 8$ ($k_d = k/4 = 2$), Agarwal's $M/G/1$ gives the same result as $M/D/1$, ignoring the self contention factor.

The total transit time for a message to a destination ($h = 1$) is

$$
\begin{aligned}
T_{\text{static}} &= T_c + T_w \\
&= nk_d + l/w + \frac{\rho}{1 - \rho}\left(\frac{l}{wk_d}\right)(1 + 1/n).
\end{aligned}
$$

The preceding cannot be used for low k (i.e., $k = 2, 3$). In this case [1], we use (n large) $M/D/1$ and:

$$T_w = \frac{\rho}{2(1 - \rho)}\frac{l}{w}$$

and

$$\rho = \frac{mk_d l}{2w}.$$

Comparing Networks

Now, in comparing networks, there are two ways a network can be limited [64]:

1. By the nodes: the number and size (lines fanout) of a node.

2. By the links or channels (wires) connecting the nodes.

We look at the node-limited networks in this section, and consider channel or wire limitation in the next section.

In comparing networks of comparable number and size of nodes, first compute the number of nodes in a network. For an indirect (baseline) network, we have:

$$\text{Switch nodes} = \lceil \log_k N \rceil \times \frac{N}{k},$$

where N is the number of compute-memory nodes to be connected and k is the number of inputs to a $k \times k$ crossbar switch at the switching node. For a direct (static, (k, n) cube) network, we have:

$$\text{Switch nodes} = N.$$

So we can compare networks of comparable numbers of switching nodes by simply selecting a $k \times k$ switch that will give us a network that best approximates N. Once we have determined k for the dynamic networks, we can adjust w, the channel width, for each network to ensure that all nodes have the same number of input and output connections.

For a static (k, n) cube,

$$\text{Fan-in plus fan-out} = 2nw.$$

For a dynamic network,

$$\text{Fan-in plus fan-out} = 2kw.$$

As Agarwal points out [6], there is one other important consideration in comparing networks: interconnect locality. Suppose that in a particular application only a fraction (L) of nodes communicate with each other, so that from a given processor only L (out of N) closest processors are potential destinations. In a direct static network, if we properly site nodes within their communications affinity group we can reduce the required number of hops. Now, define k_{dl} as the expected number of hops in a (k, n) network with locality L. Then:

$$k_{dl} = \frac{(LN)^{1/n} - 1}{2} = \frac{L^{1/n}k - 1}{2} \quad \text{for a unidirectional network,}$$

$$k_{dl} = \frac{L^{1/n}k}{4} \quad \text{for a bidirectional network.}$$

This also reduces both the latency and the occupancy.

Study 8.3   Direct (Static) Compared to Indirect (Dynamic)

This follows a similar study by Agarwal [6].

Assume we have the following network parameters:

$$
\begin{aligned}
N &= 1,024 \text{ compute nodes} \\
l &= 200 \text{ bits}
\end{aligned}
$$

$$\text{Node pins, fan-in plus fan-out} = 64$$

Dynamic, indirect: Assume we have a baseline network using 4×4 switches. This gives us:

$$\lceil \log_4 1,024 \rceil = 5 \text{ levels}$$

and each level has $1,024/4 = 256$ nodes, or a total of $5 \times 256 = 1,280$ nodes.

The channel width (w) is:

$$w = \frac{64}{2k} = 8,$$

so that

$$
\begin{aligned}
\frac{l}{w} &= \frac{200}{8} = 25 \\
T_c &= n + l/w \\
&= 5 + 25 = 30 \text{ cycles.} \\
\rho &= m\left(\frac{l}{w}\right) = m(25) \\
T_w &= \frac{\rho}{2(1-\rho)}\left(\frac{l}{w}\right)\left(1 - \frac{1}{k}\right)
\end{aligned}
$$

where $k = 4$, $l/w = 25$, and $\rho = 25m$.

So, for example, if $m = .005$ messages per cycle, then $\rho = 0.125$ and

$$T_w = \frac{.125}{2(.875)}(25)(1 - 1/4) = 1.34,$$

and the total time is 31.1 cycles.

Static, Direct (k, n) Network

As an alternative, now consider two low-dimensional, bidirectional "grid" ($n = 2$) or "cube" ($n = 3$) type networks (with closure). For about 1,024 nodes, we would have a (32,2) grid type network or a (10,3) cube type network. For the (32,2) with 64 "pins" or input/output lines, we would have $w = 64/2n = 64/4 = 16$. For the (10,3) network, $w = 64/6 = 10.7$, allowing for sake of the example a non-integer value of w.

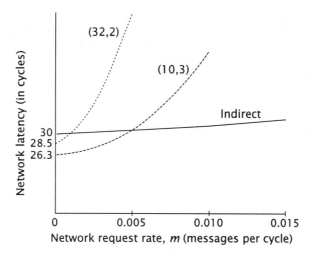

Figure 8.56 Indirect network compared with two direct networks.

So for

$$(32,2) \qquad \frac{l}{w} = \frac{200}{16} = 12.5$$

and

$$(10,3) \qquad \frac{l}{w} = \frac{200}{10.7} = 18.8$$

and

$$T_c = nk_d + l/w; \quad k_d = \frac{k}{4}$$

so that

$$(32,2) \qquad T_c = 16 + 12.5 = 28.5$$

and

$$(10,3) \qquad T_c = 7.5 + 18.8 = 26.3.$$

The waiting time is

$$T_w = \frac{\rho}{1-\rho} \left(\frac{l}{k_d w} \right) (1 + 1/n),$$

where $\rho = (mk_d)l/w$. The results are plotted in Figure 8.56.

Suppose now we include the effect of locality. Suppose we can achieve $L = 0.25$. This means that:

$$T_c = nL^{1/n}k_d + \frac{l}{w},$$

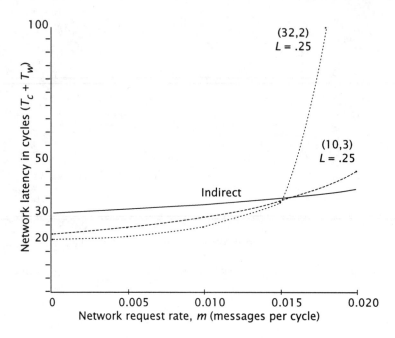

Figure 8.57 Indirect network compared with two direct networks, using locality $L = 0.25$.

For

$$(32, 2) \qquad T_c = 20.5.$$

For

$$(10, 3) \qquad T_c = 22.6.$$

For the waiting time,

$$\rho = \frac{mL^{1/n}k_d l}{2w}.$$

For $(32, 2)$ and $L = .25$, this is:

$$\rho = 50m.$$

For $(10, 3)$ and $L = .25$, this is:

$$\rho = 29.6m.$$

Now

$$T_w = \frac{\rho}{1 - \rho}\frac{l}{w}\left(\frac{1}{L^{1/n}k_d}\right)(1 + 1/n).$$

We plot $T_c + T_w$ for $L = 0.25$ and compare to the indirect network in Figure 8.57. Note that for low traffic, the static direct networks give better performance than do the more expensive indirect networks.

8.16.2   Network Dimensionality and Link-Limited Network

Networks usually are analyzed under the assumption of constant channel bandwidth. The assumption frequently is made that the link bandwidth is fixed at $w = n$ bits, or each channel is n bits wide with unit delay. Under these assumptions, higher-dimensional networks have some significant advantages. They offer more node-to-node connections than lower-dimensional networks, and have a shorter delay or diameter across the network. The number of hops, both average and maximum, is significantly reduced with higher-dimensional networks.

Dally [64] points out the inadequacy of the preceding analysis, as it ignores the complexity of the links connecting the nodes. Higher-dimensional networks must necessarily be mapped onto two or three dimensions to be realized. This mapping increases wire delays and also provides a somewhat unfair analysis advantage to the higher-dimension networks in not recognizing the costs inherent in the extra connections. As processors become smaller (the nodes), the importance of the links—the channels that connect the processors—is increased. Rather than comparing networks on distance or bandwidth, Dally proposes to compare networks based upon equal bisection width. We assume in this study, as in study 8.3, that $l = 200$. The bisection width is the minimum number of wires cut when the network is divided into two equal halves. Thus, rather than comparing networks with a constant number of nodes and node size, he compares networks with constant bisection width. In his analysis, wire density is held constant. For his analysis, the bisection width B of a k-ary n-cube with w-bit wide communications channels is:

$$B(k, n) = 2w \sqrt{N} k^{(n/2)-1} = \frac{2wN}{k}.$$

For a binary n-cube, $B(2, n) = wN$. The dynamic baseline network using 2×2 crossbars ($k = 2$) has the same bisection width as $B(2, n)$. If we use the binary n-cube as a base, then networks with lower dimensionality and the same bisection width have greater channel width. In fact, they have channel width:

$$w(k, n) = k/2.$$

EXAMPLE 8.3

Compute the bisection width of a grid (32,2). A (32,2) network has bisection width ($w = 1$) of

$$
\begin{aligned}
B(32, 2) &= \frac{2wN}{k} \\
&= \frac{2(1)1,024}{32} = 64.
\end{aligned}
$$

That is, there are 64 wires ($w = 1$) required to partition the network. Recall that the (32,2) is actually a torus, and thus the bisection of 64, not 32.

◆

EXAMPLE 8.4

Compare the bisection width of a grid (32,2) with the hypercube (2,10). If $w = 1$ for the hypercube, then the link width for (32,2) for the same bisection is

$$w(32, 2) = k/2 = 16.$$

We can check this by computing $B(2, 10)$:

$$
\begin{aligned}
B(2, 10) &= \frac{2wN}{k} \\
&= \frac{2(1)1,024}{2} = 1,024.
\end{aligned}
$$

Then

$$\frac{B(2, 10)}{B(32, 2)} = w(k, n) = \frac{1,024}{64} = 16.$$

◆

Study 8.4   Networks with Constant Bisection Width

Suppose we now consider the issue of dimensionality—which is better, a two dimensional 32×32 grid or a ten-dimensional binary hypercube? We can begin to get an answer to this question by arranging the two networks so that they have the same bisection width. We assume in this study, as in study 8.3, that $l = 200$. The bisection width of a binary 10-cube is $B(2, 10) = 2wN/2$, where we assume $w = 1$. Since $N = 1,024$, $B(2, 10) = 1,024$. The corresponding channel width for a 32×32 grid, $w(32, 2)$, is simply:

$$B(32, 2) = \frac{2w(1,024)}{32} = 64w.$$

The maximum bisection width is $64w$, and the corresponding channel width is $1,024/64$ or $w(32, 2) = k/2 = 16$. Now the average latency (without contention) through the network is calculated as:

$$T_c = nk_d + \frac{l}{w}.$$

For (2, 10), $w = 1$ and $k_d = 0.5$; while for (32, 2), $w = 16$ and $k_d = 8$. For the (2, 10) network, this corresponds to about 205 network cycles. For the (32, 2) network, we have about 28.5 cycles. Notice that the occupancy of the hypercube is the same as the occupancy of the grid. Since

$$
\begin{aligned}
\rho &= \frac{mk_d}{2} \frac{l}{w}, \\
\rho(2, 10) &= 50m \\
\rho(32, 2) &= 50m.
\end{aligned}
$$

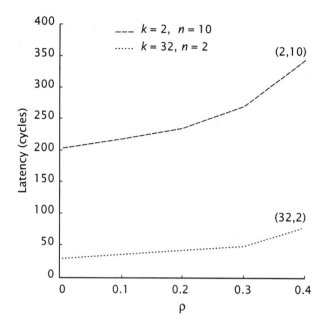

Figure 8.58   Latency vs. occupancy for 1K node networks: 32-ary 2-cube and binary 10-cube, $l = 200$ bits [64].

Since for k large we have

$$T_w = \frac{\rho}{1 - \rho} \left(\frac{l}{w k_d} \right) (1 + 1/n),$$

for (32,2) we have

$$
\begin{aligned}
T_w &= \frac{\rho}{1 - \rho} \left(\frac{200}{16(8)} \right) (1 + 1/2) \\
&= \frac{\rho}{1 - \rho} (2.34).
\end{aligned}
$$

For (10,2), k is small, so

$$
\begin{aligned}
T_w &= \frac{\rho}{2(1 - \rho)} \frac{l}{w} \\
&= \frac{\rho}{1 - \rho} 100.
\end{aligned}
$$

The results are plotted in Figure 8.58.

All this assumes that "a wire is a wire"—that there is no extra cost for mapping the hypercube onto the plane over the cost of mapping the grid onto the plane.

Dally also considers various models of delay and various types of network mapping onto the plane. For a basic model of wire delay, he shows that the low-dimensional networks significantly outperform the higher-dimensional networks of the same bisection.

Both Dally and Agarwal also note the difficulty in mapping higher-dimensional network topologies onto a plane. Higher-dimensional networks necessarily have longer interconnection distance, and hence longer propagation delay between nodes, than low-dimensional networks. This can have a significant difference on network performance and can be especially advantageous to direct low-dimensional networks. In these networks, interconnect locality has an even more dramatic effect than that discussed in the preceding section. (See problem 14.)

Wires vs. Computing Elements: Links vs. Nodes

Historically, the multiprocessor size (and hence its interconnection distance and bandwidth) was determined largely by the physical size of the computing elements or nodes. Under such circumstances, it makes sense to increase the number of links as the network increases; thus, hypercube interconnect technology is preferable to simple mesh-coupled processor interconnect topologies. As processors shrink, wires tend to dominate and determine the total interconnection delays and interconnection bandwidth. This is especially true when the wires or links that represent the interconnections between nodes are mapped onto a planar surface for implementation. Thus, as processing elements shrink in size, issues concerning the size and extent of the links determine an optimum network topology.

Networks must be implemented in two or three physical dimensions. Even if the interconnections were optical, the same principles would apply as with the wire-based network. Free-space optics, where connections are established via multifaceted holograms, may at least in part alter the wire-based analysis of network optimality [234]. After all, optical signals do not interfere with one another and, in fact, multiple optical signals can be concurrently redirected from a single hologram without losing signal integrity. Unless and until some alternative such as free-space optics is fully developed as a viable interconnect medium, wire will dominate network considerations. Even if free-space optics proves feasible, it will require a number of the same type of considerations that were present in wire-based optics. After all, even free-space optics must be implemented in three dimensions.

8.17   Hotspots and Combining

Suppose in a large network a certain memory cell is designated for the synchronization of all processor nodes. Since all N processors must synchronize to this node, even a small amount of synchronization traffic λ becomes $N\lambda$ at the node, creating a traffic hotspot and potentially saturating the node. Pfister and Norton [233] were among the first to point out this phenomenon, which they call *tree saturation*. Traffic simply saturates the weakest link in the network. Suppose N is the total number of processors (nodes), m is the probability of a processor emitting a message in a

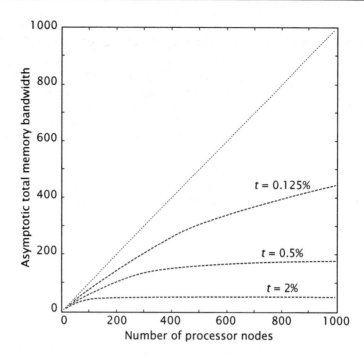

Figure 8.59   Hotspot effects for various fractions of hotspot traffic (t).

switch cycle, and t is the fraction of references directed at the hotspot. The effective request rate to the hot memory module is:

$$Nmt + m(1 - t).$$

They also compute the asymptotic limit of total communication bandwidth available as a function of the number processors in the hotspot percentage:

$$B = \frac{N}{1 + t(N - 1)}.$$

The maximum bandwidth is N messages per switch cycle.

Hotspots can have quite an effect on the system, as shown in Figure 8.59. To network a thousand processors with a hotspot traffic of 0.125% limits the system to 50% efficiency.

In order to deal with hotspots, combining networks have been proposed [110]. As messages migrate towards the hotspot, they build up traffic in the nodes in front of the hot node. Since the messages are generally performing simple commands such as `test and set`, `fetch and add`, or similar such operations, these can be combined at the intermediate node, significantly reducing traffic to the hotspot. Various types of message combining have been proposed; among the best known was the `fetch and add` proposal of the NYU Ultracomputer project [110]. Given that an update was called for, and the update was accomplished with a variable `fetch and add`, the addends could be summed in the intermediate node and the single message passed forward to the hot node for action. Returned messages (fetched) could be decomposed at the intermediate node and returned to their sources, significantly reducing the overall traffic to the hot node.

Suppose two requests are combined at a node that precedes a hotspot. Suppose these requests each wish to fetch a value and increment the value by one. The original value is fetched from memory and incremented by two after the requests are combined at the intermediate node. The original value then is returned to the intermediate node where one of the requests (the original) receives the initial value, while the subsequent request receives the value plus one.

For example, suppose a synchronization cell in memory has a value = 3 and two update requests targeted for that cell are combined at a network switch. Each request expects to fetch the current cell state and update the cell by "1." The combined request will fetch the value "3" and replace it with "5" in the cell. Then one requestor will get the return value "3" and the other will get "4."

8.18   Other Characterizations of Multiprocessors

There are a number of informal characterizations of shared-memory multiprocessor systems, which are widely used in the literature. The reader should be familiar with these terms and also the lack of precision that many of them engender.

Consider the following terms:

UMA—*uniform memory access.*

NUMA—*nonuniform memory access.*

UMA and NUMA are attempts to categorize networked shared-memory systems by the variance in the access time from processor to shared memory data. Usually, one would think that UMA would be preferred over NUMA, but this is not necessarily so, especially if the decrease in variance has come at the expense of latency. After all, one can take a NUMA network and pad out all of the fast paths to guarantee that the system will be UMA but all access will occur at the worst possible delay. Further, UMA and NUMA can be largely in the eye of the beholder. While a dynamic indirect network will generally provide a uniform access time to remote memory nodes, access to its local memory node may be significantly shorter. Is this NUMA, then, or UMA?

Other terms in common usage include the following:

NORMA—*no remote memory access,* to describe message-based multiprocessors that communicate over an interconnection network.

CC-NUMA—this represents a NUMA system with cache coherence.

COMA—*cache-only memory architecture.* Examples include DDM-1 [115] and the KSR-1 [59].

CC-NUMA could describe any of the networked systems that we looked at in the previous sections. In COMA, the nodal main memory is regarded as an enormous cache by adding a tag to each memory line and allowing memory lines to replicate. Notice that COMA is a natural progression in protocols that do not update the main memory. If the main memory need

Table 8.7 Multiprocessor machine parameters. (MP indicates message passing.)

Machine	Base Processor	Node (Cluster)	Cluster to Cluster Coherence	Interconnect	Max Processors
DASH	MIPS R3000		CD-INV	Static 2D grid	64
KSR-2	Proprietary CPU	1 processor	COMA	Ring hierarchy	32–4K
N-cube	Proprietary CPU w/14 I/O channels	1 processor	Message passing	Static hypercube	1000–8000
Intel Paragon	Intel 860	2 processors	Message passing	2D mesh	500
IBM SP2	IBM Power 2	1	Message passing	Dynamic Omega	512
Sequent S2000	Intel Pentium	30	One cluster (bus-based) Write-invalidate	Invalidate	—

not be updated, then its only function is to hold initial values. If we have a special initializing function from a tertiary memory, then we can eliminate the need for "main memory" and replace it with large nodal cache. Under such a system, a data value is completely decoupled from a physical memory location. Such a system also must have control to ensure that infrequently used values are never discarded. Notice that CC-NUMA operating under nonmemory update protocol can be made rather similar in behavior to COMA.

Symmetric multiprocessors is an operating systems concept that any processor may run the operating system. Each processor has a copy of the operating system and any processor may arrange communication among processes as required.

In *asymmetric* multiprocessors, a designated master processor controls the system and directs tasks and communications among the remaining processors.

Table 8.7 presents a picture of some network shared memory machines and some of their parameters. The reader may wish to fill in categories, or even invent new ones!

8.19   Conclusions

The appeal of multiprocessors is clear enough. As individual processors become faster and less expensive, there is great interest in arranging large ensembles of these processors to solve important single applications. However, there is probably no area of computer architecture where the application performance reality is at such variance with the linearly scaled peak performance of a multiprocessor ensemble. It can be very difficult to partition and schedule a large application over a significant number of processors. Beyond that, portions of the application that are necessarily serial or have less parallelism immediately tend to limit the potential speedup.

However, there are some applications that have a great deal of inherent parallelism. They can be readily partitioned and easily scheduled. It is somewhat illusionary, though, to point to these applications as being representative of the broader universe of applications. This is what makes the study of multiprocessors frustrating.

Over the next decade, it is expected that multiprocessors will become an increasingly important form of computer architecture. The most obvious kind of multiprocessor architecture is the shared memory multiprocessor. The shared memory paradigm allows the programmer to write processes which have a contemporary view of the entire state of the computation. This has two important consequences:

1. While it appears to make the programming process easier, the fact that there may be large delays in accessing certain parts of that memory space significantly complicates the assignment of processes to processors and the management of the memory space.

2. The hardware required to assure a coherent picture of memory to each of the processors is not insignificant. While there are many design

choices, even the less expensive choices involve significant complexity in the memory management area. More elaborate design choices, while providing additional bandwidth and ease of access to more remote portions of memory, also involve significant increases in hardware cost.

Multiprocessors may share memory by either:

1. Sharing a common data cache.

2. Sharing a common bus to memory.

3. Sharing a network which interconnects the processors to all of memory.

Clearly, shared data cache is the simplest type of multiprocessing. There are no consistency issues because data is stored in this single entity. It is also the most limiting form of multiprocessing, as rapidly the processors have to contend for a limited resource, the data cache bandwidth. A shared bus provides a small amount of additional relief; the bus bandwidth rapidly becomes a limiting resource for multiprocessor configuration. Beyond that, one can take clusters of multiprocessors which share a common bus and use these clusters as nodes in an interconnected network. While many types of networks are conceivable, and each has varying advantages in cost and performance, two issues seem to dominate determination of the most efficient network configuration. These issues are:

1. Locality.

2. The ratio of node size to link size.

If applications can be arranged to have good locality—a typical node communicates with a relatively small and known a priori subset of nodes—this can be used to great advantage. The use of locality favors those network arrangements where the processor is sited with a fraction of global memory and a switch at the same node. Networks whose nodes contain processing elements, memory, and switching are called direct networks. Indirect networks, where the switches are separate from the processing elements, clearly can take less advantage of locality than the direct networks. Since static direct networks tend to be one of the simpler forms of network, the potential use of locality would seem to favor this as the preferred mode of interconnection.

As processing elements become smaller, the wire to interconnect the processors becomes a dominant feature of the multiprocessor configuration. As wire dominates the size and performance of the network, simpler lower-dimensional network arrangements are preferred over more complex, high-dimensional arrangements, since they are easier to map onto the physical reality of a two-dimensional packaging service.

Multiprocessing is an important frontier in computer architecture. The jury is still out as to the number of processing nodes that are applicable and the overall effectiveness of large arrays of multiprocessors.

8.20   Some Areas for Further Research

There is probably no area of computer architecture that has as many open issues as the efficient use of multiprocessors. Almost every area discussed in the chapter, and many (especially in the software and language area) that we have not covered, have a long list of open issues. The partitioning and scheduling problems are known to be "hard problems." There is no known simple universal solution. Progress is made incrementally by using increasing amounts of program information either from compilers (hints as to expected behaviors) or from prior runs of programs (adaptive scheduling).

Areas such as coherence and processor interconnect are relatively easier problems, not that creating a robust and efficient protocol is an easy problem. At this time, the SCI seems to be an evolving standard coherency protocol. It is not clear that this is the most efficient protocol, but as with most things, it is usually possible to incrementally improve the efficiency of a hardware approach once its limitations have been fully identified. The great advantage of SCI is that it has received sufficient attention so that most of the hazards and races which occur in the protocol have been identified.

There are open problems in all these areas, and the reader should bear in mind that in this chapter we have just looked at shared memory multiprocessors as relatively small numbers of processors. Finer-grain processing opens a new vista of problems.

8.21   Annotated Bibliography

Multiprocessors have been around for a long time, even in configurations of 16 or more processors. (Univac LARC and Bell Labs Sentinel system are examples from the 1960s.) A good early state-of-the-art reference is by Enslow [86]. Another important early book on interconnection networks is by Wu and Feng [313]. This collects a number of the important earlier papers in the area of networking. There have been a number of valuable survey papers on hardware and software issues in shared memory multiprocessors by Milutinovic and his colleagues [236, 278, 284, 286, 287].

In developing the material in this chapter, the following papers were particularly useful:

The works of Bhuyan and Agrawal [36, 37] on the performance of interconnection networks.

Agarwal's [6] and Dally's [64] work on the evaluation of various types of interconnection networks.

Papers on the RP3 by Pfister et al. [232] for their early work on interconnection modeling, and by Pfister and Norton for their identification of hotspots [233].

A great deal of work has been done on cache coherence; a few of the more important papers are Dubois [79, 80, 81] and Archibald and Baer [21]. Among recent books that cover development in the area of multiprocessors are the books by Hwang [138], Suzuki [274], and Tomasevic and Milutinovic [285].

8.22   Problem Set

1. A certain processor (A) services jobs at a rate of 10 per second (with coefficient of variance, $c^2 = 1$). It is proposed that another processor (B) be added to the system to improve the response time ($T_w + T_s$). The available processor (B) has a service rate of 5 jobs per second ($c^2 = 1$). Jobs are to be dispatched with probability p to processor A, and with probability $1 - p$ to processor B. Use the $M/M/1$ open-queue model.

    (a) If jobs arrive at 2 per second for service, find p.

    (b) If jobs arrive at 6 per second, find p.

2. Now assume that in problem 1, the probability p can be adjusted based on queue size. Describe how p would change with Q.

3. Suppose we have four processors operating in a time multiplex SRMP. Each (L/S) processor has a four-phase instruction execution (IF – D/AG – EX/DF – PA). Since there is only one D/AG unit and one EX/DF unit, each processor accesses that unit once every four cycles. Each processor has a small integrated cache that it manages separately from the other processors. This cache has a 4% miss rate and 8-cycle miss time (1.5 refr per instruction). The execution units are fully pipelined (one operation per cycle).

    (a) For the "all in cache" (no miss) case, what is the performance of the four processors (instr per cycle)?

    (b) Considering cache misses, what is the performance of the four processors (instr per cycle)?

4. Compare the performance in 3(b) to that of a single pipelined processor (decoding one instr per cycle) with a miss rate of 1% and branch delay of 2 cycles (frequency of branch is 20%). Run-on instructions take 4 cycles of execution (run-on delay is 3 cycles) and occur with frequency 10%.

    How effective in its use of parallelism must the SRMP processor in problem 3 be to provide an overall speedup over the pipelined processor described above?

5. A certain shared bus multiprocessor (m processors) requires 8 bus cycles (processor cycle equals bus cycle) for a line transfer on a memory miss. If each processor executes at 1 CPI and has an integrated CBWA cache ($w = .5$), a miss rate of 2%, and 1.5 references per instruction,

    (a) Find the bus occupancy (ρ) for a single processor.

    (b) If we define *bus saturation* as processor time = $n \times$ bus transaction time (without waiting time), how many processors may be placed on the bus before saturation occurs?

    (c) If we have two processors on the bus, find $B(n)$ and T_w (use model with request resubmission).

6. Repeat 5(c) for four processors sharing the bus. What is the achieved bus transaction rate? What is the effect on processor performance?

7. Suppose processor bus traffic consists of three types of line accesses (CBWA): λ_I, for instruction line accesses, λ_{DL} for data line access used locally, and λ_{SH} for shared data line accesses. Find an expression for the bus traffic for N processors for

   (a) A "write-invalidate" protocol.

   (b) A "Firefly" protocol.

   Assume invalidate increases affected traffic by a factor α. Discuss conditions (relative parameter values) where one would select each protocol.

8. Evaluate the effect of the bus model with resubmissions and without resubmissions by evaluating problem 5(c) with both models.

9. Suppose we have a baseline network using 4×4 crossbar switches interconnecting 1,024 nodes. Assume $l = 200$ bits (both for request and reply), $w = 16$ bits, and $h = 1$ (wormhole routing through the switch).

   (a) How many stages are required?

   (b) What is the delay in cycles without network contention for a request to be serviced, time to go to a destination node, arrive there completely and return completely?

   (c) If m (the probability that a node makes a request or reply in a cycle) is $m = 0.015$, repeat (b) now including switch contention effects (i.e., queueing delays).

10. Our treatment of dynamic network delays utilizes an $M_B/D/1$ open-queue model. This assumes that request traffic initiated by a node is insensitive to network delay. Find an $M_B/D/1$ closed-queue model for a dynamic network switch.

11. Suppose we have a direct static $32 \times 32 = 1,024$ node network (bidirectional links) arranged as a 2D torus. If $l = 200$, $w = 32$, and $h = 1$,

   (a) What is the expected distance (number of hops between nodes)?

   (b) What is the expected delay for a message (source to destination and return, see problem 9b) without contention?

   (c) Assume m, the probability that a node makes a request or reply in a cycle, is $m = 0.015$. What is T_w per node?

   (d) What is the total expected delay (as in part b), now including queueing delay?

12. Discuss the relative advantage of update and invalidate protocols for bus-based shared memory multiprocessors.

13. Discuss the relative advantages of update and invalidate protocols for multi-node switched shared memory multiprocessors.

14. Researchers [64, 6] have noted that cycle time or network "hop" time depends on wire length. Higher-dimensional networks have larger "worst-case" wire delay when implemented in two dimensions than

have low-dimension networks. Dally [64] proposes that the network hop time can be determined as

$$T_{ch} = c_1 \left[k^{(n/2)-1} \right],$$

where c_1 is a constant.

Following study 8.3 (ignoring locality), compare networks (32,2) with (2,10). Develop a graph similar to Figure 8.57, now including the effect of wire on cycle time. Plot time in units of c_1 against network request rate for (32,2) and (2,10). Hint: Assume low occupancy (i.e., ignore the $1 - \rho$ factor). The effect of increased network cycle time is seen by the network as an increased request rate. Ignore indirect networks.

15. Repeat problem 14 for the conditions of study 8.4.

16. Assume an n-processor indirect network. Using the closed-binomial model $(M_B/D/1)$, find a relationship between achieved performance (B_{ach}) as a function of t, the hotspot traffic. (Assume 4×4 switch elements and $\delta = \rho$.)

17. Assume we have 16 processor nodes in a scalable multiprocessor connected in a bidirectional ring. Nodes are labeled from 0 to 15, and a transition from a node to an adjacent node takes one network cycle (going from 0 to 1 or from 0 to 15 takes one cycle).

    Now suppose processors 1, 3, 7, and 15 are sharing a line (and have acquired it in that order) from memory resident in node 4. If processor 2 does a write to that same line, show the directories' memory state for the SCI and CD-INV protocols

    (a) Immediately before the write takes place.

    (b) After the write takes place and is acknowledged.

18. For problem 17, using CD-INV and SCI protocols only, assume a line transmission takes 9 network cycles (latency). With wormhole routing, compute the number of network cycles. An invalidate or acknowledgement has one cycle per hop. Assume each INV and ack is a single message (no "broadcasting")

19. Repeat problem 17 for the two update protocols (CD-UP and DD-UP).

20. Repeat problem 18 for the two update protocols (CD-UP and DD-UP).

Chapter 9

I/O and the Storage Hierarchy

The processor and memory are dependent on the rest of the system, especially on input–output devices that provide the basic transport mechanism for bringing new data and programs into the processor and providing results to the user. On first inspection, the configuration and variety of special-purpose I/O devices that can be coupled to a system give the impression of a very confusing and complex process of systems design. Yet, the system performance depends on the relationship between the processor-memory and these I/O devices.

I/O is important! The access time and transport rate of I/O devices frequently limit overall system performance. The execution of various input/output functions is quite time-consuming and usually involves a great deal of processor capability in managing various I/O processes.

9.1   The Role of I/O

There are three distinct types of peripheral devices:

1. Devices that are used *primarily* to transport data between the processor and the user. These are also known as *data presentation* devices.

2. Devices that are used to communicate data from one processor to another. These include various types of network interface facilities and are referred to as *networking devices*.

3. Devices that are used to store information as part of the processor storage hierarchy. These are the basic *storage devices* of the system.

Some I/O devices fulfill multiple functions. Tape cartridges and portable disk packs are examples of devices that play a dual role. The network interface is simply the communications medium that enables the processor to reach remote peripheral devices, whether they be used for further communications or for storage.

Data transport and data presentation devices present a significantly lower workload to the processor than the storage devices. Tables 9.1 and 9.2

I/O

I/O is a generic term applied to rather distinct data movement functions that are required from the computing system. The processor has a defined storage space. The I/O system does not have such an a priori limit on the number of stored or transferred messages. The data transfer role of I/O can be further broken down into three separate functions:

1. Data presentation and acquisition.

2. Network data communications.

3. Storage devices.

Data presentation/acquisition provides the ultimate use of, and input to, processor information, while the network is responsible for moving data among processors.

Storage devices provide the higher levels of the storage hierarchy. I/O represents the archive of the data storage space that the processor may access. Most processor performance issues are related to the storage role of I/O, as most of the I/O requests come from the processor to manage storage requests.

---

illustrate some data transfer requirements for a spectrum of devices. Data transport devices either bring new information into, or remove information from, the memory hierarchy. They may directly affect the size and structure of the storage address space as seen by the processor.

While traditional data entry/data presentation devices have been rather slow compared to demands of the storage system, the situation is changing (Table 9.3). Computers are increasingly being used to manage multimedia documents consisting of:

- Graphics.

- Video ("moving pictures").

- Voice (both recognition and answerback).

Each medium requires enormous dedicated computation. Special-purpose processors have been designed to manage sophisticated graphics representations (color rendering, 3-D modeling, animation, etc.). The management of the graphic image can require up to 5–10 high-speed microprocessors.

The problem of video is simply the acceleration of the graphics problem, since a new image can be created once every 1/30th of a second (33 milliseconds). Of course, data compression and interpolation techniques can be used to significantly reduce the obvious extraordinary network load required for real-time video processing.

Voice is another very demanding data presentation format. The equivalent of 16–64 Kbps of digitized voice signals requires an extraordinary amount of processing to either create or recognize various phonemes in *real time*.

Table 9.1   Some data rates for traditional data presentation devices.

	Data Rate
Sensors	1 Bps–1 KBps
Keyboard entry	10 Bps
Communications line	30 Bps–200 KBps
CRT display	2 KBps
Line printer	1–5 KBps
Tape cartridge	0.5–2 MBps

Table 9.2   Some parameters for traditional I/O storage devices.

	Access Time	Data Rate	Capacity (bytes)
Disk	20 ms	4.5 MBps	1 GB
Tape	O (sec)^a	3–6 MBps	0.6–2.4 GB (per cartridge)

^{a}Order of seconds

Table 9.3   Some parameters for newer multimedia I/O transport devices.

	Data Rates	Maximum Delay
Graphics	1 MBps	1–5 sec
Video	100 MBps	$\approx$ 20 ms
Voice	64 Kbps (8^K Bps)	50–300 ms

Audio is one of the most demanding of the data presentation media, since it is highly user-intolerant of lapses or clips in the message presentation process. Each of these media—graphics, video, voice—represents an extraordinary challenge in processor design itself. The data they process can only be done by an ensemble of high-speed processors with associated transducers, filters, etc. (such as found in scanners and other electronic media devices). In this chapter, we treat only the role of I/O as storage in the processing system. Treatment of the various presentation media would require a separate treatise for each.

9.2   Evolution of I/O Systems Organization

The systems organization and functionality of I/O devices and their controllers have changed significantly over time. These changes have decoupled the processing of user programs from the processing of I/O requests. In the earliest I/O configurations, the processor and memory were intimately involved with the management of an I/O request [269].

In these systems, the processor-memory bus forms the basic interface to the I/O device controller. This memory bus is usually asynchronous and

---

I/O Systems Storage Management

Generally, data is distributed over many physical devices. The problem in accessing data is to design a system that is efficient in:

1. Finding the physical location of the required data.

2. Finding a path from the processor memory to the particular physical device that contains the information.

3. Accomplishing (1) and (2) without significantly interfering with the central processor's execution of user programs.

The more complex the overall system—the more processors involved, the more diverse the memory system—the more complex is the problem of effective I/O storage system design.

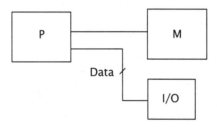

Figure 9.1   Programmed I/O. Processor waits until I/O responds to I/O request.

therefore relatively slow. The device controller interfaces to a standard memory bus protocol and assembles I/O data into proper bus protocol data units for use by the processor or memory.

The simplest protocol is programmed I/O (Figure 9.1). In this protocol, the processor, upon issuing an I/O request, enters a loop polling the I/O controller status until the data is available. When it is finally available, the controller posts a signal and data is read into the processor, which subsequently stores it in memory.

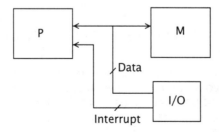

Figure 9.2   Interrupt-driven I/O. Processor continues after initiating I/O request. Interrupt from I/O allows processor to move I/O data into memory.

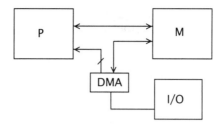

Figure 9.3 DMA-managed I/O. DMA manages the movement of data between I/O and memory.

In programmed I/O, the processor is unable to do useful work after issuing an I/O request. Thus, a simple improvement is an interrupt-driven I/O (Figure 9.2) which allows the processor to initiate the I/O request and then resume work on the user program awaiting an interrupt from the I/O device. The I/O controller interrupts the processor when the data has been retrieved. Interrupt-driven I/O, while better than programmed I/O, still suffers from several limitations [270]:

1. The CPU must still manage the I/O transfer.

2. The CPU's interrupt handling ability places a limit on the I/O transaction rate.

The direct memory access (DMA) device is a further refinement that can independently manage the interface between the memory and the I/O device and its controller (Figure 9.3). Rather than each word going to the processor and then being forwarded to memory, as in the case of interrupt-driven I/O, a block of data can be transferred from an I/O device into memory by the DMA without affecting the CPU. When the entire block transfer is complete, the DMA sends an interrupt signal to the processor so that the processor is only involved at the beginning and the end of an I/O block transfer. As I/O traffic increases, the DMA traffic from I/O device to memory may occupy a significant amount of the bus bandwidth, slowing the processor down somewhat.

9.2.1   I/O Processors/Channels

The basic problem with DMA is not so much in its functionality, but rather in the limitations inherent in the structure of a bus that supports both processor and I/O device. As processors and I/O get faster, there is a need for a specialized processor–memory bus dedicated to synchronous high-speed data transfers. The system now resembles Figure 9.4. A synchronous bus is usually under the master control of the processor or a finite-state machine in the processor. Requests from the I/O processor are made to the bus control unit and once acknowledged initiate a high-speed synchronous data transfer from I/O processor to memory. The I/O processor now becomes a type of super-DMA using the synchronous processor bus. The I/O processor itself may be a rather general-purpose microprocessor, or it may be a specially designed processor to serve the I/O function. The latter is

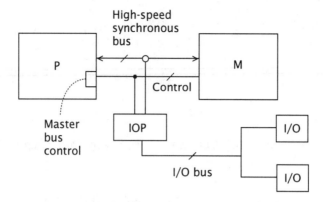

Figure 9.4 System with I/O processors.

usually called a *channel*, in mainframe parlance. Using conventional microprocessor technology for I/O processors has a number of advantages, including the ability to support many of the standard asynchronous buses that allow direct connection to previously designed I/O device controllers. We have now come almost full circle, since the I/O processor may use any of the previously discussed simple I/O systems.

Instead of using a conventional microprocessor as an I/O processor, the mainframe families use specialized I/O processors called *I/O channels* [45, 224]. Historically, there are several different types of channels:

1. The multiplexor channel. This controls many slow-speed devices. It initiates multiple requests and multiplexes the data transfers from these devices a byte at a time, assembling them at the channel for proper transmission to processor memory.

2. The selector channel. This is used for control of high-speed devices that assemble large blocks of data in the channel before transmitting the data to or from memory.

3. The block multiplex channel. This is a more recent introduction accommodating both types of channel activity within a single I/O processor/channel.

9.2.2 I/O System Support for Multiprocessors

While channels and individual controllers are associated with designated processors, some I/O devices, especially elements of the disk subsystem, must be accessible not just by one processor but by any processor in a multiprocessor ensemble. Even if a particular disk drive is available, if the channel or controller for this device is occupied by a request to another drive, the drive cannot be accessed at that time. To overcome this limitation channel subsystems with multiple sub-channels can be designed which interface to multiple high-speed synchronous buses. The processor uses the channel subsystem to access an available sub-channel and path to the desired disk without interrupting any of the other processors in the system (Figure 9.5).

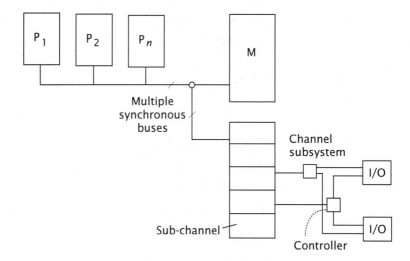

Figure 9.5   I/O channel subsystem to support multiprocessor I/O access.

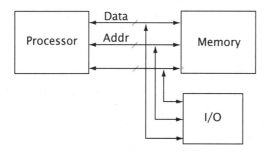

Figure 9.6   I/O subsystem.

9.3   Design of Storage Systems

In the remainder of this chapter, we concentrate on the analysis and design of storage subsystems, as it is the storage subsystem—the ensemble of disks and the I/O processors that support them—that largely determines system performance. We exclude from discussion the modern media-oriented systems, which require special-purpose processing to sustain data presentation.

To a first approximation, the I/O's subsystem is one or more control/storage devices that interface between the processor memory bus and the I/O peripheral units. (See Figure 9.6.)

9.3.1   Disk Technology

The disk drive is a modern success story. By almost any measure—data transfer, cost, and access time—significant improvements have occurred over the past several decades. Figures 9.7 and 9.8 illustrate various improvements in recording technology.

The Disk

Disk technology (and, indeed, magnetic recording technology in general) is a modern success story. Significant advances have been made in data recording density, access time, and storage costs. The goal of an OEM cost of a dollar per megabyte of disk storage will be achieved in the near future.

The problem for the systems designer is that the processor technology has outstripped several aspects of disk technology. Processing speeds have increased much more rapidly than disk access times have decreased. Some historic growth data for processors and storage are:

1. Processor speed (MIPS) increases at 2x per year.

2. Memory size (MB/die) increases at 2x per 2 years.

3. Disk density (bits/unit area) increases at 2x per 3 years.

4. Disk transfer (MBps) increases at 2x per 5 years.

5. Disk access time (ms) decreases at 2x per 10 years.

Despite this, much of the progress has been eclipsed by even more rapid improvements in processor and memory technology. In the areas of both access time and transfer rate, the processor technology has significantly overrun improvements in disk technology. It is this disparity that warrants our careful attention to the effective use of the disk. Illustrating this, Figure 9.9 projects the number of instructions executed in a 20-ms period that corresponds to a typical disk access time.

The disk remains the mainstay of the storage system because:

1. It represents nonvolatile storage.

2. Storage costs are less than one-twentieth of those of DRAM per byte.

With the advent of large, relatively low-cost main memory systems (low cost DRAM), the memory system can be used to complement the disk ensemble and maintain relatively high processing rates for the system.

9.3.2   The Disk Device

Data is stored bit-serial on the surface of a disk platter. Storage tracks are laid out in concentric circles across the surface of the platter. (See Figure 9.10.) The disk device itself consists of a stack of platters. Each platter has two surfaces for data recording. The surface of each platter is divided into tracks, and each track is further divided into sectors. The sector is the smallest addressable data unit.

The set of tracks of equal diameter on all disk surfaces is called the *cylinder*; the cylinder contains the maximum amount of information that can

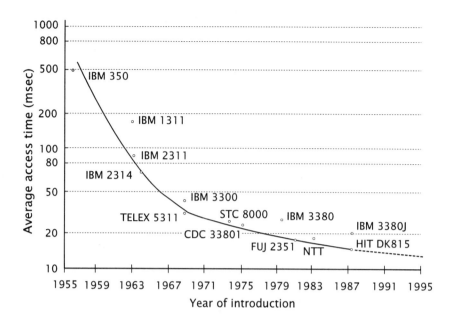

Figure 9.7   Average access time (one-half rotation delay plus seek time) of large-capacity disks (data from J. Hilbrink, NCR Journal).

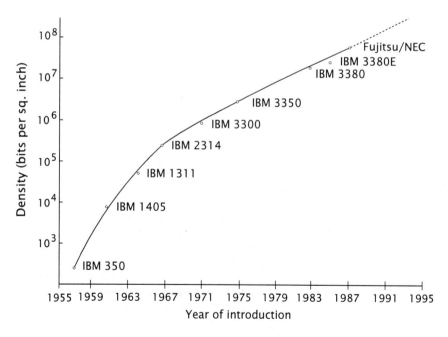

Figure 9.8   Areal density of large-capacity disks (data from J. Hilbrink, NCR Journal). Recently demonstrated areal densities have exceeded 10^9 bits per inch^2 (IBM and Fujitsu).

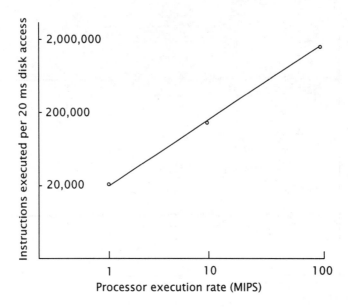

Figure 9.9 Instructions per disk access.

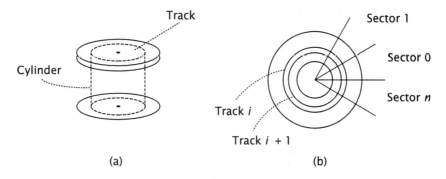

Figure 9.10 Storage tracks.

be either read or stored with a single arm assembly movement. While each surface has its own arm, all access arms move together. Only one surface is read at a time. *Seek time* is the time to position the arm at a desired track (and hence at a desired cylinder). *Latency time* is the rotational delay for the disk to move to the correct sector within a track for a given access. *Transfer time* is the time required to transfer data stored (or to be stored) on a track to or from an external buffer. It does not include seek or latency time. *Total disk access time* is the sum of seek, latency, and transfer times. Table 9.4 lists some characteristics of typical disk drives.

This fixed-track capacity model was widely implemented until recently. Many currently available drives now use a constant linear recording density, putting more bytes on the outer tracks than the inner tracks (capacity range about 2:1 outer to inner). This partitions the tracks into *zones* or unequal-size "sectors." For purposes of our analysis, we will use the older fixed-size track model.

Table 9.4 Typical drive characteristics.

	Hitachi DK516	IBM 3380	DEC RK81
No. of cylinders/device	1787 cylinders		1258
No. of tracks/cylinder	16 tracks		14
No. of sectors/track	77 sectors		52
Capacity/sector	512 bytes	512	512
Capacity	1 GB	7.5 GB	0.5 GB
Access time	15 ms	24 ms	16.6 ms

We will use a typical sector size of 512 bytes. Until quite recently, drives rotated at 3600 rpm and had a total rotational delay of 16.6 milliseconds and an expected rotational delay of half that, or 8.3 milliseconds. This assumes that the starting address of a block is uniformly distributed over a track. Currently available drives rotate at 5400 to 7900 rpm.

Seek time is more varied and complex. It is a function of the file size, the cylinder size, and the characteristics of the motor that is used to actuate the arm to move to the designated cylinder. Generally, seek time is a function of the number of tracks transited by the arm. Asymptotically, if the requests for cylinder access were uniformly distributed, we would expect that the average distance that the arm would have to travel would be $n/3$ cylinders, where n is the number of cylinders that contain user files. Several things make this an inaccurate assumption:

1. It has been observed that about half of all seeks are zero-distance.

2. Seek time is not linearly proportional to the distance the access arm travels, due to arm starting and stopping inertia.

Bitton [39] and Scranton [255] have shown that the arm movement for a high-performance voice coil motor can be approximated as:

$$\text{Seek time (in ms)} = a + b \times \sqrt{\text{seek distance in tracks}}.$$

Including the effect of zero-distance seeks mentioned before produces an estimate of expected seek time:

$$\text{Expected seek time} = 0.5 \times (a + b\sqrt{n}).$$

Table 9.5 indicates some estimates of a and b parameters for various commercial drives.

9.4   Simple I/O Transactions

Suppose we have a processor with locally attached disk. The processor executes in the user state for a while, then makes an I/O (disk) request.

Table 9.5 Some seek parameters for arm motors (seek time in ms = a + $b\sqrt{\text{seek distance}}$).

	a	b
Hitachi DK516	3.0	0.45
IBM 3380D	2.34	0.81
IBM 3380J	3.23	0.57

Models

Open-queue models are frequently used to describe disk behavior. Such models simply assume a fixed user demand on the system and then are used to predict such parameters as total response time. These models are obviously attractive because they do not require extensive knowledge of the user or processor behavior model. Their attractiveness is, of course, also their weakness. Systems simply do not continue to manufacture requests in the absence of a reply.

The primary danger in using the open-queue model is that the designer may fail to completely understand its limitations.

The same processor then manages the I/O request with system utility program(s) and resource management support programs. It finally issues the `read` or `write` command to the disk controller and then either (1) resumes user state processing (executing an alternate task) or (2) goes idle (awaiting the I/O response).

Very simple processor–I/O systems such as programmed I/O are systems at capacity: the processor effectively must wait for the I/O response before proceeding with other useful work. These systems can be adequately modeled by closed-queue models; either $M/G/1$ or, for a first estimate, the closed-queue $M/M/1$ ($c^2 = 1$). More complex systems that are not limited by I/O can often be approximated by using the open-queue model. Suppose there are multiple alternative tasks and the I/O system is responsive enough to access the required data before control is returned to the original requesting task. The overall system is unaffected by the I/O because the I/O requests are sufficiently buffered. While there is a waiting time (T_w) that a request spends in the buffer (queue), the offered request rate λ is the same as the achieved rate λ_a. In this case, we can determine the waiting time by using the open-queue model. This waiting time can be used to estimate the number of alternative tasks that must be available before the system slows down due to I/O capacity limitations (and $\lambda > \lambda_a$).

Since the system does not reach a capacity limit, an open-queue model is appropriate. Also, as there is a long time between requests, we use the Poisson arrival distribution to model the request distribution. The service distribution is not constant, so the $M/G/1$ open queue model provides the most accurate results.

In order to use the M/G/1 open queue, we need to know the coefficient of variance (c^2) associated with the service distribution. This, in turn, de-

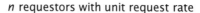

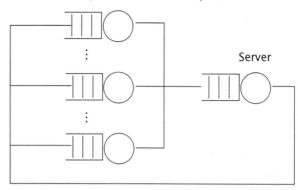

Figure 9.11   Model of multiple processors sharing a common disk server.

pends on both the distribution of file accesses (size of access, relative arm
movement required) and the characteristics of the arm itself (as discussed
earlier). For typical file and disk parameters, c^2 rarely exceeds 0.5 [219];
oftentimes, it is lower. To be conservative, we suggest using $c^2 = 0.5$ in the
absence of additional information. Then

$$T_w = \frac{\rho(1 + c^2)}{2(1 - \rho)} T_s.$$

Practical systems are a mix of open- and "closed-loop" queue models. While
the I/O occupancy is low, the system behaves as an open queue. The
achieved request rate is the same as the offered request rate, since the I/O
waiting time does not affect overall processor performance. At some point,
however, the typical system begins to experience capacity effects. Some of
the tasks are slowed down because of I/O dependency. This dependency
occurs for two reasons:

1. The waiting time becomes excessive, so that by the time the processor
   returns to the task that made an I/O request, the information to allow
   that task to proceed is still not available from the I/O system.

2. There are simply not enough tasks to mask the I/O latency, including
   waiting time. Adding additional independent tasks has its own costs.
   They occupy memory, which otherwise could be used gainfully by the
   current task. This is especially true in a virtual memory system, so
   there is a delicate balance between optimizing the virtual memory
   system, the paging system, and the system performance due to user
   file traffic.

The simplest "mixed" I/O models are called *asymptotic I/O models*. They
describe the system as being tolerant of delay to a point, but it then reaches
capacity and slows down. To develop an asymptotic I/O model, consider
an ensemble of processors requesting service from a single I/O subsystem.

Assume we have n requestors requesting service. Once a request is made,
it must be satisfied before processing proceeds (Figure 9.11).

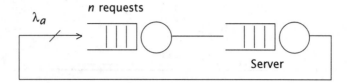

Figure 9.12   Simplified model.

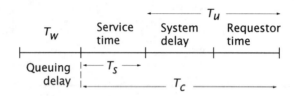

Figure 9.13   Request-service cycle.

As a further simplification, we assume that one of the serial service units (the one with the least capacity) determines the system response. We treat the other service units merely as delay centers. This is usually a reasonable assumption, as queueing delays accumulate at the *bottleneck*, or most restrictive service unit in a system. We further assume that each of the requestors has an identical Poisson request distribution. We will discuss this assumption later, as some modeling situations allow only a "finite population" of requests—unlike Poisson—to be present at any instant.

This provides us with a simplified picture of our queueing model (Figure 9.12).

Unlike open-queue models, where the request rate is independent of queueing delay, I/O–asymptotic models must recognize the effect of waiting time on request rate.

Suppose we have a request-service cycle as shown in Figure 9.13. In an open-queue model, the request rate (λ) is independent of the waiting time T_w; that is, for n requestors,

$$\lambda = \frac{n}{T_c} = \frac{n}{T_s + T_u}, \tag{9.1}$$

where T_s is the service time and T_u is the *user time* required for the requestor to prepare another request once it receives a response from the server to the prior request. T_u includes delay centers. The sum of T_s and T_u is designated T_c, the *cycle time* for a request-response in the absence of any waiting time.

In closed-loop systems (Figures 9.11 and 9.12), the waiting time T_w directly affects the achieved request rate:

$$\lambda_a = \frac{n}{T_w + T_c} = \frac{n}{T_w + T_s + T_u}. \tag{9.2}$$

Suppose we define the ratio r as

$$r = \frac{1/T_s}{1/T_u} = \frac{\mu}{1/T_u} = \frac{T_u}{T_s} \tag{9.3}$$

and the ratio f as

$$f = \frac{T_s}{T_c}.$$

The factor f is the *offered* occupancy per requestor ($n = 1$), the ratio of the offered request rate ($\lambda = 1/T_c$) to the service rate ($\mu = 1/T_s$). These factors are obviously related:

$$f = \frac{T_s}{T_c} = \frac{T_s}{T_u + T_s} = \frac{1}{\frac{T_u}{T_s} + 1} = \frac{1}{r + 1}.$$

The actual or achieved closed-loop request rate (λ_a) can also be written as:

$$\lambda_a = \frac{1 - p_o}{T_s},$$

where p_o is the probability that the system (server) is idle.

In a system with one requestor that waits until service before issuing another request, we have a special case. Our general model fails for this case, as seen following and in the next section.

When there is only one request ($n = 1$), we have ($T_w = 0$), as there can be no waiting time:

$$\lambda_a = \frac{1}{T_u + T_s} = \frac{1}{T_c}.$$

Thus,

$$p_o = 1 - \frac{T_s}{T_u + T_s} = \frac{T_u}{T_u + T_s} = \frac{r}{1 + r} \tag{9.4}$$

Similarly, the system reaches capacity or *saturation point* [166] when

$$n = 1 + r = \frac{1}{f}.$$

Increasing n (requestors) beyond this point causes the system to linearly slow down. For each additional requestor, the waiting time increases by T_s.

We can (computationally) determine the intermediate system behavior by recalling ($M/G/1$):

$$\begin{aligned} T_w &= \frac{\rho(1 + c^2)T_s}{2(1 - \rho)}, \\ \rho &= \lambda_a T_s \end{aligned}$$

so that

$$T_w = \frac{\lambda_a T_s^2(1 + c^2)}{2(1 - \lambda_a T_s)}$$

and we also have:

$$\lambda_a = \frac{n}{T_c + T_w}. \tag{9.5}$$

Substituting λ_a and solving for T_w, we get:

$$T_w^2 + (T_c - nT_s)T_w - \frac{nT_s^2(1 + c^2)}{2} = 0;$$

solving for T_w:

$$T_w = 1/2 \left\{ \sqrt{(T_c - T_s n)^2 + 2nT_s^2(1 + c^2)} - (T_c - nT_s) \right\}.$$

We can rewrite this in terms of f:

$$\frac{T_w}{T_c} = \frac{1}{2} \left\{ \sqrt{(1 - fn)^2 + 2f^2 n(1 + c^2)} - (1 - fn) \right\}. \tag{9.6}$$

and we can find ρ_a in terms of the preceding:

$$\lambda_a = \frac{n}{T_c + T_c(T_w/T_c)}. \tag{9.7}$$

$$\rho_a = \frac{\lambda_a}{\mu} = \lambda_a T_s.$$

$$\rho_a = \frac{n}{\frac{T_c}{T_s}(1 + T_w/T_c)} = \frac{nf}{(1 + T_w/T_c)}. \tag{9.8}$$

9.4.1 Multiple Servers

Suppose there are multiple disk servers (m). Now, accesses *may* or *may not* be uniformly distributed across these servers. Requests often cluster to a single file, and thus, despite the existence of multiple servers, the system may reference only one (or at least a smaller number than the physical number of servers). We will discuss this issue later in the chapter. For the moment, assume that m represents the *effective number* of independent servers. It is clear that:

Number of physical servers $\geq m \geq 1$.

Now, if requests are uniformly distributed over these m servers, the offered request rate λ is reduced by a factor of m.

So we rewrite Equation (9.5) as:

$$\lambda_a = \frac{n}{m(T_c + T_w)}.$$

Thus, for multiple servers, we rewrite equations (9.6)–(9.8) as:

$$\frac{T_w}{T_c} = \frac{1}{2} \left\{ \sqrt{(1 - nf/m)^2 + 2\frac{n}{m}f^2(1 + c^2)} - (1 - nf/m) \right\} \tag{9.9}$$

$$\lambda_a = \frac{n}{mT_c(1 + T_w/T_c)} \tag{9.10}$$

The occupancy *per server* is:

$$\rho_a = \frac{nf}{m(1 + T_w/T_c)}.$$

9.4.2   Single-Server Low Population (n)

There is a problem with our analysis for the single server ($m = 1$) with a small number (n) of tasks. It is asymptotically valid as n becomes large. The $M/G/1$ request distribution is Poisson, which implicitly assumes an *infinite* population of requests whose mean value is n per ($T_c + T_w$). This introduces significant error when n is small (especially $n < 4$) and when r is small ($r \ll 1$). When r is small, the offered occupancy is large and the effects of low n are most visible. When r is large ($r > 1$ and, e.g., $n \geq 4$), the user time quanta T_u ($r = T_u/T_s$; $r > 1$ implies $T_u > T_s$) is large with respect to T_s, and the asymptotic model naturally limits the population. When n is small, we must modify our model. Recall that:

$$\rho_a = 1 - p_0.$$

We need to find $p_0(n)$, that is, the probability that the server is idle given a population of n items in the system.

Assume a single server and service time exponentially distributed ($c^2 = 1$) with T_s as mean. Following Kobayashi [169], we define a Poisson distribution with mean R as

$$P(K,R) = \frac{R^K}{K!} e^{-R},$$

and its cumulative distribution as:

$$Q(K,R) = \sum_{i=0}^{K} P(K,R).$$

For $M/M/1$, Kobayashi shows that:

$$p_m(k) = \frac{P(k-m,r)}{Q(k,r)},$$

where $p_m(k)$ is the probability that m items are present in a system whose maximum population size in k ($0 \leq m \leq k$). This defines a truncated Poisson distribution.

Now

$$p_0(k) = \frac{P(k,r)}{Q(k,r)},$$

and since

$$
\begin{aligned}
P(k,r) &= Q(k,r) - Q(k-1,r),\\
\rho &= 1 - p_0\\
&= 1 - \frac{P(k,r)}{Q(k,r)}\\
&= \frac{Q(k-1,r)}{Q(k,r)}.
\end{aligned}
$$

This can be rewritten by factoring e^{-r} from both numerator and denominator, leaving:

$$\rho_a = \frac{1 + r + r^2/2 + r^3/3! + \cdots + r^{n-1}/(n-1)!}{1 + r + r^2/2 + r^3/3! + \cdots + r^n/n!}. \tag{9.11}$$

$$\lambda_a = \frac{\rho_a}{T_s}$$

Observe that for $n = 1$ (and $m = 1$):

$$\rho_a = \frac{1}{1+r} = f.$$

For $n = 2$:

$$\rho_a = \frac{1+r}{1+r+r^2/2},$$

and for $n = 3$:

$$\rho_a = \frac{1+r+r^2/2}{1+r+r^2/2+r^3/6}.$$

For each of the preceding cases:

$$\lambda_a = \frac{\rho_a}{T_s}$$

and

$$T_w = \frac{\lambda - \lambda_a}{\lambda_a} T_s,$$

where

$$\lambda = \frac{n}{T_s + T_u} = \frac{n}{T_c}.$$

Outside the single-server, low-population cases, the asymptotic model is generally consistent with the *exact* Kobayashi model (error usually less than 10%). It offers the following advantages:

1. It is computationally easier, especially for large n.

2. It is based on $M/G/1$, not $M/M/1$, and allows appropriate use of c^2 when known or estimated.

Figure 9.14 plots the error between the asymptotic model and the finite population model (both for $c^2 = 1$).

For the remainder of the chapter, we generally use the asymptotic model except in the special cases ($n = 1$, or $n = 2$ and $c^2 = 1$) where the exact ($M/M/1$) result is used.

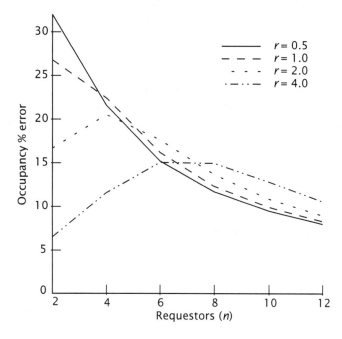

Figure 9.14   Asymptotic model error for low populations.

Model Accuracy

Accuracy in any model depends on the validity of the user parameters. A highly accurate model with inaccurate input parameters still produces an inaccurate characterization of system behavior. More complex models are susceptible to incorrect specification of input parameters.

We have tried in this chapter to choose an approximate (asymptotic) model that can be well understood by designers and can provide an initial estimate of performance across a relatively broad range of systems. This can then be the basis for initial design tradeoff studies. Later, more sophisticated simulation, or more detailed analytic studies, can provide additional system modeling detail.

9.4.3   Disk Modeling

The *disk latency time* is the sum of the seek time and the rotational delay. For purposes of our model, we assume FIFO disk access, although other request scheduling schemes (such as shortest latency time first) can significantly reduce (perhaps by a factor of two) the apparent latency time in a system. Suppose we define T_{latency} as the latency time and T_{read} as the time that a disk is busy moving a block of data into a buffer. If p is the number of blocks to be accessed, the disk service time T_s is equal to $T_{\text{latency}} + p \times T_{\text{read}}$. Depending on the system arrangement, an additional unoverlapped transfer time may be required to move a block from the disk to the buffer: $T_{\text{transfer}} = p\, T_{\text{read}}$. The arrival rate (of disk requests) λ and the service rate μ define the occupancy ρ, where

$$\mu = \frac{1}{T_s},$$

$$\lambda = \frac{1}{\text{interarrival time}},$$

$$\rho = \frac{\lambda}{m\mu},$$

where m is the number of independent disk servers, assuming that the requests are uniformly distributed across the disks. The minimum disk response time (T_R) is

$$T_R = T_s + T_w,$$

where T_w is the waiting time due to contention. In cases where the file is transferred to a buffer,

$$T_R = T_s + T_{\text{transfer}} + T_w.$$

Study 9.1   Processor Disk Models

In the following study we examine some processor–disk combinations and review the suitability and limitations of our models to various system situations.

EXAMPLE 9.1 $(n = 4, m = 1)$

Assume we have four processors $(n = 4)$, and each processor makes a disk request each 100 ms. There is one disk with $T_s = 10$ ms, $c^2 = 1$. Find λ_a, the achieved number of I/O transactions (disk accesses) per second, and the relative performance (λ_a/λ) due to disk contention.

We can solve this problem using either of our asymptotic or low-population models.

Asymptotic

$$T_s = 10 \text{ ms}$$
$$T_u = 100 \text{ ms}$$
$$T_c = 110 \text{ ms}$$
$$n = 4$$

$$f = \frac{T_s}{T_c} = \frac{10}{110} = 0.091$$

From equation 9.6,

$$\frac{T_w}{T_c} = 1/2\{\sqrt{(1 - (0.91)4)^2 + 2(0.91)^2 4(1 + 1)} - (1 - (0.91)4)\}$$
$$= 0.048$$
$$T_w = 5.3 \text{ ms}$$
$$\lambda = \frac{n}{T_c} = \frac{4}{.110} = 36.4 \text{ transactions per second}$$
$$\lambda_a = \frac{n}{m(T_c + T_w)} = \frac{4}{.115} = 34.7 \text{ transactions per second}$$
$$\text{Perf}_{rel} = \frac{\lambda_a}{\lambda} = \frac{34.7}{36.4} = 0.95.$$

Low-population

$$r = \frac{T_u}{T_s}$$
$$r = \frac{100}{10} = 10$$
$$\rho_a = \frac{1 + r + r^2/2 + r^3/6}{1 + r + r^2/2 + r^3/6 + r^4/24}$$
$$\rho_a = 0.35$$
$$\lambda_a = \mu\rho_a = \frac{1}{T_s}\rho_a$$
$$\lambda_a = 35.33$$
$$\lambda = 36.4$$
$$\text{Perf}_{rel} = \frac{\lambda_a}{\lambda} = 0.97.$$

◆

EXAMPLE 9.2   ($n = 4, m = 2$)

Now we repeat Example 9.1 for $m = 2$ and $T_s = 20$ ms. For $m \neq 1$ it is inappropriate to use the low population model. There is more contention in a system with $n = 4$, $m = 2$ than in a system with $n = 2$ and equivalent server occupancy.

Asymptotic

$$
\begin{aligned}
n &= 4, \, m = 2 \\
T_u &= 100 \text{ ms} \\
T_s &= 20 \text{ ms} \\
T_c &= 120 \text{ ms} \\
f &= \frac{T_s}{T_c} = \frac{20}{120} = 0.167.
\end{aligned}
$$

Using Equation 9.9, we get

$$
\begin{aligned}
\frac{T_w}{T_c} &= 0.076 \\
T_w &= 9.06 \text{ ms} \\
\lambda &= \frac{4}{.120} = 33.3 \text{ transactions per second} \\
\lambda_a &= \frac{4}{.129} = 31.0 \text{ transactions per second} \\
\text{Perf}_{\text{rel}} &= \frac{\lambda_a}{\lambda} = 0.93.
\end{aligned}
$$

Note: a low population model ($r = 5$, $n = 2$) predicts $\rho_a = 0.32$ and $\lambda_a = 16.2$ (or 32.4 for two drives).

◆

EXAMPLE 9.3   ($m = 4$, $T_s = 20$ MS)

We now repeat Example 9.1 for $m = 4$ and $T_s = 20$ ms.

Asymptotic

$$
\begin{aligned}
\text{From Equation 9.9,} \quad f &= 0.167 \\
\frac{T_w}{T_c} &= 0.32 \\
T_w &= 3.87 \text{ ms} \\
\lambda_a &= 32.3 \text{ transactions per second} \\
\text{Perf}_{\text{rel}} &= \frac{\lambda_a}{\lambda} = 0.97.
\end{aligned}
$$

◆

EXAMPLE 9.4   OTHER NOTES ($n < 4$, $m \neq 1$)

When $n < 4$ and $m \neq 1$, we can model only with some error (see Figure 9.14). We know the result for $n = 1$, however. Regardless of m (the processor can use only one disk at a time),

$$
\lambda_a = \frac{1}{T_c},
$$

and there is no waiting time.

◆

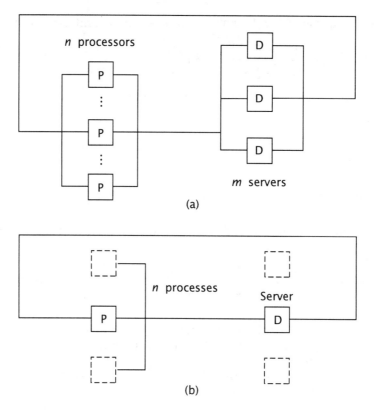

Figure 9.15   Two processor models. (a) Multiple independent processors (each server may be a cluster of disks). (b) Multiprogramming processor (usually modeled on a single server).

9.4.4   Multiprogramming Models and Inverted Servers

Our model is of multiple processors sharing a common disk server. (See Figure 9.15.) This model is also (approximately) applicable to the case of a multiprogrammed single processor (again assuming independent identically distributed tasks).

The processor makes n independent requests to a single server per T_c. No delay is encountered unless the response time is delayed (by waiting) so that the original request process is unable to proceed (because of delayed I/O data). We can model this (approximately) by simply assuming that each of the n processes (requestors) represents an independent processor. This is a rough approximation at best, and should be used with caution. When the multiprogrammed processor is fast and makes more requests to the server than the server can handle, the system saturates and the approximation is a reasonable estimate of overall performance.

Our original model has a request rate ($m = 1$) of:

$$\lambda = \frac{n}{T_u + T_s},$$

but the multiprogramming uniprocessor has a more limited request rate of:

$$\lambda = \min \left(\frac{1}{T_u}, \frac{n}{T_u + T_s} \right) = \min \left(\frac{1}{T_u}, \frac{n}{T_c} \right).$$

This assumes the system is server-limited and hence

$$T_s > T_u.$$

If $T_u > T_s$, then

$$\lambda = \min \left(\frac{1}{T_u}, \frac{n}{T_u + T_s} \right) = \frac{1}{T_u}$$

for $n \geq 2$ (this is the usual case). Now the disk is faster than the processor.

For this case, we can get reasonable performance estimates by reversing the roles of the requestor and server. After all, there is only one physical requestor and one physical server, but there are n *requests* present in the system at any one time. Clearly, the system is limited by its most restrictive element.

So for this case only (multiprogrammed uniprocessor), if $T_s \geq T_u$, we continue with the model as discussed earlier. If we have $T_u > T_s$, the system is processor-limited. In this case we have an *inverted server*, the system is limited by the capacity of the apparent requestor—which to our model, resembles the server! Thus, whenever

$$\lambda = \min \left(\frac{1}{T_u}, \frac{n}{T_c} \right) = \frac{1}{T_u} < \frac{1}{T_s} \quad \text{or } T_u > T_s,$$

we must reverse the roles of the apparent server and requestor, and T_u is interchanged with T_s. We will see an example of this shortly in study 9.2.

The worst-case error is introduced when $T_u \approx T_s$ and n is 2. Our model assumes there are two processors when in fact there are two processes residing on one processor. For this case, our model predicts an achieved occupancy of 0.5 ($r = 1$, $n = 2$); in the actual system the realized occupancy would be somewhat lower.

The approximation is increasingly valid as $T_u \ll T_s$, since the probability of a conflict in the physical processor is lessened.

Study 9.2   Multiprogrammed Processor with Single Disk

(a) 10-MIPS Processor with Disk System

Assume that we have a 10-MIPS processor that makes an I/O request every 400K user-state instructions (i.e., every 40 ms). Assume that 100K instructions are required in the system state to manage the I/O request. The processor is multiprogrammed degree 2 (i.e., has two independent user programs in memory).

The disk has an access time (to the beginning of the requested block-seek plus rotational delay) of 17.5 ms and a read time (4KB block) of 2.5 ms. Find the effective performance and the total response time for each disk access. Assume $c^2 = 1$.

The timeline of activity is:

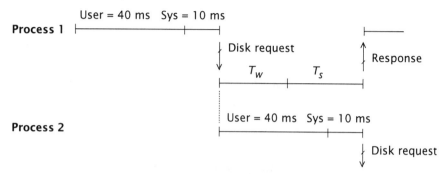

We compute system performance using our *finite-population* closed-queue model.

Here,

$$T_u = 50 \text{ ms}$$
$$T_s = 20 \text{ ms}$$
$$T_c = 70 \text{ ms}$$
$$n = 2$$
$$\lambda = \min\left(\frac{1}{T_u}, \frac{n}{T_c}\right) = 20.0 \text{ requests per second.}$$

Since $T_u > T_s$, we have an *inverted server*; the processor is modeled as the server and the disk is the requestor. Now

$$T'_u = 20 \text{ ms}$$
$$T'_s = 50 \text{ ms}$$
$$T_c = 70 \text{ ms}$$
$$n = 2$$
$$\mu = 20 \text{ items per second}$$
$$r = \frac{T'_u}{T'_s} = 0.4$$
$$\rho_a = \frac{1+r}{1+r+r^2/2} \qquad (n=2)$$
$$\lambda_a = \frac{0.95}{T_u} = \frac{0.95}{T'_s} = 18.9 \text{ requests per second.}$$

Note that the maximum capability of the processor is 1 request each 50 ms (20 items per second). We achieve 95% of this capacity.

(b) 40-MIPS Processor

Now assume that the processor in (a) is replaced by a 40-MIPS processor (i.e., four times faster); all other parameters remain the same. What is the effective speedup including the effects of I/O?

Now

$$
\begin{aligned}
T_u &= 50/4 = 12.5 \text{ ms} \\
T_s &= 20 \text{ ms} \\
T_c &= 32.5 \text{ ms} \\
n &= 2 \\
r &= 0.625.
\end{aligned}
$$

Now $T_u < T_s$, and our original model applies. Using Equation (9.11):

$$
\begin{aligned}
\rho_a &= \frac{1+r}{1+r+r^2/2} \qquad (n = 2) \\
\rho_a &= 0.89 \\
\lambda_a &= \frac{\rho_a}{T_s} = 44.5 \text{ requests per sec.}
\end{aligned}
$$

The maximum offered rate (without queueing delay) is:

$$
\lambda = \frac{n}{T_c} = \frac{2}{0.0325} = 61.5 \text{ requests per sec,}
$$

but the disk service rate is:

$$
\mu = \frac{1}{T_s} = 50 \text{ requests per sec,}
$$

which actually bounds the system performance.

The system speedup over the processor in part (a) is:

$$
\frac{\lambda_a(\text{part a})}{\lambda_a(\text{part b})} = \frac{44.5}{18.9} = 2.4.
$$

Situations in which one component of the system is significantly speeded up (as in this case) frequently realize significantly less improvement in system performance because of other hidden bottlenecks (in this case, the disk system).

Study 9.3   Network of Diskless Workstations with a File Server

A common system configuration consists of an ensemble of diskless workstations networked together to a common file server. The file server consists of an I/O processor and one or more disks. In this study, we analyze a network of such workstations (Figure 9.16).

This type of network was first studied by Lazowska et al. [179], who parameterized a diskless workstation environment under SUN/UNIX. From their

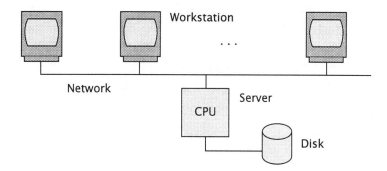

Figure 9.16   Network of diskless workstations.

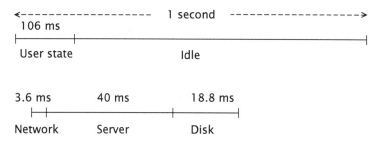

Figure 9.17   System activity per workstation request (one request per second).

measurements, they determined a baseline case that characterizes a network sharing a single disk in a software development environment. Each workstation processor executes in the user state 106 ms per second. This user state activity creates a service demand of a single 4-KB access to disk of 18.8 ms. Each I/O requires 40 ms of server processing and then an access to disk (Figure 9.17). The network bandwidth is significantly higher than either the disk or the server bandwidth. Since the server CPU capacity is significantly less than the disk capacity, the server CPU is the systems bottleneck. As a practical approximation, one can assume that the diskless workstation clients see only the server CPU in the system, as any queue builds in front of it and there will be little or no queueing in front of the disk.

In order to understand the behavior of such a network one must first realize the character of the system. With a small number of workstations, the user idle time masks any server waiting time, and the system basically performs as an open queue. This situation continues until a critical number of workstations are added to the system. At that point, the system begins to saturate—reach capacity—and additional workstations cause the achieved utilization to be less than the offered utilization, causing significant queueing delays to be visible to the client workstations.

We have three service centers:

$$T_{disk} = 18.8 \text{ ms,}$$
$$T_{server} = 40 \text{ ms,}$$

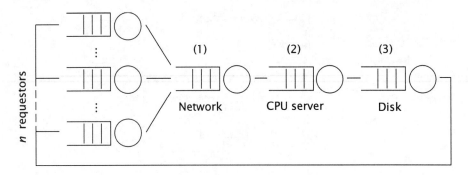

Figure 9.18   A generalized CPU–I/O model.

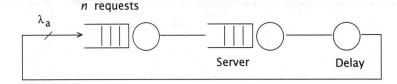

Figure 9.19   Simplified model.

$$T_{\text{network}} \quad = \quad 3.6 \text{ ms,}$$

but it is clear that the bottleneck in the system is the server CPU, since it has the least capacity. For initial analysis purposes, we treat the system as a single server (the server CPU) with a delay center of 22.4 ms to represent the disk plus network time (Figures 9.18 and 9.19). Each user has a timing relationship as shown:

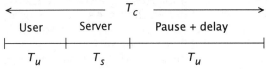

where

$$
\begin{aligned}
T_c &= 1 \text{ second} \\
T_s &= 40 \text{ ms} \\
T_u &= 960 \text{ ms (User + Pause + delay)} \\
r &= 24 \\
f &= .04.
\end{aligned}
$$

We will look at the system performance for various numbers of workstations from $n = 10$ to $n = 50$. We will use the asymptotic performance model. Let us assume the following c^2:

Unit	c^2
Server CPU	0
Disk	0.5
Network	0

Now we compute T_w/T_c using equation 9.6 for the server CPU. Table 9.6 shows the server disk and network occupancy. Its data is computed as follows.

We first regard the disk and network as constant delay counters (18.8 ms + 3.6 ms). This acts to delay requests from reaching the server CPU, but does not otherwise affect the server, $T_s = T_{s_1} = 40$ ms. Since $T_c = 1$ sec, $T_{user} = 960$ ms (sum of user time, delay, and idle time). Now we solve for the server CPU waiting time, T_{w_1}, using equation 9.6, and for λ_a using equation 9.7.

The achieved request rate, λ_a, must be the same for the server CPU, the disk, and the network. So, if ρ_2 is the disk occupancy and ρ_3 is the network occupancy, we can find:

$$\rho_2 = \frac{\lambda_a}{\mu_2} = \lambda_a T_{s_2}$$

$$\rho_3 = \frac{\lambda_a}{\mu_3} = \lambda_a T_{s_3},$$

where T_{s_2} is the disk service time (18.8 ms) and T_{s_3} is the network service time (3.6 ms).

Knowing ρ_2, ρ_3 we can find T_{w_2}, T_{w_3} by using the open-queue $M/G/1$ model:

$$T_w = \frac{\rho(1 + c^2)T_s}{2(1 - \rho)}.$$

For example, suppose we know for $n = 10$ that $\lambda_a = 9.87$ from our model of the CPU server (Equation 9.6). Then $\rho_2 = \frac{9.87}{53.18} = .1856$, and t_{w_2} can be determined using ρ_2.

Since we have additional delay ($T_{w_2} + T_{w_3}$) in the system (beyond that computed for the server CPU), the λ_a should be corrected. In our case, the correction is slight, since

$$T_{w_1} \approx T_{w_1} + T_{w_2} + T_{w_3}.$$

While we computed these delays at the various servers, they are reflected at the workstations also, since they affect λ_a. For our example, $T_c = 1$ sec and:

$$\lambda = n \text{ requestors, each making 1 request per second}$$

$$\lambda_a = \frac{n}{T_w + T_c}; \text{ solve for} T_w \text{ and set } T_c = 1$$

$$T_w = \frac{n - \lambda_a}{\lambda_a}$$

where $\lambda_a \approx \lambda_{a_1}$ as determined by the server CPU. Slowdowns in the "processing rate," or achieved request rate, are reflected as delay at the workstations (Figure 9.20). Each server is occupied at different levels, however, since

$$\rho_i = \frac{\lambda_a}{\mu_i} = \lambda_a T_{s_i}$$

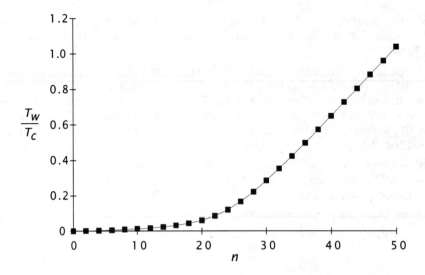

Figure 9.20   Waiting time, ratio T_w/T_c.

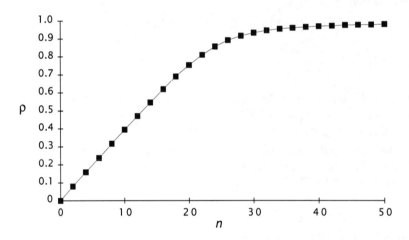

Figure 9.21   Occupancy at server CPU, $c^2 = 0$, $f = \frac{T_s}{T_c} = 0.04$. $c^2 = 0$,
$f = \frac{T_s}{T_c} = 0.04$

and the servers have different service times.

Table 9.6 agrees well with a more detailed simulation reported by Lazowska et al. [179]. Illustrating this table, Figure 9.20 shows the effect of increasing the number of workstations on the waiting time at each workstation, and Figure 9.21 shows the occupancy (utilization) of the server CPU.

Table 9.6 Network of diskless workstations (time in seconds).

	Server CPU ($c^2 = 0$)				Disk ($c^2 = 0.5$)			Network ($c^2 = 0$)			Total
n	T_{s1}	T_{w1}	λ_a	ρ_1	T_{s2}	ρ_2	T_{w2}	T_{s3}	ρ_3	T_{w3}	$T_{w1} + T_{w2} + T_{w3}$
0	0.04	0	0	0	0.0188	0	0	0.0036	0	0	0
1	0.04	0.0008	0.9992	0.04	0.0188	0.0188	0.0003	0.0036	0.0036	6E-06	0.001
10	0.04	0.013	9.8712	0.3948	0.0188	0.1856	0.0031	0.0036	0.0355	7E-05	0.016
20	0.04	0.0612	18.846	0.7538	0.0188	0.3543	0.0078	0.0036	0.0678	0.0001	0.069
30	0.04	0.2844	23.357	0.9343	0.0188	0.4391	0.0111	0.0036	0.0841	0.0002	0.296
40	0.04	0.6493	24.253	0.9701	0.0188	0.456	0.012	0.0036	0.0873	0.0002	0.662
50	0.04	1.0385	24.528	0.9811	0.0188	0.4611	0.012	0.0036	0.0883	0.0002	1.050

The Crisis in I/O

The crisis in I/O has been anticipated for some time, based upon the increasing performance of processors in the face of relatively static improvement in disk access time. This crisis has generally failed to develop, at least in the time frame it was expected to. There are a number of contributing factors to this:

1. The use of multiple disks to improve disk accessing bandwidth.

2. The use of disk cache buffers to reduce the I/O traffic to the disk storage system.

3. The use of more sophisticated I/O management techniques, including I/O processors and storage controllers.

4. The judicious use of multiprogramming in the processor.

It will require the continuing use of all of the preceding techniques, perhaps with additional techniques, to keep the crisis "wolf" from the door of the system designer.

9.4.5   Improving I/O Response and Capacity

To execute a program the processor fetches several logical data blocks from I/O that contain static program representation and data required during program execution. These data blocks consist of multiples of the disk block, which is the minimum transfer unit of the disk system. To some degree, larger block transfers reduce the number of I/Os required during program execution. With typical current systems, there is general usage for data block sizes of 4KB.

In order to avoid saturation effects, the designer can use multiprogramming with n logically independent processes. Partitioning the memory space to accommodate a multiprogrammed environment is a mixed blessing. Each process effectively has a smaller memory space. This increases the number of I/Os required to manage the working set for each program in a virtual memory system. It is very easy to create a system wherein increasing the number of active tasks decreases the overall performance as the virtual memory system begins to thrash. This is illustrated in study 9.4.

Study 9.4   Multiprogramming and Virtual Memory Effects

To illustrate the effects of multiprogramming and the resultant reduction of effective memory space on an I/O system, let us reconsider study 9.2(b). In that study, we had $n = 2$ (two active processes in the processor); the disk service time was 20 ms, and the processor request interarrival time was 12.5 ms. This was partitioned as:

$$n = 2$$

T_{user}	T_{sys}
10 ms	2.5 ms

Suppose we now operated the system without multiprogramming ($n = 1$). This effectively allows the single process access to the whole memory and reduces the I/O request rate due to paging traffic. Suppose the effect of this additional memory is to halve the paging request rate. The user time is now 20 ms (plus 2.5 ms of system time) before I/O requests. Now

$$n = 1$$

T_{user}	T_{sys}
20 ms	2.5 ms

$$T_u = 22.5 \text{ ms},$$

the disk service time (T_s) is

$$T_s = 20 \text{ ms, and}$$
$$T_u > T_s.$$

The processor is now the bottleneck and the inverted server model applies, so

$$T_s' = 22.5 \text{ ms}$$
$$T_u' = 20 \text{ ms}$$
$$r = \frac{20.0}{22.5} = .89$$

Using Equation (9.11):

$$\rho_a = \frac{1}{1 + r} = 0.53 \qquad (n = 1)$$
$$\lambda_a = \frac{.53}{T_u} = \frac{.53}{T_s'} = 23.6 \text{ requests per sec.}$$

This appears to indicate that we have a significant advantage with multiprogramming, as from study 9.2(b) the achieved request rate through the system was:

$$\lambda_a = 44.5 \qquad (n = 2),$$

but the purpose of the system is *not* simply to maximize the number of I/Os per second but rather to maximize the amount of *user computation* per second. Now let us compute the effective amount of user computation for each case ($n = 1$ and $n = 2$). To do this and understand the dynamics of each system, consider a typical one-second time period for each case. When $n = 2$:

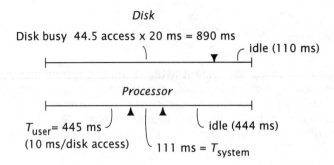

The time above the one-second timeline describes the disk activity; the time below the line describes the processor activity. For $n = 2$ the achieved processor–disk request rate, λ_a, was 44.5. This means that out of each second, the disk is busy for 44.5×20 ms = 890 ms and idle for 110 ms. The processor is executing user tasks for 44.5×10 ms = 445 ms and systems code for $44.5 \times 2.5 = 111$ ms; the remaining 444 ms the processor is idle. Thus, the processor is involved with user computation 445 ms out of each second. When $n = 1$, we have:

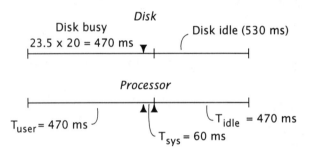

Now the processor is doing useful user computation 470 ms (23.5×20 ms) out of each second and executing systems code for about 60 ms (23.5×2.5).

We get 470 ms of user work done each second with $n = 1$ while only 445 ms of user work per second with $n = 2$. Clearly the single-program ($n = 1$) approach is preferable in this case.

Moral: Make certain you are optimizing the use of the right part of the system!

9.5   I/O Traffic and Virtual Memory Effects

The I/O traffic that a particular system and program require depends upon a number of issues, particularly:

1. The total number of I/Os that the program requires, and the average number of processor instructions between I/Os. These parameters vary considerably among programs, and are a function of the I/O block size and the management of I/O buffers.

2. Traffic due to virtual memory paging.

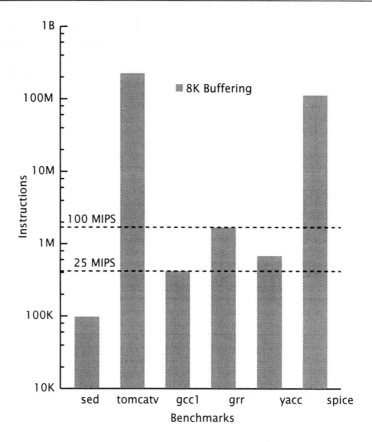

Figure 9.22   Instructions between I/O requests (from Richardson [245], see data notes).

Virtual memory traffic frequently dominates the I/O request rate. If the real memory is large compared to that required, only the basic I/O traffic (that defined by the program itself) is a factor as the virtual memory I/O traffic goes to zero. On the other hand, if the real memory is smaller than that required by a particular application, the virtual memory I/O traffic rate can easily overwhelm the basic I/O request rate.

9.5.1 Basic I/O Request Rate

Basic I/O requests represent only those accesses required to bring the static program representation into the processor for execution and subsequent data requests. This basic request rate is usually dominated by the data requests. Figure 9.22 plots the number of instructions between I/O requests assuming an 8 KB I/O buffer to prefetch requests. The six benchmarks cited represent large scientific programs and UNIX systems applications; all are run through to completion. There is an enormous variation across the programs: they vary from about 200,000 instructions between I/O requests to 700 or 800 million instructions between I/O requests. These programs are not necessarily representative of anything but perhaps the scientific environment.

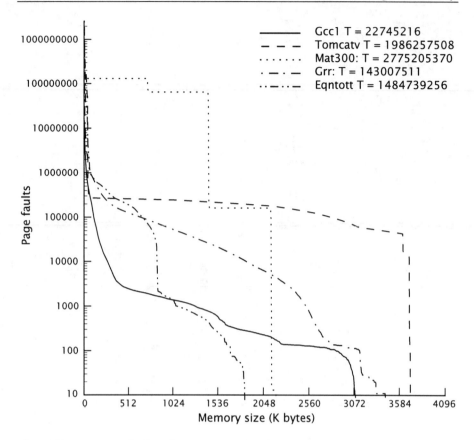

Figure 9.23   Page faults (data pages only) for various memory sizes for five benchmark programs (from Richardson [245]).

In order to get an idea of how or when these programs would be I/O limited, suppose we assume that to service these programs we have a single disk system and that a typical I/O access takes 16.3 ms (half the rotation delay for a 3600 rpm disk, 8.3 ms + 50% of 12 ms (seek) + 2 ms (transfer)). Now we can estimate when a particular program clearly becomes I/O limited as a function of CPU performance. If we take

$$\frac{\text{Instructions between I/O}}{16.3 \text{ ms}},$$

we get the processor performance at which half of the time is spent in processor execution and half waiting for I/O (assumes no multiprogramming). For our quite small sample of scientific programs, it is clear that while one program becomes I/O limited at processor performance of less than 25 MIPS, others are not I/O limited until beyond 100 MIPS.

This discussion assumes that the entire program and its data requests are brought into the processor as required and that the processor memory has ample room to hold the entire application.

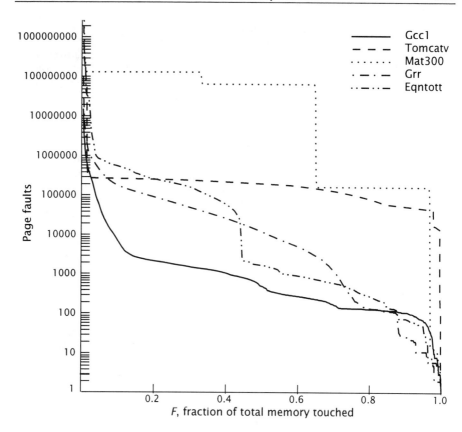

Figure 9.24   Page faults (data pages only) for normalized memory sizes, *F* (from Richardson [245]).

9.5.2   Virtual Memory I/O Traffic

Frequently the above assumption of sufficient memory to contain the entire program is not valid. The virtual memory system is used to page in active portions of the application to more efficiently use a limited memory size. This produces the other major source of I/O traffic. The smaller the memory available to an application, the more I/O traffic due to page faults. Figure 9.23 plots the number of page faults as a function of memory size for five programs. The faults included are only those due to paging. After the program and data set have been initially loaded into the processor memory, the total traffic to the I/O device is the sum of this page fault traffic plus basic I/O traffic.

Figure 9.24 shows the same information as Figure 9.23, but now the memory size is normalized to the fraction of memory required by the particular application. When the entire application fits into memory there is no paging traffic required to support program execution. Figure 9.23 has three separate regions of paging behavior:

1. The initial region from 0 to 0.1 of the required memory being available to the virtual memory system. In this region, there is severe paging activity because of a completely inadequate amount of available mem-

ory to support program execution.

2. The log linear region. In this region (from 0.1 to 0.9 of required program memory) the fault rate declines exponentially (by about a factor of 10^4) as a function of F, the fraction of total required memory currently available. Another way of describing this region is:

$$\text{Page miss rate} = K10^{-4F},$$

where K is a constant determined by the program. For example, suppose a certain program has half of its required working set available, $F = 0.5$, and its page miss rate is $K10^{-2}$. Now, if the memory available increases by one-tenth of its working set size, its miss rate falls to $K10^{-2.4}$. The relative miss rate improves by the ratio $K10^{-2.4}/K10^{-2}$, or $K10^{-.4}$; it is decreased by about a factor of 3.

3. The third region is the capture region (0.9 to 1.0 of the required memory being available). In this region, the program is completely contained in memory, and beyond this there is no virtual paging traffic.

These regions are quite variable across applications. Some applications, such as large matrices, have an almost flat region interrupted only by step functions. Apparently, there is rather little working set short of the entire program.

Figures 9.22–9.24 indicate the great difficulty in making generalizations about I/O behavior. There is a significant difference across programs, even taken from a common (scientific) application environment. Still, the systems designer is obliged to consider both the mean expected behaviors and the possible variance, and to try to create a system robust enough to handle most of the applications traffic that may present itself.

9.5.3   Disk Cache Buffers

An alternative approach without the obvious risks inherent in high degrees of multiprogramming is the use of a disk cache buffer. As we have seen in Chapter 5, caches work well for main memories. The same concept can be successfully used for disks, significantly reducing the required disk traffic. The disk cache has a similar role to the cache in a cache-memory system. It is a buffer that captures a significant fraction of the required I/O transfers, thus reducing the effective access time and the required number of disk accesses. Disk caches may be associated with a device or a storage controller or with a processor. (See Figure 9.25.)

A disk cache is a memory buffer that stores recently used portions of the disk address space. The caching unit may be anything from a sector to one or more tracks. Figure 9.26 indicates some typical miss ratios for disk caches when the buffer is in the processor memory, at the storage controller, or at the device. The system under measurement had about 50–60 disk drives and about 12–18 storage controllers with a single shared-memory CPU complex. The miss rate is best when the disk cache is in the processor memory. This comes at the expense of consistency in the backing store as, unless some further action is taken, writes made to the disk will be intercepted by the cache and not returned to provide a consistent copy

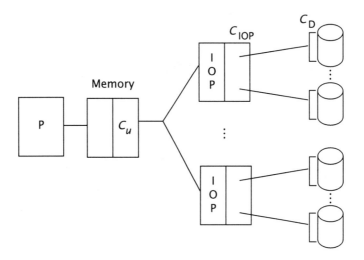

Figure 9.25 Situating the disk cache buffer. Three possible sites are illustrated. (a) C_u, at the processor memory. (b) C_{IOP}, at the storage controller (or I/O processor). (c) C_D, at the device.

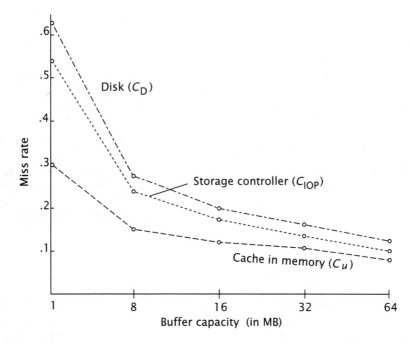

Figure 9.26 Miss rates for disk cache buffers (one track caching unit), from Smith [260].

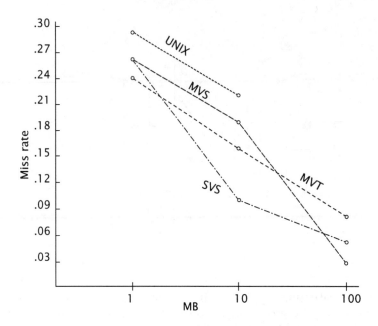

Figure 9.27   Miss rates for disk cache buffers in main memory; four different operating environments (from Smith [261] and Ousterhout et al. [223]).

until that particular cache block is replaced. Note that a write-though policy would create enormous and self-defeating traffic to the disk. However, it is possible to have writes written through the processor disk cache into a special device buffer whose only function would be to preserve consistency on subsequent accessing of a particular line.

The effectiveness of the disk cache buffers depends strongly upon the application environment and the operating system. Figure 9.27 shows three different miss ratios for two different environments using the IBM MVS, SVS, and Amdahl MVT operating systems, and then shows a UNIX operating system contrasted with the same applications running under a distributed version of UNIX called *Sprite*.

Disk caches seem effective when included as part of main memory. Their overall long-term effectiveness, however, is broadly limited by the systems environment to a lower bound on the miss rate of about .03 to .30. Generally, reductions of miss rate begin to saturate at cache sizes between about 8 and 16 megabytes (Figure 9.26).

9.5.4   Concurrent Disks

Beyond disk cache buffers, the systems designer can use ensembles of disks to provide I/O arm and transfer bandwidth for a high-performance processor complex [215]. The disk ensembles may be used in at least three different ways:

1. They may be used individually as an ensemble of disks, each containing multiple files, allowing the user to access the separate files

simultaneously (Figure 9.28).

2. Files may be distributed across multiple disks so that a particular file may be accessed concurrently by reading from the designated disks (Figure 9.29).

3. The disks may be synchronized so that reads and writes to the disk are automatically interleaved across multiple disks (Figure 9.30). Synchronized disks are matched so that each disk head is over the same data sector for all the disks.

Approach (3) is actually a hardware version of (2).

In dealing with ensembles of disks, we can attempt to improve performance by interleaving blocks across drives or by synchronizing drives to create a parallel access mechanism.

The second technique, called *file striping* or *distributed disks* (dd), simply places successive blocks on different drives up to some limit. The third technique *synchronizes* several drives (ds) so that they act in parallel. Consecutive bytes from a record are distributed over the drives up to the ds limit. Following Reddy and Banerjee [244], we notate these combinations as (q, s), where q indicates the distribution limit and s the number of disks synchronized in a cluster. For a 16-disk system, (16,1) indicates maximum (dd) distribution—16-block files (or larger) are distributed across all 16 drives. Combined arrangements are possible—for example, an (8,2) system. Here, long files (more than 8 blocks) are distributed over eight pairs of ds drives. Other configurations are possible, varying from a completely synchronized system (1,16) to 16 independent (1,1) drives. Distributing files across multiple drives has the effect of lowering the number of independent disk server mechanisms, m. Thus, distributing files reduces the service time but increases the occupancy (hence, the waiting time).

Occupancy depends on service time and m, the effective number of independent disk clusters in the system. For the moment suppose the request rate λ splits uniformly over the m independent servers. We compute traffic and occupancy on a per-server basis. Suppose a system consists of l drives. If the system consists of l multiple independent drives (1,1), then

$$m = l.$$

If a system consists of an ensemble of l disks clustered into units of s synchronized (1,s) disks (see Figure 9.31), then

$$m = \frac{l}{s}.$$

For a system of l disks clustered into units of $(q,1)$ distributed disks, the effective number of independent servers depends on characteristics of the user file. If the user file access pattern consisted only of single block file accesses, then the file accesses would be distributed across the l disks and there would be l servers, as in the independent disk case. If all file accesses were of q blocks or greater, then we would have l/q independent servers, so m depends on the access pattern (Figure 9.32). In order to describe user access behavior on distributed disks, we define the following terms (see Figure 9.33):

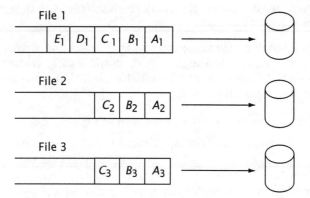

Figure 9.28   Disk ensemble of independent drives. Each file is assigned to a single device.

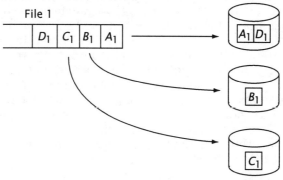

Figure 9.29   Distributing a file over multiple (three) disks. This technique, called *file striping*, assigns consecutive blocks of a single file to multiple drives.

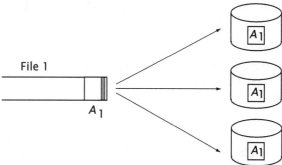

Figure 9.30   Disk synchronization (ds). Multiple drives are synchronized. Files are distributed by the *byte* on the drive, so that n drives read or write n bytes of a file simultaneously.

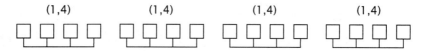

Figure 9.31 Synchronized drives; 16 drives clustered as four groups ($m = 4$) of four synchronized $(1, s)$ drives, where $s = 4$, i.e., $4 \times (1, 4)$.

If a file has f blocks, it is distributed:

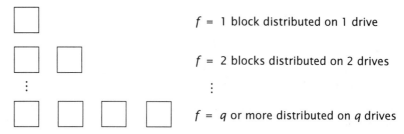

$f = 1$ block distributed on 1 drive

$f = 2$ blocks distributed on 2 drives

$f = q$ or more distributed on q drives

Figure 9.32 Distributed drives (dd): striping a file across q distributed drives.

- $E(f)$ is the expected file size (in blocks) of a file with block probability distribution function f.

- $E(f/q)$ is the expected number of blocks on each of q disks when a file with block probability distribution f is striped (dd) across the disks.

- $E(fd/q)$ is the expected number of disks to be accessed when a file of block probability distribution f is striped (dd) over q disks.

If a system consists of an ensemble of $(q,1)$ distributed disks, then the file distribution must be considered. (See Figure 9.32.) Define $E(fd/q)$ as the expected number of disks to access a file (out of q) with a block probability distribution f:

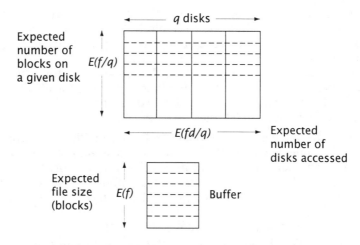

Figure 9.33 $E(f)$, $E(f/q)$, and $E(fd/q)$.

Since

$$E(fd/q) = (1) \cdot \text{Prob } (f = 1) + 2 \cdot \text{Prob } (f = 2) + \ldots + q \cdot \text{Prob } (f \geq q),$$

where Prob $(f = n)$ is the probability that a file access consists of an access to n physical disk blocks. Only one disk is accessed for $f = 1$, two disks are accessed for $f = 2$, and q disks are accessed for $f \geq q$.

Then m, the effective number of independent servers, is:

$$m = \frac{q}{E(fd/q)} \cdot \frac{l}{q} = m_q \cdot \frac{l}{q}$$

for a $(q, 1)$ system. We refer to the number of independent servers due only to distribution as m_q and $m_q = \frac{q}{E(fd/q)}$.

We can generalize for composite (q, s) systems the number of independent sub-systems, m':

$$m' = \frac{l}{q \cdot s},$$

and each (dd) subsystem is as above, so that m, the total number of independent servers, is:

$$m = m_q \cdot m'$$

$$m = \frac{q}{E(fd/q)} \cdot \frac{l}{q \cdot s}$$

Including m' in determining m is often unrealistic. Once an access is made to a file, it is highly probable that subsequent accesses will also go to it. Using m' is a *best-case* estimate of m and hence ρ. More realistic estimates will be discussed later.

In the following sections, we look at the three types of multiple disk organizations: independent, distributed (striped), and synchronized. We evaluate the T_s, T_{transfer}, and the occupancy ρ for representative configurations.

Later, we use this analysis to determine the request waiting time T_w and overall composite disk system performance. We illustrate this, following the work of Reddy and Banerjee [244], by considering a disk arrangement using 16 disk drives ($T_{\text{latency}} = 17.5$ ms, $T_{\text{read}} = 2.6$ ms for a 4KB block) and a transaction-type workload: 70% of the requests are for 1-block files, and 30% of the requests are for multiple-block files—uniformly distributed from 2 to 16 blocks. This illustrative data will later be the basis of a study of a composite disk system (studies 9.5 and 9.6).

The model of the processor(s) that uses the disk ensemble is also important. Multiple independent workstations tend to access multiple independent servers, more so than a single multiprogrammed processor. In fact, in the latter case, probably the most conservative assumption is that all requests are directed to a single file server (which itself may consist of multiple disks, $m' = 1$). In the case of multiple processors, there is an argument for assuming either (optimistically) a uniform distribution of requests over the independent servers or (conservatively) some clustering of requests about a smaller number of servers.

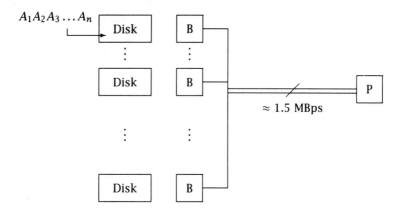

Figure 9.34   A cluster of independent disks.

9.5.5   Clusters of Independent Disks

In this configuration (Figure 9.34), we read complete files from disk to buffer, then (without overlap) transfer them from buffer to processor. (Disk read rate = buffer (B) to processor (P) transfer rate = 2.6 ms per 4-KB block.) —e.g., if file A consists of blocks $A_1, A_2, \ldots A_n$, then all blocks are assigned to a single drive and access to A would be:

Suppose we have the preceding workload, f [244], where 70% of the accesses are to files of one block and the remaining files are uniformly distributed from 2 to 16 blocks. Now the expected file length $E(f)$ is:

$$E(f) \quad = \quad \sum_{k=1}^{Max} k \cdot f(k),$$

where Max is the maximum number of blocks in f and $f(k)$ is the probability that there will be exactly k blocks in f.

For our case:

$$E(f) \quad = \quad .7(1) + .3\left(\frac{2}{15} + \frac{3}{15} + \cdots + \frac{16}{15}\right).$$

$$E(f) \quad = \quad 3.4 \text{ blocks.}$$

$$T_s \quad = \quad T_{\text{latency}} + E(f) \cdot \text{ block read time}$$

$$= \quad 17.5 + (3.4)(2.6) = 26.3 \text{ ms.}$$

$$T_{\text{transfer}} \quad = \quad 8.8 \text{ ms.}$$

If the interarrival time for requests was 40 ms and requests were uniformly

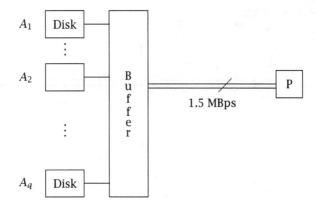

Figure 9.35 Striping files across q disks.

distributed across 16 such drives, then the occupancy per drive is:

$$\rho = \frac{1/40 \, ms}{16(1/26.3)} = 0.041.$$

9.5.6   Striping: Files Distributed across q Available Drives

Suppose a file has n blocks and it is to be distributed across q disk drives. By distributing blocks across consecutive disks (i.e., interleaving by block), we reduce the service time.

If $n \le q$, we access n drives concurrently and then read them into a common buffer. We can begin to transfer from the buffer to the processor after the first block is available. (For a file of n blocks, the disk read time = $\lceil n/q \rceil \times T_{\text{read}}$, but the buffer-to-processor transfer rate is the same as in the independent drive case and equals 2.6 ms/4-KB block. See Figure 9.35.)

Access now consists of:

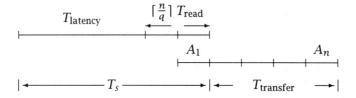

Note that we define T_{transfer} as the *unoverlapped* part of the buffer-to-processor transfer time.

Now $E(f/q)$ is the expected number of blocks that must be read to retrieve the file from a (striped) distributed disk ensemble of q disks. Thus, $E(f/1) = E(f) = 3.4$ blocks, as in the case of independent disks. For our particular workload $E(f/16) = 1$ block, since the maximum file length is 16. For $E(f/8)$, 70% of the files have one block and require one read. About one-half (actually 7/15) of the remaining 30% of the files also require a single read, as they can be distributed over eight single disks; they consist of eight or fewer blocks. The remaining 8/15 of the 30% require two disk reads. Thus:

$$E(f/8) = .7(1) + \frac{7}{15}(.3)(1) + \frac{8}{15}(.3)(2) = 1.16.$$

In general, $E(f/q)$ is

$$
\begin{aligned}
E(f/q) &= f(n \le q) + 2f(q < n \le 2q + kf(k-1)q < n \le kq) \\
E(f/q) &= \text{Prob}(n \le q) + 2\text{Prob}(q < n \le 2q) \ldots \\
&\quad + k\,\text{Prob}((k-1)q < n \le kq),
\end{aligned}
$$

where

$$k = \left\lceil \frac{n}{q} \right\rceil.$$

The service time for distributed $(q, 1)$ files on q disks is:

$$T_s = T_{\text{latency}} + T_{\text{synch}} + E(f/q) \cdot T_{\text{read}}.$$

Now all files are accessible in one block read time, although since the drives are not synchronized, there is additional block delay (T_{synch}).

Suppose we distributed the file across a (16,1) system with the previous workload (70% single blocks, 30% uniformly distributed over 2-16 blocks). Then $E(f/q) = E(f/16) = 1.0$.

Now

$$T_s = 17.5 + 2.6 + (1.0)2.6 = 22.7 \text{ ms.}$$

Blocks may be transmitted out of order, so the first block may be transmitted after one T_{read}. Transfer from buffer to processor is similar to the independent disk case (1,1), but the transfer begins as soon as the first block arrives. Thus, we have:

Now the unoverlapped transfer time is:

$$T_{\text{transfer}} = (E(f) - E(f/q))T_{\text{read}},$$

and for $E(f/16) = 1.0$ we have

$$
\begin{aligned}
T_{\text{transfer}} &= [E(f) - 1] T_{\text{read}} \\
&= [3.4 - 1]2.6 = 6.2 \text{ ms.}
\end{aligned}
$$

The occupancy depends on the number of independent units, m. On the average 3.4 units are occupied for each file; thus, the number of independent units m is:

$$m = \frac{q}{E(fd/q)} = \frac{16}{3.4} = 4.7,$$

and the (best-case) occupancy is:

$$\rho = \frac{\lambda}{m\mu} = \frac{1/40}{(4.7)1/22.7} = .12.$$

In an $(8,1)$ system, the files longer than eight blocks must be distributed over the same eight drives and require an additional read time. Now $E(f/8) = 1.16$.

$$
\begin{aligned}
T_s &= T_{\text{latency}} + T_{\text{synch}} + E(f/8) \cdot T_{\text{read}} \\
&= 23.1 \text{ ms.}
\end{aligned}
$$

Again, the transfer of the first block is assumed to be overlapped. Since the files are the same size as before, we can reduce the transfer time by the same amount we increased the service time, or by the increase in $E(f/q) \cdot T_{\text{read}}$:

$$
\begin{aligned}
E(f/16) - E(f/8) &= 0.16 \\
T_{\text{transfer}} &= 6.2 - (.16)2.6 = 5.8 \text{ ms.}
\end{aligned}
$$

The expected number of disks to be accessed is:

$$E(fd/q) = f(1) + 2f(2) + \ldots + qf(q) + qf(n > q).$$

For our case,

$$E(fd/q) = 2.68;$$

and since there are two $(8,1)$ clusters in a 16 drive system (again, the "best case" assumption):

$$
\begin{aligned}
m &= l/q \cdot \frac{q}{E(fd/q)}, \\
m &= (2)\frac{8}{E(fd/q)} = 6.0,
\end{aligned}
$$

and

$$\rho = \frac{\lambda}{m\mu} = \frac{1/40}{(6.0)(1/23.1)} = 0.096.$$

9.5.7   Disk Arrays: Files Distributed across s Synchronized (ds) Disks

Here, the s disks $(1,s)$ act as a single unit and are always accessed together. The bytes of each block are distributed across all s disks. Transfer from the buffer to the processor uses a high-speed bus and begins after the entire file is available. For a file of n blocks, the time to read the file and the buffer-to-processor transfer rate are s times faster than simpler configurations such as (1,1):

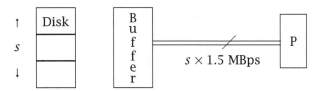

Access now consists of:

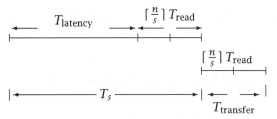

Synchronized disk (ds) files are byte-interleaved across s disks. Each block appears to be shortened by a factor of s. Since each block is distributed over all s drives, n block files are read in:

$$\text{read time} = n \cdot \frac{T_{\text{read}}}{s} \text{ for an } n\text{-block file.}$$

This assumes that the block size is at least s times the sector size (the unit of disk access). It is assumed that the buffer is fully occupied during the disk read time, so now the high-speed transfer is performed after the disk read is complete. Then

$$T_{\text{transfer}} = n \cdot \frac{T_{\text{read}}}{s}.$$

For $(1, s)$ configurations, $n = E(f)$ and

$$T_s = T_{\text{latency}} + \frac{E(f)}{s} T_{\text{read}}.$$
$$T_{\text{transfer}} = \frac{E(f)}{s} T_{\text{read}}.$$

For (1,16):

$$T_s = 17.5 + \frac{3.4}{16}(2.6)$$
$$= 17.5 + 0.55 = 18.1 \text{ ms}$$
$$T_{\text{transfer}} = 0.55 \text{ ms.}$$

For (1,8), we would have:

$$T_{\text{service}} = 17.5 + \frac{3.4}{8}(2.6)$$
$$= 18.6 \text{ ms.}$$
$$T_{\text{transfer}} = 1.1 \text{ ms.}$$

Occupancy can be computed as:

for (1,16) $\rho = \dfrac{\lambda}{m\mu}$ $(m = 1)$

$= \dfrac{1/40}{(1/18.1)} = 0.45.$

for (1,8) $\rho = \dfrac{1/40}{2(1/18.6)} = 0.23$ $(m = 2).$

9.5.8   Composite Configurations

Clusters of synchronized disks can also be striped. The analysis follows much of our earlier discussion, as illustrated in the following cases of (8,2) and (2,8).

For composite systems (q, s) where s and $q \neq 1$, the latency is extended by T_{synch} because of block starting position distribution, and the read and transfer time is shortened by s:

$$T_s = T_{\text{latency}} + T_{\text{synch}} + \frac{E(f/q)}{s} T_{\text{read}}.$$

The transfer time follows the synchronized buffer model; transfer occurs after the completion of T_s (all data is initially transferred into the buffer— no overlap):

$$T_{\text{transfer}} = E(f) \cdot \frac{T_{\text{read}}}{s}.$$

In the (8,2) case, we distribute the file over eight clusters of paired synchronized disks. The latency time is the same as the (dd) striped case, but the read time is reduced by the degree of synchronization (s). The basic latency of 17.5 ms is extended by $T_{\text{synch}} = T_{\text{read}} = 2.6$ ms to allow for the synchronization of the differing block starting points on the distributed disks. Thus,

$$\begin{aligned}
T_s &= T_{\text{latency}} + T_{\text{synch}} + \frac{E(f/q)}{s} T_{\text{read}} \\
&= 17.5 + 2.6 + \left[\frac{1.16(2.6)}{2}\right] \\
&= 21.6 \text{ ms.}
\end{aligned}$$

In computing the transfer time, we also assume an unoverlapped bus operating s times faster ($s = 2$) than the (1,1) disk. Now $E(f)$ in blocks is $0.7(1) + .3(9) = 3.4$:

$$T_{\text{transfer}} = 4.4 \text{ ms.}$$

The independence factor m is, as previously discussed:

$$m = \frac{q}{E(fd/q)} \cdot m'.$$

For (8,2) and (2,8) configurations, $m' = 1$.

Study 9.5   Open-Queue Study of Various Disk Array Configurations

We are now ready to compare the various concurrent disk configurations (and compare our results with Reddy's simulation). For this part of the study, we assume an open-queue model, and we compute the total response time based on that model.

We use the Reddy workload defined earlier as:

70% 1-block file access.
30% accesses uniformly distributed over 2–16-block file accesses.

First, we need to compute the service and transfer times for each configuration. Assuming 16 disks, we have from the preceding discussion:

Configuration	T_s	T_{transfer}
(1,1)	26.3	8.8
(16,1)	22.7	6.2
(8,1)	23.1	5.8
(4,1)	23.9	5.0
(1,16)	18.1	0.6
(1,8)	18.6	1.1
(1,4)	19.7	2.2
(2,8)	20.8	1.1
(8,2)	21.6	4.4

In order to compute ρ, we must find m, the effective number of independent disk drives. Reddy's simulation assumes that the disks are uniformly accessed. Therefore:

$$m = m_q \cdot \frac{16}{q \cdot s},$$

where

$$m_q = \frac{q}{E(fd/q)}$$

and $m_q = 1$ if $q = 1$.

Now we can approximate Reddy's workload distribution overall with a coefficient of variance of $c^2 = 0.15$. Using this and the previously discussed corresponding m factor for each configuration, we have:

Configuration	m	ρ	T_w	T_R
(1,1)	16	0.04	0.6	35.7
(16,1)	4.7	0.12	1.8	30.7
(8,1)	6.0	0.10	1.4	30.3
(4,1)	8.7	0.07	1.0	29.9
(1,16)	1	0.45	8.6	27.3
(1,8)	2	0.23	3.2	22.9
(1,4)	4	0.12	1.6	23.5
(2,8)	1.5	0.35	6.3	28.0
(8,2)	3	0.18	2.7	28.7

where T_R, the total response time, is:

$$T_R = T_s + T_{transfer} + T_w.$$

Study 9.6   Closed-Queue Study of Concurrent Disk Configurations

Now let us repeat study 9.5, but using our closed-queue model. We will assume multiprocessor requestors (n), each with the following timing:

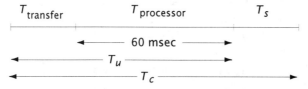

For this study, we make an important assumption on the access's behavior on distributed disks. In study 9.5, we assumed that the requests were made *uniformly to all physical servers*. In this study, we assume that the *effective number* of servers is the square root of the number of independent server classes (m'). This presumably adjusts the traffic for access patterns to frequently used files, so that now our model is shown in Figure 9.36.

We further assume a more conservative coefficient of variance of $c^2 = 0.5$. We will look at two workloads:

1. (As before) 70% 1-block file accesses, 30% accesses uniformly distributed over 2–16-block files access.

2. 30% 1-block file accesses, 70% accesses uniformly distributed over 2–16-block files access.

Using Equations 9.8 and 9.10, we can find T_w/T_c and then the λ_a, the achieved request rate *per server*. The total request–server rate for the system is:

$$\lambda_{sys} = \lambda_a \times m_{effective},$$

where $m_{effective} = m_q \sqrt{16/(q \cdot s)}$.

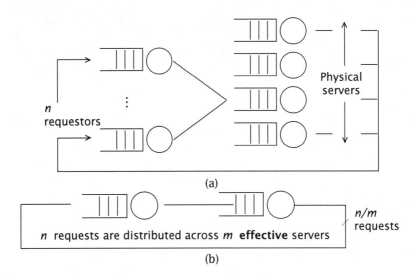

Figure 9.36   Effective number of servers.   (a) n requestors acting on m servers. (b) Asymptotic equivalent system.

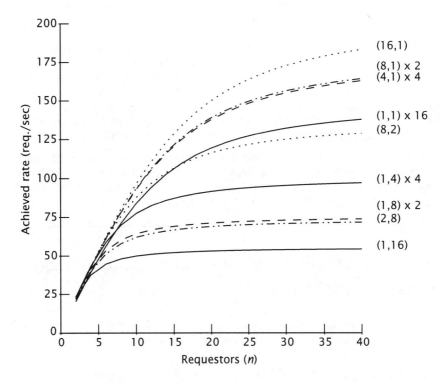

Figure 9.37   Achieved request-server rate for workload 1.

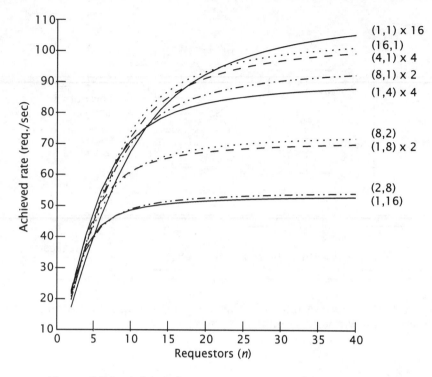

Figure 9.38   Achieved request-server rate for workload 2.

This λ_{sys} is plotted against n, the number of requestors for each workload in Figures 9.37 and 9.38. The superiority of (16,1) is largely due to our assumption about the effective number of servers. We assumed that the effective number of disk clusters was the square root of the number of physical clusters, but that concurrency within a (striped) cluster would be achieved (i.e., requests within a cluster would be uniformly distributed). A different assumption would clearly lead to different results.

In fact, one of the more interesting conclusions that can be drawn from the preceding is that array results depend heavily on user request behavior. They do not depend much on workload (access lengths) but on the way requests occur to physical servers and clusters.

9.6   Some Practical Considerations in the Design of Disk Systems

In this section, we discuss issues such as the useful design limits and practical considerations in the design and modeling of various ensembles of disks.

Our finite population model is based on the $M/M/1$ queue, where $c^2 = 1$. When n is small, it is probably appropriate to assume a relatively higher coefficient of variance. As n grows, the asymptotic model with a specified c^2 is preferred. If the file distribution and disk parameters are known, it is possible to compute the c^2. For typical configurations and typical files, Kim [162, 163] and Ogata [219] generally report the coefficient of variance to be less than .5. For the configurations cited by Reddy [244], c^2 is approximately 0.15. It would seem that for initial design purposes (especially in light of the many other assumptions made in modeling these systems), the designer could reasonably assume $c^2 = 0.5$ for large n and $c^2 = 1$ for small n ($n \leq 4$).

Another design issue touched on earlier is m', the number of independent units. For memory system design, we assume that accesses could be distributed uniformly across the low-order address bits of the memory space and hence across the interleaved memory modules. In a distributed system $(q,1)$, blocks of a file are similarly distributed across the disks, but in other disk configurations, $(1,1)$ for example, separate files are directed at separate disks. This situation much more closely resembles high-order interleaving than low-order interleaving in memory, and certainly calls into question the practical achievement of $m' = l/qs$.

It is reasonable to assume that when a file is opened there are multiple accesses to the same file—or at least a relatively small number of files— rather than that subsequent accesses are made uniformly to the file servers (m'). On the other hand, it may be somewhat severe to assume that $m' = 1$ for all cases; quite frequently, multiple files are simultaneously accessed to complete a particular transaction. A possible design position to take is that it is likely that we would achieve m':

$$m' = \sqrt{\frac{l}{qs}}.$$

Note that this indicates an effective number of independent units m as:

$$m = m_q \cdot m' = m_q \cdot \sqrt{l/q_s},$$

where m_q represents independence based on file striping:

$$m_q = \frac{q}{E(fd/q)}.$$

Before using any such arbitrary estimate, however, the designer is cautioned to carefully consider the expected behavior of the system in light of overall system specifications. In a particular case single large files may be accessed, and it is better to assume that $m' = 1$. Other distributional data on accessing patterns may be known that could be incorporated into the selection of the appropriate m'.

When the workstation-type system is being modeled with a large number of independent processors making requests on an ensemble of disk servers, it may be reasonable to simply assume that the requests are uniformly distributed across each of the servers, reducing the effect of traffic by a factor of m. However, even in this case some files (such as systems files) are accessed regularly by multiple users, and they limit the validity of the uniform distribution assumption. Depending upon the exact arrangement of the system, the designer may wish to choose an m smaller than the number of units, perhaps using the square root rule suggested before. In the case of a multiprogrammed system, especially with relatively low levels of multiprogramming (n = 2 or 3), it seems prudent to assume (in the absence of other information) that all requests are made to a single disk server at any one time. Again, the square root rule can be used if the designer has some knowledge that the requests from the various processes are being effectively distributed across at least several of the disk servers.

Disk Arrays

The rationale for disk arrays is simple: small disk drives provide storage at the same or lower cost per megabyte than a large disk drive; yet multiple small drives have multiple access mechanisms. Hence, an ensemble of drives provides the same storage as a single large drive but with multiple access paths to information contained on these drives. The down side of multiple drives replacing a single drive is reliability. Assuming that each drive, large or small, has the same failure rate, having multiple drives will significantly increase the failure rate over one large drive. The problem, then, in the effective use of disk arrays is twofold:

1. Distributing data effectively across the ensemble of small drives to use the access potential afforded by the multiple drives.

2. Judiciously introducing redundancy into the array to restore the overall disk reliability.

The difficulty with achieving the preceding requirements is that the access workload to the disk array is neither uniform nor stationary. Certain access patterns may favor a particular arrangement of drives in an array, yet later when data is accessed under a different regime, still another combination of striping and synchronization may be preferable. The designer must achieve an overall balance across a relatively diverse range of workloads to achieve a robust disk array solution.

9.7   Redundancy in Disk Arrays

Ensembles of disks may, in particular applications, provide significant performance improvement. However, multiple drives imply multiple failure points. As pointed out by Katz et al. [158], the MTBF (mean time between failures) of a disk array is:

$$\frac{\text{MTBF of a single disk}}{\text{Number of disks in the array.}}$$

This assumes that failures are independent. If a single disk has a failure rate of 30,000 hours, an array of 100 disks would have a failure rate of only 300 hours, or less than two weeks. Since the disk storage is the ultimate backing store and the only completely nonvolatile storage space in the system, its integrity is extremely important. Extra disks containing redundant information can be introduced to help preserve the integrity of the array.

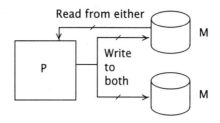

Figure 9.39   RAID1: Mirrored disk (file M is replicated on two disks).

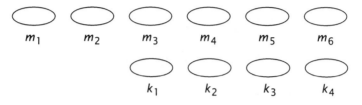

Figure 9.40   RAID2: Hamming coded file, $M = m_1, m_2, \ldots, m_6$, is distributed over multiple disks. Separate correct bits, $K = k_1, \ldots, k_4$, are maintained one on each disk.

Katz uses the term *RAID* (redundant array of inexpensive disks) to describe several techniques—in his words, "levels"—for providing redundant disks to improve the integrity of data contained on a disk array. The basic approach he describes is to decompose the array into groups, with each group having an extra redundant disk containing some check information. When a disk fails, the system detects the failure, and through the use of a *hot spare* reconstructs the information contained on the damaged disk by using the remaining valid disks in the group together with the check disk. The reconstructed information that had been on the defective disk is written to the spare disk, which on subsequent accesses to the disk array acts in place of the defective disks. At some later time during a maintenance procedure, the faulty disk is removed and a new hot spare is placed in the array in its place. Katz et al. describe six levels of RAID and the advantages and disadvantages of each in both a transaction processing environment and a supercomputer environment. The transaction environment consists of many accesses to short files, while the supercomputer access application consists of a few accesses to very large files.

In their terminology, RAID 1 consists of mirrored disks (Figure 9.39). In this approach, each data disk has a mirror disk simply replicating all the information on the original data disk. All writes to the data disk are also done to the redundant (mirror) disk. This approach was pioneered by Tandem Computers, which also replicated controllers and I/O buses. Mirroring doubles the cost of the storage system. It does not affect in any way the available read or write bandwidth.

RAID 2 is a bit-interleaved array organized much as our memory was organized in chapter 6 using Hamming codes (Figure 9.40). We still must satisfy the criteria that we have a number of correct bits such that the number of correct disks k satisfies the relationship

$$2^k \geq k + m + 1,$$

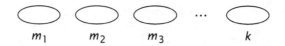

Figure 9.41   RAID3 and 4: file $M = m_1, \ldots m_n$ is distributed over n disks (bitwise in RAID3, blockwise in RAID4). A single-parity disk (k) maintains the message parity.

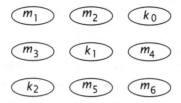

Figure 9.42   RAID5: file $M = m_1, \ldots m_n$ is distributed over n disks in a $p \times p$ array when $(p-1) \times (p-1) = n$. Parity is interleaved by sector across p disks. As above, k_0 is the parity over m_1 and m_2, k_1 is the parity for m_3 and m_4, etc.

where m is the number of data disks. If we had 10 data disks, we would need $k = 4$ redundant disks.

While reducing the cost, RAID 2 has its own difficulties. It really only suits the synchronized array (ds) described earlier. The minimum file must contain 10 data blocks, since this becomes the minimum writable unit to the disk. As observed by Katz, level 2 seems to be more useful for supercomputer-type applications and in fact is used by Thinking Machines in several of their systems.

In RAID level 3, a parity disk is introduced (Figure 9.41). This creates a type of geometric correction code discussed in Chapter 6. Data is distributed bitwise across several disks, with a final disk containing parity across the stored bit records. Failure is detected when accessing an individual disk, and the parity disk can be used to reconstruct the flawed information. Use of a parity disk requires it to be accessed on all writes, and, as with Raid 2 use, is generally suitable only for synchronized (ds) disk arrays.

RAID 4 is not unlike RAID 3, except that rather than distributing data across disks in a bitwise fashion, each disk is allocated an entire block of the record (Figure 9.41). This improves the ability of the system to access small files (e.g., 1-block files) since only one disk plus a parity disk need be engaged in the access process.

RAID Level 5 is shown in Figure 9.42. In RAID levels 3 and 4, all accesses require a parity disk, which becomes a bottleneck in the system. One can create a system of rotated parity across sectors where the parity information is now distributed across a series of disks on a sector-by-sector basis. This improves the number of simultaneous accesses that can be made to the disk array.

RAID Level 6 consists of advancing RAID level 5 to two or more dimensions of parity. Imagine now that we have several dimensions of disks in which we can create both a row and a column parity.

Interest in reliable disk operation is a natural consequence of the importance of data integrity. The problem with many of the approaches to higher levels of redundancy is that, like array configurations themselves, they are not necessarily robust with respect to varying file distributions. If a file with a particular distribution is best organized as a striped file or multiple independent files, and another file is best organized by access through a synchronized disk array, we have a significant dilemma in arranging not only the array hardware but also the redundant support mechanism to support the ensemble of disks.

9.8   Conclusions

There are many aspects of computer input/output. The I/O process represents the myriad functions: moving data in and out of a computer system, presenting it to a human user, and recognizing voice and images as well as representing the primary method for the bulk storage of large files. The primary objective of this chapter is to deal with the storage subsystem. The media and communications aspects of I/O are varied and quite important. In fact, they are of growing importance in the industry. However, each system must have a storage archive that represents all of the files accessible to a particular user. The rapid access to these files determines in large measure the performance of the system.

Despite the increasing gap between disk access time and processor performance, techniques have been developed to create systems that for many applications are not I/O bound.

Queueing models have been developed that describe I/O system response, at least asymptotically, within the obvious limitations of the assumed statistical behavior, of requests and responses. These models provide a good deal of insight into the behavior of complex processor-memory-I/O systems. The closed asymptotic $M/G/1$ model is particularly useful in describing overall systems behavior.

In order to improve I/O performance, several important techniques have been developed. The earliest and most obvious is simple processor multiprogramming—having the computer do something else (engage in another process) while the current process is waiting for I/O. This is effective enough as long as it does not significantly increase the paging rate and hence the I/O traffic required of the system. If a process has a smaller available memory because of multiprogramming, this can increase the paging rate and hence the I/O request rate.

Another approach to decreasing the I/O request rate and increasing overall performance is the use of disk cache buffers. These buffers can be effective, although they are not as robust as the use of cache memory (discussed in chapter 5). Indeed, relatively large disk cache buffers centralized at the processor (actually a part of processor/main memory) may be limited to a miss rate of 10–30%, even when as much as 16 megabytes of memory are devoted to this function.

Finally, arrays of smaller disks can be concurrently accessed to improve overall systems response. This can be most effective when the file accessing distribution is well known and represents a stable statistic. If the system must respond regularly to the access pattern coming from two different file distributions, each of quite distinct and different character, it becomes difficult or impossible to create a robust disk array solution that optimizes the performance of the system for both accessing patterns.

Since the disk arm itself is a major failure point of the system and determines to a large degree the overall mean time to failure, using multiple disks with multiple heads decreases the overall system reliability. This requires careful attention to the introduction of some degree of redundancy in the I/O system to compensate for the increased failure rate of the disk ensemble.

9.9   Some Areas for Further Research

Generally, I/O behavior remains a rather unexplored area of research. One reason is that many of the results seem to be specific to particular operating systems or particular user environments. It is difficult to generalize which results are universally applicable across a reasonable set of workloads and operating environments. Still, there may be ways to normalize the results or even to find the bounds on such issues as program request rates. Clearly, it is this understanding that is imperative in good overall systems design.

Progress on a bulk nonmechanical storage medium for I/O would have enormous consequences on I/O systems design, yet such "solid-state" disks remain something of an *El Dorado*. Even if such devices were available, however, it is not clear that we could rapidly adapt our systems and file structures to effectively use such devices. Disk arrays represent an evolutionary approach to the design of the storage system. Properly understood and properly configured, they still provide the basic method of storage system use and optimization.

9.10   Data Notes

Note 1: Figure 9.22

The benchmarks in these figures [245] are taken from the Specmark89 benchmark suite.

sedd: Stream text editor. This searches using a regular expression and does a global replace on a 1000-line C program (23M instructions).

tomcatv: Vectorizable mesh generator (2B instructions).

gcc1: Gnu, compiling a 775-line C program to assembly code.

grr: PC board router, routing an 11-layer PC board (140M instructions).

yacc: Unix compiler utility. Converts a context-free grammar into a set of tables for a simple automaton, which executes a left-recursive parsing algorithm. Building a table for a 480-line grammar.

spice: Circuit simulator, simulating a bipolar gray code counter.

mat300: Matrix multiply with 300-×-300 double precision matrices (2.8B instructions).

Eqntott: Equation minimizer. Takes 29 equations as input and produces a table of the minimal product terms as output (1.5B instructions).

9.11   Annotated Bibliography

There are many lucid introductions to I/O systems organization. Particularly recommended is Stallings [269]. There have been a number of recent papers on the issue of multimedia; particularly interesting is the special issue of *Communications of the ACM* (April 1991).

Mee and Danielle [195] and Harker [121] are particularly good treatments of recording technology and the evolution of disk storage subsystems.

Kobayashi [169] and Kleinrock [166] have the most relevant and appropriate treatment of queueing theory as it applies to processor configurations. Smith's treatment of disk cache buffers [261] is among the earliest and most comprehensive on this topic. Other relevant works in this area include Grossman, Mitsuishi and Ousterhout. Cray Research has pioneered disk striping for use in supercomputer applications [63]. Kim in her thesis [163] presents an interesting treatment of disk modeling and the statistical distributions of both disk access and service times. She further develops performance models for various disk interleaving technologies. A treatment of concurrent disk ensembles follows the terminology and treatment of Reddy [244]. His quantitative approach and evaluations are particularly valuable in validating our own models. Gray [112], Ng [216], and Salem [251] make important contributions to concurrent disk technology. Katz [158] has formalized the discussion of redundancy in disk arrays by introducing the various concepts of RAID levels; see also Patterson [229] and Lee [180].

Additional Reading

I/O System Overview

W. Stallings. *Computer Organization and Architecture: Principles of Structure and Function*. Macmillan, New York, 2nd edition, 1990.

R. Hou, G. Ganger, and Y. Patt. Issues and problems in the I/O subsystem Part I—The magnetic disk. In Milutinovic and Shriver, editors, *Proceedings of the Hawaii International Conference on System Sciences*, pages 48–57, January 1992.

R. H. Katz. High-performance network and channel based storage. *Proc. IEEE* 80(8):1238–1261, August 1992.

IEEE Computer, March 1994. This is a special issue devoted to the I/O challenge.

Proc. IEEE. Special section on the changing nature of high-speed storage. Volume 81, number 4, April 1993.

Disk Subsystem

J. M. Harker, D. W. Brede, R. E. Pattison, G.R. Santana, and L. G. Taft. A quarter century of disk file innovation. *IBM Journal of Research and Development*, pages 677–689, September 1981.

T. Teorey and T. Pinkerton. A comparative analysis of disk scheduling policies. *Communications of the ACM*, pages 177–184, March 1972.

R. A. Scranton, D. A. Thompson, and D. W. Hunter. The Access Time Myth. Research Report RC 10197, IBM, September 1983.

C. Ruemmler and J. Wilkes. An introduction to disk drive modeling. *IEEE Computer* 27(3):17–28, March 1994. (A well written paper on actual behavior of disk drives and the sensitivity to various modeling details.)

Disk Technology

C. D. Mee and E. D. Danielle. *Magnetic Recording*, Volume 1: Technology; Volume 2: Applications. McGraw Hill, NY, 1987.

D. Bitton. Arm scheduling in shadowed disks. In *Proceedings of Compcon 89*, pages 132–136, 1989.

Disk Cache Buffers

A. Smith. Disk cache—miss ratio analysis and design considerations. *ACM Transactions on Computer Systems*, 3(3):161–203, August 1985.

J. Ousterhout, H. Da Costa, D. Harrison, J. Kunze, M. Kupfer, and J. Thompson. A trace-driven analysis of the UNIX 4.2 BSD file system. In *10th Symposium on Operating System Principles*, pages 15–24, 1985.

Disk Array and Ensembles

R. Katz, G. Gibson, and D. Patterson. Disk system architecture for high performance computing. *Proceedings of the IEEE*, 77(12):1842–1858, December 1989.

K. Salem and H. Garcia-Molina. Disk striping. In *International Conference on Data Engineering*, pages 336–342, 1986.

RAID

M. Y. Kim. Synchronized disk interleaving. *IEEE Transactions on Computers*, C-35(11):978–988, November 1986.

D. Patterson, G. Gibson, and R. Katz. A case for redundant arrays of inexpensive disks (RAID). *ACM SIGMOD*, pages 109–116, May 1988.

9.12   Problem Set

1. A request is made to the Hitachi DK 516 drive outlined in Table 9.4. The new track is 30 tracks distant from the current position. The request is to move 20 sectors into a buffer. (The transfer rate is 3 MBps.) The starting block location is unknown but assumed to be uniformly

distributed over possible locations on the track. What is the total time to access and transfer the requested data?

2. In a certain system, requests to a disk system (from multiple buffered sources) arrive at the rate of one each 33 ms (λ). The disk has service time of 20 ms. Use the open-queue $M/G/1$ model ($c^2 = 0.5$) to find:

   (a) Total response time (service time plus the waiting time).

   (b) Average number of requests queued at the disk awaiting service.

3. Plot the effect of c^2 on waiting time for various values of ρ ($\rho = 0.1$, 0.2, 0.5, 0.7, 0.9). At what point(s) does c^2 contribute more than a 10% effect on total response time ($T_w + T_s$)?

4. Repeat study 9.2(a) with the following changes: $c^2 = 0.5$, $T_{user} = 20$ ms (i.e., 200K user-state instructions before an I/O request), and $n = 3$.

5. Now find the effect of a four-times-faster processor; that is, repeat study 9.2(b) using the parameters given for the previous problem, except that $c^2 = 1$.

6. Study 9.4 assumes that using $n = 2$ (two processes) residing in the same memory will double the relative paging memory miss rate and hence double the I/O request rate. At that point, multiprogramming ($n = 2$) decreases performance. At what relative paging memory miss rate (for $n = 1$) will the user performance for both $n = 1$ and $n = 2$ be the same? That is, find T_{user} ($n = 1$) so that the user time per second $n = 1$ and $n = 2$ are the same.

7. In study 9.3, suppose we increase the server processor performance by a factor of 4, but all the other system parameters remain the same. Find the disk utilization and user response time for $n = 20$. (Assume $c^2 = 0.5$ for the disk.)

8. A RAID technique is to be applied to a disk array of 18 drives (including correction drives). Suggest suitable redundancy configuration for drives with data distributed as:

   (a) (4,1).

   (b) (1,8).

   (c) (1,1).

9. Find the effect of workload on T_R using the open-queue model. Repeat study 9.5 using the alternative workload (workload #2) described in study 9.6.

10. Suppose we now apply the "square root" server (from study 9.6) to study 9.5. Again using the data of study 9.5 and the open-queue model, find T_R for each configuration if $m = m_a \cdot \sqrt{16/(q \cdot s)}$.

11. Reconsider study 9.6. Now assume

    (a) $m = 1$,

    (b) requests are uniformly distributed across servers.

    Evaluate λ_a for workload #1 for (1,1), (16,1), (1,16), and (4,4).

12. A block read request is sent to an Hitachi DK516 disk for 16 sectors, beginning with surface 3, track 23, sector 7. At the time the request is received, the active head is positioned over the start of surface 12, track 1, sector 0. If the transmission rate to the buffer is 3 MB/sec, what is the elapsed time until the data are in the buffer?

13. For study 9.2(a) and (b), what is the perceived delay per request?

14. Repeat study 9.2(a) with an 8-kB block. Assume that with an 8-kB block the processor makes a request every 700^K user-state instructions. Which block size provides better user performance?

15. Repeat study 9.5 with 50% 1-block accesses and 50% 16-block accesses.

16. A RAID storage system is to be implemented with 16 drives. These drives can be configured independently, striped, or synchronized. Configure a RAID-1, RAID-2, and RAID-5 storage system that maximizes the amount of data storage. What fraction of storage is devoted to data for each configuration?

17. The processor in study 9.2(b) is replaced with a 100-MIPS processor. Assume the memory is increased to support multiprogramming of degree 6 and the disk accesses are uniformly spread over four disk servers. Compute the achieved throughput and individual server occupancies.

18. A disk cache buffer is added to the processor in study 9.2(a). Assume a miss rate of 30%. Estimate the effect of the buffer on throughput by modifying the effective user and system time per physical disk access (miss). Assume $T_{sys} = 0$ on a cache buffer hit.

19. An additional 1 MByte memory is to be added to the processor in study 9.2(a). It can be configured as a disk buffer cache (25% miss rate), or as main memory to increase the degree of multiprogramming to three, or the block size can be doubled (thereby doubling the user instructions between disk references). Which option provides the best user performance?

20. Repeat study 9.3 with T_{disk}=35 ms for n=1 and n=10.

21. For the configuration in study 9.3, assume we distribute the disk storage throughout the workstation network. Each workstation gets a single disk with T_{disk}= 40 ms. Disk accesses are distributed uniformly over all disks in the system. Assume that each access requires 20 ms of system processing on the local processor and 20 ms on the target processor. Assume access to the local disk incurs the same network cost as a remote access. Estimate the achieved throughput and the processor and disk utilizations.

22. Repeat study 9.3 with the following modifications: Assume each workstation has a local disk. Assume 50% of user requests are to the local disks. Model the effects of the local disk by modifying the effective user and pause times per server access.

Chapter 10

Processor Studies

Good design is the product of much work. The effort involves a team of market analysts, competitive product analysts, designers, technologists, and software engineers, directed by management and financial considerations. Design is a constant series of tradeoffs between functional specifications and market requirements vs. functionality, cost, and performance. The studies we present in this chapter clearly cannot capture the man-years of effort that typify the best in processor design. The design situations we present attempt to introduce the reader to simplified design situations without making the problems overly contrived. In this chapter, we present two extended design studies. We begin with the functional specifications. These are the engineering assumptions, market considerations, and determinations that are presented to the designer as the design is begun. As in the rest of this text, we focus on the design issues in instruction sequencing in the memory hierarchy. We allocate a fraction of the design to execution resources and expect performance proportional to the amount of processor resources so dedicated.

10.1   The Baseline Mark II

This study details the design of a load/store processor to be used as the core of a high-performance workstation, the Baseline Mark II. This workstation is an improved version of the original Baseline Mark I, the only significant change being the replacement of the processor. Some minor changes to the system are planned, but none that are fundamental to the processor or system architecture, in order to maximize compatibility between the systems and to allow an easy upward migration path for customers who already own the original Baseline Mark I.

The Baseline-series workstations are targeted at the scientific and engineering communities, and are expected to be used in environments where a significant amount of the workload will be simulation and analysis—only a nominal portion of the workload will be "general-purpose applications" such as editors, databases, and so forth. Users of these machines are interested in maintaining their installed base of applications and having them run faster with newer machines. The Mark II unit is seen as meeting their needs. This study, therefore, is an extension to studies 2.3 and 4.11.

10.1.1   Design Assumptions

In order to design the new processor to be used in the Baseline Mark II, we must have some guidelines on which to base our design decisions. The following assumptions provide a basis for the use of data in earlier sections of this book:

- Cache should be adjusted for systems effects ("warm" cache).

- Use 4^{kB} pages with 1^{MB} segments.

- Out-of-order execution is not allowed.

- Run-on instructions stall the pipeline in all cases, not just those with dependencies between instructions.[1]

- The condition codes are set after the last execution cycle.

- The pipeline is dynamic.

- Arithmetic operations (integer and floating-point) are the only run-on instructions, and are not pipelined (integer add/subtract excepted).

- Wafer yield is based on the Poisson model developed in Chapter 2 and assumes a 1 defect/cm^2 defect density (ρ).

- The cache miss penalty is 5 cycles.

- The TLB miss penalty is 20 cycles.

- The memory system can support a single word access with a latency of eight cycles, and an additional three words with an additional latency of three cycles.

- General overhead is modeled as 50% of the data path area (latch 10%, bus and wiring 40%).

- Pads, pad drivers, power supply, and guard area are modeled as a 20% full chip overhead.

- Cache overhead (address tag and information bits) is modeled as a 15% area (5% tag and status bit information, 10% area mismatch penalty).

- A direct-mapped cache can support an access rate of one word per cycle, or can be pipelined to support an access rate of one word per half-cycle (for the super-pipelined processor version), and thus requires an additional 10% area penalty for pipelining the cache. A set associative cache can support an access rate of one word per two cycles (the extra is there because the request has to go through the directory first), or can be pipelined to support an access rate of one word per cycle for an additional 10% area penalty.

---

[1] This provides an upper-bound estimate. The lower bound can be generated assuming that run-on instructions stall the pipeline only when there is a data dependency, using the execution dependency distances from Table 3.20 to generate an effective penalty. However, since multiplication units are only occasionally pipelined and division units are rarely pipelined (and often use the same hardware as the multiplication unit), this lower bound is not a very useful number.

- The fabrication line for this processor uses 8-inch (20.32 cm) wafers and has a cost per wafer of $5,000, including wafer-level testing and sorting. Packaging cost for this chip is $100 per package and includes final chip-level testing.

When necessary, further assumptions will be made in order to make design decisions—an occurrence that is not infrequent in real design processes. However, these are most of the basic bookkeeping assumptions that will be required during the course of the study.

10.1.2   Design Alternatives

We use the standard area model to determine the size of the die. Table 10.1 shows the Baseline Mark I processor area breakdown, using the standard area model.

Beginning with this breakdown, we extend the processor to improve the performance of the machine. In order to understand the different tradeoffs involved, two different designs are evaluated.

- A three-quarter-scale reduction of the original baseline unit, in order to expand the cache and TLB available on-chip in the hope of increasing performance due to the reduced miss penalty. This uses the same area as the original processor.

- A super-pipelined version of the original design, which (due to conservative design practices) will be designed at full scale.

We assume no cycle time reduction for the reduced-scale processor, nor do we assume any cycle time penalty for the super-pipelined processor for simplicity. However, we will add a 10% penalty to the pipeline, cache, and TLB for the super-pipelined processor to account for the additional latch and control logic that the super-pipelined processor requires. The die overhead remains constant at the original Baseline Mark I value.

The pipeline for the original processor is shown in Figure 10.1. The pipeline for the first new design is the same as the original processor, and is shown in Figure 10.2(a). The pipeline for the second design is the half-cycle version of the original processor pipeline, and is shown in Figure 10.2(b). Since the goal of these processors is to fit into the same framework as the original processor, the times are all normalized to the original processor—thus, the reduced-scale version has a cycle time of "one cycle" and the super-pipelined version has a cycle time of "one half-cycle" for all calculations performed in the study.

10.1.3   Pipeline Timing Analysis

In order to determine what the tradeoffs are for the two design choices described in section 10.1.1, we must consider both performance and cost. This section evaluates the two pipelines for performance. We consider cost effects in the next section, using different system configurations for these two designs.

Table 10.1   Baseline Mark I area model.

Integer Unit Area Components	
Integer ALU	1.0 A
Integer register file with bypass[a]	1.15 A
Shifter	0.5 A
Incrementer	0.4 A
Program counter unit	0.85 A
TLB[b]	6.0 A
Decoder hardware	1.0 A
Cache controller	1.0 A
Bus logic	2.0 A
Store buffer	1.0 A
Load/Store byte support	0.2 A
Clock generation	1.0 A
Total integer unit area	16.1 A
Floating Point Unit Area Components	
Register file[c]	1.0 A
Adder	13.5 A
Multiplier	20.3 A
Division support[d]	3.0 A
Total floating-point unit area	37.8 A
Memory Subsystem Area Components	
16 KBI-cache[e]	53.1 A
8 KBD-cache[f]	26.6 A
Total memory subsystem area	79.7 A
Processor Overhead Area Components	
Integer unit (50%)	8.05 A
Floating-point unit (50%)	18.9 A
Memory subsystem (15%)	14.05 A
Total processor overhead area	41 A
Die Area Components	
Total processor area	174.6 A
Die overhead area (20% total processor area)	43.7 A
Total die area	218.3 A

[a] The integer register file consists of 32 single-word integer registers that are paired to support double word values.

[b] There are two TLB's, each of which is 2-way set-associative with LRU replacement and each has 128 entries (64 × 2).

[c] The floating point register file consists of 32 IEEE Single Precision registers that are paired to support Double Precision values.

[d] Additional area allows multiplier to perform division—a separate divider element would require 23.3 A, which includes both a multiplier and division support.

[e] The cache is 8[kB] direct mapped, 4 word per line (16 byte per line), write-through no write-allocate.

[f] The D-cache is a copyback cache. Both caches have 16 bytes per line and are 4-way set-associative.

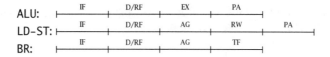

Figure 10.1   Baseline Mark I pipeline timing template.

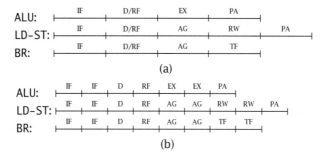

Figure 10.2   Baseline Mark II pipeline timing templates. (a) Reduced-scale processor. (b) Super-pipelined processor.

For each type of instruction pairing where there is a dependency (such as EX/EX) between the two instructions, we examine in detail the pipeline operation for each machine. The results are then tabulated and a pipeline penalty computed based on the data in Chapters 3 and 4. For each pair, the reduced-scale processor is considered first and the super-pipelined processor is considered next.

- EX/EX

  This is a sequence of any two ALU operation instructions.

  For the reduced-scale version of the processor, this sequence of instructions results in a 0-cycle delay.

  However, for the super-pipelined version of this processor there is a half-cycle delay from this sequence of instructions. This is because the execution phase of this machine occupies two cycles, and the second instruction requires the data from the first instruction and so must stall for one cycle.

- EX/AG

  This is a sequence of instructions with an ALU operation first and a load, store, or branch operation second.

For the reduced-scale version of the processor, this sequence of instructions results in a 0-cycle delay.

```
*           IF    IF    D    RF    EX    EX    PA
         |--+--+--+--+--+--+--|
* + 1    |     IF    IF    D    RF          AG    AG    RW    RW    PA
               |--+--+--+--+--  --+--+--+--+--|
```

However, since the AG and EX phases of the instruction are overlaid in the pipeline, this sequence of instructions results in a half-cycle delay.

- LD/EX

  This sequence of instructions consists of a load instruction followed by an ALU operation instruction, using data from the load.

```
*              IF         D/RF        AG         RD         PA
            |----+----+----+----|
* + 1       |         IF         D/RF                    EX         PA
                      |----+----+----|          |----+----|
```

The reduced-scale version of this processor has a one-cycle delay due to the additional cycle required to access the memory system (first-level cache).

```
*           IF    IF    D    RF    AG    AG    RD    RD    PA
         |--+--+--+--+--+--+--+--|
* + 1    |     IF    IF    D    RF                EX    EX    PA
               |--+--+--+--|    |    |    |--+--+--|
```

The super-pipelined version of this processor saves a half-cycle here for a half-cycle delay.

- EX/ST

  This sequence of instructions consists of an ALU operation instruction followed by a store instruction using data from the ALU operation.

```
*              IF         D/RF        EX         PA
            |----+----+----+----|
* + 1       |         IF         D/RF        AG         WR         PA
                      |----+----+----+----+----|
```

There is a 0-cycle delay for this sequence on the reduced-scale version of this processor.

```
*           IF    IF    D    RF    EX    EX    PA
         |--+--+--+--+--+--+--|
* + 1    |     IF    IF    D    RF    AG    AG    RW    RW    PA
               |--+--+--+--+--+--+--+--|
```

Since the result of the ALU operation is not needed for the AG phase, there is a 0-cycle delay in the super-pipelined version of this processor.

- LD/ST

  This sequence of instructions implements a memory–memory move using a load instruction followed by a store instruction.

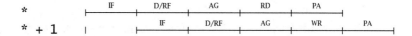

```
*              |----IF----|---D/RF---|----AG----|----RD----|----PA----|
* + 1    |          |----IF----|---D/RF---|----AG----|----WR----|----PA----|
```

The reduced-scale version of this processor has a 0-cycle delay for this sequence of instructions.

```
*           |--IF--|--IF--|--D--|--RF--|--AG--|--AG--|--RD--|--RD--|--PA--|
* + 1    |      |--IF--|--IF--|--D--|--RF--|--AG--|--AG--|      |--WR--|--WR--|--PA--|
```

The super-pipelined version of this processor has a half-cycle delay, since the write phase is slipped back a half-cycle, causing a stall to be needed.

- BRANCH (assume in-line)

This examines the pipelines for both unconditional branch (jump) and conditional branch instructions.

```
* - 1†   | ···        |----EX----|----PA----|                              † (C-Br only)
*              |----IF----|---D/RF---|----AG----|----TF----|
* + 1    |          |----IF----|---D/RF---|
T        |          |          |          |          |---D/RF---| ··· |
T + 1    |          |          |          |          |----IF----|---D/RF---| ··· |
```

For the reduced-scale version of the processor:

- Unconditional case

  There is no unconditional branch assumed to go in-line!

- Conditional case

  There is a 0-cycle delay for in-line, a 2-cycle delay for target, one unused in-line instruction fetched on branch to target, and no unused target instructions fetched on continue in-line.

```
* - 1†   | ···  |--D--|--RF--|--EX--|--EX--|--PA--|                                    † (C-Br only)
*              |--IF--|--IF--|--D--|--RF--|--AG--|--AG--|--TF--|--TF--|
* + 1    |      |--IF--|--IF--|--D--|--RF--| ··· |
* + 2    |      |      |--IF--|--IF--|--D--|--RF--| ··· |
* + 3†   |      |      |      |--IF--|--IF--|--D--|--RF--| ··· |                         † (C-Br only)
* + 4†   |      |      |      |      |--IF--|--IF--|--D--|--RF--| ··· |                  † (C-Br only)
T        |      |      |      |      |      |      |      |      |--D--|--RF--| ··· |
T + 1    |      |      |      |      |      |      |      |--IF--|--IF--|--D--|--RF--| ··· |
```

For the super-pipelined version of the processor:

- Unconditional case

  There is no unconditional branch assumed to go in-line!

- Conditional case

There is a 0-cycle delay for in-line, two half-cycle delays for target, four unused in-line instructions fetched on branch to target, and no unused target instructions fetched on continue in-line. The unused in-line instructions decrease to two as the condition dependency distance increases. This delay requires weighting according to Table 3.20, analogous to EX-EX interlock penalties, and so would be effectively reduced to 2.95^{2} unused in-line instructions instead of the (more conservative) 4, from simply analyzing the worst-case static pipeline.

- BRANCH (assume target)

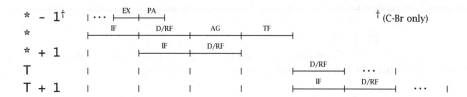

For the reduced-scale version of the processor:

- Unconditional case

There is a 2-cycle delay, and one unused in-line instruction is fetched. *Remember, there is no in-line case for an unconditional branch!*

- Conditional case

There is a 0-cycle delay for in-line, a 2-cycle delay for target, one unused in-line instruction fetched on branch to target, and no unused target instructions fetched on continue in-line.

For the super-pipelined version of the processor:

- Unconditional case

There is a 2-half-cycle delay for target and one unused in-line instruction fetched. *Remember, there is no in-line case for an unconditional branch!*

$^{2}4 \times 0.40297 + 3 \times 0.147 + 2 \times (1.0 - (0.40297 + 0.147)) = 2.95.$

Table 10.2   ALU operation costs.

Operation		Single	Double
Integer	Add	1 cycle	1 cycle
	Multiply	2 cycles	3 cycles
	Divide	16 cycles	32 cycles
Floating	Add	2 cycles	2 cycles
	Multiply	3 cycles	4 cycles
	Divide	13 cycles	27 cycles

- Conditional case

  There is a 1-cycle delay for in-line, a 2.5-cycle delay for target, two unused in-line instructions fetched for branch to target, and no unused target instructions fetched for continue in-line. These numbers are not affected by the condition dependency distance.

  This case assumes that the pending instructions are stalled on decode of a conditional branch and are continued if the in-line path is the correct one. This results in a delay of one cycle instead of the anticipated half-cycle delay, as with the majority of instructions. This is due to a half-cycle delay due to the half-cycle skew, as well as an additional half-cycle delay, which is hidden in the reduced-scale processor version, since the decode and register fetch phases are contained in the same clock cycle.

• Run-on Instructions

  These instructions consist primarily of multiplication and division instructions—since this machine is designed for engineering applications, commercial instructions (for example, those instructions operating on character and BCD data) are not included. For this machine, we use a base value for addition of one cycle for single and one cycle for double precision, for multiplication of two cycles for single and three cycles for double precision, and for division one cycle per two bits (single or double precision). Floating-point normalization is assumed to take one additional cycle over the integer time.

The results of the preceding analysis are presented in Tables 10.3 and 10.4. Using the operation distributions from Chapter 3, we can generate an estimated pipeline and branch delay penalties.

10.1.4   Pipeline Penalty Analysis

In order to determine the expected penalties from the pipelines, we need to take the data from Chapter 3 and weight the pipeline timing results from the last section accordingly.

First of all, we can estimate the probability of an instruction sequence occurring as the product of the probabilities of the two instruction types. For example, an EX/EX dependency occurs when there are two ALU operation

Table 10.3   Pipeline delay summary.

(a) Reduced-Scale Processor

Sequence	Delay
EX/EX	0 cycles
EX/AG	0 cycles
LD/EX	1 cycle
EX/ST	0 cycles
LD/ST	0 cycles

(b) Super-Pipelined Processor

Sequence	Delay
EX/EX	$\frac{1}{2}$ cycle
EX/AG	$\frac{1}{2}$ cycle
LD/EX	$1\frac{1}{2}$ cycle
EX/ST	0 cycles
LD/ST	$\frac{1}{2}$ cycle

Table 10.4   Branch delay summary (in cycles)

(a) Reduced-Scale Processor

Branch type $\left(\begin{smallmatrix}\text{assumed}\\\text{path}\end{smallmatrix}\right)$	Penalty When	
	Taken	Not Taken
Unconditional	2 cycles	—
Conditional (in-line)	2 cycles	0 cycles
Conditional (target)	2 cycles	0 cycles

(b) Super-Pipelined Processor

Branch type $\left(\begin{smallmatrix}\text{assumed}\\\text{path}\end{smallmatrix}\right)$	Penalty when	
	Taken	Not Taken
Unconditional	$2\frac{1}{2}$ cycles	—
Conditional (in-line)	$2\frac{1}{2}$ cycles	0 cycles
Conditional (target)	$2\frac{1}{2}$ cycles	1 cycles

instructions. However, the number of cycles that are actually penalty cycles is not constant—it is a linear function of the distance between the two dependent instructions. The greater the distance between the two instructions, the less the actual penalty, with the worst penalty being when the two instructions are sequential. Table 3.20 shows the distribution of distances between two dependent ALU operation instructions, and Table 3.19 shows the distribution of distances between an ALU operation and an address generate phase of an instruction. For simplicity, we assume that load and store instructions follow the same distribution as the two ALU operations.

From Chapter 4, we know that the actual penalty from a given instruction is found by applying the equation:

$$P = \sum_{\text{all dependencies } i} w_{\text{dependency } i} \times d_{\text{dependency } i},$$

where $P_{1,2}$ is the total penalty between the instructions over all possible dependency distances. The pipeline delay for any given instruction pair is

Table 10.5 Branch excess instruction fetch summary.

(a) Reduced-Scale Processor

Branch type $\left(\begin{smallmatrix}\text{assumed}\\\text{path}\end{smallmatrix}\right)$	Excess When	
	Taken	Not Taken
Unconditional	1	—
Conditional (in-line)	1	0
Conditional (target)	1	0

(b) Super-Pipelined Processor

Branch type $\left(\begin{smallmatrix}\text{assumed}\\\text{path}\end{smallmatrix}\right)$	Excess When	
	Taken	Not Taken
Unconditional	2	—
Conditional (in-line)	4	0
Conditional (target)	2	0

$d_{\text{dependency } i}$, and this is weighted by the probability ($p_{\text{dependency } i}$) that there is a dependency at that distance.

For the reduced-scale processor, there is only one case that has a penalty—a load instruction followed by an ALU operation instruction. In this case, the above equation reduces trivially as:

$$P_{\text{LD/EX}} = p_0 \times 1 = p_0 = 0.403,$$

which gives a penalty of 0.403 cycles after weighting. Note that instruction i_1 is the load instruction and instruction i_2 is the ALU operation instruction.

For the super-pipelined processor, there are a number of cases that have nonzero penalties. Consider the same case as before; in the super-pipelined processor, this sequence of instructions has a delay of one half-cycle, corresponding to three instructions, all of which are issued on the half-cycle. In this case, the same equation now reduces to:

$$P = p_0 \times 1\frac{1}{2} + p_1 \times 1 + p_2 \times \frac{1}{2} = 0.605 + 0.147 + 0.018 = 0.770,$$

which gives a penalty of 0.770 cycles. Note that $d_{\text{dependency } i}$ (delay penalty) is in terms of half-cycle instead of one-cycle increments—this is an artifact of using half-cycle instruction issue in the super-pipelined processor. The results of weighting the penalties based on distance functions are shown in Table 10.6, in the column "Weighted Delay."

To compute branch delays, we have to consider two cases—whether the in-line or target path is the assumed path. To do this, we can calculate the break-even probability of branches that actually go to the target instruction path, and then make our selection of guessed path appropriately.

The break-even point for predicting the branch path is found using the equation:

$$P_{\text{break-even}} \times \delta_t^t + (1 - P_{\text{break-even}}) \times \delta_i^t$$
$$= \quad P_{\text{break-even}} \times \delta_t^i + (1 - P_{\text{break-even}}) \times \delta_i^i,$$

where $P_{\text{break-even}}$ is the probability indicating that it does not matter whether or not the branch is taken. The penalty in either case would be identical.

$\delta_{\text{actual}}^{\text{predicted}}$ is the cycle penalty for the specified case of predicted and actual branch directions, with t being the taken direction and i being the in-line direction. This then simplifies to the equation:

$$P_{be} = \frac{\delta_i^i - \delta_i^t}{\left(\delta_i^i - \delta_i^t\right) - \left(\delta_t^i - \delta_t^t\right)}.$$

When P_{actual} (the probability that the branch is actually taken) is less than or equal to the calculated $P_{\text{break-even}}$, then the appropriate path to guess is in-line, and when it is greater, then the appropriate path is target. This does not consider the case where there are hints in the branch instructions that can be used to assist the choice of branch paths.[3] Using this equation, we can calculate the break-even point for the reduced-scale processor as follows:

$$P_{\text{break-even}} = \frac{0 - 0}{(0 - 0) - (2 - 2)} = \frac{0}{0} = \text{Undefined.}$$

This is undefined, and it is easy to see that since the branch condition is always known before the next instruction enters execution, any choice is the same here. For the super-pipelined processor, however, we get the following:

$$P_{\text{break-even}} = \frac{0 - 1}{(0 - 1) - \left(2\tfrac{1}{2} - 2\tfrac{1}{2}\right)} = \frac{1}{1} = 1.$$

Here it is clear that there can never be a probability P such that it is better to choose the target path; even if all branches are predicted to go to target, this is only the break-even point, and there is no loss when guessing in-line![4]

This argument ignores the additional bus traffic[5] due to continuing to fetch the in-line case—not a problem in the Baseline-series workstations, but a potential problem in any design that has several devices contending for the bus (as in a common-bus, shared-memory multiprocessor system). One solution for these designs would be to continue fetching the in-line path until there is a memory system fault—either a cache or TLB miss or protection violation—and then to stall the pipeline. This solution is a typical one for

---

[3] Although in these cases there is nothing to be gained by this knowledge, since guessing in-line is never worse than guessing target.

[4] This is only the case because all branches are going to target anyway, and thus there is no difference between the penalties for guess in-line and go to target, and guess target and go to target. When there is even one single not-taken branch, then it is better to guess in-line and save the 1-cycle penalty in this one case.

[5] The bus traffic is considered in Chapter 9.

Table 10.6   Weighted pipeline delay summary.

(a) Reduced-scale Processor

Sequence	Weighted Delay	Prob.	Eff. Delay
EX/EX	0.000 cycles	0.152	0.000
EX/AG	0.000 cycles	0.238	0.000
LD/EX	0.403 cycles	0.118	0.047
EX/ST	0.000 cycles	0.069	0.000
LD/ST	0.000 cycles	0.052	0.000
Branch	1.264 cycles	0.130	0.164
Run-on			0.600
		Total	0.811

(b) Super-pipelined Processor

Sequence	Weighted Delay	Prob.	Eff. Delay
EX/EX	0.201 cycles	0.152	0.030
EX/AG	0.050 cycles	0.238	0.012
LD/EX	0.769 cycles	0.118	0.091
EX/ST	0.000 cycles	0.069	0.000
LD/ST	0.201 cycles	0.052	0.010
Branch	1.580 cycles	0.130	0.205
Run-on			0.600
		Total	0.948

any kind of speculative execution in processors, and continuing to execute the in-line case of a branch is a simple and common example of speculative execution.

In both of these cases, it is clear that there is no advantage to assuming the target path when a branch is encountered. In many cases, the analysis is not so clear, and a full analysis must be performed, as in study 4.7.

Now, from Table 3.10, we can calculate the effective penalty for both processors using the delays for branches going either in-line or to target—assuming in-line prediction. For the reduced-scale processor, we have a 2-cycle penalty for unconditional branches, which are 20% of the distribution; a 0-cycle penalty for conditional to in-line, which is 36.8% of the distribution; and a 2-cycle penalty for conditional to target, which is 43.2% of the distribution. This gives a weighted branch penalty of 1.264 cycles for branches—and since branches comprise 13% of the instruction mix (Table 3.4), this gives an aggregate penalty of 0.164 cycles for all branches. Similarly, for the super-pipelined processor we get an aggregate penalty of 0.185 for all branches.

Finally, for run-on delays, we use the same assumption of 0.6 cycles that is used in study 4.3 as a simplification—the actual problem is difficult to determine analytically, since there are many possible code sequences that must be considered. For our purposes, the assumption provides a feel for the magnitude of the problem while not overcomplicating the overall solution.

In order to determine the overall penalty of the two pipelines, we need to weight the penalties determined above with the engineering (scientific) environment instruction distribution values from Chapter 3. We use these values to determine the actual pipeline penalty for this instruction mix, using:

$$P_{\text{pipeline}} = \sum_{\forall d \in \text{dependencies}} w_d \times P_d,$$

where P_{pipeline} is the total penalty when considering the distribution weight (w_d) in the instruction mix and the penalty (P_d) as calculated in Table 10.3. The results of these calculations are displayed in Table 10.6.

Note that although the reduced-scale version of the processor has a lower delay than the super-pipelined version, the cycles per instruction are significantly greater, since the base cycle time for the reduced-scale version is 1 cycle and for the super-pipelined version, $\frac{1}{2}$ cycle. Thus, we get an effective CPI of 1.811 cycles for the reduced-scale version and 1.448 cycles for the super-pipelined version—a reduction of 20%!

If this were all the analysis necessary to make a decision, then the result would be complete and conclusive: choose the super-pipelined processor. Unfortunately, there are yet two additional factors to consider—the cost of memory accesses, and the cost of fabrication for both processors. For the reduced-scale processor, the cache is increased into the available space (keeping the same die size), and for the super-pipelined, it remains the same size as in the original version of the processor (with a slightly larger die size to handle the additional latch overhead and cache access rate).

10.1.5   Cache and Memory Analysis

The original Baseline Mark I processor used a split cache as its on-chip cache. The DTMRs for the instruction cache and data cache are 0.05 (Figure 5.30) and 0.08 (Figure 5.27), respectively. The miss rate for each cache is then calculated by using the equation:

$$\text{MR} = \text{DTMR} \times f_{\text{mapping}} \times f_{\text{system}}.$$

In the case of the instruction cache, the values for f_{mapping} and f_{system} are 1.04 (Figure 5.10) and 1.75 (Figure 5.14), respectively. This yields a miss rate of 9.1%. For the data cache, on the other hand, the values for f_{mapping} and f_{system} are 1.04 (Figure 5.10) and 1.65 (Figure 5.14). This results in a miss rate of 13.7%. From Table 5.6, the number of data reads/instr is 0.33, while the number of data writes/instr is 0.235. As a result, the effective miss rate for the I- and D-caches is calculated to be 16.8% ((1)(0.091) + (.235 + .33) (0.137)). The effective not-in-TLB rate for both TLBs is 1.02% ((1)(0.65%)+ (.235 + .33)(0.65%)).

The miss penalty is then calculated using the hit and miss penalties, which are 0 and 5 cycles, respectively. Thus, we get a miss penalty of 5 cycles $\times$ 16.8% = 0.84 cycles. The not-in-TLB rate for a 2×64 = 128-entry TLB is found in Figure 5.46 and is 0.65%. The not-in-TLB penalty is found similarly to the cache miss penalty and is 20 cycles ×0.0102% = 0.204 cycles.

With the reduced-scale processor version, the original processor area of 174.6 A is effectively increased to 232.8 A—this adjustment takes into account the reduction to three-quarter scale and allows all calculations to be made using the nominal full-scale values. All the components on the chip (besides the TLB and cache and their overheads) occupy 71.85 A (16.1 + 37.8 + 41 − 6 − 14.05 − 3). This leaves us with 160.95 A (232.8 − 71.85) for the cache, TLB, and their overhead. This area is not large enough to permit doubling the caches and the TLBs. So we will consider doubling the I-cache to 32 KB while leaving the D-cache at 8 KB. Since we have doubled the I-cache, we also double the TLB associated with it. The 32-KB I-cache and the 8-KB D-cache occupy 132.8 A. Their overhead constitutes an additional 23.8 A ($\frac{15}{85}$ × 132.8). The TLBs now occupy 9 A (6 + 3), while their overhead is 4.5 A. So the new cache + TLB configuration consists of 170.1 A (132.8 + 23.8 + 9 + 4.5). Thus, the total processor area of the reduced-scale processor is now 241.95 (170.1 + 71.85). When scaled back down, this implies a total actual area of 181.5 A. Including the 20% die overhead area, this gives a total die area of 226.9 Å, which still fits in the 230 A die originally specified for the Mark I Baseline processor.

By redoing the calculations for the enlarged I-cache (32 KB), we find that it has a DTMR of 0.03 (Figure 5.30). The miss rate is now reevaluated with an f_{mapping} of 1.04 (Figure 5.14) and an f_{system} of 1.75 (Figure 5.22). It is found to be 0.0546, or 5.46%. The effective miss rate for both the I-cache and the D-cache is 13.2%, and the miss penalty is 0.66 cycles. The not-in-TLB rate for the D-cache (128 entries) is 0.65%, while the not-in-TLB rate for the I-cache (256 entries) is 0.39%. This yields an effective not-in-TLB rate of 0.76% ((1)(0.39%) + (0.235 + 0.33)(0.65%))—hence, a miss penalty of 0.151 cycles.

The super-pipelined processor uses the same basic configuration as the original Mark I unit, but includes an additional 10% pipeline latch overhead that affects the total processor area but not the die overhead. Thus, we get an increase of 17.5 A over the original design for a total processor area of 218.3 A + 17.5 A = 235.8 A. Note that this makes both processors essentially the same as far as area considerations go.[6]

Since the super-scalar cache is the same as the cache in the original Mark I processor, it has a 16.8% miss rate and thus a 0.84 cycle miss penalty. The TLB is also the same as the TLB in the Mark I processor, and it has an effective 1.02% not-in-TLB rate with a .204 cycle not-in-TLB penalty.

The memory results are summarized in Table 10.7, and the overall processor results are in Table 10.8.

10.1.6 Cost-Performance Analysis

We now have all the information from which to compute the actual cost and performance for these two processors.

The fabrication cost of all three processors—the original Mark I as well as

---

[6]There will be subtle differences between final chip costs due to variations in die production and yields, as is seen in section 10.1.6.

Table 10.7   Memory system delays.

Miss Penalty	Reduced-Scale	Super-Pipelined
Cache	0.670 cycles	0.895 cycles
TLB	0.080 cycles	0.130 cycles
Total Memory	0.750 cycles	1.025 cycles

Table 10.8   Processor system instruction cycle summary.

Delay Source	Reduced-scale	Super-pipelined
Instruction	1.000 cycles	0.500 cycles
Pipeline	0.795 cycles	0.928 cycles
Memory	0.750 cycles	1.025 cycles
Total	2.545 cycles	2.453 cycles

the reduced-scale and super-pipelined processors—is now easy to determine. First, using the Poisson model, we get a yield of:

$$Y = e^{-\frac{218.3\ A}{100\ A/cm^2} \times 1\ defects/cm^2} = 11.3\%.$$

The 8-inch wafer gives a total die count of:

$$A = \frac{218.3\,A}{100\,A/cm^2} = 2.183\ cm^2$$

$$N = \left\lfloor \frac{\pi}{4A}\left(d - \sqrt{A}\right)^2 \right\rfloor = \left\lfloor \frac{\pi}{4 \times 2.183}\left(20.32 - \sqrt{2.183}\right)^2 \right\rfloor$$
$$= \lfloor 127.7 \rfloor = 127.$$

Since there is an 11.3% yield, we get a total of $127 \times 0.113 = 14.4$ average good dies per wafer. The cost per chip is thus the packaging cost for a chip plus the net cost per die, or

$$\text{Cost per chip} = \$100 + \frac{\$5,000}{14.4} = \$447.2$$

for the Baseline Mark I processor. Similarly, for the reduced-scale and super-pipelined processers, respectively, we get yields of 10.3% and 9.5%, areas of 2.269 cm and 2.359 cm, wafer counts of 122 and 117, average good dies per wafer of 12.6 and 11.1, and costs per chip of $496.8 and $550.5. Thus, the reduced-scale processor costs $49.6 (11.1%) more, and the super-pipelined processor $103.3 (23.1%) more, than the original processor.

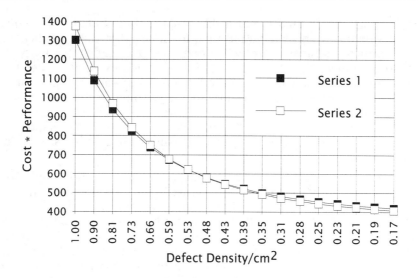

Figure 10.3 Tradeoff between reduced-scale and super-pipelined illustrated learning curve.

By looking over the calculations performed, it does not seem immediately clear which processor is the better choice. While the cost per chip for the reduced-scale processor is \$496.8, the cost per chip for the super-pipelined CPU is \$550.5 (roughly 10% more). On the other hand, the super-pipelined processor outperforms the reduced-scale with CPIs of 2.492 cycles and 2.622 cycles, respectively. By combining the two factors (cost and performance), we may be able to determine which processor to invest in. So we find the cost–performance product of the reduced scale to be 1302.6 \$-cycles, while that for the super-pipelined is 1371.8 \$-cycles. We may then conclude, on this basis, that the reduced-scale processor would be a better investment. Some further analysis may prove otherwise. If one considers the effect of the learning curve on the design process, then after some amount of time (in a year's time, maybe), the cost–performance of the super-pipelined processor may be less than that of the reduced-scale. Consider, for example, a 10% decrease in defect density/month. Then, according to Figure 10.3, in less than a year's time, the super-pipelined will turn out to be a better choice. Then again, in this business, both processors may be obsolete in a year's time!

Several questions must be considered before making a final choice of processors: what is the technical difficulty of designing, verifying, fabricating, and testing these parts? What changes might be made to the system in the future that might change the outcome? What are the scalability considerations between the two processor designs that might affect future performance enhancements?

While the reduced scale processor is already scaled down in feature size, the super-pipelined processor has much tighter timing constraints and is potentially more affected by unwanted clock skew than is the reduced-scale processor. The greater sensitivity to clock characteristics in the super-pipelined processor requires more careful design and simulation during development to ensure that the design can be reliably fabricated. With today's design tools, this is not a difficult problem, but it does require more development and simulation time to ensure that these verifications are performed. Because the pipeline operates at a higher frequency due to the super-pipelining, testing the product also requires higher-speed test equipment on the fabrication and production floors—and will possibly require the purchase of higher-performance equipment to meet the testing requirements. For purposes of this study, we will ignore these issues, but they must be evaluated in a real design situation to ensure that engineering does not design a product that cannot be easily or cheaply transferred into manufacturing.

One aspect of manufacturing that this discussion has not addressed is that the cost of the processor does not necessarily have a significant effect on the price of the final system, which is driven by both manufacturing and marketing issues. Assuming that marketing has no impact on the initial price estimate, using a 3- to 5-times markup will provide a typical approximation to this initial price. These two processors give $149 to $455 and $310 to $516 differences in price between the original system using the Baseline Mark I processor and the two options for the Baseline Mark II processor. This difference, not more than $500, is clearly not too significant for a $5,000 to $10,000 workstation. Even if one processor cost double the other processor, the result would still be insignificant. The lesson here is that processors have a minor effect on the final price of the system and, although the cost of a given component is important, it may not necessarily be the most important factor in component selection. As a *caveat*, this is often true only when comparing very similar components—for example, comparing a high-performance and a low-performance processor also requires comparing the costs of the supporting design elements, whereas comparing two comparable-performance processors need consider only the costs of the two processors.

Another aspect of the selection is in the response of the system to future changes in the overall Baseline system—for example, improving the physical or virtual memory systems performance while keeping the processor the same. This is a significant problem that should be considered before making a final selection. Looking at the performance calculations, we can specify the performance of the machines as:

$$P_{\text{reduced-scale}} = 1.811 + 0.132P_{\text{cache-miss}} + 0.0076P_{\text{page-fault}}$$

$$P_{\text{super-pipelined}} = 1.448 + 0.168P_{\text{cache-miss}} + 0.0102P_{\text{page-fault}},$$

and solving for the break-even performance point, we get

$$P_{\text{cache-miss}} = 10.08\overline{33} - 0.07222P_{\text{page-fault}}.$$

Figures 10.4, 10.5, and 10.6 show the performance for these processors, with varying page fault penalties for three cases. Figure 10.4 is representative of performance with the addition of a second-level cache off-chip that reduces the effective first-level cache miss rate from 5 cycles to 2.5 cycles; Figure 10.5 is the current configuration, and Figure 10.6 is a configuration with a lower-performance memory system installed and a first-level cache miss rate of 7.5 cycles. In the first two cases, it is clear that for almost any credible page fault penalty, the super-scalar processor is a clear winner—the

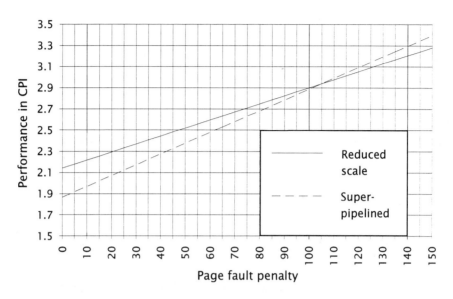

Figure 10.4   Performance with 2.5-cycle cache miss penalty.

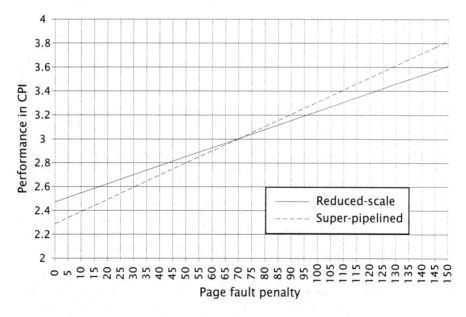

Figure 10.5   Performance with 5-cycle cache miss penalty.

Figure 10.6   Performance with 7.5-cycle cache miss penalty.

more so, the faster the memory system appears to the processor. However, when reducing the performance of the memory system, it is clear that the memory system becomes the determining factor for performance—if the memory system appears "slow" to the processor, then the super-pipelined processor is a slight loser. In fact, for page fault penalties greater than 30 cycles, the super-pipelined processor is never better than the reduced-scale processor. Whether or not this poses a problem is determined by marketing's goals and engineering's ability to scale up memory system performance with processor performance—if marketing has plans for offering systems with lower performance than the current 5-cycles memory system penalty, there may be justification for developing both processors; if marketing plans to offer only systems with increased memory system performance, there is little question that the super-pipelined processor is the better choice to pursue, provided that the designers account for a learning curve that reduces the defect density in a reasonable amount of time.

It is clear that a myriad of design choices is available and that these choices are not based purely on engineering and performance considerations. However, given a set of constraints that must be met, an estimation of the expected performance is fairly easy to work through using data of the sort provided here. The data may be acquired from a number of different sources (as is the data in this book) or may be specifically measured for the application at hand—it makes no difference to the application of the data. Calculations as performed in this study, however, should be used as coarse predictions of performance. More accurate results may be needed to base final design decisions on, and will require much more detailed and careful calculations and measurements, possibly including a full processor and system simulation to adequately gauge the tradeoffs.

10.2   Area Performance Analysis of Processors

As integrated circuit density increases, computer architects face the interesting problem of how best to utilize the available die size given cost and performance constraints. It is now commonplace to have more than 3 million transistors on a single chip with over 500 pins. Table 2.3 details some of the state-of-the-art implementations currently available.

The architect faces the complex problem of how to balance performance against complexity and design time. Since the lifetime of a microprocessor is about two years, the architect must examine ways to use the advances in IC technology and design a microprocessor that fits the needs of the target market in terms of performance, power consumption, and cost. It is an exciting challenge to define a new architecture or to extend an older architecture at the instruction level.

Are the added capabilities adequately utilized by the workload? Instruction sets change in response to technology and anticipated application needs. Some recent examples of this evolution are the shift to 64-bit architectures and the inclusion of instructions to enhance graphics operations. The software effort of revamping the architecture requires redevelopment of the operating system and compiler, and can be a lengthy effort. To accommodate backward compatibility, hardware and software emulations are frequently run. This comes at a cost: an example is the Intel Pentium, where reportedly more than 15% of the area is used to support emulation.

With added performance and complexity comes higher cost for the processor chip. Is the customer willing to pay for the increased performance?

10.2.1   The Problem

The previous study evaluated and compared two possible incremental changes:

- Pipeline redesign.
- Cache expansion.

This study looks at different implementations, as it is possible to mix and match different configurations of the core processor, floating point unit, memory hierarchy, and external bus interfaces using predefined modules. Using such a modular design style has many advantages. A company can create a family of processors with different cost, performance, and power utilization at the "press of a button." "Press of a button" is definitely an oversimplification, since there are specific techniques that must be used to reduce cost and power. Having a family of processors based on different configurations of modules offers the company the luxury of attacking different market segments: scientific servers, workstations, PCs, laptops, and the embedded processing market.

This study details the design of a load/store processor to be used as the core of a high-performance system. It could be the processing engine of a scalable multiprocessor system. A specific goal of this study is to investigate how varying the feature size, thus increasing or decreasing the transistor count, affects the CPI of the different implementations. This also gives the designer a sense of the future direction of microprocessors.

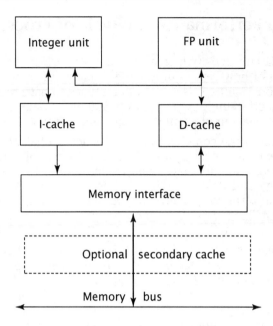

Figure 10.7 Baseline block diagram.

Suppose we have just been told that our process engineers have derived an improved process which decreased the minimum feature size to 0.75μ. We are given the task of designing the highest-performance microprocessor based on this new process. The instruction set is to remain unchanged to maintain software compatibility. Most modules of a baseline processor have been designed and used by a previous processor designed using a technology with 1μ feature size. The only modifications allowed to these modules are data-path widths and controls. Our task is to efficiently use the additional transistors (area) available to us. A decision was made to consider three possible configurations with identical area and cycle time constraints:

1. Single-issue processor (akin to our baseline) with a branch adder and expanded cache. The high-level block diagram is shown in Figure 10.7, and the processor organization is shown in Figure 10.8.

2. Superscalar processor that inspects four instructions and issues up to two instructions every cycle.

3. Two baseline processors, each possessing its own I-cache and sharing one D-cache. The high-level block diagram is shown in Figure 10.9.

The key element of this study is selecting the optimum cache and memory organizations for each configuration. The best-performing measure in CPI is selected. An optional 256KB direct-mapped secondary cache is available with a cost increase of 20%. In order to justify the addition of secondary cache, the designers need to demonstrate an accompanying increase in performance of greater than 20%.

The second objective of this study is to look at the optimum evolution path as one scales the technology. Along with the 0.75μ feature size, we

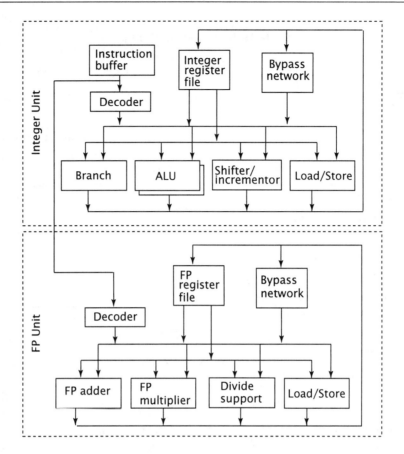

Figure 10.8 Processor organization.

also investigate how additional reductions in feature size affect the CPI of the three implementations. The feature sizes that we investigate are 1.0μ, 0.75μ, 0.6μ, 0.5μ, 0.4μ, and 0.3μ. The additional area resulting from each scaling is allocated to cache.

10.2.2 Specifications

In solving any complex problem, whether academic or industrial, the first step is to clearly define all specifications and make some simplifying assumptions. What assumptions do we make, and how do we know we are not masking some important parameters? It is critical to review some of our assumptions once we arrive at some results and evaluate whether further refinements are necessary.

Process specifications:

Process	0.75μ
Defect Density	1 defect/cm^2
Yield	10%

Table 10.9   Given conditions.

Area (from Study 2.3)	
Total chip area	230 mm^2
I/O pad overhead	20%
Latch overhead	10% of Integer and FP units
Bus overhead	40% of Integer and FP units
Aspect ratio mismatch overhead	10% of cache area

Base CPI (given)	
Implementation type	Base CPI
Baseline processor	1.47
Superscalar processor	0.833
Multiprocessor processor	0.795

References per instruction (given)	
Instruction references	1 (approximation)
Data Read references	0.31
Data Write references	0.20

Timing specifications (given)	
Cycle time	8 ns
Memory T_{access}	96 ns
Memory T_{cycle}	60 ns
Memory T_c	16 ns
Memory T_{bus}	8 ns
On-chip cache access	8 ns
L2 cache T_{access}	24 ns

Memory specifications (given)	
Memory size	64MB
Types	4M $\times$ 8b
Fast sequential page mode	Available
Interleaving	To be determined

TLB specifications (given)	
Number of entries	128
Associativity	2 way
Page size	4KB
TLB miss rate	0.0065 (Table 5.48)
TLB miss penalty	20 cycles

Secondary cache specifications (given)	
Size	256KB
Organization	Direct-mapped

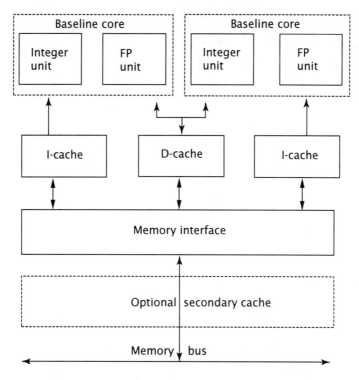

Figure 10.9   Multiprocessor block diagram.

Pipeline specifications (study 4.11):

Instruction type				
ALU	IF	D/RF	EX	PA
LD/ST	IF	D/RF	AG	PA
BR/BC	IF	D/AG	TIF	

Superscalar specifications:

- 2 integer ALUs.

- Pipelined FP unit.

- 1 branch adder.

- 1 L/S unit.

- Register file with 2 Read and 2 Read/Write ports.

- Additional bypassing muxes.

- Doubled instruction buffer size.

- Doubled decoder hardware size.

Dual-issue combinations:

- 2 integer ops.

- 1 FP and 1 integer op.

- 1 FP multiply and 1 FP addition.

- 1 branch.

- 1 L/S only.

Multiprocessor specifications:

- Two baseline processors.

- Two I-caches.

- Two I-TLBs.

- One shared D-cache.

- One shared D-TLB.

10.2.3   Assumptions

- For copyback cache, assume dirty line ratio of 50%.

- For the multiprocessor shared data cache, use multiprogrammed environment = 2, Q = 100 as an approximation. The only adjustment required is for set size.

- Secondary cache implementations increase system costs by 20%.

- Additional branch adder reduces specified CPI by 0.08 for baseline processor, as computed in study 4.11.

- The processor's intended environment is scientific.

- Physical address space is 64MB.

- Each cache tag includes an additional 4-bit control field (for cache coherency and line replacement purposes).

- Two memory interface designs to choose from for all possible implementations due to pin limitations. Either 32b or 64b physical words can be utilized with 64b implementation, adding 5% to system cost.

10.2.4   The Design

Let us take a moment to develop the analytical tools required to arrive at a reasonable conclusion. In this section, we develop the various design choices to be considered and analytical models to be used. In the next section, we present the data derived based on the analysis for each one of the possible implementations.

Given the above specification and assumptions, the next step is to define what we have to work with and what choices need to be made. Since the task is to optimize performance, we start with a brief review of CPU performance.

Table 10.10   Bandwidth requirements.

	Baseline	Superscalar	Multiprocessor
Peak issue rate	1	2	2
Peak Instruction bw(MB/s)	500	1000	1000
Average Instr. bw(MB/s)	340	600	629
Average Data Read/cycle	0.224	0.396	0.42
Average Data Read bw(MB/s)	112	198	210
Average Data Write/cycle	0.16	0.282	0.296
Average Data Write bw(MB/s)	80	141	148

Basics of Performance

Execution time = Instruction count/program $*$ CPI $*$ cycle time.

Since all three implementations use the same optimizing compiler, the first parameter, Instruction/Program, remains constant. This implies that the compiler does not resolve pipeline dependencies by installing NOP instructions to delay instruction. All conflicts are resolved in hardware. The third parameter also is assumed to be constant at 8 ns. We have to be wary of this assumption, since we assume that none of the modules we are modifying is part of the critical path and does not become a critical path at any time in the future. An example of this is selecting the associativity during the cache design. Selecting a cache with higher associativity does not penalize us in cycle time. This leaves us with the task of optimizing the CPI. For this study, the freedom of design lies in the design of the memory hierarchy. Since the core processor has been preselected, this fixes the various CPI components of the pipeline:

- Procedural dependencies.

- Data conflicts.

- Resource conflicts.

The remaining CPI components are mostly related to the memory hierarchy design. To facilitate this, the area available for cache design needs to be evaluated for each implementation.

Bandwidth Calculations

It is useful to do some approximate calculations prior to proceeding (Table 10.10). Since we are running at 8 ns per cycle or 125 MHz, the processor's bandwidth requirement is obvious. The memory hierarchy design needs to take this into account, or it becomes the limiting factor. As we go from baseline to superscalar to multiprocessor implementation, a key design goal is to supply sufficient bandwidth. Of course, because of area and cost limitations, we may not be able to satisfy some target requirements, and this determines the best implementation.

Table 10.11   Given area specifications.

Feature size	0.75μ
Defect density	1 per cm^2
Yield	10%
Control overhead	20%
Aspect ratio overhead	10%
Latch overhead	10%
Bus overhead	40%

Area Modeling

Fortunately, area statistics for our baseline model are available. These are given in study 2.3. (Note the added branch adder plus its overhead.) A quick summary is provided in Tables 10.12-10.14.

Description of Calculations

Each module is shown with its corresponding area utilization in "A," where "A" is defined as 1481 **rbe** and each **rbe** is 675 f^2. The various units that belong in the baseline processor are summed up. The only addition in this implementation is the branch adder, which was added to enhance the CPI. After obtaining the total area for both integer and floating-point units, the overhead for both latches and buses for communication is added. These are 10% and 40% of the units, respectively. As indicated, the baseline implementation requires 82.35 A (80.9 A as in study 2.3, plus 1 A for branch adder and about 0.57 A for branch adder overhead). It is given that the die area is 230 mm^2. To account for peripheral area such as I/O pads, 20% of the die area is subtracted, which gives us 184 mm^2. Now we must convert the available area from mm^2 to units of A:

$$\text{Area}(A) = (\text{area})\ \text{mm}^2/(1481 * 675 * f * f * 0.001 * 0.001).$$

Subtracting the baseline area and deducting 10% for aspect mismatch gives the area available for cache plus directory. A similar analysis is used for superscalar and multiprocessor implementations of the chip. The basic parameters are given in Tables 10.11-10.14.

Based on the area calculations in Tables 10.12-10.14, we explore different cache configurations for the available area.

General Buffer Design

Whenever data needs to be sent from one entity to another, a simple solution is synchronous communication: when one entity is ready to send and the other to receive, the data element is transferred. If more flexibility is required, a buffer needs to be introduced to allow asynchronous communication. A buffer allows processes of similar bandwidth to proceed in

Table 10.12   Baseline processor area.

Integer ALU	1.00	Added branch adder	1.00
Integer register	1.00	FP RegFile	1.
Shifter	0.50	FP adder	13.5
Incrementor	0.40	FP multiplier	20.3
PC unit + Bypass	1.00	Divide Support	3.
2 TLBs	6.00	F-P Unit	37.8
Decode + Control	1.00		.
Cache controller	1.00	Latches overhead	5.49
Bus logic	2.00	Bus overhead	21.96
Stored buffer + Bypass	1.00	Total baseline	82.35
Load/store	0.20		.
Clock generator	1.00	Die area	230.
Integer Unit	16.10	Area available	184.
		Area in "A"	335.11
		Option 1	.
		Remaining area	252.76
		−10% aspect ratio	25.28
		Cache area	227.48
		Cache bits	561,116.96
		Cache KB	68.50

spite of differences in transient performance or latency (e.g., IB runout). Buffers are useless if the average bandwidth of the entities is very different. In this case, the performance of the entities degrades to that of the lower bandwidth process.

Instruction Buffer Design

Before exploring cache design, we need to account for the effect of instruction buffer given the available area just computed. In designing a buffer, we may design it either for mean request rate or for the maximum request rate. Designing a buffer to accommodate only the mean request rate allows us to trade off buffer size against the probability of overflow. We must evaluate the consequences of overflow and decide whether it is tolerable in terms of overall processor performance. For the instruction reference traffic, we assumed a mean instruction traffic of 1 inst ref/cycle (i.e., 1 IF/I) for the baseline processor. Since the maximum throughput of the pipeline is one, the maximum instruction traffic is at least one instruction word per cycle, not including the branch reference traffic.

In-line instruction references dominate performance and should be designed for the maximum request rate, since the I-buffer fetches whenever the cache is free and the buffer is not full. The designer needs to ensure the following:

Table 10.13   Superscalar processor area.

Integer ALU	1.00	FP RegFile	1
Integer register	1.00	FP adder	13.5
Shifter	0.50	FP multiplier	20.3
Incrementor	0.40	Divide support	3
PC unit	1.00	FP unit	37.8
2 TLBs	6.00	Added pipeline	12
Decode + control	1.00	Total FP	49.8
Cache controller	1.00		
Bus logic	2.00		
Stored buffer + bypass	1.00		
Load/store	0.20		
Clock generator	1.00		
Integer unit	16.10		
Added branch adder	1.00	Latches	7.062
Additional integer unit	1.00	Bus	28.248
Additional buffer	1.00		
Additional decoder	1.00		
Added port/RegFile	0.32		
Added bypass network	0.40		
Total integer	20.82	Total superscalar	105.93
		Remaining area	229.18
		10% aspect ratio	22.92
Die area	230	Cache area	206.26
Area available	184	Cache bits	508,769.36
Area in "A"	335.11	Cache KB	62.11

1. The bandwidth from the primary cache to the I-buffer meets or exceeds the maximum request rate of the processor.

2. There are enough entries in the I-buffer to avoid buffer runout.

3. The I-buffer consists of one or several instruction registers that hold the current instruction being decoded, an alternate path buffer, and a primary path buffer.

From the preceding requirements, the important design parameters of the I-buffer are:

- The width of the memory interface and the access time per I-fetch.

- The number of in-line and alternate path buffers.

- Branch instruction frequency, behavior, and branch management scheme.

Table 10.14   Multiprocessor area.

Integer ALU	1.00	FP multiplier	20.3
Integer register	1.00	Divide support	3
Shifter	0.50	FP unit	37.8
Incrementor	0.40	2x FP unit	75.6
PC unit	1.00		
2 TLBs	6.00	Latches	10.68
Decode + control	1.00	Bus	42.72
Cache controller	1.00		
Bus logic	2.00	Total multiprocessors	160.20
Stored buffer + bypass	1.00		
Load/store	0.20	Die area	230
Clock generator	1.00	Area available	184
Integer unit	16.10	Area in "A"	335.11
Added branch adder	1.00		
		Remaining area	174.91
2x integer unit	34.20	10% aspect ratio	17.49
Remove one TLB	3.00	Cache area	157.41
Total integer	31.20		
FP RegFile	1	Cache bits	388,289.96
FP adder	13.5	Cache KB	47.40

In-Line Traffic

The in-line reference traffic is calculated as follows:

$$I_{\text{in-line}} = (1/m) * \text{IF access time} * \text{instr/IF},$$

where m is the number of cycles between instruction issues, IF access time is the number of cycles required per access, and instructions per IF is the width of the interface between the I-cache and the I-buffer. For the baseline case:

$$m = 1 \text{ (maximum of 1 instruction decoded per cycle).}$$
$$\text{IF access time} = 1 \text{ cycle.}$$
$$\text{Instructions per IF} = 1 \text{ or 2 (interface width of 4 or 8 bytes).}$$

Instr/IF	I (in-line)
1	1
2	0.5

Branch Traffic

With the additional branch adder, we save a cycle in cache access, since we have removed the conflict with ALU operations and branch target address computation (AG), which is generated during the decode stage. We opt to use the static prediction strategy, since the required hardware cost is small and the accuracy achieved is 60 to 70%. For unconditional branch, the added reference traffic is:

$$\text{Excess I-traffic on BR} = \text{Prob (BR)} \; [N_1 \frac{I}{P}],$$

where N_1 is the number of in-line instructions fetched before the branch is decoded, and BR is the frequency of an unconditional branch. For our pipeline layout, N_1 is one cycle. From study 4.11, the branch profile is:

BR	2.6%	
BC	10.4%	with 54% to target

The added reference traffic is:

$$\text{Excess I-traffic on BC}$$
$$= \text{Prob} (BC) \left[\text{Prob (c.p.)} [N_2 \frac{I}{P}] + (1 - \text{Prob (c.p.)}) [N_3 \frac{I}{P}] \right],$$

where N_2 is the number of unused instructions fetched given a correct prediction, and N_3 is the number of unused instructions fetched given an incorrect prediction.

For our pipeline and branch prediction scheme, $N_2 = 0$ and $N_3 = 1$. The width of the I-buffer–I-cache interface is critical for high performance. The basic idea is that we must meet or exceed the maximum bandwidth requirements of the instruction issue logic. Decreasing the width results in higher reference traffic, leading to a greater number of misses and higher CPI.

Write Buffer Design

Before proceeding to cache design, another integral part of the memory hierarchy design deserves consideration. The aforementioned I-buffer provides the interface between the instruction execution stream and the storage providing the instructions, whereas the write buffer can serve a multitude of purposes:

1. Since write traffic tends to be temporal, a write buffer can filter out some write traffic by eliminating identical write requests by updating the write buffer instead of writing directly to memory.

2. Write buffer alleviates the latency differences between the processor and off-chip memory. The processor can write to the write buffer instead of waiting to gain ownership of the memory interface bus and completing the write to memory prior to processing more instructions.

Data Reference Traffic

Data reference traffic has different behavior from instruction traffic, which tends to exhibit more spatial locality (sequential). Data is explicitly loaded into register prior to use for a L/S machine; thus, the size of references should be the size of a data word.

Type	Data Read/cycle	Data Write/cycle
Baseline	0.31	0.200
Superscalar	0.54	0.357
MP	0.57	0.374

Perfect versus Real Buffers

In evaluating performance, the effect of data reference traffic on performance needs to be evaluated. By assuming a perfect buffer, a majority of the performance degradation due to data stores can be removed. A perfect buffer is a buffer that is arbitrarily large enough such that the probability of overflow tends to zero. If the occupancy of memory is low, such an assumption may be a valid one. Ultimately, the bandwidth of the off-chip memory must be greater than that of the reference traffic, or a closed-queue situation will occur where the request rate of the processor has to be slowed down to that of the service rate.

Since data store traffic is usually less than read traffic (instr read + data read) and is not as critical to performance, we can choose to design the write buffer based on either maximum or average traffic. The actual amount of write traffic depends on the cache management strategy and is discussed in the next section.

There are three ways to view the data reference data. Obviously, 0.20 data read/cycle is an average, since we cannot have 0.20 data read references. For maximum traffic, we could feasibly have a sequence of data stores, thus giving one data write per cycle. On the other end of the spectrum, we can compute the average number of data stores per cycle. For the baseline CPI of 1.47, the data store per cycle rate is $0.20/1.47 = 0.16$ stores/cycle. Thus, assuming 0.20 data stores/cycle seems to be a reasonable midpoint as long as we design our write buffer sufficiently large to handle a short period of peak traffic.

Management of the Buffer

In addition to deciding the size of the write buffer, there are various design decisions regarding the management of buffers and memory accesses. These decisions affect the processor in terms of the number of stall cycles during memory references.

There are three classifications:

- Simple: all data in the write buffer must be written to memory before processing the read request. In other words, reads cannot bypass writes. For CBWA caches, the replaced line, if dirty, has to be written out before the read can proceed.

- Read Bypass Write: read request can bypass all writes in buffer; checking must be done to ensure that the current read request data is not in the write buffer already, to maintain consistency. For CBWA caches, the replaced line, if dirty, can be transferred to the write buffer concurrently with issuing the read request to memory. The processor restarts once the entire line is read into the cache.

- Read Bypass with Wrap Around: In addition to allowing a read to bypass writes, this scheme allows the missed word to be accessed first instead of waiting for the entire line to be returned to cache from memory; thus, the CPU can resume processing as soon as the first word is returned.

Based on the preceding description, we analyze all three cases for CBWA policy and the latter two for the WTNWA policy. Since WTNWA does not have line writes, the simple scheme does not apply. The basic idea behind schemes 2 and 3 is to reduce the time the processor is waiting for read data. For these cases, it is possible to have contention between previous read and write requests in progress and the current read request. The implications of the different schemes on CPI are presented in the CPI section, and a performance comparison is done in the analysis section.

Cache Design

Unified versus Split

Given a fixed area to implement the cache, we can first qualitatively consider whether to use the unified or the split cache scheme. Unified cache offers a lower overall miss rate, but we must consider the amount of contention delay due to conflicting data and instruction accesses. A split cache offers higher bandwidth, since separate data paths exist for instruction and data accesses. However, we must provide the additional area required for the data paths and a higher overall miss rate. As a rough approximation, we assume that for a split cache 10% of the cache area is utilized by data paths.

Unified Cache Contention Modeling

In a unified cache, the designer must evaluate the performance penalty resulting from contention at the cache interface that is due to conflicts between data accesses and instruction accesses. In calculating the contention, one needs to take the actual CPI into consideration, since many of the instruction requests are from branches that degrade the CPI of the processor. Only in-line reference stream and executed instructions need to be considered, since an instruction that is not executed cannot result in contention. We can model the contention as performed in study 5.4. However, we must break the analysis into CBWA and WTNWA cases.

CBWA

For CBWA, the data traffic needs to include both data fetch and data store, since, unlike WTNWA, both access the cache. Since the on-chip cache can be accessed every cycle, we should take CPI into account and calculate the probability of contention per cycle:

$$\text{Contention/cycle} = \frac{(\text{In-line IF/cycle}) * (\frac{DF+DS}{I})}{\text{CPI}^2} = 0.118$$

Table 10.15   CBWA and WTNWA specifications.

	Read Hit	Read Miss	Write Hit	Write Miss
CBWA	Read word from cache	Load line from memory Write replaced line to memory if dirty	Write word to cache	Read line from memory Write replaced line to memory if dirty Write word to cache
WTNWA	Read word from cache	Load line from memory	Write word to memory Invalidate cache line	Write word to memory

Assuming the penalty due to contention is one cycle, the additional CPI is $0.118 \times 1.47 = 0.173$.

WTNWA

$$\text{Contention/cycle} \quad = \quad \frac{(\text{In-line IF/cycle}) * (\text{DF/cycle})}{CPI^2} = 0.0717$$

$$\text{Additional CPI} \quad = \quad 0.0717 \times 1.47 = 0.105$$

Based on the preceding penalty, we need to compare the performance due to contention versus the performance lost due to smaller split cache and higher miss rate.

Write-Through versus Copyback

A choice must be made between WTNWA and CBWA for the write policy. The responses with respect to the different requests of these schemes is briefly described in Table 10.15.

The characteristics of memory traffic generated by the two schemes are quite different. With the CBWA scheme, all the memory traffic generated is lines, whereas the WTNWA scheme generates line traffic during a read miss and a word write to memory during every write.

Traffic Modeling

To provide a more quantitative view of memory traffic difference between the implementation choices, the following simple model has been developed. We present two additional models for a Write Assembly Cache (WAC) and a WTNWA first-level cache with a CBWA secondary cache. The factors important in this model are:

- T_{word} is the word access time (T_{access}).
- Cache miss ratio (MR).
- % of total lines that are dirty (W).
- Reference traffic patterns.

To calculate $T_{\text{line access}}$, see equation 6.3.

The schemes we consider are:

- Write-Through No Write Allocate (WTNWA)

- Copy Back Write Allocate (CBWA)

- Write-Through with a Write Assembly Cache (WAC)

- Write-Through with CBWA Secondary Cache (WTWSC)

With Secondary Cache

The secondary cache is assumed to be CBWA and has a fixed line size of 128 bytes. The sizes of the secondary cache vary across different feature sizes from a minimum of 256KB to 2MB in order to maintain a reasonable size ratio between the level-1 cache and the secondary cache. The first-level cache associated with the secondary cache is WTNWA.

$$
\begin{aligned}
\text{Line accesses/cycle} \;&=\; \text{(IF/cycle)} * \text{secondary cache.MR} \\
&\quad + \text{(DF + DS)}/\text{I} * (1 + \text{W}) \\
&\quad * \text{(secondary cache.MR)}. \\
\text{Word access/cycle} \;&=\; 0. \\
\text{Total bus time/cycle} \;&=\; \text{Line accesses/cycle} * T_{\text{line}}(128B). \\
\text{Total offered occupancy} \;&=\; \text{(Total bus time/cycle)/cycle time.}
\end{aligned}
$$

The difference between CBWA and WTNWA is in the write traffic generated. The write-through scheme generates a word write with every processor write request, and the CB scheme generates line writes to write dirty replaced lines back to memory.

The basic question is which scheme generates more memory references, and this question is answered quantitatively later. We calculate the total offered occupancy for the data traffic and present the data in the analysis section.

Bus saturation occurs when the offered occupancy of the bus is greater than one. Occupancy is defined as the ratio between the traffic that is offered by the CPU (Offered Traffic) and the maximum traffic that can be handled by the memory bus (Achieved Traffic). A rule of thumb for the bus designer is to keep the occupancy of the bus below 0.5. The intuitive reasoning is probabilistic. Since there are different reference streams (data read, data write, instruction read), it is possible for these to conflict with each other, resulting in CPU stalls in certain cases. The quantitative analysis of this involves the references per cycle of the different streams, the bus time of each reference, the traffic filtering effect of caches, and the buffering effect of write buffers.

When occupancy is $\ll 1$, a probabilistic model can be used to derive the average wait time due to contention. This contention time is added to memory access time and results in higher CPI. When occupancy is > 1, the processor has to slow down to match the bandwidth of the bus, since achieved occupancy can never exceed one.

From the preceding relations, it is quite obvious that below a certain miss rate, the write-through traffic dominates all traffic to memory. Write-through caches have an advantage over copyback caches, since memory is always consistent with cache. However, memory traffic can be exceedingly high. Increasing the physical word size to memory increases memory bandwidth, but does not help the situation with write-through traffic, since write-through traffic consists of single words.

From the previous analysis, main memory cannot support the write-through traffic, so another solution needs to be considered. One such alternative is to use a Write Assembly Cache (WAC). Data show that a Write Assembly Cache of 16 8-byte lines can reduce the relative write traffic to 30%. Adding a write assembly cache serves two purposes:

- It filters out repeated writes to the same line.

- It converts single-word transfers to more efficient line transfers.

Since a WAC is unique to the write-through cache, we must evaluate its cost to compare the merits of the different write policies. Based on data given in section 5.13, 16 8-byte lines can filter about 70% of the write traffic. The area of this Write Assembly Cache is calculated as follows:

$$
\begin{aligned}
\text{Cache bits} &= 16 * 8 * 8 = 1024 \text{ bits} \\
\text{Tag bits} &= (\log_2 (\text{memory size/write assoc. cache size}) \\
&\quad + 2 \text{ control bits} + 2\text{-bit assoc.} * 16 \text{ lines} \\
&= (19 + 2 + 2) * 16 = 368 \text{ bits} \\
\text{Total (bytes)} &= 174 \text{ bytes}
\end{aligned}
$$

This is small when compared to the cache size. The write cache size becomes bigger as the write traffic increases for the superscalar and multiprocessor implementations.

With the addition of a secondary cache, the traffic to the memory bus is reduced, since it serves as a filter between L1 traffic and the memory bus. We verify this later.

CPI

Different combinations of CBWA and WTNWA and different buffer management schemes have different implications for the overall CPI. For the analysis below, a "perfect write buffer" is assumed, since the effect of write traffic is analyzed separately.

With the WTNWA configuration, we consider two buffer management schemes.

Scheme 1: In a read miss, the entire line must be fetched in prior to the resumption of processing.

Scheme 2: In a read miss, wraparound is used so the first word is returned first, and processing continues while memory finishes loading the rest of the line into cache.

From chapter 6:

$$T_{\text{m.miss}} = \text{Time memory is busy due to a read request}$$

$$
\begin{aligned}
T_{\text{c.miss}} &= \text{Time processor is stalled due to a read miss} \\
T_{\text{write.mem}} &= \text{Time memory is busy due to a write miss} \\
T_{\text{write.c}} &= \text{Time processor is stalled due to a write miss} \\
T_{\text{busy}}\,(\text{Read}) &= T_{\text{m.miss}} - T_{\text{c.miss}}.
\end{aligned}
$$

This is the time period where CPU is free to make further requests while the memory is still busy.

For write buffer number 1:

$$
\begin{aligned}
T_{\text{m.miss}} &= T_{\text{line}} \\
T_{\text{c.miss}} &= T_{\text{line}} \\
T_{\text{write.mem}} &= \max(T_{\text{access}}, T_{\text{cycle}}) \\
T_{\text{write.c}} &= 0 \\
T_{\text{busy}}\,(\text{Read}) &= 0.
\end{aligned}
$$

Since $T_{\text{busy}}(\text{Read}) = 0$, no memory contention can occur due to a read blocking another read. However, a write that is being serviced can block a read request, and is accounted for in $T_{\text{w.interference}}$.

$$
T_{\text{w.interference}} = (1 - (1 - (\text{IF+DF})/\text{cycle})^{\frac{T_{\text{write.mem}}}{\text{cycle time}}})(\text{DS}/\text{cycle})(T_{\text{write.mem}}/2).
$$

The first term, $1 - (1 - \text{Reads}/\text{cycle})^{T_{\text{write.mem}}/\text{cycletime}}$, is the probability of a read request during the number of cycles it takes to process the write request. The second term, Writes/cycle, is the probability of a write request during any cycle. The third term, $T_{\text{write.mem}/2}$, is the average waiting time of a read request.

After including the write interference time, the time to process a read is:

$$
T_{\text{c.miss}} = T_{\text{line}} + T_{\text{w.interference}}.
$$

For write-through cache with buffer 2, we have the following:

$$
\begin{aligned}
T_{\text{m.miss}} &= T_{\text{line}} \\
T_{\text{c.miss}} &= T_{\text{access}} \\
T_{\text{write.mem}} &= \max(T_{\text{access}}, T_{\text{cycle}}) \\
T_{\text{write.c}} &= 0
\end{aligned}
$$

For this case, a read in progress can block an upcoming read, since $T_{\text{busy}} = T_{\text{line}} - T_{\text{access}}$. As a result, we must also include $T_{\text{r.interference}}$ in the final read processing time of memory.

$$
\begin{aligned}
T_{\text{r.interference}} = {} & \frac{1}{2}T_{\text{busy.D}}^{2}\,(\text{D-cache.MR} * (\text{DF}/\text{cycle}/\text{cycle time}) \\
& + \frac{1}{2}T_{\text{busy.I}}^{2}\,\text{I-cache.MR} * (\text{IF}/\text{cycle}/\text{cycle time}))
\end{aligned}
$$

For CBWA, there are three combinations shown in Table 10.16.

Table 10.16   Cache/memory interface options.

Option 1	Option 2	Option 3
Write dirty line to memory	Fetch new line	Fetch missing word first
Fetch new line	Start processor	Start processor
Start processor	Write dirty line to buffer	Finish line fetch and write dirty line to buffer
$T_{\text{m.miss}} = (1 + w)T_{\text{line}}$	$T_{\text{m.miss}} = (1 + w)T_{\text{line}}$	$T_{\text{m.miss}} = (1 + w)T_{\text{line}}$
$T_{\text{c.miss}} = (1 + w)T_{\text{line}}$	$T_{\text{c.miss}} = T_{\text{line}}$	$T_{\text{c.miss}} = T_{\text{access}}$
$T_{\text{busy}} = 0$	$T_{\text{busy}} = wT_{\text{line}}$	$T_{\text{busy}} = (1 + w)T_{\text{line}} - T_{\text{access}}$

For CBWA, there are three combinations shown in Table 10.16.

Line Size

Line size is the unit of transfer between cache and memory. The selection of line size is critical for processor performance. Altering the line size affects the following:

- Cache miss rate.

- Memory traffic.

- Tag memory size for cache directory.

Increasing or decreasing the line size is a decision based on balancing cache miss rate, memory traffic, and tag memory size. Increasing the line size decreases the miss rate due to the enhanced spatial locality of the cache (sequential address request). However, the decreases in miss ratio become smaller as we increase the line size further, since the cache is losing its temporal locality (fewer lines). The optimum point is reached when the effect of decreasing the miss ratio no longer compensates for the increase in T_{line}. Increasing the line size decreases the number of lines in the cache, thus decreasing the overhead of tag memory associated with each line. With small caches, if we increase the line size too much, we hurt the temporal locality of the cache, since we tend to replace lines too often due to the low number of lines available.

Tag Memory Modeling

A physical address is broken into the following:

Tag	Index	Offset

Direct Map Cache

$$\text{Tag bits} = \log_2 (\text{mem size/cache size}).$$
$$\text{Index bits} = \log_2 (\text{number of lines}).$$
$$\text{Offset bits} = \log_2 (\text{number of bytes/line}).$$

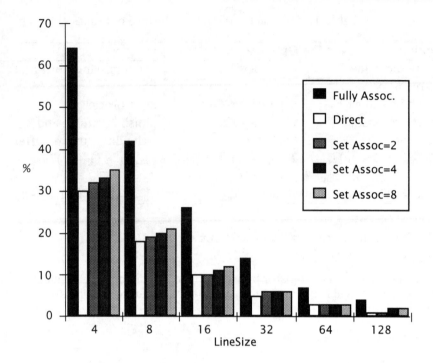

Figure 10.10   Percent total cache area used for cache tags.

Set Associative Cache

$$\text{Tag bits} \quad = \quad \log_2(\text{mem size/cache size}) + \log_2(\text{degree of assoc.}).$$
$$\text{Index bits} \quad = \quad \log_2(\text{number of lines/degree of associativity}).$$
$$\text{Offset bits} \quad = \quad \log_2(\text{number of bytes/line}).$$

Fully Associative Cache

$$\text{Tag bits} \quad = \quad \log_2(\text{mem size/cache size}) + \log_2(\text{number of lines}).$$
$$\text{Index bits} \quad = \quad 0.$$
$$\text{Offset bits} \quad = \quad \log_2(\text{number of bytes/line}).$$

For tag memory, four bits are added as control bits. In addition, the direct-mapped cache requires only one comparator, while the set-associative requires as many comparators as its degree of associativity. The fully associative cache requires a content-addressable memory (CAM) as its directory, since every line is a candidate. These memory bits are modeled as 2 **rbe** each.

Figure 10.10 shows the tag memory area for different configurations and line sizes. The fully associative is prohibitively expensive for small line sizes, so set associativity of eight is chosen.

Table 10.17 shows an example of the analysis carried out across different cache organizations (direct, associative, split versus unified cache) and line

Table 10.17   Sample area/cache analysis (fully associative cache).

Line Size	4	8	16	32	64	128
Cache size (KB)	64	64	64	64	64	64
Lines	16384	8192	4096	2048	1024	512
Tag bits/line	28	23	22	21	20	19
Tag memory size (KB)	112	46	22	10.5	5	2.375
Total cache size (KB)	176	110	86	74.5	69	66.375
% cache overhead	64%	42%	26%	14%	7%	4%
Does it fit?	False	False	False	False	False	True
Cache miss rate	0.095	0.052	0.03	0.019	0.011	0.007
Split cache area	184.8	115.5	90.3	78.225	72.45	69.69375
Does split cache fit?	False	False	False	False	False	False

sizes. It compares the resulting total area to the available area for cache and narrows down the possible organizations.

Given a certain target data cache size, the smaller line size implementations simply do not fit in the given area. Set associativity of 8 gives us the greatest reduction in cache miss ratio, yet provides a relatively low tag memory overhead. Increasing line sizes has the greatest effect in reducing tag memory overhead.

Associativity

In this study, we assume that the cache implementation is not the critical path of the processor. Increasing the associativity does not penalize cycle time. What we can consider is the area cost due to associativity, along with the cost of comparators. We consider the cases of direct-mapped, 2,4,8 set associative, and fully associative. More associativity reduces the miss rate, but also results in larger tag memory comparator and muxing cost.

Memory Design

Memory Modeling

The memory design has been simplified because of the various assumptions. Since the DRAM chip we are required to use is $4M * 8$ with memory size of 64 MB, we can determine the possible interleaving factors:

Physical Word Size	Interleaving
32b	4
64b	2

The performance increase with wider interface has to be greater than 5% in order to outweigh the 5% cost. Once the interleaving is determined, T_{line} can be calculated for different line sizes:

$$T_{\text{line}} = T_{\text{access}} + T_{\text{page}}(\lceil L/m \rceil - 1) + T_{\text{bus}}((L - 1) \bmod m).$$

Secondary Cache

Another decision is whether the addition of a secondary cache boosts performance by more than 20%, to overcome its higher cost of 20%. With the addition of the second-level cache, CPI computation is as follows:

CPI.2nd cache =
    CPI.Base + TLB.penalty
    + DR/cycle $*$ D − cache.MR $*$ (T_{access}.L2 + (L/W − 1)T_{cycle}.L2)
    + Cache.L2.MR/D − cache.MR $*$ T_{line}/cycle time
    + I − cache.MR $*$ IR/cycle $*$ (T_{access}.L2 + (L/W − 1)Tcycle.L2)
    + Cache.L2.MR/I − cache.MR $*$ T_{line}/cycle time.

The following assumptions were made in generating the preceding model:

- Inclusion.

- The secondary cache is CBWA.

- The secondary line size is 128 bytes.

Of course, there may be cases of contention in the second-level cache, as in a unified cache, but since the on-chip cache and write assembly cache are able to filter out most of the requests, we assume that instruction references do not collide with data references in the analysis.

A secondary cache serves as intermediate storage between the processor and main memory. It buffers the processor from traffic on the memory bus and can reduce the amount of traffic on the bus. This is especially critical in a multiprocessor system where we want to avoid bus saturation and isolate coherent traffic from the processor. Most secondary caches are managed using CBWA to reduce write traffic on the shared bus. To reduce coherent traffic interference, the first-level cache is WTNWA to keep the secondary cache consistent with the first-level cache.

Bus Contention Model

When a bus is accessed by multiple users, one can have contention among the users. A simple model is one that takes into account the occupancy of the bus by users. We follow the model presented in chapter 6.

10.2.5   Analysis

The previous section detailed the models and qualitative discussion of various implementation options. In this section, we present results of the analysis. Of course, only a small part of the data can be presented because of space limitations. Most of the data shown is for the 0.75μ case, and we discuss results from the other feature sizes.

Table 10.18   CPI summary without memory traffic scaling.

Size	Baseline	CPI	Superscalar	CPI	Multiprocessor	CPI
0.75μ	64K-U	1.957	48K-U	1.918	8I/8I/16D	2.37
	32I/32D	1.851	16I/32D	1.693	16I/16I/8D	1.977
			32I/16D	1.533		
1.0μ	24k-U	2.158	16K-U	2.514	2I/2I/2D	5.08
	16I/8D	2.12	8I/8D	2.33		
	8I/16D	2.17				
0.6μ	64I/48D	1.786	64I/32D	1.324	32D/32I/32I	1.403
	48I/64D	1.795	32I/64D	1.382	48D/16I/16I	1.634
0.5μ	96I/64D	1.763	128I/32D	1.306	48D/48I/48I	1.326
	128I/32D	1.781	96I/64D	1.239	64D/32I/32I	1.348
0.4μ	256-U	1.854	256-U	1.547	128D/64I/64I	1.182
	128I/128D	1.737	128I/128D	1.176		
0.3μ	512-U	1.84	512-U	1.51	256D/128I/128I	1.124
	256I/256D	1.72	256I/256D	1.145		

Cache Design Options

After calculating the area available for cache, we proceed with the selection of the cache configuration that results in the optimum CPI. One of the problems is that the area may not fall squarely into 2^nKB boundaries. Industry implementations use different associativities to accommodate this problem, but this explodes the number of configurations.

The effect of nonbinary associativity is better utilization of the available area, but it should have only a second-order effect on CPI. The cache configurations with their respective CPI are as shown in Table 10.18.

Some general observations can be made from Table 10.18:

1. The unified cache does not perform as well as split cache when contention is taken into account.

2. Since the processor core size shrinks with feature size, all implementations tend to have similar cache sizes at smaller feature sizes.

3. The multiprocessor requires at least three separate caches due to the requirement of having split instruction caches. This results in a higher I-cache miss rate, compared to the superscalar case.

Write Buffer Management

Recall the CPI section where we discussed different write buffer management schemes. For CBWA and WTNWA, there are three schemes and two schemes, respectively, with the first being the simplest. In order to evaluate

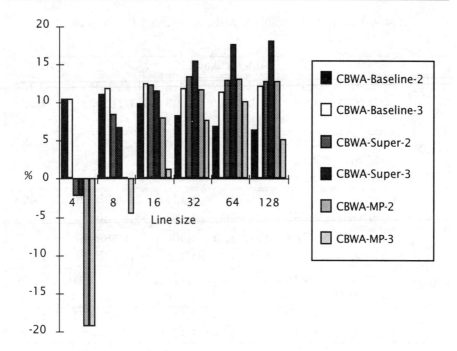

Figure 10.11 Percent CPI improvement of CBWA buffer management schemes 2 and 3 relative to scheme 1 for 0.75μ. (Write policy–Configuration–Buffer management scheme.)

which scheme to use, the CPI versus line size of each scheme was calculated. Figures 10.11 and 10.12 detail the performance improvement of schemes 2 and 3 relative to buffer management scheme 1.

Physical Word Size

A decision needs to be made with regard to the width of the memory bus. We calculate the effect of increasing the memory bus for both CBWA and WTNWA, and the results are displayed in Figures 10.13–10.15.

These figures exhibit an interesting point. The increase in bus width brings a large return in CPI reduction for the CBWA case but not for the WTNWA case. It is somewhat intuitive that increasing bus width reduces T_{line} but does nothing for T_{access}. Since WTNWA traffic is dominated by the write traffic as the miss ratio is reduced, its performance is not enhanced by a reduction in T_{line}.

Another interesting question is why the improvement reaches a peak for the MP-CBWA case at line size = 16 and reduces after that. This is due to the small cache area for the multiprocessor implementation. CPI reaches a peak at smaller line sizes.

For CBWA implementation, it is worthwhile in all cases to implement a wider memory interface, since the performance benefit is greater than 5% for reasonable line sizes.

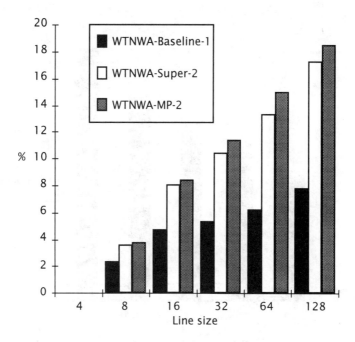

Figure 10.12   Percent CPI improvement of WTNWA buffer management scheme 2 relative to scheme 1 for 0.75μ. (Write policy–Configuration–Buffer management scheme.)

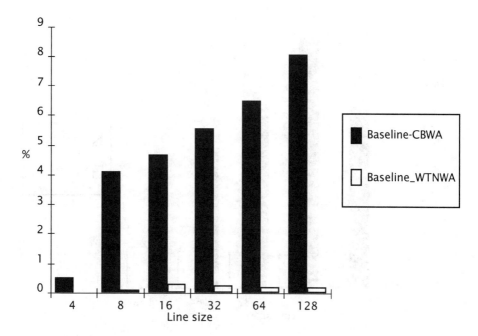

Figure 10.13   Percent CPI improvement of 64b memory bus relative to 32b memory bus for a 0.75μ baseline processor.

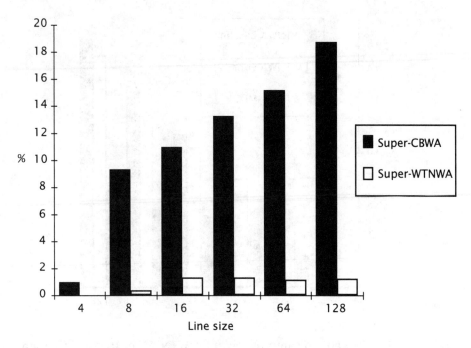

Figure 10.14   Percent CPI improvement of 64b memory bus relative to 32b memory bus for a 0.75μ superscalar processor.

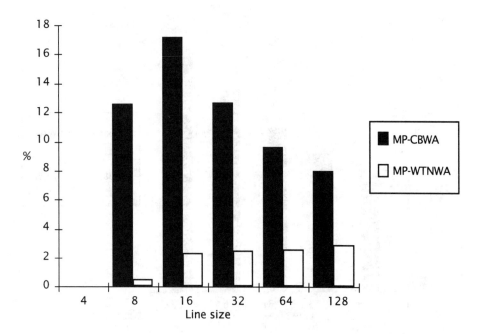

Figure 10.15   Percent CPI improvement of 64b memory bus relative to 32b memory bus for a 0.75μ multiprocessor.

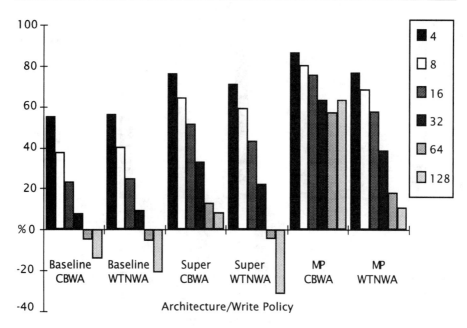

Figure 10.16 Percent CPI improvement of implementations with secondary cache relative to implementation without secondary cache for 1.0μ across different line sizes.

Secondary Cache

The effect of adding secondary cache to CPI across the different line sizes, write policy, and architecture is shown for the 1.0μ and 0.3μ cases. These cases are selected in order to show the benefits of secondary cache as feature sizes shrink.

From the data in Figure 10.16, it is beneficial to add a secondary cache only with shorter line size. A question arises from these data: Why is the improvement negative for the baseline case at large line sizes?

This is due to the assumption that was made in the design of the secondary cache. Figure 10.16 compares the best CPI without secondary cache with the CPI implemented with a secondary cache. This negative improvement is due to the fact that the implementation with secondary cache uses a simple write buffer management scheme. As a result, for the CBWA case, $T_{c.miss} = (1+w)T_{line.128}$ (we first need to write back the dirty line and wait for the entire read line to be returned prior to the resumption of processing).

Therefore, for the baseline case (which has the biggest level-1 cache and the smallest reference traffic), as the line size is increased, the best CPI (buffer management scheme 3) without secondary cache is lower than with secondary cache.

We would expect the situation to get worse for the 0.3μ case, since the miss rate of the level-1 cache is now even lower (a much larger on-chip cache), and the ratio of size between the first-level and secondary caches is only four. This is shown in Figure 10.17 for the 0.3μ case.

Based on these data, the addition of a secondary cache is not warranted, since the performance improvement does not exceed 20% for higher line

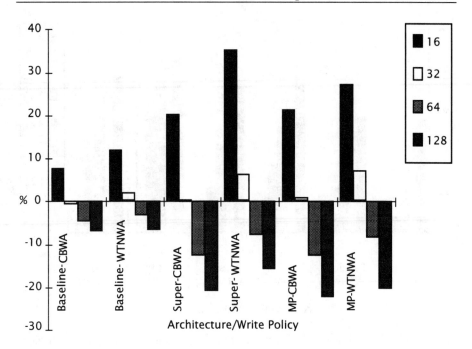

Figure 10.17 Percent CPI improvement of implementations with secondary cache relative to implementations without secondary cache for 0.3μ across different line sizes.

sizes. However, we have not taken memory traffic into account, and secondary cache plays an important part in reducing memory traffic.

Traffic and Line Size

Traffic on the memory bus is critical to overall system performance. When the offered bandwidth exceeds the achieved bandwidth, the memory bus dictates the performance of the overall system. The effect of bus traffic on a multiprocessor system is even more severe. Four main implementations can be considered:

- Write-Through No Write Allocate cache.

- Copy Back Write Allocate cache.

- Write-Through No Write Allocate cache with a Write Assembly cache.

- WTNWA with the addition of a secondary cache.

Now 8 ns of bus time are available to each instruction, and the offered bus time has to be below that to avoid significant performance degradation. The data are presented in two ways. We first compare to the total offered occupancy for each implementation, and we then break down the traffic of each implementation into different reference streams to get a better idea of the types of traffic on the bus and how they change with increasing line size.

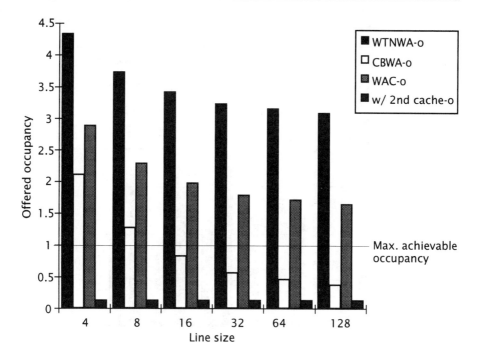

Figure 10.18   Baseline cache management policy/traffic analysis for 0.75μ.

A glance at the results tells us that the WTNWA implementation has the highest offered occupancy among the four implementations. Even at a size of 128 bytes, the offered traffic is three times more than the available bandwidth. We show the adverse effect this has on overall performance as we take bus saturation into account in the CPI analysis. These data rule out the use of a WTNWA cache, since the bus has become the limiting resource even without multiple processors on the bus. In a multiprocessor system, we select either the CBWA with large line size or the WTNWA implementation with a secondary cache. Figure 10.19 shows that traffic is higher for the multiprocessor implementation. In the multiprocessor implementation, it is even more important to have a secondary cache to reduce bus traffic.

As Figure 10.20 for WTNWA shows, as line size is increased, the traffic from both data and instruction read references is reduced, but the data write traffic remains constant. In this implementation, the CPU performance is bus saturated.

Figure 10.21 gives the traffic breakdown for the CBWA implementation. One can see that as line size increases, reducing the cache miss ratio, a significant reduction in all three streams of traffic occurs. At a line size of 128 bytes, the bus occupancy is kept below 0.5, and processor performance degradation due to the bus contention among the three reference streams should be small.

Figure 10.22 shows the traffic breakdown of the WAC case. In using the write assembly cache, the data write traffic is converted from word traffic to the more efficient line traffic. Data from chapter 5 show that the WAC can filter out 70% of the write traffic. The write traffic is reduced, but still dominates the overall reference traffic.

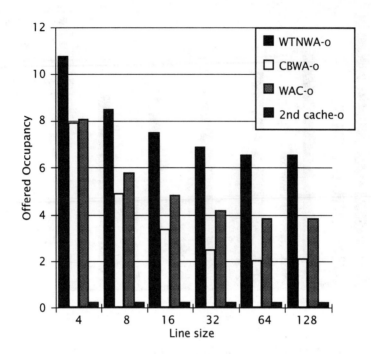

Figure 10.19   Multiprocessor cache management policy/traffic analysis for 0.75μ.

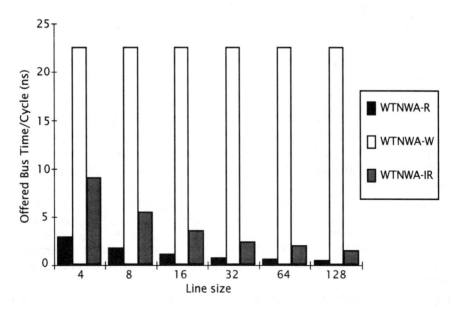

Figure   10.20 Baseline   WTNWA   traffic   breakdown   for   0.75μ. (Configuration–Reference type.)

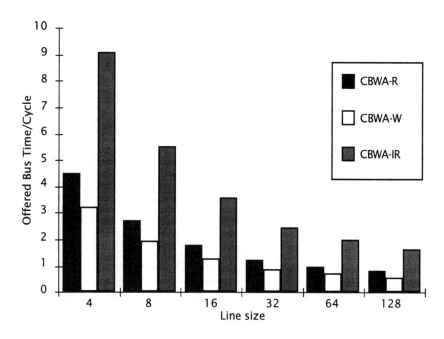

Figure 10.21   Baseline CBWA traffic breakdown for 0.75μ. (Configuration–Reference type.)

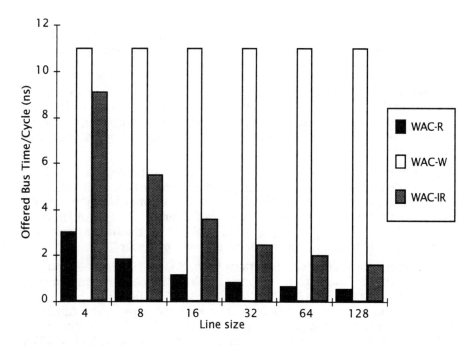

Figure 10.22   Baseline WAC traffic breakdown for 0.75μ. (Configuration–Reference type.)

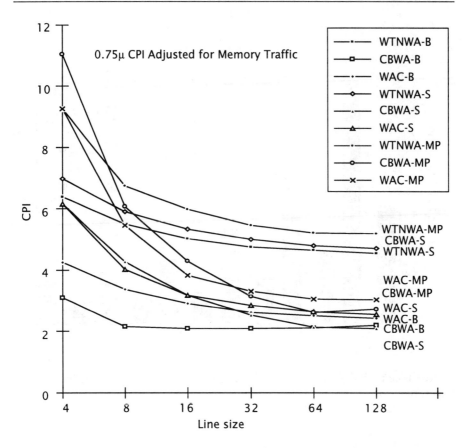

Figure 10.23 CPI/cache management policy summary for 0.75μ. (Write policy–Configuration: B = Baseline, S = Superscalar, MP = Multiprocessor.)

In order to prevent the bus from becoming the system bottleneck, we can pick either the CBWA or the implementation with secondary cache. The total offered occupancy has to be kept below the maximum achievable occupancy. As we decrease the feature size, the situation is improved because larger caches reduce the bus traffic.

The CPI models that we used previously assumed a "perfect write buffer." These models for CPI are valid as long as bus occupancy is kept below one and a sufficiently large write buffer exists. However, when bus occupancy is above one, the bus saturates and we must consider total traffic and degrade CPI accordingly. Figure 10.23 shows the final CPI for the 0.75μ implementations with bus traffic taken into account when necessary.

Many useful conclusions can be drawn from Figure 10.23. The best-performing configurations are the superscalar and the baseline implementation with CBWA cache at a line size of 128 bytes. The fact that the baseline implementation comes out relatively even with the superscalar can be attributed to its larger cache and smaller need for bandwidth. Another interesting point is that the worst-performing implementations are all WTNWA, with WTNWA-MP being the worst. It is also notable that increasing the line size has less beneficial effect on WTNWA than on the other implementations. This is due to the fact that most of its traffic is word writes and the

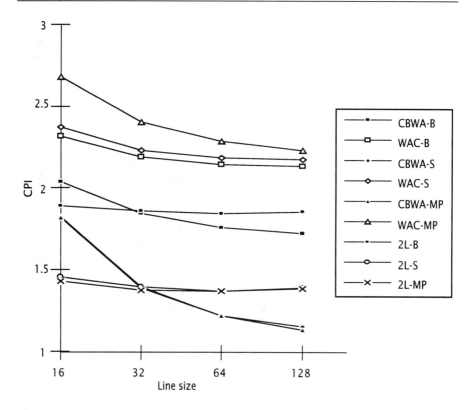

Figure 10.24   CPI/cache management policy summary for 0.30μ. (Write policy–Configuration. 2L indicates use of 2 levels on chip cache.)

initial access time cannot be amortized, as in the case of line accesses.

Figure 10.24 shows the same analysis for the 0.3μ implementation. In this case, the best performance is multiprocessor with CBWA. This is a reversal from the 0.75μ implementation, where the multiprocessor generally performed the worst. This graph does not include the WTNWA cases, since we have concluded that those are not feasible implementations. However, the secondary cache implementations are shown. Again, the question is, why does the secondary cache perform worse than the CBWA implementation at larger line sizes? As described earlier, this is due to the simple buffer implementation associated with the secondary cache.

The main difference between the 0.3μ and the 0.75μ implementations is that the first-level cache is now sufficiently large to supply the bandwidth demands of the multiprocessor implementation. There is also much less degradation of CPI due to bus saturation (except in the case of WTNWA implementation).

Multiprocessor Bus Contention

The data in Figure 10.25 show the effect of bus contention in a multiprocessor system. The data presented are based on the following configuration:

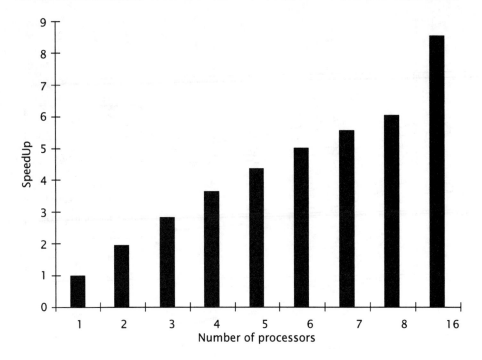

Figure 10.25   Speedup relative to one processor.

Baseline Processor with CBWA Cache	
Level one cache miss ratio	0.01
Level one cache line size	128 bytes
$T_{\text{service.L2}}$	348 ns

In a multiprocessor system, given an application that can be partitioned appropriately, we generally want to have linear increases in performance. This means that as we scale the system from 1 to N processors, the performance of the N processor system should be N times that of the single processor system. However, this usually is not true in real life, and one of the limitations is the shared memory bus.

As can be seen from Figure 10.25, the increase in performance decreases as the amount of bus contention increases. This contention is taken into account by incorporating the wait time in the memory access time.

CPI versus Feature Size

Figure 10.26 shows the best CPI across feature sizes. At the 1μ feature size, the bandwidth supplied is not sufficient to match that of the multiprocessor implementation. This results in a dramatic drop in CPI for the multiprocessor case as we go from 1μ to 0.75μ. It can also be observed that the increasing cache size does not help the baseline CPI much after 0.75μ. With this observation, one should consider moving to either superscalar or multiprocessor architecture. This coincides with what is happening in the industry. To decide between the superscalar and multiprocessor cases is a

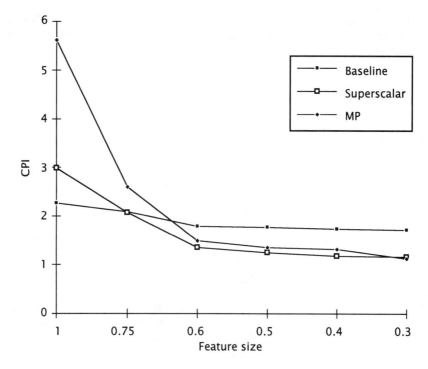

Figure 10.26   CPI versus feature size summary.

different story. The multiprocessor implementation has a higher demand for bandwidth, and it is at a disadvantage due to the requirement for split I-cache. The CPI of the two implementations is roughly equalized at 0.3μ. The slow decrease of CPI after 0.6μ points out the fact that architects should consider other architectures at this point, such as higher-number-issue superscalar or higher multiprocessor implementations. However, steps must be taken to provide memory bandwidth so that the memory bus does not become the limiting factor.

10.3   Study Results

Some observations can be made based on results in the previous section. Performance gain due to scaling of technology levels out for our three implementations at different points. For the baseline case, insignificant gains are achieved as one scales below 0.75μ. For the superscalar and multiprocessor implementations, the reduction of gains occurs at 0.6μ. This should gives designers a hint for the future. As technology scales to below 0.6μ, architects need to explore higher-issue superscalars and more than two multiprocessors on a single chip. The benefits of larger on-chip caches decline as these caches reach 128K (total) and beyond. One alternative that should be considered is on-chip secondary cache.

The biggest issue facing architects is the widening gap between processor speed and memory latency. Based on our analysis, only the CBWA and secondary cache implementations are feasible. A simple bus-based memory interface quickly becomes the system bottleneck. Higher-bandwidth implementations such as crossbar switches would be required to force down contention.

10.4   Conclusions

There is no conclusion to the design process—merely a termination. Design iteration follows iteration, each improving our understanding of the design tradeoffs of cost and performance. At some point, the design is "frozen" so that implementation can be completed. At that point, the designer can only hope that the component parameters, which are changing as time goes by, are correctly predicted. Mispredicted parameters, overlooked functional assumptions or interactions, flaws, etc., create sleepless nights for the designer. Each is repaired or "featured" (a feature is sometimes a flaw that we learn to live with), hopefully with minimum impact on the implementation.

At the end, the design team, having learned the lessons for the current project, moves on to the next design… which has new technology, marketing, cost, etc., assumptions. The rapid change in the computer design field diminishes, but does not negate, the value of "the last project's" lessons. In each case, however, the better the understanding and the better the analysis, the better the resulting design.

Appendix A

DTMR Cache Miss Rates

The following cache data is a more complete tabularization of the chapter 5 cache performance data.

A.1 Basic DTMR

This is the basic cache data (misses per reference) for each of integrated, data, and instruction caches. It follows the work of A. Smith, with extensions (discussed in chapter 5).

Table A.1 DTMR for integrated cache.

Line Size	4	8	16	32	64	128
Cache Size						
1KB	0.4500	0.3000	0.2000	0.1500	0.1500	0.1500
2KB	0.4000	0.2600	0.1700	0.1200	0.0950	0.0880
4KB	0.3200	0.1900	0.1200	0.0800	0.0600	0.0480
8KB	0.2300	0.1400	0.0750	0.0500	0.0320	0.0240
16KB	0.1900	0.1000	0.0600	0.0350	0.0240	0.0180
32KB	0.1200	0.0700	0.0400	0.0250	0.0150	0.0090
64KB	0.0950	0.0520	0.0300	0.0190	0.0110	0.0070
128KB			0.0200	0.0120	0.0070	0.0045
256KB			0.0190	0.0085	0.0045	0.0028
512KB			0.0150	0.0062	0.0038	0.0019
1024KB			0.0100	0.0050	0.0028	0.0012

Table A.2   DTMR for data cache.

Line Size	4	8	16	32	64	128
Cache Size						
1KB	0.2900	0.2100	0.1550	0.1500	0.1500	0.1700
2KB	0.2750	0.1850	0.1200	0.0900	0.0850	0.0820
4KB	0.2500	0.1700	0.0950	0.0700	0.0550	0.0480
8KB	0.2100	0.1350	0.0800	0.0550	0.0370	0.0310
16KB	0.1800	0.0950	0.0600	0.0390	0.0260	0.0190
32KB	0.1100	0.0650	0.0400	0.0250	0.0180	0.0115
64KB			0.0300	0.0190	0.0110	0.0075
128KB			0.0250	0.0130	0.0075	0.0045
256KB			0.0230	0.0110	0.0055	0.0032
512KB			0.0190	0.0093	0.0047	0.0027
1024KB			0.0170	0.0084	0.0042	0.0023

Table A.3   DTMR for instruction cache.

Line Size	4	8	16	32	64	128
Cache Size						
1KB	0.5000	0.3000	0.1950	0.1400	0.1000	0.0800
2KB	0.4000	0.2300	0.1600	0.0950	0.0650	0.0550
4KB	0.2800	0.1700	0.0950	0.0630	0.0440	0.0310
8KB	0.1850	0.1000	0.0600	0.0380	0.0240	0.0180
16KB	0.1650	0.0820	0.0500	0.0300	0.0190	0.0120
32KB	0.0900	0.0550	0.0300	0.0180	0.0098	0.0065
64KB			0.0210	0.0120	0.0066	0.0040
128KB			0.0195	0.0098	0.0055	0.0030
256KB			0.0190	0.0090	0.0045	0.0026
512KB			0.0018	0.0080	0.0036	0.0020
1024KB			0.0016	0.0070	0.0029	0.0015

Table A.4   Adjustment for DTMR associativity (Tables A.1–A.3).

	Line Size	16	32	64
	Direct	1.5200	1.6100	1.7000
256K cache	2-way	1.1700	1.2000	1.2200
	4-way	1.0500	1.0600	1.0700
	Direct	1.5000	1.5600	1.6400
128K cache	2-way	1.1700	1.1900	1.2000
	4-way	1.0500	1.0500	1.0500
	Direct	1.4500	1.5100	1.5700
64K cache	2-way	1.1700	1.1700	1.1800
	4-way	1.0500	1.0500	1.0500
	Direct	1.4300	1.4400	1.5100
32K cache	2-way	1.4500	1.1400	1.1400
	4-way	1.0400	1.0400	1.0400
	Direct	1.3500	1.3800	1.4600
16K cache	2-way	1.1300	1.1300	1.1300
	4-way	1.0400	1.0350	1.0400
	Direct	1.3200	1.3500	1.4600
8K cache	2-way	1.1200	1.1300	1.1500
	4-way	1.0400	1.0350	1.0400
	Direct	1.2900	1.3500	0.4500
4K cache	2-way	1.1100	1.1200	0.1400
	4-way	1.0300	1.0300	0.0300
	Direct	1.2700	1.3300	1.4500
2K cache	2-way	1.0900	1.1200	1.1400
	4-way	1.0200	1.0300	1.0400
	Direct	1.2600	1.3400	1.4600
1K cache	2-way	1.0900	1.1100	1.1300
	4-way	1.0200	1.0400	1.0400

A.2   Associativity Adjustments

Use Table A.4 to adjust Tables A.1–A.3 for non-fully-associative caches. For our purposes, set associative caches that are 8-way set associative or higher are treated as being fully associative.

Use Table A.5 to adjust all remaining cache data (Tables A.6–A.56) for low levels (1, 2, and 4-way) of associativity.

Table A.5   Associativity adjustment for Tables A.6–A.56.

Unadjusted MR	< 1%	1–2%	2–6%	6-12%	12–25%
Direct	1.6500	1.5200	1.3800	1.3700	1.3300
2-way	1.2100	1.1700	1.1400	1.1300	1.1100
4-way	1.0600	1.0500	1.0400	1.0300	1.0300

A.3   User + System

Tables A.6–A.8 provide cache data for user programs with operating system service routines.

Table A.6   User + system, fully associative, integrated cache.

Cache	Line Size			
Size	16	32	64	128
1024	0.273	0.211	0.1639	0.1636
2048	0.244	0.178	0.1274	0.1105
4096	0.185	0.127	0.0845	0.0650
8192	0.132	0.0825	0.0509	0.0358
16384	0.104	0.0629	0.0379	0.0246
32768	0.069	0.041	0.0245	0.0151
65536	0.049	0.0295	0.0192	0.0127
131072	0.031	0.0182	0.0117	0.0082
262144	0.026	0.0128	0.0071	0.0046

Table A.7   User + system, fully associative, data cache.

Cache	Line Size			
Size	16	32	64	128
1024	0.1550	0.1500	0.1500	0.1700
2048	0.1200	0.0900	0.0850	0.0820
4096	0.0950	0.0700	0.0550	0.0480
8192	0.0861	0.0592	0.0398	0.0333
16384	0.0712	0.0463	0.0308	0.0226
32768	0.0520	0.0325	0.0234	0.0150
65536	0.0429	0.0272	0.0158	0.0107
131072	0.0385	0.0200	0.0115	0.0069
262144	0.0379	0.0182	0.0091	0.0053

Table A.8   User + system, fully associative, instruction cache.

Cache	Line Size			
Size	16	32	64	128
1024	0.1950	0.1400	0.1000	0.0800
2048	0.1600	0.0950	0.0650	0.0550
4096	0.0950	0.0630	0.0440	0.0310
8192	0.0645	0.0409	0.0258	0.0193
16384	0.0594	0.0356	0.0225	0.0143
32768	0.0390	0.0234	0.0127	0.0084
65536	0.0300	0.0172	0.0094	0.0057
131072	0.0300	0.0151	0.0085	0.0046
262144	0.0300	0.0149	0.0074	0.0043

A.4   Transaction-Based Systems

This environment is also referred to as "cold-start." Multiple processes are resident in memory, and control passes to a new process after the execution of Q instructions. Control *does not* return (statistically) while any of the original program's working set is in the cache.

Table A.9   Cold start, line size 16, fully associative, integrated cache.

Cache	Q				
size	100	1000	10000	20000	100000
1024	0.3325	0.2818	0.2739	0.2735	0.2731
2048	0.3312	0.2604	0.2455	0.2445	0.2438
4096	0.3311	0.2317	0.1910	0.1881	0.1858
8192	0.3311	0.2224	0.1464	0.1394	0.1335
16384	0.3311	0.2222	0.1293	0.1179	0.1076
32768	0.3311	0.2222	0.1187	0.0986	0.0764
65536	0.3311	0.2222	0.1180	0.0948	0.0618
131072	0.3311	0.2222	0.1180	0.0947	0.0552
262144	0.3311	0.2222	0.1180	0.0947	0.0549

Table A.10   Cold start, line size 32, fully associative, integrated cache.

Cache	Q				
size	100	1000	10000	20000	100000
1024	0.2638	0.2172	0.2113	0.2109	0.2107
2048	0.2590	0.1901	0.1790	0.1784	0.1778
4096	0.2585	0.1580	0.1302	0.1284	0.1269
8192	0.2585	0.1450	0.0912	0.0870	0.0834
16384	0.2585	0.1444	0.0775	0.0705	0.0645
32768	0.2585	0.1444	0.0694	0.0575	0.0454
65536	0.2585	0.1444	0.0687	0.0545	0.0360
131072	0.2585	0.1444	0.0687	0.0543	0.0309
262144	0.2585	0.1444	0.0687	0.0543	0.0305

Table A.11   Cold start, line size 64, fully associative, integrated cache.

Cache	Q				
size	100	1000	10000	20000	100000
1024	0.2065	0.1687	0.1645	0.1642	0.1640
2048	0.1948	0.1362	0.1283	0.1279	0.1275
4096	0.1926	0.1046	0.0867	0.0857	0.0848
8192	0.1925	0.0905	0.0559	0.0535	0.0514
16384	0.1925	0.0896	0.0461	0.0422	0.0388
32768	0.1925	0.0896	0.0399	0.0330	0.0263
65536	0.1925	0.0896	0.0394	0.0314	0.0222
131072	0.1925	0.0896	0.0394	0.0311	0.0182
262144	0.1925	0.0896	0.0394	0.0311	0.0176

Table A.12   Cold start, line size 128, fully associative, integrated cache.

Cache	Q				
size	100	1000	10000	20000	100000
1024	0.1944	0.1669	0.1640	0.1638	0.1637
2048	0.1628	0.1165	0.1111	0.1108	0.1106
4096	0.1532	0.0778	0.0663	0.0657	0.0651
8192	0.1531	0.0606	0.0387	0.0373	0.0361
16384	0.1531	0.0588	0.0294	0.0271	0.0252
32768	0.1531	0.0588	0.0241	0.0200	0.0162
65536	0.1531	0.0588	0.0237	0.0190	0.0142
131072	0.1531	0.0588	0.0237	0.0186	0.0114
262144	0.1531	0.0588	0.0237	0.0186	0.0105

Table A.13   Cold start, line size 16, fully associative, data cache.

Cache	Q				
size	100	1000	10000	20000	100000
1024	0.4240	0.2246	0.1631	0.1590	0.1558
2048	0.6749	0.2230	0.1324	0.1263	0.1213
4096	0.6749	0.2224	0.1152	0.1056	0.0972
8192	0.6749	0.2010	0.1118	0.1024	0.0907
16384	0.6749	0.2224	0.1104	0.0955	0.0774
32768	0.6749	0.2224	0.1103	0.0943	0.0663
65536	0.6749	0.2224	0.1103	0.0942	0.0642
131072	0.6749	0.2224	0.1103	0.0942	0.0640
262144	0.6749	0.2224	0.1103	0.0942	0.0640

Table A.14   Cold start, line size 32, fully associative, data cache.

Cache	Q				
size	100	1000	10000	20000	100000
1024	0.3336	0.1885	0.1541	0.1520	0.1504
2048	0.4727	0.1595	0.0981	0.0941	0.0908
4096	0.4727	0.1574	0.0821	0.0762	0.0713
8192	0.4720	0.1353	0.0781	0.0710	0.0623
16384	0.4727	0.1574	0.0739	0.0626	0.0502
32768	0.4727	0.1574	0.0736	0.0609	0.0410
65536	0.4727	0.1574	0.0736	0.0608	0.0393
131072	0.4727	0.1574	0.0736	0.0608	0.0389
262144	0.4727	0.1574	0.0736	0.0608	0.0389

Table A.15   Cold start, line size 64, fully associative, data cache.

Cache	Q				
size	100	1000	10000	20000	100000
1024	0.2838	0.1700	0.1520	0.1510	0.1502
2048	0.3279	0.1239	0.0892	0.0871	0.0854
4096	0.3279	0.1147	0.0626	0.0589	0.0558
8192	0.3182	0.1029	0.0563	0.0497	0.0422
16384	0.3279	0.1143	0.0493	0.0412	0.0332
32768	0.3279	0.1143	0.0489	0.0395	0.0276
65536	0.3279	0.1143	0.0489	0.0393	0.0241
131072	0.3279	0.1143	0.0489	0.0393	0.0237
262144	0.3279	0.1143	0.0489	0.0393	0.0237

Table A.16   Cold start, line size 128, fully associative, data cache.

Cache	Q				
size	100	1000	10000	20000	100000
1024	0.2560	0.1799	0.1710	0.1705	0.1701
2048	0.2424	0.1043	0.0843	0.0832	0.0822
4096	0.2422	0.0853	0.0523	0.0502	0.0484
8192	0.2113	0.0808	0.0440	0.0394	0.0347
16384	0.2422	0.0834	0.0347	0.0291	0.0240
32768	0.2422	0.0834	0.0336	0.0262	0.0177
65536	0.2422	0.0834	0.0336	0.0260	0.0153
131072	0.2422	0.0834	0.0336	0.0260	0.0146
262144	0.2422	0.0834	0.0336	0.0260	0.0146

Table A.17   Cold start, line size 16, fully associative, instruction cache.

Cache	Q				
size	100	1000	10000	20000	100000
1024	0.3898	0.2320	0.1989	0.1969	0.1954
2048	0.5023	0.2123	0.1657	0.1629	0.1606
4096	0.5023	0.1969	0.1094	0.1024	0.0965
8192	0.5006	0.1839	0.0989	0.0854	0.0697
16384	0.5023	0.1965	0.0886	0.0754	0.0629
32768	0.5023	0.1965	0.0878	0.0714	0.0482
65536	0.5023	0.1965	0.0878	0.0713	0.0446
131072	0.5023	0.1965	0.0878	0.0713	0.0446
262144	0.5023	0.1965	0.0878	0.0713	0.0446

Table A.18   Cold start, line size 32, fully associative, instruction cache.

Cache	Q				
size	100	1000	10000	20000	100000
1024	0.2655	0.1602	0.1421	0.1410	0.1402
2048	0.3226	0.1292	0.0987	0.0968	0.0954
4096	0.3226	0.1187	0.0701	0.0666	0.0637
8192	0.3161	0.1090	0.0596	0.0520	0.0436
16384	0.3226	0.1180	0.0525	0.0448	0.0376
32768	0.3226	0.1180	0.0517	0.0416	0.0283
65536	0.3226	0.1180	0.0517	0.0415	0.0253
131072	0.3226	0.1180	0.0517	0.0415	0.0251
262144	0.3226	0.1180	0.0517	0.0415	0.0251

Table A.19   Cold start, line size 64, fully associative, instruction cache.

Cache	Q				
size	100	1000	10000	20000	100000
1024	0.1793	0.1107	0.1011	0.1005	0.1001
2048	0.1988	0.0835	0.0669	0.0660	0.0652
4096	0.1988	0.0740	0.0476	0.0458	0.0444
8192	0.1874	0.0687	0.0370	0.0323	0.0273
16384	0.1988	0.0724	0.0319	0.0275	0.0236
32768	0.1988	0.0724	0.0306	0.0241	0.0156
65536	0.1988	0.0724	0.0306	0.0239	0.0139
131072	0.1988	0.0724	0.0306	0.0239	0.0138
262144	0.1988	0.0724	0.0306	0.0239	0.0138

Table A.20   Cold start, line size 128, fully associative, instruction cache.

Cache	Q				
size	100	1000	10000	20000	100000
1024	0.1282	0.0855	0.0806	0.0803	0.0801
2048	0.1278	0.0641	0.0559	0.0555	0.0551
4096	0.1275	0.0492	0.0331	0.0320	0.0312
8192	0.1138	0.0476	0.0255	0.0228	0.0201
16384	0.1275	0.0469	0.0202	0.0174	0.0149
32768	0.1275	0.0469	0.0190	0.0147	0.0099
65536	0.1275	0.0469	0.0189	0.0145	0.0083
131072	0.1275	0.0469	0.0189	0.0145	0.0080
262144	0.1275	0.0469	0.0189	0.0145	0.0080

Table A.21   Integrated cache, warm start, line size 16, fully associative, MP 2.

Cache size	Q				
	100	1000	10000	20000	100000
1024	0.3049	0.2808	0.2739	0.2735	0.2731
2048	0.2786	0.2567	0.2454	0.2445	0.2438
4096	0.2416	0.2161	0.1907	0.1880	0.1858
8192	0.1922	0.1780	0.1445	0.1389	0.1335
16384	0.1372	0.1406	0.1222	0.1156	0.1075
32768	0.1068	0.1073	0.0965	0.0893	0.0758
65536	0.0702	0.0730	0.0730	0.0702	0.0588
131072	0.0492	0.0502	0.0513	0.0508	0.0452
262144	0.0318	0.0320	0.0335	0.0341	0.0349

Table A.22   Integrated cache, warm start, line size 32, fully associative, MP 2.

Cache size	Q				
	100	1000	10000	20000	100000
1024	0.2424	0.2167	0.2113	0.2109	0.2107
2048	0.2133	0.1882	0.1790	0.1783	0.1778
4096	0.1760	0.1494	0.1300	0.1283	0.1269
8192	0.1319	0.1170	0.0903	0.0867	0.0834
16384	0.0866	0.0887	0.0739	0.0694	0.0644
32768	0.0643	0.0649	0.0577	0.0530	0.0451
65536	0.0422	0.0440	0.0437	0.0417	0.0347
131072	0.0296	0.0302	0.0306	0.0300	0.0260
262144	0.0182	0.0183	0.0192	0.0195	0.0192

A.5   Multiprogrammed (Warm Cache) Environment

This environment is similar to the transaction environment, except that control returns to a program after MP processes have each executed Q instructions.

Table A.23   Integrated cache, warm start, line size 64, fully associative, MP 2.

Cache	Q				
size	100	1000	10000	20000	100000
1024	0.1937	0.1685	0.1645	0.1642	0.1640
2048	0.1619	0.1353	0.1283	0.1279	0.1275
4096	0.1260	0.1003	0.0867	0.0856	0.0848
8192	0.0884	0.0746	0.0555	0.0534	0.0514
16384	0.0541	0.0552	0.0444	0.0417	0.0388
32768	0.0390	0.0392	0.0339	0.0308	0.0262
65536	0.0248	0.0259	0.0264	0.0253	0.0216
131072	0.0193	0.0197	0.0193	0.0189	0.0160
262144	0.0118	0.0119	0.0125	0.0125	0.0117

Table A.24   Integrated cache, warm start, line size 128, fully associative, MP 2.

Cache	Q				
size	100	1000	10000	20000	100000
1024	0.1897	0.1668	0.1640	0.1638	0.1637
2048	0.1452	0.1162	0.1111	0.1108	0.1106
4096	0.1055	0.0761	0.0663	0.0657	0.0651
8192	0.0681	0.0527	0.0385	0.0372	0.0361
16384	0.0387	0.0382	0.0287	0.0269	0.0252
32768	0.0257	0.0257	0.0211	0.0190	0.0162
65536	0.0155	0.0163	0.0168	0.0161	0.0140
131072	0.0129	0.0130	0.0127	0.0123	0.0104
262144	0.0082	0.0083	0.0086	0.0085	0.0076

Table A.25   Integrated cache, warm start, line size 16, fully associative, MP 3.

Cache	Q				
size	100	1000	10000	20000	100000
1024	0.3176	0.2813	0.2739	0.2735	0.2731
2048	0.3048	0.2585	0.2454	0.2445	0.2438
4096	0.2906	0.2233	0.1908	0.1881	0.1858
8192	0.2612	0.1983	0.1454	0.1391	0.1335
16384	0.2161	0.1770	0.1255	0.1167	0.1075
32768	0.1461	0.1484	0.1063	0.0935	0.0761
65536	0.1060	0.1111	0.0914	0.0806	0.0602
131072	0.0697	0.0725	0.0724	0.0671	0.0495
262144	0.0525	0.0529	0.0552	0.0533	0.0428

Table A.26 Integrated cache, warm start, line size 32, fully associative, MP 3.

Cache	Q				
size	100	1000	10000	20000	100000
1024	0.2519	0.2169	0.2113	0.2109	0.2107
2048	0.2336	0.1891	0.1790	0.1783	0.1778
4096	0.2143	0.1533	0.1301	0.1283	0.1269
8192	0.1812	0.1293	0.0908	0.0868	0.0834
16384	0.1380	0.1114	0.0755	0.0700	0.0645
32768	0.0904	0.0909	0.0628	0.0550	0.0452
65536	0.0640	0.0670	0.0537	0.0471	0.0353
131072	0.0418	0.0432	0.0424	0.0390	0.0281
262144	0.0295	0.0296	0.0300	0.0292	0.0236

Table A.27 Integrated cache, warm start, line size 64, fully associative, MP 3.

Cache	Q				
size	100	1000	10000	20000	100000
1024	0.1995	0.1686	0.1645	0.1642	0.1640
2048	0.1759	0.1357	0.1283	0.1279	0.1275
4096	0.1534	0.1023	0.0867	0.0856	0.0848
8192	0.1220	0.0815	0.0557	0.0534	0.0514
16384	0.0870	0.0685	0.0452	0.0419	0.0388
32768	0.0552	0.0547	0.0365	0.0318	0.0263
65536	0.0401	0.0414	0.0316	0.0279	0.0219
131072	0.0247	0.0266	0.0261	0.0236	0.0170
262144	0.0192	0.0192	0.0184	0.0178	0.0141

Table A.28 Integrated cache, warm start, line size 128, fully associative, MP 3.

Cache	Q				
size	100	1000	10000	20000	100000
1024	0.1919	0.1668	0.1640	0.1638	0.1637
2048	0.1530	0.1163	0.1111	0.1108	0.1106
4096	0.1243	0.0769	0.0663	0.0657	0.0651
8192	0.0931	0.0562	0.0386	0.0372	0.0361
16384	0.0609	0.0460	0.0291	0.0270	0.0252
32768	0.0376	0.0355	0.0224	0.0194	0.0162
65536	0.0267	0.0267	0.0196	0.0173	0.0141
131072	0.0166	0.0178	0.0166	0.0149	0.0109
262144	0.0128	0.0127	0.0121	0.0116	0.0088

Table A.29 Integrated cache, warm start, line size 16, fully associative, MP 10.

Cache	Q				
size	100	1000	10000	20000	100000
1024	0.3290	0.2817	0.2739	0.2735	0.2731
2048	0.3257	0.2600	0.2455	0.2445	0.2438
4096	0.3234	0.2297	0.1910	0.1881	0.1858
8192	0.3192	0.2169	0.1462	0.1394	0.1335
16384	0.3155	0.2125	0.1284	0.1176	0.1076
32768	0.3059	0.2059	0.1157	0.0974	0.0764
65536	0.2915	0.1973	0.1117	0.0914	0.0614
131072	0.2556	0.1818	0.1065	0.0878	0.0538
262144	0.2278	0.1717	0.1026	0.0847	0.0519

Table A.30 Integrated cache, warm start, line size 32, fully associative, MP 10.

Cache	Q				
size	100	1000	10000	20000	100000
1024	0.2610	0.2171	0.2113	0.2109	0.2107
2048	0.2531	0.1899	0.1790	0.1783	0.1778
4096	0.2487	0.1569	0.1301	0.1284	0.1269
8192	0.2416	0.1412	0.0911	0.0869	0.0834
16384	0.2346	0.1366	0.0770	0.0704	0.0645
32768	0.2208	0.1311	0.0678	0.0569	0.0453
65536	0.2017	0.1239	0.0650	0.0527	0.0358
131072	0.1574	0.1106	0.0617	0.0504	0.0303
262144	0.1156	0.0961	0.0575	0.0475	0.0288

Table A.31 Integrated cache, warm start, line size 64, fully associative, MP 10.

Cache	Q				
size	100	1000	10000	20000	100000
1024	0.2048	0.1687	0.1645	0.1642	0.1640
2048	0.1902	0.1361	0.1283	0.1279	0.1275
4096	0.1830	0.1040	0.0867	0.0856	0.0848
8192	0.1740	0.0883	0.0559	0.0534	0.0514
16384	0.1644	0.0843	0.0459	0.0421	0.0388
32768	0.1481	0.0801	0.0391	0.0327	0.0263
65536	0.1357	0.0763	0.0375	0.0305	0.0221
131072	0.1022	0.0681	0.0358	0.0292	0.0180
262144	0.0645	0.0551	0.0328	0.0274	0.0167

Table A.32 Integrated cache, warm start, line size 128, fully associative, MP 10.

Cache	Q				
size	100	1000	10000	20000	100000
1024	0.1938	0.1669	0.1640	0.1638	0.1637
2048	0.1604	0.1165	0.1111	0.1108	0.1106
4096	0.1458	0.0776	0.0663	0.0657	0.0651
8192	0.1353	0.0595	0.0387	0.0373	0.0361
16384	0.1220	0.0555	0.0293	0.0271	0.0252
32768	0.1028	0.0521	0.0237	0.0199	0.0162
65536	0.0946	0.0495	0.0227	0.0186	0.0142
131072	0.0709	0.0445	0.0218	0.0177	0.0113
262144	0.0416	0.0351	0.0200	0.0167	0.0101

Table A.33 Data cache, warm start, line size 16, fully associative, MP 2.

Cache	Q				
size	100	1000	10000	20000	100000
1024	0.1833	0.2040	0.1627	0.1590	0.1558
2048	0.1614	0.1636	0.1309	0.1259	0.1213
4096	0.1246	0.1272	0.1098	0.1039	0.0971
8192	0.1200	0.1032	0.1018	0.0983	0.0904
16384	0.0871	0.0874	0.0867	0.0840	0.0763
32768	0.0717	0.0731	0.0716	0.0699	0.0619
65536	0.0521	0.0528	0.0551	0.0555	0.0532
131072	0.0430	0.0433	0.0445	0.0450	0.0459
262144		0.0387	0.0393	0.0397	0.0412

Table A.34 Data cache, warm start, line size 32, fully associative, MP 2.

Cache	Q				
size	100	1000	10000	20000	100000
1024	0.1968	0.1816	0.1540	0.1520	0.1504
2048	0.1526	0.1322	0.0975	0.0939	0.0908
4096	0.0965	0.0988	0.0799	0.0756	0.0712
8192	0.0899	0.0763	0.0727	0.0689	0.0622
16384	0.0602	0.0608	0.0589	0.0561	0.0497
32768	0.0468	0.0479	0.0468	0.0453	0.0388
65536	0.0326	0.0332	0.0349	0.0352	0.0335
131072	0.0273	0.0275	0.0279	0.0278	0.0273
262144		0.0201	0.0206	0.0209	0.0218

Table A.35   Data cache, warm start, line size 64, fully associative, MP 2.

Cache size	Q				
	100	1000	10000	20000	100000
1024	0.2104	0.1679	0.1520	0.1510	0.1502
2048	0.1500	0.1141	0.0891	0.0871	0.0854
4096	0.0920	0.0844	0.0618	0.0586	0.0558
8192	0.0839	0.0633	0.0533	0.0486	0.0422
16384	0.0410	0.0423	0.0402	0.0377	0.0330
32768	0.0313	0.0321	0.0320	0.0309	0.0267
65536	0.0236	0.0240	0.0241	0.0237	0.0209
131072	0.0158	0.0159	0.0166	0.0168	0.0164
262144	0.0116	0.0116	0.0119	0.0121	0.0123

Table A.36   Data cache, warm start, line size 128, fully associative, MP 2.

Cache size	Q				
	100	1000	10000	20000	100000
1024	0.2254	0.1794	0.1710	0.1705	0.1701
2048	0.1516	0.1013	0.0843	0.0832	0.0822
4096	0.0895	0.0720	0.0520	0.0501	0.0484
8192	0.0714	0.0561	0.0428	0.0390	0.0347
16384	0.0348	0.0352	0.0303	0.0276	0.0239
32768	0.0231	0.0238	0.0228	0.0213	0.0173
65536	0.0151	0.0155	0.0160	0.0158	0.0138
131072	0.0108	0.0109	0.0112	0.0112	0.0105
262144	0.0070	0.0070	0.0072	0.0073	0.0075

Table A.37   Data cache, warm start, line size 16, fully associative, MP 3.

Cache size	Q				
	100	1000	10000	20000	100000
1024	0.2280	0.2133	0.1629	0.1590	0.1558
2048	0.2675	0.1871	0.1317	0.1261	0.1213
4096	0.1984	0.1620	0.1123	0.1047	0.0972
8192	0.1200	0.1248	0.1062	0.1002	0.0906
16384	0.1447	0.1306	0.0970	0.0890	0.0768
32768	0.1056	0.1040	0.0890	0.0810	0.0639
65536	0.0873	0.0863	0.0793	0.0731	0.0580
131072	0.0783	0.0773	0.0721	0.0673	0.0539
262144	0.0770	0.0760	0.0709	0.0659	0.0520

Table A.38 Data cache, warm start, line size 32, fully associative, MP 3.

Cache	Q				
size	100	1000	10000	20000	100000
1024	0.2373	0.1849	0.1540	0.1520	0.1504
2048	0.2259	0.1438	0.0978	0.0940	0.0908
4096	0.1567	0.1206	0.0809	0.0759	0.0713
8192	0.0900	0.0921	0.0751	0.0699	0.0622
16384	0.0942	0.0892	0.0653	0.0590	0.0499
32768	0.0662	0.0683	0.0581	0.0520	0.0398
65536	0.0553	0.0551	0.0504	0.0460	0.0360
131072	0.0407	0.0402	0.0409	0.0395	0.0323
262144	0.0369	0.0364	0.0360	0.0349	0.0292

Table A.39 Data cache, warm start, line size 64, fully associative, MP 3.

Cache	Q				
size	100	1000	10000	20000	100000
1024	0.2382	0.1689	0.1520	0.1510	0.1502
2048	0.2028	0.1186	0.0892	0.0871	0.0854
4096	0.1377	0.0966	0.0622	0.0588	0.0558
8192	0.0849	0.0764	0.0547	0.0491	0.0422
16384	0.0650	0.0629	0.0441	0.0392	0.0331
32768	0.0477	0.0489	0.0388	0.0345	0.0271
65536	0.0324	0.0339	0.0328	0.0300	0.0224
131072	0.0237	0.0244	0.0254	0.0244	0.0194
262144	0.0184	0.0182	0.0188	0.0190	0.0167

Table A.40 Data cache, warm start, line size 128, fully associative, MP 3.

Cache	Q				
size	100	1000	10000	20000	100000
1024	0.2386	0.1796	0.1710	0.1705	0.1701
2048	0.1843	0.1027	0.0843	0.0832	0.0822
4096	0.1270	0.0778	0.0522	0.0501	0.0484
8192	0.0801	0.0652	0.0433	0.0392	0.0347
16384	0.0527	0.0493	0.0322	0.0283	0.0239
32768	0.0346	0.0353	0.0271	0.0234	0.0175
65536	0.0232	0.0242	0.0220	0.0197	0.0145
131072	0.0150	0.0154	0.0163	0.0156	0.0122
262144	0.0108	0.0110	0.0116	0.0116	0.0101

Table A.41   Data cache, warm start, line size 16, fully associative, MP 10.

Cache size	Q				
	100	1000	10000	20000	100000
1024	0.3530	0.2219	0.1630	0.1590	0.1558
2048	0.5507	0.2138	0.1323	0.1263	0.1213
4096	0.5103	0.2067	0.1145	0.1054	0.0972
8192	0.4935	0.1773	0.1104	0.1019	0.0907
16384	0.4606	0.1989	0.1073	0.0939	0.0772
32768	0.3949	0.1906	0.1055	0.0912	0.0657
65536	0.3513	0.1843	0.1039	0.0898	0.0627
131072	0.3258	0.1802	0.1030	0.0890	0.0618
262144	0.3219	0.1795	0.1029	0.0889	0.0615

Table A.42   Data cache, warm start, line size 32, fully associative, MP 10.

Cache size	Q				
	100	1000	10000	20000	100000
1024	0.3044	0.1877	0.1541	0.1520	0.1504
2048	0.3924	0.1556	0.0980	0.0940	0.0908
4096	0.3552	0.1478	0.0819	0.0761	0.0713
8192	0.3054	0.1219	0.0773	0.0707	0.0623
16384	0.3051	0.1391	0.0718	0.0618	0.0501
32768	0.2540	0.1315	0.0700	0.0588	0.0407
65536	0.2266	0.1268	0.0685	0.0575	0.0385
131072	0.1792	0.1168	0.0664	0.0560	0.0373
262144	0.1643	0.1130	0.0656	0.0554	0.0367

Table A.43   Data cache, warm start, line size 64, fully associative, MP 10.

Cache size	Q				
	100	1000	10000	20000	100000
1024	0.2716	0.1697	0.1520	0.1510	0.1502
2048	0.2904	0.1227	0.0892	0.0871	0.0854
4096	0.2589	0.1100	0.0625	0.0588	0.0558
8192	0.1626	0.0952	0.0559	0.0495	0.0422
16384	0.2085	0.1000	0.0480	0.0407	0.0332
32768	0.1809	0.0950	0.0464	0.0383	0.0275
65536	0.1382	0.0863	0.0448	0.0370	0.0237
131072	0.1058	0.0774	0.0428	0.0357	0.0227
262144	0.0838	0.0690	0.0411	0.0344	0.0220

Table A.44 Data cache, warm start, line size 128, fully associative, MP 10.

Cache	Q				
size	100	1000	10000	20000	100000
1024	0.2517	0.1798	0.1710	0.1705	0.1701
2048	0.2263	0.1039	0.0843	0.0832	0.0822
4096	0.2039	0.0835	0.0523	0.0502	0.0484
8192	0.1267	0.0766	0.0439	0.0393	0.0347
16384	0.1533	0.0736	0.0341	0.0290	0.0240
32768	0.1221	0.0673	0.0319	0.0255	0.0176
65536	0.0955	0.0613	0.0305	0.0244	0.0151
131072	0.0640	0.0512	0.0284	0.0231	0.0140
262144	0.0488	0.0435	0.0267	0.0219	0.0135

Table A.45 Instruction cache, warm start, line size 16, fully associative, MP 2.

Cache	Q				
size	100	1000	10000	20000	100000
1024	0.2575	0.2265	0.1988	0.1969	0.1954
2048	0.2115	0.1934	0.1654	0.1628	0.1606
4096	0.1611	0.1452	0.1077	0.1019	0.0965
8192	0.1599	0.1133	0.0922	0.0830	0.0696
16384	0.0658	0.0701	0.0717	0.0688	0.0625
32768	0.0599	0.0594	0.0570	0.0547	0.0461
65536	0.0391	0.0399	0.0418	0.0419	0.0384
131072	0.0301	0.0304	0.0319	0.0328	0.0340
262144		0.0307	0.0310	0.0315	0.0324

Table A.46 Instruction cache, warm start, line size 32, fully associative, MP 2.

Cache	Q				
size	100	1000	10000	20000	100000
1024	0.1947	0.1581	0.1420	0.1410	0.1402
2048	0.1470	0.1200	0.0985	0.0968	0.0954
4096	0.1001	0.0916	0.0694	0.0664	0.0637
8192	0.0948	0.0718	0.0567	0.0510	0.0435
16384	0.0419	0.0447	0.0440	0.0417	0.0374
32768	0.0360	0.0361	0.0344	0.0328	0.0273
65536	0.0235	0.0241	0.0250	0.0248	0.0222
131072	0.0172	0.0174	0.0182	0.0185	0.0187
262144		0.0152	0.0155	0.0158	0.0165

Table A.47 Instruction cache, warm start, line size 64, fully associative, MP 2.

Cache size	Q				
	100	1000	10000	20000	100000
1024	0.1427	0.1099	0.1011	0.1005	0.1001
2048	0.1039	0.0797	0.0669	0.0660	0.0652
4096	0.0692	0.0614	0.0473	0.0457	0.0444
8192	0.0645	0.0488	0.0357	0.0319	0.0273
16384	0.0268	0.0289	0.0277	0.0261	0.0235
32768	0.0229	0.0226	0.0206	0.0192	0.0152
65536	0.0128	0.0132	0.0140	0.0139	0.0123
131072	0.0095	0.0096	0.0100	0.0103	0.0104
262144	0.0085	0.0085	0.0087	0.0087	0.0089

Table A.48 Instruction cache, warm start, line size 128, fully associative, MP 2.

Cache size	Q				
	100	1000	10000	20000	100000
1024	0.1111	0.0852	0.0805	0.0803	0.0801
2048	0.0826	0.0628	0.0559	0.0555	0.0551
4096	0.0556	0.0436	0.0330	0.0320	0.0312
8192	0.0476	0.0355	0.0250	0.0226	0.0201
16384	0.0204	0.0211	0.0182	0.0168	0.0149
32768	0.0146	0.0148	0.0134	0.0123	0.0098
65536	0.0085	0.0088	0.0091	0.0089	0.0075
131072	0.0058	0.0058	0.0061	0.0062	0.0061
262144	0.0046	0.0047	0.0048	0.0049	0.0051

Table A.49 Instruction cache, warm start, line size 16, fully associative, MP 3.

Cache size	Q				
	100	1000	10000	20000	100000
1024	0.3026	0.2291	0.1988	0.1969	0.1954
2048	0.3027	0.2018	0.1655	0.1628	0.1606
4096	0.2221	0.1666	0.1085	0.1021	0.0965
8192	0.1600	0.1374	0.0953	0.0841	0.0697
16384	0.1203	0.1119	0.0787	0.0717	0.0627
32768	0.0786	0.0820	0.0696	0.0619	0.0471
65536	0.0610	0.0632	0.0590	0.0538	0.0411
131072	0.0606	0.0602	0.0543	0.0493	0.0384
262144	0.0632	0.0627	0.0557	0.0501	0.0376

Table A.50   Instruction cache, warm start, line size 32, fully associative, MP 3.

Cache size	Q				
	100	1000	10000	20000	100000
1024	0.2211	0.1591	0.1421	0.1410	0.1402
2048	0.2005	0.1242	0.0986	0.0968	0.0954
4096	0.1466	0.1028	0.0697	0.0665	0.0637
8192	0.0950	0.0843	0.0581	0.0515	0.0435
16384	0.0735	0.0683	0.0476	0.0431	0.0375
32768	0.0475	0.0505	0.0415	0.0366	0.0278
65536	0.0360	0.0375	0.0347	0.0315	0.0236
131072	0.0305	0.0303	0.0294	0.0273	0.0213
262144	0.0299	0.0297	0.0282	0.0261	0.0201

Table A.51   Instruction cache, warm start, line size 64, fully associative, MP 3.

Cache size	Q				
	100	1000	10000	20000	100000
1024	0.1573	0.1103	0.1011	0.1005	0.1001
2048	0.1343	0.0815	0.0669	0.0660	0.0652
4096	0.1000	0.0668	0.0474	0.0458	0.0444
8192	0.0649	0.0558	0.0363	0.0321	0.0273
16384	0.0478	0.0429	0.0295	0.0268	0.0236
32768	0.0274	0.0302	0.0247	0.0213	0.0154
65536	0.0226	0.0223	0.0197	0.0177	0.0130
131072	0.0171	0.0170	0.0165	0.0152	0.0118
262144	0.0150	0.0149	0.0145	0.0137	0.0109

Table A.52   Instruction cache, warm start, line size 128, fully associative, MP 3.

Cache size	Q				
	100	1000	10000	20000	100000
1024	0.1183	0.0854	0.0805	0.0803	0.0801
2048	0.0987	0.0634	0.0559	0.0555	0.0551
4096	0.0753	0.0461	0.0330	0.0320	0.0312
8192	0.0530	0.0402	0.0253	0.0227	0.0201
16384	0.0330	0.0293	0.0191	0.0171	0.0149
32768	0.0201	0.0209	0.0157	0.0134	0.0098
65536	0.0143	0.0142	0.0124	0.0111	0.0079
131072	0.0093	0.0095	0.0096	0.0090	0.0069
262144	0.0086	0.0086	0.0084	0.0080	0.0063

Table A.53   Instruction cache, warm start, line size 16, fully associative, MP 10.

Cache	Q				
size	100	1000	10000	20000	100000
1024	0.3654	0.2313	0.1988	0.1969	0.1954
2048	0.4486	0.2098	0.1657	0.1629	0.1606
4096	0.4088	0.1893	0.1092	0.1023	0.0965
8192	0.3130	0.1705	0.0980	0.0851	0.0697
16384	0.3555	0.1759	0.0862	0.0745	0.0628
32768	0.2947	0.1649	0.0834	0.0691	0.0479
65536	0.2514	0.1557	0.0809	0.0672	0.0438
131072	0.2513	0.1557	0.0805	0.0666	0.0431
262144	0.2584	0.1573	0.0808	0.0668	0.0431

Table A.54   Instruction cache, warm start, line size 32, fully associative, MP 10.

Cache	Q				
size	100	1000	10000	20000	100000
1024	0.2535	0.1599	0.1421	0.1410	0.1402
2048	0.2872	0.1280	0.0987	0.0968	0.0954
4096	0.2626	0.1147	0.0700	0.0666	0.0637
8192	0.1763	0.1020	0.0593	0.0519	0.0436
16384	0.2194	0.1052	0.0513	0.0444	0.0376
32768	0.1797	0.0983	0.0491	0.0404	0.0281
65536	0.1469	0.0915	0.0475	0.0390	0.0249
131072	0.1328	0.0881	0.0465	0.0382	0.0242
262144	0.1309	0.0876	0.0464	0.0381	0.0240

Table A.55   Instruction cache, warm start, line size 64, fully associative, MP 10.

Cache	Q				
size	100	1000	10000	20000	100000
1024	0.1736	0.1106	0.1011	0.1005	0.1001
2048	0.1801	0.0830	0.0669	0.0660	0.0652
4096	0.1662	0.0722	0.0475	0.0458	0.0444
8192	0.1052	0.0651	0.0369	0.0322	0.0273
16384	0.1358	0.0648	0.0313	0.0274	0.0236
32768	0.1023	0.0588	0.0291	0.0234	0.0156
65536	0.0826	0.0541	0.0279	0.0224	0.0137
131072	0.0755	0.0522	0.0272	0.0218	0.0133
262144	0.0670	0.0495	0.0267	0.0215	0.0131

Table A.56 Instruction cache, warm start, line size 128, fully associative, MP 10.

Cache size	Q				
	100	1000	10000	20000	100000
1024	0.1257	0.0855	0.0806	0.0803	0.0801
2048	0.1198	0.0639	0.0559	0.0555	0.0551
4096	0.1107	0.0485	0.0331	0.0320	0.0312
8192	0.0769	0.0457	0.0255	0.0228	0.0201
16384	0.0872	0.0421	0.0199	0.0173	0.0149
32768	0.0674	0.0382	0.0181	0.0144	0.0099
65536	0.0507	0.0340	0.0172	0.0136	0.0082
131072	0.0418	0.0313	0.0164	0.0131	0.0078
262144	0.0389	0.0302	0.0162	0.0129	0.0076

Appendix B

SPECmark vs. DTMR Cache Performance

Figure B.1 compares the DTMR miss rate with the actual miss rate derived from the SPECMARKII benchmark suite [98]. Note the consistently lower miss rate estimated from the SPECMARKII.

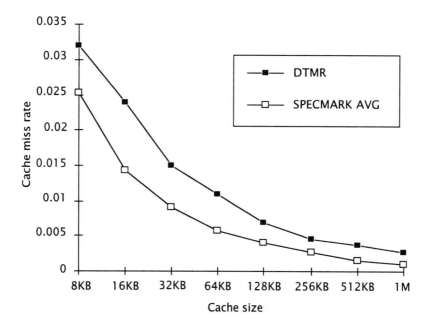

Figure B.1   Comparing DTMR and SPECMARK cache miss ratios.

DTMR versus SPECMARKII Cache Miss Rate

Unified Cache
Line Size = 64
Associativity = 8
(SPECMARKII results are the average of the benchmarks.)

Appendix C

Modeling System Effects in Caches

C.1 Cold Start Cache

Our miss rates for cold start caches are computed from a stochastic model based on Haikala's work [116, 117]. Haikala's basic model assumes fully-associative LRU caches. An application program always starts with a cold-start cache and runs for a geometric distributed interval of an average of Q memory references before task switches. The entire cache is flushed at task switch. Cache behavior is modeled as a Markov chain. For a cache of n lines, the Markov chain has $n+1$ states: $S_0, \ldots, S_n$ (Figure C.1). The cache is said to be in the state S_i when it contains only i valid lines. The probability that a task switch occurs before the next memory reference is e. If there is no task switch and the next memory reference is a cache hit, the cache remains in the same state. Otherwise a cache miss occurs and a new line is brought into the cache. The cache state then changes from S_i to S_{i+1} unless the cache state is already in S_n. When a cache is in S_n, it remains there until task switch. Since the cache is fully associative and uses LRU replacement, the probability that the next memory reference is a cache miss is the same as the miss rate of a warm-start cache of i lines, MR_i^{warm}. By solving the stationary state probabilities of the Markov chain, $P_0, \ldots, P_n$, the cache miss rate MR_n can be determined from the following equations:

$$P_0 = e$$

$$P_i = P_{i-1} * \frac{1 - H_{i-1} - e}{1 - H_i} \qquad \text{for } i > 0$$

$$MR_n = \sum_{i=1}^{n} MR_i^{\text{warm}} * P_i$$

Haikala has shown that miss rates calculated from the preceding Markov chain model are at most 12% off simulation results.

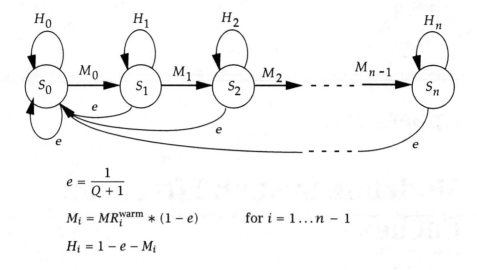

$$e = \frac{1}{Q+1}$$

$$M_i = MR_i^{\text{warm}} * (1 - e) \qquad \text{for } i = 1 \ldots n - 1$$

$$H_i = 1 - e - M_i$$

Figure C.1   The Markov chain cold-start cache model.

We adopt Haikala's basic model to compute cold start misses for different task switch intervals. In our computation, the warm-start cache miss rates are determined from DTMR.

C.2   Cache Misses in Multiprogramming Environment

We extend the stochastic cold-start cache model to compute cache miss rates in multiprogramming environment. If needed, fully associative LRU caches are assumed. All multiprogramming programs' cache behaviors are assumed statistically the same and have DTMR as their warm-start cache miss rates. Similar to the cold-start cache modeling, each program runs for a geometric distributed interval of an average of Q memory references before task switches to other program. However, cache is not flushed at task switch. Next time when the program is scheduled to resume execution, some valid memory lines (known as foot prints) may remain in the cache.

We model the multiprogramming effect by a two-dimensional Markov chain. For a cache of n lines, the Markov chain has $2n$ states (Figure C.2). Besides the n states (S_0, ..., S_n) as defined in the cold-start cache model, n new states (X_0, ..., X_n) are introduced to model the effect of other programs on the cache. When other programs are running and the cache still contains i valid lines, the cache is said in the state X_i. All other programs can be viewed just as another program (the equivalent program) and the cache behaves as if it contains $n - i$ lines for the equivalent program. For a multiprogramming level of N, other programs (so is the equivalent program) will run for an interval of an average of $(N - 1) * Q$ memory references before task switches back to the program. When the program resumes execution,

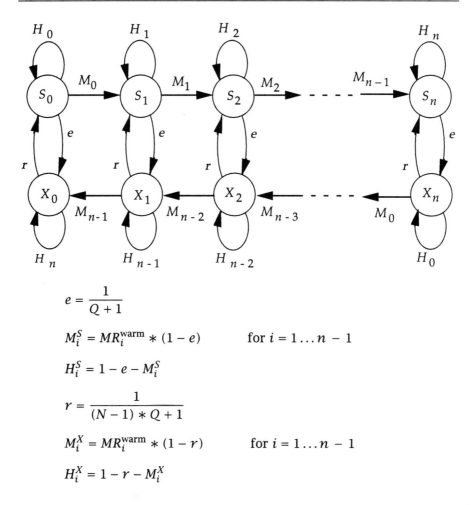

$$e = \frac{1}{Q+1}$$

$$M_i^S = MR_i^{\mathrm{warm}} * (1 - e) \qquad \text{for } i = 1 \ldots n - 1$$

$$H_i^S = 1 - e - M_i^S$$

$$r = \frac{1}{(N-1) * Q + 1}$$

$$M_i^X = MR_i^{\mathrm{warm}} * (1 - r) \qquad \text{for } i = 1 \ldots n - 1$$

$$H_i^X = 1 - r - M_i^X$$

Figure C.2   The Markov chain for modeling multiprogramming effect.

the cache state changes from its current state, say, X_i to S_i. After solving the stationary state probabilities of the two-dimensional Markov chain, cache miss rates can be computed from the following equation:

$$MR_n = \frac{\sum_{i=1}^{n} MR_i^{\mathrm{warm}} * P_i^S}{\sum_{i=1}^{n} P_i^S}.$$

Appendix D

New DRAM Technologies

Here we review recent advances in DRAM technology and summarize by both chip level and system level comparisons. Data abstracted from Przybylski [238].

Throughout the past two decades, various trends in memory designs have become apparent.

- DRAM size has quadrupled every 3 years. (60% growth per year.)

- Little change in the interface design resulted in low bandwidth growth.

- Row access time has decreased aproximately 7% every year.

- Column access has decreased approximately 25% every year.

- Processor demand on memory has increased despite heavy use of cache.

- Bandwidth per bit has declined 25% per year.

The above data lead to a critical problem—the need to increase the bandwidth per bit. With this need in mind, new architectures, whether evolutionary or revolutionary, have been designed to deal with the bandwidth problem.

D.1 Typical Performance Enhancements

- Use of block transfers. Basically, once a row has been fetched into the sense amps, the entire row is available for column access. As a result, the sense amps can be used as a cache to hold an entire row of data.

- Use of page mode (static column mode).

- Use of newer packages provides better pin-out density and electrical properties.

- Use of low voltage electrical interfaces.

- Use of synchronized interface.

- Use of new bus or ring interfaces.

D.2   Enhanced DRAM

Enhanced DRAM incorporates operational changes to the standard data bus and a multiplexed address bus controlled by RAS and CAS to increase the operating frequencies, and cycle by cycle efficiency of the standard interface. Particular attention has also been given to improve the performance of the row cache. EDRAMs provide fast access times and through intelligent design, hide precharge time during burst transfers. It is also designed so that writes do not need to disturb the row cache, and the interface is available prior to the actual completion of the DRAM write. The problems with EDRAMs are the limited number of suppliers, TTL signaling levels, and asynchronous interface.

D.3   Synchronous DRAM

Synchronous DRAMs are DRAM that conforms to the EIA/JEDEC JC42.3 DRAM standard. SDRAM retains the multiplexed address bus, but adds a high speed clock to synchronize all the required operations. For synchronous DRAMs, all timing is specified in terms of cycles of the chip operating frequencies instead of the delays (ns) in conventional DRAMs. SDRAM also employs a two bank scheme to improve the sustained bandwidth. The two bank scheme incorporates pipelining and alternates between the two banks to enhance the access time.

D.4   Cache DRAM

The secondary cache (SRAM) is placed on the DRAM ICs. Therefore, CDRAM is a DRAM with a small embedded SRAM. As a result, CDRAMs can be very fast with a cycle time of 10ns. CDRAMs can provide high peak bandwidth, since some overlapping of SRAM and DRAM operations can occur. CDRAM also provides a low latency access without the high cost of a discrete secondary cache. However, incorporating a cache greatly complicates the tasks of the memory controller.

D.5   Rambus DRAM

Rambus is a small company founded in 1989 to develop a new high bandwidth DRAM interface. Their design abandons the conventional pin-level interface: separate data bus and multiplexed address bus. A single byte-serial bus transfers control, addresses, as well as data. Rambus specifies both physical (wire length) and electrical characteristics of the interface so that incorporation into a system requires conformance to their new interfaces. Rambus has the following features:

- 500MB/sec per channel.
- Vertically mounted DRAMs.
- Physically constrained bidirectional bus.
- Reduced voltage swing.
- Synchronous design.
- Dual bank row-caching.

Some of the advantages of Rambus DRAMs are high bandwidth with small number of chips, large row caches, and good match for frame buffer design. Some of the disadvantages of Rambus DRAMs are its high latency, need to incorporate proprietory macros for bus interface, and the byte serial to word parallel conversion delay.

D.6   Ramlink DRAM

Ramlink is a standard developed by the IEEE Computer Society. The working group applied the techniques adopted in Scalable Coherent Interface (SCI) to develop a ring-topology interconnect memory device. Ramlink also used a high speed byte-wide bus, as in the case of RAMBUS. However, instead of a single short bus, Ramlink uses a ring topology with point-to-point links. As in RAMBUS, Ramlink also has maximum bandwidth of 500MB/s interfaces. The advantage of Ramlink is that it is non-proprietory with a general interconnect. It does not have a physically constrained interconnect bus structure. The disadvantages are longer latency access and lack of availability.

D.7   Chip Level Summary

TTL voltage levels are logic 0 for 0.8 volt or below, and logic 1 for 2.0 volts or above. Low voltage TTL (LVTTL) changes the maximum input voltage requirement. Rambus Signalling logic (RSL) specifies a 600mv swing centered at 2.2 volt. Low-voltage differential signalling (LVDS) specifies a 250mv differential swing centered anywhere between 0 and 2v.

Table D.1 Chip Level Comparisons

	EDRAM	SDRAM	CDRAM	RDRAM	RAMLINK
Vendor	Nippon Steel	NEC,Samsung Mitsubishi	Mitsubishi Samsung	Toshiba NEC Fujitsu	None
Pin-Level Interface	Enhanced Asynchronous RAS/CAS	Synchronous RAS/CAS	Synchronous RAS/CAS and SRAM address	High-Speed Synchronous 9-bit bus	High-Speed Synchronous 8/9 bit ring
Package[a]	28 SOJ	50 TSOP	44 TSOP	32 SVP	unspecified
Size	4Mb	16Mb	4Mb	4Mb	unspecified
Organization	x1,x4	x4, x8,x9 x16, x18	x4,x16	x9	unspecified
Row-Cache	1 row x 2kb	1row x 4kb	256 x 64	2 row x 9kb	unspecified
Row Access Time	35 ns	70 ns	70 ns	152 ns	unspecified
Row Cache Access Time	15 ns	30 ns	10 ns	36 ns	unspecified
Peak Per-Pin Bandwidth	66Mb/s	100Mb/s	500Mb/s	500Mb/s	
Peak Device Bandwidth	264Mb/s	800Mb/s	500Mb/s	4.5Gb/s	4.5Gb/s
Supply Voltage	5v	3.3v	5v,3.3v	5v	unspecified
Interface Voltage	TTL	LVTTL	TTL, LVTTL	RSL	LVDS

[a]Packaging terms: SOJ—small-outline J-lead package. TSOP—thin, small-outline package. SVP—surface vertical package.

Appendix E

$M/G/1$ **Queues**

The derivation of the $M/G/1$ is generally straightforward, but somewhat distracting in the context of chapter 6. We present a (somewhat) informal derivation here, originally based on the work of Kendall [160]. There are many variations of the derivation, e.g. [166, 169]. We follow a simplified derivation from Goode and Machol [106]. We define the following random variables:

$$
\begin{aligned}
t_i &= \text{Time between successive arrivals } i \text{ and } i - 1 \\
r_i &= \text{Number of arrivals during a time interval } t_i \\
n_i &= \text{Queue length, including item in service at the end of } t_i
\end{aligned}
$$

We write the expection (mean) of each of the preceding as $E(t_i) = E(t)$, $E(r_i) = E(r)$, $E(n_i) = E(n)$. Also recall that

$$
\begin{aligned}
T &= E(t) = \text{Service time} = \frac{1}{\mu} \\
N &= \text{Mean queue length} = \text{Expected value of } n_i = E(n).
\end{aligned}
$$

The derivation assumes that $\rho < 1$ and that the process is stationary—i.e., statistically invariant over time. For our purposes, this means

$$
\frac{dp(n)}{dt} = 0,
$$

where $p(n)$ is the probability of a queue size of n. Thus, $E(n)$ is not a function of time ($E(n_1) = E(n_2)$).

The requirement that $\rho < 1$ is a necessary result of stationarity. If $\rho > 1$, the queue size would grow as a function of time.

Now consider items $C_1, C_2 \ldots$ awaiting service at the moment that item C_0 completes service. We designate the queue length (including the item in service) after C_0 leaves as n_0. Suppose it takes time T_1 for the next item (C_1) to be served. The number of items that arrive when C_1 is being served is r_1. When C_1 completes service and departs, the queue length will be n_1. Now

$$
n_1 = n_0 + r_1 - 1.
$$

This assumes that $n_0 \neq 0$ and hence C_1 actually enters and leaves the server. If $n_0 = 0$ then

$$n_1 = n_0 + r_1 \qquad (n_0 = 0),$$

as no item entered or left the server. We combine these as

$$n_1 \quad = \quad n_0 + r_1 - 1 + \delta_0, \tag{E.1}$$

where δ_0 is the probability that $n_0 = 0$. δ_0 has only two values: $\delta_0 = 0$ when $n_0 \neq 0$ and $\delta_0 = 1$ when $n_0 = 1$, so that $n_0 \delta_0 = 0$ and $\delta_0^2 = \delta_0$. Now find $E(\delta)$, which lies between 0 and 1:

$$
\begin{aligned}
E(n_i) &= E(n_0) + E(r_i) - 1 + E(\delta_0) &\tag{E.2}\\
E(\delta) &= E(\delta_0) = 1 - E(r_1) = 1 - E(r) \\
\text{and } E(n_1) &= E(n_0) = E(n)
\end{aligned}
$$

by the stationarity assumption.

Now $E(r)$ is the expected number of arrivals during a service time; i.e.,

$$E(r) = \lambda E(t) = \frac{\lambda}{\mu} = \rho,$$

so that

$$E(\delta) = 1 - \rho.$$

The expectation that the server is idle, $E(\delta)$, is

$$
\begin{aligned}
E(\delta) &= \quad \text{Prob}\,(n = 0) = 1 - \rho \quad \text{and} \\
\text{Prob}\,(n > 0) &= \quad \rho.
\end{aligned}
$$

Now suppose we generalize equation E.1 for time intervals i and $i - 1$ and we square both sides of equation E.1.

$$n_i^2 = n_{i-1}^2 + (r_i - 1)^2 + \delta_{i-1} + 2n_{i-1}(r_i - 1) + 2\delta_{i-1}(r_i - 1).$$

Taking the expcted value of both sides,

$$
\begin{aligned}
E(n_i^2) &= \quad E(n_{i-1}^2) + E((r_i - 1)^2) + E(\delta_{i-1}) + E((2n_{i-1}(r_i - 1)) \\
&\quad + E(2\delta_{i-1}(r_i - 1)),
\end{aligned}
$$

again by stationary $E(n_i^2) = E(n_{i-1}^2)$. Also, since $n_{i-1}, r_i, \delta_{i-1}$ are independent and $E(r_i) = E(r)$, etc., we have

$$0 = E((r - 1)^2) + E(\delta) + 2E(n)E(r - 1) + 2E(\delta)E(r - 1).$$

Now, since $E(r) = \rho, E(\delta) = 1 - \rho, E(n_0) = E(n)$, we have

$$
\begin{aligned}
0 &= \quad E(r^2) - 2\rho + 1 + 1 - \rho + 2E(n)(\rho - 1) + 2(1 - \rho)(\rho - 1) \\
2E(n)(1 - \rho) &= \quad E(r^2) - 3\rho + 2 + 2[-\rho^2 + 2\rho - 1] \\
&= \quad E(r^2) - 2\rho^2 + \rho \\
E(n) &= \quad \frac{E(r^2) - 2\rho^2 + \rho}{2(1 - \rho)}
\end{aligned}
$$

so that

$$N = E(n) = \rho + \frac{E(r)^2 - \rho}{2(1 - \rho)}. \tag{E.3}$$

The equation E.3 is valid for an arbitrary arrival time distribution (i.e., $G/G/1$).

Suppose we now assume a Poisson type arrival distribution; then from chapter 6, section 6.4.1:

$$P(k) = \frac{(\lambda T)^k}{k!} \epsilon^{-\lambda T}$$
$$P(r_i) = \frac{(\lambda T)^{r_i}}{r_i!} \epsilon^{-\lambda T_i},$$

where r_i is the number of arrivals during T_i. The mean of this distribution is $E(r_i) = \lambda T_i$ and the variance $(\sigma_{r_i}^2)$ is also λT_i. From probability theory,

$$\sigma_{r_i}^2 = E(r_i^2) - |E(r_i)|^2$$
$$E(r_i^2) = \sigma_{r_i}^2 + |E(r_i)|^2.$$

Taking the expectation over all i,

$$E(r^2) = \lambda E(T) + \lambda^2 E(T^2).$$

But, from probability theory (σ_T^2 is the variance of T_i):

$$E(T^2) = \sigma_T^2 + |E(T)|^2 = \sigma_T^2 + \frac{1}{\mu^2}.$$

Then

$$E(r^2) = \frac{\lambda}{\mu} + \lambda^2(\sigma_T^2 + \frac{1}{\mu^2}) = \rho + \lambda^2\sigma_T^2 + \rho^2$$

and substituting into equation E.3:

$$\begin{aligned}
N = E(n) &= \rho + \frac{\rho^2 + \lambda^2\sigma_T^2}{2(1 - \rho)} \tag{E.4}\\
&= \rho + \frac{\rho^2(1 + (\lambda^2\sigma_T^2/\rho^2))}{2(1 - \rho)}\\
&= \rho + \frac{\rho^2(1 + \mu^2\sigma_T^2)}{2(1 - \rho)}.
\end{aligned}$$

Since the coeficient of service variance $c^2 = \mu^2\sigma_T^2$,

$$N = \rho + \frac{\rho^2(1 + c^2)}{2(1 - \rho)}. \tag{E.5}$$

Little's result applied to equation E.5 gives the $M/G/1$ form for T_w as used in chapter 6.

Appendix F

Some Details on Bus-Based Protocols

The following tables present further details on the bus and CPU actions that are to be taken for each type of CPU memory action in order to ensure memory coherency. We include the Synapse protocol, not covered in chapter 8. This has also been widely discussed in the literature.

The protocols presented are:

1. Write-invalidate [107].

2. Synapse [95].

3. Illinois [225].

4. Berkeley [157].

5. Firefly [21].

6. Dragon [191].

Table F.1   Write-invalidate CPU actions.

State	Read Hit	Write Hit	Read Miss	Write Miss
Invalid	N/A	N/A	Issue bus read. Next state = Valid.	Issue bus write miss. Next state = Dirty.
Valid	Supply data to processor. Next state = Valid.	Issue bus invalidation. Write data. Next state = Dirty.	Issue bus read. Next state = Valid.	Issue bus write miss. Next state = Dirty.
Dirty	Supply data to processor. Next state = Dirty.	Write data, no delay. Next state = Dirty.	Write old line to memory. Issue bus read. Next state = Valid.	Write old line back to memory. Issue bus write miss. Next state = Dirty.

Table F.2   Write-invalidate bus actions.

State	Bus Read	Bus Write Miss	Bus Invalidation
Invalid	No Action	No Action	No Action
Valid	No Action.	Supply data from memory. Next state = Invalid.	Next state = Invalid.
Dirty	Supply data and update memory. Next state = Valid.	Supply data and update memory. Next state = Invalid.	N/A

Table F.3   Synapse CPU actions.

State	Read hit	Write hit	Read miss	Write miss
Invalid	—	—	Submit request to read line from main memory. If cache receives a negative acknowledge, resubmit the request. Next state = Valid.	Submit bus write miss request. If the cache receives a negative acknowledge, resubmit the request. Next state = Dirty.
Valid	Supply data to processor. Next state = Valid.	Submit bus write miss request. If the cache receives a neg. acknowledge, resubmit the request. Next state = Dirty.	Submit request to read line from main memory. If cache receives a negative acknowledge, resubmit the request. Next state = Valid.	Submit bus write miss request. If the cache receives a negative acknowledge, resubmit the request. Next state = Dirty.
Dirty	Supply data to processor. Next state = Dirty.	Supply data to processor. Next state = Dirty.	Write old line back to memory. Submit request to read line from main memory. If cache receives a negative acknowledge, resubmit the request. Next state = Valid.	Write old line back to memory. If cache receives a negative acknowledge, resubmit the request. Next state = Dirty.

Table F.4   Synapse bus actions.

State	Bus Read	Bus Write Miss
Invalid	No action.	No action.
Valid	No action.	Next state = Invalid.
Dirty	Write data back to main memory, send negative acknowledge. Next state = Invalid.	Write data back to main memory, send negative acknowledge. Next state = Invalid.

Table F.5   Illinois CPU actions.

State	Read Hit	Write Hit	Read Miss	Write Miss
Invalid	N/A	N/A	Issue bus read. If data is from memory, next state = Valid-Exclusive; otherwise next state = Shared.	Issue bus write miss. Write data to cache. Next state = Dirty.
Valid-Exclusive	Supply data to processor. Next state = Valid-Exclusive.	Write, no delay. Next state = Dirty.	Issue bus read. If data is from memory, next state = Valid-Exclusive; otherwise next state = Shared.	Issue bus write miss. Write data to cache. Next state = Dirty.
Shared	Supply data to processor. Next state = Shared.	Issue bus invalidation. Write data. Next state = Dirty.	Issue bus read. If data is from memory, next state = Valid-Exclusive; otherwise next state = Shared.	Issue bus write miss. Write data to cache. Next state = Dirty.
Dirty	Supply data to processor. Next state = Dirty.	Write, no delay. Next state = Dirty.	Write old line to memory. Issue bus read. If data is from memory, next state = Valid-Exclusive; otherwise next state = Shared.	Write old line back to memory. Issue bus write miss. Write data to cache. Next state = Dirty.

Table F.6   Illinois bus actions.

State	Bus Read	Bus Write Miss	Bus Invalidation
Invalid	No Action	No Action	No Action
Valid-Exclusive	Supply data. Next state = Shared.	Supply data. Next state = Invalid.	N/A
Shared	If highest priority, supply data. Next state = Shared.	If highest priority, supply data. Next state = Invalid.	Next state = Invalid.
Dirty	Supply data and update memory. Next state = Shared.	Supply data. Next state = Invalid.	N/A

Table F.7 Berkeley CPU actions.

State	Read Hit	Write Hit	Read Miss	Write Miss
Invalid	N/A	N/A	Issue bus read. Next state = Valid.	Issue bus write miss. Write data to cache. Next state = Dirty.
Valid	Supply data to processor. Next state = Valid.	Issue bus invalidation. Write data to cache. Next state = Dirty.	Issue bus read. Next state = Valid.	Issue bus write miss. Write data to cache. Next state = Dirty.
Shared-Dirty	Supply data to processor. Next state = Shared-Dirty.	Issue bus invalidation. Write data. Next state = Dirty.	Write old line to memory. Issue bus read. Next state = Valid.	Write old line to memory. Issue bus write miss. Write data to cache. Next state = Dirty.
Dirty	Supply data to processor. Next state = Dirty.	Write, no delay. Next state = Dirty.	Write old line to memory. Issue bus read. Next state = Valid.	Write old line to memory. Issue bus write miss. Write data to cache. Next state = Dirty.

Table F.8 Berkeley bus actions.

State	Bus Read	Bus Write Miss	Bus Invalidation
Invalid	No Action	No Action	No Action
Valid	No Action.	Next state = Invalid	Next state = Invalid
Shared-Dirty	Supply data. Next state = Shared-Dirty	Supply data. Next state = Invalid	Next state = Invalid
Dirty	Supply data. Next state = Shared-Dirty	Supply data. Next state = Invalid	N/A

Table F.9 Firefly CPU actions.

State	Read Hit	Write Hit	Read Miss	Write Miss
Invalid	N/A	N/A	Issue bus read. If data is from memory, next state = Valid-Exclusive, otherwise next state = Shared.	Issue bus write miss. Write data to cache. If data is from memory, next state = Dirty; otherwise next state = Shared and write data to memory. and other caches sharing it.
Valid-Exclusive (or Read Private)	Supply data to processor. Next state = Valid-Exclusive.	Write data, no delay. Next state = Dirty.	Issue bus read. If data is from memory, next state = Valid-Exclusive; otherwise next state = Shared.	Issue bus write miss. Write data to cache. If data is from memory, next state = Dirty; otherwise next state = Shared and write data to memory and other caches sharing it.
Shared	Supply data to processor. Next state = Shared.	Write data to mem. and other caches. If no other caches Shared, next state = Valid-Exclusive, otherwise next state = Shared.	Issue bus read. If data is from memory, next state = Valid-Exclusive, otherwise next state = Shared.	Issue bus write miss. Write data to cache. If data is from memory, next state = Dirty, otherwise next state = Shared and write data to memory and other caches sharing it.
Dirty	Supply data to processor. Next state = Dirty.	Write data, no delay. Next state = Dirty.	Write old line to memory. Issue bus read. If data is from memory, next state = Valid-Exclusive; otherwise next state = Shared.	Write old line to memory. Issue bus write miss. Write data to cache. If data is from memory, next state = Dirty; otherwise next state = Shared and write data to memory and other caches sharing it.

Table F.10   Firefly bus actions.

State	Bus Read	Bus Write Miss	Bus Write
Invalid	No Action	No Action	No Action
Valid-Exclusive	Supply data on bus. Next state = Shared.	Supply data on bus and get updated. Next state = Shared.	N/A
Shared	Supply data on bus. Next state = Shared.	Supply data on bus and get updated. Next state = Shared.	Get updated. Next state = Shared.
Dirty	Supply data (and update memory). Next state = Shared.	Supply data (and update memory) and get updated. Next state = Shared.	N/A

Table F.11　Dragon CPU actions.

State	Read Hit	Write Hit	Read Miss	Write Miss
Invalid	N/A	N/A	Issue bus read. If shared, next state = Shared-Clean; otherwise next state = Valid-Exclusive.	Issue bus write miss. Write data to cache. If shared[a], next state = Shared-Dirty, issue bus write[b]; otherwise next state = Dirty.
Valid-Exclusive (or Read Private)	Supply data to processor. Next state = Valid-Exclusive.	Write data to cache. Next state = Dirty.	Issue bus read. If shared, next state = Shared-Clean; otherwise next state = Valid-Exclusive.	Issue bus write miss. Write data to cache. If shared, next state = Shared-Dirty, issue bus write; otherwise next state = Dirty.
Shared-Clean	Supply data to processor. Next state = Shared-Clean.	Issue bus write. If shared, Next state = Shared-Dirty; otherwise next state = Dirty.	Issue bus read. If shared, next state = Shared-Clean; otherwise next state = Valid-Exclusive.	Issue bus write miss. Write data to cache. If shared, next state = Shared-Dirty, issue bus write; otherwise next state = Dirty.
Shared-Dirty	Supply data to processor. Next state = Shared-Dirty.	Issue bus write. If shared, next state = Shared-Dirty; otherwise next state = Dirty.	Write old line to memory. Issue bus read. If shared, next state = Shared-Clean; otherwise next state = Valid-Exclusive.	Write old line to memory. Issue bus write miss. Write data to cache. If shared, issue bus write, next state = Shared-Dirty; otherwise next state = Dirty.
Dirty	Supply data to processor. Next state = Dirty.	Write, no delay. Next state = Dirty.	Write old line to memory. Issue bus read. If shared, next state = Shared-Clean; otherwise next state = Valid-Exclusive.	Write old line to memory. Issue bus write miss. Write data to cache. If shared, issue bus write, next state = Shared-Dirty; otherwise next state = Dirty.

[a]i.e., if any other cache has the data.
[b]This updates all other caches sharing it.

Table F.12   Dragon bus actions.

State	Bus Read	Bus Write Miss	Bus Write
Invalid	No Action	No Action	No Action
Valid-Exclusive	Next state = Shared-Clean.	Get updated. Next state = Shared-Clean.	N/A
Shared-Clean	Next state = Shared-Clean.	Get updated. Next state = Shared-Clean.	Get updated from bus. Next state = Shared-Clean.
Shared-Dirty	Supply data. Next state = Shared-Dirty.	Supply data. Get updated. Next state = Shared-Clean.	Get updated from bus. Next state = Shared-Clean.
Dirty	Supply data. Next state = Shared-Dirty.	Supply data. Get updated. Next state = Shared-Clean.	N/A

Bibliography

[1] S. Abraham and K. Padmanabhan. Performance of direct binary n-cube networks for multiprocessors. *IEEE Transactions on Computers*, 38(7):1000–1111, July 1989.

[2] R. D. Acosta, J. Kjelstrup, and H. C. Torng. An instruction issuing approach to enhancing performance in multiple functional unit processors. *IEEE Transactions on Computers*, C-35:815–828, September 1986.

[3] S. V. Adve and M. D. Hill. Weak ordering—a new definition. In *Proceedings of the 17th International Symposium on Computer Architecture*, pages 2–14, 1990.

[4] A. Agarwal. *Analysis of Cache Performance of Operating Systems and Multiprogramming*. PhD thesis, Computer Systems Laboratory, Stanford University, May 1987. Published as CSL-TR-87-332.

[5] A. Agarwal. Performance tradeoffs in multithreaded processors. VLSI Memo 89-566, MIT Laboratory for Computer Science, September 1989.

[6] A. Agarwal. Limits on interconnection network performance. *Transactions on Parallel and Distributed Systems*, 2(4):398–412, October 1991.

[7] A. Agarwal, P. Chow, M. Horowitz, J. Acken, A. Salz, and J. Hennessy. On-chip instruction caches for high performance processors. *Advanced Research in VLSI, Proceedings of the 1987 Stanford Conference*, pages 1–24, 1987.

[8] A. Agarwal, J. Hennessy, and M. Horowitz. Cache performance of operating system and multiprogramming workloads. *ACM Transactions on Computer Systems*, 6(4):393–431, November 1988.

[9] A. Agarwal, B. Lim, and D. Kranz. APRIL: A processor architecture for multiprocessing. In *Proceedings of the 17th International Symposium on Computer Architecture*, pages 104–114, 1990.

[10] A. Agarwal, R. Simoni, M. Horowitz, and J. Hennessy. An evaluation of directory schemes for cache coherence. In *Proceedings of the 15th International Symposium on Computer Architecture*, 1988.

[11] C. Alexander, W. Keshlear, and F. Cooper. Cache memory performance in a Unix environment. *Computer Architecture News*, 14(3):41–70, June 1986.

[12] K. Alnaes, E. Kristiansen, D. Gustavson, and D. James. Scalable coherent interface. In *Proceedings of the IEEE International Conference on Computer Systems and Software Engineering*, Tel Aviv, 1990.

[13] D. Alpert, D. Carberry, M. Yamamura, Y. Chow, and P. Mak. A 32-bit processor chip integrates major system functions. *Electronics*, pages 113–119, July 14 1983.

[14] G. Amdahl. Validity of single processor approach to achieving large scale computing capabilities. In *Proceedings of the Spring Joint Computer Conference*, pages 483–485. AFIPS, April 1967.

[15] G. M. Amdahl. The structure of System/360, Part III: Processing design unit design considerations. *IBM Systems Journal*, 3(2):144–164, 1964.

[16] G. M. Amdahl, G. A. Blaauw, and F. P. Brooks, Jr. Architecture of the IBM System/360. *IBM Journal of Research and Development*, 8(2):87–101, April 1964.

[17] D. W. Anderson, F. J. Sparacio, and R. M. Tomasulo. The IBM System/360 model 91: Machine philosophy and instruction-handling. *IBM Journal of Research and Development*, 11(1):8–24, 1967.

[18] S. F. Anderson, J. G. Earle, R. E. Goldschmidt, and D. M. Powers. The IBM System/360 model 91 floating-point execution unit. *IBM Journal of Research and Development*, 11(1):34–53, January 1967.

[19] T. E. Anderson. The performance of spin lock alternatives for shared-memory multiprocessors. *IEEE Transactions on Parallel and Distributed Systems*, 1(1):6–16, January 1990.

[20] T. E. Anderson, H. M. Levy, B. N. Bershad, and E. D. Lazowska. The interaction of architecture and operating system design. In D. Patterson, editor, *ASPLOS-IV Proceedings*, pages 108–120, Santa Clara, CA, April 1991. ACM.

[21] J. Archibald and J.-L. Baer. Cache coherence protocols: Evaluation using a multiprocessor simulation model. *ACM Transactions on Computer Systems*, 6(4):273–298, November 1986.

[22] J.-L. Baer and W.-H. Wang. Architectural choices for multi-level cache hierarchies. *Proceedings of the 1987 International Conference on Parallel Processing*, pages 258–261, 1987.

[23] J.-L. Baer and W.-H. Wang. On the inclusion properties for multi-level cache hierarchies. In *Proceedings of the 15th Annual International Symposium on Computer Architecture*, pages 73–80, May 1988.

[24] D. H. Bailey. A high-performance fast Fourier transform algorithm for the Cray-2. *Journal of Supercomputing*, 1(1):43–60, 1987.

[25] L. Balady and C. Kuehner. Dynamic space sharing in computer systems. *Communications of the ACM*, 12(5), May 1969.

[26] G. Baldwin. Towards an assembly language standard. *IEEE Micro*, August 1984. IEEE P694 Working Group.

[27] U. Banerjee. *Dependence Analysis for Supercomputing*. Kluwer Academic Publishers, Norwell, MA, 1988.

[28] R. Barton. A new approach to the functional design of a digital computer. In *Proceedings of the Western Joint Computer Conference*, pages 393–396. AFIPS, 1961.

[29] F. Baskett and A. J. Smith. Interference in multiprocessor computer systems with interleaved memory. *Communications of the ACM*, 19(6):327–334, June 1976.

[30] C. G. Bell, R. Cady, H. McFarland, B. Delagi, J. O'Loughlin, R. Noonan, and W. Wulf. A new architecture for mini-computers: The DEC PDP-11. In *Proceedings of AFIPS SJCC*, volume 36, pages 657–675, 1970.

[31] C. G. Bell, J. C. Mudge, and J. E. McNamara. *Computer Engineering*, chapter 17: VAX-11/780, William D. Strecker. Digital Press, 1978.

[32] C. G. Bell, J. C. Mudge, and J. E. McNamara. *Computer Engineering: A DEC View of Hardware System Design*. Digital Press, Bedford, MA, 1978.

[33] James E. Bennett. Personal communication, 1993.

[34] D. Bhandarkar and D. W. Clark. Performance from architecture: Comparing a RISC and a CISC with similar hardware organization. In *Proceedings of ASPLOS-IV*, pages 310–319. ACM, April 1991.

[35] D. P. Bhandarkar. Analysis of memory interference in multiprocessors. *IEEE Transactions on Computers*, C-24(9):897–908, September 1975.

[36] L. Bhuyan and D. Agrawal. Design and performance of generalized interconnectgin networks. *IEEE Transactions on Computers*, C-32(12):1081–1090, December 1983.

[37] L. Bhuyan, Q. Yang, and D. Agrawal. Performance of multiprocessor interconnection networks. *IEEE Computer*, 22(2):25–37, February 1989.

[38] J. S. Birnbaum and W. S. Worley, Jr. Beyond RISC: High-precision architecture. *Hewlett-Packard Journal*, (36), August 1985.

[39] D. Bitton. Arm scheduling in shadowed disks. In *Proceedings of Compcon 89*, pages 132–136, 1989.

[40] G. A. Blaauw. The structure of System/360, Part V: Multi-system organization. *IBM Systems Journal*, 3(2):181–195, 1964.

[41] G. A. Blaauw and F. P. Brooks, Jr. The structure of System/360, Part I: Outline of the logical structure. *IBM Systems Journal*, 3(2):119–135, 1964.

[42] W. Brantley, K. McAuliffe, and J. Weiss. RP3 processor-memory element. In *International Conference on Parallel Processing*, pages 782–789, 1985.

[43] Brian K. Bray and M. J. Flynn. Write caches as an alternative to write buffers. Technical Report CSL-TR-91-470, Stanford University, April 1991.

[44] G. Bronson and H. Silver. *32-Bit Microprocessors: A Primer Plus*. Advanced Technology Series. AT&T, Indianapolis, 1988.

[45] D. T. Brown, R. L. Gibson, and C. A. Thorn. Channel and direct access device architecture. *IBM Systems Journal*, 11(3):186–199, 1972.

[46] W. Buchholz. *Planning a Computer System*. McGraw-Hill, New York, 1962.

[47] R. P. Case and A. Padegs. Architecture of the IBM System/370. *Communications of the ACM*, 21(1):73–96, January 1978.

[48] L. M. Censier and P. Feautrier. A new solution to coherence problems in multicache systems. *IEEE Transactions on Computers*, C27(12):1112–1118, December 1978.

[49] D. Y. Chang, D. J. Kuck, and D. H. Lawrie. On the effective bandwidth of parallel memory. *IEEE Transactions on Computers*, C-26(5):480–489, May 1977.

[50] J. H. Chang, H. Chao, and K. So. Cache design of a sub-micron CMOS System/370. *Proceedings of the 14th Annual International Symposium on Computer Architecture*, pages 208–213, 1987.

[51] J. Cho, A. J. Smith, and H. Sachs. The memory architecture and the cache and memory management unit for the Fairchild Clipper processor. Technical Report UCB/CSD 86/289, Computer Science Division, U.C. Berkeley, 1986.

[52] D. W. Clark. Measurement and analysis of instruction use in the VAX 11/780. In *Proceedings of the 9th Annual Symposium on Computer Architecture*, pages 9–17, Washington, DC, April 1982. IEEE Computer Society Press.

[53] D. W. Clark. Cache performance in the VAX-11/780. *ACM Transactions on Computer Systems*, 1(1):24–37, February 1983.

[54] D. W. Clark and J. S. Emer. Performance of the VAX-11/780 translation buffer: Simulation and measurement. *ACM Transactions on Computer Systems*, 3(1):31–62, February 1985.

[55] W. Connors, V. Mercer, and T. Sorlini. S/360 instruction usage distribution. IBM Technical Report TR 00.2025, May 1970.

[56] C. J. Conti, D. H. Gibson, and S. H. Pitowsky. Structural aspects of the System/360 Model 85, Part I: General organization. *IBM Systems Journal*, 7(1):2–14, 1968.

[57] R. W. Cook and M. J. Flynn. System design of a dynamic microprocessor. *IEEE Transactions on Computers*, C-19(3):213–222, March 1970.

[58] Intel Corporation. The Intel 8086 Family User's Manual. Intel Corp., Santa Clara, CA, 1980.

[59] KSR Corporation. KSR-1 overview. Internal report, KSR, 170 Tracer Lane, Waltham, MA 02154, 1991.

[60] L. Cotton. Maximum rate pipelined systems. In *Proceedings of the Spring Joint Computer Conference*, pages 581–586. AFIPS, 1969.

[61] Harvey G. Cragon. An evaluation of code space requirements and performance of various architectures. *Computer Architecture News*, 7(5):5–21, February 1979.

[62] J. H. Crawford and P. P. Gelsinger. *Programming the 80386*. Sybex, Alameda, CA, 1987.

[63] Cray Research. Cray X-MP and Cray-1 Computer Systems: Disk Systems Hardware Reference Manual, Volume H0077. 1440 Northland Drive, Mendota Heights, MN 55120, 1985.

[64] W. J. Dally. Performance analysis of k-ary n-cube interconnection networks. *IEEE Transactions on Computers*, 39(6), June 1990.

[65] Subrata Dasgupta. *Computer Architecture: A Modern Synthesis* (Two volumes). Wiley, New York, 1989.

[66] J. W. Davidson and R. A. Vaughan. The effect of instruction set complexity on program size and memory performance. *Proceedings of the 2nd International Conference on Architecture Support for Programming Languages and Operating Systems (ASPLOS II)*, pages 60–64, October 1987.

[67] B.D. de Dinechin. A ultra fast Euclidean division algorithm for prime memory systems. In *Proceedings of Supercomputing '91*, pages 56–65. IEEE, November 1991.

[68] P. J. Denning. The working set model for program behavior. *CACM*, 11(5):323–333, May 1968.

[69] P. J. Denning. Virtual memory. *Computing Surveys*, 2(3):153–189, September 1970.

[70] P. J. Denning. Segmentation and the design of multiprogrammed computer systems. *Journal of the ACM*, 12(4):589–602, October 1979.

[71] J. Dennis. Segmentation and the design of multiprogrammed computer systems. *Journal of the ACM*, 12(4), October 1965.

[72] J. A. DeRosa and H. M. Levy. An evaluation of branch architectures. In *Proceedings of the 14th Annual Symposium on Computer Architecture*, pages 10–16, June 1987.

[73] D. Ditzel and R. McLellan. Register allocation for free: the C machine stack cache. In *Proceedings of the Symposium on Architectural Support for Programming Languages and Operating Systems*, pages 48–56, New York, March 1982. ACM.

[74] K. M. Dixit. New CPU benchmark suites from SPEC. *SPEC Newsletter*, 4(1), February 1992.

[75] R. Dowsing. *Introduction to concurrency using Occam*. Van Nostrand Reinhold, London, 1988.

[76] P. K. Dubey, , and M. J. Flynn. A bubble propagation model for pipeline performance. *Journal of Parallel and Distributed Computing*, 23(3):330–337, December 1994.

[77] P. K. Dubey and M. J. Flynn. Optimal pipelining. *Journal of Parallel and Distributed Computing*, 8:10–19, 1990.

[78] Pradeep K. Dubey. *Exploiting Fine-Grain Concurrency: Analytical Insights in Superscalar Processor Design*. PhD thesis, Purdue University, August 1991.

[79] M. Dubois, C. Scheurich, and F. Briggs. Memory access buffering in multiprocessors. In *Proceedings of the 13th International Symposium on Computer Architecture*, pages 434–442, 1986.

[80] M. Dubois, C. Scheurich, and F. Briggs. Synchronization, coherence and event ordering in multiprocessors. *IEEE Computer*, 21(2), 1988.

[81] M. Dubois and S. Thakkar, editors. *Scalable Shared-Memory Multiprocessors*. Kluwer Academic, Boston, 1992.

[82] M. C. Easton and R. Fagin. Cold-start vs. warm-start miss ratios. *Communications of the ACM*, 21(10):866–872, October 1978.

[83] S. Eggers. *Simulation Analysis of Data Sharing in Shared Memory Multiprocessors*. PhD thesis, University of California at Berkeley, 1989. Comp. Sci. Division Tech. Report UCB/CSD 89/501.

[84] S. Eggers and R. Katz. A characterization of sharing in parallel programs and its applicability to coherency protocol evaluation. Technical Report Report No. UCB/CSD 87/387, University of California at Berkeley, December 1987.

[85] R. J. Eickemeyer and J. H. Patel. Performance evaluation of on-chip register and cache organizations. *Proceedings of the 15th Annual International Symposium on Computer Architecture*, pages 64–72, May 1988.

[86] P. H. Enslow, editor. *Multiprocessors and Parallel Processing*. Wiley, New York, 1974.

[87] W. Feller. *An Introduction to Probability Theory and Its Application*, volume 1. Wiley, New York, 1968.

[88] P. M. Fenwick. Some aspects of the dynamic behavior of hierarchical memories. *IEEE Transactions on Computers*, C-34(6):570–573, June 1985.

[89] J. A. Fisher. Very long instruction word architectures and the ELI-512. In *Proceedings of the 10th Symposium on Computer Architecture*, pages 140–150. ACM, 1983.

[90] I. Flores. Derivation of a waiting time factor for a multiple band memory. *Journal of the ACM*, 11:265–282, July 1964.

[91] M. J. Flynn. Trends and problems in computer organization. In *Proceedings of IFIP Congress*, pages 2–10. North-Holland, Amsterdam, 1974.

[92] M. J. Flynn and L. W. Hoevel. Execution architecture: The DELtran experiment. *IEEE Transactions on Computers*, C-32(2):156–175, February 1983.

[93] M. J. Flynn and L. W. Hoevel. Measures of ideal execution architectures. *IBM Journal of Research and Development*, 28(4):356-369, July 1984.

[94] M. J. Flynn, C. L. Mitchell, and J. M. Mulder. And now a case for more complex instruction sets. *IEEE Computer*, 20(9):71-83, September 1987.

[95] S. J. Frank. Tightly coupled multiprocessor systems speed memory access times. *Electronics*, 57(1):164-169, January 1984.

[96] J. Fu, J. Keller, and K. Haduch. Aspects of the VAX 8800 C box design. *Digital Technical Journal*, (4):41-51, February 1987.

[97] S. H. Fuller, P. Shaman, D. Lamb, and W. E. Burr. Evaluation of computer architectures via test programs. In *Proceedings of AFIPS*, volume 46, pages 147-160, 1977.

[98] J. Gee, M. Hill, D. Pnevmatikatos, and A. Smith. Cache performance of the SPEC92 benchmark suite. *IEEE Micro*, 13(4):17-27, August 1993.

[99] J. Gee and A. Smith. The performance impact of vector processor caches. In *Proceedings, 25th Hawaii International Conference on System Sciences*, volume 1, pages 437-448, January 1992.

[100] S. K. Ghandi. *VLSI Fabrication Principles: Silicon and Gallium Arsenide.* Wiley Interscience, New York, 1983.

[101] K. Gharachorloo, D. Lenoski, J. Laudon, P. Gibbons, A. Gupta, and J. Hennessy. Memory consistency and event ordering in scalable shared-memory multiprocessors. In *Proceedings of the 17th Annual International Symposium on Computer Architecture*, pages 15-26, May 1990.

[102] D. H. Gibson. Considerations in block-oriented systems design. In *Proceedings of AFIPS*, volume 30, pages 75-80, 1967.

[103] J. C. Gibson. The Gibson mix. Technical Report TR 00.2043, IBM Systems Development Division, Poughkeepsie, NY, 1970.

[104] D. B. Glasco, B. A. Delagi, and M. J. Flynn. Update-based cache coherence protocols for scalable shared-memory multiprocessors. In *Proceedings of the 27th Annual Hawaii International Conference on System Sciences*, volume 1, pages 534-545, January 1994.

[105] R. H. Gonter. Comparison of the Gibson mix with UMASS mix. Publication No. TN/RCC/004, University of Massachusetts Research Computing Center, 1969.

[106] H. H. Goode and R. E. Machol. *Systems Engineering.* McGraw-Hill, New York, 1957.

[107] J. R. Goodman. Using cache memory to reduce processor-memory traffic. In *Proceedings of the 10th International Symposium on Computer Architecture*, pages 124-131. IEEE, June 1983.

[108] J. R. Goodman. Cache consistency and sequential consistency. Technical Report 61, IEEE SCI committee, March 1989.

[109] J. R. Goodman and W.-C. Hsu. On the use of registers vs. cache to minimize memory traffic. *Proceedings of the 13th Annual International Symposium on Computer Architecture*, pages 375-383, 1986.

[110] A. Gottlieb, R. Grishman, C. Kruskal, K. McAuliffe, L. Rudolph, and M. Snir. The NYU Ultracomputer—designing an MIMD shared memory parallel computer. *IEEE Transactions on Computers*, C-32(2):276-290, February 1983.

[111] A. Gottlieb, B. Lubachevsky, and L. Rudolph. Basic techniques for efficient coordination of cooperative sequential processors. *ACM Transactions on Programming Languages and Systems*, pages 164-189, April 1983.

[112] J. Gray, B. Horst, and M. Walker. Parity striping of disk arrays: Low-cost reliable storage with acceptable throughput. In *Proceedings of the 16th VLDB Conference*, pages 148-161, August 1990.

[113] C. J. Grossman. Cache–DASD storage design for improving system performance. *IBM Systems Journal*, 24(3/4):316-334, 1985.

[114] J. L. Gustafson. Re-evaluating Amdahl's law. *Communications of the ACM*, 31(5):532-533, May 1988.

[115] E. Hagersten, A. Landin, and S. Haridi. DDM—A cache-only memory architecture. *IEEE Computer*, 25(9):44-54, September 1992.

[116] I. J. Haikala. Cache hit ratios with geometric task switch intervals. In *Proceedings of the 11th Annual International Symposium on Computer Architecture*, pages 364-371, Ann Arbor, MI, June 1984.

[117] I. J. Haikala. Program behavior in memory hierarchies. PhD thesis (Technical Report A-1986-2), CS Dept., University of Helsinki, 1986.

[118] T. G. Hallin and M. J. Flynn. Pipelining of arithmetic functions. *IEEE Transactions on Computers*, pages 880-886, August 1972.

[119] C. Hamacher, Z. Vranesic, and S. Zaky. *Computer Organization*. McGraw-Hill, New York, 3rd edition, 1990.

[120] D. Hammerstrom. *Analysis of Memory Addressing Architecture*. PhD thesis, University of Illinois, July 1977.

[121] J. M. Harker, D. W. Brede, R. E. Pattison, G. R. Santana, and L. G. Taft. A quarter century of disk file innovation. *IBM Journal of Research and Development*, pages 677-689, September 1981.

[122] E. A. Hauck and B. A. Dent. Burroughs' B6500/B7500 stack mechanism. In *Proceedings of AFIPS*, volume 32, pages 245-251, 1968.

[123] J. Hayes. *Computer Architecture and Organization*. McGraw-Hill, New York, 1988.

[124] W. Helbig and V. Milutinovic. The RCA's DCFL E/D MESFET GaAs 32-bit experimental RISC machine. *IEEE Transactions on Computers*, 36(2):263-274, February 1989.

[125] H. Hellerman. On the average speed of a multiple-module storage system. *IEEE Transactions on Computers*, C-15:670, August 1966.

[126] J. L. Hennessy, N. Jouppi, F. Baskett, and J. Gill. MIPS: A VLSI processor architecture. In *Proceedings of the CMU Conference on VLSI Systems and Computations*, pages 337-346. Computer Science Press, October 1981.

[127] J. L. Hennessy and D. A. Patterson. *Computer Architecture: A Quantitative Approach*. Morgan Kaufmann, San Mateo, CA, 1990.

[128] W. Hilf and A. Nausch. *The M68000 Family*, volume 1 of *Motorola Solid-State Electronics Series*. Prentice-Hall, Englewood Cliffs, NJ, 1989.

[129] M. D. Hill. *Aspects of Cache Memory and Instruction Buffer Performance*. PhD thesis, University of California, Berkeley, 1987. Published as TR UCB/CSD 87/381.

[130] M. D. Hill. A case for direct-mapped cache. *IEEE Computer*, pages 25-40, December 1988.

[131] C. Hoare. Monitors: An operating system structuring concept. *Communications of the ACM*, 17(10):549-557, October 1974.

[132] R. W. Hockney and C. R. Jesshope. *Parellel Computers 2*. Adam Hilger, Philadelphia, 1988.

[133] R. Hou, G. Ganger, and Y. Patt. Issues and problems in the I/O subsystem Part I—The magnetic disk. In Milutinovic and Shriver, editors, *Proceedings of the Hawaii International Conference on System Sciences*, pages 48–57, January 1992.

[134] P. Y. T. Hsu and E. S. Davidson. Highly concurrent scalar processing. In *Proceedings of the 13th Annual Symposium on Computer Architecture*, pages 386–395, June 1986.

[135] J. Huck. *Comparative Analysis of Computer Architectures*. PhD thesis, Stanford University, May 1983. CSL-TR-83-243.

[136] J. C. Huck and M. J. Flynn. *Analyzing Computer Architectures*. IEEE Computer Society Press, New York, 1989.

[137] K. Hwang. *Computer Arithmetic: Principles, Architecture, and Design*. Wiley, New York, 1978.

[138] K. Hwang. *Advanced Computer Architecture: Parallelism, Scalability, Programmability*. Computer Engineering Series. McGraw-Hill, 1993.

[139] K. Hwang and F. Briggs. *Computer Architecture and Parallel Processing*. Computer Organization and Architecture series. McGraw-Hill, New York, 1984.

[140] IBM Corporation. IBM System/360 Principles of Operation. Technical Report GA22-6821-4, 1970.

[141] IBM Corporation. IBM System/360 System Summary. Technical Report GA22-6810-8, 1970.

[142] IBM Corporation. IBM System/360 and System/370 Model 195, Functional Characteristics, 5th edition. Technical Report GA22-6943-4, file no. S/360 S/370-01, 1975.

[143] IBM Corporation. IBM System/370 Principles of Operation. Technical Report GA22-77000, 1978.

[144] American National Standards Institute. An American National Standard: IEEE Standard for Binary Floating-Point Arithmetic, 1988. ANSI/IEEE Standard No. 754.

[145] Intel Corporation. iAPX 432 VLSI General Data Processor. Document No. 171873, Intel Corp., Santa Clara, CA, 1981.

[146] K. E. Iverson. *A Programming Language*. Wiley, New York, 1962.

[147] D. James. *Cache and Interconnect Architectures in Multiprocessors*, chapter SCI (Scalable Coherent Interface). Kluwer Academic Publishers, Boston, 1989. M. Dubois and S. Thakkar, Editors.

[148] D. James. The Scalable Coherent Interface: Scaling to high-performance systems. In *Spring Compcon '94 Digest of Papers*, pages 64–71, San Francisco, February 1994. IEEE.

[149] W. M. Johnson. *Superscalar Microprocessor Design*. Prentice-Hall, Englewood Cliffs, NJ, 1991.

[150] N. P. Jouppi and D. W. Wall. Available instruction-level parallelism for superscalar and superpipelined machines. In *Proceedings of ASPLOS III*, pages 272–282, April 1989.

[151] J. R. Jump and S. Lakshmanamurthy. NETSIM: A general-purpose interconnection network simulator. In *International Workshop on Modeling, Analysis and Simulation of Computer and Telecommunication Systems*, pages 121–125, January 1993.

[152] G. Kane. *MIPS R2000 RISC Architecture*. Prentice-Hall, Englewood Cliffs, NJ, 1986.

[153] G. Kane. *MIPS RISC Architecture*. Prentice-Hall, Englewood Cliffs, NJ, 1988.

[154] G. Kane and J. Heinrich. *MIPS RISC Architecture*. Prentice-Hall, Englewood Cliffs, NJ, 1992.

[155] A. H. Karp and H. P. Flatt. Measuring parallel processor performance. *Communications of the ACM*, 33(5):539–543, May 1990.

[156] M. Katevenis. *Reduced Instruction Set Computer Architecture for VLSI*. MIT Press, Cambridge, MA, 1985.

[157] R. Katz, S. Eggers, D. Wood, C. Perkins, and R. Sheldon. Implementing a cache consistency protocol. In *Proceedings of the 12th International Symposium on Computer Architecture*, pages 276–283. IEEE, 1985.

[158] R. H. Katz, G. A. Gibson, and D. A. Patterson. Disk system architecture for high performance computing. *Proceedings of the IEEE*, 77(12):1842–1858, December 1989.

[159] R. M. Keller. Look ahead processors. *Computing Surveys*, 7(4):177–195, December 1975.

[160] D. G. Kendall. Some problems in the theory of queues. *Journal of the Royal Statistical Society*, 13(2):151–185, 1951.

[161] T. Kilburn, D. B. G. Edwards, M. J. Lanigan, and F. H. Sumner. One-level storage system. *IRE Transactions on Electronic Computers*, EC-11(2):223–235, April 1962.

[162] M. Y. Kim. Synchronized disk interleaving. *IEEE Transactions on Computers*, C-35(11):978–988, November 1986.

[163] M. Y. Kim. *Synchronously Interleaved Disk Systems*. PhD thesis, Polytechnic Institute of New York, 1987.

[164] E. F. Klass. *Pushing the Limits of CMOS Technology by Using Wave Pipelining*. PhD thesis, Delft University of Technology, September 1994.

[165] F. Klass and J. M. Mulder. Use of cmos technology in wave pipelining. In *Proceedings of the Fifth International Conference on VLSI Design*, pages 303–308, Bangalore, India, January 1992.

[166] L. Kleinrock. *Queueing Systems*. Wiley, 1975. Two volumes.

[167] D. Knuth. An empirical study of Fortran programs. Technical Report STAN-CS-70-186, Stanford University, 1970.

[168] F. Kobayashi, Y. Watanabe, M. Yamamoto, A. Anzai, A. Takahashi, T. Daikoku, and T. Fujita. Hardware technology for Hitachi M-880 processor group. In *Proceedings of the Electronic Components and Technologies Conference*, pages 693–703, 1991.

[169] H. Kobayashi. *Modeling and Analysis: An Introduction to Systems Performance Evaluation Methodology*. Addison-Wesley, Menlo Park, CA, 1978.

[170] M. Kobayashi. Dynamic profile of instruction sequences for the IBM System/370. *IEEE Transactions on Computers*, C-32(9):859–861, 1983.

[171] P. M. Kogge. *The Architecture of Pipelined Computers*. McGraw-Hill, New York, 1981.

[172] C. Kruskal and M. Snir. The performance of multistage interconnection networks for multiprocessors. *IEEE Transactions on Computers*, C-32(12), December 1983.

[173] D. Kuck, P. Budnik, S. Chen, D. Lawrie, R. Towle, R. Strebendt, E. Davis, J. Han, P. Kraska, and Y. Muraoka. Measurements of parallelism in ordinary Fortran programs. *IEEE Computer*, 7(1):37–46, January 1974.

[174] D. Kuck, Y. Muraoka, and S. Chen. On the number of operations simultaneously executable in Fortran-like programs and their resulting speedup. *IEEE Transactions on Computers*, C-21:1293–1310, December 1972.

[175] S. R. Kunkel and J. E. Smith. Optimal pipelining in supercomputers. In *Proceedings of the 13th Annual Symposium on Computer Architecture*, pages 404–411, 1986.

[176] M. Lam. Software pipelining: An effective scheduling technique for VLIW machines. In *Proceedings of SIGPLAN '88 Conference on Programming Language Design and Implementation*, pages 318–328, June 1988.

[177] L. Lamport. How to make a multiprocessor computer that correctly executes multiprocess programs. *IEEE Transactions on Computers*, C-28(9):690–691, September 1979.

[178] D. Lawrie. Access and alignment of data in an array processor. *IEEE Transactions on Computers*, C-24(12):1145–1154, December 1975.

[179] E. Lazowska, J. Zahorjan, D. Cheriton, and W. Zwaenepoel. File access performance of diskless workstations. *ACM TOCS*, 4(3):238–268, August 1986.

[180] E. Lee and R. Katz. Performance consequences of parity placement in disk arrays. In *4th International Conference on Architectural Support for Programming Languages and Operating Systems*, pages 190–199, 1991.

[181] J. K. F. Lee and A. J. Smith. Analysis of branch prediction strategies and branch target buffer design. *IEEE Computer*, 17(1):6–22, January 1984.

[182] R. B. Lee. *Performance Characterization of Parallel Processor Organizations*. PhD thesis, Stanford University, May 1980.

[183] R. B. Lee. The Hewlett-Packard Precision architecture. *IEEE Computer*, 22(1):78–91, January 1989.

[184] D. Lenoski, J. Laudon, K. Gharachorloo, W. Weber, A. Gupta, J. Hennessy, M. Horowitz, and M. Lam. The Stanford DASH multiprocessor. *IEEE Computer*, 25(3):63–79, March 1992.

[185] H. M. Levy and D. W. Clark. On the use of benchmarks for measuring system performance. *Computer Architecture News*, 10(6):5–8, 1982.

[186] C. Z. Loboz. *An Analysis of Program Execution: Issues for Computer Architecture*. PhD thesis, The Australian National University, July 1990.

[187] A. Lunde. Empirical evaluation of some features of instruction set processor architecture. *Communications of the ACM*, 20(3):143–153, March 1977.

[188] W. L. Lynch. *The Interaction of Virtual Memory and Cache Memory*. PhD thesis, Stanford University, October 1993. CSL-TR-93-587.

[189] M. MacDougall. Instruction-level program and process modeling. *IEEE Computer*, 17(7):14–26, July 1984.

[190] D. Marple and A. El Gamal. Area-delay optimization of programmable logic arrays. In *Proceedings of the 4th MIT Conference on Advanced Research in VLSI*, pages 171–194, April 1986.

[191] E. McCreight. The Dragon computer system: An early overview. Technical report, Xerox Corp., September 1984.

[192] S. McFarling and J. Hennessy. Reducing the cost of branches. In *Proceedings of the 13th Annual Symposium on Computer Architecture*, pages 396–403, June 1986.

[193] K. McNeeley and V. Milutinovic. Emulating a CISC with a RISC. *IEEE Micro*, 7(1):60–72, February 1987.

[194] C. Mead and L. Conway. *Introduction to VLSI Systems*. Series in Computer Science. Addison-Wesley, Reading, MA, 1980.

[195] C. D. Mee and E. D. Danielle. *Magnetic Recording*, volume 1: *Technology*; Volume 2: *Applications*. McGraw-Hill, NY, 1987.

[196] Military computer architectures: A look at the alternatives. *IEEE Computer*, 10(10), October 1977. (Special issue).

[197] R. E. Miller. *Switching Theory: Sequential Circuits and Machines*, volume 2. Wiley, New York, 1965.

[198] V. Milutinovic, D. Fura, and W. Helbig. An introduction to GaAs microprocessor architecture for VLSI. *IEEE Computer*, 19(3):30–42, March 1986.

[199] V. Milutinovic, N. Lopez-Benitez, and K. Hwang. A gaas-based microprocessor architecture ofr real-time applications. *IEEE Transactions on Computers*, C-36(6):714–727, June 1987.

[200] C. Mitchell. *Processor Architecture and Cache Performance*. PhD thesis, Stanford University, June 1986. CSL-TR-86-296.

[201] C. L. Mitchell and M. J. Flynn. A workbench for computer architects. *IEEE Design & Test*, 5(1):19–29, February 1988.

[202] C. L. Mitchell and M. J. Flynn. The effects of processor architecture on memory traffic. *ACM Transactions on Computer Systems*, 8(3):230–250, August 1990.

[203] A. Mitsuishi, T. Mizoguchi, and T. Miyachi. Performance evaluation for buffer-contained disk units. *Systems and Computers in Japan*, 16(5):32–40, 1985.

[204] T. Mudge, H. Al-Sadoun, and B. Makrucki. Memory-interference model for multiprocessors based on semi-Markov processes. *IEE Proceedings*, 134, Part E(4):203–214, July 1987.

[205] T. Mudge, J. Hayes, G. Buzzard, and D. Winsor. Analysis of multiple bus interconnection networks. In *Proceedings of the International Conference on Parallel Processing*, pages 228–232. IEEE, 1984.

[206] J. Mulder. *Tradeoffs in Data-Buffer and Processor-Architecture Design*. PhD thesis, Stanford University, December 1987. CSL-TR-87-345.

[207] J. M. Mulder, N. T. Quach, and M. J. Flynn. An area model for on-chip memories and its application. *Journal of Solid State Circuits*, 26(2), February 1991. Also published as CSL-TR-90-413.

[208] T. E. Muller and W. S. Bartky. A theory of asynchronous circuits. Technical Report 75, University of Illinois Digital Computer Laboratory, November 1956.

[209] T. E. Muller and W. S. Bartky. A theory of asynchronous circuits. Technical Report 78, University of Illinois Digital Computer Laboratory, March 1957.

[210] B. Murphy. Cost–size optima of monolithic integrated circuits. *Proceedings of the IEEE*, 52(12):1537–1545, December 1964.

[211] W. Murray. *Computer and Digital System Architecture*. Prentice-Hall, Englewood Cliffs, NJ, 1990.

[212] G. J. Myers. The case against stack-oriented instruction sets. *Computer Architecture News*, August 1977.

[213] G. J. Myers. *Advances in Computer Architecture*. Wiley, New York, 1978.

[214] D. Nagle, R. Uhlig, T. Mudge, and S. Sechrest. Optimal allocation of on-chip memory for multiple-api operating systems. In *Proceedings of the 21st Annual International Symposium on Computer Architecture*, pages 358-369, April 1994.

[215] S. Ng. Some design issues of disk arrays. In *Proceedings of COMPCON*, pages 137-142, Spring 1989.

[216] S. Ng, D. Lang, and R. Selinger. Tradeoffs between devices and paths in achieving disk interleaving. In *Proceedings of the 15th International Symposium on Computer Architecture*, pages 196-201, 1988.

[217] Tin-Fook Ngai. *Run-time Resource Management in Concurrent Systems*. PhD thesis, Department of Electrical Engineering, Stanford University, January 1992. CSL-TR-92-504.

[218] A. Nicolau and J. Fisher. Measuring the parallelism available for very long instruction word architectures. *IEEE Transactions on Computers*, C-33:968-976, November 1984.

[219] M. Ogata and M. Flynn. A queuing analysis for disk array systems. Technical Report CSL-TR-90-443, Computer Systems Lab, Stanford University, August 1990.

[220] O. Olukotun, T. Mudge, and R. Brown. Performance optimization of pipelined caches. *IEEE Transactions on Computers*, 1994. To appear.

[221] E. Organick. *Computer Systems Organization: The B5700/B6700 Series*. Academic Press, New York, 1973.

[222] E. Organick and J. Hinds. *Interpreting Machines: Architecture and Programming of the B1700/B1800 Series*. North-Holland, New York, 1978.

[223] J. Ousterhout, H. Da Costa, D. Harrison, J. Kunze, M. Kupfer, and J. Thompson. A trace-driven analysis of the UNIX 4.2 BSD file system. In *Proceedings of the 10th Symposium on Operating System Principles*, pages 15-24, 1985.

[224] A. Padegs. The structural of System/360, Part IV: Channel design considerations. *IBM Systems Journal*, 3(2):165-180, 1964.

[225] M. Papamarcos and J. Patel. A low overhead coherence solution for multiprocessors with private cache memories. In *Proceedings of the 11th International Symposium on Computer Architecture*, pages 348-354. IEEE, 1984.

[226] J. H. Patel. Performance of processor-memory interconnections for multiprocessors. *IEEE Transactions on Computers*, C-30(10):771-780, October 1981.

[227] Y. N. Patt, W.-M. Hwu, and M. Shebanow. HPS, A new microarchitecture: Rationale and introduction. In *Proceedings of the 18th Annual Workshop on Microprogramming*, pages 103-108, December 1985.

[228] D. Patterson and D. Ditzel. The case for the reduced instruction set computer. *Computer Architecture News*, 8(6):25-33, October 1980.

[229] D. Patterson, G. Gibson, and R. Katz. A case for redundant arrays of inexpensive disks (RAID). *ACM SIGMOD*, pages 109-116, May 1988.

[230] D. A. Patterson and C. H. Sequin. RISC-1: A reduced instruction set VLSI computer. In *Proceedings of the 8th Annual Symposium on Computer Architecture*, pages 443-458, May 1981.

[231] B. L. Peuto and L. J. Shustek. Current issues in the architecture of microprocessors. *IEEE Computer*, pages 20-25, February 1977.

[232] G. Pfister, W. Brantley, D. George, S. Harvey, W. Kleinfelder, K. McAuliffe, E. Melton, V. Norton, and J. Weiss. The IBM Research parallel processor prototype (RP3): Introduction and architecture. In *Proceedings of the International Conference on Parallel Processing*, pages 764–789. IEEE, August 1985.

[233] G. F. Pfister and V. A. Norton. "Hot spot" contention and combining in multistage interconnection networks. *IEEE Transactions on Computers*, pages 943–948, October 1985.

[234] T. M. Pinkston. *The GLORI Strategy for Multiprocessors: Integrating Optics into the Interconnect Architecture*. PhD thesis, Stanford University, December 1992. CSL-TR-92-552.

[235] C. Polychronopoulos, M. Girkar, M. Haghighat, C. L. Lee, B. Leung, and D. Schouten. Parafrase-2: An environment for parallelizing, partitioning, synchronizing, and scheduling programs on multiprocessors. In *Proceedings of the 1989 International Conference on Parallel Processing*, pages 39–48, 1989. Volume 2 of 3.

[236] J. Protic, M. Tomasevic, and V. Milutinovic. A survey of distributed shared memory systems. In *Proceedings of the Hawaii International Conference on System Sciences*, Maui, Hawaii, January 1995.

[237] S. Przybylski, M. Horowitz, and J. Hennessy. Characteristics of performance-optimal multi-level cache hierarchies. In *Proceedings of the 16th Annual Symposium on Computer Architecture*, pages 114–121, June 1989.

[238] S. A. Przybylski. *New DRAM Technologies*. MicroDesign Resources, ?, 1994.

[239] G. Radin. The 801 minicomputer. In *Proceedings of the Symposium on Architectural Support for Programming Languages and Operating Systems*, pages 39–47, Palo Alto, CA, March 1982.

[240] M. R. Ransford. MC 68040 cache design study. *NCR Journal*, 3(2), December 1989.

[241] B. R. Rau. *Program Behavior and the Performance of Memory Systems*. PhD thesis, Stanford University, July 1977.

[242] B. R. Rau, D. Yen, W. Yen, and R. Towle. The CYDRA 5 departmental supercomputer. *IEEE Computer*, 22:12–35, January 1989.

[243] C. V. Ravi. On the bandwidth and interference in interleaved memory systems. *IEEE Transactions on Computers*, C-21:899–901, August 1972.

[244] A. L. N. Reddy and P. Banerjee. An evaluation of multiple-disk I/O systems. *IEEE Transactions on Computers*, 38(12):1680–1690, December 1989.

[245] K. J. Richardson and M. J. Flynn. TIME: Tools for input/output and memory evaluation. In V. Milutinovic, editor, *25th Hawaii International Conference on System Sciences*, pages 58–66. IEEE, January 1992.

[246] E. M. Riseman and C. C. Foster. The inhibition of potential parallelism. *IEEE Transactions on Computers*, C-21:1405–1411, December 1972.

[247] G. Rossmann and B. Rau. System/360 program statistics. Internal Report, Palyn Associates, San Jose, CA, January 1974.

[248] G. E. Rossmann. Personal communication.

[249] R. M. Russell. The CRAY-1 computer system. *Communications of the ACM*, 21(1):63–72, January 1978.

[250] James W. Rymarczyk. Coding guidelines for pipelined processors. In *Proceedings of the Symposium on Architectural Support for Programming Languages and Operating Systems*, pages 12–19. ACM, March 1982.

[251] K. Salem and G. Garcia-Molina. Disk striping. In *International Conference on Data Engineering*, pages 336–342, 1986.

[252] Vivek Sarkar. *Partitioning and Scheduling Parallel Programs for Execution on Multiprocessors*. PhD thesis, Stanford University, April 1987. CSL-TR-87-328.

[253] D. Sasha and M. Snir. Efficient and correct execution of parallel programs that share memory. *ACM Transactions on Programming Languages and Systems*, pages 282–312, April 1988.

[254] C. Scheurich and M. Dubois. Correct memory operation of cache-based multi-processors. In *Proceedings of the 14th International Symposium on Computer Architecture*, pages 234–243, 1987.

[255] R. A. Scranton, D. A. Thompson, and D. W. Hunter. The access time myth. Research Report RC-10197, IBM, September 1983.

[256] L. J. Shustek. *Analysis and Performance of Computer Instruction Sets*. PhD thesis, Stanford University, May 1978. STAN-CS-78-658.

[257] D. P. Siewiorek, C. Gordon Bell, and A. Newell. *Computer Structures: Principles and Examples*. Computer Science Series. McGraw-Hill, New York, 1982.

[258] M. L. Simmons and H. J. Wasserman. Performance evaluation of the IBM RISC System/6000: Comparison of an optimized scalar processor with two vector processors. In *Proceedings of Supercomputing '90*, pages 132–141. IEEE, 1990.

[259] A. J. Smith. Cache memories. *ACM Computing Surveys*, 14(3):473–530, September 1982.

[260] A. J. Smith. Cache evaluation and the impact of workload choice. In *Proceedings of the 12th International Symposium on Computer Architecture*, pages 64–73, June 1985.

[261] A. J. Smith. Disk cache: Miss ratio analysis and design considerations. *ACM Transactions on Computer Systems*, 3(3):161–203, August 1985.

[262] A. J. Smith. Line (block) size choices for CPU cache memories. *IEEE Transactions on Computers*, C-36(9):1063–1075, September 1987.

[263] B. Smith. Architecture and applications of the HEP multiprocessor computer system. *SPIE*, 298:241–248, 1988.

[264] J. E. Smith. A study of branch prediction strategies. In *Proceedings of the 8th Annual Symposium on Computer Architecture*, pages 135–148, May 1981.

[265] J. E. Smith and A. R. Pleszkin. Implementation of precise interrupts in pipelined processors. In *Proceedings of the 12th International Symposium on Computer Architecture*, pages 36–44, June 1985. Published in SIGARCH 13(3).

[266] M. D. Smith, M. Johnson, and M. A. Horowitz. Limits on multiple instruction issue. In *Proceedings of ASPLOS III*, pages 290–320, April 1989.

[267] G. S. Sohi and S. Vajapeyam. Instruction issue logic in high-performance inter-ruptible pipelined processors. In *Proceedings of the 14th Annual Symposium on Computer Architecture*, pages 27–34, June 1987.

[268] M. Squillante and E. Lazouska. Using processor-cache affinity information in shared-memory multiprocessor scheduling. *IEEE Transactions on Parallel and Distributed Systems*, 4(2):131–143, February 1993.

[269] W. Stallings. *Computer Organization and Architecture: Principles of Structure and Function*. Macmillan, New York, 2nd edition, 1990.

[270] W. Stallings. *Reduced Instruction Set Computers*. Tutorial. IEEE Computer Society Press, Los Alamitos, CA, 2nd edition, 1990.

[271] H. S. Stone, editor. *Introduction to Computer Architecture*. Computer Science Series. SRA, Chicago, 2nd edition, 1980.

[272] H. S. Stone. *High-Performance Computer Architecture*. Electrical and Computer Engineering Series. Addison-Wesley, Reading, MA, 2nd edition, 1990.

[273] W. D. Strecker. *Analysis of the Instruction Execution Rate in Certain Computer Systems*. PhD thesis, Carnegie-Mellon University, Pittsburgh, PA, 1970.

[274] N. Suzuki. *Shared memory multiprocessing*. MIT Press, Cambridge, MA, 1992.

[275] Y. Tamir and C. H. Sequin. Strategies for managing the register file in RISC. *IEEE Transactions on Computers*, C-32(11):977–989, 1983.

[276] A. S. Tanenbaum. *Structured Computer Organization*. Series in Automatic Computation. Prentice-Hall, Englewood Cliffs, NJ, 1976.

[277] A. S. Tanenbaum. Implications of structured programming for machine architecture. *Communications of the ACM*, 21(3):237–243, March 1978.

[278] I. Tartalja and V. Milutinovic. A survey of software solutions for maintenance of cache consistency in shared memory multiprocessors. In *Proceedings of the Hawaii International Conference on System Sciences*, Maui, Hawaii, January 1995.

[279] T. Teorey and T. Pinkerton. A comparative analysis of disk scheduling policies. *Communications of the ACM*, pages 177–184, March 1972.

[280] Manu Thapar. *Cache Coherence for Scalable Shared Memory Multiprocessors*. PhD thesis, Stanford University, May 1992. CSL-TR-92-522.

[281] J. E. Thornton. *Design of a Computer: The Control Data 6600*. Scott, Foresman and Co., Glenview, IL, 1970.

[282] G. S. Tjaden. *Representation and Detection of Concurrency Using Ordering Matrices*. PhD thesis, Johns Hopkins University, 1972.

[283] G. S. Tjaden and M. J. Flynn. Detection and parallel execution of independent instructions. *IEEE Transactions on Computers*, C-19:889–895, October 1970.

[284] M. Tomasevic and V. Milutinovic. A simulation study of snoopy cache coherence protocols. In *Proceedings of the HICSS*, pages 427–436, Koloa, Hawaii, January 1992.

[285] M. Tomasevic and V. Milutinovic. *The Cache Coherence Problem in Shared-Memory Multiprocessors: Hardware Solutions*. IEEE Computer Society Press, 1993.

[286] M. Tomasevic and V. Milutinovic. Hardware approaches to cache consistency in shared memory multiprocessors: Part 1. *IEEE Micro*, October 1994.

[287] M. Tomasevic and V. Milutinovic. Hardware approaches to cache consistency in shared memory multiprocessors: Part 2. *IEEE Micro*, December 1994.

[288] R. M. Tomasulo. An efficient algorithm for exploiting multiple arithmetic units. *IBM Journal of Research and Development*, 11(1):25–33, January 1967.

[289] J. Torrellas, J. Hennessy, and T. Weil. Analysis of critical architectural and program parameters in a hierarchical shared-memory multiprocessor. *Performance Evaluation Review*, 18(1):163–172, May 1990.

[290] J. Torrellas, A. Tucker, and A. Gupta. Benefits of cache-affinity scheduling in shared-memory multiprocessors. *Performance Evaluation Review*, 21(1):272–274, June 1993.

[291] S. G. Tucker. Microprogram control for System/360. *IBM Systems Journal*, 6(4):222–241, 1967.

[292] A. K. Uht. An efficient hardware algorithm to extract concurrency from general-purpose code. In *Proceedings of the 19th Annual Hawaii International Conference on System Sciences*, pages 41–50, 1986.

[293] S. Ungar. *Asynchronous Sequential Switching Circuits*. Wiley Interscience, New York, 1969.

[294] S. Ungar and C. Tan. Clocking schemes for high-speed digital systems. *IEEE Transactions on Computers*, C-35(10):880–895, October 1986.

[295] M. Upton, T. Huff, T. Mudge, and R. Brown. Resource allocation in a high clock rate microprocessor. In *Proceedings of the Conference on Architectural Support for Programming Languages and Operating Systems*, pages 98–109, October 1994.

[296] A. J. van de Goor. *Computer Architecture and Design*. Addison-Wesley, 1989.

[297] K. Wagner. A survey of clock distribution techniques on high speed computer systems. Technical Note CSL-TN-86-309, Stanford University, December 1986.

[298] J. Wakerly. *Microcomputer Architecture and Programming*. Wiley, New York, 1989.

[299] D. M. H. Walker. *Yield Simulation for Integrated Circuits*. International Series in Engineering and Computer Science. Kluwer Academic Publishers, Boston, 1987.

[300] S. Waser and M. Flynn. *Introduction to Arithmetic for Digital Systems Designers*. Holt, Rinehart and Winston, New York, 1982.

[301] W. J. Watson. The TI ASC: A highly modular and flexible super computer architecture. In *Proceedings of AFIPS*, volume 41, part 1, pages 221–228, 1972.

[302] R. Wedig. *Detection of Concurrency in Directly Executed Language Instruction Streams*. PhD thesis, Stanford University, June 1982.

[303] S. Weiss and J. E. Smith. Instruction issue logic in pipelined supercomputers. In *Proceedings of the 11th Annual Symposium on Computer Architecture*, pages 110–118, June 1984.

[304] C. Wiecek. A case study of VAX-11 instruction set usage for compiler execution. In *Proceedings of the Symposium on Architectural Support for Programming Languages and Operating Systems*, pages 177–184, New York, March 1982. ACM.

[305] M. V. Wilkes. The best way to design an automatic calculating machine. In *Manchester University Computer Inaugural Conference*, Ferranti, Ltd., London, 1951.

[306] M. V. Wilkes. Slave memories and dynamic storage allocation. *IEEE Transactions on Electronic Computers*, EC-14(2):270–271, February 1965.

[307] B. Wilkinson. Comments on "Design and analysis of arbitration protocols". *IEEE Transactions on Computers*, 41(3):348–351, March 1992.

[308] M. Wolfe. *Optimizing Compilers for Supercomputers*. PhD thesis, MIT, 1982.

[309] D. Wong, G. De Micheli, and M. Flynn. Designing high-performance digital circuits using wave pipelining: Algorithms and practical experiences. *IEEE Transactions on Computer Aided Design of Integrated Circuits*, 12(1):25–46, January 1993.

[310] D. Wong, G. De Micheli, and M. Flynn. Designing high-performance digital circuits using wave pipelining. In *Proceedings of VLSI '89*, pages 241–252, Munich, Germany, August 1989.

[311] D. C. Wong. *Techniques for Designing High-Performance Digital Circuits Using Wave Pipelining.* PhD thesis, Stanford University, August 1991. Also published as CSL-TR-92-508, February 1992.

[312] C.-L. Wu and T.-Y. Feng. On a class of multistage interconnection networks. *IEEE Transactions on Computers*, pages 696–777, August 1980.

[313] C.-L. Wu and T.-Y. Feng. *Interconnection Networks for Parallel and Distributed Processing.* Tutorial. IEEE Computer Society Press, Washington DC, 1984.

[314] T.-Y. Yeh and Y. N. Patt. Two-level adaptive training branch prediction. In *Proceedings of the 24th Annual International Symposium on Microarchitecture*, pages 51–61, November 1991.

[315] T.-Y. Yeh and Y. N. Patt. Alternative implementations of two-level adaptive branch prediction. In *Proceedings of the 19th Annual International Symposium on Computer Architecture*, pages 124–134, May 1992.

[316] D. Yen, J. Patel, and E. Davidson. Memory interference in synchronous multiprocessor systems. *IEEE Transactions on Computers*, C-31:1116–1121, November 1982.

Index

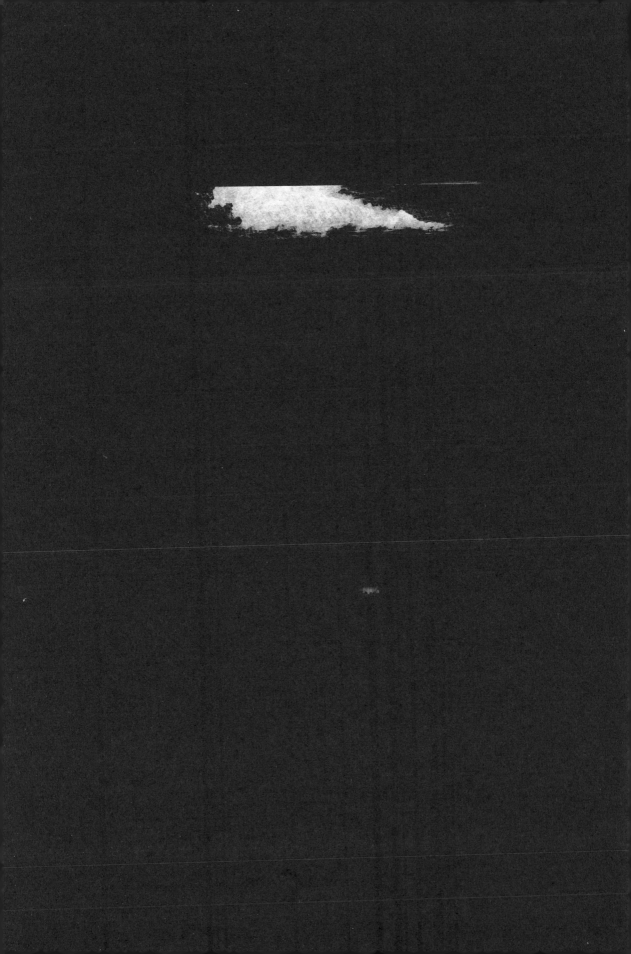